Matthew Parkin, Claire Brown, Melissa Lorenz and Jules Robson

Cambridge International AS and A Level

Marine Science

Coursebook

CAMBRIDGE
UNIVERSITY PRESS

University Printing House, Cambridge CB2 8BS, United Kingdom

One Liberty Plaza, 20th Floor, New York, NY 10006, USA

477 Williamstown Road, Port Melbourne, VIC 3207, Australia

314–321, 3rd Floor, Plot 3, Splendor Forum, Jasola District Centre, New Delhi – 110025, India

79 Anson Road, #06 -04/06, Singapore 079906

Cambridge University Press is part of the University of Cambridge.

It furthers the University's mission by disseminating knowledge in the pursuit of education, learning and research at the highest international levels of excellence.

www.cambridge.org
Information on this title: www.cambridge.org/9781316640869 (Paperback)

© Cambridge University Press 2017

First published 2017

20 19 18 17 16 15 14 13 12 11 10 9 8 7

Printed in Dubai by Oriental Press

A catalogue record for this publication is available from the British Library

ISBN 978-1-316-64086-9 Paperback

Contents

How to use this book   vi
Introduction   viii

1   AS   Scientific method   1

1.1   The history of the scientific method   2
1.2   Steps in the scientific method   2
1.3   Scientific theories   6
1.4   Steps in planning valid laboratory-based
        experiments   6
Summary   7
Exam-style questions   7
Case study: Barnacle distribution   8

2   AS   Marine ecosystems and biodiversity   9

2.1   An aquatic home   10
2.2   Fundamental principles of marine ecology   10
2.3   Symbiosis within marine ecosystems   12
2.4   Feeding relationships   14
2.5   Food chains and food webs   15
Practical: Intertidal zonation studies   18
Maths skills: Mean, median, mode and range   19
2.6   Succession   22
2.7   Environment and biodiversity   24
Case study: Our deep-sea pharmacy   25
2.8   Specialised and generalised ecological niches   27
Summary   29
Exam-style questions   29
Extended case study: Southern Ocean ecosystem   32

3   AS   Energetics of marine ecosystems   36

3.1   Where does the energy for life come from?   37
3.2   Productivity   37
Practical: Investigating the compensation point   41
Practical: Measuring primary productivity of grass   44
Case study: The Peruvian anchoveta fishing
industry   46
3.3   Energy transfer   47
Maths skills: Interpreting energy diagrams and
calculating percentage efficiency   49
3.4   Illustrating feeding relationships   51
Summary   53
Exam-style questions   53
Extended case study: The Gulf of Mexico dead
zone   56

4   AS   Nutrient cycles in marine ecosystems   58

4.1   Cycling of elements through the ecosystem   59
4.2   Nutrient cycles   59
4.3   Processes that add nutrients to the
        surface water   61
4.4   Processes that remove nutrients from
        the surface layer   63
4.5   Examples of marine nutrient cycles   65
Practical: Simple investigations into the exchange
of carbon dioxide between the atmosphere and the
ocean   67
Practical: Investigating the nitrogen cycle in a fish
tank   70
Case study: The Redfield ratio   74
Maths skills: Plotting and interpreting graphs   75
Summary   77
Exam-style questions   78
Extended case study: The importance of salmon
to the growth of trees   79

5   AS   Coral reefs and lagoons   82

5.1   Coral seas   83
5.2   Coral physiology   83
5.3   Physical factors necessary for coral growth   84
5.4   Types of reef   85
5.5   Reef erosion   87
Case study: Reef destruction through human
interference   89
Practical: The effect of acidity on calcium
carbonate   92
5.6   Reconstructing the history of coral reefs   92
Maths skills: Radiocarbon dating   94
Summary   95
Exam-style questions   96
Extended case study: Crown-of-thorns starfish on
Indo-Pacific reefs   97

6   AS   The ocean floor and the coast   99

6.1   How the Second World War changed marine
        science   100
6.2   Plate tectonics   100
6.3   Plate boundaries   102
6.4   Hydrothermal vents   105
6.5   Seabed   106

iii

6.6 Isostasy   107
6.7 The littoral zone   108
Maths skills: Measuring biodiversity on a rocky shore   112
Practical: Sediment-settling tube   116
Case study: Mangrove benefits, loss and restoration   116
Summary   118
Exam-style questions   118
Extended case study: Estuary loss in South Florida   119

7 AS **Physical and chemical oceanography**   **122**
7.1 Understanding the ocean   123
7.2 Chemical oceanography and the chemical composition of seawater   123
Case study: Dead Sea   127
Practical: Creating a halocline   131
7.3 Physical oceanography   132
Maths skills: Graphing and interpreting tidal data   134
Summary   141
Exam-style questions   142
Extended case study: Biomagnification in Minamata Bay   144

8 A **Physiology of marine primary producers**   **146**
8.1 The foundation of marine life   147
8.2 The basics of productivity   147
Practical: Separating out photosynthetic pigments by chromatography   149
Practical: The effect of light colour on photosynthesis rate   153
8.3 Factors affecting the rate of photosynthesis and the law of limiting factors 155
Maths skills: Calculating volumes and rates and using significant figures 158
8.4 Adaptations of different primary producers   159
Case study: The uses of seaweeds   166
Summary   167
Exam-style questions   167
Extended case study: Marine algal blooms and red tides: natural causes, pollution and global warming 170

9 A **Aspects of marine animal physiology**   **173**
9.1 A variable environment   174
9.2 Respiration   174
9.3 Gaseous exchange   176
Practical: Investigating the effect of surface area : volume ratio on the rate of diffusion 183
Maths skills: Surface area : volume ratios and rearranging formulae   184

9.4 The regulation of salinity   185
Practical: Identification of the isotonic point of potato cells   187
Case study: Red and white muscles in fish   190
Summary   190
Exam-style questions   191
Extended case study: The Aral Sea, an ecological catastrophe   194

10 A **Marine animal reproductive behaviour**   **197**
10.1 The cycle of life   198
10.2 Life cycles of marine organisms   198
Practical: The surface preferences of oyster spats   213
Maths skills: Analysing data   214
10.3 Fertilisation methods and parental care   216
Case study: The strange life cycle of the ceratoid deep-sea angler fish 219
Summary   220
Exam-style questions   220
Extended case study: The Elwha River Restoration Project   223

11 A **Fisheries management**   **226**
11.1 The impact of fishing   227
11.2 Sustainable fishing and the North Sea fishing fleet   227
11.3 Regulating sustainable fishing   231
Practical: Estimating fish ages in a population   242
11.4 Methods of monitoring and enforcement   243
Maths skills: Comparing data   246
11.5 Sociological impacts of fishing policies   249
11.6 Rehabilitation of stocks   249
Case study: Salmon hatcheries in North America   251
Summary   252
Exam-style questions   252
Extended case study: Sustainable rock lobster fishing in West Australia 255

12 A **Aquaculture**   **258**
12.1 Feeding the world   259
12.2 Extensive and intensive aquaculture   259
12.3 Specific examples of aquaculture   261
Practical: The effects of aquaculture conditions on the growth rate of fish 265
Maths skills: Frequency tables, pie charts and histograms   266
12.4 Sustainable aquaculture   268
12.5 Minimising the negative effects of aquaculture   276

Contents

Case study: Saving the mangroves of Vietnam
with organic shrimp farming 278
Summary 280
Exam-style questions 280
Extended case study: Offshore cobia and mutton
snapper production in the Bahamas 282

13 A Human impact on marine ecosystems 284
13.1 The impact of humans 285
13.2 The oil industry 285
13.3 Desalination plants 288
13.4 Agriculture 290
Practical: The effect of mineral ions on
eutrophication 291
13.5 Sewage and refuse 292
Case study: Dumping New York's sewage
into the north-west Atlantic 294
13.6 Dredging 295
13.7 The bioaccumulation and biomagnification
of toxins 297
Maths skills: Standard form, decimal places
and accuracy 299
13.8 Global warming and human activity 301
13.9 Effects of wrecking ships for dive sites 306
Summary 307
Exam-style questions 308
Extended case study: The *Deepwater Horizon*
oil spill in the Gulf of Mexico 311

14 A Marine conservation and ecotourism 315
14.1 Successful conservation 316
14.2 Conservation: what it is and why it
is necessary 316
14.3 Successful conservation 322
Case study: Sea bream protection in the
Adriatic Sea 326

14.4 Coastal communities 327
Practical: Reporting on the effectiveness of a
conservation project 336
Maths skills: Significant figures and when
to use them 337
Summary 338
Exam-style questions 338
Extended case study: Trouble in paradise, the
Chagos Islands marine protected area 342

15 A Marine biotechnology 346
15.1 The biotechnological age 347
15.2 Biotechnology 347
15.3 Selective breeding 348
Practical: Extracting DNA from organisms 354
15.4 Genetic engineering 354
Case study: Pollution indicators and pets:
the story of the GloFish 362
Maths skills: Measuring gradients of straight
lines and curves 363
Summary 365
Exam-style questions 366
Extended case study: Using genetic engineering
to control invasive species 368

Answers to self-assessment questions 373
Answers to practical activity questions 387
Answers to case study questions 392
Answers to maths skills questions 396
Answers to exam-style questions 401
Answers to extended case study questions 418
Glossary 426
Acknowledgements 434
Index 435

v

How to use this book

Learning outcomes set the scene for each chapter, help with navigation through the Coursebook and indicate the important concepts in each topic.

Key terms boxes contain clear and straightforward definitions of the most important terms in each topic.

An **Opening discussion** brings the subject of each chapter to life, sparking discussion in class and encouraging students to read around the topic.

Self-assessment questions throughout each chapter allow students to quickly check their knowledge and understanding, and track their own progress. Answers to these questions are provided at the back of the book.

Practical activities boxes throughout the book provide opportunities for students to conduct their own investigations and develop their practical skills.

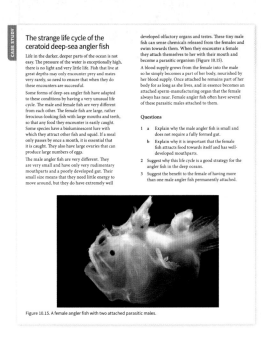

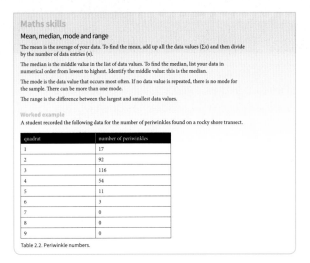

Every chapter contains a **Case study** covering a real world scenario that illustrates relevant aspects of the syllabus, with questions to develop students' higher-order thinking skills.

Maths skills boxes contain background information, worked examples and extra practice questions to provide students with more opportunities to develop the necessary mathematical skills they will need during the Marine Science course.

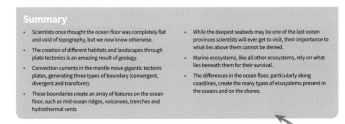

A **Summary** is included at the end of each chapter, providing a recap of the key concepts.

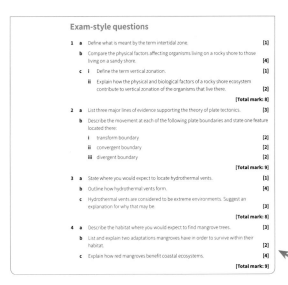

Students can use the **Exam-style questions** at the end of each chapter to check their knowledge and understanding of the whole topic and to practise answering questions that use a similar style to those they will encounter in their exams.

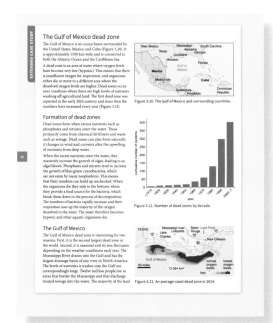

Each chapter contains an **Extended case study** – these are longer case studies related to more complex real world settings in order to provide students with opportunities to practise higher-order thinking skills and to prepare for their examinations.

Introduction

This first edition of the *Cambridge International AS and A Level Marine Science Coursebook* has been written to help you acquire the knowledge and skills required by the Cambridge International Examinations AS and A level Marine Science examination (9693). It provides full coverage of the syllabus for examinations from 2017 onwards.

The chapters are arranged in the same sequence as the syllabus. Chapters 1 to 7 cover the AS material and chapters 8 to 15 cover the full A Level material. The Cambridge International A Level examination assumes that you have a full knowledge of the AS course, including the scientific method covered in Chapter 1.

Each chapter has similar features to help you, including: key terms, maths skills, self-assessment questions, exam-style questions, practical activities and case studies that look at real-life scenarios. Look at the How to use this book section for more information about each feature.

The AS and A Level examinations use a range of question styles, some of which require factual recall and others that require you to think about unfamiliar examples and apply your knowledge. Working through the questions in this coursebook, and checking your answers against those provided in the back of the book, will help you to develop your answer-writing skills. Although the book is arranged as a series of discrete chapters, it is important to remember that the topics in these chapters link to each other.

Practical skills are an important part of the marine science course. You will develop these skills as you perform experiments and other practical work related to the topic you are studying. Each chapter contains practical activities for you to carry out. The exam-style questions at the end of each chapter include practical questions similar to those posed in exams and Chapter 1 explains the nature of scientific investigation.

Marine science is a unique and engaging subject that requires you to have an understanding of subjects such as biology, geography, geology, physics, chemistry and even sociology. This coursebook will cover material from all of these areas and look at both established knowledge and some of the recent exciting developments in our understanding of the marine world. It will help you to appreciate topical issues, such as the effects of human activity, by looking at real case studies. People study marine science for a variety of reasons: a route into further study through marine science courses at universities; to help develop careers that are linked to the seas such as fishing, aquaculture or tourism; or simply for pure interest in our marine world. Whatever reasons you have for studying marine science, we hope you enjoy learning about this fascinating subject. Now read on and let us get started!

Chapter 1
Scientific method

Learning outcomes

By the end of this chapter, you should be able to:

- describe the steps in the scientific method
- explain how observations and questions are used to formulate a hypothesis
- use the scientific method to design experiments to test a hypothesis
- ensure that experimental results are valid by identifying independent, dependent and control variables
- explain how to make the results of an experiment reliable
- choose appropriate equipment to make accurate measurements and reduce the uncertainty in experimental results.

1.1 The history of the scientific method

The Ancient Greek philosopher Aristotle is believed to be the first person who realised that it is necessary to take measurements in order to increase our knowledge. More than 2000 years have passed since he made this suggestion and scientific enquiry is still based on his idea. The philosophers and scholars who followed him added to his idea and refined it so that we now have a standard way to carry out scientific enquiry. In the Middle Ages a monk named Roger Bacon described a scientific method that he used to investigate nature. He made observations, formulated a **hypothesis** and carried out experiments. This sequence of events in scientific enquiry is probably familiar to most of us today. Galileo has been called the father of modern science and he also contributed to the development of the scientific method. He began to standardise measurements so that experimental results could be checked by other people.

The scientific method requires a logical approach in order to collect measurable results. Measurements are taken in an experiment designed to test a hypothesis. The results will then be used to either support or contradict the hypothesis. Because experimental data are naturally variable there will often be uncertainties in the results. The level of uncertainty can be reduced by ensuring that large numbers of accurate measurements are taken. **Variables** other than the one being investigated should be kept constant or, if this is not possible, measured. If enough evidence is gathered to support a hypothesis, then it may become a **theory**.

In this chapter you will begin to consider the use of the scientific method to formulate and test hypotheses. You will also learn how to plan controlled experiments to collect results to support or **refute** a hypothesis.

KEY TERMS

Hypothesis: an explanation of an observation that can be tested through experimentation

Variable: a condition in an experiment that can be controlled or changed

Theory: a well-substantiated explanation of an aspect of the natural world that has been repeatedly tested and confirmed through observation and experimentation

Refute (a hypothesis): submitting evidence that shows that a hypothesis is not correct

1.2 Steps in the scientific method

There are several steps in the scientific method that should be followed whenever an experiment is planned (Figure 1.1). It is important to remember that the scientific method is a process. Even if a hypothesis is supported, ideas can change in the future if new observations are made.

Observations, questions and hypotheses

The first stage in the process is making observations. For example, you might observe that phytoplankton are found in the upper layers of the ocean. Initial observations are often **qualitative** rather than **quantitative**. This means that they are descriptive rather than having an amount or numerical value. In this case, the position of the phytoplankton is observed and its position in the ecosystem is described. A hypothesis is then formulated to try and explain the observation. A hypothesis is one possible answer to the question 'why?'. Your question might be: Why are the phytoplankton observed in the upper layers of the ocean? So your hypothesis could be that phytoplankton need light to grow. At this stage a **prediction** can also be made. A prediction states what you think will happen in the experiment and is linked to the hypothesis. To continue with the same example, your prediction might be: The more light phytoplankton are given, the more they will grow.

KEY TERMS

Qualitative data: descriptive data about a variable, for example colour or behaviour

Quantitative data: numerical data that give the quantity, amount or range of a variable, for example concentration of oxygen or number of eggs laid

Prediction: a statement of the expected results in an experiment based on the hypothesis being tested

Testing the hypothesis

The next stage is to design an experiment to test your hypothesis. The experiment needs to produce quantitative data that can be evaluated and used to support or refute (disprove) the hypothesis. All experiments involve variables:

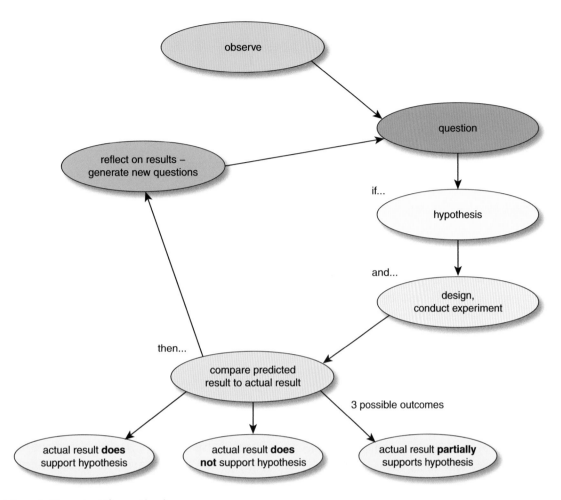

Figure 1.1. Steps in the scientific method.

these are the conditions that can be changed. The **independent variable** is the one that is changed during the experiment and the **dependent variable** is the one that is measured. To test your hypothesis that phytoplankton need light to grow you would need to change the light intensity. You would then measure the growth of the phytoplankton at different light intensities. This could be done by counting samples of the cells under a microscope.

KEY TERMS

Independent variable: the variable being changed in an experiment

Dependent variable: the variable being measured in an experiment

Control group: a group within an experiment or study that receives exactly the same treatment as the experimental groups with the exception of the variable being tested

Control variables: variables that are not being tested but that must be kept the same in case they affect the experiment

A **control group** should normally be included in the experiment. The control group is treated in the same way as the experimental groups apart from the independent variable. This gives you results to use as a comparison. If you are testing the hypothesis that phytoplankton need light to grow, the control group would be phytoplankton that are given no light. To obtain valid results, all variables other than the independent variable must be kept the same. If more than one variable is changed at the same time it would be impossible to say which one caused any changes in the measurements. The variables that are kept the same are the **control variables**. A control variable is any variable that could affect the dependent variable. Important examples to consider when deciding on the control variables are:

- temperature

- carbon dioxide concentration

- oxygen concentration

- pH

- light intensity
- light wavelength.

Obviously these can only be controlled if they are not the independent variable and there may be other controls depending on the experiment being carried out.

It is much more difficult to control the variables in field-based experiments than in laboratory-based experiments. Clearly you cannot control the temperature or amount of light available on a seashore, for example. To help analyse the results, measurements should be taken of any variable that might affect the dependent variable. These are generally the same variables that would be controlled in the laboratory, for example the pH or light intensity. These are measured at the same sampling sites as the dependent variable and recorded. Any trends or patterns in the results can then be related to changes in these measurements as well as to changes in the independent variable. You may also see these variables referred to as **confounding variables**. A confounding variable is something that could affect the results of the experiment but that cannot be controlled.

To make sure that the results are **reliable** each treatment needs to be repeated. You can then calculate mean values for your measurements. It also allows you to identify any **anomalous** results that could affect your conclusions. Anomalous results are individual results that do not fit the pattern of the rest of the data. They may be caused by errors in measurement or difficulties in controlling the variables. It can be difficult to tell whether an anomalous result is due to natural variation within the variable being measured or genuine problems with the data. For this reason repeated readings are important to help to identify any anomalies by comparing them with the other readings taken at the same point in the experiment.

> **KEY TERMS**
>
> **Confounding variable:** a variable that could affect the dependent variable. In laboratory experiments these are the variables that must be controlled. In field experiments they are normally just measured and recorded
>
> **Reliable:** results that can be replicated by other people
>
> **Anomaly:** a result or observation that deviates from what is normal or expected. In experimental results it normally refers to one repeated result that does not fit the pattern of the others

> **SELF-ASSESSMENT QUESTIONS**
>
> 1 Copy and complete Table 1.1 to summarise the different variables in an experiment.
>
> | type of variable | description |
> | --- | --- |
> | independent | |
> | dependent | |
> | control | |
> | confounding | |
>
> Table 1.1. Types of variables.
>
> 2 A student observes that there are more algae growing in a fish tank in summer than in the winter. Suggest a hypothesis to explain this and predict the results of an experiment to investigate it.

Uncertainty in data

It is sometimes difficult to be certain about the results of experiments because the measurements will vary to some extent. If an experiment is reliable, it can be repeated by other people and similar results obtained. This decreases the uncertainty about the results. Controlling all variables apart from the independent variable also reduces uncertainty because you know that only the independent variable could have altered the measurements. Finally, all measurements must be taken as accurately as possible. This means choosing the most appropriate equipment to take the measurements and then reading the results properly. For example, when measuring liquids the **meniscus** is used. The meniscus is the curve in the upper surface of a liquid that is held in a container. A concave meniscus curves downwards and is seen when measuring the volume of water, for example. A convex meniscus curves upwards and is seen in mercury thermometers. In both cases it is the centre of the meniscus that is the point used to take the measurement. The meniscus must also be at eye level so that it can be read accurately (Figure 1.2). The correct equipment to measure a liquid is normally a measuring cylinder and the smallest appropriate size should be chosen. Measuring 8 cm³ in a 10 cm³ cylinder is more likely to be accurate than using a 200 cm³ cylinder because it will be easier to read the correct value from the scale. For volumes of liquid that are less than 10 cm³, a pipette or a syringe would be more accurate.

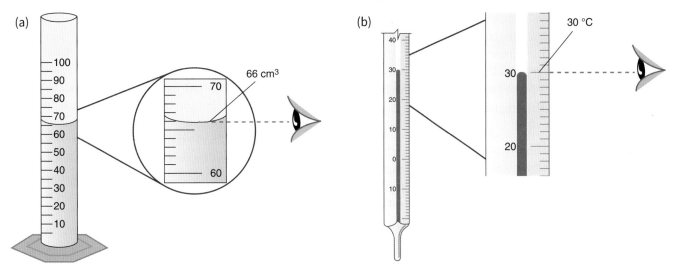

Figure 1.2. Reading the meniscus at eye level (a) in a measuring cylinder and (b) on a thermometer.

KEY TERM

Meniscus: the curve in the upper surface of a liquid inside a container. It is caused by surface tension and can be concave or convex

SELF-ASSESSMENT QUESTIONS

3 Suggest the most appropriate equipment to measure the following accurately.

   a   86 cm³ of water

   b   0.5 cm³ of water

   c   The mass of seaweed found in 1 m²

4 Figure 1.3 shows three measurements of volume being taken.

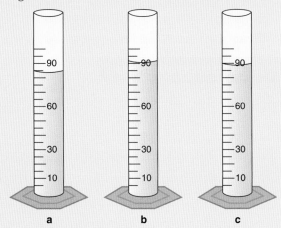

Figure 1.3. Three different measurements of the volume of liquids.

Describe how you would accurately read off the amount of liquid in each cylinder and write down the volume contained in each one.

Analysing the results

During any experiment, the results must be clearly and accurately recorded. The best way to do this is in a results table. This should be drawn before the experiment begins and must have space to fit in all the data to be collected. Normally, the independent variable is placed in the first column of the table. All the columns should have headings that describe the variables and state the units that will be used to measure them (Table 1.2).

light intensity / lux	number of algae present in sample after 2 days		
	trial 1	trial 2	trial 3
0			
2000			
4000			
6000			
8000			
10 000			

Table 1.2. A results table for an experiment investigating the effect of light intensity on the growth of algae.

The first stage in analysing the results is to calculate a mean from each set of repeated measurements. If one repeat is obviously different to the others and does not fit the pattern it may be an anomaly. Anomalies that have been caused by random errors in measurements can be ignored when calculating the mean. Standard deviation can also be calculated, which is a measure of the spread of data around the mean (see the Maths skills box in Chapter 10).

The larger the standard deviation, the larger the range of the data. Percentages, rates and rates of change may also be calculated depending on the experiment (see the Maths skills box in Chapter 3). Often, a graph will be drawn to show the data more clearly and to see whether there is a relationship between the dependent and independent variables (see the Maths skills box in Chapter 4).

Once the data have been analysed a conclusion can be drawn. This should be a statement describing the results and any patterns obtained. The data obtained during the experiment are used to illustrate each point. The trends and patterns in the results should then be explained and linked back to the prediction. In general, the more accurate the measurements taken, and the less variation there is within repeated results, the more valid the conclusions will be.

A good conclusion will come from an experiment with the following features:

- repeated readings are taken
- anomalous results are identified and explained
- sufficient measurements of the dependent variable are made to show a clear pattern
- other variables are controlled and recorded
- the measurements of the variables are made accurately using appropriate equipment.

Evaluation of the hypothesis

If the results match the prediction, they support the hypothesis. If the results do not quite match the prediction, they do not support the hypothesis and it may need to be refined. If the results are completely different to the original prediction, they may be used to refute the hypothesis. This means arguing that the hypothesis is incorrect. You may then need to generate new questions by observing the data and making a new hypothesis that explains all of the data you now have. Alternatively, the original hypothesis may be refined to include the new observations.

5 Explain what an anomalous result is.

6 Describe the relationship between the prediction and the results if those results support a hypothesis.

1.3 Scientific theories

If a hypothesis is consistently supported by the results of many observations and experiments, it may become a scientific theory. Theories are intended to be accurate models of the world that can be used to predict what will happen in different situations. Theories can be modified as new observations and experimental data are collected. Examples of theories that are discussed later in this book are the theory of plate tectonics and the Darwin–Dana–Daly theory of atoll formation. Both of these theories started as hypotheses and only became theories when large amounts of evidence were found to support the original hypothesis.

1.4 Steps in planning valid laboratory-based experiments

Once a hypothesis and prediction have been made, an experimental approach to testing them must be planned. In order to obtain accurate results and to make valid conclusions, you should take the following steps.

1 Decide on the independent variable and the range of values to use.

2 List all the control variables that could affect the experiment and that must therefore be kept the same.

3 Decide how to keep the control variables the same.

4 Decide how many repeats to carry out.

5 Decide the timescale of the experiment.

6 Plan which measurements to take of the dependent variable and which equipment to use to do so accurately.

7 Distinguish between a hypothesis and a theory.

8 Suggest two control variables for each of the following investigations.

  a The effect of temperature on the growth of algae.

  b The effect of pH on the number of zooplankton.

  c The effect of light intensity on the growth of seagrass.

Summary

- The scientific method is a series of steps that are used to investigate scientific phenomena.

- Observations are made first and used to formulate a hypothesis.

- A prediction is made based on the hypothesis.

- An experiment is planned to test the hypothesis by changing the independent variable and measuring the dependent variable.

- All other variables must be controlled in order to obtain valid results.

- There may be uncertainties in the results because of variability in the data and the accuracy of measurements.

- If the results match the prediction, they support the hypothesis.

- If the results do not match the prediction, they refute the hypothesis.

- A hypothesis that is supported by many sets of observations and experimental results may become a theory.

Exam-style questions

1 Design a laboratory-based experiment to test the hypothesis that algae need light to grow. **[6]**

[Total mark: 6]

2 An investigation into the growth of coral at different temperatures was carried out. Samples of coral were grown in the laboratory at different temperatures and the increase in surface area was measured in $cm^2\ week^{-1}$. The results are shown in Table 1.3.

temperature / °C	increase in surface area / $cm^2\ week^{-1}$			mean increase in surface area / $cm^2\ week^{-1}$
	trial 1	trial 2	trial 3	
14	0.3	0.5	0.2	0.33
16	0.6	0.6	0.8	
18	0.8	0.9	1.1	0.93
20	1.4	0.1	1.3	1.35
22	1.6	1.5	1.8	1.63
24	1.7	1.4	1.8	1.63

Table 1.3. Growth of coral at different temperatures.

a i Calculate the missing mean for 16 °C. **[2]**

ii Identify the anomalous result in the table. **[1]**

iii Describe the pattern shown by the results. **[2]**

b The researchers devised the following hypothesis to explain the results: Coral grows faster at higher temperatures.

i Explain whether the results support or refute the hypothesis. **[2]**

ii Give two factors that should have been controlled during the experiment. **[2]**

c Design a laboratory-based experiment to investigate the effect of salinity on the growth of coral. **[6]**

[Total mark: 15]

3 A field-based experiment was carried out that investigated the distribution of two different species of fish in an estuary.

a Suggest three environmental factors that could affect the distribution of fish in an estuary. **[3]**

b These factors cannot be controlled during the experiment. Explain what should be done instead. **[2]**

[Total mark: 5]

Barnacle distribution

A student made the observation that two species of barnacle appeared to be distributed unevenly on a rocky shore. She noticed one species (*Chthamalus stellatus*) living nearer the high water mark than the other (*Semibalanus balanoides*). She decided to investigate her observation using the scientific method and so formulated a hypothesis. Her hypothesis stated that *Chthamalus stellatus* was more able to resist drying out than *Semibalanus balanoides* (Figure 1.4)

Figure 1.4. Barnacles growing on rocks.

She marked out a 50 mm² area just above the low-water mark and counted the number of each species that was present. She then repeated this at 5 m intervals from the low-water mark to the high-water mark at the top of the shore.

Her results are shown in Table 1.4.

distance from low water mark / m	number of *Semibalanus balanoides*	number of *Chthamalus stellatus*
0	12	0
5	9	8
10	11	0
15	6	0
20	0	10

Table 1.4. Distribution of two species of barnacle on the shore.

The student concluded that her results supported her hypothesis. Some of the other students in her class were not sure and argued that there were problems with her results and with her method.

Questions

1 State the independent and dependent variables in this investigation.

2 It is often difficult to control variables when not in the laboratory: suggest a variable that the student could have controlled.

3 Which result do you think is most likely to be anomalous and why?

4 Suggest what might have caused the anomalous result.

5 Suggest how the experiment could be improved.

6 Do you agree with her conclusion?

Chapter 2
Marine ecosystems and biodiversity

Learning outcomes

By the end of this chapter, you should be able to:

- understand and use the key terms ecosystem, community, habitat, ecological niche, succession, biodiversity, population, species, producer, consumer, predator, prey, trophic level, food chain and food web
- describe types of interspecific marine relationship, including mutualism and parasitism
- explain how fluctuations in populations of predator and prey may be linked
- define the key term shoaling and explain its benefits, using examples
- use examples from deep-sea vents and whale-fall ecosystems to describe succession
- understand how the biodiversity of marine environments is affected by how stable and extreme they are, and provide examples
- explain the terms specialised and generalised niches and provide marine examples
- explain the relationship between the breadth of ecological niches and level of biodiversity
- apply what you have learnt to new, unfamiliar contexts.

2.1 An aquatic home

From space, the Earth appears blue because water dominates the surface of our planet. There are five **oceans** on Earth today: the Arctic, Atlantic, Indian, Pacific and Southern. These oceans cover approximately 70% of the globe and their marine ecosystems are crucial for life on Earth. Oceans are where life evolved more than 3.5 billion years ago and they are home to an enormous biodiversity of sea creatures.

The interface between the oceans and the land has also proved crucial to shaping the planet we live on. Competition within life in the oceans, as well as changes in its temperatures and salinity, propelled some marine plants and animals to start colonising the land over 425 million years ago. The **seas** are where the oceans and land meet, producing a variety of coastline habitats (such as sandy, rocky, muddy). Marine biologists have also investigated the estuarine interface, where seas extend inland to meet the mouth of a river. In **estuaries** fresh water and seawater are mixed by the daily and seasonal rhythm of tides. Many marine organisms start their life here before venturing out to spend their adult life in the ocean.

The term ecology is derived from the Greek word 'oikos' meaning 'house'. Marine ecology is the study of marine organisms in their homes or habitats. Marine ecologists study the connections between marine organisms and their environments and aim to understand the factors that control the distribution and abundance of life in the oceans. To do this, it is important to understand the range of relationships between organisms. Ecologists also strive to understand how marine organisms are adapted to their aquatic environment and how both they and humans can alter that environment.

KEY TERMS

Ocean: a continuous mass of seawater on the Earth's surface, its boundaries formed by continental land masses, ridges on the ocean floor or the equator

Sea: a continuous mass of seawater on the Earth's surface, part of the ocean, that is partially enclosed by land, so seas are found where the ocean and land meet

Estuary: a partially enclosed, tidal, coastal body of water where fresh water from a river meets the salt water of the ocean

2.2 Fundamental principles of marine ecology

Ecosystems

Life on Earth can be divided into subunits called **ecosystems**. An ecosystem is all the living organisms in an area plus the non-living environmental factors that act on them.

The **biotic** components of an ecosystem are the living factors, such as producers, consumers and decomposers. Biotic components also include feeding relationships, for example predator–prey relationships, which can be shown as food chains and webs. The **abiotic** components of a marine ecosystem are the environment's geological, physical and chemical features:

- geological features include substrate type, topography and suspended sediment

- physical features include temperature, exposure to wind and sunlight wave action, tides, currents, hydrostatic pressure, light intensity and wavelength

- chemical features include organic nutrients, pH, salinity, oxygen, carbon, nitrogen and phosphorus.

KEY TERMS

Ecosystem: the living organisms and the environment with which they interact

Biotic: the living parts of an ecosystem, which includes the organisms and their effects on each other

Abiotic: the environment's geological, physical and chemical features, the non-living part of an ecosystem

Habitat: the natural environment where an organism lives

Habitat

A **habitat** is the natural environment where organisms live. Habitats are areas in which organisms can find food, protection, shelter and a mate. Marine environments form a range of habitats in estuaries, on the shoreline and in shallow and deep ocean water. Estuaries are brackish areas where fresh and salt water mix. Sediments from streams often settle in estuaries, creating a number of important habitats where marine species can feed and breed. These habitats include swampy areas called wetlands, mangrove forests and salt marshes.

The habitat an organism occupies can be defined by where it lives and how it moves. For example:

- planktonic organisms, such as phytoplankton and zooplankton, drift in ocean currents

- nektonic organisms, such as fish, marine reptiles and mammals, can actively swim

- benthic organisms, such as tube worms, starfish, crabs and sea cucumbers, live on the seabed.

Some organisms cross from one habitat to another during their life cycles. For example, crabs and clams both start out as planktonic larvae but become benthic adults.

Habitats are not always geographical; for example, parasitic worms live inside their host species.

Species

A **species** is defined as a group of similar organisms that can interbreed naturally to produce fertile offspring. Each species is given a name composed of two parts, both of which are in Latin. This naming system is called the binomial system of nomenclature. It was first formulated in 1736 by Carolus Linnaeus, a Swedish botanist. The first part of the name refers to the genus, and the second part refers to the species. The genus is given a capital letter, whereas the species is always lower case. In print, a binomial always appears in italic. For example, the Latin binomial name for the Galapagos penguin is *Spheniscus mendiculus*. When you write a binomial name by hand, you should underline it, for example <u>Spheniscus mendiculus</u>.

KEY TERMS

Species: a group of similar organisms that can interbreed naturally to produce fertile offspring

Population: all the individuals of the same species that live at the same place and time

Population

A **population** is all the organisms of the same species that live at the same place at the same time, and are able to reproduce. For example, the squat lobsters living off Otago, New Zealand, are a population. Similarly, all the salmon in the Atlantic Ocean make up the Atlantic salmon population.

The number of individuals in any population often increases and decreases. Population increases are caused by reproduction or by new individuals joining the population area. Population decreases are caused by death or by individuals leaving the population area.

The largest population that can be sustained by the available resources is called the carrying capacity. If some resources are less than optimal, or get completely used up, they are called limiting factors and result in reduced growth in the population. Limiting factors can be either biotic or abiotic. Biotic limiting factors include competition and predation. Abiotic limiting factors affect growth, survival and reproduction, and include living space, food, water temperature, pH and light intensity.

Community

A **community** is an association of all the different populations of species occupying a habitat at the same time. An example is the mollusc community on a Californian rocky shore, which would include all the different species of molluscs living in this habitat. Biomes are communities that extend over large areas of the globe and are classified according to the predominant vegetation. Marine biomes include intertidal, rocky, sandy and muddy shores, coral reefs and the seabed. Each biome has a characteristic community.

Biodiversity

Biodiversity describes the enormous variation in organisms living on the Earth. Life on Earth evolved in the marine environment, the seas and oceans, which have an extremely high biodiversity.

KEY TERMS

Community: all the different populations occupying a habitat at the same time

Biodiversity: a measure of the numbers of different species present

Ecological niche: the role of a species within an ecosystem

Ecological niche

Ecological niche is defined as the role of a species within an ecosystem. The term also takes into account interrelationships with other organisms.

- Feeding relationships: for example, both sperm whales and killer whales are top predators. Sperm whales consume predominantly squid, whereas killer whales consume a wider variety of prey, including elephant seals and baleen whales. These two species of whale therefore occupy different ecological niches.

11

- Spatial relationships: two species may have the same feeding relationships but occupy that niche in different parts of the ocean. For example, if a prey species is found throughout the water column, one predator may feed on it in the surface photic zone (where there is light) while another feeds deeper down in the aphotic zone (where there is no light).

- Temporal relationships: two species may have the same feeding relationships but occupy the niche at different times, for example if a prey species is found in the same location throughout each day, one predator may feed at night (nocturnal) while another feeds in the daytime (diurnal).

2.3 Symbiosis within marine ecosystems

Symbiosis literally means 'living together'. The term refers to an interspecies relationship between two or more organisms from different species living in close physical association. The smaller partner in the symbiosis is called the symbiont and the larger one is called the host.

There are many forms of symbiosis including:

- **mutualism**, when both species benefit from the relationship

- **parasitism**, when one organism (the parasite) benefits at the expense of the host.

Other types of interspecies relationship include:

- **competition**, when both species are negatively affected by trying to fill the same ecological niche

- **predation**, feeding that involves hunting, killing and eating another animal.

KEY TERMS

Mutualism: a relationship between two different organisms where both organisms benefit

Parasitism: a relationship between two organisms where the parasite obtains benefit at the expense of the host

Competition: a relationship between two organisms where both species are negatively affected by trying to fill the same ecological niche

Predation: a relationship between two organisms where a predator hunts, kills and eats a prey animal.

Marine mutualism

Examples of marine mutualism include:

- coral and zooxanthellae

- chemosynthetic bacteria and tube worms

- cleaner fish and shrimps and their hosts.

Coral and zooxanthellae

The tissues of corals are host to symbiotic single-celled algae called zooxanthellae (see Chapter 5).

Zooxanthellae photosynthesise and provide the coral with nutrients such as oxygen and glucose:

zooxanthellae photosynthesis:
carbon dioxide + water → glucose + oxygen

As the coral grows, it respires aerobically and provides the zooxanthellae with the carbon dioxide required for photosynthesis:

coral polyps aerobic respiration:
glucose + oxygen → carbon dioxide + water

The zooxanthellae are provided with a safe habitat with a large surface area for maximum absorption of light. They also obtain other minerals from the coral's waste products: nitrogenous compounds are used to make proteins, ATP and DNA, and phosphates are used for DNA, ATP and membranes.

Chemosynthetic bacteria and tube worms

Tube worms (for example *Riftia* and *Tevnia* species) are associated with deep-sea vents (see Chapter 3). They live in the 'midnight' or aphotic zone where there is no light. Because there is no light, photosynthesis is not possible so photoautotrophic producers cannot survive in this zone. Tube worms have followed a very different evolutionary pathway compared with photoautotrophic producers. They host colonies of chemosynthetic bacteria that produce organic matter from the chemicals available at deep-sea vents. These symbiotic chemosynthetic bacteria live in an organ inside the tube worm called the trophosome. The plume at the tip of a tube worm takes in hydrogen sulfide, carbon dioxide and oxygen. Carbon dioxide and hydrogen sulfide are carried in the blood of the tube worm to the chemosynthetic bacteria in the trophosome (Figure 2.1).

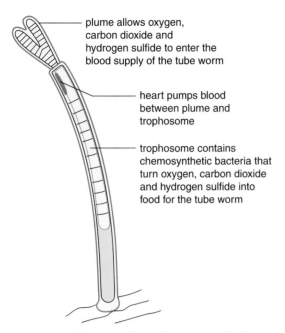

plume allows oxygen, carbon dioxide and hydrogen sulfide to enter the blood supply of the tube worm

heart pumps blood between plume and trophosome

trophosome contains chemosynthetic bacteria that turn oxygen, carbon dioxide and hydrogen sulfide into food for the tube worm

Figure 2.1. Chemosynthetic bacteria and tube worm mutualism.

In this way the chemosynthetic bacteria gain a safe environment and nutrients while the tube worms use the organic matter for cellular respiration to create the ATP energy they require to grow. The tube worms form part of the food chain for other organisms colonising the vent, such as polychaete worms, octopuses, giant clams, mussels, limpets, crabs and vent fish. Eventually, a complex community consisting of many different species is established.

Cleaner fish, shrimps and grouper

Cleaning stations are often located on the top of a coral head. Reef fish, sea turtles and sharks congregate to have parasites removed by numerous species of cleaner fish (especially wrasses and gobies) and cleaner shrimps. When the host animal approaches a cleaning station, it opens its mouth wide as a signal to the cleaner species. The cleaner species then remove and eat the parasites from the host's skin, mouth and gills. The cleaners benefit by gaining nutrients from the dead skin and parasites that they remove. They also gain protection from predators while they are cleaning. The host fish benefit from reduced infection.

Other examples of cleaning mutualism include:

- pilot fish cleaning sharks
- Pacific cleaner shrimps and bluesteak cleaner wrasses cleaning eels.

Marine parasitism

Parasitism is a relationship in which the parasites obtain benefit at the expense of the host.

Finding the next host is paramount for a parasite, and a large portion of a parasite's energy is used for reproduction. Parasites can be divided into two main groups: ectoparasites and endoparasites.

Ectoparasites

Ecotoparasites live on the outside of their host. The salmon louse is a species of copepod that is an ectoparasite on Pacific salmon (Figure 2.2). The lice attach to the skin, fins and gills of juvenile and adult salmon, and feed off the mucus or skin. The parasite can be fatal to juvenile salmon. For adult salmon, the lice can carry diseases between wild and farmed salmon (for example infectious salmon anemia, which can lead to the collapse of fish farms).

Other ectoparasitic copepods feed on the body fluids of flying fish and spread disease. Others attach to the eyes of Greenland sharks and cause inflammation, which reduces the shark's vision and its ability to survive and reproduce.

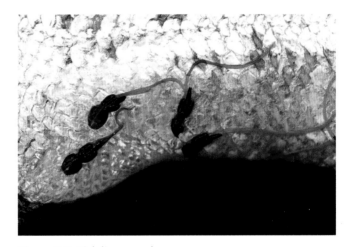

Figure 2.2. Fish lice on salmon.

Endoparasites

Endoparasites live inside their host, for example in the digestive system, attached to gills or in muscle tissue. They are considered to be parasites because they may weaken the host individual. Nematodes or roundworms are common endoparasites in tuna (Figure 2.3).

Another example of an endoparasite is the small tapeworm that derives food and shelter by living in the guts of whales.

13

Figure 2.3. Endoparasites living on the gills of a tuna.

2.4 Feeding relationships

Producers

Producers provide food for virtually all other organisms in food chains and food webs. As autotrophs, they are 'self-feeders' and synthesise organic 'food' from simple inorganic compounds and an energy source. There are two types of producer:

- **photoautotrophs**, which use light energy
- **chemoautotrophs**, which use chemical energy.

> ### 🔑 KEY TERMS
>
> **Producer:** an organism that can produce its own food energy
>
> **Photoautotroph:** a producer that uses light energy to produce its own food energy
>
> **Chemoautotroph:** a producer that uses chemical energy to produce its own food energy

Photoautotrophs

Photoautotrophs use pigments (for example chlorophyll) to trap light energy from the Sun, in the light-dependent stage of photosynthesis. Marine photoautotrophs include seagrass, mangroves, seaweed, kelp, cyanobacteria and phytoplankton. Phytoplankton include diatoms and dinoflagellates and are essential to life on Earth because they produce half of the world's oxygen and are a major sink for carbon dioxide. Diatoms are single-celled organisms with a silicon shell. Dinoflagellates can form enormous ocean blooms or red tides that are sometimes visible from space.

Chemoautotrophs

Chemoautotrophs use energy from the oxidation of sulfur in hydrogen sulfide to make their own food energy. Aerobic chemoautotrophs (such as mutualistic bacteria that live in tube worms) need oxygen, whereas anaerobic chemoautotrophs (such as bacteria that live in deep-sea vent sediment) do not need oxygen. Chemoautotroph producers will be covered in greater details in Chapters 3 and 6.

aerobic chemosynthesis $CO_2 + H_2O + H_2S \rightarrow (CH_2O) + H_2SO_4$

anaerobic chemosynthesis $CO_2 + 6H_2 \rightarrow (CH_2O) + CH_4 + H_2O$

> ### SELF-ASSESSMENT QUESTIONS
>
> 1 Using the following symbols, complete Table 2.1 showing different interspecies relationships.
>   - 0, species is unaffected
>   - −, species is harmed
>   - +, species benefits
>
> | | host | symbiont |
> |---|---|---|
> | mutualism | | |
> | parasitism | | |
> | competition | | |
> | predation | | |
>
> Table 2.1. Different interspecies relationships.
>
> 2 Name and explain the main similarity and difference between the two ways that producers can synthesise food energy.
>
> 3 Concentrations of phytoplankton are lower in Antarctica's Southern Ocean than oceans closer to the equator. How might the abiotic conditions of the Southern Ocean inhibit photosynthesis?

Consumers

The term **consumer** refers to an organism that obtains its energy requirements by feeding on other organisms. The rate at which consumers convert the chemical energy of their food into their own biomass is called secondary productivity.

Consumers include:

- predators (for example sharks) that kill and eat prey animals (for example fish)
- herbivores that eat plants (for example manatees)

- suspension feeders that filter the water for food (for example mussels)
- grazers that scrape algae (for example limpets, sea urchins and parrot fish).

Zooplankton are important consumers and include copepods, foraminifera and krill. Copepods are small herbivores that feed on diatoms. Foraminifera are single-celled animals with calcium carbonate shells. Krill are shrimp-like carnivores that feed on other zooplankton species and phytoplankton. Krill are important food sources for birds, fish, seals and baleen whales.

KEY TERMS

Consumer: an animal that feeds on other organisms to gain its food energy

Food chain: a way of describing the feeding relationships between organisms

Food web: a way of describing how food chains are interrelated in an ecosystem

Trophic level: a position in a food chain or food web

2.5 Food chains and food webs

A **food chain** shows the linear sequence of organisms feeding on other organisms. A series of interlinked food chains forms a multi-branched **food web**. In food chains and food webs, arrows represent the direction in which energy, biomass and nutrients are transferred. The term **trophic level** refers to the 'feeding level' in a food chain or web. Producers occupy the first trophic level, primary consumers occupy the second trophic level, secondary consumers occupy the third trophic level, and so on.

producer → primary consumer → secondary consumer → tertiary consumer → quaternary consumer

1st trophic level → 2nd trophic level → 3rd trophic level → 4th trophic level → 5th trophic level

Primary (first level) consumers are also known as herbivores. Secondary (second level) consumers are carnivores that feed on herbivores. Tertiary (third level) or quaternary (fourth level) consumers are carnivores that feed on carnivores. If carnivores are at the end of a food chain, they are called top predators. Organisms can be grouped into different consumer types depending on the specific food chain being discussed. For example, an omnivore feeds on plants (making it a primary consumer) and other consumers (making it a secondary consumer).

Detritivores (for example worms, fish, crabs, starfish and urchins) eat detritus (dead and decaying material). This makes it easier for decomposers (for example bacteria and fungi) to convert the organic molecules in detritus back to inorganic nutrients. Detritivores and decomposers both gain their energy from recycling the nutrients and energy in detritus (see Chapter 4).

Food webs illustrate how species feed on a number of other species so that they are not dependent on one food source. As a result, if the population of one prey species declines, alternative sources of food are still available. Food webs can also be used to illustrate the different feeding relationships that one species might have at different stages of its life cycle. For example, herring change the prey they feed on as they develop from young fish into mature adults.

Predators and their prey

Predator–prey relationships are an integral part of the niche of a consumer. A **predator** is an animal that catches, kills and eats another animal. Predators are secondary, tertiary and quaternary consumers in food chains. Marine predators include sharks as well as carnivorous fish that eat plankton (planktivores) or fish (piscivores). Predators have adaptations such as speed, agility, camouflage, teeth, poison and the ability to hunt in packs.

Prey are animals that are eaten by predators. Survival adaptations for prey animals include camouflage, defensive spines, the ability to hide in safe places and the ability to flee.

Some predator–prey relationships are an example of coevolution, where the predator and prey species have evolved together in response to changes in each other's morphology and physiology.

Predator–prey relationships are crucial for keeping a healthy balance of populations within the ecosystem. For example, without starfish (Figure 2.4a) there would be no natural predators to control the numbers of mussels, sea urchins and **shellfish**. Left unchecked, these organisms can destroy a kelp forest. Similarly, butterfly fish (Figure 2.4b)

KEY TERMS

Predator: an animal that kills and eats animals for food

Prey: an animal that is eaten by predators

Shellfish: aquatic invertebrates that are used as food, including shelled molluscs, crustaceans and echinoderms, such as bivalves, crabs, lobsters and sea urchins are herbivores that prey on marine algae growing on coral reefs. Without this crucial predator–prey relationship, the algae would overgrow the coral and limit the light reaching the zooxanthellae. This would eventually kill the coral.

Figure 2.4. (a) Starfish; (b) butterfly fish.

Population changes in predator–prey relationships

The predator population is usually smaller than its prey population. This is because individual predators often have a larger biomass than individual prey, and there is a significant loss in energy between trophic levels.

The availability of food is a major limiting factor that affects the location and numbers of predators in an ecosystem. The

spatial distribution of predators is often linked to their prey. For example, predators such as swordfish, sharks and gannets follow their sardine prey along their annual migration route. But predator and prey locations are not always linked. For example, a predator may have many alternative prey species and not closely follow prey that is a minor source of food energy.

Organisms in an ecosystem are interdependent, so when one species changes in population size, other species in the community may also be affected. When the availability of food (the number of prey organisms) increases, the number of predators also increases. This is because when predators have more food energy available, they have an increased chance of surviving and reproducing. The opposite is also true: when the number of prey decreases, the number of predators also decreases.

For example, if a fish population increases because it finds a new food source, the predator shark population also increases because the sharks have more food. If the fish population decreases because of over-fishing, the population of sharks also reduces because the sharks have less food. Conversely, if the shark population decreases as a result of sickness, the fish population would experience less predation and increase.

Lionfish

The numbers of prey and predators in interrelated populations fluctuate through time, with the number of predators lagging behind the number of prey. An example of this interrelationship can be seen between the predatory lionfish and the native Atlantic Ocean fish species that they prey on. An increase in the population of predatory lionfish causes a reduction in native fish stocks. When the fish stocks are too low to sustain the increased lionfish population, lionfish numbers begin to decrease. The drop in predatory lionfish therefore 'lags behind' the drop in numbers of its prey. A reduction in the lionfish population results in less predation of the Atlantic fish, and the fish population begins to recover. After a time lag, the rising prey population results in an increase in the predatory lionfish population. These oscillations in the predator–prey cycle continue with decreasing amplitude until a more stable ratio of predators to prey is reached (Figure 2.5).

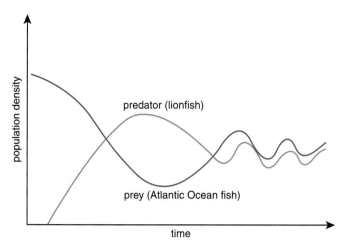

Figure 2.5. Predator–prey relationship for lionfish and Atlantic Ocean fish.

Crown-of-thorns starfish

The crown-of-thorns starfish predates corals on the Great Barrier Reef. The numbers of predators (starfish) and prey (corals) have fluctuated over a 25-year period (Figure 2.6). Between years 4 and 16, the coral population (measured by percentage cover) decreased from 52% to 6%. This led to a reduction in the relative number of starfish from 16 to 3. The drop in starfish numbers did not start until year 10: there was a time lag of 6 years between the drop in coral prey and the drop in starfish predators. The time lag resulted in a maximum number of predators as the prey population was in decline. The coral recovered between years 16 and 25 because the relative numbers of starfish were low. From 21 years, as the coral cover increased, the relative number of starfish also began to increase. Again there was a time lag between the increase in coral cover and the increase in relative number of starfish.

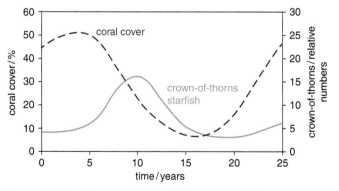

Figure 2.6. Predator–prey graph for crown-of-thorns starfish and coral cover.

KEY TERM

Keystone species: a consumer that affects biodiversity to a greater extent than would be expected from its population numbers

Keystone species

Keystone species are consumers that affect biodiversity to a greater extent than would be expected from their population numbers. Keystone species are likely to occur near the top of the food chain, although they are not necessarily the top predator. Keystone species control other species by means of predation and competition. They may also be capable of ecosystem engineering by physically modifying the habitat. Keystone species are important in conservation programmes that focus resources on maintaining such species, rather than attempting to protect and manage all endangered species in a habitat that is at risk.

Starfish are an example of a keystone species in coral reef communities. Starfish (for example *Pisaster ochraceus*) are not top predators, because they are prey for sharks, rays and sea anemones. Starfish themselves feed on a range of species, including sea urchins and mussels. If starfish are removed, mussel and sea urchin populations increase dramatically, because those species have no other natural predators. An explosion in the mussel population would drive out other molluscs (for example limpets, chitons and barnacles) by outcompeting them for the limited space available on reefs (competitive exclusion). An increased sea urchin population would feed unhindered on the coral and lead to a decrease in coral biomass. Starfish thus promote biodiversity by controlling mussel and sea urchin populations. They are key to the delicate interrelationship between other organisms within the coral reef community. Without starfish, the ecosystem biodiversity would be significantly reduced.

SELF-ASSESSMENT QUESTIONS

4 Over-fishing of cod in seas off Maine, USA, led to a population explosion of one of its prey, sea urchins. The rapid increase in sea urchin numbers nearly wiped out kelp forests in the area, the habitat for lobsters. Predict and explain what would consequently happen to the lobster population.

5 Sea urchins are considered a delicacy in many parts of the world (for example Japan and New Zealand). How could fisherman in Maine have responded to the change in populations in question 4?

17

PRACTICAL ACTIVITY 2.1

Intertidal zonation studies

Introduction

The intertidal (littoral) part of a rocky shore has distinct zones (for example low tide, mid-tide, high tide and splash zones) where specific groups of organisms are found. The species commonly found in each zone are those that are best adapted to the abiotic and biotic conditions of that zone. Field work using a quadrat and transect line can be performed to investigate these zonation patterns. By collecting quantitative and qualitative data about the relative abundance of species between high- and low-tide marks, you can determine which organisms are found in each zone of a rocky shore (Figure 2.7). This method can also be used to study sandy and muddy shores.

Equipment

- Tape measure, 30 m
- Quadrats or other sampling equipment
- Species identification chart
- Recording sheets (in a waterproof folder)

Figure 2.7. Students taking a rocky shore transect of Buckleton's Beach, New Zealand.

Method

- Look at local tide charts and time the field trip for 1 h either side of low tide.
- Lay out a tape measure to mark your transect route. The transect should be perpendicular to the water's edge, from high tide to low tide.

- Use a quadrat to sample the rocky shore organisms. Typically, a quadrat is a square 30–50 cm in length with a marked grid of ten squares by ten squares.
- Use a species identification chart to identify common organisms on your rocky shore. Choose four species to collect data for.
- Choose the number of sampling points, for example if you are doing a 20 m transect line, you may decide to take 11 quadrat samples, i.e. one for every 2 m, starting at high tide (0 m).
- There are a number of ways to record your data. For each species you must use the same method for all the transect lines sampled. To be able to calculate averages, it is important to repeat the transect three to five times at different points along the rocky shore.
- For large fauna (for example chitons) the simplest method is to count the total number of organisms in your quadrat. Alternatively, if numbers are large (for example periwinkles or barnacles), then an estimate can be made by counting the number in a quarter of the quadrat and multiplying this value by 4.
- For plant species (for example seaweed) vegetation percentage cover can be estimated using the 10 × 10 quadrat grid. Alternatively, abundance can be recorded using the ACFOR scale:

  A = ABUNDANT (greater than / equal to 30%)

  C = COMMON (20–29%)

  F = FREQUENT (10–19%)

  O = OCCASIONAL (5–9%)

  R = RARE (1–4%)

- Abiotic data (for example temperature, pH or salinity) may also be recorded along the transect line. You may wish to use a data logger probe for this.
- On your record sheet there should be a column for any features that may affect the abundance of species (for example if the quadrat is in or near a rock pool or crevice).
- You may wish to record the height of each quadrat above low tide. These data can then be used to plot the profile of the rocky shore.
- A sketch map of the rocky shore should also be drawn showing the position of your transect lines. This may be useful when comparing zonation patterns with different coastal characteristics (for example more exposed versus less exposed to wave action).

Conclusions

- Use of percentage cover estimates and the ACFOR scale for vegetation coverage is a qualitative measure and hence more subjective than quantitative data.
- Kite diagrams (Figure 2.8) can be used to show the zonation patterns graphically.
- Secondary data, for example records from previous years' field trips, can be used to investigate whether there are any zonation changes over time or whether zonation patterns are dependent on the time of year.

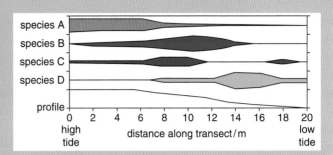

Figure 2.8. A kite graph representing zonation patterns on a rocky shore. Biotic data are shown as kites and abiotic data as lines. Y axis is relative and will vary for each species. For example plants may be measured in percentage of cover, while animals may be measured in number.

Maths skills

Mean, median, mode and range

The mean is the average of your data. To find the mean, add up all the data values (Σx) and then divide by the number of data entries (n).

The median is the middle value in the list of data values. To find the median, list your data in numerical order from lowest to highest. Identify the middle value: this is the median.

The mode is the data value that occurs most often. If no data value is repeated, there is no mode for the sample. There can be more than one mode.

The range is the difference between the largest and smallest data values.

Worked example

A student recorded the following data for the number of periwinkles found on a rocky shore transect.

quadrat	number of periwinkles
1	17
2	92
3	116
4	54
5	11
6	3
7	0
8	0
9	0

Table 2.2. Periwinkle numbers.

To work out the mean number of periwinkles recorded:

$\Sigma x = 17 + 92 + 116 + 54 + 11 + 3 + 0 + 0 + 0 = 293$

Mean = $\Sigma x / n = 293 / 9 = 33$ (0 decimal places)

The median is the middle value, so you have to rewrite the list in order from lowest to highest:

0, 0, 0, 3, 11, 17, 54, 92, 116

There are nine data values in the list, so the middle one will be the fifth data value. The median is therefore 11.

The mode is the number that is repeated more often than any other. The mode for this data set is 0 because it is repeated three times.

The largest data value in the list is 116, and the smallest is 0, so the range is 116−0 = 116

Questions

1 Trophic level transfer efficiency (TLTE) measures the amount of energy that is transferred between trophic levels. TLTE is calculated by:

TLTE = energy trophic level^{n+1}/ energy trophic level^{n} × 100

trophic level^{n+1} is the trophic level above trophic level^{n}

Figure 2.9 shows a pyramid of energy for a marine ecosystem (in arbitrary units).

Calculate the TLTE for:

a phytoplankton – zooplankton

b zooplankton – herring

c mackerel – tuna

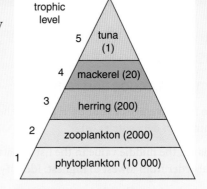

Figure 2.9. Pyramid of energy for a marine ecosystem (in arbitrary units).

2 Calculate, to the nearest whole number, the mean, median, mode and range for the list of TLTE values given in Table 2.3.

energy trophic level^{n}	energy trophic level^{n+1}	TLTE / %
seal	polar bear	4
krill	blue whale	4
squid	Weddell seal	4
arctic cod	Weddell seal	4
copepod	arctic cod	8
krill	arctic cod	10
krill	squid	10
arctic cod	squid	10
diatom	krill	12
krill	copepods	15
diatom	copepod	20

Table 2.3. TLTE values.

Shoaling

If fish come together in an interactive, social way, they are said to be **shoaling**. The fish adjust their behaviour to remain close to the other fish in the group. Shoaling fish can be of one species (a school) or include fish of different sizes and of mixed species. Fish in a shoal function in a coordinated way even though they appear to have no leader. The individual fish tend to keep a constant distance between each other, turning, stopping and starting in near perfect unison. The shape of a shoal depends on the type of fish and what the fish are doing. Fast-moving shoals usually form a wedge shape, while shoals that are feeding tend to become circular. Shoals that are travelling can form long thin lines, squares or ovals. For example, mullet can form 'chains' of shoals 100 km long.

> **KEY TERM**
>
> **Shoaling:** when fish swim together in a group

Why fish shoal

The formation of a shoal has a number of advantages to the fish.

- Small fish (for example sardines, herrings, anchovies and menhaden) are preyed on by larger predators (for example tuna, sharks, dolphins, sea birds, seals and whales). The small fish compensate for their size by forming shoals as a defence against predators. These shoals can become huge when migrating across open oceans. The synchronised movement of large shoals of fish may confuse a predator: the shoal may split into several groups or surround the predator. This makes it difficult for the predator to concentrate on just one fish. Some shoals form 'bait balls' to protect themselves from predators. The fish at the centre are relatively protected whereas those on the outside are more vulnerable. Tightly shoaling fish usually have silvery sides (like anchovies) and may swim to produce a wave-like effect on the outside of the shoal to confuse predators further.

- With so many eyes, it is more likely that a predator will be seen. Fear chemicals are then secreted that help alert other individuals in the shoal when an attack is imminent.

- With large numbers of fish, there are many eyes to search for food, so the time taken to find food is decreased. Fish in shoals share information by closely monitoring each other's behaviour. The feeding behaviours of one fish quickly stimulate food-searching behaviour in other members of the shoal.

- Shoaling also leads to a reproductive advantage. The close proximity of males and females increases the chance of finding a mate or fertilising externally released eggs.

- During migrations, swimming efficiency is improved because most of the fish can take advantage of the slipstream produced by the fish in front. This reduces the water resistance (drag) for the fish swimming behind so the shoal can swim faster and save energy.

There are also disadvantages of shoaling.

- Some predators are more efficient at attacking shoals than individual fish.

- The large numbers of fish swimming close together cause excretory waste to build up, while oxygen and food supplies are depleted.

However, there must be a net survival advantage to shoaling otherwise this behaviour would not have been evolutionarily successful. The energy saved by shoaling can be used to increase an individual's potential to survive, reproduce and pass on its gene alleles to the next generation.

Examples of shoaling

- **Sardines** are small, oily fish related to herrings. Sardines are a shoaling forage fish that form 'bait balls' (Figure 2.10) to minimise their chance of being taken by predators. Individual sardines are more likely to be eaten than a large group swimming together.

- **Herring** are forage fish whose small shoals aggregate together into much larger shoals during migration. In the North Atlantic, up to 3 billion fish can be in one shoal. Herring shoals have precise arrangements that allow them to maintain a constant speed. Herring shoals react rapidly to predators because they have excellent hearing.

- **Skipjack tuna** are predatory shoalers that swim in large groups of up to 50 000 individuals when migrating to find food. Simultaneous attack by large numbers of tuna helps break up the sardine 'bait balls' that they prey on. Skipjack tuna sometimes shoal with other tuna species or other fish of similar size. Shoaling improves the tuna's chance of finding prey because there are more individuals to sense the prey.

21

Figure 2.10 A 'bait ball' of bluelined snapper.

2.6 Succession

The term **succession** refers to the gradual process of change that occurs in community structure over a period of time. This temporal change in the composition of species in a particular area is predictable and can be measured by ecologists. There are three stages in succession (Figure 2.11).

- Colonising stage: the first community of organisms to colonise a new habitat appears (a pioneer community).

- Successionist stage(s): stage(s) in which the biodiversity or species richness in a community increases during succession. Communities move through several different successionist stages. A seral stage is a stage when a new species successfully establishes within the community. The halosere is the entire range of communities that succeed one another at a salt-water site.

- Climax stage: a complex community of many species is finally formed. Over time, producers, consumers and decomposers change. Gradually, the community changes less and less frequently until the structure and species composition become stable. This is the climax community.

Types of succession

There are two types of succession: primary succession and secondary succession.

Primary succession occurs in newly formed habitats where there has never been a community before. The new habitat is a bare substrate with no life present. These new habitats can be natural, for example new islands formed as a result of underwater volcanic eruptions. Alternatively, the new habitats can be unnatural, as a result of human activity, for example the structure of a deep-sea oil rig.

Secondary succession occurs on sites that have previously supported a community that is now no longer there, for example because of habitat destruction caused by a cyclone or tsunami.

KEY TERM

Succession: the change in community structure over time

Coral reefs

Both primary and secondary succession occur on coral reefs. Primary succession occurs as a volcano erupts and

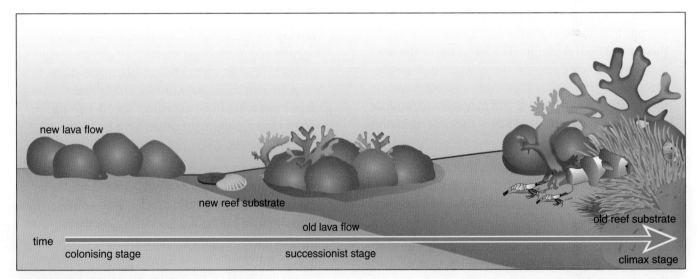

new lava flow

new reef substrate

old lava flow

old reef substrate

time

colonising stage   successionist stage   climax stage

Figure 2.11. Primary succession in a coral reef.

lava creates a new habitat with no plant life (Figure 2.11). Coral is the first to colonise and grow on the lava flow, so is a pioneer species. Coral reefs also undergo secondary succession, for example after an area of the reef has been removed by deep-sea trawlers.

Hydrothermal vents

A hydrothermal vent is a gap in the Earth's surface that releases geothermally heated water.

Succession occurs around hydrothermal vents in deep oceans. Hot water forced from hydrothermal vents brings up nutrients from the rocks beneath the seabed. The first organisms to grow near the vent fluid are chemosynthetic archaebacteria. Tube worms (*Tevnia* species) are early pioneer species that inhabit a hydrothermal vent, forming symbiotic relationships with the archaebacteria. *Tevnia* is later replaced by the much larger (up to 2 m long) and faster-growing *Riftia* tube worms. The nutrients produced by the tube worms allow other organisms to colonise the

vent (for example polychaete worms, octopuses, clams, limpets, crabs, mussels, hagfish and vent fish). Eventually, a complex climax community consisting of many different species is established (Figure 2.12).

Whale fall

A whale-fall community is formed when a whale dies and sinks to the ocean floor (Figure 2.13). The pioneer species of this community are detritivores, such as sharks, hagfish and amphipods. They eat the decaying flesh of the carcass. Within a year, most of the whale's flesh will have been removed. Crabs, small fish, snails and worms then eat the organic leftovers in the sediment. When only the skeleton remains, heterotrophic bacteria decompose the oils in the whale bones. The decomposition of the whale's body enriches the surrounding sediments with nutrients. Decomposition also releases compounds that serve as energy sources for chemosynthetic archaebacteria. Mussels, clams, snails, crabs and worms feed on these bacteria.

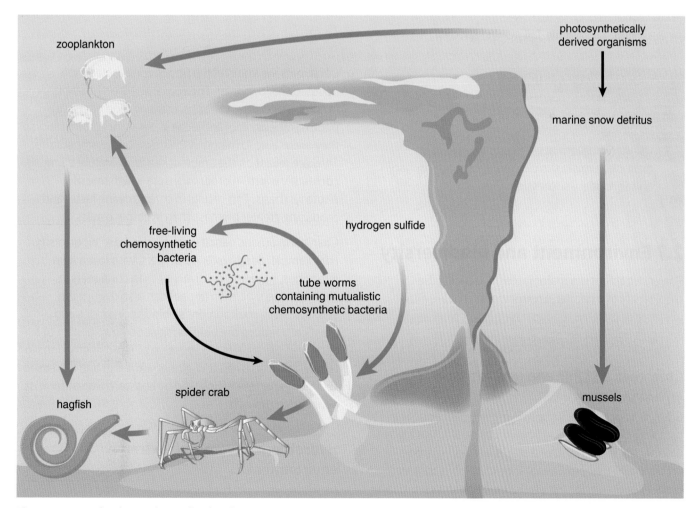

Figure 2.12. Hydrothermal vent food web.

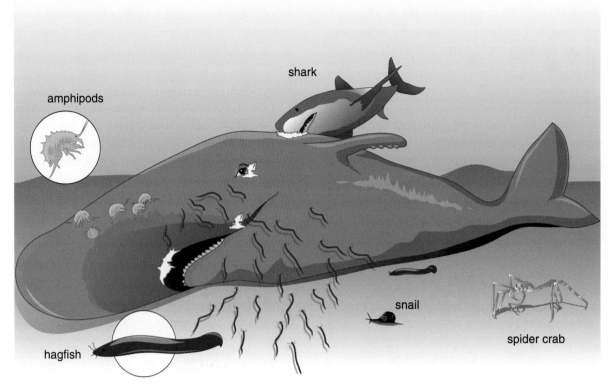

Figure 2.13. Whale-fall pioneer species.

6 Compare and contrast succession at hydrothermal vents and whale falls.

7 Using hydrothermal vent communities as an example, explain the difference between primary and secondary succession.

2.7 Environment and biodiversity

The environment is a major factor influencing the biodiversity of a habitat. Environments that are either unstable or extreme tend to have a lower biodiversity than environments that are stable and not extreme.

Coral reef: a stable and non-extreme environment

Coral reefs occupy less than 1% of the ocean floor, but contain more than 25% of known marine life. This high biodiversity is the result of a stable and non-extreme environment that provides abiotic conditions that are close to optimum for the producers. A vibrant community of producers provides the foundation for long food chains and a diverse food web.

Coral reefs are found in the photic zone in clear non-polluted shallow water. The zooxanthellae symbionts in coral are photoautotrophs, creating food energy by photosynthesis. Zooxanthellae in coral are ectothermic, so they are unable to maintain their own body temperature. They are reliant on the ambient sea temperature being constantly warm, in order to ensure a high rate of photosynthesis. This results in coral growing faster and producing greater biomass than in colder waters.

Changes in abiotic conditions can decrease biodiversity. For example, deep-water coral reefs, with lower light intensities, have less biodiversity than coral reefs in shallow waters. Human impact can also disrupt the stability of the environment's abiotic conditions and drastically reduce the biodiversity and functionality of a coral reef. Coral reefs are sensitive to rapid fluctuations in temperature (as a result of global warming) and increased sediment and toxicity (caused by coastal deforestation or agricultural run-off).

Hydrothermal vents: an extreme environment

Hydrothermal vent communities are located in an environment that is extreme because the abiotic conditions, including toxins, temperature, pH, hydrostatic pressure and light, are outside the zone of tolerance for most organisms.

The hot water from a hydrothermal vent contains dissolved minerals from the Earth's crust below the vent. As the hot vent water meets the cold oceanic water, it rapidly cools, causing the dissolved minerals to solidify. The high concentration of hydrogen sulfide gas, as well as minerals such as copper, lead, zinc and sulfur, create an environment that is toxic to most organisms. The water surrounding hydrothermal vents can reach temperatures as high as 320 °C with a pH as acidic as 2.8. To survive here, the chemosynthetic bacteria have specialised enzymes that can resist denaturing of their active sites. The bacterium *Thermus aquaticus* has an optimum temperature range of 75–80 °C.

Hydrothermal vents can occur at depths of up to 4 km. Few organisms can live at this depth because the hydrostatic water pressure may be up to 300 atmospheres. Deep hydrothermal vents are also in the aphotic zone. Producers that require light for photosynthesis are unable to grow here, so there is less energy and fewer nutrients to support consumers further up the food chain.

As few organisms are adapted to live in the extreme conditions, hydrothermal vents have a low biodiversity.

CASE STUDY

Our deep-sea pharmacy

The World Health Organization (WHO) estimates that antibiotic treatments add an average of 20 years to all of our lives. But since the introduction of penicillin in 1942, our society's overuse of antibiotics has led to the emergence of many more antibiotic-resistant strains of bacteria. These untreatable superbugs mean that what were once considered to be easily treated infections are becoming fatal again. In 2013, more patients died of MRSA (methicillin-resistant *Staphylococcus aureus*) than of AIDS (acquired immune deficiency syndrome).

Many pharmaceutical drugs are derived from plants, animals, fungi or bacteria. The European Union PharmSea initiative has provided £9.5 million to research a variety of marine organisms to discover whether they can supply the next superdrug with antibiotic, anti-cancer or anti-inflammatory properties.

Deep-sea trenches are the largest unexplored habitat on Earth. Trenches are inhabited by extremophile organisms with unique and unusual biochemistry, allowing them to survive in severe temperatures, pressure and pH. Marine scientists are bioprospecting a number of these ocean trenches (Figure 2.14), including the Kermadec Trench off New Zealand, the Mariana

25

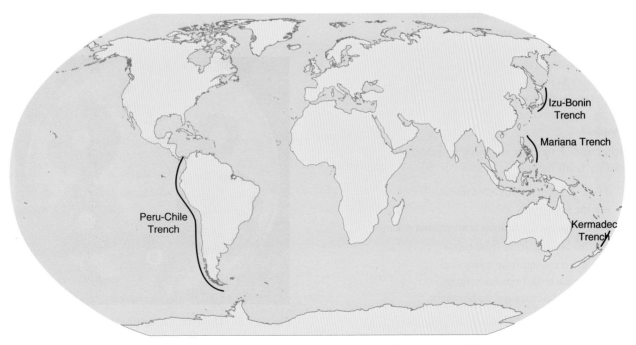

Figure 2.14. The location of deep-sea trenches, which provide habitats for extremophile organisms.

Trench in the western Pacific, the Izu-Bonin Trench off Japan and the Peru–Chile Trench.

Engineers access the benthic sediment either by deep-sea submarines or dropping a long coring device to the ocean floor. It takes at least 4 h for the coring apparatus to sink to the seabed at a depth of 8000–11 000 m.

Organisms in the trench sediment are pressure-sensitive and need high-pressure chambers to survive and grow in laboratories at sea-level. Researchers extract and test the bioactive compounds produced by these organisms for medicinal properties. Zebrafish are used to test new medicines as they have a similar physiology to humans.

Dermacoccus abyssi is a bacterium retrieved from sediment in the Mariana Trench. This organism produces dermacozines, a new biochemical that may help protect against the parasite that causes African sleeping sickness.

Lake Hodgson is a fresh-water lake in Antarctica. It is another source of microbes that may provide future medicinal drugs. This lake has been sealed beneath 4 m of ice for at least 11 000 years. Analysis of sediment taken from beneath the subglacial waters has shown that about a quarter of the DNA present comes from previously unknown species.

Marine organisms living on the benthic floor of more shallow waters may also be potential sources of medicinal drugs. Such organisms can be collected by dredging, scuba diving or snorkelling. For example, three species of Australian sea sponges have been found to produce chemicals called chondropsins. The drug potential of chondropsins is related to their ability to inhibit certain enzymes that play a role in the development of bone cancer, Alzheimer's disease, viral infections, diabetes and cardiovascular disorders.

Other discoveries that are currently undergoing medical trials include:

- a pain-relief drug harvested from marine cone snails
- schizophrenia medication from marine worms
- wound-healing drugs from corals
- anti-cancer drugs from a range of marine bacteria, bryozoans, fungi, tunicates, molluscs and nudibranchs.

Figure 2.15 shows the proportional uses of beneficial chemicals derived from marine organisms.

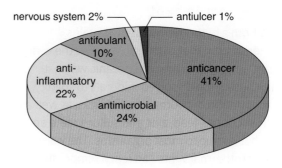

Figure 2.15. Use of beneficial chemicals derived from marine organisms.

Questions

1   What is the mean of the data shown in Figure 2.15?

2   Australian sea sponges act as mutualistic hosts for bacteria that produce chondropsins. Explain how the sponge and bacteria both benefit by living together.

3   Figure 2.16 shows different strains of marine bacteria (A–F) that have been harvested from sponges. The sponge-derived bacteria produce powerful antibiotics against a range of drug-resistant bacteria. The effect of the antibiotic can be measured by the radius of its inhibition zone. An inhibition zone is an area where bacteria cannot grow because of the production of an antibiotic. On Figure 2.16 it is measured by the diameter of no bacteria around each disc (A–F). Explain which drug-resistant antibiotic-producing strain (A–F) is the most effective in this figure.

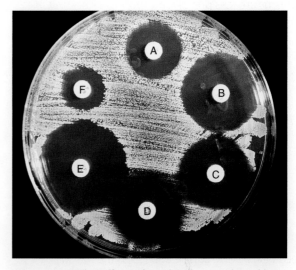

Figure 2.16. The effect of antibiotics produced by different strains of sponge-derived bacteria (A–F).

Sand on a reef slope: an unstable but non-extreme environment

Reef slopes are the steep, sometimes vertical, walls at the front (fore) of a reef. These fore-reef zones absorb most of the energy and damage from incoming waves and stormy seas. This means the sandy substrate of a reef slope is easily eroded by currents, waves and wind, and it is difficult for marine plants to grow there. Lack of biomass in primary producers and the usual loss of energy between trophic levels means that food chains are short and the environment cannot support species at higher trophic levels.

The organisms that can successfully use the reef slope sand habitat include animals that burrow into the sand, such as worms, clams, sand fleas and crabs. Although the physical conditions are not extreme, they are constantly changing so the environment is described as unstable. Not many marine organisms are adapted to survive in such condition, so biodiversity is low.

Rocky shore: a stable and non-extreme environment

Like coral reefs, rocky shores are a stable, non-extreme environment. They support a greater number of species than sandy shores because they are better at resisting wave action and erosion. The rock provides a good attachment surface for molluscs and seaweeds, so there is less chance of the organisms being washed away. Rocky shores also provide protective habitats such as rock pools and crevices. They are less porous than sandy shores so organisms are less prone to drying out and dying from desiccation.

> **SELF-ASSESSMENT QUESTIONS**
>
> **8** Explain why hydrothermal vents have low biodiversity.
>
> **9** Explain why rocky shores have a higher biodiversity than hydrothermal vents.

2.8 Specialised and generalised ecological niches

An ecological niche can be defined as the role of an organism in an ecosystem. Marine organisms may have either a specialised or a generalised niche in their specific environments.

Specialised ecological niches

If an organism can survive only within very narrow physical, biological or chemical parameters, it is considered to have a very specialised niche. Organisms with a specialised niche have a narrow range of food requirements or live in a specific habitat. Coral reefs have a high number of organisms with specialised niches, such as butterfly fish and emperor angelfish. Butterfly fish are territorial and live closely associated with a specific area of coral. They are highly adapted to surviving on coral reefs. For example, they have thin snouts to reach into the crevices of rocks to feed on the corals and sea anemones. Emperor angelfish live in Indo-Pacific ocean reefs and have a specialised niche, feeding on coral sponges as well as parasites and dead skin from larger fish.

Generalised ecological niches

Generalised niches are held by organisms that can exploit a wide range of habitats and food sources. Marine examples include the northern bluefin tuna. This fish follows the nutrient-rich cold ocean currents feeding on a wide range of prey, including fish, rotifers, molluscs, squid and crustaceans. Unlike many cold-blooded animals, tuna can increase their body temperature compared with the temperature of the surrounding ocean. As a result, tuna are able to swim rapidly and tolerate a broad range of water temperatures. This ensures that tuna can inhabit a broad thermal niche and be found throughout the Atlantic Ocean.

Another marine organism that has a generalised niche is the bottlenose dolphin, whose diet includes a large variety of fish and squid species and whose habitat extends throughout the world's oceans except for the polar regions. Similarly, mako sharks are opportunistic feeders, eating a range of shoaling fish such as tuna and mackerel (Figure 2.17). Sharks can live in a wide range of different conditions, surviving at different temperatures and depths. They can move easily between habitats and hence hunt in different prey locations.

Figure 2.17. Mako shark.

High biodiversity and narrow ecological niches

High biodiversity means that many different species live within one ecosystem. Each species has its own niche or ecological role within the ecosystem. Niches are determined by factors such as habitat, food, reproduction and behaviour. All of these factors are sources of competition between species.

Competition is a relationship between organisms that strive for the same resources in the same place. There are two different types of competition:

- intraspecific competition, which occurs between individuals of the same species (for example two male fish of the same species competing for female mates in the same area)

- interspecific competition, which occurs between members of different species (for example predators of different species competing for the same prey).

Interspecific competition can lead to overlap between ecological niches. The species that is less well adapted has access to fewer resources and is less likely to survive and reproduce: this could lead to the species becoming extinct. However, interspecific competition more often leads to greater niche adaptations and niche specialisation.

The fundamental niche is the niche of a species where that species experiences no competition with others. The fundamental niche can also be defined as the tolerance range for all important abiotic conditions, within which individuals of a species can survive, grow and reproduce. But all organisms are part of complex food webs, sharing the ecosystem with other species, and all competing for the same biotic and abiotic resources. As these resources are limited, this leads to interspecific competition.

The competitive exclusion principle predicts that, in a stable ecosystem, no two species can be in direct competition with each other. If the niches for two species are identical, one species will die out as a result of interspecific competition. For example, if an introduced species is added to an existing marine habitat then the new species may have the same niche as a native species (for example two top predators feeding on the same prey at the same time in the same habitat). Interspecific competition between the two species will occur, as they compete for this niche. One of the two species will be better at hunting the prey, therefore will thrive and increase in population size. The population of the other species will be less ecologically or reproductively viable, eventually dying out.

Coral reefs

Coral reefs are home to many different species, including corals, fish, anemones, turtles, crabs, sharks and dolphins. Estimates of the number of reef species worldwide are between 600 000 and more than 9 million. A survey by the Smithsonian National Museum of Natural History found that coral heads with a surface area of 6.3 m^2 have 525 different species of crustacean. This is almost as many crab species as found in all of the seas of Europe.

The high biodiversity of coral reefs results from high productivity and each organism is intrinsically linked to the other animals, plants and microorganisms in the food web. The nutrient and energy flow between trophic levels is highly efficient. With so many species in such small areas, organisms avoid competition by narrowing their ecological niches.

All species living in the same habitat do something slightly different compared with the other species in order to narrow their niche and so prevent competitive exclusion. For example, if two species share the same food source, they may feed at different times (one species feeding at night, another feeding in daylight); this is temporal separation. Alternatively, a niche may be narrowed by spatial separation, for example, different fish species living at different levels of the reef to avoid competing for food.

The coral reef environment is stable and not extreme, it has high productivity and high biodiversity. When there is a high biodiversity, the realised niche of each species narrows to reduce interspecific competition. As the productivity is high, there is still sufficient energy and resources for species to survive and reproduce.

Low biodiversity and ecological niches

The open sea has fewer species and therefore lower biodiversity. Species such as tuna and sharks are able to exploit a wider range of food sources and hence have more general realised niches. This is a result of there being less interspecific competition in the open sea. If a species narrows its realised niche in a region of low biodiversity, the energy and resources available for it to grow may be insufficient, leading to less reproduction, and eventually the species dying out.

In unstable ecosystems, for example where there are regular tropical cyclones and tornados, the instability can interfere with competitive exclusion, allowing other species to have a chance in the habitat and hence increasing biodiversity. An example of this can be seen on rocky shores where strong storms regularly remove competitively dominant mollusc species, allowing other normally competitively excluded species to survive.

In an area where there is a lot of one species, such as a large school of fish, the strain on resources is a lot larger, so the species must expand its realised niche, feeding on organisms that might not otherwise be part of the diet.

Summary

- The structure of marine ecosystems can be described using the key terms environment and habitat.

- The key terms species, population, community and biodiversity help us describe the organisms that live in marine habitats.

- There are a variety of roles, or niches, that organisms perform in their aquatic environment. These include producers, consumers and decomposers.

- The feeding connections between different organisms can be described using food chains, food webs and trophic levels.

- The biological, chemical and physical parts of the environment are linked by energy and nutrient flows.

- There is a rich variety of relationships between species. These include mutualism, parasitism, competition and predator–prey.

- Shoaling is an example of the importance of studying fish biology and behaviour.

- How stable or extreme a habitat is helps determine the complex and delicate balance of life it supports. This leads to variation in the number and type of niches, as well as biodiversity, that exists between coral reefs, hydrothermal vents, sandy and rocky shores.

Exam-style questions

1 **a** Explain what is meant by each of the following terms.

    i Population [1]

    ii Community [1]

    iii Trophic level [1]

    iv Species [1]

    v Ecosystem [1]

  b Many forage fish species (for example sardines or herrings) form shoals.

    i Discuss the advantages of shoaling. [4]

    ii Discuss the disadvantages of shoaling. [2]

[Total mark: 11]

2 Figure 2.18 below shows the interdependence of ocean temperature and predator–prey cycles.

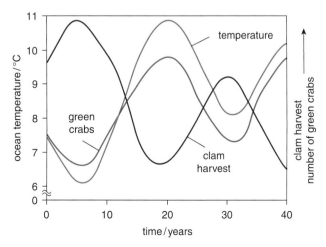

Figure 2.18. The interdependence of ocean temperature and predator–prey cycles.

29

   a Use Figure 2.18 to find the range of ocean temperatures. **[1]**

   b How might global warming affect the green crab population? **[1]**

   c Describe the relationship between the green crabs and clams and suggest an explanation for this relationship. **[3]**

   d Explain how populations of marine predators may be spatially linked to their prey. **[2]**

   e Suggest how ecologists could have collected the green crab data. **[4]**

(Total mark: 11)

3 Figure 2.19 shows a marine food web.

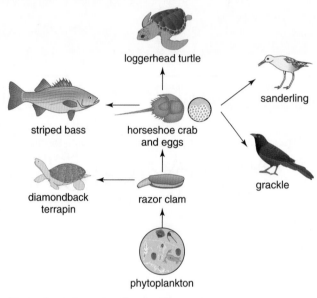

Figure 2.19. A marine food web.

   a What is the primary source of energy for this food web? **[1]**

   b Write a food chain based on the food web including a tertiary consumer. **[2]**

   c Explain what the arrows between organisms represent. **[2]**

   d With reference to Figure 2.19, explain the term predator. **[2]**

   e Suggest one biotic factor, other than predation, that may affect the horseshoe crab population. **[1]**

   f Ecologists studied a total of 130 horseshoe crabs and found 10 with ciliate parasites. Explain the term parasite. **[3]**

(Total mark: 11)

4 **a** Describe the relationship between coral and zooxanthellae. **[3]**

   b Define succession. **[1]**

   c Outline the succession that leads to the formation of a coral reef. **[3]**

   d Discuss why coral reefs contain narrow ecological niches. **[4]**

(Total mark: 11)

5   Figure 2.20 shows a food web for the Arctic.

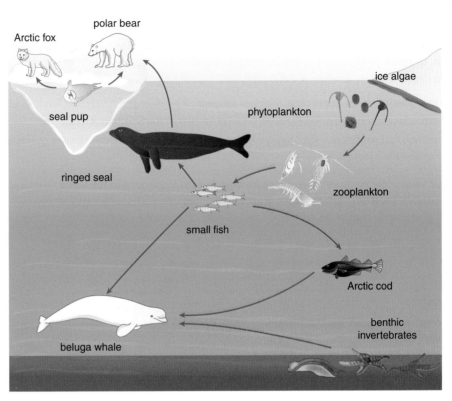

Figure 2.20. An Arctic food web.

a   Draw a food chain with polar bears as a quaternary (4th level) consumer.   **[1]**

b   Beluga whales are hunted in Canadian Alaskan and Russian Arctic regions for their meat, blubber and skin. Explain how this could affect the population numbers of each of the other species in the food chain: phytoplankton – zooplankton – small fish – Arctic cod – beluga whale.   **[4]**

c   A study of the stomach contents of seals found that they included a variety of invertebrate prey: 73 crabs, 55 clams, 47 snails, 32 amphipods and 18 shrimps. Calculate the mean percentage of invertebrates in the stomachs.   **[1]**

d   Discuss the effects of global warming on the following species:

   i   polar bear   **[1]**

   ii   ice algae   **[1]**

e   When moulting, seals spend time out on ice packs while replacing their fur and skin. In 2011, several species of ice-dependent seals were found dead or sick with abnormal coats. Discuss why some scientists believe abnormal coats may be linked to global warming.   **[2]**

f   In 2015, global warming led to the seal-hunting season in north-western Alaska being the shortest in memory. The season lasted less than a week, compared with the usual 3 weeks. Why might this have been caused by decreased ice packs?   **[1]**

(Total mark: 11)

Southern Ocean ecosystem

The Southern Ocean encircles the Antarctic and encompasses between 10 and 20% of the global ocean area, including the Earth's largest current, the Antarctic circumpolar current. The Southern Ocean is not uniform in either productivity or biodiversity. Localised changes in ice coverage, seabed topography and oceanic currents create a range of different habitats including:

- the permanently open ocean zone, which is nutrient rich but has relatively low levels of photosynthesis
- the seasonal ice zone, which is the most productive part of the Southern Ocean
- the coastal and continental shelf zone, which contains a permanent ice pack zone characterised by large phytoplankton blooms.

The food webs of the Southern Ocean are among the most important in the world. They support a wide range of local organisms from algae to large animals such as whales, seals and penguins (Figure 2.21). You can refer to this figure as you read on about the producers, consumers and microorgansims in this ecosystem.

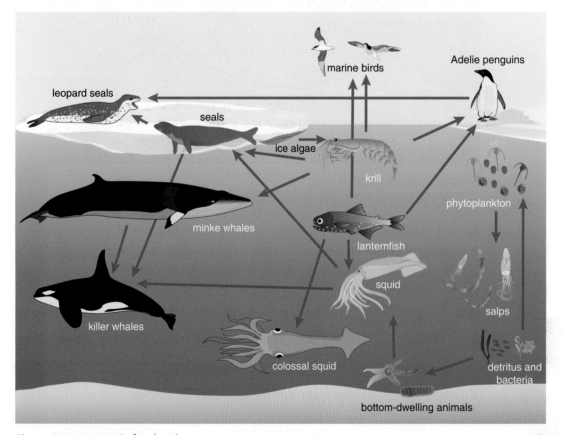

Figure 2.21. Antarctic food web.

Producers

Open ocean waters are rich in single-celled organisms that have different cellular characteristics from animal and plant cells. These organisms are called protoctists and include phytoplankton (for example diatoms, cyanobacteria and dinoflagellates). These are the producers that organisms in higher trophic levels depend on. Phytoplankton can be divided into three groups depending on their size:

- picoplankton (2.0–2 μm)
- nanoplankton (2–20 μm)
- microplankton (20–200 μm).

The ocean water around Antarctica is often frozen and covered by ice for long periods of time. Under the ice, the light intensity is too low for phytoplankton to photosynthesise but algae can grow and are an important food source for herbivorous zooplankton, for example krill. There are also more than 700 species of seaweed found in Antarctica's shallow coastal waters. Water temperature and depth are important limiting factors that control seaweed distribution.

Consumers

Zooplankton are consumers that feed on phytoplankton. Some zooplankton species complete the whole of their life cycles as plankton (haloplankton) while other species are only planktonic in their larval stages (meroplankton).

Melting ice in spring and summer produces a layer of less saline water on the Southern Ocean's surface, together with increased nutrients and sunlight. These changes in abiotic conditions lead to a massive increase in phytoplankton, known as a bloom. The phytoplankton blooms feed krill and other herbivorous zooplankton, which subsequently become very abundant. Krill can produce swarms that contain 30 000 individuals per cubic metre. They form a major amount of the biomass in the Southern Ocean.

Krill are a group of about 80 different species of crustaceans. The main species in the Southern Ocean is Antarctic krill. Antarctic krill have a high reproductive capacity: the females can lay up to 10 000 eggs. Krill form a vital part of Antarctic food chains, being consumed by a variety of organisms, including fish, birds, squid, whales, seals and penguins. Krill are also a target species for commercial fisheries and over-harvesting of krill can lead to a decrease in the krill population. This allows the population of phytoplankton to produce even larger phytoplankton blooms. These large blooms can produce toxins harmful to other organisms in the ecosystem.

Zooplankton besides krill include copepods, salps and larval fish. Like krill, copepods are crustacea that can produce very high populations. In the waters around King George Island they can form up to 87% of the summer zooplankton biomass. Copepods are an important food source for fish, which are then eaten by seals, penguin and sea birds.

Salps are planktonic sea squirts that can produce huge colonies and filter vast amounts of phytoplankton (Figure 2.22). Salps are eaten by fish that are in turn consumed by squid and then Southern bluefin tuna. Salp populations increase and krill populations decrease in years when ocean temperatures and currents cause the sea ice to retreat.

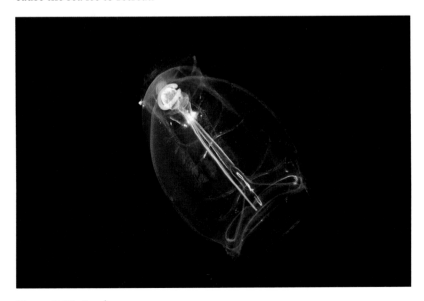

Figure 2.22. A salp.

The Southern Ocean contains extremely few fish. Most live in coastal benthic waters (for example Antarctic cod) and very few are found in open waters (for example lanternfish).

Antarctic squid are one of the most important species in the Southern Ocean food web, with a total biomass of 110 million tonnes. Squid are a major component of the diets of seals and killer whales. The main diet of Antarctic squid is not krill but lanternfish that have fed mainly on copepods. Squid populations can fluctuate dramatically, so are highly susceptible to over-fishing.

Benthic habitats provide rich habitats for an array of bottom-dwelling animals. These include filter feeders (for example anemones, soft corals, sea squirts, molluscs and tube worms) and mobile scavengers and predators (for example sea urchins, starfish, giant sea spiders and ribbon worms) (Figure 2.23).

Figure 2.23. Giant sea spider.

Microorganisms

Microorganisms (for example bacteria and viruses) form a crucial link in the Southern Ocean's food web. Coastal and continental shelf areas of Antarctica have rich benthic bacterial communities. Water temperatures of the continental shelf are generally low and stable. Oxygen (from photosynthesis) and organic matter (from detritus) is produced in seasonal pulses by the biotic communities in the surface water. Bacteria feed on dissolved organic matter and, as decomposers, they break down detritus and remobilise inorganic nutrients for the growth of phytoplankton. Bacteria are consumed by protoctists, who are in turn eaten by zooplankton.

Viral infection accounts for about 50% of the death of marine bacteria and may be one of the major sources of dissolved organic matter in the sea. Viruses are also capable of inhibiting phytoplankton growth by up to 80%.

Questions

1. a. Under the ice shelf the main producer is algae rather than phytoplankton. Explain why algae can photosynthesise under the ice far better than phytoplankton.

   b. When snow covering the ice sheet blows away, there is an increase in oxygen bubbles trapped under the ice. Explain why this occurs.

   c. Suggest why cracks in the sea ice may be important to the survival of penguins.

2 Using data from Figure 2.21:

   a Draw a food chain for krill that has a quaternary consumer.

   b Why can krill can be considered to be a keystone species for the Southern Ocean?

3 Global warming is decreasing the amount of sea ice around Antarctica and leading to a change in penguin populations. Some penguin species are increasing in population size while others are declining.

   a Adelie penguins on Anvers island have lost 70% of their population or 10 000 breeding pairs in the past 30 years. To the nearest 1000, calculate the original number of Adelie penguins in this population.

   b Gentoo penguins are increasing in numbers and are breeding on the Antarctic peninsula for the first time in 800 years. Adelie penguins are dependent on krill whereas gentoo penguins have a more flexible diet feeding on squid and fish. Describe how the differing niches of the two penguin species may affect their chances of surviving.

   c Adult Emperor penguins need 3-4 weeks of solid sea ice in order to replace worn out feathers (moult). Feathers help keep the birds insulated, waterproof and free from skin infections. During a warm period in the 1970s, the population of Emperor penguins on the coast of Adelie land declined by 50%. Suggest a reason why.

   d In winters when it is colder, the survival rate of Emperor penguins increases but they lay fewer eggs. Suggest a reason why.

4 A reduction in sea ice as a result of global warming results in reduced numbers of phytoplankton. Suggest reasons why this leads to a reduction in benthic organisms.

Chapter 3
Energetics of marine ecosystems

Learning outcomes

By the end of this chapter, you should be able to:

- explain how the energy in sunlight is captured during photosynthesis
- explain how the energy in dissolved minerals can be captured by chemosynthesis
- compare and contrast the processes of photosynthesis and chemosynthesis
- describe the relationship between photosynthesis and respiration
- calculate gross primary productivity and net primary productivity and explain the meaning of each of these terms
- describe different methods that can be used to measure productivity
- explain how high productivity influences the food chain
- calculate the energy losses along food chains and give the reasons for these losses
- calculate the efficiency of energy transfer between trophic levels
- give reasons for differences in the efficiency of energy transfer
- illustrate food chains by drawing pyramids of number, biomass or energy
- apply what you have learnt to new, unfamiliar contexts.

3.1 Where does the energy for life come from?

All life on Earth is dependent on the energy that can be fixed into carbohydrates by **autotrophic** organisms. An autotroph is able to make its own food by forming organic substances from simple inorganic molecules. In marine ecosystems, the autotrophs are either **photosynthetic** or **chemosynthetic**. Photosynthetic organisms capture the Sun's energy, whereas chemosynthetic organisms are able to use the energy in chemicals that are dissolved in the water.

Photosynthesis can only take place in the sunlit upper layer of the ocean. About 90% of all marine life is therefore found in this area. The ability of the chemosynthetic organisms to produce carbohydrates is an important adaptation to living in extreme conditions. The hydrothermal vents where they are found have no light so photosynthesis is not possible. Until the vent communities were discovered in the 1970s, it was thought that the only way in which energy would reach the lower parts of the ocean was when organisms died and fell to the bottom.

Other organisms have to obtain their energy by feeding on the autotrophs. These are known as **heterotrophic** organisms or consumers. The **primary productivity** of an ecosystem relates to how much energy is fixed into **carbohydrates** (new organic matter). The most productive ecosystems per unit area are estuaries, swamps and marshes. However, the most productive ecosystems overall are the oceans, because they cover such a high proportion of the Earth's surface. Over a billion people rely on marine ecosystems for their food. Although we tend to think that increased productivity is always an advantage, this is not always true. Marine dead zones are areas where the productivity has reached such a peak that the ecosystem becomes unbalanced. Eventually oxygen levels are reduced and there is very little life.

KEY TERMS

Autotroph (autotrophic): an organism that can capture the energy in light or chemicals and use it to produce carbohydrates from simple molecules such as carbon dioxide

Photosynthesis (photosynthetic): the process of using light energy to synthesise glucose from carbon dioxide and water

Chemosynthesis (chemosynthetic): the production of organic compounds by bacteria or other living organisms using the energy derived from reactions with inorganic chemicals

Heterotroph (heterotrophic): an organism that cannot make its own food and instead relies on consuming other organisms; all animals, fungi and protozoans are heterotrophic, as well as most bacteria

Primary productivity: the rate of production of new biomass through photosynthesis or chemosynthesis

Carbohydrate: organic compounds occurring in living tissues that contain carbon, hydrogen and oxygen, for example starch, cellulose and sugars; carbohydrates can be broken down in the process of respiration to release energy

37

3.2 Productivity

Primary productivity is the rate of production of new biomass (living material) by autotrophic organisms through either photosynthesis or chemosynthesis (Figure 3.1). It allows light or chemical energy to be fixed into useable organic molecules, and as such is the basis of all food chains and food webs. In all ecosystems illuminated by the Sun, the main way in which energy is fixed is through photosynthesis. On land the majority of photosynthesis is carried out by green plants, but in the oceans it is mainly carried out by **phytoplankton**. Most of these tiny algae are single-celled and simply float with the current in water. As well as the phytoplankton there are also much larger algae (macroalgae), such as kelp and rooted plants called seagrass. These organisms are all photoautotrophs: they make their own food using light energy. You will learn about the adaptations of each of these producers in Chapter 8.

Photosynthesis

Photosynthesis is a process in which the inorganic compounds carbon dioxide and water are combined to produce glucose. Glucose is a useable organic compound. Oxygen is produced as a byproduct.

carbon dioxide + water → glucose + oxygen

The energy to do this comes from sunlight and must be absorbed by pigments in the plants or algae.

KEY TERM

Phytoplankton: microscopic photosynthetic organisms that live in the upper, sunlit layers of water

(a)

(b)

(c)

Figure 3.1. Important producers in marine ecosystems: (a) phytoplankton; (b) seagrass; (c) kelp.

The most common pigment is **chlorophyll**, which is found in organelles called chloroplasts (Figure 3.2). You can read more about the different pigments needed for photosynthesis in Chapter 8.

> **KEY TERM**
>
> **Chlorophyll:** a pigment found in plants and algae that is used to absorb sunlight for photosynthesis

Figure 3.2. Single-celled alga with green chloroplasts visible.

Factors affecting photosynthesis

The rate of photosynthesis can be affected by several different factors. These include:

- nutrients
- amount of light
- temperature
- concentration of carbon dioxide.

In a marine environment, the most important factors are likely to be the availability of nutrients and light.

Temperature and carbon dioxide

Clearly there is always an abundance of water, and the water contains dissolved carbon dioxide. Although temperature affects the rate of the reactions taking place during photosynthesis, the temperature of the ocean is much more stable than air temperature on land.

Nutrients

Algae and plants both need nutrients in the form of mineral ions in order to grow. A lack of a particular nutrient therefore affects the rate of productivity of new biomass because it affects the rate of growth. Nutrient availability is discussed in more detail in Chapter 4.

Light

The layer of the ocean that has enough light for photosynthesis is relatively thin compared with the total depth. This sunlit zone is called the photic zone and all photosynthesis must take place here (Figure 3.3). This means that the vast majority of the biomass in the open ocean is contained within the upper 200 m of water.

Water both absorbs and scatters the sunlight. The amount of light reflected will depend on the state of the water. When there are waves, more light is reflected because the waves act like lenses and focus the light. When the light penetrates the surface of the water it is refracted because light travels more slowly in water than in the air. Finally, solid particles within the water also scatter and absorb the light. The availability of light within the water and methods to measure the light penetration are discussed further in Chapter 8.

The absorption of sunlight by the water also increases the temperature of the water. When the temperature increases, the molecules of water have more kinetic energy and are moving more quickly so the water is less dense and therefore more buoyant than cold water. The thin layer of warm water floats on top of the colder deep water and the transition between the two is called the **thermocline**. It can also be referred to as a **pycnocline**, which is simply related to the different densities of the layers rather than the temperature. There is little mixing between the two layers because a source of energy (such as wind) is needed to push the warm water down. This is very important to the phytoplankton as it keeps them floating near the surface where they have access to light.

KEY TERMS

Thermocline: a boundary between two layers of water with different temperatures

Pycnocline: a boundary between two layers of water with different densities

Deep chlorophyll maximum: the maximum concentration of chlorophyll below the surface of a body of water

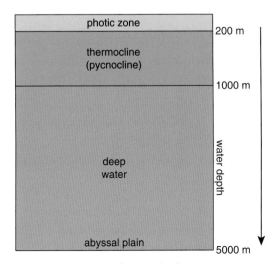

Figure 3.3. Layers of water in the ocean.

Without the thermocline, there would be much more mixing of the water and currents would carry the phytoplankton down and away from the light. This would reduce the rate of photosynthesis and therefore the productivity. However, the thermocline also prevents nutrient-rich water from mixing with the upper layers and therefore limits the productivity. Generally the deeper the water the higher the nutrient levels but the lower the light. There is normally a point near the thermocline where the productivity is highest as there is enough light for photosynthesis and enough nutrients for growth. This level is known as the **deep chlorophyll maximum** (DCM) because it is the area with the highest concentration of chlorophyll.

The light varies with the seasons, particularly at high latitudes. In spring the average length of the day and the intensity of light both increase. This is clearly an advantage in terms of photosynthesis, and productivity is therefore higher in spring and summer than it is in winter. Often it is nutrient availability that limits the rate of photosynthesis in spring and summer, and light which limits it during autumn and winter.

SELF-ASSESSMENT QUESTIONS

1 State the two ways in which new biomass is produced in the ocean.

2 Explain why ocean productivity is limited to the first 200 m in depth.

Chemosynthesis

There are some ecosystems, such as those found around hydrothermal vents, where light is not available for productivity. Chemosynthesis is a process where carbon dioxide is turned into useable organic molecules using the energy stored in dissolved chemicals. The chemicals dissolve in heated water in the undersea crust as it makes its way back to the surface to emerge from the vents. Chemoautotrophs are species of bacteria that are able to make their own food using chemical energy. There are several species of chemosynthetic bacteria, including *Beggiatoa* and *Thiothrix* species. Each species uses different chemicals as their energy source and produces different sugars. One common pathway is:

hydrogen sulfide + oxygen + carbon dioxide → sugar + water + sulfur

Chemosynthetic bacteria were first discovered in hydrothermal vents in the ocean floor in 1977. The vents are found at depths varying from around 2000 m in the Galapagos

Ridge to 7700 m in the Mid-Atlantic Ridge. Clearly at these depths there is no light, there are no phytoplankton and therefore there can be no photosynthesis. Chemosynthesis is the only way in which life is possible in such an inhospitable environment. The species able to survive here are all examples of **extremophiles**, which means that they are able to survive very harsh conditions. At these vents there is extremely high pressure, as well as water temperatures that can vary from 2 °C to 400 °C.

Chapter 2 discusses the symbiotic relationship between giant tube worms (*Riftia* species) and chemosynthetic bacteria (Figure 3.4). Up to 75% of animal species at hydrothermal vents depend on mutualistic relationships with chemosynthetic bacteria for at least some of their food. For example, mussels at these vents have mutualistic bacteria living in their gills but also filter feed.

Figure 3.4. Giant tube worms at hydrothermal vents have a symbiotic relationship with chemosynthetic bacteria.

KEY TERMS

Extremophile: an organism that is adapted to survive extreme temperature, pressure, salinity or pH

Respiration: the process by which all living things release energy from their food by oxidising glucose

Similarities and differences between photosynthesis and chemosynthesis

Both photosynthesis and chemosynthesis use carbon dioxide and require an energy source to produce sugars. In photosynthesis, oxygen is produced as a byproduct whereas in chemosynthesis the byproducts vary depending on the chemicals that are used, although sulfur is often produced. There is therefore only one possible equation for photosynthesis compared with several different equations for chemosynthesis. In both processes the sugars produced

are used to provide metabolic energy through **respiration**, or built up into the other chemicals needed by the organism.

SELF-ASSESSMENT QUESTIONS

3 Explain why the organisms living at hydrothermal vents are called extremophiles.

4 Copy and complete Table 3.1 to compare photosynthesis and chemosynthesis in ocean ecosystems.

feature	process	
	chemosynthesis	photosynthesis
energy source		
products		
type of organism		
main location in ocean		

Table 3.1. Photosynthesis and chemosynthesis.

Respiration

Respiration is the process by which all living things release the chemical energy stored in organic molecules such as carbohydrates. This energy is then used to carry out all the different metabolic reactions within the organism. Aerobic respiration requires a supply of oxygen and glucose and produces carbon dioxide and water.

glucose + oxygen $\rightarrow$ carbon dioxide + water

As well as the useable energy the organism needs, respiration produces heat energy, which is lost to the environment.

The link between photosynthesis and respiration

Primary productivity is the amount of new biomass made by the producers, but not all of this is available for the consumers to eat. Some of the carbohydrate produced is not stored but is oxidised in respiration to provide energy. **Gross primary production** (GPP) is the amount of energy that primary producers are able to fix in a given length of time and within a given area. **Net primary production** (NPP) is the amount left over to create new biomass after respiration (R) has been taken into account. This can be shown by the following equation:

$$NPP = GPP - R$$

It is this net primary production that is available to pass on to the consumers. **Secondary production** is the amount of biomass produced by heterotrophs after eating the producers. Hence the more productive an ecosystem, the more energy is available to pass along the food chain. In the marine environment, there is no large-scale accumulation of biomass as there is in savannahs and forests on land. However, the reproductive rate of the phytoplankton is very high so there is a constant source of new organisms to photosynthesise. Carbon dioxide from the atmosphere dissolves in the water and is then available for photosynthesis. When it is fixed into glucose it is stored as phytoplankton biomass. Much of this 'locked up' carbon dioxide sinks to the floor of the ocean when organisms die. This process is discussed in detail in Chapter 4.

 KEY TERMS

Gross primary production: the amount of light or chemical energy fixed by producers in a given length of time in a given area

Net primary production: the amount of energy that is left over after respiration to be made into new plant biomass

Secondary production: the rate of production of new biomass by consumers, using the energy gained by eating producers

PRACTICAL ACTIVITY 3.1

Investigating the compensation point

The compensation point is the light intensity at which respiration is equal to photosynthesis. Below this point producers use more carbohydrate in respiration than they can produce in photosynthesis so their biomass decreases.

Hydrogencarbonate indicator is red in atmospheric conditions but turns yellow if the amount of carbon dioxide increases and purple if the amount decreases.

Apparatus
- Four boiling tubes with bungs
- 150 cm³ hydrogencarbonate indicator
- 20 cm³ measuring cylinder
- Pondweed such as *Cabomba* (available from aquatic shops) or seaweed if available
- Boiling tube rack
- Square of aluminium foil 15 cm × 15 cm
- Square of muslin cloth 15 cm × 15 cm
- Bench lamp
- Elastic bands

Method
- Pour a small amount of indicator into each boiling tube, swirl it around and then pour away; do the same with the measuring cylinder.
- Carefully wrap one of the tubes in the foil and secure with an elastic band.
- Wrap a second tube in muslin cloth and secure with elastic bands.
- Measure 20 cm³ of indicator into each boiling tube.
- Place equally sized pieces of pondweed into each of the wrapped tubes and one of the unwrapped tubes.
- Leave the fourth tube empty apart from the indicator.
- Place bungs into each tube.
- Leave the tubes in the boiling tube rack with a bench lamp shining on them for at least 1 h.
- Copy out the results table and predict the colour of the indicator in each tube.
- Remove the wrapping on the tubes and record the colour of the indicator in your results table.

Risk assessment
Hydrogencarbonate indicator should be freshly made by qualified staff using a fume cupboard.

To make the stock solution
- Dissolve 0.20 g of thymol blue and 0.1 g of cresol red in 20 cm³ of ethanol.
- Dissolve 0.85 g of sodium hydrogencarbonate in about 200 cm³ of freshly boiled distilled water.
- Add the ethanol solution from the first step and dilute to 1000 cm³ with water.

→

When it is ready to use:

- Dilute the stock solution ten times with freshly boiled distilled water.

- Bubble air through the diluted solution to equilibrate it with atmospheric carbon dioxide.

Avoid exhaling near the solution as it is very sensitive to changes in carbon dioxide concentration.

Precautions should also be taken to avoid burns or dazzle from a hot bench lamp.

Safety glasses should be worn in case of cold indicator splashing onto the hot light bulb and causing it to shatter.

Prediction and results

Predicted and observed results

tube	predicted colour	observed colour
unwrapped with pondweed		
wrapped in muslin with pondweed		
wrapped in foil with pondweed		
unwrapped but empty		

Table 3.2. Results.

Conclusions

1. Why was it important to rinse all the equipment in the indicator before the experiment is started?
2. What was the reason for the tube without any pondweed in it?
3. Why did the tubes need to have bungs in?
4. How well did your results match your predictions? Were there any results that surprised you?
5. Explain the colour in each of your tubes.
6. Suggest a way to extend the investigation to make it more precise or to investigate photosynthesis further.

Measuring productivity

There are several ways in which primary productivity can be estimated:

- using the rate of photosynthesis of producers
- using the rate of increase in the biomass of producers
- looking at the amount of chlorophyll in an ecosystem.

For example, the higher the rate of growth of producers, the higher the amount of chlorophyll present. Net primary production and gross primary production are usually given as units of energy per unit area per unit of time, for example $kJ\ m^{-2}\ year^{-1}$. However, the units used vary depending on the method of measurement chosen.

Rate of photosynthesis

The rate of photosynthesis can be found by looking at the change in either the oxygen or carbon dioxide concentrations. If photosynthesis is taking place, there will be a decrease in the concentration of carbon dioxide and an increase in the concentration of oxygen.

Because the majority of marine producers are single-celled phytoplankton, they are easy to keep in a closed system such as a bottle. If a bottle is placed in the light, both photosynthesis and respiration will take place. If a bottle is in the dark, there will be no photosynthesis but respiration will continue. If you assume that the rate of respiration remains relatively constant, you can compare the readings of bottles kept in the dark and light to work out the rate of photosynthesis (Figure 3.5). The levels of oxygen in the water can be measured with a dissolved oxygen sensor. You need to take three readings:

- the initial reading before the experiment begins
- the reading in the light bottle at the end of the experiment
- the reading in the dark bottle at the end of the experiment.

The results would be tabulated as shown in Table 3.3.

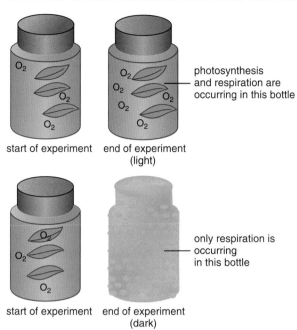

start of experiment   end of experiment
(light)

photosynthesis and respiration are occurring in this bottle

only respiration is occurring in this bottle

start of experiment   end of experiment
(dark)

Figure 3.5. The light- and dark-bottle method for measuring productivity. The LH bottles represent start of experiment and RH bottles represent end of experiment.

bottle	amount of oxygen / mg dm^{-3} h^{-1}
start of experiment	6
end of experiment in the light	16
end of experiment in the dark	1

Table 3.3. A sample set of results from the light- and dark-bottle method.

The amount of oxygen in the light bottle increases because the rate of photosynthesis is higher than the rate of respiration. In the dark bottle, the only process taking place is respiration so the amount of oxygen in this bottle decreases.

The net primary production is therefore the difference between the oxygen in the bottle at the start and the oxygen in the light bottle at the end. The respiration is the difference between the oxygen at the start and the oxygen in the dark bottle at the end. The gross primary production is the difference between the light and dark bottles at the end of the experiment.

In this example:

NPP = 16 − 6 = 10 mg O_2 dm^{-3} h^{-1}

Respiration = 6 − 1 = 5 mg O_2 dm^{-3} h^{-1}

GPP = 16 − 1 = 15 mg O_2 dm^{-3} h^{-1}

This technique can be extended to investigate the effect of light on productivity. Samples are removed from different depths in the water and placed into pairs of light and dark bottles. The bottles are then suspended at the same depth the samples were removed from. The calculations are carried out as described to work out the net primary production, gross primary production and respiration at each depth.

The productivity generally increases as you move down towards the deep chlorophyll maximum, and then decreases as the amount of light begins to limit the rate of photosynthesis (Figure 3.6). At the point where the rates of respiration and photosynthesis are equal, there is no change in the amounts of carbon dioxide or oxygen and the net productivity is zero. The light intensity at this depth is known as the **compensation point**. Below this depth, there is still light available but producers are unable to survive because the rate of respiration would be greater than the rate of photosynthesis. This part of the photic zone is sometimes called the disphotic zone. Around 90% of marine life is therefore found above the depth of the compensation point. This upper area, with sufficient light for photosynthesis is called the euphotic zone.

KEY TERM

Compensation point: the light intensity at which the rate of photosynthesis and the rate of respiration are equal

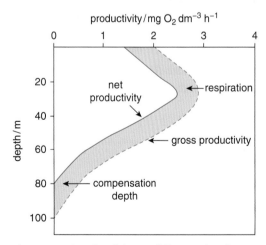

Figure 3.6. Productivity at different depths as measured by the light- and dark-bottle method.

Changes in biomass

A second way to measure productivity is to look at the rate of accumulation of biomass. This can be achieved by harvesting producers after a set amount of time, drying them to remove variations in the water content, and then finding the mass. If you know the size of the area the producers came from, you can then work out the biomass per unit area per year to give an estimate of the net primary production. As the producers would have been respiring while growing, you are unable to measure the gross primary production. There are difficulties with this method however, as you cannot measure the biomass that has already been consumed by heterotrophic organisms. This may also be true for the light- and dark-bottle method if small heterotrophic organisms are not sieved out before the experiment begins.

Satellite imagery

The other main way in which scientists monitor the productivity of the oceans is by using satellite imagery to measure the colour of the surface layers of water. This can be used to follow the changes in chlorophyll concentration and therefore the amount of producers present (Figure 3.7).

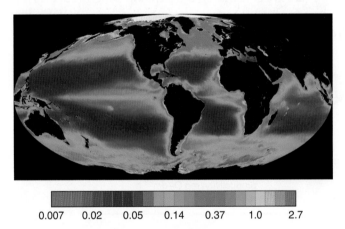

0.007	0.02	0.05	0.14	0.37	1.0	2.7

Figure 3.7. False-colour picture showing annual mean amount of chlorophyll *a* in the oceans (NASA *aqua modis*).

From Figure 3.7 you can see that the most productive areas are in the tropics and at the higher latitudes, which are shown in green and orange. The least productive areas, shown in pink and blue, tend to be where there is a smaller supply of nutrients from the deeper waters, perhaps because of wind patterns. Of course, there are problems with this method of measurement too because the relationship between chlorophyll concentration and biomass is not fixed. It depends on the individual species present and their adaptations.

The satellites can indicate only relatively shallow depths and certainly cannot penetrate the entire euphotic zone where production is taking place. However, the satellite images give a very useful summary of differences in productivity and enable scientists to monitor any changes. Recently, researchers at Sheffield University discovered that water from melting giant icebergs in the Southern Ocean contains nutrients that increase the growth of the local phytoplankton. These giant icebergs are more than 18 km in length. Scientists studied the satellite images and found that the increased productivity caused by these icebergs lasts for at least a month after they pass through an area and extend for hundreds of kilometres.

SELF-ASSESSMENT QUESTIONS

5 Explain the difference between gross primary production and net primary production.

6 a If the GPP = 53 kJ m^{-2} year^{-1} and the NPP = 31 kJ m^{-2} year^{-1} calculate the amount of energy used in respiration.

  b Explain why organisms need to respire.

PRACTICAL ACTIVITY 3.2

Measuring primary productivity of grass

Primary productivity is the rate of production of new biomass. It is this biomass that is available to pass to the next trophic level through feeding. In this experiment, grass is grown with and without light and the biomass is found using two different methods. This allows you to estimate the net primary productivity of the grass plants. This experiment takes 3–4 weeks.

Apparatus

- Potting compost
- Grass seeds (for example rye grass), readily available from garden centres and online
- two plastic germination trays (also available from garden centres and online)
- Aluminium foil
- Balance

- Drying oven or blotting paper and plant press
- Spoons or small trowels
- Light source

Method

- Label the trays 'light' and 'dark'.
- Fill both germination trays with the potting compost until three-quarters full.
- Scatter the grass seed on top of the soil so that there is approximately 5 mm between each seed.
- Cover the seeds with a thin layer of compost.
- Leave the trays in sunlight or under lamps.
- Water regularly and grow for about 2 weeks until the seedlings are around 3 cm tall.
- Carefully remove all the plants from a 50 mm × 50 mm area.
- Remove as much of the soil as possible and weigh the plants, recording the wet mass in a copy of the results table.
- Place the plants in a drying oven for 48 h at 95 °C. If no oven is available they can be dried for the same length of time using blotting paper and a plant press.
- Weigh the plants and record the dry mass in your results table.
- Carefully cover the tray labelled dark with aluminium foil.
- Leave both trays for another week, remembering to water regularly.
- Carefully remove another 50 mm × 50 mm area of plants from each tray and record the wet masses in your table.
- Dry each sample using the same method as before and record the dry masses in your table.
- Complete the calculations and answer the questions.

Risk analysis

There are few risks associated with this experiment. Care should be taken with compost to avoid accidentally ingesting it.

Results and analysis

	light tray	dark tray
initial wet mass / g		n/a
final wet mass / g		
initial dry mass / g		n/a
final dry mass / g		

Table 3.4. Results.

Final mass in the light – initial mass = net primary productivity.

Final mass in the dark – initial mass = respiration (will be negative as the plants lose mass).

Gross primary productivity = net primary productivity + respiration (use the figure, ignoring the – sign).

Do these calculations for both the wet and dry masses.

All the masses were taken from areas of 2500 mm^2 so you can convert them to g m^{-2} by multiplying your answers by 400. The units of time depend on how long you leave the seedlings between the two measurements but it will probably be g m^{-2} week^{-1}.

Conclusions

1 What is the difference in your calculations using wet and dry masses?

2 What does the tray in the dark show you?

3 Why did you need to harvest and weigh plants at the beginning of the experiment?

4 Compare your results with the rest of your class. Which method gave you the most reliable results? Why do you think this is?

5 What assumptions have you made during this practical?

The influence of changes in productivity on the food chain

The higher the productivity, the more biomass accumulated by the producers and therefore the more biomass available for the consumers to eat. This means that, in general, higher productivities lead to more abundant populations of consumers, or longer food chains. The most productive areas of the oceans tend to be those areas with high levels of nutrients from upwelling. In tropical areas, there are high levels of light but it is also warm, which leads to a strong thermocline and little mixing of nutrients from deeper waters. In contrast, polar waters are nutrient rich because it is very cold and there is therefore only a weak thermocline. However, productivity is only high in the summer when the light levels are higher.

There does come a point when productivity can be too high. This leads to effects that are similar to the process of eutrophication seen in fresh-water ecosystems. If the levels of nutrients increase too much or too rapidly, phytoplankton may rapidly increase in a phenomenon known as an **algal bloom**.

In these circumstances, up to 5 million cells per litre can be produced, which is very damaging to the ecosystem. This density of algae is so high that it can clog the gills of fish so that they are unable to obtain enough oxygen. Once the algal cells die they are broken down by decomposers such as bacteria so there is also an increase in bacterial populations. The bacteria respire and grow and use up the oxygen in the water, which can lead to **hypoxic** conditions (lacking oxygen). This also kills heterotrophic organisms because without oxygen they cannot respire.

If the algal species involved also produce toxins, the effects can be even worse because the organisms that ingest them will be poisoned. This can cause mass mortality in aquatic organisms such as dolphins, manatees and whales, as well as food poisoning in people who eat contaminated shellfish. You can read more about these harmful algal blooms in Chapter 8.

KEY TERMS

Algal bloom: a rapid increase in a population of algae

Hypoxic: an area of water with a low concentration of dissolved oxygen

SELF-ASSESSMENT QUESTIONS

7 a Evaluate the use of different methods to measure ocean productivity.

 b Explain why giant icebergs increase productivity of the oceans.

8 a Explain why it can be damaging for nutrient levels in water to increase too much.

 b Suggest why waters at high latitudes normally have higher productivity than tropical waters.

CASE STUDY

46

The Peruvian anchoveta fishing industry

Anchovies are small forage fish found in the open ocean away from the seabed or the shore. A forage fish is a fish that is used by other predators for food. Anchovies are mainly filter feeders: water is taken in through the mouth and zooplankton is filtered out by the gill rakers. Forage fish are an important part of the food chain. They provide food for:

- larger fish such as tuna and salmon
- mammals like dolphins and whales
- sea birds including gulls and pelicans.

The Peruvian anchoveta fishery is the biggest single species fishery in the world. Anchoveta are a species of anchovy that live for up to 3 years and can grow to be 20 cm in length (Figure 3.8).

Figure 3.8. Peruvian anchoveta.

In the 1960s, catches of anchoveta off the coast of Peru were more than 10 million tonnes year^{-1}. In 1971, the catch was 13.1 million tonnes (Figure 3.9). In 1972, the industry collapsed because of over-fishing and the El Niño phenomenon. El Niño is a change in the trade winds in the Pacific Ocean. These winds normally stimulate upwelling of cold, nutrient-rich waters into the warmer sunlit water above. During an El Niño year, the thermocline deepens, which effectively blocks the cooler water underneath from mixing with the warm water at the top. Lack of nutrients therefore limits the primary productivity in the sunlit zone, leading to reductions in the numbers of fish.

After the collapse of the anchoveta populations, the industry shifted to fishing sardines for several years until the waters cooled again and anchoveta numbers increased (Figure 3.9). There was another reduction in numbers during an El Niño event in the early 1980s, but by the mid-1990s the catch was back up to 12.5 million tonnes. In 2014, only 2.2 million tonnes were caught after the second fishing season was cancelled because of the El Niño phenomenon.

It is not just the fishing industry that is affected by El Niño. Guano (excrement from sea birds) is an important fertiliser. When there are fewer fish, there is less food for the sea birds, which are their predators, and therefore less guano is produced.

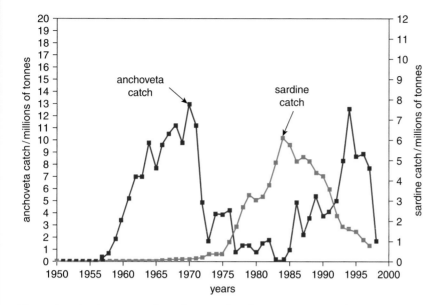

Figure 3.9. Anchoveta and sardine catches between 1950 and 2000.

Questions

1 Explain how a reduction in the nutrients in the upper layers of the ocean could lead to a decrease in the numbers of forage fish such as anchoveta.

2 Anchoveta feed on large zooplankton whereas sardines feed mainly on phytoplankton. Use this information to suggest why sardine numbers are less likely to collapse during an El Niño event.

3 Look at the graph in Figure 3.9 and suggest two years other than 1971 that could have had El Niño events. Explain your answer.

3.3 Energy transfer

Only a small amount of the radiation from the Sun is fixed by the Earth's producers. Some of the radiation never reaches the producers because it is reflected back into space. Of the light that does reach the ocean, some is absorbed, reflected or scattered by the water.

The remainder is available to the producers but even then it cannot all be used. Some is the wrong wavelength for the pigments of producers to absorb. Chlorophyll, for example, absorbs red and blue light but reflects green light (which is why it appears to be green). Of the light that is the correct wavelength, some will miss the chloroplasts and still not be absorbed (Figure 3.10).

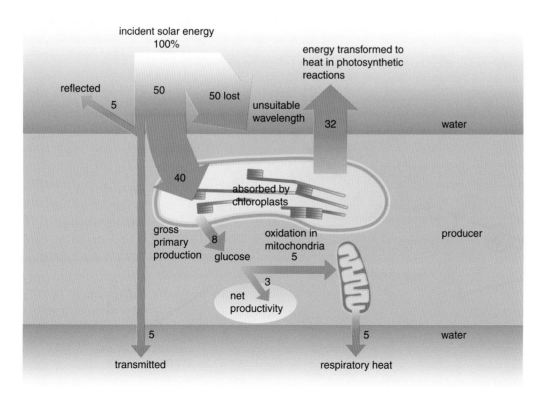

Figure 3.10. The fate of light energy falling on producers in the ocean.

The process of photosynthesis itself is not completely energy efficient. During the various chemical reactions that must take place, energy is lost as heat. Worldwide it has been estimated that producers such as green plants and phytoplankton fix about 0.06% of the total energy radiating from the Sun. But this figure can be as high as 1% in aquatic ecosystems and 2–3% on land.

Producers need some of the carbohydrates they produce for respiration. This means that only the net production of biomass is available to the next trophic level. The energy stored in biomass is passed to heterotrophic organisms when they ingest, digest and absorb the nutrients from the producers. These nutrients can then be assimilated into new biomass. If the producers are phytoplankton, then the entire cell is usually ingested by the primary consumers, passing on all the available energy. However, in the case of macroalgae and rooted plants like seagrass, there are parts of the producer that are not eaten (the roots, for example). The energy stored in these areas is therefore not available to the next trophic level, although it may later re-enter the ecosystem through decomposition when the plant dies.

Secondary production is the production of new biomass by the consumers. It can involve animals eating the phytoplankton, macroalgae and seagrass, or animals eating other animals. Decomposers such as bacteria and fungi break down dead organic matter to obtain the nutrients they need. This also releases nutrients back into the ecosystem (see Chapter 4). Secondary production depends on:

- the biomass available in the producers
- the amount of energy lost through respiration by the consumers
- the amount of energy lost in waste products such as urine (Figure 3.11).

Most salt-water fish only lose small amounts of urine and excrete most of their nitrogenous waste through their gills in the form of ammonia. Undigested food is egested as faeces.

These energy transfers can also be expressed as a formula: $C = P + R + F + U$

Where C is the energy consumed, R is the energy used in respiration, F is the energy in faeces, U is the energy in urine and other excreted waste products of metabolism, and P is the energy left over for the production of new biomass by the animal.

The energy of production (P) is then available to pass on to the next trophic level.

The efficiency of energy transfer

The efficiency of the energy transfer can be expressed as a percentage. This can be shown as:

$$\frac{\text{energy transferred to new trophic level}}{\text{energy in previous trophic level}} \times 100$$

For example, if the energy radiating from the Sun is 1 600 000 kJ m^{-2} year^{-1} and phytoplankton captures 153 000 kJ m^{-2} year^{-1} in photosynthesis, the efficiency is:

153 000 ÷ 1 600 000 × 100 = 9.6%

If 12 856 kJ m^{-2} year^{-1} is then passed to the zooplankton that make up the next trophic level, the efficiency is:

12 856 ÷ 153 000 × 100 = 8.4%

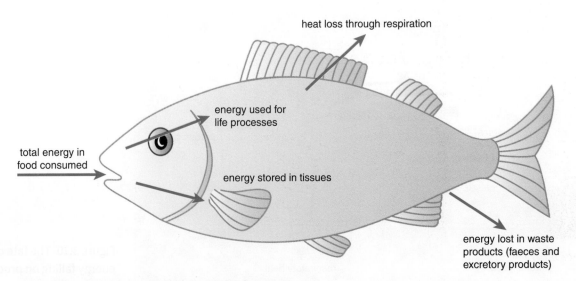

Figure 3.11. Energy transfer into and out of a consumer.

Typically the efficiency of transfer between trophic levels is around 10%, but it varies depending on:

- how much of the food is eaten

- how easy it is for the consumer to digest and assimilate the nutrients

- how much energy is used for movement

- how much is lost in the waste products of metabolism.

Some organisms are easier to digest and assimilate than others: generally, consumers find it easier to assimilate the energy in other animals than the energy in producers. If it is easier to assimilate the energy, then more of it will be passed to the next consumer. In addition, some organisms at each trophic level escape being eaten and the energy stored in their biomass will never pass to the next level.

Most fish are **ectothermic**, which means that their body temperature varies with the environmental temperature. The ocean sunfish, for example, is a secondary consumer that eats zooplankton, tiny animals present in the water that feed on the phytoplankton. The ocean sunfish is ectothermic and does not use energy in respiration to keep its body temperature higher than that of the surrounding water.

Tuna are **endothermic**, which means that they must expend energy maintaining their body temperature. Tuna occupy two trophic levels in the same food web, as secondary consumers eating zooplankton, and as tertiary consumers eating small crustaceans that have already fed on the zooplankton.

Small sharks feed on both the sunfish and the tuna but the efficiency of energy transfer is higher from the sunfish. Assuming that the sunfish and tuna take in similar amounts of energy, the tuna use more of this in respiration to keep warm so there is less to pass to the sharks. In general, the efficiency of transfer from ectothermic organisms ranges from 5% to 15% and from endothermic organisms ranges from 1% to 5%. The efficiency of transfer between the different trophic levels determines how many levels there are in the ecosystem. The higher the efficiency of transfer, the more trophic levels the ecosystem can support.

KEY TERMS

Ectothermic: an organism that maintains its body temperature by exchanging heat with its surroundings

Endothermic: an organism that maintains its body temperature by generating heat in metabolic processes

SELF-ASSESSMENT QUESTIONS

9 The total solar energy falling on phytoplankton is 1 000 000 kJ m^{-2} year^{-1} and the efficiency of transfer to the phytoplankton is 1%.

   a Calculate the GPP.

   b If 30% of the GPP is used in respiration, then what is the NPP?

10 Describe the factors that determine how efficient the transfer of energy is.

49

Maths skills

Interpreting energy diagrams and calculating percentage efficiency

Energy diagrams are another way of showing the flow of energy through an ecosystem (Figure 3.12). They show the energy entering the ecosystem from the Sun, moving through producers and being lost as a result of respiration and excretion. The main point to remember is that all the energy has to go somewhere, so the values on the arrows going into a box must always equal the sum of the values on those coming out. The units can be given as kJ m^{-2} year^{-1} or simply arbitrary units. Arbitrary units are relative units of measurement to allow comparison. For example, if there is twice as much energy in producers as in primary consumers the arbitrary units could be 5 and 10 or 50 and 100, it does not matter.

→

Worked example

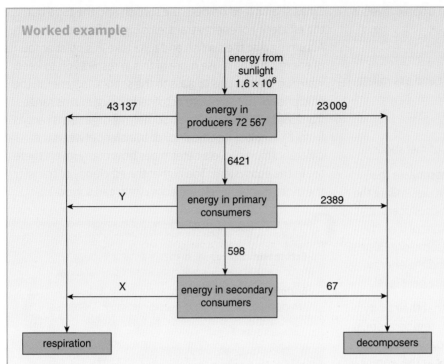

Figure 3.12. Worked example of an energy flow diagram (units are kJ m^{-2} year^{-1}).

1   How much energy is being lost in respiration by the secondary consumers?

Remember that the energy entering the secondary consumers must equal the energy leaving.

From the diagram you can see that 598 kJ m^{-2} year^{-1} enters the secondary consumers (the 'in arrow'); 67 kJ m^{-2} year^{-1} ends up being passed to the decomposers. On this diagram the only other arrow is the respiration arrow (labelled X). So the energy lost in respiration, X, must be equal to 598 – 67 = 531 kJ m^{-2} year^{-1}.

You can check your answer by making sure the arrows add up. So in this case the 'in arrow' is 598. The 'out arrows' are 531 and 67, which added together do add up to 598.

2   What is the efficiency of energy transfer between the Sun (solar energy) and producers?

To calculate the efficiency of energy transfer you always work out a percentage. This allows you to compare different ecosystems where the initial energy inputs might be different. The percentage is the energy that is transferred divided by the energy that was in the previous trophic level and then multiplied by 100. So in this case the energy transferred to the producers was 72 567 kJ m^{-2} year^{-1} and the energy in the previous trophic level (the Sun) was 1.6 × 10^6 kJ m^{-2} year^{-1}. So the efficiency of transfer is:

(72 567 ÷ 1.6 × 10^6) × 100 = 4.53%

You may also be given similar information in the form of a pyramid of energy. In this case, just use the figures in the pyramid in your percentage calculation. Always divide the figure in any particular tropic level by the figure for the previous level and then multiply by 100. For example: (energy in primary consumers / energy in producers) × 100.

Questions

1   a   Calculate the amount of energy used in respiration (Y) by primary consumers.

    b   Calculate the efficiency of energy transfer between producers and primary consumers.

2 The pyramid of energy in Figure 3.13 shows the energy in a marine food chain. It is not drawn to scale and the energy is given in arbitrary units.

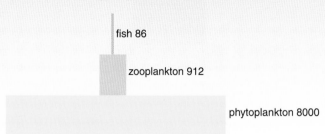

fish 86

zooplankton 912

phytoplankton 8000

Figure 3.13. Pyramid of energy showing energy in arbitrary units.

a Use the information in Figure 3.13 to calculate the efficiency of energy transfer between the phytoplankton and the zooplankton.

b Use the information in Figure 3.13 to calculate the efficiency of energy transfer between the zooplankton and the fish.

c The average efficiency of transfer between producers and primary consumers is 10%. Suggest why the transfer in this pyramid between phytoplankton and zooplankton is more efficient than this.

3.4 Illustrating feeding relationships

You can show the relationships between the different trophic levels using pyramids of number, biomass and energy. These are like bar charts but are made up of horizontal bars arranged in a pyramid shape to show a particular food chain. They can be drawn to scale or simply sketched to give an idea of the changes as energy is transferred along the food chain. Producers are always at the bottom, followed by primary consumers, secondary consumers and tertiary consumers. Although energy is transferred to decomposers once the producers and consumers die, it is not often shown on the pyramid.

Pyramids of number

A **pyramid of numbers** simply shows the number of organisms present in each trophic level at a particular moment in time. The size of each horizontal bar is proportional to the number of organisms. In theory this should be quite simple but in practice it is actually rather difficult. It is often hard to estimate accurately the number of organisms present, and even once this has been achieved it can be difficult to show them to scale. For example, a typical oceanic food chain is:

phytoplankton → zooplankton → herring → mackerel → mahi mahi → shark

There could be millions of cells of phytoplankton and only one or two sharks. Finding a scale to show this is impossible. For this reason many pyramids of numbers are sketched rather than drawn to scale (Figure 3.14). In addition, much of the phytoplankton is consumed very quickly after it is produced. Thus if the numbers present in an ecosystem are counted after most have been eaten, the pyramid will be inverted (upside down) and it will look as though there are fewer phytoplankton than zooplankton. The number of organisms in an ecosystem will also vary depending on factors such as the time of year or the amount of fishing. This means that the pyramid can only show the numbers in each trophic level at a particular moment in time. Using pyramids of number also does not take into account the size of organisms, which can lead to odd-looking pyramids. For example, if several small parasites feed on one large fish you will see an inverted pyramid.

 KEY TERM

Pyramid of numbers: a diagram that shows the number of organisms in each trophic level of a food chain

Pyramids of biomass

Instead of finding the number of each organism you could measure their total biomass. This overcomes the difficulties of having organisms of different sizes, such as the parasites in the last example. It does not, however, solve the issues caused by phytoplankton being eaten before they can be measured. It is possible that the

51

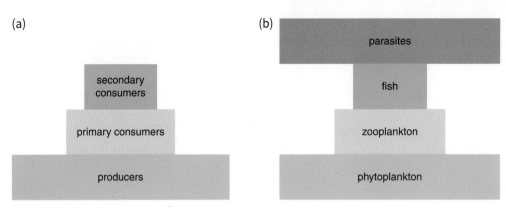

Figure 3.14. (a) A generalised pyramid of numbers; (b) A pyramid of numbers for a marine ecosystem showing small parasites feeding off a large fish.

biomass of organisms within an ecosystem could increase or decrease after measurements are taken which will make the pyramid inaccurate.

It is difficult to find the biomass of each trophic level accurately. Organisms vary in the amount of water they contain, and this water does not contribute to their biomass. For this reason dry mass should be used, with the water removed by evaporation. Clearly to do this the organisms must be killed, and it is therefore undesirable to measure the biomass of the entire food chain. Instead there are conversions available to change the mass of living material into dry mass. This still means that every individual must be found and weighed. Alternatively, the dry mass of a sample can be taken and then multiplied by the total number of organisms to give the total average dry mass. Both of these methods will give an estimate of the total biomass but neither of them will be completely accurate.

A **pyramid of biomass** may still be inverted as the total amount of biomass in phytoplankton at any one time is small because they are eaten very quickly. However, their reproductive rate is very high so they reproduce quickly enough to provide enough biomass to maintain the population of consumers. In other words the amount of biomass is low but the rate of production of biomass

is high. This snapshot view of the biomass at a particular moment in time is known as the standing crop (Figure 3.15).

Pyramids of energy

A **pyramid of energy** shows the rate of production of biomass rather than the standing crop, and is therefore always pyramid shaped (Figure 3.16). It involves finding the energy in each trophic level of the food chain, which is a complex procedure. Data is collected over a long period of time, normally a year. Often conversion tables are used that will convert dry biomass into energy production. The units for pyramids of energy are $kJ\ m^{-2}\ year^{-1}$ so it will not be a standing crop but a measurement of the energy available over the entire year. Although pyramids of energy are the most difficult to produce, they are probably the most useful in terms of understanding the ecosystem.

> **KEY TERMS**
>
> **Pyramid of biomass:** a diagram that shows the biomass present in each trophic level of a food chain
>
> **Pyramid of energy:** a diagram that shows the amount of energy in each trophic level of a food chain

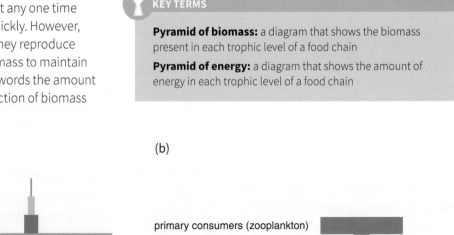

Figure 3.15. (a) Pyramid of biomass showing the decrease in biomass through the food chain; (b) Inverted pyramid of biomass showing the problems caused by the standing crop of rapidly reproducing phytoplankton.

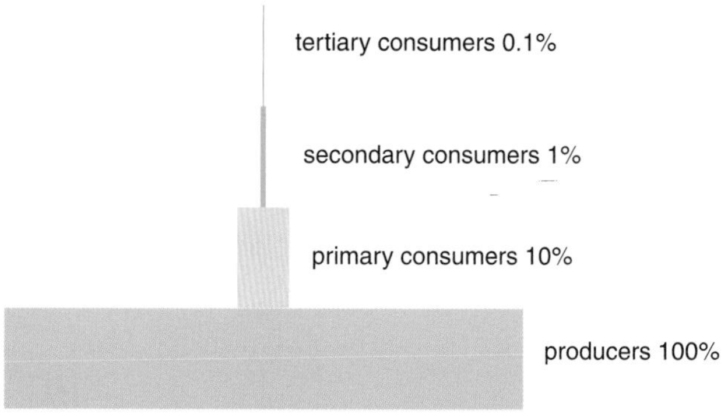

tertiary consumers 0.1%

secondary consumers 1%

primary consumers 10%

producers 100%

Figure 3.16. A generalised pyramid of energy showing the approximate transfer between tropic levels.

SELF-ASSESSMENT QUESTIONS

11 What are the drawbacks of using pyramids of number?

12 Why is it best to use dry mass to produce pyramids of biomass?

13 Describe what an inverted pyramid is and explain what might cause it.

Summary

- Energy enters marine ecosystems in two main ways: either through photosynthesis or chemosynthesis.

- Photosynthesis is carried out by producers such as phytoplankton, seaweeds and seagrasses.

- In photosynthesis, light energy is used to fix carbon dioxide into carbohydrates.

- Chemosynthesis is carried out by bacteria at hydrothermal vents, which are able to convert energy in chemicals dissolved in the water into carbohydrates.

- Productivity is the rate of production of new biomass by the autotrophs, which depends on various factors including the amount of light and the availability of nutrients.

- Productivity can be measured by measuring the rate of photosynthesis, looking at changes in biomass or by using satellite images that show the amount of chlorophyll in the oceans.

- If productivity is too high this can cause an algal bloom, which reduces the amount of oxygen in the water and damages the ecosystem.

- Not all of the energy from the Sun is fixed by producers, some is reflected by the water, some is the wrong wavelength for chlorophyll to absorb, and some simply does not reach a producer.

- Some of the energy fixed into carbohydrates is used in respiration, or lost through excretion, the rest is available to be passed to the next trophic level.

- The efficiency of this transfer varies but is normally around 10%.

- You can show the transfer of energy by drawing pyramids of number, biomass or energy.

- Pyramids of energy are the most difficult to draw but give us the most information about the food chain.

Exam-style questions

1 **a** **i** Describe what is meant by the term productivity. [3]

ii Give three factors that can affect the productivity. [3]

iii Briefly describe a simple method to measure productivity. [3]

b Explain why productivity is increased during the spring and summer. [4]

[Total mark: 13]

2 **a** Describe the process of photosynthesis. **[4]**

b **i** Why does photosynthesis not occur at hydrothermal vents on the ocean floor? **[2]**

ii Describe how energy enters the ecosystem found at the hydrothermal vents. **[4]**

c The solar energy falling on the ocean is 1.7×10^6 kJ m^{-2} year^{-1} and the phytoplankton are able to use 18 754 kJ m^{-2} year^{-1} of this.

i Calculate the percentage of the Sun's energy that is used by phytoplankton. Show your working. **[2]**

ii Explain why 100% of the energy is not used. **[3]**

[Total mark: 15]

3 Study the graph below.

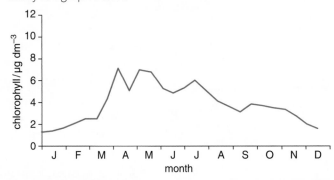

Figure 3.17. Chlorophyll concentrations on the California coast in 2001.

a Describe the shape of the graph. **[3]**

b Explain why the amount of chlorophyll increases in March. **[5]**

c Suggest and explain what will happen to the population of zooplankton in March and April. **[2]**

d Within this ecosystem, herring feed on the zooplankton and mackerel feed on the herring. There are 809 phytoplankton, 37 zooplankton, 11 herring and 1 mackerel. Draw the pyramid of numbers for this food chain. **[3]**

[Total mark: 13]

4 Study the graph below.

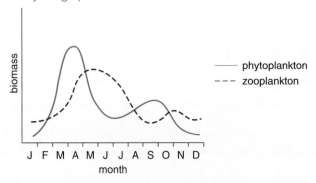

Figure 3.18. The biomass of phytoplankton and zooplankton round the Norwegian coast over the course of a year.

a Sketch a pyramid of biomass to show the phytoplankton and zooplankton in March. **[2]**

b Explain why there is normally more biomass in the producers than in the consumers. **[3]**

c Describe how the pyramid of biomass would be different in July. **[2]**

d Explain why the pyramid of biomass would be different in July. **[1]**

[Total mark: 8]

5 Figure 3.19 shows a food chain from a marine ecosystem. The figures show the energy in each trophic level in winter in arbitrary units.

phytoplankton 5000	→	zooplankton 589	→	sardine 61	→	tuna 4

Figure 3.19. A food chain from a marine ecosystem showing the energy in each trophic level in arbitrary units.

a Calculate the efficiency of the transfer of energy between the phytoplankton and the zooplankton. Show your working. **[2]**

b Explain why there is less energy in the consumers than in the producers. **[3]**

c **i** Suggest what would happen to the energy in each level during summer. **[3]**

ii Suggest what might happen to the food chain if fertilisers from coastal farmland drain as run-off into the water. **[3]**

[Total mark: 11]

6 **a** **i** Explain the difference between gross primary production and net primary production. **[3]**

ii The gross primary production in an ecosystem is 78 935 kJ m^{-2} year^{-1} and the energy lost in respiration is 23 674 kJ m^{-2} year^{-1}. Calculate the net primary production. **[2]**

b Explain why measurements of productivity in kJ m^{-2} year^{-1} are a more accurate representation of what is happening in the ecosystem than measurements of biomass. **[2]**

[Total mark: 7]

The Gulf of Mexico dead zone

The Gulf of Mexico is an ocean basin surrounded by the United States, Mexico and Cuba (Figure 3.20). It is approximately 1500 km wide and is connected to both the Atlantic Ocean and the Caribbean Sea.

A dead zone is an area of water where oxygen levels have become very low (hypoxic). This means that there is insufficient oxygen for respiration, and organisms either die or move to a different area where the dissolved oxygen levels are higher. Dead zones occur near coastlines where there are high levels of nutrients washing off agricultural land. The first dead zone was reported in the early 20th century and since then the numbers have increased every year (Figure 3.21).

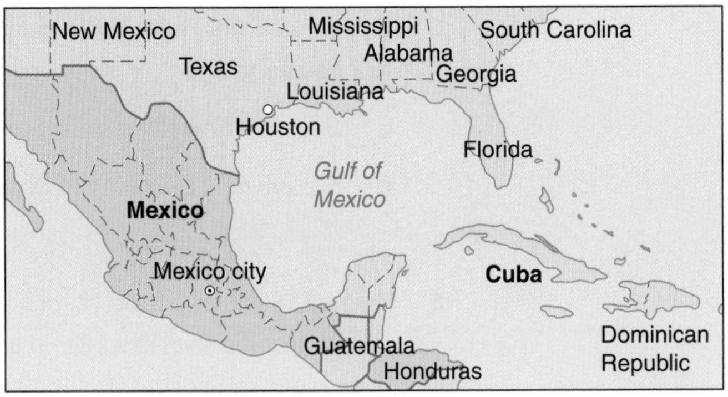

Figure 3.20. The Gulf of Mexico and surrounding countries.

Formation of dead zones

Dead zones form when excess nutrients such as phosphates and nitrates enter the water. These primarily come from chemical fertilisers and waste such as sewage. Dead zones can also form naturally if changes in wind and currents alter the upwelling of nutrients from deep water.

When the excess nutrients enter the water, they massively increase the growth of algae, leading to an algal bloom. Phosphates and nitrates tend to increase the growth of blue-green cyanobacteria, which are not eaten by many zooplankton. This means that their numbers can build up unchecked. When the organisms die they sink to the bottom, where they provide a food source for the bacteria, which break them down in the process of decomposition. The numbers of bacteria rapidly increase and their respiration uses up the majority of the oxygen dissolved in the water. The water therefore becomes hypoxic and other aquatic organisms die.

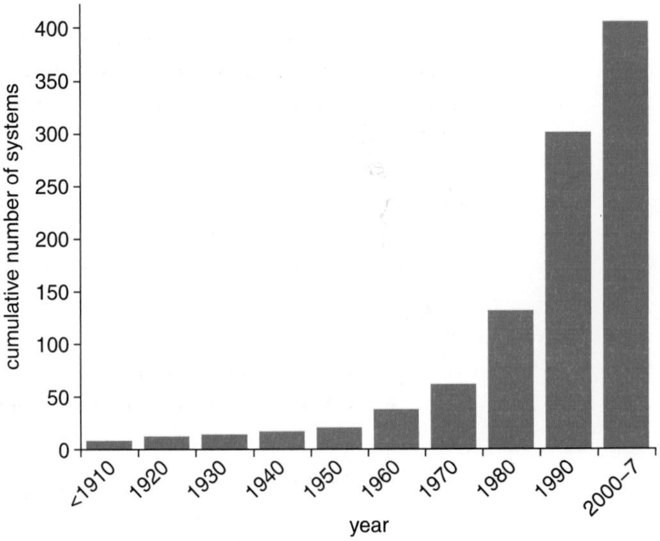

Figure 3.21. Number of dead zones by decade.

The Gulf of Mexico

The Gulf of Mexico dead zone is interesting for two reasons. First, it is the second largest dead zone in the world. Second, it is seasonal and its size fluctuates depending on the weather conditions each year. The Mississippi River drains into the Gulf and has the largest drainage basin of any river in North America. The levels of nutrients it washes into the Gulf are correspondingly large. Twelve million people live in areas that border the Mississippi and that discharge treated sewage into the water. The majority of the land

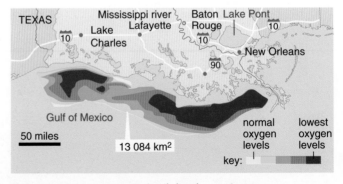

Figure 3.22. An average-sized dead zone in 2014.

near the Mississippi is farmland so rainwater constantly washes fertilisers into the water. About 1.7 million tonnes of nutrients are released into the Gulf of Mexico from the Mississippi every year. In the spring and summer this causes algal blooms and the development of the dead zone. The size of the dead zone varies; on average it is around 13 000 km^2 but it has been as large as 22 000 km^2 (in the summer of 2002). During times of heavy flooding the dead zone tends to be very large. In the late summer of 1998 the dead zone disappeared because there was a severe drought and the amount of water entering the Gulf decreased significantly. Figure 3.22 shows the size of the dead zone in an average year.

The fresh water flowing into the Gulf from the Mississippi is less dense than the seawater and so forms a layer on the top. This means that the deeper water, where the hypoxia occurs, is cut off from a resupply of oxygen from the atmosphere. The dead zone therefore persists until the water mixes again, either because of a hurricane or when cold fronts form in the autumn and winter.

The effects of the dead zone

The seafood industry in the Gulf of Mexico is very important. The Gulf provides the United States with the majority of its farmed oysters and shrimp, as well as being a source for several types of fish. The National Oceanic and Atmospheric Administration (NOAA) has estimated that the dead zone costs the tourism and fishing industries \$82 million year^{-1}. When fish move out of the dead zone because of the lack of oxygen, fishers have to travel further to catch them. This costs both time and money. Shrimp are often unable to escape the dead zone and instead are simply killed, reducing the population and making them harder to catch in the future.

Reducing the size of the dead zone

The main way to reduce the size of any dead zone is to reduce the level of nutrients entering the water. In 1997 the Gulf of Mexico Watershed Nutrient Task Force was formed with the aim of reducing the average size of the dead zone to 5000 km^2. Strategies that can be used include reducing the use of inorganic fertilisers on farms, as well as altering the timing of their use to avoid leaching by rainwater. Management of flood plains is important because an increased area of flood plains means that less floodwater makes its way into the Gulf and nutrient-rich sediment is captured. Farmers are being encouraged not to drain wetlands but to leave them in their natural state to improve soil quality and reduce erosion. Waste treatment processes are being improved to reduce the discharge of nutrients into the water and to avoid animal waste entering waterways at all.

Questions

1 Describe how a dead zone forms.

2 Suggest why the number of dead zones has increased since they were first discovered.

3 Explain why the Gulf of Mexico dead zone varies in size each year.

4 Explain why the Gulf of Mexico dead zone is seasonal.

5 Summarise the control measures being taken to reduce the size of the Gulf of Mexico dead zone and explain how each measure works.

Chapter 4
Nutrient cycles in marine ecosystems

Learning outcomes

By the end of this chapter, you should be able to:

- describe the general processes that take place within a nutrient cycle
- explain what is meant by a reservoir within a nutrient cycle
- describe and explain the processes that add nutrients to the surface water of the ocean
- describe the processes that remove nutrients from the surface water of the ocean
- summarise the nitrogen, carbon, magnesium, calcium and phosphorus cycles as a simple diagram
- state the uses of each of the above nutrients in living organisms
- plot and interpret accurate graphs of experimental results
- apply what you have learnt to new, unfamiliar contexts.

4.1 Cycling of elements through the ecosystem

Nutrient cycles are some of the most important processes that occur in any ecosystem. They show the movement of **nutrients** that are essential for life, such as nitrogen, carbon and phosphorus. These nutrients are used by living organisms and are moved through the food chain by feeding. When organisms die the nutrients are recycled by **decomposers** and return to inorganic forms. The inorganic forms remain in the environment, sometimes for millions of years, before being converted back into organic forms to be used once again, thus continuing the cycle.

The ocean is an important **reservoir** for these elements, which means that they may be held there for long periods of time. Microorganisms are able to fix inorganic substances into organic molecules, which enables them to be used by other organisms. In this way the nutrients are moved from the **abiotic** part of the cycle to the **biotic**. The nutrients may then be removed temporarily from the cycle if they sink to the ocean floor as faeces, or after the organism has died. Some will be incorporated into coral reefs and others will be removed from the ocean altogether by harvesting. Inorganic molecules are returned to the ocean by various processes, including dissolving directly into the water, **run-off** from the land and **upwelling**.

Chapter 3 discussed the effect of nutrient concentration in the ocean. Up to a certain point, the more nutrients present, the more productive the environment. When there

are too many nutrients the productivity can increase too fast and the ecosystem is damaged. Recently, it has been suggested that artificially altering the nutrient balance in the oceans could increase productivity and therefore increase the amount of carbon dioxide used in photosynthesis. This has been proposed as a solution to the increasing levels of carbon dioxide in the atmosphere. However, this solution may have unintended consequences, such as decreasing the pH of the water and damaging animals with shells. It could also lead to harmful algal blooms as discussed in Chapters 3 and 8.

KEY TERMS

Nutrient cycles: the movement and exchange of elements that are essential to life, from inorganic molecules, through fixation and then into living organisms, before being decomposed back into inorganic molecules

Nutrient: a chemical that provides what is needed for organisms to live and grow

Decomposers: bacteria and fungi that break down dead organic matter and release the nutrients back into the environment

Reservoir: part of the abiotic phase of the nutrient cycle where nutrients can remain for long periods of time

Abiotic: the environment's geological, physical and chemical features, the non-living part of an ecosystem

Biotic: the living parts of an ecosystem, which includes the organisms and their effects on each other

Run-off: the flow of water from land caused by precipitation

Upwelling: the movement of cold, nutrient-rich water from deep in the ocean to the surface

4.2 Nutrient cycles

Nutrient cycles are the essential movement and recycling of the elements that are necessary for organisms to live and grow. Globally, the carbon and nitrogen cycles are probably the best known and most clearly understood, but there are many other elements that are important. These include phosphorus, calcium and magnesium. In this chapter you look at why each of these is necessary for life, as well as the mechanisms that add them or remove them from the oceans.

All nutrient cycles have a biotic and an abiotic phase (Figure 4.1). A nutrient moves from the abiotic to the biotic phase when it is absorbed and **assimilated** by producers.

For example carbon dioxide (an inorganic molecule and therefore part of the abiotic cycle) is fixed during photosynthesis into glucose. This can later be converted into the other molecules needed by the producer, for example starch. It has been assimilated and is now part of the biotic cycle. During the biotic phase nutrients are moved from one organism to the next by feeding. So nutrients move along the food chain from the producers to the consumers. Some will be lost from each organism

KEY TERM

Assimilation: the conversion of a nutrient into a useable form that can be incorporated into the tissues of an organism

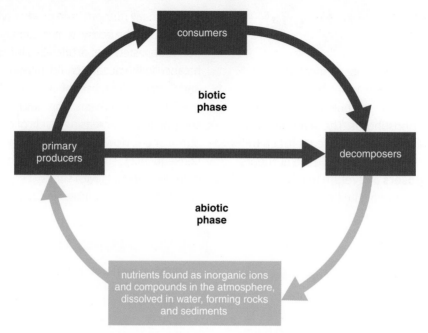

Figure 4.1. A generalised nutrient cycle showing the movement from the biotic to the abiotic phases.

by egestion and excretion and the rest will remain within organic compounds until the organism dies. After death, organisms must be broken down by decomposers, which results in nutrients returning to their inorganic form and therefore the abiotic part of the cycle. During this part of the cycle nutrients can be found dissolved in water, as gases in the atmosphere, or forming sediment that can later become rocks.

Reservoirs in nutrient cycles

A reservoir is part of the abiotic phase of the nutrient cycle where elements can remain for long periods of time. The ocean is an important reservoir for many elements. The **residence time** is the average time a particle spends in a system. Average residence times for nutrient ions in the ocean tend to be very long because some of them fall to the bottom in faeces or dead organisms. They can remain in sediment on the ocean floor for thousands or even millions of years (Table 4.1)

The time the same nutrients spend in just the surface layer of the ocean is much shorter because the nutrients are constantly being used and recycled by the organisms

nutrient	average residence time / years
phosphate (phosphorus)*	20 000–100 000
magnesium	17 000 000
hydrogencarbonate** (carbon)*	100 000
nitrogen	2 000
calcium	1 000 000

*Where the nutrient is found as an ion, the element is given in parentheses

**Sometimes called bicarbonate

Table 4.1. Approximate residence times for different nutrients in the ocean.

living there. This surface reservoir is of particular importance because it enables the high productivity of phytoplankton. Nutrient availability is often the main limiting factor after light intensity for growth of producers.

Phytoplankton are found in the surface layer of the ocean where there is plenty of light. It is therefore the concentration of nutrients that determines the rate of growth. The higher the rate of growth of phytoplankton, the higher the rate of photosynthesis and therefore the higher the productivity. The productivity of the

---

KEY TERM

Residence time: the average time that a particle spends in a particular system

phytoplankton determines how much energy can be transferred to the next trophic level (see Chapter 3). In general, the amounts of nitrogen and phosphorus limit the rate of growth because they are found in the lowest concentrations in the water. This means that there is usually slightly less than is needed by the producers. If the concentrations increase, the productivity increases. The average concentrations of ions dissolved in the water at the ocean surface are shown in Table 4.2.

ion	average concentration in seawater / ppm
chloride	19 345.00
sodium	10 752.00
sulfate	2701.00
magnesium	1295.00
calcium	416.00
hydrogencarbonate	145.00
nitrate	0.50
phosphate	0.07

Table 4.2. Average concentrations of some of the ions found dissolved in seawater.

SELF-ASSESSMENT QUESTIONS

1 a Describe what is meant by the words biotic and abiotic with reference to nutrient cycles.

  b Explain how nutrients move from the abiotic to the biotic part of a nutrient cycle.

2 a Describe how nutrients move within the biotic part of the cycle.

  b Name two places where you would find nutrient ions within the abiotic part of a nutrient cycle.

4.3 Processes that add nutrients to the surface water

There are three main processes that add nutrients to the reservoir within the surface water. These are:

- dissolving in the water from the atmosphere
- upwelling
- run-off.

The relative importance of these processes depends on each nutrient. For nutrients present in high concentrations in the atmosphere, dissolving will add more to the reservoir than run-off, for example.

Dissolving of atmospheric gases

Nitrogen and carbon are both present in the Earth's atmosphere and are therefore both able to dissolve directly into the water. Nitrogen is present in the form of nitrogen gas, N_2, and carbon as carbon dioxide gas, CO_2. The amount of gas that can dissolve in the water depends on several factors. These include the:

- temperature of the water
- atmospheric concentration of each gas
- amount of mixing of water at the surface.

In some areas there will be more gas dissolving in the water than there is diffusing back into the atmosphere. These areas are known as **sinks**.

In other areas it will the other way around, and more gas will diffuse into the atmosphere than is dissolving into the water. These areas are called **sources**. Generally the overall concentration tends to remain at an equilibrium, with the same amount dissolving into the ocean as is removed by diffusion back into the atmosphere (Figure 4.2).

KEY TERMS

Sink: an area where there is a net loss of material (for example where more gas dissolves into the ocean than diffuses into the atmosphere)

Source: an area where there is a net gain of material (for example where more gas diffuses into the atmosphere than dissolves in the ocean)

Upwelling

Upwelling involves cold water from the deep ocean being brought to the surface. These deep waters have higher concentrations of nutrients than those at the surface because of the tendency for the remains of living things to sink. So faecal matter and dead organisms sink from the surface layers to the deeper parts of the ocean. Here they may be broken down by decomposers and the nutrient ions returned to the water. During upwelling this nutrient-rich water rises to the surface where it effectively fertilises the surface layers and increases productivity. Areas with high levels of coastal upwelling tend to be the

61

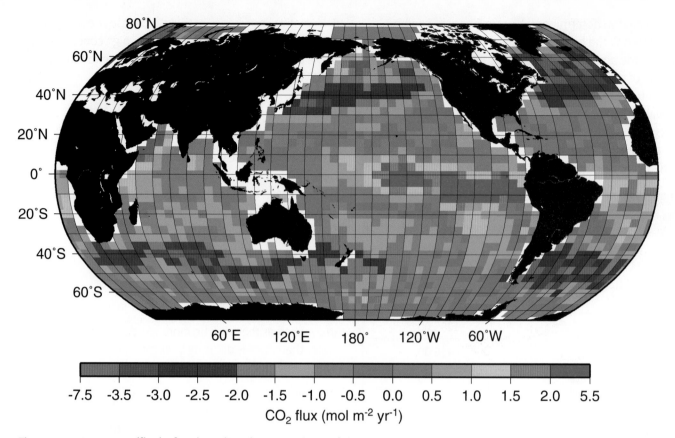

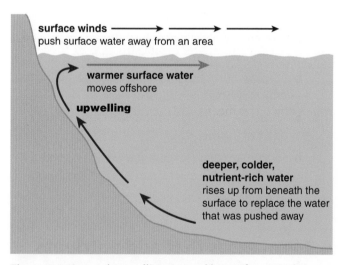

Figure 4.2. Movement (flux) of carbon dioxide into and out of the ocean over the course of a year. Purple and blue areas are carbon sinks; yellow and red areas are carbon sources; green areas are at an equilibrium, with the same amount of carbon dioxide dissolving as being released.

most productive and have high catches of commercially important fish. It has been estimated that 25% of fish are caught from just 5% of the ocean where there are high levels of upwelling.

Coastal upwelling is caused when winds blow parallel to the shore (Figure 4.3). This displaces the warm surface water, which moves further offshore and has to be replaced by water from deeper in the ocean. Other mechanisms of upwelling are discussed in Chapter 7. If the wind is moving in the opposite direction and drives the water towards the coastline, it is also possible for downwelling to occur. This of course removes nutrients from the surface layers of the ocean.

Figure 4.3. Coastal upwelling caused by surface winds.

Run-off

Run-off is part of the water cycle in which water flows into streams and rivers and from there to the ocean. During the water cycle, water evaporates from rivers, lakes, oceans and streams. It condenses into clouds in the atmosphere and from there falls on the land as precipitation (Figure 4.4). Some of the precipitation enters the soil in a process called **infiltration**. The rate of infiltration is affected by the characteristics of the soil. Sandy soil, which

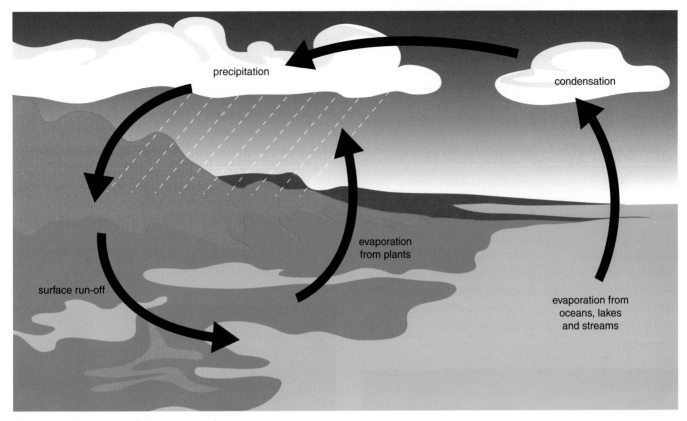

Figure 4.4. Summary of the water cycle.

is formed from large particles with relatively large gaps between them, has a high infiltration rate, compared with clay soil, which has a low infiltration rate. The higher the infiltration rate, the lower the rate of surface run-off. In other words, the more impermeable the ground, the more surface run-off there is.

As the water flows towards the sea it **leaches** nutrients from the soil. This means that water-soluble nutrient ions dissolve in the water. Run-off can also collect other substances as it flows, such as oil, heavy metals, pesticides and sewage. These all end up in the ocean. Excess nutrients in run-off can lead to marine dead zones (Chapter 3) and harmful algal blooms (Chapter 3, and discussed in more detail in Chapter 8).

 KEY TERMS

Infiltration: part of the water cycle where water soaks into the soil from ground level and moves underground

Leaching: a process during which water-soluble nutrients are removed from the soil and dissolve in water that is flowing to the sea (run-off)

SELF-ASSESSMENT QUESTIONS

3 What effect do you think upwelling would have on a food web?

4 Explain why nitrogen and carbon dioxide dissolve in the water from the atmosphere, but not phosphate.

4.4 Processes that remove nutrients from the surface layer

The main way in which nutrients are removed from the surface layer is through uptake and assimilation by producers. They fix the inorganic ions into useable organic compounds that are fed on by consumers. In this way the nutrients are able to move through the food chain. For example, phytoplankton take up nitrate ions and use them to produce amino acids. These are then built up into proteins that form part of the phytoplankton structure. Zooplankton eat the phytoplankton and digest these proteins, using the amino acids released in digestion to produce their own proteins. Small fish then eat the zooplankton and the process continues. Once the nutrients have entered the food chain there are different paths they can take. Some sink to the floor as **marine snow**, some are incorporated into coral reefs, and some are removed by harvesting.

KEY TERM

Marine snow: particles of organic material that fall from surface waters to the deeper ocean

Marine snow

Marine snow is the name given to the particles of organic matter that fall from the surface of the ocean to the deeper water. It is made up of faeces from the organisms living in the surface layers, as well as dead animals, phytoplankton and zooplankton. It is called marine snow because that is what it looks like, small white particles floating in the water (Figure 4.5).

Figure 4.5. Marine snow in the water.

This continuous fall of organic matter provides food for many organisms that live deeper in the ocean. Some of it is fed on by zooplankton and fish as it falls, some is eaten by filter feeders much deeper down. Much of it is not eaten at all and forms part of the sediment at the bottom of the ocean. Some of the nutrients in the sediment are released into the water by processes such as erosion and dissolving, others remain in the sediment for many years.

SELF-ASSESSMENT QUESTIONS

5   Describe the process that removes nutrients from the water and allows them to enter the food chain.

6   Describe what forms marine snow and explain where the majority of it ends up.

Incorporation into coral reefs

Coral polyps secrete a hard shell made from calcium carbonate to protect themselves and the zooxanthellae that live within them. Figure 4.6 shows some of the structures produced by coral. Coral eat tiny zooplankton and digest them to gain the nutrients they need. The zooplankton have previously gained their nutrients from phytoplankton. Any type of nutrient can be incorporated into the living parts of the reef and the other organisms that live there. But the hard shells last even after the living part has died. Coral reefs are very large and can last for a very long time, so the nutrients contained in them are removed from the cycling process for a long time. Most established coral reefs are between 5000 and 10 000 years old. Reef formation is discussed in Chapter 5.

Figure 4.6. Structures produced by coral polyps.

Harvesting

Harvesting refers to the removal of marine species by humans. In 2016, it was estimated that the global fish catch in 2010 had been 109 million metric tonnes. This is 30% higher than had been previously thought. Other species are also harvested, including crustaceans such as crabs and lobsters, molluscs such as mussels and squid, and macro-algae such as seaweeds. All the nutrients present in these species are removed when they are harvested from the ocean. However, many of the nutrients eventually find their way back to the ocean through the normal cycling of nutrients. For example, fish may be eaten and digested by humans and some of the nitrogen-containing compounds are then lost in urine, which ends up in sewage. In many areas, sewage is released into rivers and oceans after only being partially treated. In some areas, raw sewage is released. In this way, the nitrogen-containing compounds present in the original fish return to the ocean.

4.5 Examples of marine nutrient cycles

The processes discussed so far that take place in marine nutrient cycles can all be summarised in the same diagram (Figure 4.7).

Nutrients enter the reservoir of dissolved nutrients in the surface layer by dissolving, run-off and upwelling, and are removed by uptake by producers. Once in the food chain nutrients can sink, become incorporated into coral reefs or be harvested. Each nutrient is needed for a different purpose within organisms, and each nutrient cycle is slightly different.

KEY TERM

Dissociation (dissociates): a reversible chemical change where the molecules of a single compound separate into two or more other substances

The carbon cycle

Carbon is needed by living things because it is the basis of all organic materials. Carbohydrates such as glucose and starch; lipids; proteins; and nucleic acids such as DNA are all based on chains of carbon molecules. Carbon enters the biotic phase of the cycle through the fixation of carbon dioxide in photosynthesis. Carbon dioxide is then released through respiration by all living things.

The main way carbon enters the ocean is by dissolving of carbon dioxide gas from the atmosphere. Carbon dioxide dissolves in water to form carbonic acid (H_2CO_3). This then **dissociates** into hydrogencarbonate ions (HCO_3^-) and hydrogen ions (H^+) in a reversible reaction. Hydrogencarbonate dissociates further into carbonate ions (CO_3^{2-}) and hydrogen ions (H^+). So in solution there is a dynamic equilibrium between carbon dioxide, hydrogencarbonate and carbonic acid. In seawater 89% of the dissolved inorganic carbon is found as hydrogencarbonate, 10% is carbonate and 1% is dissolved carbon dioxide.

65

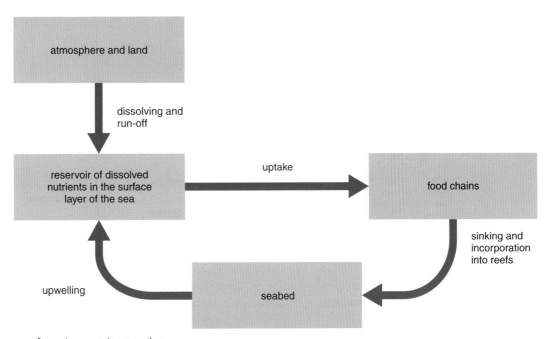

Figure 4.7. A summary of marine nutrient cycles.

The reactions in this equilibrium are:

carbon dioxide + water ⇌ carbonic acid
$$CO_2 + H_2O \rightleftharpoons H_2CO_3$$

carbonic acid ⇌ hydrogencarbonate ion + hydrogen ion
$$H_2CO_3 \rightleftharpoons HCO_3^- + H^+$$

hydrogencarbonate ion ⇌ carbonate ion + hydrogen ion
$$HCO_3^- \rightleftharpoons CO_3^{2-} + H^+$$

The algae and photosynthetic bacteria that make up the phytoplankton are able to take in dissolved forms of carbon dioxide and use it in photosynthesis. It is fixed into glucose, which can then be used to form other compounds needed by the phytoplankton. When the phytoplankton are eaten by zooplankton, the carbon-containing compounds are broken down during digestion. The zooplankton then assimilate them into their own biomass. This process is repeated when the zooplankton are eaten by other consumers.

At each stage, the organisms are respiring so they release carbon dioxide back into the water. From here it can diffuse back into the atmosphere. When the organisms die, some of the organic matter is broken down by decomposing bacteria and returns to the water as dissolved inorganic carbon. Some of the organic matter falls to the ocean floor as marine snow, where it may remain for long periods of time (Figure 4.8).

The flux of carbon between the ocean and the atmosphere is around 90 gigatons year[1]. In other words, the same amount of carbon dioxide dissolves into the ocean as diffuses back into the atmosphere. However, there are also approximately 2 gigatons of carbon each year added to the ocean through human activities such as burning fossil fuels. This makes the oceans a very important carbon sink in terms of reducing atmospheric carbon dioxide. But the risk is that the ocean will become more acidic because of the extra carbonic acid formed. It has been estimated that since the 18th century, the pH of the ocean has decreased by 30%. This can have negative effects on the ecosystem. For example, a low pH triggers chemical reactions that decrease the concentration of carbonate ions; this makes it more difficult for corals to produce their calcium carbonate skeleton. This can also affect other species with calcified shells, including oysters and clams. If the water becomes even more acidic, it can dissolve the coral skeletons and the shells of other organisms, making them weaker and more vulnerable to damage.

Some scientists have suggested that artificially fertilising the ocean with iron would increase the productivity of the phytoplankton and mean that more carbon dioxide could be absorbed. This has been put forward as a possible way to reduce the amount of carbon dioxide in the atmosphere. The theory is that, since iron is often a limiting factor for phytoplankton growth, adding more will cause increased growth rates and thus increased use of carbon

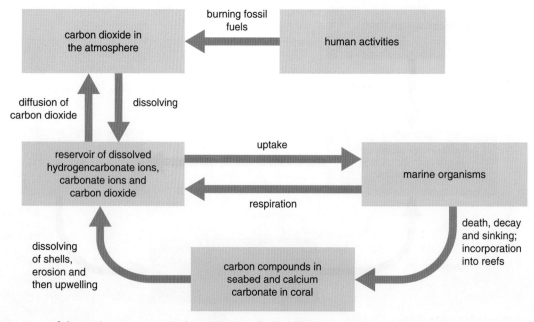

Figure 4.8. Summary of the main processes in the marine carbon cycle.

dioxide. This process is known as ocean seeding or iron fertilisation. Trials have shown that ocean seeding does increase the growth of phytoplankton but there are risks to this procedure. If the productivity increases too much, a harmful algal bloom could take place. The long-term effects of altering the ecosystem in this way are not clearly understood. If more carbon dioxide is absorbed, the pH of the water could decrease further, causing harm to many different species.

PRACTICAL ACTIVITY 4.1

Simple investigations into the exchange of carbon dioxide between the atmosphere and the ocean

Introduction

High concentrations of carbon dioxide dissolve into seawater from the atmosphere. When carbon dioxide dissolves in water it forms carbonic acid. As levels of carbon dioxide in the atmosphere increase, more is dissolving in the ocean, which decreases the pH. This can cause problems for marine organisms with hard shells, as the shells can start to dissolve. In these simple investigations you will use an egg to represent a marine organism with a shell. As with marine organisms, eggs have shells made from calcium carbonate. You will also add carbon dioxide to samples of water and record how long it takes the water to become acidic.

Apparatus
- Raw chicken eggs
- Acetic acid or white vinegar
- $3 \times 250 \, cm^3$ beakers
- $100 \, cm^3$ beaker
- Goggles
- Universal indicator solution
- Seawater (if real seawater is unavailable, a substitute can be made by dissolving approximately 30 g of sodium chloride in $1 \, dm^3$ of water)
- Tap water (fresh water)
- Drinking straws
- Stopwatch
- Marker pen for labelling beakers or sticky labels

Method
- Examine a raw egg and record your observations in a copy of Table 4.3.
- Carefully place a raw egg into a $250 \, cm^3$ beaker and cover with the acetic acid or white vinegar.
- Fill the $100 \, cm^3$ beaker with water and place it on top of the egg to keep it submerged.
- Leave for 24 h.
- Carefully remove the smaller beaker and pour the acid away.

- Remove the raw egg, rinse it with tap water, and record your observations.
- Place $100 \, cm^3$ of seawater into a $250 \, cm^3$ beaker and label it.
- Place $100 \, cm^3$ of tap water into another $250 \, cm^3$ beaker and label it.
- Add a few drops of universal indicator to each beaker.
- Blow gently through the drinking straws into each water sample and time how long it takes for the colour of the indicator to change to yellow, which shows that an acid has been produced.
- Record your results in a copy of Table 4.4.

Risk assessment

Goggles should be worn to protect the eyes from acid and universal indicator. Hands should be washed after handling raw eggs or coming into contact with acid or indicator, both of which are irritants.

Results

observations before the experiment	observations after leaving egg in acid

Table 4.3. Egg experiment results.

type of water	time taken to become acidic / s
seawater	
fresh water	

Table 4.4. Exchange of carbon dioxide between the atmosphere and water.

Conclusions

1. What was the main difference in the egg after it was placed in acid?
2. What implications does this have for coral and other marine organisms with hard shells as the ocean becomes more acidic?

→

3 Why does the universal indicator turn yellow when you blow into the water?

4 Which type of water is able to absorb more carbon dioxide without becoming acidic?

5 What does this suggest about the relative importance of seawater and fresh water as carbon sinks?

6 Why do large bodies of water in nature not become acidic this quickly?

7 Suggest ways in which you could extend the exchange of carbon dioxide investigation.

The nitrogen cycle

Nitrogen is needed to form amino acids, which are built into proteins. It is also a component of nucleic acids such as DNA. The nitrogen cycle is more complex than the carbon cycle because most producers are unable to take in nitrogen gas from the atmosphere. The organisms that are able to take in molecular nitrogen (N_2) must convert it into useable forms. In the marine environment this takes place through the action of **diazotrophs** (Figure 4.9). Diazotrophs are bacteria and archaea that can convert molecular nitrogen to substances such as ammonia (NH_3).

KEY TERM

Diazotroph: an organism that is able to grow without external sources of fixed nitrogen because it is able to fix nitrogen gas into substances like ammonia

Figure 4.9. *Trichodesmium*, a genus of marine diazotroph showing its filaments of cells, which are able to fix molecular nitrogen.

Nitrogen fixation requires a nitrogenase enzyme, which needs low levels of oxygen to function. Species that carry out nitrogen fixation therefore need specialised cells with lower than normal oxygen concentrations. *Trichodesmium* have cells that are specialised for nitrogen-fixing rather than carbon-fixing (through photosynthesis). Lack of photosynthesis means the cells have lower oxygen levels.

When the ammonia produced from nitrogen fixation dissolves in water, it forms ammonium ions (NH_4^+), which the phytoplankton are able to take in and convert to protein. Phytoplankton can also take in nitrite ions (NO_2^-) and nitrate ions (NO_3^-) but the oxygen must first be removed, which requires energy. However, because nitrite and nitrate are present in the water in higher concentrations than ammonia, many phytoplankton species do take in most of their nitrogen in these forms.

The proteins made by phytoplankton will be passed to consumers where they are digested by the consumers into amino acids and used to build the consumers' proteins. When consumers and producers die, the proteins are broken down into amino acids by **saprophytic** bacteria and fungi. The amino acids are converted back into ammonia by ammonifying bacteria. Ammonia can then be oxidised into first nitrites and then nitrates in a process known as nitrification.

KEY TERM

Saprophytic (saprophyte): decomposers that feed on dead organic matter ('death eater')

The conversion of ammonia to nitrites is carried out by species of bacteria from the genus *Nitrosomonas,* and from nitrites to nitrates by bacteria from the genus *Nitrobacter*. These species are chemoautotrophic (like the bacteria found at hydrothermal vents) and gain energy from the reaction. The final type of bacteria involved in the nitrogen cycle is the denitrifying bacteria, which convert ammonia and nitrates back into nitrogen gas (N_2). This reduces the amount of nitrogen available for phytoplankton to use and, because nitrogen is normally a limiting factor for growth, reduces productivity.

Nitrates are also added to the oceans by upwelling and run-off, particularly of nitrogen-based fertilisers (Figure 4.10).

SELF-ASSESSMENT QUESTIONS

9 Give one positive and one negative effect of increased levels of carbon dioxide dissolving in the ocean.

10 Copy and complete Table 4.5 to show the types of bacteria involved in the nitrogen cycle and their functions.

type of microorganism	function in the nitrogen cycle
diazotrophs	
saprophytic bacteria	
ammonifying bacteria	
nitrifying bacteria	
denitrifying bacteria	

Table 4.5. Bacteria and the nitrogen cycle.

The magnesium cycle

Magnesium is needed by producers to synthesise the photosynthetic pigment chlorophyll. Magnesium is found in rocks such as dolomite (calcium magnesium carbonate) and enters water through erosion and weathering. It is also used in many chemical industries and is found in fertiliser. The main way in which it enters the ocean is therefore through run-off after being leached from the soil. Once the magnesium is taken in by phytoplankton it is used to form chlorophyll, which is essential for photosynthesis. Chlorophyll is a large and complex molecule with a magnesium ion at its centre.

The main way in which magnesium ions are removed from the water is by deposition in the sediment at the bottom of the ocean (Figure 4.11). Because magnesium is present in every living cell, it is also removed by harvesting living organisms from the ocean, and incorporation into the organisms in coral reefs.

69

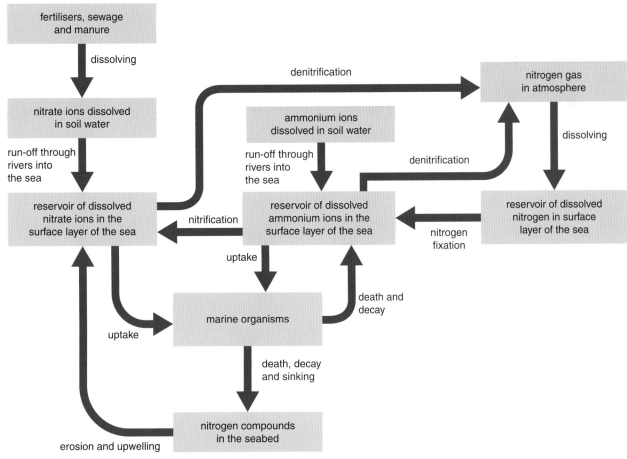

Figure 4.10. Summary of the main processes in the marine nitrogen cycle.

Investigating the nitrogen cycle in a fish tank

The nitrogen cycle is an important nutrient cycle both on land and in the sea. Most fish excrete their nitrogenous waste in the form of ammonia. This can cause them problems in an enclosed environment such as a fish tank. If the levels of ammonia increase too much, their gills and skin will be damaged. In an established aquarium this is less of a problem as levels of bacteria build up and start to cycle the nitrogen. Some species convert ammonia to nitrite and some convert the nitrite to nitrate. In this experiment you will use a fish tank without any fish and monitor the cycling of ammonia into nitrite and nitrate. All the equipment can be purchased easily from pet stores and aquatic shops. The test strips can be bought from the same suppliers as well as cheaply online. You can use an aquarium that you already own but you must use new gravel as old gravel will already have colonies of bacteria. This is a long-term investigation that will take a few minutes every week for several weeks.

Apparatus

- Fish tank with air pump (approximately 1 gallon capacity)
- Gravel (2.5 kg bag)
- Two live aquarium plants
- Test strips for ammonia, nitrite and nitrate
- Small pieces of raw fish or prawns
- The foot of a pair of tights
- Elastic band

Method

- Rinse the gravel and place it in the bottom of the tank to a depth of 2–4 cm.
- Set up the air pump according to the instructions and add the live plants.
- Use the test strips to test for the levels of ammonia, nitrite and nitrate and record the results in a copy of Table 4.6.
- Place the raw fish or prawns into the bottom of a sock or pair of tights and close with an elastic band.
- Place this into the fish tank.
- Test the water approximately every 3 days for at least 3 weeks, longer if you can.

- Record the results in a copy of Table 4.6, making sure that you include enough space for all the readings you are planning to take. The units you use will depend on the test kit you purchase and will need to be added to the heading of your table.

Risk assessment

Hands should be washed after handling raw fish and prawns and after testing the water.

date	ammonia concentration	nitrite concentration	nitrate concentration

Table 4.6. Results.

Analysis

Plot a graph to show the concentration of each nutrient against time in days. You can plot three lines on the same graph if you include a key, or you can draw three separate graphs.

Conclusions

1. Describe the shape of your graphs.
2. Explain the shape of your graphs.
3. Why did you put fish or prawns into the tank?
4. Where did the bacteria come from to convert the nutrients from one form to another?
5. Did you have any anomalous or unexpected results?
6. Suggest an explanation for your answer to question 5.
7. Using your results, explain how long you think aquariums should be set up before fish are introduced.

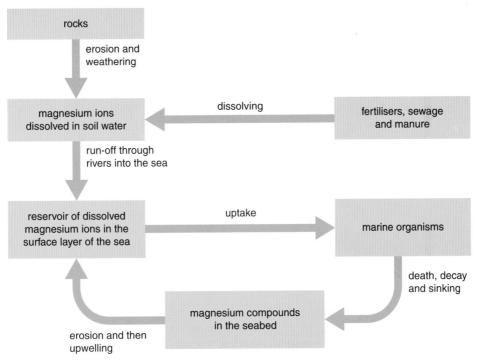

Figure 4.11. Summary of the main processes in the marine magnesium cycle.

The calcium cycle

Calcium is necessary to build healthy bones, coral and teeth so is needed by many marine animals. Rainwater reacts with carbon dioxide gas in the atmosphere to form carbonic acid. This extracts calcium from calcium-rich rocks such as limestone, marble and dolomite and forms calcium hydrogencarbonate. This dissolves in the water and enters the ocean through surface run-off. Phytoplankton such as coccolithophores use the calcium to produce scales called coccoliths from calcium carbonate (Figure 4.12). The scales are transparent and so do not disrupt photosynthesis. It has been suggested that the scales protect the cells from predators or from osmotic changes within the cells. The production of the scales also increases the rate of photosynthesis as carbon dioxide is produced as a byproduct of the precipitation of the calcium carbonate.

Coccolithophores are eaten by zooplankton, passing the calcium to the animals. After they die, they fall to the ocean floor and become part of the sediment (Figure 4.13). Chalk is formed from coccolithophores that were deposited millions of years ago. As the seabed subsided, the sediment was subjected to heat and pressure, which formed it into rocks. The white cliffs of Dover in England are a famous example of chalk produced in this way from coccolithophores (Figure 4.14).

Figure 4.12. Magnified picture of a coccolithophore.

The phosphorus cycle

Phosphorus is necessary for all living things to form nucleic acids such as DNA. It is also essential for bones in vertebrates. The major environmental source of phosphorus is rocks such as apatite. Phosphorus attaches to soil particles and is therefore added to the water through soil erosion rather than being in solution. Phosphates are also found in fertilisers, manure and sewage, which also contribute to run-off.

71

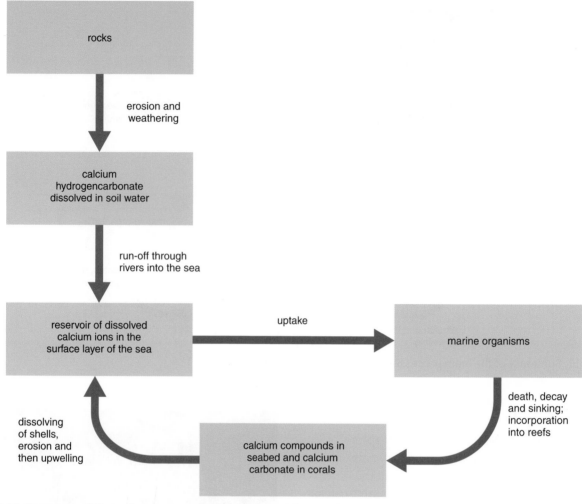

Figure 4.13. Summary of the main processes in the marine calcium cycle.

Figure 4.14. The white cliffs of Dover in England.

Along with nitrogen, phosphorus is an important limiting factor for growth of phytoplankton and therefore photosynthesis and productivity. Once phytoplankton take in the phosphorus, it is assimilated into DNA and also phospholipids in the cell membranes. There is now evidence that many species of phytoplankton are able to alter the composition of their cell membranes depending on the amount of phosphorus in the water. This enables them to survive even when phosphorus levels are low. Animals eat the phytoplankton and incorporate the phosphorus into their own membranes and DNA. When the phytoplankton and animals die, they are either broken down by decomposers, which releases the phosphorus back into the water, or they fall to the bottom of the ocean and become part of the sediment (Figure 4.15).

SELF-ASSESSMENT QUESTIONS

11 Copy and complete Table 4.7 to show the uses of the main nutrients.

nutrient	biological use
nitrogen	
carbon	
magnesium	
calcium	
phosphorus	

Table 4.7. Uses of the main nutrients.

12 Suggest what type of weather conditions could lead to an increase in the amount of phosphorus in surface run-off.

73

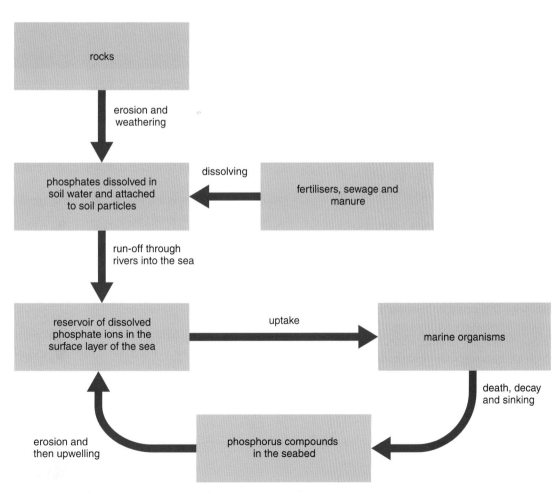

Figure 4.15. Summary of the main processes in the marine phosphorus cycle.

The Redfield ratio

In the 1930s, Alfred Redfield reported that he had taken samples from various depths in the Pacific, Atlantic and Indian oceans and measured the concentrations of dissolved nutrient ions (Figure 4.16). He also compared many samples taken by other people. He discovered that the ratio of nitrate to phosphate in most of his samples was consistently around 20:1. Later this ratio was refined to 16:1 and expanded to include carbon, which occurs at a ratio of 106:16:1 with nitrate and phosphate. The same ratio was found inside the phytoplankton that lived in the water. In other words, the composition of the water and the phytoplankton appeared to be not only the same but consistent across many different areas and depths. Redfield suggested that the reason for the stability of the ratio could be the cycling of nitrogen from abiotic to biotic sources. This helped scientists understand how the run-off of nutrients from coastal areas leads to algal blooms. The Redfield ratio is still in use today because it helps our understanding of all the major nutrient cycles in the ocean. Deviations from the ratio can be caused by increased run-off of nutrients into the water and by changes in nitrogen fixation and denitrification. Aquarium owners can also use the ratio to monitor the nutrients present in the water and thus control the levels of algae.

More recently, it has been discovered that, although the average ratio of carbon to nitrogen to phosphorus in phytoplankton conforms to the Redfield ratio of 106:16:1, it actually varies within individual species. Species that are adapted to living in low nutrient levels tend to have a higher nitrogen to phosphate ratio. Species that are adapted for exponential growth and that form the basis of algal blooms have a lower nitrogen to phosphate ratio. This could be because the proteins and chlorophyll necessary for photosynthesis are high in nitrogen and low in phosphates. DNA and RNA, which are necessary for growth, contain more equal amounts of nitrogen and phosphate. So the ratio within an organism depends on the strategy it has adopted for survival and the

Figure 4.16. Alfred Redfield.

adaptations within its cells. It may be that the average Redfield ratio found in phytoplankton reflects the balance between the two different survival strategies. This would mean that alterations in global nutrient cycles would also alter the proportions of different phytoplankton species, which could have implications for the rest of the food chain.

Questions

1 Describe what will happen to the Redfield ratio if excess nitrates enter the water through the run-off of fertilisers.

2 What effect would this have on the types of phytoplankton that grow and their ratio of nitrate to phosphate?

3 Explain why you think that scientists continue to monitor the Redfield ratio in seawater.

Maths skills

Plotting and interpreting graphs

Plotting graphs is an important skill because graphs help us to visualise and better understand data. The data on a line or scatter graph should be plotted with the independent variable (the one that has been changed) on the x-axis. The dependent variable (the one that has been measured during the experiment) should be on the y-axis. A sensible scale should be used for each axis, for example 2 units per square of graph paper. The graph should fill at least ¾ of the available space on the graph paper and also be easy to plot and read the data afterwards. Scales that involve 3 units per square are difficult to plot and even more difficult for someone else to interpret and so should be avoided. It is not always necessary to start the scale at zero, but if the scale starts with another number this should be indicated by drawing two lines through the axis. Both the x and y axis need to be labelled with a description of the variable and the units that have been used.

When the points have been plotted, a line can be drawn. On a scatter graph this will be a line of best fit, showing the relationship between the two variables. Try to make sure that equal numbers of points are on either side of the line. For a line graph in biology, the line will often simply be straight lines drawn with a ruler between the points. This is because the actions of living organisms make it difficult to tell what happens between each point. A smooth curve of best fit can be drawn if there is reason to believe that the intermediate points would fall on the curve.

To interpret a graph it is important to both describe and explain what the data are showing. Think of describing a graph as answering the question: What do you see? You should state the key points that can be seen and give data from the graph to illustrate your answer. Explaining a graph by contrast means answering the question: Why does it happen? You should give the reasons for the shape of the graph and any changes that you see.

Worked example

The data in the table show the fertiliser consumption per hectare in the USA.

year	fertiliser consumption per hectare / kg
1880	1.4
1890	1.9
1900	2.9
1913	5.8
1922	7.0
1937	8.7
1957	23.4
1999	108.3

Table 4.8. Fertiliser consumption per hectare in the USA.

1 Plot a graph to show this data.

Remember that the independent variable must be on the x-axis, which in this case is the year. The dependent variable is the fertiliser consumption, and this should be on the y-axis: remember to include the units (kg). The points should be joined with a straight line because you cannot predict what might have happened in the intervening years.

A graph of these data should look something like Figure 4.17.

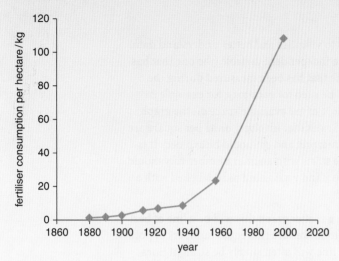

Figure 4.17. Fertiliser consumption in the USA from 1880 to 1999.

2   Describe the shape of the graph.

Remember, to describe you need to say what is happening and quote figures from the data. So a description of this graph needs to include the slow increase between 1880 and 1922, followed by a much more rapid increase to 108.3 kg hectare^{-1} in 1999.

3   Suggest an explanation for the shape of the graph.

One possible explanation is the increase in availability of commercially prepared fertiliser. Another explanation could be that the price decreased or that increased demands for food meant that more fertiliser had to be used to increase crop yields.

Questions

1   The data in Table 4.9 show the amount of phosphate fertilisers used between 1975 and 2005.

year	amount of phosphate fertiliser used / tonnes
1975	124 000
1980	87 000
1985	62 000
1990	38 000
1995	27 000
2000	27 000
2005	22 000

Table 4.9. Phosphate fertiliser use between 1975 and 2005.

a   Plot these data as a graph on graph paper.
b   Describe the shape of the graph.

2 The graph in Figure 4.18 shows the increase in the amount of carbon dioxide measured in the atmosphere in America.

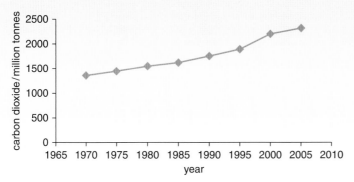

Figure 4.18. Changes in carbon dioxide concentration in America between 1970 and 2005.

a Describe the graph.

b Suggest one human activity that could increase the amount of carbon dioxide in the atmosphere.

c Suggest the effect of increasing carbon dioxide in the atmosphere on the concentration of carbon dioxide dissolved in seawater.

Summary

- Nutrient cycles show the movement of nutrients through the abiotic and biotic parts of the ecosystem.

- In the abiotic stage nutrients are found as gases in the atmosphere, as well as dissolved in water and as part of rocks.

- An important reservoir of dissolved nutrients is found in the upper layers of the ocean.

- Nutrients move to the biotic phase through uptake and assimilation by producers such as phytoplankton.

- When phytoplankton are eaten, organic compounds containing the nutrients are digested and absorbed by consumers and then assimilated into consumer biomass.

- From here they can be removed from the ecosystem altogether by harvesting.

- Once organisms die they can sink to the bottom of the ocean, where they form part of the sediment.

- Nutrients can also become incorporated into coral reefs.

- More nutrients are added to the reservoir in the surface layers by dissolving from the atmosphere, running-off the land or upwelling from nutrient-rich deeper waters.

- The main nutrients are:
  - nitrogen, which is needed for proteins
  - carbon, which is found in all organic molecules including glucose and lipids
  - magnesium, which is needed for chlorophyll
  - calcium, which is needed for bones, shells and coral
  - phosphorus, which is needed for DNA and bone.

Exam-style questions

1   The diagram in Figure 4.19 shows the marine magnesium cycle.

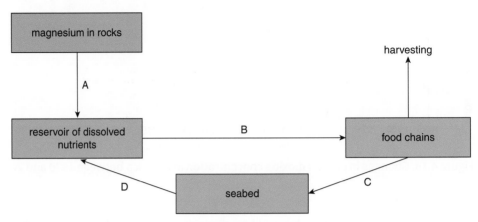

Figure 4.19. The marine magnesium cycle.

a   Name the process shown by arrow D.   **[1]**

b   Describe how the magnesium found in rocks on land ends up in sediments on the seabed.   **[4]**

c   i   Suggest what will happen to the concentration of magnesium over time.   **[1]**

   ii   Provide an explanation for your answer.   **[3]**

   [Total mark: 9]

2   **a   i**   Describe how nutrient-rich water from deep in the ocean enters the reservoir of nutrients at the surface.   **[2]**

   ii   Suggest two other ways in which nutrients enter surface waters.   **[2]**

   b   i   Suggest a benefit of increased nutrients in surface waters.   **[2]**

   ii   Suggest how increased nutrients in surface waters could be harmful.   **[2]**

   [Total mark: 8]

3   **a   i**   State how carbon dioxide enters surface water from the atmosphere.   **[1]**

   ii   Describe the effect this has on the pH of the water.   **[2]**

   iii   Name a biological compound that contains carbon.   **[1]**

   b   i   Give two ways in which phosphorus can enter surface water.   **[2]**

   ii   Describe the effect of increasing phosphorus levels on producers.   **[3]**

   [Total mark: 9]

4 a Fill in Table 4.10 to show the uses of different nutrients. **[3]**

nutrient	biological use
nitrogen	
calcium	
phosphorus	

Table 4.10. The uses of different nutrients.

b i Describe the process of run-off. **[3]**

ii Describe the effect of run-off of nitrogen fertilisers on producers. **[3]**

iii Explain how this will affect the consumers in the food chain. **[2]**

[Total mark: 11]

5 a Describe how calcium in limestone on land can be incorporated into coral. **[5]**

b i Give one biological use of calcium apart from in coral. **[1]**

ii Why does the level of calcium in the seawater stay constant? **[4]**

c i Name a nutrient whose levels are increasing in seawater. **[1]**

ii Suggest an explanation for this increase. **[2]**

[Total mark: 13]

79

The importance of salmon to the growth of trees

Harvesting by humans is an important way in which nutrients are removed from the marine environment. However, nutrients are also removed by migrations of marine organisms such as salmon (Figure 4.20) to fresh-water areas where they are eaten by predators like bears and eagles. Pacific salmon spend most of their life at sea. The juveniles tend to feed on zooplankton and the adults feed on krill and smaller fish such as herring. In this way the nutrients from the water that are taken up by the phytoplankton end up being assimilated by the salmon.

Figure 4.20. Adult Pacific salmon.

EXTENDED CASE STUDY

Each year salmon return to the freshwater streams and lakes where they were born in order to breed (Figure 4.21). For successful reproduction, the fish need the streams to be shaded by trees so that the water is not too warm. Warm water also contains less oxygen, which would mean that fewer of the eggs would be able to survive. The trees help to prevent soil erosion, stopping sediment from entering the streams and keeping the water clear for the salmon. Large populations of insects live in the leaves and needles of trees that provide food for the young salmon once they hatch. The trees are therefore important for the survival of the salmon. The majority of the trees that grow in these forests tend to be conifers such as spruce.

What has become clear is that not only do the salmon need the trees, but the trees need the salmon. As millions of salmon move through the waters of the Pacific Northwest coast of the USA, they provide huge amounts of food for bears and eagles (Figure 4.22). It has been estimated that each bear fishing in British Columbia, for example, can catch 700 salmon during the spawning period. Although the bears kill the salmon in the water, they move away from the water to eat. Roughly half of each salmon carcass is consumed by the bear, with the rest feeding scavenger species and insects.

Figure 4.21. Spawning Pacific salmon moving upstream.

Figure 4.22. Bear catching salmon.

The nitrogen compounds from the decomposing salmon carcasses eventually find their way into the soil as part of the nitrogen cycle. Proteins are broken down and converted into nitrates by a series of different types of bacteria. Proteins are broken down into amino acids by decomposers. The amino acids are then converted to ammonia in the process of ammonification. Ammonia is then converted to nitrite and finally nitrate by nitrifying bacteria. The trees take in the nitrates through their roots and are able to use it to form amino acids which are then built up into plant proteins. As nitrate is normally a limiting factor for plant growth, increasing the level of nitrates increases the growth of the trees. The fish provide up to 120 kg nitrogen per hectare of forest, which enables the trees to grow up to three times faster than they would without the added nitrates.

Researchers have used different isotopes of nitrogen to investigate the uptake of nitrates from the salmon. Isotopes are forms of the same element that have different numbers of neutrons and therefore different relative atomic masses, although they have the same chemical properties. The nitrogen 15 isotope is far more abundant in marine ecosystems than in terrestrial ecosystems and so can be used as a marker for the nitrogen that has come from marine sources. Small samples of wood can be extracted from the tree trunk and the isotopes compared. Using this method, it has been shown that larger trees have higher levels of nutrients that originate in the salmon than smaller trees. In addition, the closer the tree is to the spawning sites, the higher the levels of nutrients from the salmon. In this way a positive feedback loop is formed. The more salmon that are deposited, the better the trees grow, and the better the trees grow, the better the conditions in the stream for the spawning of salmon (Figure 4.23).

Figure 4.23. Spruce trees growing near a river in Montana.

This has important implications for conservation of both salmon and forests, as each helps the other to survive. Since the 1990s there have been sharp declines in the numbers of Pacific salmon, which could cause problems not only for the bears that feed directly on them, but for the growth of trees. This would of course also affect all the other species that live in and around the forests, and which need the spruce trees for their habitat. Eventually it would also affect the salmon themselves, as fewer trees would mean worse conditions for spawning. Therefore, in order to conserve the salmon populations the forests must be protected, and in order to conserve the forests there need to be enough salmon spawning each year.

Questions

1 a Explain why the growth of trees is important for the survival of salmon.

   b Explain how the salmon increase the growth of the trees.

2 a Researchers have used different isotopes of nitrogen to trace nutrients derived from marine sources. Describe the possible route from the ocean to a tree of a nitrogen atom contained in an ammonia molecule.

   b Most of the nitrogen appears to come from the salmon carcasses abandoned by the bears. Suggest another way that extra nitrogen is provided by the salmon.

3 Name another nutrient present in the salmon and suggest where it would be found within the salmon.

4 Suggest a type of organism other than the trees that would benefit from the nitrogen within the salmon.

5 a Suggest how some of the nitrogen in the forest is returned to the marine ecosystem.

   b Why must salmon and forest conservation take place at the same time?

Chapter 5
Coral reefs and lagoons

Learning outcomes

By the end of this chapter, you should be able to:

- explain and provide evidence supporting the Darwin–Dana–Daly theory of atoll formation
- connect how coral grows and survives with the Darwin–Dana–Daly theory
- explain what can cause a change from reef growth to reef erosion
- explain how reefs can reduce the energy of waves and help protect shores and anchorages, and the negative effects of reef erosion
- discuss the effects of artificial reefs on shores and anchorages
- describe and differentiate between the methods used to discover the history of reefs and the effects of sea-level changes on reefs
- apply what you have learnt to new, unfamiliar contexts.

5.1 Coral seas

Clear, blue waters surround the world's 284 300 km² of coral reef ecosystems. Reef structures are, arguably, one of the greatest intersections between the physical structure of an environment and the organisms that live there. Just as in tropical rainforests, in coral reef communities the living organisms in the environment actually provide the structure necessary for the many microhabitats of the community to exist. These microhabitats provide homes to thousands of marine species. The species surviving on a coral reef, as well as the coral itself, create one of the most beautiful and biodiverse communities on our planet: a community that is reliant on the physiology of the coral animal for health and survival.

One of the most well-known coral reef systems is the Great Barrier Reef off the coast of Queensland, Australia. This reef system is home to over 2900 individual coral reefs housing more than 2000 species of animals, from corals to whales.

Unfortunately, this beautifully biodiverse community, like other coral reefs worldwide, is under attack.

Climate change, pollution and reef erosion are happening at rates that are dangerous for the world's coral reefs. Over 90% of the corals living on the Great Barrier Reef are suffering from a disease called **coral bleaching**. More than 20% of those corals affected have already died because of the loss of nutrients caused by the bleaching. Coral bleaching tends to happen in areas with rising water temperatures and increased levels of pollution. Recovering from the disease is possible but not easy. It is vital that we begin the process of cleaning up our oceans and reducing our ecological impact in order to give the coral communities their best chance at survival.

 KEY TERM

Coral bleaching: the loss of symbiotic algae from the tissues of corals as a result of environmental factors

5.2 Coral physiology

All corals belong to a special phylum of organisms called cnidarians. Animals in this phylum are found in aquatic ecosystems, primarily marine, and all capture food using stinging cells called cnidocytes. The presence of these stinging cells in coral polyps indicates a close relationship with sea anemones and jellyfish.

Like anemones, corals live their entire adult life as polyps. Polyps are the sessile (non-moving) life stage of coral animals. Polyps tend to be simple in appearance, just a cylinder of epidermal tissue with tentacles surrounding a mouth. This mouth leads to a simple, sac-like stomach, or gastrovascular cavity, made of tissue designed to secrete enzymes for digestion. Polyps may live individually or in giant colonies capable of building reefs. There are two major categories of corals: those that build reefs, **hermatypic** corals, and those that do not build reefs, **ahermatypic** corals.

 KEY TERMS

Ahermatypic: soft corals that do not build reefs
Hermatypic: hard corals capable of reef-building
Zooxanthellae: symbiotic, photosynthetic dinoflagellates living within the tissues of many invertebrates

83

Ahermatypic corals are routinely referred to as soft corals because they are flexible and do not create stony skeletons, using proteins for support instead. Soft corals resemble plants, trees or fans, and generally do not maintain a symbiotic relationship with **zooxanthellae**, photosynthetic dinoflagellates that can be found in the tissues of corals and many other marine invertebrates. Some examples of soft corals are sea whips, sea fans and gorgonians.

Hermatypic corals, or hard corals, are the reef-building group of corals. Within this group, the coral polyps always live in colonies and always include zooxanthellae (Figure 5.1). These colonies begin when a single planktonic coral larvae settles on a hard substrate. Once the larvae has attached, it goes through metamorphosis to become a coral polyp. If this original polyp survives and thrives, it will reproduce asexually through a process called budding. Budding happens when the initial polyp grows a clone of itself. As a result of this process, typically all polyps in a coral colony are genetically identical to the founder polyp. In order to cement themselves to the substrate, each polyp secretes calcium carbonate ($CaCO_3$) onto the substrate. When an older polyp dies, a new polyp will grow in its place, adding another layer of calcium carbonate to the structure. Eventually, this process creates a limestone skeleton that can form many different shapes and provides the framework of the coral reef. Because coral polyps are so tiny, it can take billions of polyps to form a reef.

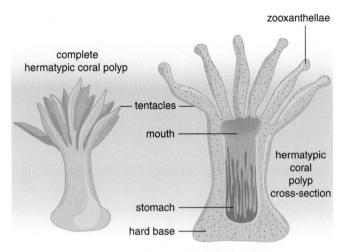

Figure 5.1. Hermatypic coral polyp with symbiotic zooxanthellae.

It is important to note that hermatypic corals would probably be unable to build reefs without the symbiotic relationship they maintain with zooxanthellae. Zooxanthellae are microscopic, single-celled dinoflagellates that live within the tissue of hard corals (Figure 5.1). Using the carbon provided by the coral host, zooxanthellae perform photosynthesis to generate organic material that can then be passed on to the coral. Without the extra nutrition provided by zooxanthellae, corals would be unable to secrete enough calcium carbonate to build the skeleton of the reef. The zooxanthellae provide enough food for the coral in clear, sunny waters so that often the coral can survive without eating. Coral are predators, however, even if zooxanthellae support them. Coral polyps use their tentacles filled with cnidocytes to prey on microscopic zooplankton floating in the water near them.

5.3 Physical factors necessary for coral growth

In 1842 Charles Darwin published a book called *Coral Reefs* based on his observations aboard the HMS *Beagle* between November 1835 and April 1836. This book would become central to the discussion of how coral reefs form and the environment necessary for their unimpeded growth. In the book, Darwin included a map of all the known coral reefs. This map showed where in the world coral reefs are most likely to be found: between 30° north and 30° south of the equator. It is interesting to note that, despite a lack of modern equipment, Darwin's map, and the observations

that formed it, are still largely accurate today. Darwin also distinguished between three major types of reef (fringing, barrier and atoll) and how each is formed, which you will find out about in the following section.

Coral reefs are reliant on several physical factors for healthy growth and colonisation, particularly an appropriate temperature, water clarity and suitable depth. When mapping out coral reef distribution (Figure 5.2), scientists can hypothesise which reefs will have the highest growth rates by evaluating the presence, or lack, of these vital physical factors. As the combination of these factors is prevalent within an area referred to as the 'tropics', this is where coral reefs are most likely to be found.

The most important physical factor for corals is temperature. Hard corals are limited to waters with temperatures ranging between 16 °C and 35 °C (61–95 °F). Corals growing in water with temperatures at either end of this range tend to be less healthy and grow less quickly than those in water of the preferred range of 23–25 °C (73–77 °F). Because of the warm temperatures needed for successful coral growth, you would expect to find coral reefs located exclusively in the tropics between 30 °N and 30 °S of the equator. However, some areas outside this zone, such as Florida and southern Japan, are also able to support healthy coral reefs. This is because there are warm water currents flowing along the continental shelf in those areas.

A suitable depth of water is needed for healthy coral growth. While all corals grow in the subtidal zone, those present in areas within 20 m of the surface tend to have the fastest growth rate. Because of the symbiotic nature of coral's relationship with photosynthetic zooxanthellae, you do not find coral reefs in deeper water because there is insufficient light. Those corals that do not use zooxanthellae may be found in deeper waters with warm enough temperatures.

In order for zooxanthellae to photosynthesise efficiently, sunlight must be able to reach the coral polyps at sufficient levels. Therefore, water clarity is also vital to the health and growth of coral reefs. If the light is unable to reach the coral polyps, the zooxanthellae cannot produce the organic material necessary for the coral to build up the reef. This reduces overall growth and potentially stresses the coral, which is why clear water without silt or an excess of nutrients is needed for rapid coral growth. An abundance of nutrients may lead to an algal bloom that can cloud the surrounding water and reduce light penetration. An excess of small sediments, like silt, also causes turbidity, or cloudiness, within the water.

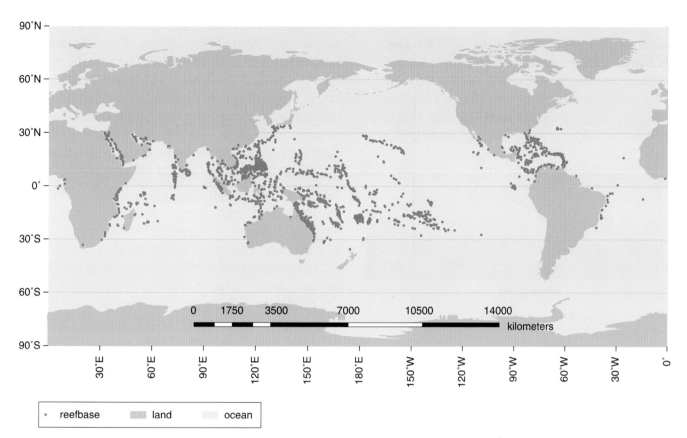

Figure 5.2. A map of the world's coral reefs.

85

Salinity and substrate are determining factors in the success of a coral reef. Corals must have an appropriate rocky surface for attachment. Coral larvae cannot attach to sand or other unstable materials, so the larvae tend to attach to denser materials. The basaltic rocks of undersea mountains and other hard surfaces along the continental shelf provide excellent attachment sites for the larvae. Corals are not adapted to freshwater or brackish conditions. For this reason, they do not do well near river mouths or other areas linked with fresh water or run-off flowing into the sea.

A final physical factor determining coral health is pH. Scientists use pH to determine how acidic or basic a substance is on a logarithmic scale of 0–14. Acidic substances have a pH below 7; neutral substances have a pH around 7; basic substances have a pH above 7. For healthy growth in coral reefs to occur, the ocean should be slightly basic, with a pH between 8.1 and 8.5. Waters with lower pH levels stress the corals and cause bleaching.

If a coral larva has found a location that meets all of these requirements, it will thrive and begin the process of reef-forming. Coral polyps will continue to add to existing coral skeletons, growing outwards for thousands of years. If the seabed subsides, or sinks, the coral polyps

will tend to grow vertically to maintain the appropriate depth for photosynthesis. This will also occur if there is sea-level rise, as when polar ice caps melt adding water to the ocean.

SELF-ASSESSMENT QUESTIONS

1   Explain why coral reefs are most commonly found within 30 °N and 30 °S of the equator.

2   Suggest which physical factors are linked most closely with the symbiotic relationship coral has with zooxanthellae. Support your answer with evidence.

5.4 Types of reef

Geomorphology is a term used to describe the scientific study of landforms and the processes involved in creating those landforms. While aboard the HMS *Beagle*, Charles

 KEY TERM

Geomorphology: the study of the characteristics, origin and development of landforms

Darwin studied the geomorphology of coral reefs. In doing so, Darwin observed three fairly distinct types of reef: **fringing reefs**, **barrier reefs** and **atolls**. In his book *Coral Reefs*, Darwin writes about the differences between these three reefs and how they are all connected. Since Darwin's time, a fourth reef type has been categorised: **patch reefs** (Figure 5.3). However, whether or not this is a true fourth category is debated.

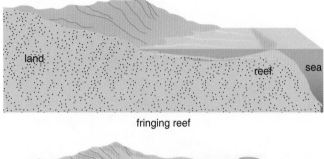

fringing reef

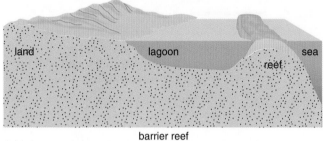

barrier reef

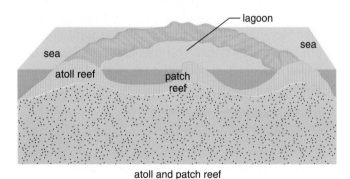

atoll and patch reef

Figure 5.3. Different reef formations.

KEY TERMS

Fringing reef: a reef close to and surrounding newer volcanic islands or that borders continental landmasses

Barrier reef: a reef separated by a lagoon from the land mass with which it is associated

Atoll: a coral reef somewhat circular in shape with a central lagoon

Patch reef: small, isolated reef usually located within the lagoon of a barrier reef

---

Darwin hypothesised that all reefs begin as fringing reefs. Fringing reefs form along the edges of continental landmasses, islands and oceanic volcanoes. Fringing reefs are separated from the shoreline by narrow, shallow lagoons. Rocky shorelines are the best substrate for the initial placement of the larvae, but a soft bottom will do as long as there is at least one hard place to cement to. Fringing reefs are the most commonly seen and explored because they tend to be easy to reach. This nearness to shore makes them vulnerable to excessive sediment, run-off containing pollutants and fresh water, and human disturbance.

Barrier reefs are similar to fringing reefs in that they lie along the shoreline of a larger landmass. Barrier reefs are separated from land by deeper, wider lagoons and may be up to 97 km from the shore. A lagoon is a shallow, sheltered body of water that typically has a soft sediment bottom. Fringing reefs may even exist within the lagoon created between the barrier reef and the shoreline. Portions of barrier reefs may have grown so that the water above is very shallow, making them dangerous for boats to travel over them.

Typically found between fringing reefs and barrier reefs are patch reefs. Patch reefs are the smallest of the reef types and they tend to grow vertically from the continental shelf or lagoon floor as an isolated formation within the lagoons formed by barrier reefs. The size of patch reefs can vary based on age and location, but they rarely have the vertical height needed to reach the water's surface. It has been argued that patch reefs are actually just a formation within a barrier reef and should not be placed in a separate category.

The final category of reefs are atolls. An atoll is a coral reef that develops as a ring around a central lagoon. Atolls vary in size from 1 to 32 km in diameter. Most atolls can be found in the tropical Indian Ocean and the west and central Pacific Ocean; they are rare in Caribbean and Atlantic oceans. Atolls vary drastically from fringing and barrier reefs in their location. Typically, atolls are found kilometres from any visible land in incredibly deep water. This enormous distance provided a challenge to the scientists of Darwin's day. These scientists, including Darwin, wanted to be the first to determine how atolls formed.

Darwin–Dana–Daly theory of atoll formation

After much observation and consideration on his HMS *Beagle* voyage, Darwin was certain he had worked out how atolls were formed. According to Darwin, the type of reef seen was dependent on time. He described a fringing reef as the first, which would lead to a barrier reef and subsequently end up as an atoll. After Darwin released his hypothesis of atoll formation, it was supported and modified by two leading geologists of the day: James Daly and Reginald Dana.

The Darwin–Dana–Daly theory of atoll formation can be summarised as follows. Coral larvae begin to colonise the basaltic rocks along the coastline of a recently emerged oceanic volcano (sea mount). The corals continue to grow and colonise, creating a fringing reef around this island. The island then begins to erode at the top and sinks slowly beneath the sea. (It has since been discovered that tectonic activity is responsible for this sinking.) As the island sinks and erodes, a lagoon begins to form and grow between the reef and the island. Once the lagoon has grown sufficiently, the reef is classified as a barrier reef. This reef continues to grow around the area where the island had been, despite the continuous sinking of the island. Eventually, the island sinks entirely below the surface of the water, leaving behind a ring of coral, an atoll, with a relatively shallow lagoon in the centre (Figure 5.4).

This theory has since been supported by data from multiple sources. As an example, when scientists took drilling cores of the Bikini Atoll in the Pacific Ocean, the data showed that coral age increased with depth. Those corals located at the base of the atoll, nearly 1200 m deep, were 50 million-year-old fossilised coral species, while those at the surface were living modern species. After testing the substrate under the fossilised corals, scientists found volcanic rock, supporting the idea that the original corals settled along the edges of a recently emerged volcanic island. As these fossil corals, now located more than 1000 m below the surface, could only have grown in shallow waters, this provides even more evidence supporting the idea that the island sank over time.

SELF-ASSESSMENT QUESTIONS

3 Compare and contrast the three major types of reefs: fringing reefs, barrier reefs and atolls, paying particular attention to formation and age.

4 Summarise the evidence used to support the Darwin–Dana–Daly theory of atoll formation.

5.5 Reef erosion

A healthy coral reef in a location where all physical factors are being met can expect to accumulate between 3 and 15 m of calcium carbonate every 1000 years. The largest of the coral species are the slowest growing, often only adding between 5 and 25 mm of calcium carbonate a year. The faster growing corals, such as staghorn corals, can add as much as 20 cm to their branches per year. According to current geological estimates, most modern coral reef systems are between 5000 and 10 000 years old. This slow growth rate of healthy corals is one reason why **reef erosion** can be so detrimental.

When a coral reef begins to lose more calcium carbonate each year than it accumulates, it is undergoing reef erosion. There are many causes of reef erosion, both biological and

KEY TERM

Reef erosion: the gradual wearing away of a coral reef by the action of living organisms (bioerosion) and physical factors, such as storms

87

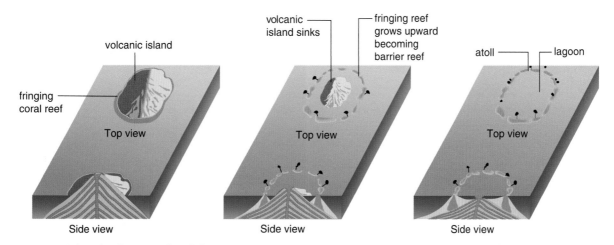

Figure 5.4. An aerial and side view of atoll formation.

physical. Biological causes of reef erosion, often referred to as bioerosion, include the predation of coral by organisms such as the parrotfish, butterflyfish and the crown-of-thorns starfish. Physical causes of reef erosion include storms, exposure to air and ocean acidification.

Both parrotfish and butterfly fish are avid predators of coral polyps among coral reefs. Butterfly fish tend to be specialists, eating only a few particular species of polyps. Parrotfish, on the other hand, are grazers that eat coral polyps in order to get to the algae living within them. Parrotfish will use their beak-like teeth to bite off portions of rock or coral reef, which they swallow whole. Their bodies then digest all of the organic material (i.e. the algae) located within the coral polyps and release the indigestible calcium carbonate as faeces. This process leads to an overall loss of calcium carbonate present on the reef, causing reef erosion.

The crown-of-thorns starfish (*Acanthaster planci*) has been a serious threat to corals in the Indo-Pacific region for the last 50 years. These coral predators have seen multiple population booms and are considered to be the greatest cause of coral mortality on the Great Barrier Reef. There are several hypotheses about what causes an outbreak of crown-of-thorns starfish, but the most likely is nutrient-rich run-off as a result of the overuse of fertilisers combined with the removal of predators. These nutrients, primarily nitrogen and phosphorus, tend to cause plankton blooms where crown-of-thorns starfish larvae thrive. Without predatory fish to control the population of larvae, the larvae metamorphose into adult starfish and devour the reef.

Physical damage to reefs during low tide can also be extensive. Because corals need to be in subtidal regions, any exposure to air can be dangerous. During spring tides, the lowest of the tides can leave coral reefs exposed to the air, causing the corals to desiccate

or overheat. When the coral polyps die, they may be replaced with algae or slowly eroded.

Storms are another major source of reef erosion. The turbulence caused by hurricanes, typhoons and tropical storms can be extensive. Typically, the damage is caused by breakage of the coral itself or a scouring of the coral by abrasive sediments that are being swirled through the normally calm waters. Evidence of the damage to the Great Barrier Reef caused during cyclone Ita is shown in Figure 5.5.

Corals can generally recover from hurricane damage but the time the recovery takes is influenced by several factors, including:

- the amount of coral rubble remaining after the storm
- the sediment stirred up by turbulence
- the growth of algae competing for attachment surfaces within the reef
- run-off, which may bring toxins, lower the salinity of the water and increase nutrients, encouraging an algal bloom.

For example, Hurricane Hattie destroyed a 43 km stretch of barrier reef off the coast of British Honduras in 1961. At the time it was estimated that 80% of the Belize Barrier Reef was damaged by this storm. While the reef has since recovered, scientists at the time believed it would take between 25 and 100 years for the ecosystem to repair itself.

Over the last 300 million years the pH of the world's oceans has been slightly basic, at an average pH of 8.2. However, within the last 200 years, since the Industrial Revolution, it has dropped to 8.1. This drop seems tiny, but the pH scale is logarithmic, so a 0.1 drop represents a 25% increase in acidity. This process is called **ocean acidification**. The gases in our atmosphere (especially carbon dioxide) dissolve at the ocean surface (see Chapter 7). This creates higher levels of carbonic acid (H_2CO_3), lowering the overall pH of the

Figure 5.5. A portion of the Great Barrier Reef before and after the category five tropical cyclone Ita passed through in 2014.

ocean. This acidity is having an abnormally large impact on coral reefs that use calcium carbonate in the manufacture of their skeletons. Ocean acidification prevents corals from absorbing all of the calcium carbonate they need to build their skeletal structures. This can lead to the skeletons themselves dissolving in the more acidic water.

KEY TERM

Ocean acidification: a reduction in the pH of the ocean over an extended period time, caused primarily by uptake of carbon dioxide from the atmosphere

CASE STUDY

Reef destruction through human interference

While most reef erosion happens naturally through bioerosion and physical factors such as storms, quite a bit is also caused by human interference. Human interference can take many forms. Fishing, tourism and coral harvesting are probably the most well-known causes of destruction of coral reefs worldwide.

Fishing near a coral reef makes sense economically considering the vast biodiversity of a healthy reef system. However, this can pose several problems. If the fishermen are not careful, they can easily anchor their boats on a portion of the reef or run their boat over the top of the shallower portions of the reef. This also applies to boats chartered for tourists and cruise liners. For example, a single cruise ship destroyed 3150 km^2 of reef in Fiji in 2006.

Additionally, fishing methods and practices, such as dynamite and cyanide, can be especially dangerous for coral reefs. These methods are used to stun fish so that they are easy to catch at the surface in handheld nets (Figure 5.6). The blast of the dynamite will explode portions of the reef, causing permanent damage. Cyanide fishing is only meant to stun larger fish for easier catching, but actually kills smaller organisms like coral polyps. Over-fishing of large predatory fish on the reef has also led to an average decrease in fish size on most of the world's reefs and large-scale ecosystem change on some reefs. When the larger predatory fish or herbivorous fish are removed from the coral reef system, there is nothing to keep algae or coral predators, like crown-of-thorns starfish, from overtaking the reef.

Figure 5.6. A young man dynamite fishing in the Philippines.

The harvesting of coral is one human interference that is not accidental. Many uninformed tourists break off pieces of the reef to take home as souvenirs, but damage is also often caused by local businesses. Black coral can be polished and is sold as jewellery in many parts of the world. Other pieces of coral are dried out and sold to people as decorative items for their homes. On a large-scale, this harvesting causes a lot of damage to reefs over time.

Questions

1   Using your knowledge of average coral growth, describe the damage the cruise ship mentioned previously caused in ecological terms.

2   Suggest a possible reason why over-fishing can lead to erosion on coral reefs.

3   With specific reference to hermatypic and ahermatypic corals, explain which type you think is most commonly harvested and why.

Coral bleaching and climate change

The term **climate change** refers to changes in global or regional climate patterns and more specifically to the changes that have been seen since the late 20th century. Many studies have found a correlation between the rate of climate change and rising levels of carbon dioxide in our atmosphere as a result of fossil fuel use. Climate change has two primary impacts on ocean ecosystems: a rise in sea surface temperatures and a lowering of pH levels.

KEY TERM

Climate change: changes in global or regional climate patterns, especially changes that have been seen since the late 20th century

Coral bleaching occurs when hard corals become stressed by environmental factors, particularly rising water temperature and acidity. This stress causes the coral polyps to reject their symbiotic zooxanthellae. Because the zooxanthellae contain all the pigments that give the coral polyps their colour, the bright white calcium carbonate skeleton of the reef becomes visible (Figure 5.7). This change from yellows and browns to white is called bleaching. While bleached, corals are not adding to their calcium carbonate skeletons, so reef growth stops. If the bleaching event lasts too long the corals will die as a result of lack of nutrients and poor conditions. There have been multiple mass bleaching events around the world since the mid-1990s.

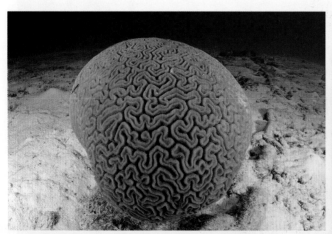

Figure 5.7. A healthy coral and a bleached coral in the Florida Keys.

Impacts of reef erosion and artificial reefs

While many people see coral reefs as beneficial only in terms of biodiversity in the ocean, they are also of benefit to onshore habitats. Coral reefs absorb on average 97% of the energy of waves coming into shore. Wave height is also reduced, on average by 84%. These reductions in wave energy and height have important implications for the shoreline. By reducing the oncoming wave energy, coral reefs are able to protect the shoreline from erosion caused by strong waves. Preventing erosion of the shoreline and reducing wave height helps to protect anything on the shore from being damaged during storms and being lost to the sea as a result of erosion. Those ecosystems that exist along the shoreline, for example mangroves, also benefit from reduced wave action and serve as nurseries for marine organisms.

Healthy coral reefs also help protect boats and **anchorages**. Many coastal communities provide breakwaters to create anchorages, areas where people anchor their boats. These breakwaters can be expensive. However, where there is a healthy coral reef, the reduced wave action means there is less need for a breakwater, reducing the cost to the community. Additionally, the anchorage itself is safer for boats because the coral reduces turbulence in the area, calming the waters. The reduction in erosion and cost of breakwaters means areas with healthy coral reefs have a significant economic advantage over those areas without.

Those areas with coral reefs suffering from reef erosion are therefore at an economic disadvantage. Coastal properties and shores are at a greater risk of exposure to the damaging effects of waves, particularly during tropical cyclones. The loss of shoreline and greater damage by storm surges can cost human communities millions of dollars to repair. This is why many communities are creating **artificial reefs**. In addition to increasing biodiversity and ecological stability, artificial reefs provide many of the other benefits of healthy coral reefs. Artificial reefs help reduce wave energy and height, behaving as a submerged breakwater. This protects anchorages and boats from damage, and shorelines from erosion.

Artificial reefs are human-made structures designed to recreate a coral ecosystem. Typically these reefs are placed in areas that do not have an appropriate substrate for larval attachment. Many different materials have been used to create artificial reefs, including specially designed non-toxic concrete, sacks filled with sand, stone blocks and even sunken ships. Figure 5.8 illustrates one type of artificial reef: the reef ball. The USS *Oriskany*, a retired aircraft carrier, was sunk off the Panhandle of Florida with the intention of creating an artificial reef in 2006. The ship was overhauled to ensure no toxins (for example paints or oils) would seep from it into the marine environment. Since its sinking, the *Oriskany* has become a popular diving location to see reef fish.

KEY TERMS

Anchorage: [boats] the portion of a harbour or estuary used for ships to anchor; [organisms] location on a substrate where a sessile organism attaches and lives

Artificial reef: an artificial underwater structure built to mimic the characteristics of a natural reef

Figure 5.8. Commercially available artificial reef balls.

Artificial reefs provide a physical structure for coral, sponges and algae to colonise. Once these sessile animals have become attached and begun to colonise, many different species of fish are attracted to the area. After several years, it should be impossible to tell that the reef was once an artificial construct, it will so closely resemble a genuine coral reef. At the Cancun Underwater Museum in Mexico, British artist Jason de Caires Taylor has created an art installation with more than 400 sculptures of humans designed to become artificial reefs. Even as these artificial reef sculptures are colonised, they may retain some of their original identity.

PRACTICAL ACTIVITY 5.1

The effect of acidity on calcium carbonate

Apparatus

- 12 small limestone rocks per group
- 3×500 cm³ beakers
- pH paper or other pH testing device
- Water, preferably distilled water
- Acetic acid (vinegar)
- Sodium hydrogencarbonate (baking soda)
- Scale

Method

- Rinse all the rocks until all dust is removed. Allow to dry.
- Place 240 cm³ of vinegar in one 500 cm³ beaker.
- Test the acidity of the solution using pH paper. Record the acidity level.
- Add water to the vinegar until the pH is between 4 and 5.
- Place 240 cm³ of vinegar in a second 500 cm³ beaker.
- Add small amounts of sodium hydrogencarbonate until the pH is between 8 and 9.
- Place 400 cm³ of water in the third 500 cm³ beaker.
- Divide the dried limestone rocks into three groups.
- Weigh the total mass of each group and record the results.

- Place one group of weighed rocks into each beaker.
- Leave the mixtures overnight.
- After 24 h, remove the rocks from each solution, rinse and dry them but keep the three groups separated. Weigh each group again.

Results and analysis

Copy Table 5.1 and enter your data. Calculate the percentage difference between the initial mass and the second mass for each group of rocks.

$$\frac{\text{final} - \text{initial}}{\text{initial}} \times 100 = \text{percent difference}$$

Generate an appropriate graph of the results. Decide whether you should have a bar graph or a line graph.

Conclusions

1. What is the independent variable in this study? What is the dependent variable?
2. Is there a control present? If so, which mixture represents the control?
3. Compare your data with other people's data. Are there similarities or trends in the data? What are they?
4. How does this information relate to coral reefs?

mixture	pH	initial mass / g	mass after 24 h / g	% difference
water				
vinegar				
sodium hydrogencarbonate				

Table 5.1. Results table for effect of pH on calcium carbonate.

5.6 Reconstructing the history of coral reefs

Using what we now know about the geomorphology of coral reef structures, scientists are able to determine a reef's age and history with modern techniques. Of primary interest to these scientists are changes in species composition and growth patterns of the reef. The evidence gained from these techniques helps us understand the Earth's geological and climatological history in order to

better predict the results of modern-day climate change through modelling.

Deep drilling of coral reefs is designed to provide cylindrical cores of calcium carbonate and biological material. Scientists use specialised equipment to drill into the cores and remove long cylinders of the coral skeleton intact (Figure 5.9), making these cores an excellent timeline of coral growth. The cores are analysed to determine the history of species that existed on a reef and estimate

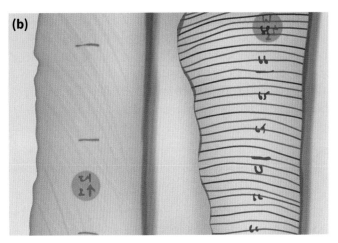

Figure 5.9. (a) Coral scientists use a pneumatic drill to remove a cylinder of past coral; (b) a drawing of a core sample labelled to show the horizontal growth lines.

the reef's approximate growth rate. Like a tree, corals continually grow outwards, so when a core of a coral reef is taken, scientists can see 'bands' of growth: layers of calcium carbonate laid down by the different generations of polyps through time. The width of these bands is dependent on water temperature, nutrient availability and other environmental conditions. Using information from deep drilling, scientists can generate hypotheses and correlations relating growth and environmental conditions of the past.

> **KEY TERM**
>
> **Radiocarbon dating:** a process used to estimate the age of organic material by measuring the radioactivity of its carbon content (also called carbon dating)

Radiocarbon dating, also referred to as carbon dating or carbon-14 dating, is another method used to analyse the history of coral reefs. Carbon dating determines the age of organic materials by comparing the proportions of the radioactive isotope of carbon (^{14}C) with the non-radioactive form of the carbon element (^{12}C). The technique relies on biomass being passed through food webs.

Radiocarbon (^{14}C) is being continuously created within our atmosphere when ultraviolet (UV) rays interact with atmospheric nitrogen. Once created, the ^{14}C joins with oxygen to create a radioactive form of carbon dioxide capable of diffusing into the ocean. When producers (for example zooxanthellae) photosynthesise, they take up carbon from the surrounding environment, including the radioactive carbon. After photosynthesis, the zooxanthellae pass the newly made organic materials

containing ^{14}C to the coral host. The coral polyps can then use this ^{14}C to create calcium carbonate in order to build their skeleton framework. Once the carbon has been deposited, it begins to go through radioactive decay, reducing the amount of ^{14}C present in the sample. The half-life of ^{14}C is 5730 years, which means that every 5730 years half of the ^{14}C in the sample will have decayed. Using this information, it has been determined that carbon dating can be successfully used on samples 50 000 years old or younger (Figure 5.10).

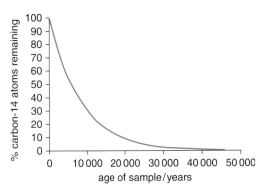

Figure 5.10. Graph of the decay of carbon-14.

Carbon dating allows coral scientists to judge accurately the age of a particular reef or place on a reef. Because the growth of coral is particularly dependent on the availability of light for rapid growth, scientists know that most hard corals prefer to be within 20 m of the ocean surface. However, in places like Bikini Atoll, fossil corals have been found in waters more than 1200 m deep. Using carbon dating and deep drilling, scientists have been able to show that the coral polyps grow slowly in layer after layer on top of older pieces of the reef, continuously growing vertically

93

over the course of hundreds of thousands of years. This evidence supports the theory that the initial substrate of the coral colony must have slowly been sinking from its original location close to the surface. This sinking of the seabed is called **subsidence** and the Darwin–Dana–Daly theory of atoll formation is reliant on the idea that ocean volcanoes can sink.

KEY TERM

Subsidence: sinking of land

Sea-level rise and fall is another phenomenon that coral reefs have to survive. During interglacial periods, when the ice caps are melting, sea-levels tend to be higher than during ice ages. This is because, during an ice age, the cold weather freezes the ocean water, locking it in ice and reducing the overall depth of the ocean. When sea-levels are high, coral reefs must grow vertically to remain within 20 m of the surface for the best light. When sea-levels

drop, however, the coral reef is exposed to air and dies. The best evidence of these changes in sea-level is present in fossilised corals that occur above sea-level. Several fossilised corals have been examined recently in Mexico. Scientists were able to correlate the growth and death of these corals with the sea-level changes between ice ages.

SELF-ASSESSMENT QUESTIONS

5 Describe the major factors leading to reef erosion.

6 Explain the role of artificial reefs in the preservation of shorelines.

7 Suggest a reason why surfers at popular surfing locations may protest against the installation of an artificial reef designed to protect the shoreline.

8 How are modern scientists using carbon dating and deep drilling to support early theories like the Darwin–Dana–Daly theory of atoll formation?

Maths skills

Radiocarbon dating

As discussed in this chapter, scientists routinely use carbon dating to determine the age of coral reefs and other organic materials. This information can then be analysed to estimate changes in sea-level or subsidence of the seabed. In order to begin this process, scientists need a few key pieces of information:

- ^{14}C decays at a constant rate once the organism has died
- ^{14}C has a half-life of 5730 years, meaning that for every 5730 years, half of the remaining sample of ^{14}C has decayed.

Worked example

If a coral sample has 100 g of ^{14}C when the organism dies, then after 5730 years the sample will only contain 50 g of ^{14}C. After another 5730 years pass, there will only be 25 g of ^{14}C remaining. This pattern will continue until there is only a tiny amount of ^{14}C remaining in the sample. So, using N_0 to represent the original amount of ^{14}C within a sample, you can determine the amount left after multiple half-lives have passed.

To determine one half-life: $\frac{1}{2} \times N_0 = \frac{N_0}{2}$

Assuming 5000 g for N_0, that means: $\frac{1}{2} \times 5000 = \frac{5000}{2} = 2500\ g$

To determine two half-lives: $\frac{1}{2} \times \frac{1}{2} \times N_0 = \left(\frac{1}{2}\right)^2 \times N_0 = \frac{N_0}{4}$

Assuming 5000 g for N_0, that means: $\frac{1}{2} \times \frac{1}{2} \times 5000 = \left(\frac{1}{2}\right)^2 \times 5000 = \frac{5000}{4} = 1250\ g$

half-lives that have passed	years from present	percentage of original ^{14}C remaining	amount of original ^{14}C remaining / g
0	0	100	5000
1	5730	50	2500
2		25	1250
3			
4			
5			
6			

Table 5.2. Half-life of ^{14}C.

Questions

1   Using the information, complete Table 5.2.

2   Generate a line graph with an appropriate scale showing the relationship between 'years from present' and 'percentage of original ^{14}C remaining'. Make sure to place your data on the appropriate axes.

3   As a coral scientist, you have recently been sent a core sample from the Great Barrier Reef in Australia. Comparing the oldest portion of the coral sample with the newest, you discover that the oldest pieces of coral contain only 60% of the ^{14}C contained in the modern sample. Using that information, estimate how old this portion of the reef is and discuss your reasoning.

Summary

- The coral animal is unique in its ability to create colonies that span thousands of years and generations, and create geological structures inhabited by thousands of other organisms.

- These structures can take the form of a fringing reef, barrier reef or atoll.

- Regardless of type, coral reefs increase the biodiversity on our planet and health of our oceans.

- Coral reefs provide many benefits to our coastlines, which are easily disturbed when the reef begins to suffer from erosion.

- Using technology, scientists are now able to study coral reefs as historical records of climate change and sea-level rise.

- These characteristics make coral reef ecosystems vital to our planet's future.

Exam-style questions

1 **a** Describe each of the following reef types:

    i Fringing reef [2]

    ii Barrier reef [2]

    iii Atoll [2]

  b Outline the Darwin–Dana–Daly theory of atoll formation. [4]

[Total mark: 10]

2 **a** List and describe three reasons why artificial reefs are beneficial to shorelines. [6]

  b In order to determine the best placement for artificial reefs, developers must take certain physical factors into consideration. Explain which factors are most important when determining placement of a coral reef for healthy growth. [6]

  c Most artificial reefs are now constructed from a pH neutral cement material. Explain why scientists prefer this material to old truck tyres, abandoned planes and ships. [4]

[Total mark: 16]

3 A survey was taken in 2000 of the percentage of coral cover in the Florida Keys of Islamorada and Key West. Another survey was taken in 2005 to determine coral cover after the 2004 hurricane season, and again in 2010. The results of these studies are shown in Table 5.3.

year	percentage cover of corals	
	Islamorada	Key West
2000	62	60
2005	43	35
2010	57	42

Table 5.3. Percentage of coral cover in the Florida Keys of Islamorada and Key West.

  a Using the data in Table 5.3, compare the coral cover of both locations between 2000 and 2010. [2]

  b Calculate the percentage increase in coral coverage between 2005 and 2010. Show your working. [2]

  c Suggest two reasons why the corals in Key West are not recovering as quickly as those in Islamorada. [2]

[Total mark: 6]

4 a Describe the relationships shared by the following pairs of organisms:

  i Coral polyps and zooxanthellae. [2]

  ii Butterflyfish and coral polyps [2]

 b Explain how parrotfish lead to reef erosion. [3]

[Total mark: 7]

5 a Describe how increased carbon dioxide in our atmosphere is related to ocean acidification. [3]

 b Explain how limiting nutrients, such as nitrogen and phosphorus, can have both *positive* and *negative* impacts on coral growth. [4]

 c Suggest one reason why coral reefs are not usually found in upwelling areas. [1]

[Total mark: 8]

Crown-of-thorns starfish on Indo-Pacific reefs

The crown-of-thorns starfish (*Acanthaster planci*) is a naturally occurring venomous predator found on coral reefs in the Indo-Pacific Ocean. This predator is an important part of the food web on these reefs. On healthy reefs, it tends to feed on only the fastest growing corals, such as staghorn and plate corals. It may seem that any coral predation is negative, but by feeding on these fast-growing corals, the crown-of-thorns starfish provides a mechanism for the slower growing coral species to develop into well-established colonies. This increases the coral biodiversity on the reef, which in turn provides more niches for other organisms to occupy, increasing the overall biodiversity of a reef.

However, the crown-of-thorns starfish has got a bad reputation as a destroyer of reefs because of several 'outbreaks' that have occurred in the last 50 years. Not everyone agrees on how to define an 'outbreak' of crown-of-thorns starfish. Although, one easy-to-use definition comes from the Great Barrier Reef Marine Park Authority. According to them, when there is a high level of coral cover, 'an outbreak is considered to have occurred when there is roughly more than 15 starfish per hectare'. Outbreaks of crown-of-thorns starfish have been cited as one of the most significant threats to the Great Barrier Reef. An outbreak may last over a decade as the crown-of-thorns starfish spread along the reef southwards.

Causes of outbreaks

Many studies have been conducted to determine what causes these outbreaks and it seems that multiple factors are involved before an outbreak occurs. Large female crown-of-thorns starfish are capable of producing up to 65 million eggs during the spawning season, but this is not unusual for invertebrates. Therefore, other causes must have a role in an outbreak. Initially, there needs to be an overall increase in certain limiting nutrients, particularly nitrogen and phosphorus, in the ecosystem. Generally, an increase in these nutrients is seen when fertiliser used on land is washed into the sea as run-off. When these nutrient levels are high, phytoplankton blooms provide more food for crown-of-thorns starfish larvae. As more larvae are well-sustained in this juvenile stage, an unusual number of larvae settle and metamorphose to become adult crown-of-thorns starfish.

→

However, as larvae and adults, crown-of-thorns starfish have natural predators. So, a second factor that must come into play for an outbreak to occur is a reduction in crown-of-thorns starfish predators. Not much is known about the larval predators, although many scientists hypothesise that corals themselves are the best predators of larval crown-of-thorns starfish. Adults are preyed on by giant triton snails (Figure 5.11), humphead Maori wrasse, starry pufferfish and titan triggerfish. When these animals are over-fished for either food or aquaria, then the reef can easily become overwhelmed by too many starfish.

Figure 5.11. A giant triton snail attacks while a crown-of-thorns starfish tries to dine on a piece of the coral reef.

On the Great Barrier Reef, and elsewhere, it appears that outbreaks of crown-of-thorns starfish happen cyclically. According to the Great Barrier Reef Marine Park Authority, outbreaks happen approximately every 15–17 years, with the latest outbreak occurring in 2010. There have been four major outbreaks on the Great Barrier Reef since the 1960s, and the crown-of-thorns starfish are probably responsible for up to 36% of the coral damage, making the crown-of-thorns starfish the greatest cause of coral damage on the Great Barrier Reef.

Questions

1   Outline the causes of crown-of-thorns starfish outbreaks.
2   Describe how a loss of coral through reef erosion during a tropical cyclone may lead to an outbreak of crown-of-thorns starfish.
3   Explain how poor fishing practices and waste management are contributing factors to outbreaks of these starfish.
4   Explain when and how crown-of-thorns starfish can be beneficial to the coral reef ecosystem.

Chapter 6
The ocean floor and the coast

Learning outcomes

By the end of this chapter, you should be able to:

- explain and provide evidence supporting the theory of plate tectonics
- demonstrate how tectonic processes produce features along the ocean floor, such as trenches, mid-ocean ridges, hydrothermal vents, abyssal plains and volcanoes
- demonstrate how tectonic processes create natural disasters such as volcanic eruptions, earthquakes and tsunamis
- explain why pressurised, hot, nutrient-rich water arises from hydrothermal vents
- explain the process and effects of isostasy
- describe how erosion and sedimentation create the different habitats found within the littoral zone, including estuaries, deltas, and rocky, sandy and muddy shores
- explain how the physical environment influences littoral communities, including mangrove forests
- apply what you have learnt to new, unfamiliar contexts.

6.1 How the Second World War changed marine science

The shore is where people first fall in love with the sea. Coastal environments are some of the most studied marine environments worldwide, because they are easily accessible for scientists interested in the biodiversity of our oceans. Conducting studies and experiments on the coast is easy because you need no special equipment to get there and it is easy to return to the same spot to repeat surveys. A love of the coast is not restricted to scientists, however: whenever you spend a sunny day relaxing at the beach, you are enjoying a small piece of the littoral zone.

While scientists may have started by studying the sea from dry land, they soon wanted to know what lies below the large bodies of water that dominate our planet. Images of the Kraken and other sea monsters swam through the minds of many sailors for thousands of years, as they wondered what really lay below the keels of their ships.

Unfortunately for those seafarers, it was not until the 20th century that technology became advanced enough to allow us to see what lies on the seabed, even though the technology used to explore the seabed was actually designed with another purpose in mind.

During the Second World War, many countries needed to be able to detect enemy submarines in the ocean. New technology was needed to make this possible, and that is why SONAR (an acronym for **so**und **n**avigation **a**nd **r**anging) was invented. SONAR enables scientists to map the ocean floor, and some amazing discoveries have been made using SONAR data. Instead of flat, barren plains stretching from shore to shore, scientists found mountain ranges dividing oceans in half and trenches sinking deeper than the highest mountains. This technology, followed quickly by SCUBA (**s**elf-**c**ontained **u**nderwater **b**reathing **a**pparatus), has been used for studies throughout the oceans, changing preconceived notions and providing evidence for new theories about the geology of our planet.

6.2 Plate tectonics

The history behind the theory of plate tectonics

In 1912, a German scientist named Alfred Wegener proposed an unusual theory regarding our planet to the geologists of his day. Wegener based his theory on evidence from multiple disciplines of science, such as geology and palaeontology. While looking at studies performed by other scientists, Wegener realised that identical fossilised plants and animals had been found on the coasts of different continents separated by oceans. When comparing geological structures (for example mountains) between continents, he found evidence that the rock layers in South Africa match those in Brazil. Between Europe and North America, he discovered that the structure of the Appalachian Mountains in the United States closely matches that of the mountains in the West Highlands of Scotland. Wegener then argued that the shape of the coastlines with matching geological features – South America and Africa, North America and Europe – fit together like pieces of a jigsaw puzzle. Using these observations, Wegener developed his theory of **continental drift**. This theory claims that, more than 300 million years ago, all the continents on Earth were joined as a single landmass Wegener named Pangea. Over the course of millions of years, Pangea began to split and its pieces have been slowly moving further and further away from each other since then.

Unfortunately for Wegener, his theory was not well received. In spite of the evidence he presented, his peers were not convinced that continental drift was happening or had ever happened. This was partly because Wegener did not suggest a clear mechanism by which continents moved. He proposed continents ploughed through the oceanic crust as an iceberg moves through water. Other scientists pointed out that this would change the shape of the continents, refuting the evidence Wegener was relying on to support his theory. Scientists at the time insisted on the idea of non-moving continents with long-gone land bridges for animals and plants to cross. It was another 50 years before other scientists were able to discover enough evidence to determine what was really happening. This evidence led them to new discoveries in the fields of geology, morphology and ecology of the oceans.

KEY TERM

Continental drift: a theory supporting the possibility that continents are able to move over Earth's surface

KEY TERMS

Plate tectonics: the process where large sections ('plates') of the Earth's crust are in constant movement over the fluid mantle, causing earthquakes and volcanoes at the borders between the plates

Lithosphere: the outermost layer of the Earth's crust

Asthenosphere: a nearly liquid layer made of the uppermost part of the mantle

Mantle: a region of molten rock within the interior of the Earth, between the core and the crust

The theory of plate tectonics

In the 1960s, the continental drift theory was revised as new evidence came to light. The revised theory included a mechanism for how the continents were actually moving across the surface of our planet, a factor missing from Wegener's original theory. The new theory – the theory of **plate tectonics** – suggests that the outermost layer of the Earth's crust, the **lithosphere**, is made up of many different plates called tectonic plates. Each of these plates floats independently on the nearly liquid **asthenosphere**, a layer made of the uppermost part of the **mantle** (Figure 6.1).

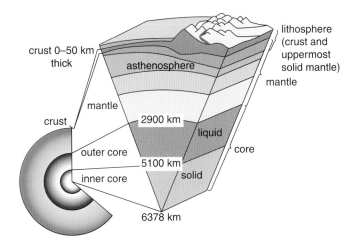

Figure 6.1. A diagram of the Earth's interior.

Evidence supporting the theory of plate tectonics

Seabed spreading

Many lines of evidence supporting plate tectonics have been discovered by scientists since the theory was first proposed. The concepts used by Wegener to support continental drift, of coastlines 'fitting' together and fossils being spread over multiple continents, also support the theory of plate tectonics. However, after the invention of

SONAR, new evidence of plate boundaries came to light on the bottom of the ocean.

The data collected while looking for submarines showed mountains and trenches lining the edges of plate boundaries. These geological features created a clear map of where the tectonic plates line up. Marie Tharp, a geologist and oceanic cartographer, and her partner Bruce Heezen, a geologist, collaborated for 20 years to collect ocean floor mapping data in order to create an accurate, scientific map of the seabed. This map (Figure 6.2), called the World Ocean Floor, revolutionised Earth science after its publication in 1977, because of the prominent presence of the mid-ocean ridge. This map is responsible for convincing many scientists to accept the theory of plate tectonics and seabed spreading.

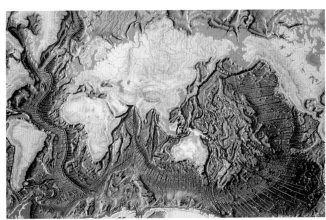

Figure 6.2. The World Ocean Floor by Marie Tharp and Bruce C. Heezen.

Magnetic polarity reversal

More evidence supporting the theory of plate tectonics was discovered after the Second World War had ended. Scientists began studying magnetism on the ocean floor using magnetometers created to locate submarines during the war, as SONAR had been. The evidence they found surprised them. The magnetic field of the ocean floor was laid out in alternating stripes of normal polarity and reversed polarity.

The fact that the ocean floor was magnetic was not the surprise. Sailors had known for more than 100 years that the basaltic rocks lining the ocean floor were magnetic. It was the striped pattern that was unexpected. Further research showed that the striped pattern had an origin around the mid-ocean ridges, where the crust is weakest and magma often pushes through (Figure 6.3). This magma held the explanation.

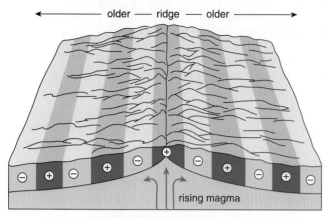

Figure 6.3. Seabed spreading and magnetic reversal.

Basaltic rocks, the type commonly found on the seabed, are an example of an igneous rock. Igneous rocks are created when molten magma from a volcanic eruption cools and hardens. Within igneous rocks is a naturally magnetic iron material called magnetite, which is why basalt is magnetic. When molten magma first reaches the Earth's surface, the particles of magnetite within it align with the Earth's magnetic field. Once the magma begins to harden, the magnetite is locked in place, holding information about the Earth's magnetic field at the time the rock was formed. Scientists have found that the Earth's magnetic field reverses on average every 250 000 years, changing magnetic north to magnetic south. This information, when applied to the ocean floor, provides unique evidence in support of the theory of plate tectonics.

At divergent boundaries, where mid-ocean ridges form, scientists now know the seabed is spreading because of magma rising from the mantle and hardening into igneous rocks. When the magnetic properties of the rocks at these boundaries were measured, scientists confirmed that the rocks lay in alternating stripes of magnetic polarity radiating away from the boundary in parallel lines. These stripes differed in width based on the length of time between each reversal, providing the strongest evidence in support of seabed spreading and plate tectonics.

SELF-ASSESSMENT QUESTIONS

1 Compare the theory of continental drift with the theory of plate tectonics.
2 List the major lines of evidence for the theory of plate tectonics.

6.3 Plate boundaries

In order for lithospheric (tectonic) plates to move, the asthenosphere must be moving as well. This movement is caused by **convection currents** within the mantle. Convection currents happen when the molten rock of the mantle moves because of density changes in the rock caused by temperature differences. In other words, as the molten rock is heated, it becomes less dense as the molecules spread out. The less dense rock moves upwards in the mantle towards the crust in order to float on top of the denser rock. Then, as the rock begins to cool, it begins to sink towards the warmer core. This forms a circular cell of flowing molten rock capable of moving the lithospheric plate lying on top of it. Because the plates are heavy and the convection currents in the asthenosphere move so slowly, the plates move only 2–5 cm year^{-1}. However, even this small movement causes the plates to meet and form three types of boundary: convergent, divergent and transform. Each boundary type has identifiable characteristics and geological features (Figure 6.4).

KEY TERMS

Convection current: the movement of fluids or air based on density differences caused by differing temperature

Convergent boundary: when two or more tectonic plates come together

Subduction: the process where one lithospheric plate slides below another at a convergent plate boundary

Trench: a long, narrow and deep depression on the ocean floor with relatively steep sides, caused by convergent plate boundaries

Volcano: a mountain or hill with a crater or vent through which lava, rock fragments, hot vapour and gas are being forced from the Earth's crust

Earthquake: a sudden release of energy inside the Earth that creates seismic waves usually caused by movement of tectonic plates or volcanic activity

Tsunami: a seismic sea wave created by an underwater earthquake or volcanic event, not noticeable in the open ocean but building to great heights in shallow water

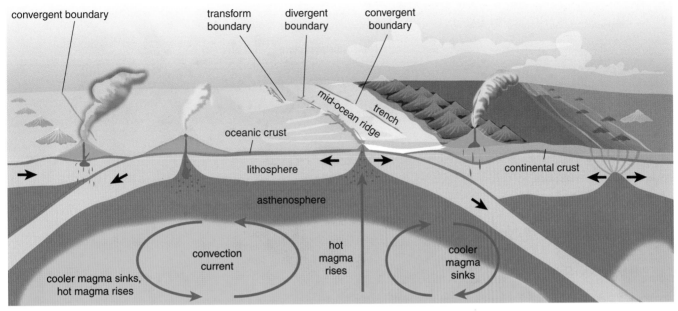

Figure 6.4. Visual representation of plate boundaries and their features.

Convergent boundaries and their features

Convergent boundaries form when two tectonic plates are moving towards each other. These boundaries form **subduction** zones where one plate, typically a denser oceanic plate, slides underneath the other, less dense, continental plate. These areas are known as destructive zones. This is because, as the denser oceanic plate slides below the continental plate, it is destroyed by the heat of the asthenosphere and returns to the molten mantle. Common features along subduction zones are **trenches, volcanoes, earthquakes** and **tsunamis**.

Trenches are long, narrow, deep canyons in the seabed. Trenches only occur at subduction zones within convergent boundaries. The deepest part of the ocean, Challenger Deep, exists within the Marianas Trench in the western Pacific Ocean. Challenger Deep is 11 033 m deep, which is deeper than Mount Everest is tall (8848 m).

A volcano is formed when an opening in the Earth's crust allows gases and molten rock to escape from the mantle. Volcanoes that rise above sea-level form new islands like those in the Hawaiian and Philippines archipelagos. However, many volcanoes are located under the ocean's surface, creating new seabed when the magma cools after erupting. Of these underwater volcanoes, most lie along the convergent plate boundaries surrounding the Pacific Ocean. Together, they create what is known as the Ring of Fire (Figure 6.5). The areas that border the Ring of Fire are

hotspots for volcanic and seismic activity. Volcanoes can also be found at divergent boundaries and areas where the crust is very thin.

Earthquakes occur after there has been a sudden release of energy from the movement of the Earth's crust. When two plates are moving past each other, at either a convergent or transform boundary, they may get stuck. When this happens, the pressure for them to move builds and builds until movement finally happens, releasing stored potential energy in a sudden burst. This burst of energy releases seismic waves that move through the lithosphere making everything on top of the crust shake. Volcanoes are also capable of causing an earthquake when they release enormous amounts of energy during an eruption.

Sudden releases of energy on the seabed, either through an earthquake or a volcanic eruption, can lead to tsunamis. Tsunamis are long-wavelength, high-energy waves created by seismic activity. When an earthquake releases its stored energy on the seabed, it moves all the water lying above. The water holds on to this energy and moves very quickly but unnoticeably through deep ocean water. However, as the tsunami reaches shallow, coastal waters, the wave slows down and grows exponentially in height. These large, high-energy waves can be incredibly destructive. Tsunamis are sometimes called 'tidal waves' but this is inaccurate because the tides have nothing to do with the creation of tsunamis.

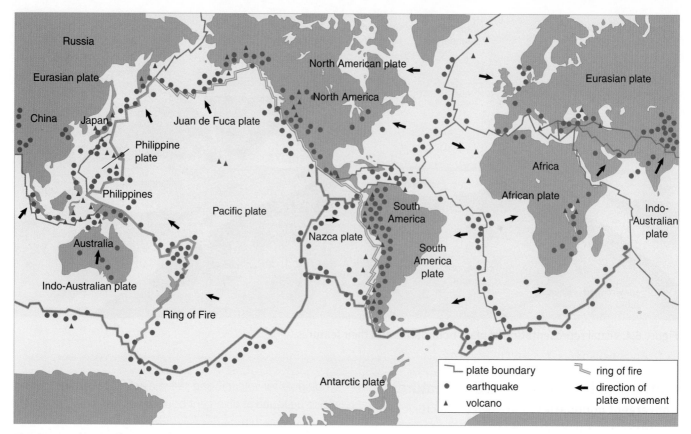

Figure 6.5. The Pacific Ring of Fire with tectonic plate movement.

Divergent boundaries and their features

Divergent boundaries are areas where the tectonic plates are moving away from each other and allowing molten magma from the mantle to push through to the crust. These areas are considered to be constructive zones. As the magma, driven by convection currents, pushes through the opening in the crust, it spreads out and solidifies in the cold ocean waters at the bottom of the sea. The new rocks created through this process eventually build up and form underwater mountain ranges called **mid-ocean ridges**. As these mid-ocean ridges continue to build new crust, there is an eventual movement away from the divergent boundary, causing seabed spreading. Seabed spreading helps to move tectonic plates towards convergent boundaries on the opposite side of the planet. This process, over the course of millions of years, is responsible for a shrinking Pacific Ocean and growing Atlantic Ocean. Located within these mid-ocean ridges are volcanoes and hydrothermal vents, which are discussed in further detail later in this chapter.

> ### KEY TERMS
>
> **Divergent boundary:** where two tectonic plates are moving away from each other
>
> **Mid-ocean ridge:** a mountain range with a central valley on an ocean floor at the boundary between two diverging tectonic plates, where new crust forms from upwelling magma
>
> **Transform boundary:** when two plates are moving in an antiparallel direction, creating friction between them
>
> **Abyssal plain:** a flat, sandy region of the ocean floor found between trenches and the continental rise

Transform boundaries and their features

Transform boundaries are areas where two plates slide laterally next to each other. No crust is created or destroyed at transform boundaries. However, transform boundaries are areas of great seismic activity. The increased friction between plates at these boundaries causes small cracks called faults to form. The pressure that builds up in these fault lines can lead to earthquakes and tsunamis. The most common ocean feature found along transform boundaries are **abyssal plains**, which are discussed in the section on the seabed.

3 Describe how tsunamis are formed.

4 How are divergent and convergent boundaries related to the rock cycle?

KEY TERMS

Hydrothermal vent: an area where cold ocean water that has seeped into the Earth's crust is superheated by underlying magma and forced through vents in the ocean floor

Figure 6.6. A hydrothermal vent along the Juan de Fuca Ridge in the northern Pacific Ocean.

6.4 Hydrothermal vents

Hydrothermal vent systems were discovered in 1977 along the Galapagos Rift in the Pacific Ocean by scientists from Woods Hole Oceanographic Institute (WHOI) using the deep sea submersible *Alvin*. Hydrothermal vents (Figure 6.6) occur in deep ocean water, usually 2000 m or more below sea-level, within mid-ocean ridge systems. At this depth, the pressure is over 200 atmospheres and there is no light. These are unique circumstances for the development of an ecosystem.

Hydrothermal vents are formed when cold ocean water seeps through cracks in the thin crust surrounding divergent boundaries (Figure 6.7). As the water moves through the crust to an area directly over a magma chamber, it dissolves minerals (for example iron, copper and zinc sulfides) from the rocks, turning it black. Once heated by the magma, the water reaches temperatures well over 100 °C but never boils because of the extreme pressure in the region. This superheated water then escapes the crust through a fissure above.

105

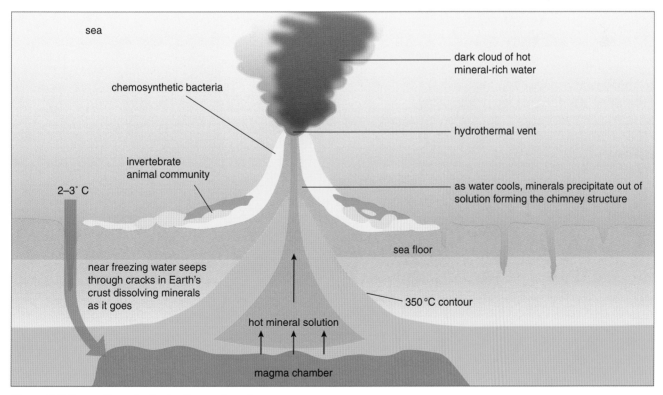

Figure 6.7. Formation of a hydrothermal vent.

As the superheated water meets the near freezing water on the ocean floor it begins to cool. As the water cools, the minerals precipitate out of solution. This means the minerals form solids, which settle near the fissure, piling on top of each other. This forms a chimney, or vent, for the superheated water that can be up to 60 m high. These hydrothermal vents release water at temperatures over 350 °C. They are often referred to as 'black smokers' because of the black smoke-like look the water has as it escapes from the chimney. The chemicals contained in the water are the basis for energy capture, chemosynthesis, in these dark waters (see Chapter 2).

SELF-ASSESSMENT QUESTIONS

5   Why do you think it took until 1977 for scientists to discover hydrothermal vents?

6   Would you describe this environment as extreme? Why or why not?

6.5 Seabed

The ocean floor is divided into specific regions based on physical structure and location. The **continental margin** comprises approximately 28% of the ocean floor. This region of the ocean floor divides the thin, but dense, oceanic crust from the thicker, less dense, continental crust located at the edge of continents. Within the continental margin are three distinct zones (Figure 6.8).

- The **continental shelf** is the flat, shallow area extending from the shore to the continental slope. This area tends to be featureless because of the deposition of sediments as a result of wave action. The average width of continental shelves is 70 km, but they range from 20 km to 1500 km. The widest continental shelves happen in areas where there is little tectonic action taking place.

- The **continental slope** begins where the continental shelf ends. This region is a fairly steep area of the

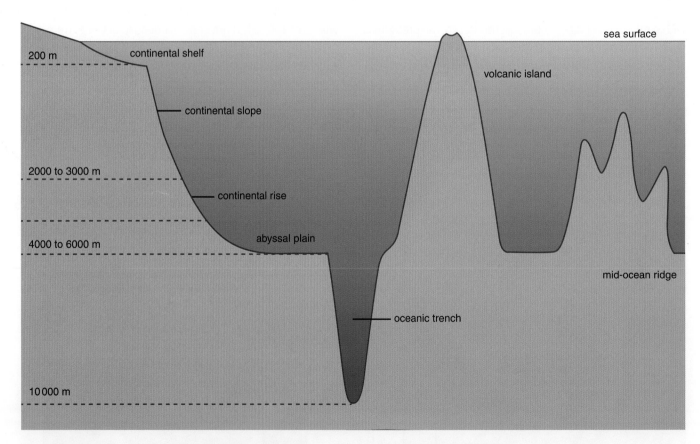

Figure 6.8. Diagram of the seabed, not drawn to scale.

seabed that descends into the ocean basins. This area is even steeper when located near a convergent boundary because of the presence of trenches.

- The **continental rise** is a narrow edge to the continental slope connecting the continental slope to the seabed.

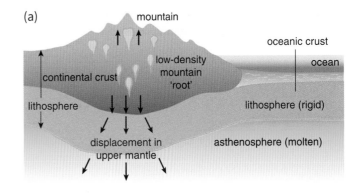

KEY TERMS

Continental margin: the submerged area next to a continent, which includes the continental shelf, continental slope and continental rise

Continental shelf: a gently sloping surface that extends from the low tide line to the continental slope, typically where a great deal of sand deposits

Continental slope: a relatively steep sloping surface between the continental shelf and the continental rise

Continental rise: a gently sloping surface at the base of the continental slope where sand deposits

---

Leading from the continental rise are incredibly flat areas of the ocean floor called abyssal plains. These areas are located at depths between 3000 and 6000 m below sea-level and can typically be found between the continental rise and a mid-ocean ridge. Abyssal plains make up more than 50% of the Earth's total surface area. This flat plain is formed when the uneven, rocky surface of the seabed is slowly covered in sand and decomposing organic matter that sinks to the bottom of the ocean.

6.6 Isostasy

The term **isostasy** means 'weighing the same'. In geology, isostasy refers to the buoyancy of different rock layers as they float on other layers. The buoyancy of each rock type is determined by its density and thickness. This concept explains why the Earth's crust is able to float on the denser molten rock of the mantle the way an ice cube floats in a glass of water. Figure 6.9 shows this process in stages.

KEY TERM

Isostasy: a process similar to buoyancy but related to the Earth's crust floating on the flexible mantle

---

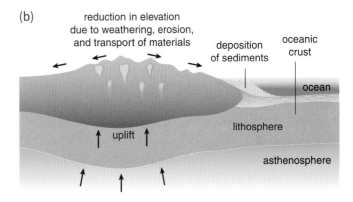

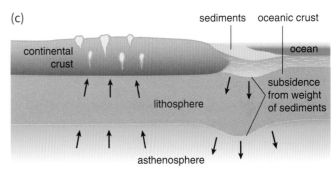

Figure 6.9. Process of isostasy and how shallow seas are formed.

Isostasy allows scientists to create a model of the Earth representing the way each rock layer floats on the underlying mantle. Table 6.1 shows the approximate densities of the Earth's rock layers for reference. Both continental crust and oceanic crust float on the mantle because they have a lower density than the rock in the mantle. However, the continental crust tends to float higher on the mantle than the oceanic crust. This is because, even though the continental crust is a thicker layer of rock, its density is lower than that of oceanic crust.

layer	density / g cm⁻³
continental crust	2.7–3.0
sediments on continental shelf	2.4
oceanic crust	3.0–3.3
mantle	3.3–5.7

Table 6.1. Densities of the Earth's rock layers.

During the last ice age, much of the planet's ocean water was frozen as ice, lowering sea-levels worldwide. These lower sea-levels meant that most, if not all, of the continental shelf regions were above water at the time. Now that these areas are back under water, they form the base of shallow seas at the outermost edge of continents. Remember, the continental shelf is a relatively shallow area of the ocean covered in sediments as a result of the erosion of rocks on the continents. The depth of water in these areas is controlled by two factors:

- changes in sea-level as a result of the melting or freezing of sea ice

- changes in land height as a result of isostatic changes.

SELF-ASSESSMENT QUESTIONS

7   Would you expect the continental shelf near a convergent plate to be wide or narrow? Why?

8   How does isostasy create shallow seas during non-ice age time periods?

6.7 The littoral zone

The area of the ocean most commonly studied is that of the **littoral zone**. This is the area of the shore where land meets sea and is also known as the intertidal zone. The littoral zone is the area between the high water mark during spring tides and the lowest part of the shore that is permanently submerged. This area of the ocean is varied and is categorised according to:

- the shape of the shore

- wave action and erosion

- the substrate that makes up the shore

- the organisms that live there.

KEY TERMS

Littoral zone: the benthic, or bottom, zone between the highest and lowest spring tide shorelines, also referred to as the intertidal zone

Morphology: the study of the forms of things

Morphology of the littoral zone

The shape of the sea shore depends primarily on the geology of the land lying closest to the shore and the level of exposure to erosion on that shore. This means that sea shores may be nearly flat areas covered in fine particles of mud or nearly vertical areas with large rocks. Scientists studying the different shape and make-up of sea shores are studying the **morphology** of that shore. The two factors that scientists focus on when studying morphology are the slope of the shore and the size of the sediment found on the shore. Table 6.2 shows some different categories and diameters of sediments commonly found on sea shores.

particle type	diameter / mm
silt	0.002–0.02
fine sand	0.02–0.2
coarse sand	0.2–2.0
gravel (small stones)	>2.0

Table 6.2. Diameters of common sediment types.

Rocky shores

Rocky shores are areas of shore that are characterised by the presence of a rocky substrate (Figure 6.10). Rocky shores vary widely in slope from nearly vertical cliff faces to wide flat expanses of rocks. The size of the rocks making up the shore also varies from very large boulders to much smaller pieces of gravel and pebbles.

Figure 6.10. A rocky shore with tide pools in Cozumel, Mexico.

Geologically speaking, rocky shores tend to be made of primarily granite or igneous rocks, which are incredibly resistant to weathering and take a much longer time to break down than softer rocks such as sandstone. Rocks along these shores often exist in a gradient, with the largest rocks occurring farthest from the water at the high-water mark and the smallest rocks occurring nearer the low-water mark. Scientists believe this gradient is caused by the pounding of waves wearing away those rocks closest to the water line first and not being able to reach those farther up the shore. It is not surprising that these shores are the most resistant to erosion even though they also tend to be the most open and exposed.

Sandy shores

A normal sandy shore is made of loose deposits of sand (silica), small pieces of gravel and shells. Sandy shores are formed by the **erosion** of sandstone and **deposition** of sediments by the waves. Sandy shores are constantly in motion as the ocean moves the sand up and down the beach. These shores tend to have a gradual slope towards the ocean.

KEY TERMS

Erosion: a natural process where material is worn away from the Earth's surface and transported elsewhere

Deposition: a geological process where sediments, soil and rocks are added to a landform or land mass

Muddy shores

Muddy shores are found in protected regions and are shores least exposed to erosion. There tends to be no slope on muddy shores, giving rise to the name mud flat. A lack of erosion and little to no water movement allows the deposition of a layer of very fine silt particles and organic materials.

Estuaries

Estuaries form in sheltered or partially enclosed areas where fresh water and salt water meet; this mix of water is called brackish. Because these areas are sheltered from the erosive action of waves, the bottom is often made of fine sand and silt that falls out of suspension when the water is still. The water in estuaries is very murky, with high turbidity as a result of the fine sediments. Other names for estuaries include bays, lagoons, sounds and sloughs.

KEY TERMS

Estuary: a partially enclosed, tidal, coastal body of water where fresh water from a river meets the salt water of the ocean

Delta: a low-lying triangular area at the mouth of a river formed by the deposition of sediments

Deltas

Deltas form at the mouth of a river where it meets the sea. These shores are named after the Greek letter delta (Δ) because they usually have a triangular shape (Figure 6.11). As a river flows towards its mouth, it picks up sediment along the way. The river begins to widen as it approaches the sea, slowing down the speed of the water. When the water slows enough, the sediments begin to settle on the bottom of the river. Over time, these sediments deposit and accumulate into sandbars and other small landmasses, forming a wide fan-shaped structure resembling a branching tree. If the landmasses build up enough, it is possible for the delta to form new tributary channels of the river. The most well-known river deltas are the:

- Mississippi River Delta, leading to the Gulf of Mexico in the United States

- Nile River Delta, draining into the Mediterranean Sea in Egypt.

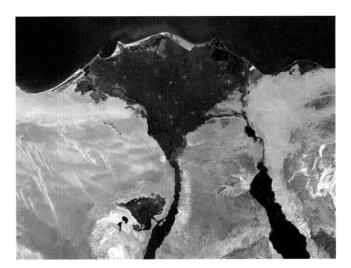

Figure 6.11. Nile River Delta.

Ecosystems of the littoral zone

Ocean ecosystems are a product of the environment in which they exist. Many abiotic factors, including temperature, exposure to air, stability of the substrate and salinity, have a role in the formation of an ecosystem. These and others are responsible for the development of the many ecosystem types located within the littoral zone.

This chapter focuses on the formation of the three ecosystems that can develop in the littoral zone of oceans: rocky shores, sandy shores and mangroves.

Rocky shores

Living on a rocky shore is not easy. Organisms have a lot to contend with, including fluctuating temperatures, wave action and exposure to air based on the tides. Other factors that they have to adapt to are the slope of the shore, what type of rocks make up the substrate, whether the habitat is in a temperate or tropical region, and how much sunlight is available at any time during the year. It may therefore come as a surprise to you that rocky shores are typically habitats with significant biodiversity (Figure 6.12).

In spite of the difficulties organisms may face living on a rocky shore, these areas provide habitat and stability to a multitude of species within the littoral zone. The rocky substrate provides many places for organisms to attach to, a necessity for survival in a place where waves can wash organisms and substrate away. Algae, barnacles, sea anemones and many species of mollusc make their home attached to the rocky surface. The need for safe anchorage makes space, not food or light, the main resource that organisms compete for in this ecosystem.

In order to reduce competition for space, species in rocky shore ecosystems space themselves vertically on the rocks in a pattern called **zonation**. To determine the upper limit of a species' zone, scientists look for physical factors affecting survival: temperature tolerance and length of time the species can spend out of water before **desiccation**. To find the lower level of a species' zone, scientists look at biological factors: competition between other species and predation. The intertidal zone on a rocky shore can be divided into three major areas (Figure 6.13).

Figure 6.12. Rocky shore flora and fauna at Cannon Beach, Oregon.

KEY TERMS

Zonation: a separation of organisms in a habitat into definite zones or bands according to biological and physical factors, common in rocky shore habitats

Desiccation: the process of drying out or losing moisture

- High-tide zone: this area only has water during high tides. Organisms here must be able to withstand long periods of time without water or food. These organisms risk desiccation or drying out. Typical organisms located in this zone include chitons, crabs, isopods and barnacles.

- Middle-tide zone: this area is exposed to air twice a day at low tide, so organisms must have a coping method to deal with desiccation. Typical organisms in this zone include limpets, periwinkles and mussels.

- Low-tide zone: this area is usually covered with water, except during the lowest spring tides (Chapter 7). Organisms found here have very few adaptations for living outside water and dry out or overheat easily. Typical organisms found here include seaweed, algae, sea stars, sea urchins, sea anemones and oysters.

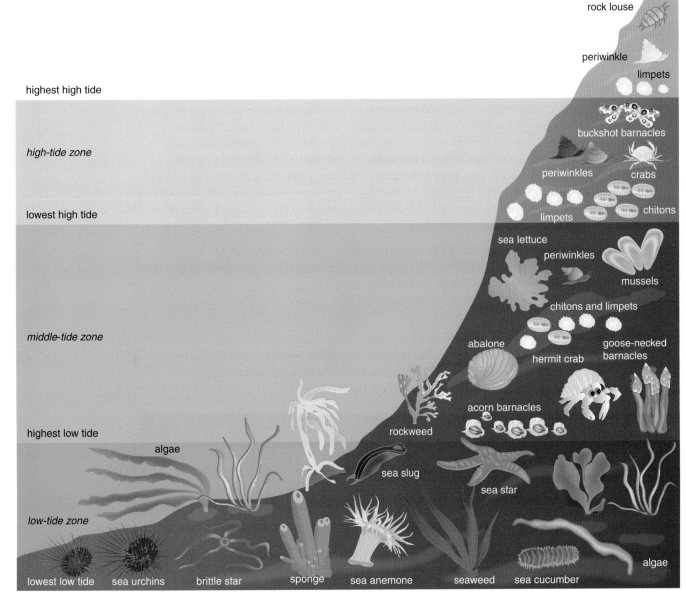

Figure 6.13. Diagram of zonation patterns on a rocky shore.

Within each of these zones, tide pools may exist. Tide pools form when seawater fills a particularly low spot in the rocks during low tides (Figure 6.10). Tide pools are important for organisms in the higher zones to survive because they create an area where they can cool down, carry out gaseous exchange and feed. As the tide comes back in, the water in the tide pool is replaced and refreshed so there are few problems with increased salinity or decreased oxygen.

Sandy shores

Sandy shores produce a unique set of circumstances for organisms to deal with. The most difficult factor organisms have to be adapted for is the ever-shifting substrate. Sandy shores are incredibly unstable, as a single wave or gust of wind can remove a lot of the fine sand the organisms live on. Most organisms therefore deal with this situation by living *in* the substrate rather than *on* the substrate. Organisms found on a sandy shore tend to be burrowers or **infauna**, such as ghost crabs, cockles and other bivalves, and annelid worms like ragworms and lugworms. These challenges explain why sandy shores tend to have low biodiversity compared to rocky shores.

> **KEY TERM**
>
> **Infauna:** animals living within the sediments of the ocean floor, river or lake beds

Maths skills

Measuring biodiversity on a rocky shore

The quadrat survey is a commonly used method for biodiversity studies as it allows scientists to create a standard unit of area for studying the distribution of an organism over a large area. A quadrat is normally square in shape, but can be rectangular or circular, depending on the needs of the study. The size of the quadrat also varies depending on the study. For instance, when determining tree biodiversity in a forest, the quadrat may be 10 m² because of the size of the study species; in a rocky intertidal zone, the quadrat may only be 0.25 m² because much smaller organisms are being studied. Quadrat surveys are useful in rocky intertidal areas because the majority of organisms located there are slow-moving, attached to the substrate or plants.

Scientists use a method of random sampling to determine where to place the quadrat when conducting a survey. This prevents any bias affecting the data. The counts from each quadrat are then averaged to reach an approximate number for the entire area.

Worked example

Scientists were conducting a quadrat survey on a rocky shore in Vancouver, BC, Canada. They were specifically investigating the abundance of leather stars (*Dermasterias imbricate*) and the Pacific blue mussel (*Mytilus trossulus*) along the shore. Square quadrats of 1 m² were used to measure the abundance in ten randomly selected locations (see Table 6.3).

sample area	1	2	3	4	5	6	7	8	9	10
number of leather stars in 1 m²	3	15	0	8	4	17	12	1	2	9
number of mussels in 1 m²	20	49	9	47	12	100	48	10	16	32

Table 6.3. Results of 1 m² sample area calculations.

Standard deviation

Often scientists include standard deviation in their results when they analyse their data. Standard deviations tell you how spread out the numbers in a data set are. The smaller the standard deviation, the closer the numbers are to the mean. This can tell you, for example, how variable a population is within a community. The equation for standard deviation is:

$$S = \sqrt{\frac{\sum(x-\bar{x})^2}{n-1}}$$

These symbols all relate to the different steps you need to complete to find the standard deviation. This equation can be broken down into stages. The standard deviation (S) for the leather star data given in Table 6.3 is calculated as shown below.

- Calculate the mean value ($\bar{x}$) for the leather star population:

$$\bar{x} = \frac{(3+15+0+8+4+17+12+1+2+9)}{10} = 7.1$$

- Then for each quadrat, subtract the mean ($\bar{x}$) from its number (x) and square the result, giving you: $(x - \bar{x})^2$. So for quadrat 1: $(3 - 7.1)^2 = 16.8$.

Table 6.4 shows the results of this step for all 10 quadrats.

sample area	1	2	3	4	5	6	7	8	9	10	mean
number of leather stars in 1 m²	3	15	0	8	4	17	12	1	2	9	7.1
$(x - \bar{x})^2$	16.8	62.4	50.4	0.8	9.6	98.0	24.0	37.2	26.0	3.61	32.9

Table 6.4. Working out the mean values for the leather stars.

- The next step is to calculate $\sum(x - \bar{x})^2$ by adding all of the $(x - \bar{x})^2$ values. So, $\sum(x - \bar{x})^2 = 328.81$
- Then, divide your value for $\sum(x - \bar{x})^2$ by $(n-1)$, where n is the number of values you have (10, in this case). This should provide you with a value of 36.53.
- Finally, take the square root of your calculated value.
- Using this equation, your standard deviation should be 6.04.

Questions

1 a Calculate the mean numbers per m² for the mussels, using the data in Table 6.3.

   b Calculate the standard deviation for the population of mussels.

2 Based on your knowledge of rocky intertidal zone communities, predict which quadrats were placed in the lower intertidal zone and which were placed in the upper intertidal zone.

Organisms on a sandy shore also show vertical zonation patterns similar to those on a rocky shore (Figure 6.14). Once again, the area inhabited by an organism is determined by both physical and biological factors, such as predation and the ability to resist drying out. The primary difference between zonation on rocky shores and sandy shores is that it is less noticeable on sandy shores because of the burrowing nature of the organisms that live here.

Because there is no place for attachment on a sandy shore, seaweeds cannot survive here. The only producers that may occur on a sandy shore are phytoplankton brought in by the tides. Therefore most of the organisms on sandy shores are detritivores that collect organic material from between sand grains as they burrow. This is particularly the case on coasts where sand is mixed with muddy deposits. However, a sand and mud shore is more stable than a shore of sand alone, so more biodiversity is present.

Mangroves

Mangroves are trees that prefer to live in coastal or estuarine environments between latitudes 25 °N and 25 °S.

There are more than 110 species of mangrove, many of which are found in Indonesia where mangrove biodiversity is highest. These trees survive in saline habitats because of the lack of competition from other plants. Mangroves tend to form woodland habitats that provide the basis for incredibly biodiverse habitats. Areas where mangroves grow are referred to as mangrove swamps, mangrove forests or just mangroves.

Within a coastal or estuarine habitat, there are two primary physical factors that mangroves have to contend with that can impact their survival:

- high salt content in the water
- low oxygen content in the substrate.

High salt content

Mangroves have several adaptations for dealing with the high salt content of coastal and estuarine waters. Red mangroves (*Rhizophora mangle*) have two methods for living in salt water. The first method begins at the roots, which have become nearly impermeable to salt because

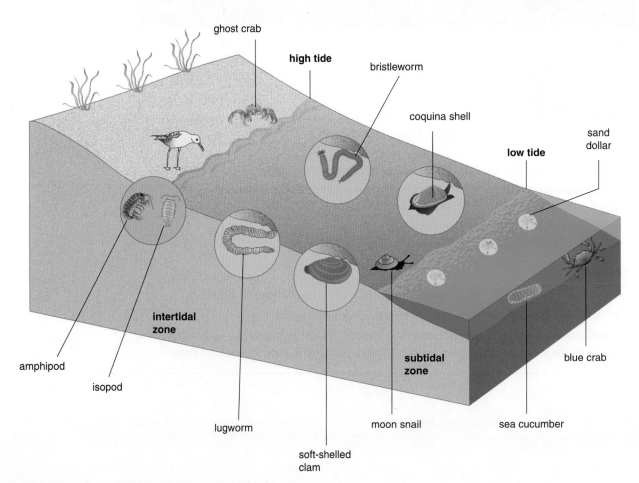

Figure 6.14. Common zonation patterns on a sandy shore.

of a very efficient filtration method. Some scientists have hypothesised the use of a 'sacrificial leaf', where red mangroves deposit excess salts that make it past the filtration system. However, other studies dispute this hypothesis. Black mangroves (*Avicennia germinans*) expel salt through pores on the underside of their leaves.

Anoxic soil

Red mangroves use prop roots to hold themselves above the water level at high tide and absorb the oxygen they need through their bark. Black mangroves do not possess prop roots. Instead their roots are specially designed with pneumatophores that act as snorkels and stick up out of the water. These pneumatophores allow the roots of the tree to breathe even during high tides (Figure 6.15).

Figure 6.15. Black mangrove (*Avicennia germinans*) tree with pneumatophores protruding from the water at high tide.

The root systems of red mangroves are called prop roots because they primarily exist above the substrate and prop up the tree. The unusual design of prop roots allows them to have a specific function in this ecosystem as well as serve the traditional purpose of tree roots (Figure 6.16). Prop roots help prevent erosion by storms such as hurricanes and reduce wave energy, similar to a coral reef. This feature of mangroves is why they are protected in Florida in the United States and why they are being replanted in many places in Indonesia. Because these roots provide a cage-like structure under the water at high tide and collect sediment, many organisms find a home among the roots. Algae, oysters, sponges, crabs, barnacles, fish and other crustaceans all live among mangrove roots, making mangrove a keystone species in this environment.

Figure 6.16. Illustration of red mangrove (*Rhizophora mangle*) showing how the prop roots retain sediments and act as a habitat for local species.

The extensive root system also makes mangroves unique in their ability to grow their own habitat. When a mangrove tree produces seeds, or propagules, they float around in the ocean for a period of time (each species requires a specific length of time). Eventually, the propagule will come to rest on a piece of land and begin to root. In some cases the 'land' is just a sand bar or area of high **sedimentation**. Once the propagule takes root, a new mangrove tree begins to form. The roots of the newly formed tree begin to act as a trap for sediment and slowly build an island as more mangrove colonise the trapped sediment.

KEY TERM

Sedimentation: the act or process of depositing sediment from a solution (e.g. seawater)

SELF-ASSESSMENT QUESTIONS

9 What is the primary difference between an estuary and a delta?

10 Why are rocky shores able to house more biodiversity than sandy shores?

11 How do the roots of the red mangrove work to create an ecosystem?

115

PRACTICAL ACTIVITY 6.1

Sediment-settling tube

Purpose

Sediment-settling tubes are used to determine how quickly different diameter sediments settle when water stops moving.

Materials

- One clear plastic tennis ball can with lid, or a 45 cm clear plastic watertight tube with PVC caps on both ends
- Four containers, one each containing:
  - diatomaceous earth
  - sand
  - soil
  - pebbles
- Enough water to fill the tube
- Electrical or duct tape
- Timer or stopwatch

Method

- Make sure the tube is capped at one end.
- Pour material from the four containers into the tube.
- Add water to fill the tube up to near the top.
- Place the remaining cap on the open end and secure with tape.
- Shake the tube so that all the material is mixed in the water.
- Set the tube down on a flat surface and allow the material to settle.
- Start timing as soon as the tube is set down.
- Time how long it takes for all of the material to settle to the bottom.

Conclusions

1 How does this tube represent the sedimentation seen on different types of shore?

2 Based on this tube and your knowledge of substrate types, rank the shores (sandy, rocky, muddy) from greatest to least amount of wave action, and explain your ranking.

3 Using what you know about mangroves and this demonstration, explain why mangroves play a vital role on sandy shores.

Mangrove benefits, loss and restoration

Mangroves are found in tropical and subtropical areas around the world. Several species of mangrove trees will live in a typical mangrove swamp, depending on the tolerance of each species to salinity and anoxic soil. Those species that are able to spend the longest time submerged, and with the greatest tolerance for salinity, will grow best nearest the sea. The other species will grow in zones up the shore based on their tolerance of these factors.

Benefits of mangroves

There are many ecological and financial benefits to mangroves growing along a coastline. Mangroves act as a buffer for coastal regions against tropical cyclones and other heavy storms by creating a wave break. The roots of the mangroves closest to the shore, particularly red mangroves, help prevent erosion by holding sediment in place. These root systems prevent the need for **beach renourishment** along exposed coasts, saving millions of dollars.

Ecologically speaking, mangrove forests are a natural way of fighting global climate change. Mangroves absorb carbon dioxide, the primary greenhouse gas released through the burning of fossil fuels, and store it in their extensive root systems. In tropical ecosystems, mangrove forests are the most carbon-dense forests. Mangrove forests in Indonesia contain over 3 billion metric tonnes of carbon within the soil, living trees, roots and dead branches.

 KEY TERM

beach renourishment: the process of dumping sand from another location onto an eroding shoreline to create a new beach or to widen the existing beach.

Deforestation

The world's largest area of mangrove forest, nearly 3 million hectares, is located in Indonesia, a mangrove biodiversity hot spot. Since 1980, Indonesia has lost approximately 40% of its mangrove forest, compared with a global destruction rate of 20%. This gives Indonesia the reluctant honour of the fastest rate of mangrove destruction worldwide. Worse, the deforestation of these areas is responsible for 42% of the global greenhouse emissions released as a result of the destruction of coastal ecosystems (for example marshes, mangroves and seagrasses).

There are several causes of mangrove loss globally: logging, conversion of land to agriculture, and devastation of land as a result of pollution, such as oil spills. The primary cause of mangrove loss in Asia, however, is aquaculture, particularly shrimp farming. Between 1988 and 2008 the world production of shrimp from these farms rose drastically from 500 000 metric tonnes to 2.8 million metric tonnes. Indonesia, China and Vietnam have destroyed huge swathes of mangroves in order to support this industry, despite the fact that doing so has harmed other local industries and fishermen in the region.

Reforestation

Many governments have come to realise that the financial benefits of having intact mangrove forests outweigh the needs of one particular industry (Figure 6.17). Coastline protection, the addition of new land through the natural sedimentation process created by the mangrove root system, and nursery services for young fish, all have financial value to the countries involved. Studies showing how vital intact mangrove systems are to ecosystems and services have convinced governments that reforestation is necessary to protect their populations from rising sea-levels and tropical cyclones. The government of Belize, realising the financial importance of their mangrove forests (over US$150 million year^{-1}), has implemented strict regulations to protect

mangroves from deforestation. At a loss of only 2% over the last 30 years, their regulations are considered to be successful.

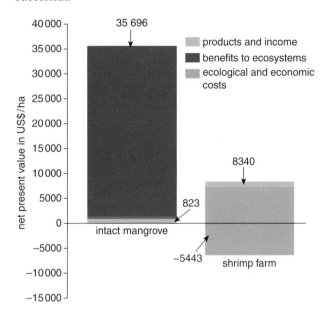

Figure 6.17. Comparing the economic and social value of mangroves and shrimp farms.

The governments of Vietnam and Indonesia have begun to take steps to restore their mangrove forests. In both cases, an emphasis has been placed on repairing local economies using mangrove forest restoration. People are encouraged to replant mangroves in order to improve local fishing and provide construction materials, pulp for paper and ecotourism.

Questions

1   Explain how mangrove forests slow down climate change.

2   Calculate the difference between the total net value (both social and economic) of intact mangroves and shrimp farms.

3   Imagine you are a conservationist working to convince a local government to rebuild the mangrove forest. Write a speech to the government explaining why intact mangrove forests are better for the economy than shrimp farming.

117

Summary

- Scientists once thought the ocean floor was completely flat and void of topography, but we now know otherwise.

- The creation of different habitats and landscapes through plate tectonics is an amazing result of geology.

- Convection currents in the mantle move gigantic tectonic plates, generating three types of boundary (convergent, divergent and transform).

- These boundaries create an array of features on the ocean floor, such as mid-ocean ridges, volcanoes, trenches and hydrothermal vents

- While the deepest seabeds may be one of the last ocean provinces scientists will ever get to visit, their importance to what lies above them cannot be denied.

- Marine ecosystems, like all other ecosystems, rely on what lies beneath them for their survival.

- The differences in the ocean floor, particularly along coastlines, create the many types of ecosystems present in the oceans and on the shores.

Exam-style questions

1 a Define what is meant by the term intertidal zone. **[1]**

 b Compare the physical factors affecting organisms living on a rocky shore to those living on a sandy shore. **[4]**

 c i Define the term vertical zonation. **[1]**

 ii Explain how the physical and biological factors of a rocky shore ecosystem contribute to vertical zonation of the organisms that live there. **[2]**

[Total mark: 8]

2 a List three major lines of evidence supporting the theory of plate tectonics. **[3]**

 b Describe the movement at each of the following plate boundaries and state one feature located there:

 i transform boundary **[2]**

 ii convergent boundary **[2]**

 iii divergent boundary **[2]**

[Total mark: 9]

3 a State where you would expect to locate hydrothermal vents. **[1]**

 b Outline how hydrothermal vents form. **[4]**

 c Hydrothermal vents are considered to be extreme environments. Suggest an explanation for why that may be. **[3]**

[Total mark: 8]

4 a Describe the habitat where you would expect to find mangrove trees. **[3]**

 b List and explain two adaptations mangroves have in order to survive within their habitat. **[2]**

 c Explain how red mangroves benefit coastal ecosystems. **[4]**

[Total mark: 9]

5   *Tevnia* are a species of tube worms typically found at hydrothermal vent ecosystems. These marine invertebrates have free-swimming planktonic larvae and eventually grow into adults that form a symbiotic relationship with chemosynthetic bacteria. Researchers wanted to determine if high pressure attracted the tube worm larvae to settle in that ecosystem. Three containers of seawater were set up. Each container was kept at a different pressure: 0 atm (to represent sea-level), 100 atm (to represent a mid-level depth in the ocean) and 250 atm (to represent the pressure at a hydrothermal vent). Approximately 250 larvae were released into each container. Temperature, pH and salinity were carefully controlled. After 3 days, the numbers of larvae that had settled within each container were counted. The results are shown in Table 6.5.

container	number of tube worm larvae settled
0 atm	15
100 atm	87
250 atm	95

Table 6.5. Number of tube worm larvae settled in each container.

a   Using the data in Table 6.5, describe the effect of pressure on the attachment of *Tevnia* larvae.   **[2]**

b   The attachment of *Tevnia* is also affected by other factors, including pH.

Outline a laboratory-based experiment to determine whether pH plays a role in settlement of *Tevnia*.   **[5]**

[Total mark: 7]

Estuary loss in South Florida

Estuaries in Florida

Estuaries are an important ecosystem in the marine environment of Florida, USA. These areas, where fresh water from rivers joins salt water from the sea, provide habitat for more than 70% of the fish, crustaceans and shellfish that are important commercially and recreationally to Florida. These organisms primarily spend time in the estuaries when they are newly hatched or juveniles, as the adults return to estuaries in order to breed.

Because of the inflow of nutrient-rich fresh water from the rivers, estuaries are highly productive ecosystems. Phytoplankton, algae and seagrasses can all be found in estuaries, where the access to nutrients and sunlight in the shallow water increases the rate of photosynthesis. These producers then provide energy in the form of food to other organisms higher up the food chain. When the producers die, detritivores break down the remains, adding even more nutrients to the environment. All of this energy and nutrition combine to create an excellent nursery area for small fish and invertebrates.

Lake Okeechobee and its drainage problem

Lake Okeechobee, located in South Florida, is the seventh largest fresh-water lake in the United States. Its area is more than 1900 km², but it is a very shallow lake with an average depth of only 2.7 m. It is an integral part of the Everglades ecosystem that provides Florida with its fresh water. However, as water flows from the Kissimmee River into Lake Okeechobee it carries tonnes of fertiliser and pesticide waste from farms upstream.

Historically, when too much water entered Lake Okeechobee, the lake would overflow and send water down into the Everglades with vital nutrients. However, that flow was changed after two devastating hurricanes moved over a newly settled South Florida. In 1926, the Great Miami Hurricane killed 300 people after moving inland. Just 2 years later, in 1928, the Okeechobee hurricane hit Florida. After moving over land, the hurricane passed over Lake Okeechobee, causing a storm surge that drove water over the minimal mud dike. This flooded the neighbouring towns, killing thousands (the exact number is not known because of poor residential records).

After these hurricanes cost so many lives, the US Army Corps of Engineers built a flood control system, including the Herbert Hoover dike, to prevent damage from future storm surges. The dike was expanded a few years later to accommodate larger storms. Since then the dike has prevented most of the outflow from Lake Okeechobee into the Everglades system, holding on to vital nutrients and water.

Lake Okeechobee and Florida's estuaries: what's the connection?

Too little water

Because water that flows into Lake Okeechobee is kept there instead of being allowed to flow out as it naturally should, an incredible amount of pesticides, fertilisers and sediment has built up on the bed of Lake Okeechobee. In 2007, a severe drought affected South Florida and the water levels in Lake Okeechobee dropped to historic lows. Many parts of the lake bed were exposed and accessible to people and wildlife. Water management officials thought removing the mud would help restore the lake's substrate to a sandy bottom and increase water clarity, making the water healthier. Officials tested the mud to see if it could be used in agriculture as a compost, but discovered that it contained high levels of toxins such as arsenic. The mud was therefore considered to be too toxic for agricultural or commercial use, making its disposal a challenge. It was not until Tropical Storm Fay in 2008, when 1.2 m of rain raised the water levels in Lake Okeechobee, that some improvement was seen in the lake quality.

Too much water

Since 2008, the water levels in Lake Okeechobee have continued to rise as a result of storms and the seasonal rain of South Florida. Unfortunately, the lake can only contain so much water before the 70-year-old dike holding back its waters is in danger of being damaged. The US Army Corps of Engineers tries to keep the lake level between 3.8 m and 4.7 m to reduce the strain on the dike; but in years like 2016, when rain levels are abnormally high, maintaining these levels becomes impossible without draining the lake. Additionally, flood water from the sugar plantation fields that surround Lake Okeechobee is directed into the lake, adding more polluted water and sediment to the already toxic mix. Since 2013, the US Army Corps of Engineers has had to pump billions of gallons of polluted water from Lake Okeechobee to prevent damage to the Herbert Hoover dike. If the dike is destroyed and the waters from Lake Okeechobee overflow into the five neighbouring counties, the potential damage and loss of life could rival that seen when the levees in New Orleans broke during Hurricane Katrina in 2005.

When draining Lake Okeechobee, water managers send water from the lake into two major canal systems, one to the east and one to the west. To the east the water drains into the St Lucie River estuary, and to the west the water drains into the Caloosahatchee River estuary. In both cases the normal inflow of fresh water into the estuary is elevated and causes incredible damage to the estuary ecosystems, and the ecosystems they are connected to, such as the Indian River Lagoon.

Damage to the estuaries

As billions of gallons of water are pumped out of Lake Okeechobee and into estuaries on both the east and west coasts of Florida, residents, environmentalists, scientists and policy-makers are all wondering if this is the right thing to do. The evidence of pollution is clear: aerial photos show a mass of brown water entering the clear blue waters of the estuary. However, pollution is not the only risk to the estuaries caused by these releases: the lack of salt in the water can cause just as many issues for the aquatic life of the region.

Estuaries rely on the inflow of fresh water from rivers to combine with the salty seawater from the ocean to reduce salinity. The organisms living in estuaries are adapted to living in this medium salinity, brackish water. Too much fresh water coming into the estuaries reduces the salinity to dangerous levels for many of the plants and animals found in these waters. These reduced salinity levels are the most likely cause of multiple fish-kill events and a massive die-off of seagrasses and oyster beds lining the estuary bottom. Additionally, a number of (potentially toxic) algae blooms cloud the water whenever large releases of water from Lake Okeechobee enter the estuaries (Figure 6.18).

While too little salinity is a problem for those estuaries on the east and west coasts of central Florida, too much salinity has become a problem for Florida Bay in the south. By not allowing fresh water to drain naturally through the Everglades, Florida Bay is unable to maintain its historical salinity levels. In February 2016, Florida's Governor, Rick Scott, asked the US Army Corps of Engineers to raise the water levels in canals flowing southwards to divert water from Lake Okeechobee away from the central estuaries and allow it to flow south. While this will do nothing to fix the pollution problem, it will reduce fresh-water outflow to the east and west by sending it south towards the Everglades and Florida Bay.

Figure 6.18. Algal bloom where water from Lake Okeechobee meets the water of the Caloosahatchee River Estuary.

Possible solutions

Unfortunately, there are no ready solutions in the near future to handle the billions of gallons of water necessary to reduce water levels, and protect the estuaries and the people who are connected to Lake Okeechobee. Some relief should come in 2019 when the US Army Corps of Engineers plans to have completed a reservoir designed to hold some of the necessary water. In the meantime, politicians are asking for relief from the federal government; but that is unlikely to be successful because any positive outcome will not be seen immediately, and decision-makers like to see quick results.

Questions

1   How could this outflow of fresh water affect not only the estuary the river leads to, but also the environment outside the estuary?

2   How do you think these water releases affect Florida's economy? Make sure to discuss both the economy related to the coast and estuaries, and the economy related to agriculture.

3   The release of water from Lake Okeechobee has already been held responsible for the die-off of seagrasses within the affected estuaries. How does this die-off impact upon the available energy within these ecosystems?

4   Beyond repairs to the Herbert Hoover dike, what other repairs or changes need to be made to improve the water quality and quantity flowing from Lake Okeechobee?

Chapter 7
Physical and chemical oceanography

Learning outcomes

By the end of this chapter, you should be able to:

- explain how volcanic activity, run-off and dissolved gases affect the chemical composition of seawater
- describe how evaporation and precipitation affect the salinity of seawater
- explain how temperature and salinity create gradients and layers within the ocean, and how those layers can be mixed
- explain why different concentrations of dissolved oxygen exist within bodies of water
- discuss how tides are formed and influenced by many factors
- explain how ocean currents and upwelling are caused
- explain the causes and effects of El Niño events in the Pacific Ocean
- describe how monsoon winds are formed in the Indian Ocean
- explain the cause and impact of tropical cyclones
- apply what you have learnt to new, unfamiliar contexts.

7.1 Understanding the ocean

When scientists study chemical and physical oceanography, they are really studying the forces that make the entire ocean able to function. On the surface, chemical and physical oceanography appears to be merely the study of the ocean's chemistry and physical properties. While that is an accurate definition, it does not touch on the real purpose for studying these fields: most people study the chemistry of water and forces within the ocean to understand how they make life possible. How can organisms exist in waters with nearly zero dissolved oxygen? How can the flooding rains that are blown in with the monsoons be a benefit to the communities affected? How does the ocean moderate the world's climate? What causes the tides that control the mating behaviour of so many animals? All of these questions and thousands more have been answered by studying how the ocean functions.

This chapter covers a broad range of topics under the very large umbrella of chemical and physical oceanography. From minerals dissolved in the ocean's waters to the destructive winds of tropical cyclones and everything in between, chemical and physical oceanography explain many of the mysteries of marine science. However, the most important aspect of all these individual pieces is how they fit together. When scientists study coral reefs, they cannot just study the individual polyps that make up the reef. They must also look at the nutrients available in the water: are there too many or too little? They must look at the run-off entering the ocean from the coast: is it toxic? If so, how toxic? They need to study sea surface temperatures in order to predict both coral bleaching and tropical cyclones. In all aspects of ocean life, the environment around an organism is of paramount importance to its survival.

7.2 Chemical oceanography and the chemical composition of seawater

Chemical oceanography is the study of ocean chemistry and the behaviour of those chemicals found within the ocean. Surprisingly, 'only' studying the chemicals found within the ocean is not particularly limiting. Nearly every element in the Periodic Table has been located, in some form, within the ocean's vast waters. Understanding the movement of these chemicals requires a fundamental knowledge of ocean circulation, climate and the interactions between the atmosphere, geosphere and hydrosphere on this planet.

KEY TERMS

Salinity: a measure of the quantity of dissolved solids in ocean water, represented by parts per thousand, ppt or ‰

Evaporation: a change in state from liquid to gas below the boiling point of a substance

Salinity

When studying chemical oceanography, traditionally you start by looking at the **salinity** of seawater. Salinity is a measure of the concentration of salts within a body of water. There are two methods commonly used to determine the salinity of a water sample.

- Total dissolved solids (TDS)
  Using this traditional method, a scientist **evaporates** a known volume of water and then weighs the solids left behind. This method is not particularly good for use in the field because of the equipment and time needed.

- Electrical conductivity
  This more modern method is faster and easier to use when out in the field. An electric current is passed between two metal plates, and how well the current moves between the plates is measured. The more dissolved salts (solutes) in the water, the greater the conductivity (ease of flow) between the plates. The information gained from electrical conductivity can be used to estimate the total dissolved solids.

The unit used for salinity is parts per thousand (ppt or ‰). This unit was originally derived using TDS. Scientists would take 1000 g of seawater and evaporate it. The solutes left behind, usually ions called salts, were then weighed, making them the 'parts' that make up 1000 g of water. After hundreds of years of water samples, scientists now know that the average salinity of the open ocean is 35‰.

Composition of seawater

The first true scientific study of the open ocean happened between the years of 1872 and 1876 on HMS *Challenger*. This 70 000 km scientific voyage was the first of its kind.

Led by Charles Wyville Thomson, the Royal Society of London purchased an old warship and retrofitted it with scientific laboratories. These laboratories enabled scientists aboard to collect data in the fields of natural history and chemistry. More than 4000 new species of marine life were discovered on this journey, along with vital chemical oceanography.

When the *Challenger* returned home in 1876, the water samples taken during the voyage were sent to William Dittmar. After analysing the samples, Dittmar discovered the same six ions made up the majority of the solutes in seawater (Table 7.1). Additionally, he found that, regardless of the concentration of salts in the water, the ions were always present in the same percentages. He termed this phenomenon the 'theory of constant proportions'.

From Table 7.1, you can see that the majority of the salts in the ocean are sodium and chloride. This should not be a surprise as seawater tastes like table salt, which is a common name for sodium chloride (NaCl). Other ions, such as sulfate, magnesium, calcium and potassium, play vital roles in the biology of the ocean. Many other ions are also present but in such small concentrations that they are called micronutrients (for example nitrogen, phosphorus and hydrogencarbonate). Dittmar's theory of constant proportions holds true for the open ocean and, generally, for coastal regions.

However, further research has found that ion concentrations can be changed by local events, such as atmospheric **dissolution**, volcanic eruptions and run-off (Figure 7.1). These are the three major sources of ions in the world's ocean, and each is discussed in this chapter.

Effect of atmospheric dissolution on the chemical composition of seawater

Gases in the atmosphere (nitrogen, carbon dioxide and oxygen) are in a state of equilibrium with the gases dissolved in ocean water. As the concentration of a particular gas in the atmosphere increases (carbon dioxide, for instance), the concentration of that gas in seawater also rises. Mixing, as a result of turbulence and wave action, works to maintain this equilibrium. The more turbulence there is, the easier it is for gases in the atmosphere to dissolve into the ocean. This can lead to higher concentrations of carbon dioxide and oxygen within the first 200 m depth of the ocean than are found in the atmosphere. Factors contributing to the concentration of gases in seawater include the following.

- The solubility of the gas
  Solubility refers to the ability for a particular solute, like carbon dioxide, to dissolve in a solvent, like seawater. Carbon dioxide is very soluble in seawater because of its ability to form carbonic acid, a weak acid, when introduced to water. Oxygen, while more soluble than nitrogen, is less soluble than carbon dioxide. Oxygen and nitrogen are less soluble because they do not chemically combine with the water molecules. This means that the level of carbon dioxide held by seawater is higher than that of oxygen and nitrogen.

- The temperature of the seawater
  Cold water is able to hold more gas than water at warmer temperatures. This means that water found near the poles will hold more oxygen than water found in the tropics (Table 7.2).

KEY TERM

Dissolution: the dissolving of a solute into a solvent

KEY TERM

Solubility: the ability of a solute to dissolve into a solvent

ion	mean concentration in seawater / parts per thousand (‰)	Ratio of ion : total salts / percentage (%)
chloride (Cl^-)	19.35	55.04
sodium (Na^+)	10.75	30.61
sulfate (SO_4^{2-})	2.70	7.68
magnesium (Mg^{2+})	1.30	3.69
calcium (Ca^{2+})	0.42	1.16
potassium (K^+)	0.38	1.10

Table 7.1. Concentrations of the six most common ions in seawater.

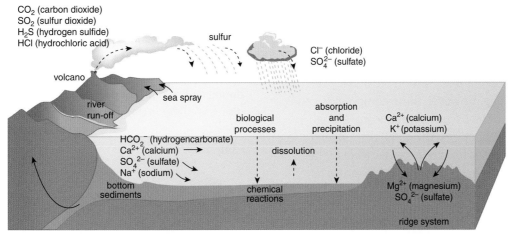

Figure 7.1. How chemicals get into our oceans: atmospheric dissolution, volcanic activity and run-off.

temperature of water / °C	concentration of dissolved oxygen / mg dm^{-3}
0	14.6
5	12.8
10	11.3
15	10.2
20	9.2
25	8.4

Table 7.2. Relationship between temperature and the maximum concentration of dissolved oxygen in fresh water.

- The salinity of the seawater
  Gases are able to dissolve better into water with lower levels of salinity. Therefore you would expect to find higher levels of oxygen in an estuary than in the open ocean or the Dead Sea.

- The presence of organisms in the seawater
  Organisms play a large role in determining how much of each gas is found in the different layers of the ocean. Nitrogen gas that is dissolved can be transformed into ammonia by nitrogen-fixing bacteria. This makes the nitrogen easier to use for other organisms. At the surface, producers take in dissolved carbon dioxide for use in photosynthesis. Consumers and producers both use dissolved oxygen for respiration.

Effect of volcanoes on the chemical composition of seawater

When volcanoes above sea-level erupt, they pour tonnes of hot ash into the atmosphere. Within that ash are many minerals and gases that impact our oceans. In particular,

carbon dioxide (CO_2), sulfur dioxide (SO_2), hydrogen sulfide (H_2S) and hydrogen chloride (HCl) leave the volcano mixed with the particulates of ash. When these gases enter the atmosphere they mix with atmospheric water, especially water already condensed into a cloud. When the cloud becomes **precipitation**, the dissolved gases rain down into the ocean as part of the hydrological cycle. The addition of these ions into the water changes the ion concentration for a brief time.

Volcanoes that are still submerged can also impact upon the ion concentrations of the seawater around them. These volcanoes, located at either convergent or divergent plate boundaries, erupt releasing the same gases into the water. Submerged volcanoes have been releasing hydrogen chloride and chlorine gas into the ocean since the ocean was first formed. In fact, they have released so much chlorine gas they are considered to be the primary source of chloride ions found in today's seawater.

KEY TERMS

Precipitation: water that falls from the atmosphere to the Earth's surface as rain, sleet, snow or hail

Run-off: the flow of water from land caused by precipitation

Effect of run-off on chemical composition of seawater

Run-off is water that flows over the Earth's surface due to precipitation or melting snow or ice. As this water flows over city streets or through farmers' fields, it dissolves many substances and carries them along. These substances could include vital nutrients, pesticides, fertilisers, oils and other pollutants. Eventually, most of this water, as part of the hydrological cycle, finds its way to the oceans, either directly or by first flowing into a river. So, while run-off is not considered a pollutant, it is capable of carrying many types of pollution into the ocean.

Many of the pollutants carried by run-off have a very low concentration in the water and are initially seen as non-threatening. However, these compounds can be absorbed into the tissues of producers through uptake. Once this happens, the pollutant concentration increases as it passes from one trophic level to the next within a food chain. This process is known as **biomagnification**.

KEY TERM

Biomagnification: the increasing concentration of a substance, such as a toxic chemical, in the tissues of organisms at successively higher levels in a food chain

Since the Industrial Revolution, many examples of biomagnification have come to light. In the United States, the use of a pesticide known as DDT was responsible for the near extinction of several predatory bird species, including the bald eagle. Another example comes from Minamata city in Japan.

Fertilisers carried to the ocean can also pose a unique risk to marine ecosystems. Most chemical fertilisers contain a mixture of nitrogen and phosphorus. Both of these nutrients are necessary for the growth and health of plants, including algae and phytoplankton, and are normal in the ocean in low concentrations. Nitrogen and phosphorus are considered to be limiting factors in marine ecosystems because their low concentrations helps control the population of producers. However, chemical fertilisers contain very high concentrations of these elements and, when dissolved in run-off, their presence can disrupt local coastal ecosystems. Excessive fertiliser in run-off is a primary cause for harmful algal blooms (HABs) that can be toxic to both the environment and humans.

Effects of evaporation and precipitation on salinity

While 35‰ is the average salinity of ocean water, the actual salinity at any given location does vary. In areas with fresh-water run-off or melting glaciers, for example, the salinity may be much lower. This lower salinity is caused by the addition of water, rather than the removal of salts. Precipitation (for example rain or snow) also lowers the salinity of a body of water by diluting the salt in the seawater with incoming fresh water. Estuaries are a great example of salinity varying throughout a body of

water. Near the mouth of the river within an estuary, the water is considerably less saline than the water nearest the ocean. The water lying at the top of the water column in an estuary is also fresher than water on the bottom. This means that salinity levels within an estuary change during high and low tides (Figure 7.2). This phenomenon is discussed later in this chapter.

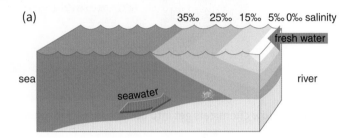

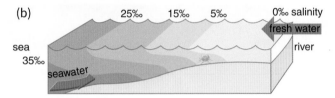

Figure 7.2. Salinity levels in an estuary at (a) high tide and (b) low tide.

Salinity higher than 35‰ is often found in regions with above-average evaporation rates and a limited fresh-water inflow. When the salts are even more concentrated, the water is described as **hypersaline**. One example of a hypersaline environment is the Dead Sea, an inland sea found between Jordan and Israel. The salinity levels are ten times that of the open ocean. Salinity is so high that salt coats the beach as a result of evaporation (Figure 7.3).

KEY TERMS

Hypersaline: when a body of water has a salinity level greater than 35‰

Dissolved oxygen (DO): oxygen that has dissolved into water

Dissolved oxygen and the oxygen minimum layer

The concentration of **dissolved oxygen (DO)** varies throughout the ocean. As mentioned above, both temperature and salinity affect the concentration of dissolved oxygen in the ocean. The higher the water temperature, the lower the oxygen concentration. Also, the higher the salinity, the lower the dissolved oxygen concentration, although this difference is slight.

Figure 7.3. Dead Sea salt crystallises along the shore and looks like snow.

Dead Sea

The Dead Sea is a hypersaline lake located in the Middle East in the Jordan Rift Valley. On its eastern shore lies the country of Jordan, while its western shore borders Israel and the West Bank. At 377 m deep, the Dead Sea is considered to be the deepest hypersaline lake in the world. This depth also helps make the Dead Sea the lowest elevation on land, at 423 m below sea-level.

This 50 km long and 15 km wide body of water is considered to be one of the saltiest places on Earth. The salinity of the water in the Dead Sea ranges from 280 to 350‰. The salinity varies depending on the time of year and where in the water column the measurement was taken. Measurements taken nearest the surface tend to be higher because of the high evaporation rates in the desert-like conditions of the Jordan Rift Valley. As typical ocean water contains salinity levels of only 35‰, the waters of the Dead Sea are, on average, 8.5 times as salty.

For thousands of years, the Dead Sea has been a vacation destination. The salty waters are rumoured to have healing powers because of its mineral content. Swimming here is really just floating on the incredibly dense waters. According to historical rumour, the first health spa was located at the Dead Sea for Herod I (37–34 BCE).

It is ironic that the Dead Sea is considered to be a place of health and healing considering that salinity levels make it impossible for most animals to live there. Only a few species of archaea, bacteria and fungi are capable of making their homes in the Dead Sea on a continuous basis. However, during 1980, a particularly rainy winter reduced the salinity so much that a new type of algae became established and turned the waters red.

Today, the Dead Sea is used to produce a major component of fertilisers: potash. Potash is the common name for potassium chloride and it has been mined from the Dead Sea since 1929. In order to remove potash from the waters of the Dead Sea, shallow evaporation pools have been created in the southernmost portion of the lake (Figure 7.4). This allows sunlight to evaporate water from the brine and leave the salts behind. The waters of the Dead Sea are replenished by the Jordan River. However, in order to make these pools successful, the southern end of the Dead Sea has had several barricades, or dikes, built to prevent water from the Jordan River from flowing in naturally. This allows the corporations mining the potash, such as Dead Sea Works, to control rainwater flow.

Unfortunately, this evaporation process, which has been happening for nearly 100 years, has caused a severe drop in water levels. Between 1970 and 2006, the water levels in the Dead Sea dropped an average 1 m year^{-1}. This reduction

has been followed by a drop in groundwater, leading to sinkholes, when the underground salt structures collapse.

Questions

1   Potassium is a minor component in seawater. When seawater is evaporated, which minerals would you expect to find the most of?

2   Evaporation is a major factor in the salinity of the Dead Sea. What role does it play in the ocean?

3   How does the increased salinity of the Dead Sea due to the fertiliser industry impact upon the microscopic organisms that live there?

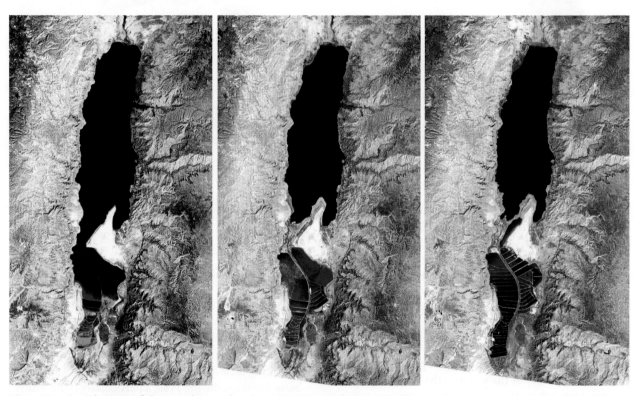

Figure 7.4. Aerial views of the Dead Sea taken in 1972, 1989 and 2011.

The area of the ocean with the greatest concentration of dissolved oxygen is the top 100 m of the ocean, known as the surface layer. Within this layer, the dissolved oxygen concentration can reach 'supersaturation'. This means there is more oxygen dissolved in the seawater than it would normally be able to carry. Two major factors work together to increase the amount of dissolved oxygen to supersaturation level: the motion of the water and photosynthesis by producers. The more turbulent the water, the more oxygen is mixed into it by the movement of the waves. Meanwhile, producers, like phytoplankton and algae, use photosynthesis to create glucose and generate oxygen as a byproduct. This oxygen adds to the amount of dissolved oxygen in the surface layer. Dissolved oxygen is removed from this layer by the respiration of organisms.

Below the surface layer of the ocean, the concentration of dissolved oxygen changes dramatically. As the depth of the ocean increases, the level of dissolved oxygen decreases until it reaches the **oxygen minimum layer**. The oxygen minimum layer typically occurs at a depth of around 500 m, but has been found anywhere between 100 and 1000 m deep depending on location. Some organisms are capable of living within the oxygen minimum zone, despite the lack of dissolved oxygen, but they do need special adaptations for survival. Most of the organisms found here are fairly inactive, which reduces their need for oxygen. The gills of the fish in this area are incredibly efficient at extracting oxygen from water, even at the low levels present in this layer. Additionally, many of the organisms here have a very oxygen-efficient form of hemoglobin, a blood protein responsible for carrying oxygen throughout the body.

After reaching the oxygen minimum layer, the oxygen concentration begins to increase deeper into the ocean. Three reasons exist for this subtle increase in oxygen (Figure 7.5).

- First, the organisms found below the oxygen minimum layer are in an area with very few food resources. This lack of food reduces the need for the organisms to respire, so they survive with less oxygen.

- Second, the solubility of oxygen increases as the temperature decreases. As you go deeper into the ocean, the temperature decreases to near-freezing.

The lower temperature means oxygen is more likely to stay dissolved in the water.

- Third, as pressure increases, the solubility of oxygen increases. For every 10 m you sink into the ocean, the pressure increases by one atmosphere. This pressure keeps the water and oxygen molecules packed closely together, allowing for greater solubility of the oxygen.

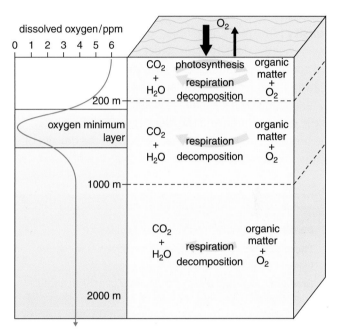

Figure 7.5. Oxygen minimum layer in the eastern tropical Pacific Ocean and the biological processes responsible.

KEY TERM

Oxygen minimum layer: the layer within the ocean where the concentration of dissolved oxygen is at its lowest, typically found between 100 and 1000 m deep

SELF-ASSESSMENT QUESTIONS

1   What are the three most important gases in seawater, biologically speaking? How do they impact upon life in the ocean?

2   How do volcanoes and run-off change the composition of the world's ocean?

Layers in the ocean

From the surface, the ocean appears to be a uniform mass of water. Through the many scientific studies that have taken place since the *Challenger* expedition, scientists now know that the water in the ocean is anything but uniform. Temperature, salinity and density change with depth, creating layers within the sea.

Density

Density is the mass of an object divided by its volume. The higher the density of an object, the lower it will sit in a container of water. So, when discussing density in seawater, the denser the water is, the lower it will sit in the water column. The least dense water will rise to the surface of the water column and the densest water will sink to the bottom. Two main variables determine the density of water: temperature and salinity.

> **KEY TERMS**
>
> **Density:** the mass per unit volume of a substance
>
> **Thermocline:** a boundary between two layers of water with different temperatures
>
> **Gradient:** the rate of increase or decrease of a characteristic relative to another
>
> **Halocline:** a layer of water below the mixed surface layer where a rapid change in salinity can be measured as depth increases

Temperature

Temperature is the factor most responsible for changes in density. As temperature increases, density decreases. This is why, when looking at a profile of the water column in the ocean, the warmest water sits on top of the water column. This warm layer is fairly shallow and it sits on top of colder, denser water. Between the two layers is an area where the temperature abruptly changes, known as the **thermocline** (Figure 7.6). Water at the surface may reach 25 °C or higher in tropical seas, but is more likely to be 1 °C at depths of 2000 m or more. In polar seas, the temperature **gradient** is less drastic. In these areas, the surface water is likely to be about 10 °C and cools with depth to about 1 °C, with only a very faint thermocline, if one is present at all.

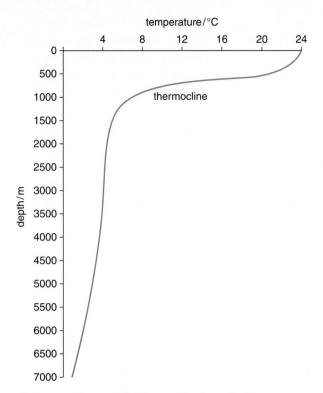

Figure 7.6. Thermocline in a typical tropical sea.

Salinity

Salinity has less of an impact on density than temperature, but the interaction between salinity and temperature makes it worth mentioning. As salinity in the ocean increases, so does the density of the water. Therefore, water with the lowest density floats on top of water with higher densities. This is why in an estuary, fresh water sits above the salt water. Between the less saline, and therefore less dense, surface waters and the more saline, more dense, bottom waters, there is an area where salinity changes significantly with depth. This area is called the **halocline**.

This would indicate that the saltiest water in the ocean is at the seabed. For the most part this is true, but there is one exception: tropical seas. In tropical seas between 30° N and 30° S, the temperatures create high evaporation rates at the surface. This results in a very warm, but also very salty, layer across the surface of the ocean. This layer floats on the surface, in spite of its increased salinity, because the temperature is so high. Just below that layer, the salinity profile shows a steep decrease in salinity, the halocline, until 750 m, followed by a slow increase, as expected (Figure 7.7).

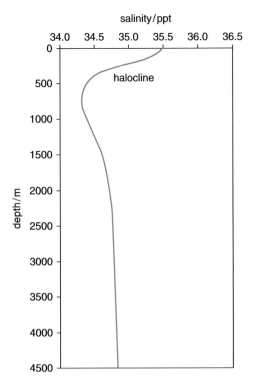

Figure 7.7. Typical halocline in a tropical sea.

Mixing of the layers

The surface layer of the ocean, from zero to 200 m deep, is the best-mixed area of the ocean. As the wind blows across the surface of the ocean, currents and turbulence are created. This water movement mixes the first 200 m of the ocean, making it fairly uniform in both temperature and salinity.

Mixing of the layers within the ocean can also be density driven. For example, if the surface of the ocean cools, the density of the water will increase. As the density increases, the water sinks, carrying with it all the nutrients and dissolved gases that it contained at the surface, mixing with the higher density water that is rising.

SELF-ASSESSMENT QUESTIONS

3   What impact do temperature and salinity have on density?

4   Sketch what you would expect the thermocline to look like in an Arctic environment.

131

PRACTICAL ACTIVITY 7.1

Creating a halocline
This practical demonstrates how a halocline forms in marine ecosystems. It can be modified to create a thermocline using hot and cold water.

Materials
- Small aquarium or clear, rectangular container capable of holding 2 litres of liquid
- Scale
- Two 1 dm³ beakers
- 35 g salt, any type
- Blue food colouring
- Red food colouring

Method
- Prepare salt water (35 ppt).
  - Weigh 35 g of salt using the scale.
  - Place the salt into one of the 1 dm³ beakers.
  - Place this beaker onto the scale.
- Add water until the scale reads 1000 g (approximately 4 cups of water).
- Add a few drops of blue food colouring and mix until consistent.
- Prepare fresh water.
  - Place 1 dm³ of water into the second beaker.
  - Add a few drops of red food colouring and mix until consistent.
- Place fresh water into the aquarium and let it settle till calm.
- Slowly add salt water along the side of the aquarium.

Conclusions
1   As you are adding the salt water to the aquarium, what do you notice?
2   Why do you think this is happening?
3   Predict what would happen if a volume of hot, salty water was added to the tank.
4   Is there a halocline in your aquarium? Sketch a diagram of your aquarium to indicate where it is.

7.3 Physical oceanography

When studying physical oceanography, a scientist must take into account many physical factors that are in fact completely outside the ocean. Physical oceanography involves the gravitational pull of the Moon and Sun, the atmosphere, and the uneven heating of Earth's largely water-based surface. All these pieces of the global environment play a part in the formation of and changes within the marine environment.

Tides

A **tide** is the regular rise and fall of bodies of water as dictated by the gravitational interactions of the Moon, Earth and Sun. Tides can be found in all coastal areas as well as large lakes. Most coastal areas have tides with an interval of 12.5 h, creating two high tides and two low tides each day. Tidal patterns like this are called **semi-diurnal** and the tides are easy to predict. Areas with only one high tide and one low tide each day have a **diurnal** tidal pattern.

> **KEY TERMS**
>
> **Tide:** the periodic rise and fall of the surface of the ocean resulting from the gravitational pull of the Moon and Sun
>
> **Semi-diurnal:** occurring twice daily
>
> **Diurnal:** occurring daily

Tidal range

Tidal range, or tidal amplitude, is the difference in height between the low-water mark and the high-water mark on a coastline (Figure 7.8). Tidal range varies all over the world and from day to day. This variance is due to the gravitational effects of the Moon, Earth and Sun as well as physical features of the coastline where the tide is occurring.

Spring and neap tides

Spring tides create the greatest tidal range for coasts. These tides are not reliant on seasons, but rather on phases of the Moon. Spring tides occur during the phases of new moon (when the Moon is dark) and full moon. So a spring tide can be predicted to happen twice a month.

During spring tides, the Earth, Moon and Sun are in a straight line, with either the Earth between the Sun and Moon or the Sun and Moon on one side of Earth (Figure 7.9). This alignment amplifies the gravitational effects the Moon and Sun have on Earth, creating what is often called a larger than usual ocean bulge. This results in the highest of the high tides and the lowest of the low tides.

Neap tides have the smallest tidal range, with the highest low-tide marks and the lowest high-tide marks. During these tides, the Sun and Moon are at a right angle to each other, with the Earth as the pivot point (Figure 7.9). Neap tides occur during the first- and third-quarter moon phases. During this time the Sun and Moon are pulling the ocean in opposite directions, creating a smaller than average ocean bulge.

> **KEY TERMS**
>
> **Tidal range:** the difference in height between the high-tide mark and the low-tide mark over the course of a day, also called the tidal amplitude
>
> **Spring tide:** a tide that occurs when the Sun and Moon are aligned, causing the largest tidal range
>
> **Neap tide:** a tide that occurs when the Moon and Sun are at right angles from each other, causing the smallest tidal range

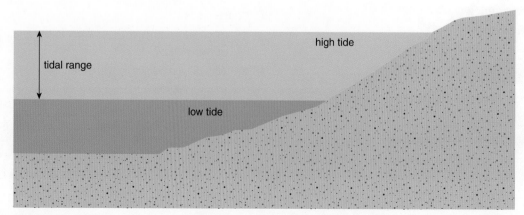

Figure 7.8. How to determine tidal range.

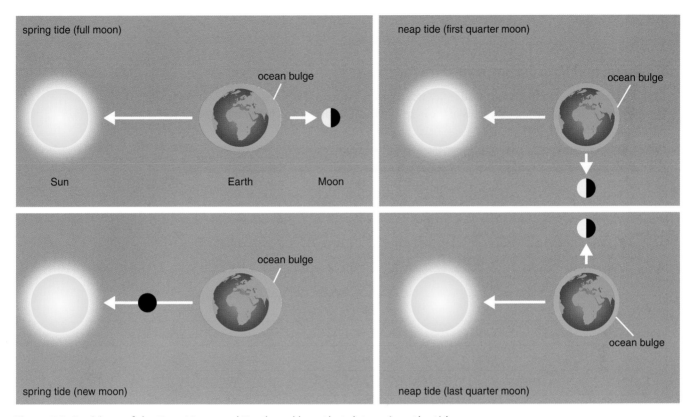

Figure 7.9. Positions of the Sun, Moon and Earth and how that determines the tide.

Physical factors affecting tidal range

Depending on the type of tide, as well as certain physical factors, the tidal range in different parts of the world can vary from 12 m to nearly nothing. The factor with the greatest influence on the tidal range is the coastline itself. The slope of the coast and the size of the body of water it contains, combined with local weather conditions, all influence the tidal range.

The shape of the coastline plays a large role in the size of the tidal range. If the tide is entering a particularly narrow channel (for example a river mouth or entrance to an estuary), the tidal height is increased because the water is being forced into a smaller area. If, however, the tide is happening along an open beach, the tidal height is much smaller because the same volume of water is more spread out.

An extreme example of the coastline changing the tidal amplitude is the Bay of Fundy in Canada, home to the highest tidal range in the world. The average spring tide range here is 14.5 m. The highest water level recorded in the Bay of Fundy, 21.6 m, occurred during the tropical cyclone Saxby Gale in 1869, providing evidence of another physical factor affecting tides: the weather.

Weather is a major factor in tide heights. In particular, changes in wind and air pressure can have incredible effects on tidal range. During a tropical cyclone, air pressure is much lower than usual, allowing water to swell. There are also high winds capable of pushing water onto the shore. Combined, these two factors are capable of creating a **tidal surge**, which is a dangerous rising of water higher than the predicted levels of the tide.

KEY TERM

Tidal surge: the coastal flood or tsunami-like phenomenon of rising water, associated with low pressure weather systems, also called a storm surge

Open ocean, seas and lakes

In the open ocean, tidal ranges are small, approximately 0.6 m. For the most part, the difference between high and low tide is unnoticeable, unless you enter the continental margin, where the water begins to get shallow. Small bodies of water, like the Mediterranean or Red Sea, also have tidal ranges, but they are minimal. Small tidal ranges even occur in large lakes, such as Lake Superior in the northern United States, but the effect is usually masked by the winds blowing across the lake.

Maths skills

Graphing and interpreting tidal data

Graphing data sets is an important skill in science. Equally important is being able to determine what the data mean. The following data set is of the height of the tides above and below mean sea-level for Barcelona, Spain (Table 7.3).

date	high-tide level / m	low-tide level / m	tidal range / m
1 June	0.55	0.50	0.05
2 June	0.59	0.46	
3 June	0.66	0.31	
4 June	0.76	0.13	
5 June	0.90	−0.06	
6 Jun	0.98	−0.23	
7 June	1.05	−0.37	
8 June	1.13	−0.46	
9 June	1.18	−0.50	
10 June	1.19	−0.48	
11 June	1.15	−0.42	
12 June	1.05	−0.31	
13 June	0.90	−0.17	
14 June	0.72	−0.02	
15 June	0.53	0.12	
16 June	0.34	0.25	

Table 7.3. Height of tides above and below mean sea-level in Barcelona, Spain.

Worked example

Tidal range is determined by subtracting the low-tide value from the high-tide value.

$$\text{high tide} - \text{low tide} = \text{tidal range}$$

As an example, 1 June has been completed for you: 0.55 − 0.50 = 0.05

Questions

1   Before setting up a graph, calculate the tidal range for each date and complete Table 7.3.

2   a   Using standard graphing paper, create a graph representing the change in tidal range over time. Make sure your independent variable (date) is on the x-axis and your dependent variable (tidal range) is on the y-axis.

    b   Using your knowledge of tides, circle the date(s) of the spring tide(s) on your graph and explain why you chose that date(s).

    c   Using your knowledge of tides, draw a square around the date(s) of the neap tide(s) on your graph and explain why you chose that date(s).

KEY TERMS

Current: a continuous physical movement of water caused by wind or density

Coriolis Effect: a force that results from the Earth's rotation that causes objects or particles in motion to deflect to the right in the Northern Hemisphere and to the left in the Southern Hemisphere

Currents

Within any large body of water, you will find **currents**. In the ocean, currents are the continuous movement of seawater in a particular direction. Currents carry with them nutrients, dissolved gases and heat. Organisms can use currents to travel from place to place. Currents are created by different physical forces acting on the water, such as wind, the **Coriolis Effect**, temperature, salinity and tides. There are two major types of currents in our oceans: surface currents and deep-water currents.

Surface currents

Surface currents are typically driven by the wind. These currents are steady and dependable as a result of global wind patterns caused by an uneven heating of the Earth's surface by the Sun. Areas with large amounts of solar radiation (for example the equator) have excess heat in the air, causing it to rise in the atmosphere. As that air rises, it

begins to lose some of its heat energy until it begins to sink in areas with less radiation and cooler temperatures. This movement of air in convection currents forms predictable winds, leading to constant surface sea currents at different latitudes (Figure 7.10).

In the Northern Hemisphere, these currents tend to have a clockwise spiral, while in the Southern Hemisphere they have a counter-clockwise spiral. These spiral patterns are caused by the Coriolis Effect. The Coriolis Effect is a result of the Earth's rotation. As an object moves across the rotating Earth, the object swerves slightly to the left or right rather than travelling in a straight line. So, as wind blows the seawater across the ocean surface the rotation of the Earth actually deflects the water at a 45° angle. That is why wind and currents have spiral patterns away from the equator in both hemispheres (Figure 7.11).

Deep currents

Deep-water currents (thermohaline circulation) are driven by differences in density caused by salinity and temperature. These currents happen along the ocean floor and cannot be detected by satellite imagery the way surface currents can. The movement of these currents over the planet is called the 'global conveyor belt' (Figure 7.12). These slow-moving currents carry a huge volume of water: more than 100 times the flow of the

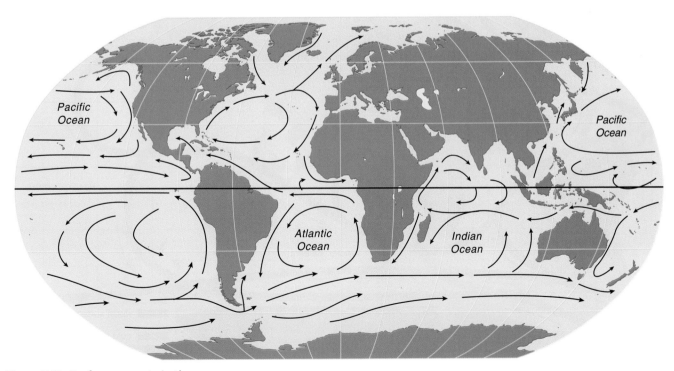

Figure 7.10. Surface currents in the ocean.

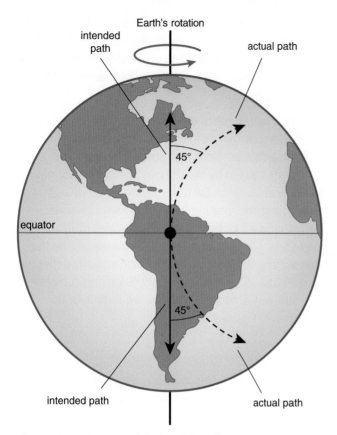

Figure 7.11. Diagram of the Coriolis Effect on objects moving over the Earth's surface.

Amazon River. The global conveyor belt starts at the North Pole when the cold water freezes into sea ice, leaving behind the salts, which do not freeze. This now denser water downwells, causing a mixing of the water column, until it reaches the bottom of the ocean. The water then begins moving south through the Atlantic Ocean towards Antarctica. In Antarctica, it picks up more cold water and then splits. One part of the belt goes towards the Indian Ocean and the other towards the Pacific Ocean. In the Indian Ocean, this cold water moves northwards towards the equator, bringing nutrients to the eastern African coasts. The water warms as it moves towards the equator, so it begins to rise to the surface. When the water cannot rise any longer, it loops back through the south Indian Ocean as a warm surface current.

The cold water in the Pacific Ocean moves through the equator toward the northern Pacific. As this water warms it also rises, becoming a warm surface current along the western coast of North America. This warm current then wraps around the northern coast of Australia and reconnects with the Indian Ocean portion of the global conveyor belt. Together, these warm currents flow through the Atlantic Ocean back towards the North Pole, where the entire process will begin again.

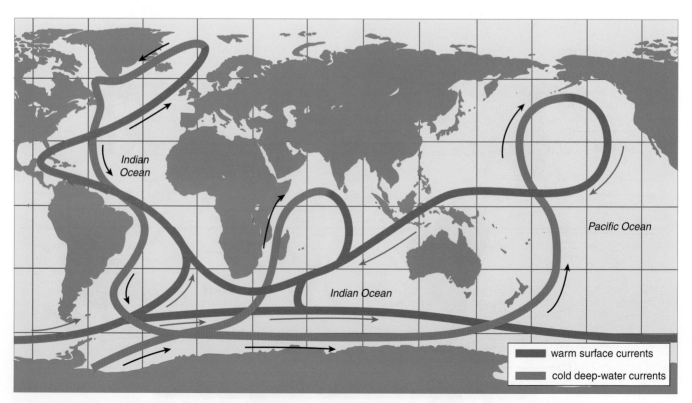

Figure 7.12. Thermohaline circulation (the global conveyor belt) showing the distribution of heat worldwide.

KEY TERM

Upwelling: the movement of cold, nutrient-rich water from deep in the ocean to the surface

Upwelling

Upwelling is the movement of cold, nutrient-rich water from the seabed vertically to the ocean's surface. Upwelling can be caused by winds forcing the warmer surface water away from the coastline and creating a low pressure zone that brings colder water to the surface (Figure 7.13). Upwelling can also be caused by the topography of the seabed. A mid-ocean ridge, or sea mount, can deflect a cold water current upwards causing upwelling. This movement of nutrient-rich water upwards acts as fertiliser for surface waters, increasing the productivity of producers in the area.

An excess of producers and biomass then increases the biomass of consumers, making areas with upwelling very healthy ecosystems with a lot of biological productivity.

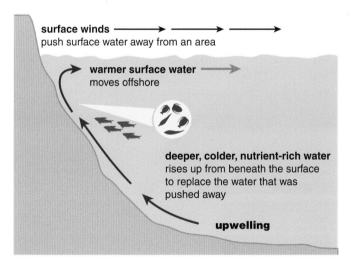

Figure 7.13. The process of upwelling as a result of surface winds.

SELF-ASSESSMENT QUESTIONS

5   If you owned a seaside home and a bad storm brought heavy winds and high surf to your coastline, would you prefer it to be during a new moon or a quarter moon? Why?

6   Compare and contrast a current and a tide.

El Niño Southern Oscillation

Normal conditions

Under normal conditions (Figure 7.14), currents flowing north along the west coast of South America bring cold, nutrient-rich water towards the equator. This flow of water is part of the global conveyor belt. As strong south-westerly winds blow water away from the coast of South America, the cold, nutrient-rich water moves toward the surface, causing upwelling and high levels of productivity off equatorial South America. This leads to large numbers of small fish (for example anchovies and sardines), which support a substantial fishery industry, along with many species of sea birds and large marine consumers.

However, on the other side of the Pacific, these westerly winds push large amounts of warm water towards Australia and Asia. The water levels in the western Pacific Ocean are about 0.5 m higher than those found in the eastern Pacific Ocean. The warm water that has been pushed west evaporates, creating massive storm clouds and bringing large amounts of much-needed rain to Australia and Asia, while keeping the eastern Pacific fairly dry.

KEY TERM

El Niño: a warm current that develops off the coast of Ecuador around December, which can cause widespread death within local food chains

El Niño conditions

Every 3–5 years (sometimes as long as 7 years), the weather pattern in the Pacific Ocean changes. The change is referred to as **El Niño** or the El Niño Southern Oscillation (ENSO). The prevailing trade winds that normally blow from east to west along the equator stop blowing in their normal pattern. Instead these winds reduce, preventing warm water and moist air from moving to the west (Figure 7.15). The warm water builds up along the coast of South America, stopping the upwelling that usually occurs when the Humboldt Current brings cold water to the surface. Indonesia and Australia experience drought conditions, because of a reduction in rainfall, while Peru and the eastern Pacific experience increased rainfall.

Without the upwelling off the South American coast, there is no fresh supply of nutrients or colder water to reduce surface temperatures. As a result, many cold-water species die and primary productivity goes into a steep decline due to lack of nutrients. The lack of producers impacts upon every other level of the local food webs.

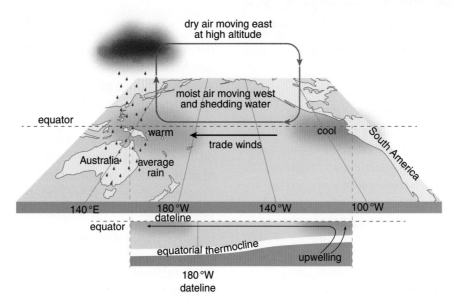

Figure 7.14. Normal weather conditions in the equatorial Pacific Ocean.

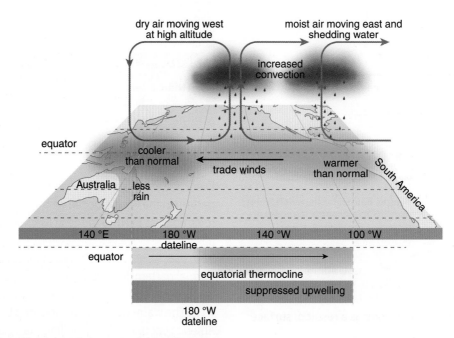

Figure 7.15. El Niño conditions in the equatorial Pacific Ocean.

This causes both the ecosystems and the fishing industries to fail during these times.

El Niño is a naturally occurring phenomenon, but its exact cause is not known. A problem with determining the cause is that not all El Niño years begin or progress in the same way. There has been some speculation that climate change is an exacerbating factor in the increasing occurrence of El Niño conditions, but it is unlikely that this is the only factor involved.

Major El Niño events

Scientists use the Oceanic Niño Index (ONI) to identify El Niño events. The ONI tracks average sea-surface temperature in the equatorial Pacific region in 3-month increments. If there are five consecutive overlapping 3-month periods with sea-surface temperatures at or more than +0.5 °C above average temperatures, they consider it to be an El Niño event. There have been a few 'very strong' El Niño events in the past few decades according to the ONI.

- 1982–83: sea-surface temperatures rose to 2.1 °C above average and caused massive flooding along the eastern Pacific basin.

- 1997–98: the strongest El Niño event recorded so far, sea-surface temperatures rose 2.3 °C above the average temperature.

- 2015–16: scientists believe this event may equal or surpass the 1997–98 event, sea-surface temperatures had risen 2.3 °C above the average sea-surface temperature by May 2016.

Monsoons

Asia is widely considered to be the largest continent. Because of its size, Asia is home to a multitude of biomes and climate conditions. From the warm, wet rainforest in south-east Asia to the cold, dry deserts in northern Asia, nearly every climate can be found in this large region. One feature of the climate in southern Asia is the **monsoon**. Monsoons are seasonal winds that come from the Indian Ocean.

> **KEY TERM**
>
> **Monsoon:** seasonal winds in India that blow from the south-west during the summer and the north-east during the winter

Monsoons are created by the uneven heat capacity of land and sea. During the summer months (May–August), the land absorbs solar radiation much faster than the Indian Ocean, creating a large temperature difference (Figure 7.16). The air over the landmass is then heated as the warmth from the land is re-radiated to the atmosphere. This air rises as its density decreases and draws in the denser, warm, humid air that was lying over the Indian Ocean. The wind created by this vacuum blows from the south-west and brings thunderstorms and torrential rain. Summer monsoons account for 80% of the yearly rainfall in India, causing flooding while also supporting their primary agricultural crops like rice and cotton.

In September, the temperature difference between the land and ocean begins to even out, reducing the winds. By October, and through the winter months, the oceans hold more heat than the landmass. This means the saturated air over the ocean begins to rise and become less dense. In order to fill the vacuum left by this rising air, cool, dry air from the landmass begins to blow toward the ocean from the north-east. The wind blowing from the north-east is called the 'post-monsoon'. All the moisture evaporated from the ocean remains over the ocean, where rainstorms

(a)

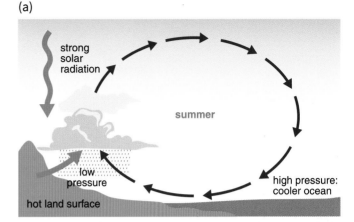

(b)

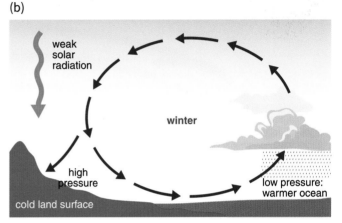

Figure 7.16. Monsoon winds during summer and winter.

release the water back into the ocean. Meanwhile the Asian landmass is left with drought conditions until the summer monsoons return.

Tropical cyclones

In the Indian and south Pacific oceans, large storm systems with wide, low-pressure centres, strong winds (over 120 km h^{-1}) and heavy rains are called **tropical cyclones**. Elsewhere, storms with the same physical structure and method of formation have different names. In the North Atlantic and north-east Pacific, these storms are called **hurricanes**. In the north-west Pacific, they are called **typhoons**. In this book, these storms are all called tropical cyclones.

> **KEY TERMS**
>
> **Tropical cyclone:** a localised, intense low-pressure wind system that forms over tropical oceans with strong winds
>
> **Hurricane:** a tropical cyclone with wind speeds of more than 120 km h^{-1}, generally applied to those occurring in the Atlantic Ocean and northern Pacific Ocean
>
> **Typhoon:** a tropical cyclone in the Indian Ocean or western Pacific Ocean

139

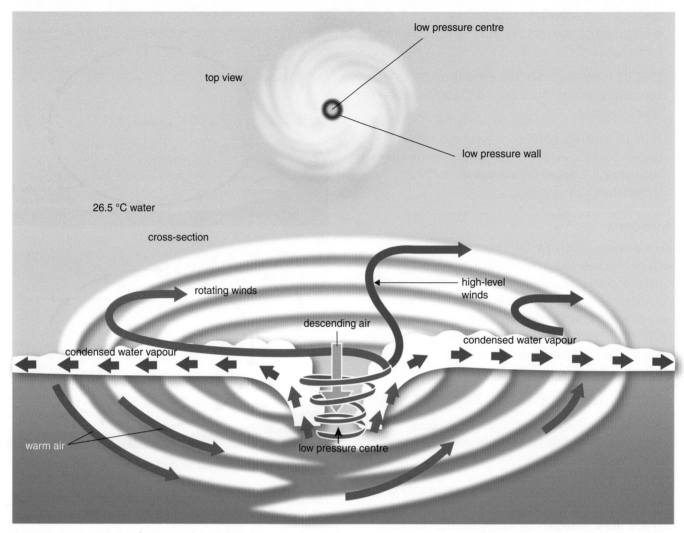

low pressure centre

top view

low pressure wall

26.5 °C water

cross-section

rotating winds

high-level winds

descending air

condensed water vapour

condensed water vapour

warm air

low pressure centre

Figure 7.17. Formation of a tropical cyclone.

Formation

Everywhere in the world, these storms always form under the same conditions. For a tropical cyclone to form, there must be a large body of warm water (temperatures higher than 26.5 °C). As the air over this warm water heats up, it begins to rise because of its decreasing density, even as it is filled with water vapour through evaporation. This rising air creates a low-pressure area, often called 'the eye', over the water, drawing in cooler air. The cooler air begins to create winds as it too warms and rises, drawing evaporated water vapour with it. Once risen, the water vapour in the warm air **condenses** and releases large amounts of stored energy in the form of heat (**latent heat**). This heat energy works to warm even greater amounts of air, causing even more evaporation and drawing in larger winds and fuelling the development of a tropical cyclone (Figure 7.17).

KEY TERMS

Condensation (condense): when water changes from vapour to liquid, the energy needed to maintain the vapour state is released into the atmosphere

Latent heat: the quantity of heat gained or lost per unit of mass as a substance undergoes a change of state (for example vapour to liquid)

This system of warming and rising begins to spin because of the rotation of the Earth and the Coriolis Effect. As the air rises, it does so at a 45° angle from the winds coming into the low-pressure zone. In the Northern Hemisphere, cyclones rotate counter-clockwise; in the Southern Hemisphere, they rotate in a clockwise direction.

This spinning system of high winds and latent heat is not stationary. As the prevailing winds blow the warm water currents that feed these storms, they also push the storms in the same direction. In the northern Atlantic, for example, hurricanes are pushed by the north-east trade winds from the western coast of Africa across the Atlantic towards the Gulf of Mexico. Scientists use computer-based models to predict the path or 'track' of the storm.

Impacts on coastal communities

The high winds and torrential rains of tropical cyclones can be incredibly dangerous and destructive to the communities – both human and ecological – within their path. The wind during a tropical cyclone often blows steadily over 90 km h^{-1} and can gust up to 280 km h^{-1}. Such high winds destroy coastal properties and cause incredible damage to the built environment. Huge waves erode shorelines and damage moored boats.

Storm surges (drastic, unpredictable increases in sea-level) and heavy rainfall often accompany tropical cyclones. Between the storm surges and increased precipitation, flooding is inevitable in low-lying coastal areas. These floods are capable of causing many drownings within the storm area.

Ecologically speaking, these storms have both positive and negative impacts. The storms and accompanying storm surges lead to erosion, loss of shoreline and loss of coral reefs (see Chapter 5). However, the heavy rainfall may happen in places with a dry, arid climate. The influx of rain helps the people and organisms in the area survive. Additionally, storm surges carry many nutrients to coastal communities. This means that the reservoir of nutrients stored in the coastal waters is refilled. Producers in the affected area are no longer limited by a scarcity of nutrients and overall productivity is increased.

> **SELF-ASSESSMENT QUESTIONS**
>
> 7 Describe how wind patterns are related to the El Niño Southern Oscillation.
>
> 8 How could El Niño lead to increased numbers of tropical cyclones?

141

Summary

- Chemical and physical oceanography share a connection that allows life to survive on this planet.

- Upwelling is caused by physical factors (for example temperature differences) that can change the chemical make-up of coastal ecosystems by bringing in fresh nutrients.

- These nutrients increase productivity in the area and support incredibly biodiverse food webs and major fishing industries.

- The average salinity of the ocean is 35‰.

- The salinity and gaseous dissolution of seawater vary depending on environmental and physical conditions such as temperature, density and pressure.

- Chemicals and gases enter the ocean through dissolution, run-off and volcanic eruptions.

- Layers form in the ocean based on temperature and salinity differences, creating varying degrees of density. The denser a layer is, the lower in the water column it will be.

- As temperature increases, dissolved oxygen decreases, except where there are a large number of producers photosynthesising.

- Spring tides have the greatest tidal range and happen when the Moon, Sun and Earth are in a straight line.

- Neap tides have the smallest tidal range and happen when the Moon and Sun are at right angles to each other.

- The uneven heating of the Earth creates winds that blow the water of the ocean, creating currents.

- The Earth rotates, forcing the winds and currents to move at a 45° angle (the Coriolis Effect), creating a circular pattern.

- El Niño happens when there is less cool water and therefore warmer conditions in the eastern Pacific, so upwelling off the western South American coast is suppressed. Cooler than normal conditions prevail in the western Pacific.

- Monsoons are seasonal winds that bring flooding in the summer and drought in the winter.

- Tropical cyclones form over warm water in areas with a low-pressure centre and bring strong winds and heavy rains.

- Tropical cyclones are also known as hurricanes and typhoons.

Exam-style questions

1 a Outline the principles behind the Coriolis Effect. **[4]**

b Explain the impact of the Coriolis Effect on tropical cyclones. **[3]**

c Table 7.4 shows the air pressure at different distances from the centre of a tropical cyclone.

distance from centre of cyclone / km	air pressure / millibars
100	980
80	976
60	970
40	964
20	956
0	916
20	956
40	964
60	970
80	976
100	980

Table 7.4. Air pressure at different distances from the centre of a tropical cyclone.

i Plot these data on a graph. **[4]**

ii Explain why the lowest pressure is at the centre of the cyclone. **[2]**

[Total mark: 13]

2 a Figure 7.18 compares normal and El Niño conditions in the Pacific.

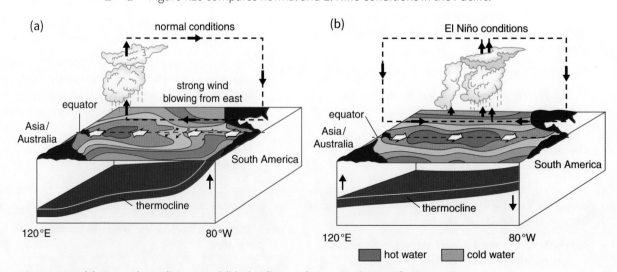

Figure 7.18. (a) Normal conditions and (b) El Niño conditions in the Pacific Ocean.

> **i** With reference Figure 7.18, compare El Niño conditions with normal conditions in the equatorial Pacific. **[2]**
>
> **ii** Using Figure 7.18, explain why there is a smaller fish harvest in El Niño years. **[6]**
>
> **b** Outline how the weather conditions in an El Niño year can influence the formation of tropical cyclones in the Pacific Ocean. **[3]**
>
> **[Total mark: 11]**

3 **a** Compare summer monsoons in India with those in winter. **[8]**

    b Discuss the impacts of monsoons on the people of India. **[2]**

[Total mark: 10]

4 **a** Figure 7.19 displays the depth distribution of dissolved oxygen and carbon dioxide in the ocean.

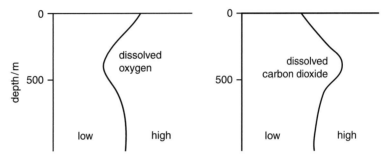

Figure 7.19. Depth distribution of dissolved oxygen and dissolved carbon dioxide in the ocean.

> **i** With reference to Figure 7.19, describe how the oxygen minimum layer forms. **[5]**
>
> **ii** Describe what is happening in the carbon dioxide graph of Figure 7.19. **[2]**
>
> **iii** Suggest a reason for these data. **[2]**
>
> **[Total mark: 9]**

Biomagnification in Minamata Bay

Minamata, Japan, is a small town on the western coast of Kyushu, the southernmost island in Japan's archipelago. Historically, this town was a fishing and farming village where the people were typically rural and poor. The majority of the people living there consumed the fish and shellfish caught in Minamata Bay, the estuary the town was built on.

Environmental damage

In 1932, the Chisso Corporation, a local employer of more than 20 years, moved a new industry into Minamata. Because of increasing demand, a factory for acetaldehyde was built on the shores of Minamata Bay by the Chisso Corporation. Acetaldehyde is an essential ingredient in plastic production, a relatively new technology at the time. A necessary component in the process used to make acetaldehyde is the heavy metal mercury. Unfortunately, the mercury used in this process also became part of the untreated waste water that was released into Minamata Bay.

While we now know that releasing untreated waste water into a water source is not a good idea, this was a common practice at the time. People did not have the scientific knowledge we now do to understand the environmental impacts these chemicals could have. For instance, people did not know that, when mercury was released into Minamata Bay, it was forming the compound methylmercury chloride, or simply methylmercury. They also did not know that this new compound was slowly being absorbed by the phytoplankton in the bay and working its way into the food web (see Chapter 2).

Mercury is a dangerous substance to have in a food web. Methylmercury chloride is even more dangerous because it is a compound capable of biomagnification. This means that, when eaten, methylmercury is not excreted or digested as most chemicals and foods typically are. Instead, the compound is stored in the different tissues of the organism that ingested it. These tissues, full of toxins, are then passed on to the next organism in the food chain as biomass. So, the further you go up the food chain, the more concentrated methylmercury becomes in the tissues of the organisms of Minamata Bay (Figure 7.20). These organisms include the humans reliant on the bay for sustenance.

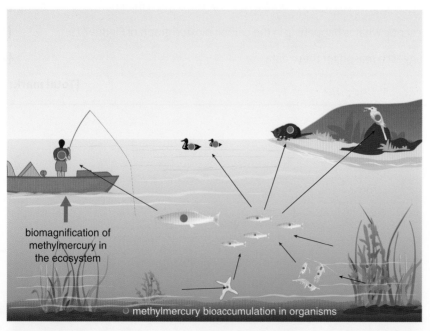

biomagnification of methylmercury in the ecosystem

methylmercury bioaccumulation in organisms

Figure 7.20. Biomagnification of methylmercury in Minamata Bay. The red dots represent the proportional concentration of methylmercury in the tissues of organisms.

Despite the elevated toxin levels in the bay's organisms, the results of the mercury toxicity were not immediately noticed. In fact, it was decades before people really began noticing the evidence that there was a problem. Of course, by then, many people in the town were already affected.

Evidence of toxicity

By the 1950s, fish began floating in Minamata Bay. Chisso paid the fisherman for any possible damage to the water of the bay, so this was overlooked. However, about this time local cats began acting very strangely. They began walking and swaying on two legs, giving an appearance of dancing, hence the name 'dancing cat disease' became popular. This dancing movement often left the cats disoriented, causing them to fall into the waters of Minamata Bay. When people saw this, they said the cats were committing suicide.

In the early 1950s, symptoms of the dancing cat disease began to appear in humans within the village. People began to have trouble walking and performing simple, everyday tasks, such as buttoning up a shirt. The symptoms progressed to paralysis, hearing loss, aphasia, convulsions and, in severe cases, death.

In 1956, there was an epidemic of the disease in the village. Scientists were called in to discover the cause of this debilitating disease. By the end of the year, evidence of mercury toxicity in the shellfish of Minamata Bay led researchers to discover that heavy metal poisoning was the cause of this disease. By measuring mercury levels in the tissues of organisms (Table 7.5) from the bay, cats and infected humans, scientists were able to create a clear chain of evidence for mercury poisoning. However, it was not until the 1960s that scientists were able to identify conclusively the Chisso Corporation's factory as the source of the mercury poisoning.

organism	mercury concentrations in tissue samples / ppm
oyster	5.6
grey mullet (fish)	10.6
china fish	24.1
crab	35.7
cat (liver)	up to 145.5
human (liver)	up to 70.5

Table 7.5. Mercury concentrations in tissue samples of organisms living in or near Minamata Bay.

Questions

1   Using Table 7.5, create a food chain of at least four animals illustrating how the toxins moved from one organism to the next.

2   Estuaries, like Minamata Bay, are usually sheltered areas with a narrow opening to the ocean. How do you think this amplified the biomagnification issue here?

3   Define biomagnification in your own words.

4   How does Table 7.5 support the conclusions of scientists that mercury toxicity was the cause of dancing cat disease?

Chapter 8
Physiology of marine primary producers

Learning outcomes

By the end of this chapter, you should be able to:

- explain the important role of primary producers in marine environments
- explain why different habitats are characterised by different primary producers
- describe the process of photosynthesis and how it is affected by limiting factors
- explain how accessory pigments are used by marine primary producers to use different wavelengths of light at different depths of the ocean
- apply what you have learnt to new, unfamiliar contexts.

8.1 The foundation of marine life

All food chains and food webs in the world's oceans ultimately require a source of energy. There are two main sources of energy for these food webs: light from the Sun and hydrogen sulfide from deep-sea hydrothermal vents. All food webs begin with organisms that can trap or fix this energy and convert it into energy stored in organic chemicals such as **carbohydrates**. This ability to take inorganic molecules and use energy to create organic molecules is called **autotrophic nutrition**. The roles of **primary producers** are to fix carbon and provide **habitats** for other organisms. They also shape environments by fixing the substrate and providing shelters and **nursery grounds** for other species of animal. Photosynthesis also produces oxygen gas, without which organisms would be unable to **respire**. Without producers in an **ecosystem**, there would be no food chain, very little atmospheric oxygen and a loss of habitat for many animals. This chapter looks at the process and importance of primary productivity in marine ecosystems.

KEY TERMS

Carbohydrate: organic compounds occurring in living tissues that contain carbon, hydrogen and oxygen, for example starch, cellulose and sugars; carbohydrates can be broken down in the process of respiration to release energy

Autotroph (autotrophic): an organism that can capture the energy in light or chemicals and use it to produce carbohydrates from simple molecules such as carbon dioxide

Primary producer: organisms that produce biomass from inorganic compounds, in almost all cases these are photosynthetically active organisms

Habitat: the natural environment where an organism lives

Nursery ground: important habitats of oceanic water where young fish and other species find food and shelter from predators, for example mangroves

Respiration: the process by which all living things release energy from their food by oxidising glucose

Ecosystem: the living organisms and the environment with which they interact

8.2 The basics of productivity

The majority of primary productivity in the world's seas and oceans is the result of **photosynthesis**. It is the process by which green plants, photosynthetic protoctists such as **diatoms** and **dinoflagellates**, and photosynthetic bacteria such as **cyanobacteria**, gain their energy from sunlight. Organisms that convert light energy into chemical energy in the form of organic chemicals are the basis of most of the world's food webs. Without photosynthesis, there would be almost no way to bring energy into the planet's ecosystems and life on Earth would be all but extinct.

Photosynthesis requires light energy to be trapped by pigments such as chlorophyll. This trapped energy is then used by the producer to produce glucose and oxygen (a byproduct) from carbon dioxide and water. Carbon is fixed into organic compounds and energy is taken from sunlight and converted into chemical energy in the form of organic compounds. The chemical process occurs in many steps and is controlled by a large number of **enzymes**.

The basic equation for photosynthesis is:

$$6\,CO_2 + 6\,H_2O \rightarrow C_6H_{12}O_6 + 6\,O_2$$

carbon dioxide + water $\rightarrow$ glucose + oxygen

The cells of producers contain **chloroplasts**, the organelles that carry out photosynthesis.

KEY TERMS

Photosynthesis (photosynthetic): the process of using light energy to synthesis glucose from carbon dioxide and water protoctists

Diatom: group of unicellular algae found in phytoplankton, characterised by silica skeletons

Dinoflagellate: group of unicellular algae found in phytoplankton, characterised by the presence of two flagella

Cyanobacteria: group of photosynthetic bacteria found in marine and fresh water

Enzyme: a protein produced by a living organism that acts as a catalyst in a specific reaction

Chloroplast: the photosynthetic cell organelle found in eukaryotes

Endosymbiosis: a theory that suggests that chloroplasts were originally independent photosynthetic bacteria that were taken in by other cells

Chloroplasts

Different types of chloroplast are found in different species of producers, although they all have some common features. The structure of chloroplasts provides clues about their origins, which is thought to involve a process called **endosymbiosis**. All chloroplasts contain their own DNA and ribosomes, and show structural similarities to a group of photosynthetic bacteria called cyanobacteria. It is thought that, at some point, cyanobacteria were engulfed by other cells but were not broken down, so were able to live within these cells. Eventually, the cyanobacteria lost their independence and became chloroplasts.

The majority of green algae and plants have chloroplasts similar to the general structure shown in Figure 8.1.

> **KEY TERMS**
>
> **Thylakoid:** a flattened, membrane-bound, fluid-filled sac that is the site of the light-dependent reactions of photosynthesis in a chloroplast granum
>
> **Stroma:** the fluid part of a chloroplast in which the carbohydrates are synthesised
>
> **Ribosome:** cell organelle involved in protein synthesis

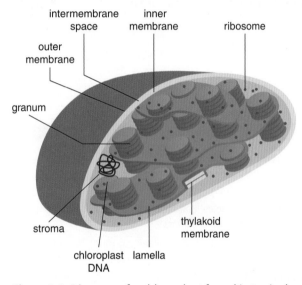

Figure 8.1. Diagram of a chloroplast found in typical green plants and algae.

Chloroplasts are covered with two membranes, one of which is probably a legacy of the original bacterial ancestor and the other a legacy of the ancestral host cell. Inside the chloroplast is an extensive network of membranes called **thylakoids**. These have stacked areas called grana, which contain the photosynthetic pigments. The thylakoid membranes are where light energy is trapped, and the extensive network ensures that a large surface area is exposed to the light. Surrounding the thylakoid membranes is a fluid called the **stroma**. This contains many chemicals and enzymes and is where glucose and other sugars are synthesised. The stroma also contains **ribosomes**, DNA and other substances, such as insoluble starch granules and lipid droplets.

> **KEY TERMS**
>
> **Primary pigment:** photosynthetic pigment that is directly involved with photosynthesis
>
> **Chlorophyll (*a* and *b*):** green pigments responsible for light capture in photosynthesis in algae and plants
>
> **Accessory pigment:** a pigment that is not essential for photosynthesis but that absorbs light of different wavelengths and passes the energy to chlorophyll si such as chlorophyll *b*, carotenoids and xanthophylls
>
> **Carotenoid:** a yellow, orange or red plant pigment used as an accessory pigment in photosynthesis
>
> **Xanthophyll:** a yellow or brown plant pigment used as an accessory pigment in photosynthesis

The primary and accessory pigments found in producers

The thylakoid membranes contain a range of different pigments that absorb light. The **primary pigment** that is most important in photosynthesis is **chlorophyll *a***, but there are many other **accessory pigments**, including **chlorophyll *b***, the **carotenoids** and **xanthophylls**. The chlorophylls give most plants their green colour. Different species of producer often have different accessory pigments depending on their particular habitats, and this will be discussed later in this chapter.

You can separate and identify different pigments by carrying out paper chromatography. In chromatography, the pigments are extracted from the producers and dissolved in a solvent. The extract is then placed on a strip of chromatography paper and the wick of this placed into more solvent. As the solvent moves up the paper, the pigments dissolve and are carried up the paper. Pigments that are more soluble travel faster and so run further up the paper, as shown in Figure 8.2.

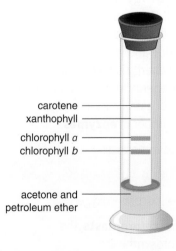

Figure 8.2. Separation of photosynthetic pigments by chromatography.

PRACTICAL ACTIVITY 8.1

Separating out photosynthetic pigments by chromatography

There are many chromatography techniques that can be used to extract and separate out the photosynthetic pigments, some more complex than others. This method can be adapted for different solvents.

Apparatus required

- 250 cm³ beaker (or similar sized glass jar)
- Very fine bore pipette or glass capillary tube
- Washed sand
- Chromatography paper (such as Whatman's number 1), which should be cut into strips that are long enough to hang into the base of the beaker with the top folded
- Propanone
- About 1 g of fresh plant (for example grass or seaweed) material, which should be as fresh as possible
- Scissors
- Pestle and mortar
- Pencil
- Splint or straw

Method

- Using the scissors, cut up the grass or other producer into small pieces and place them into the mortar.
- Add a few pinches of washed sand and, using the pestle, grind the grass until a pulp is produced.
- Add between 4 and 8 cm³ propanone and continue grinding until a dark green solution begins to form. If the solution is pale, add more grass and continue to grind. If the pulp has little free solution, add more propanone.
- When a dark green solution of propanone is produced, leave the mixture to settle for about 1 min. If a centrifuge is available, the propanone can be decanted into centrifuged tubes and the solid debris 'spun down' to remove it, leaving a very clear propanone solution.
- Take the chromatography paper and draw a pencil line 20 mm from the base of the paper.
- Using the fine pipette or capillary tube, draw up a small quantity of the pigment extract from the mortar and carefully make a spot in the centre of the pencil line on the paper. Dry the spot for a few seconds and repeat the process in exactly the same place. The aim is to place as much pigment in as small a spot as possible. If the paper

is not allowed to dry, the solution will diffuse across the paper, making too large a spot.

- Place a small amount of propanone into the beaker and suspend the chromatography paper into the solvent taped onto the splint or straw, as shown in Figure 8.3. It is essential that the solvent does not rise over the spot. The experiment should now be left until the pigments have separated.

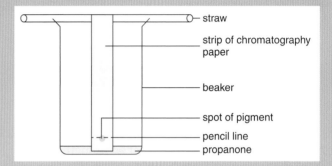

Figure 8.3. Setting up the chromatography paper in solvent.

- When the pigments have separated clearly, use a pencil to mark the highest distance that the solvent has reached.
- Remove the chromatography paper and leave it to dry.

Risk assessment

- Propanone is flammable and an irritant so no naked flames should be present and safety glasses must be worn, particularly when grinding.
- Capillary tubes are made of thin glass, which is easy to break and get in your eyes. Safety glasses should be worn and care should be taken when handling them.

Results

R_f values need to be calculated to identify the pigments. To calculate R_f values, use a ruler to measure the distance that the solvent has moved from the origin and then measure the distance the centre of each spot of pigment has travelled. The R_f value is calculated using the formula:

$$R_f = \frac{\text{distance moved by pigment}}{\text{distance moved by solvent}}$$

Use Table 8.1 of standard R_f values for pigments separated in propanone to identify each pigment.

149

→

pigment	colour	R$_f$ value
chlorophyll *a*	green	0.45
chlorophyll *b*	blue/green	0.65
xanthophyll	yellow/brown	0.71
phaeophytin	grey	0.83
carotene	yellow	0.95

Table 8.1. R$_f$ values for different pigments in propanone solvent.

Conclusions
Use Table 8.1 to identify each pigment on your chromatograph.

Absorption and action spectra

Different colours of light have different wavelengths. The different pigments found in producers absorb light wavelengths of slightly different colours. The **absorption spectrum** of a pigment shows the amount of light of each wavelength that a particular pigment absorbs. The absorption spectra of chlorophylls *a* and *b* and carotene are shown in Figure 8.4. The graph shows clearly the two peak areas of absorption of both chlorophylls around the blue and red ends of the spectrum. Most plants are green in colour because they reflect or transmit green light but absorb light in the red and blue areas of the spectrum. The overall absorption spectrum of a particular producer will be the combined absorption spectra of all its pigments.

An **action spectrum** shows the actual effect of different light wavelengths on the rate of photosynthesis. It can be obtained by measuring the rate of photosynthesis of a producer at different light intensities. The shapes of action and absorption spectra are usually the same. This means that the light wavelengths used in photosynthesis are the same ones that are absorbed (Figure 8.5). Details of a simple practical for seeing this are given later.

KEY TERMS

Absorption spectrum: a graph of the absorbance of different wavelengths of light by a compound such as a photosynthetic pigment

Action spectrum: a graph showing the effect of different wavelengths of light on a process, for example on the rate of photosynthesis

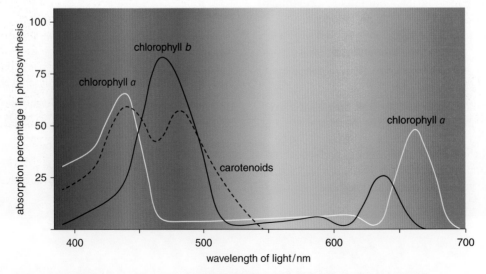

Figure 8.4. Absorption spectra of chlorophyll *a*, chlorophyll *b* and carotenoids.

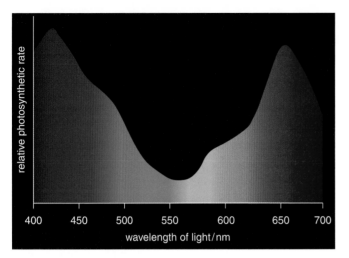

Figure 8.5. Photosynthetic action spectrum for a typical producer.

The pigments present in different species of marine primary producers are linked to the depth of water that they inhabit. Different light wavelengths penetrate to different depths in the water, so the wavelengths of light available to a particular producer depend on the depth it inhabits.

1 Explain what is meant by the terms absorption spectrum and action spectrum.

2 In 1882, Theodor Engelmann carried out an experiment to investigate the effect of light wavelength on the rate of photosynthesis of the filamentous alga, *Spirogyra*. He placed a filament of the alga on a microscope slide with some aerobic bacteria that moved towards areas of higher oxygen concentration. He used a prism to illuminate the algal filament with different wavelengths of light and then observed the movement of the bacteria.

   a Suggest why aerobic bacteria that move towards oxygen were used.

   b State what the production of oxygen by the chloroplasts shows.

   c Explain the results shown in Figure 8.6.

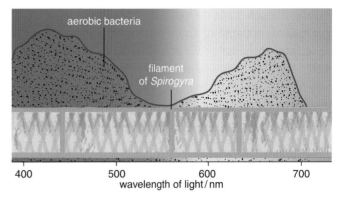

Figure 8.6. Results from Englemann's experiment showing which parts of the algal filament the aerobic bacteria have migrated towards.

Light penetration in water: wavelength and turbidity

There are two main factors that affect how deep in the water light can penetrate:

- the wavelength, or colour, of light

- the amount of particulate material, known as turbidity, in the water.

Light wavelength

Figure 8.7 shows the maximum depths to which different wavelengths of light penetrate. It also demonstrates that all wavelengths of light penetrate further in less turbid, open ocean waters than coastal waters.

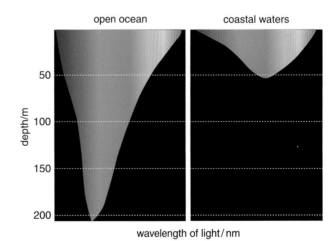

Figure 8.7. Penetration of different light wavelengths in clear ocean waters and turbid coastal waters.

151

Blue light reaches the deepest parts of the ocean, up to a maximum depth of about 200 m, while red light penetrates the least and is absorbed by the surface water within the first 10 m. Any producers living below 10 m only receive light from the blue and green areas of the spectrum. Chlorophylls *a* and *b* and carotene absorb very little light from the green area of the spectrum, which creates a potential problem. Red and brown algae are adapted to live in these depths, possessing accessory pigments such as xanthophyll and a group of pigments called phycobilins. Phycobilins are pigments that are bound to proteins, forming protein–pigment complexes called phycobiliproteins. There are several different phycobiliproteins, the main two being phycoerythrin and phycocyanin; their absorption spectra are shown in Figure 8.8.

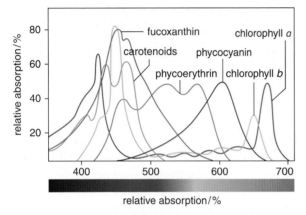

Figure 8.8. Absorption spectra of chlorophylls *a* and *b*, fucoxanthin (a xanthophyll found in algae), carotenoids, phycoerythrin and phycocyanin.

These accessory pigments enable red and brown algae to absorb light from the yellow and green areas of the spectrum. This increases their rate of photosynthesis in depths where there is no red light. Red and brown algae with these pigments are able to compete and survive better at these depths than green algae, which lack these accessory pigments.

SELF-ASSESSMENT QUESTIONS

3   Explain why a diver's red oxygen tank appears black in deeper water.

4   It has been suggested that it is energetically very costly to produce phycoerythrin and phycocyanin. Suggest why algae found at the surface do not contain these pigments.

Turbidity

Large amounts of sediment, particles or even living organisms such as plankton, reduce light penetration. The cloudiness or clarity of the water is known as **turbidity**. Estuarine and coastal water generally has a greater turbidity than open ocean water so light is less able to penetrate to lower depths (Figure 8.7). Light penetration can easily be measured by using a piece of apparatus known as a Secchi disc. This is a white 30 cm circular metal or plastic disc attached to a rope. The disc is lowered into the water until it is no longer visible and the length of rope recorded. The disc is then raised and the length of rope when the disc becomes visible measured (Figure 8.9). An average distance is then calculated using the two values.

KEY TERM

Turbidity: the cloudiness of water or other fluids due to the presence of particles. It affects the penetration of light

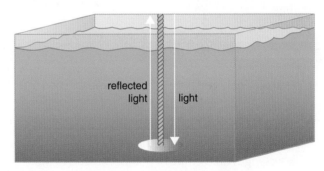

Figure 8.9. Use of a marine Secchi disc to detect water turbidity.

In areas of ocean with high turbidity and low light penetration, producers are less able to live at lower depths because they are unable to photosynthesise.

SELF-ASSESSMENT QUESTIONS

5   Explain why coastal waters have lower light penetration than open ocean.

6   Suggest why an average distance is calculated for visibility of the Secchi disc rather than relying on the distance it immediately becomes no longer visible.

The effect of light colour on photosynthesis rate

Apparatus

- Fresh, healthy pond weed with good quality leaves; *Cabomba* is the best plant to use and is usually available from aquatic shops
- Boiling tube
- Bench lamp
- 1% sodium hydrogencarbonate solution
- Coloured cellophane (red, blue, orange, yellow and green)
- Boiling tube rack
- Dissecting scissors

Method

- Take an approximately 5 cm long piece of *Cabomba* with one cut stem and carefully cut the cut end of the stem at a 45° angle.
- Place the *Cabomba* into the boiling tube with the cut end pointing upwards. It may be necessary to weigh the plant down with a paper clip.
- Cover the plant entirely with 1% sodium hydrogencarbonate indicator solution.
- Place the boiling tube in the boiling tube rack and place the lamp 10 cm away from the boiling tube.
- Switch on the lamp and switch off all other lighting in the room (there needs to be a reasonable gap between any other experiments going on and all the main lighting in the room should be turned off and any blinds or curtains drawn).

- Leave the plant illuminated for 5 min; during this time check that it is producing a stream of bubbles from the cut end of the stem. The rate will vary between different plants.
- Count the bubbles that emerge from the end of the stem for an appropriate period of time, for example 1–5 min. If the stream of bubbles is rapid, use a shorter time period; for a slower stream of bubbles increase the time. Record the number of bubbles and the time period.
- Record the number of bubbles for two more time periods. There is no need to wait between readings.
- Repeat the experiment after wrapping cellophane of different colours around the boiling tube. Each time the cellophane colour is changed, the plant will need 5 min to adjust to the colour of light.

Risk assessment

There is a risk of cold water being splashed onto the hot light bulb causing the glass to shatter, so safety glasses should be worn.

Results and analysis

- Copy Table 8.2 and enter your results, calculating the mean rates of bubble production.
- Produce an appropriate graph of the results. You will need to decide whether to draw a bar chart or line graph.

colour of light	number of bubbles of oxygen counted			time period	rate of production of oxygen / bubbles min^{-1}
'white'					
red					
orange					
yellow					
green					
blue					

Table 8.2. Results table for effect of light colour on the rate of photosynthesis.

Conclusions

1 Why was it important to wait 5 min before beginning a count with a new colour?

2 Describe and explain the pattern shown by your graph. Ensure that you include references to the absorption of light and the photosynthetic pigments.

3 Figure 8.10 shows a more accurate method of determining rate of photosynthesis. Explain why it would produce more accurate results than the method you have used.

4 In the ocean, red light is absorbed by the surface water. Using your results, explain how brown and red algae are adapted to survive in deeper water and why green algae, which generally possess the same pigments found in *Cabomba*, are largely restricted to the surface water.

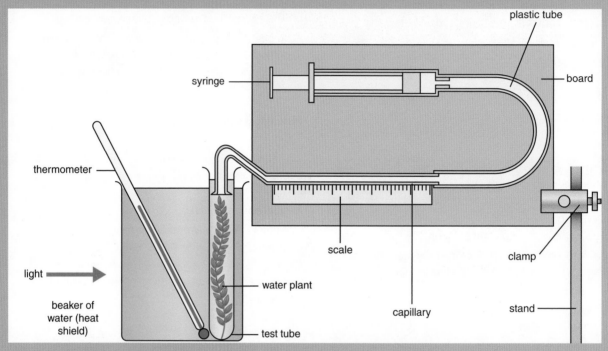

Figure 8.10. A photosynthometer (also called the Audus apparatus).

Productivity and depth of water

There are three distinct zones in marine waters that relate to the depth of light penetration and productivity. The upper layer of water, where there is high light penetration, is called the euphotic zone. This zone may extend to about 200 m in clear water or only about 5 m in turbid water. Producers are able to photosynthesise effectively in this zone. Below the euphotic zone is the disphotic zone, often referred to as the twilight zone. This zone has some blue light but at a low intensity and ranges from between 15 m in highly turbid water to 1000 m in very clear water. No producers are found here, despite the presence of some light. Below the disphotic zone is the aphotic zone, where less than 1% of the surface light reaches. There are no producers here that use photosynthesis as a method of primary productivity. The zones are shown in Figure 8.11.

To understand why there are no producers in the disphotic zone, despite the presence of light, you need to consider the processes of photosynthesis and respiration.

If you look at the basic equations for photosynthesis and respiration, it becomes immediately obvious that they are exact opposites.

Photosynthesis: $6\,CO_2 + 6\,H_2O \rightarrow C_6H_{12}O_6 + 6\,O_2$

Respiration: $C_6H_{12}O_6 + 6\,O_2 \rightarrow 6\,CO_2 + 6\,H_2O$

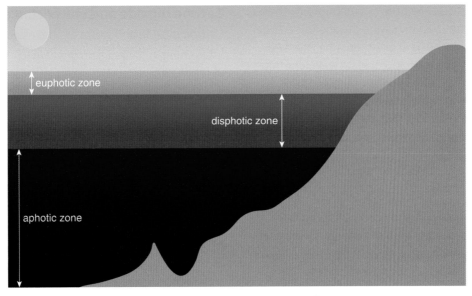

Figure 8.11. The euphotic, disphotic and aphotic zones of the ocean.

Photosynthesis builds up glucose, which has energy from light locked into it. The glucose is converted into other compounds, such as starch and protein, which are used for storage and growth. Respiration releases the energy in the glucose by oxidation.

The total amount of energy fixed by a plant into chemical compounds by photosynthesis is the **gross primary productivity** (GPP). This is not all available for growth as the plant has to use some of the glucose in respiration (R) to release energy for active processes. **Net primary productivity** (NPP) is a measure of what energy the plant is able to fix into its chemical compounds and use for growth. It is calculated using the formula:

net primary productivity (NPP)
= gross primary productivity (GPP) – respiratory loss (R)

It is clear that, if a producer is to grow, its rate of photosynthesis must exceed its rate of respiration. In the euphotic zone, the light intensity is sufficient to enable a rate of photosynthesis that is greater than the rate of respiration, so that the NPP has a positive value. In the disphotic zone, despite the producers being able to photosynthesise, the average rate is lower than that of respiration, so the NPP value is negative, resulting in the producers being unable to grow. If the rate of respiration equals the rate of photosynthesis, the producer is said

to be at the compensation point and there is no net production of glucose. There may be periods during a summer day when the rate of photosynthesis exceeds the rate of respiration but over an extended period, such as a year, the mean rate of respiration is higher.

155

KEY TERMS

Gross primary productivity: the amount of light or chemical energy fixed by producers in a given length of time in a given area

Net primary productivity: the amount of energy that is left over after respiration to be made into new plant biomass

8.3 Factors affecting the rate of photosynthesis and the law of limiting factors

Several external factors affect the rate of photosynthesis:

- light intensity

- light wavelength

- temperature

- carbon dioxide concentration.

As these abiotic factors affect the rate of photosynthesis, they affect the distribution of marine producers. In order to maximise photosynthesis, a plant must be exposed to sufficient light intensity of appropriate wavelengths, must be kept at a relatively warm temperature and must be supplied with sufficient carbon dioxide and water. In practice, the factors that are in the least supply restrict the rate of photosynthesis: this is the law of **limiting factors**.

Light intensity

Light provides the energy for photosynthesis. The more light energy that is available, the more energy can be used to make glucose. Light energy is absorbed by chlorophyll and this harvested energy is used to combine carbon dioxide with water to make sugars. The higher the light intensity, the faster the rate of photosynthesis. This can be measured by the increasing rate of oxygen production.

Light wavelength

As you have already seen, producers contain pigments that absorb the light. Depending on the pigments present, different wavelengths of light are absorbed. Most producers are unable to absorb certain colours of light, such as green. Many contain accessory pigments, such as phycoerythrin, phycocyanin, and xanthophyll, which enable them to absorb additional light wavelengths.

Temperature

A suitable temperature is essential to maximise the rate of photosynthesis. Carbon dioxide and water molecules are combined by the action of enzymes. These molecules constantly move in random directions and react when they collide with each other. As the temperature rises, kinetic energy (the energy of movement) increases, so they move faster. Faster moving particles collide more frequently, so photosynthesis becomes faster. If the temperature rises too high, the enzymes denature, causing the reaction to slow down to almost zero.

KEY TERM

Limiting factor: the one factor, of many affecting a process, that is nearest its lowest value and hence is rate limiting. Photosynthesis rate is usually limited by light intensity, temperature and / or carbon dioxide concentration

Carbon dioxide and water concentrations

Carbon dioxide and water are the essential raw materials for photosynthesis. If they are in short supply, the rate of photosynthesis is reduced. If their concentrations increase, they collide more frequently with the enzymes involved in photosynthesis, and the rate of photosynthesis increases. In practice, water is not considered to be a limiting factor because it is rarely in short supply.

It is easy to measure the effects of these factors on photosynthesis by measuring the rate of production of oxygen by an aquatic plant such as *Cabomba*.

A typical experimental setup is shown in Figure 8.10. The water plant is placed into a boiling tube in a solution of sodium hydrogencarbonate, which provides a source of carbon dioxide for photosynthesis. The cut end of the stem is arranged below a capillary tube so that oxygen produced by photosynthesis collects in the tube. The plastic tube and capillary are also filled with sodium hydrogencarbonate. The tube containing the plant is placed into a water bath and a light source is placed next to it. The beaker of water prevents the lamp heating up the plant.

When oxygen has been collected for a set period of time, the syringe is used to draw up the bubble of oxygen and line it up against the scale so that the length of it can be measured. The limiting factors can be changed using methods shown in Table 8.3.

limiting factor	method of altering factor
light intensity	set light source at different, measured, distances from plant
light wavelength	place coloured filters in front of light source
temperature	change temperature of water bath and measure with thermometer
carbon dioxide concentration	alter concentration of sodium hydrogencarbonate solution

Table 8.3. Altering different limiting factors.

Figure 8.12 shows how you can present the effects of changing limiting factors.

(a)

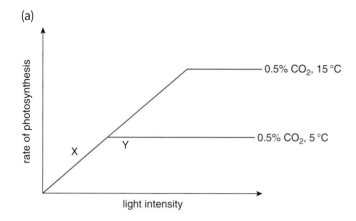

(b)

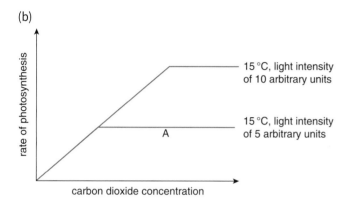

(c)

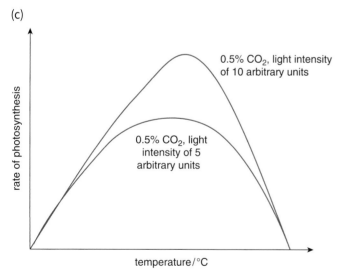

Figure 8.12. The effects of increasing (a) light intensity, (b) carbon dioxide concentration and (c) temperature on the rate of photosynthesis.

Figure 8.12a shows the effect of increasing light intensity and temperature on the rate of photosynthesis of a producer. Over section X of the graph, the rate of photosynthesis increases as the light intensity increases at both 5 °C and 15 °C. This means that over these light intensities, the light intensity must have been the limiting factor.

At Y on the graph, increasing the light intensity at 5 °C has no more effect on the rate of photosynthesis as the graph has now levelled off. This means that light is no longer a limiting factor and something else must be. Increasing the temperature to 15 °C from 5 °C increases the rate of photosynthesis, so at point Y temperature must be the limiting factor.

In Figure 8.12b, you can see that increasing the concentration of carbon dioxide has a similar effect as increasing the light intensity on the rate of photosynthesis.

The effect of increasing temperature gives a slightly different shaped graph (Figure 8.12c). As the temperature increases, the rate of photosynthesis increases until another factor limits the rate of photosynthesis. If the temperature continues to rise, however, the rate of photosynthesis eventually drops. This is caused by **denaturation** of the enzymes.

157

KEY TERM

Denaturation: the loss of shape of enzymes, resulting in a loss of activity, usually the result of heating to a high temperature

An understanding of limiting factors can help you understand how producer growth increases under certain climatic conditions. For optimal growth, marine producers require a high light intensity for a long period of time, high carbon dioxide levels and a warm temperature. Phytoplanktonic blooms often occur when these conditions are optimal and primary productivity increases rapidly. These phytoplanktonic blooms underpin many food chains: marine species, such as whales, have migration patterns that ensure their arrival at a particular location at the time when the blooms occur to maximise productivity.

Maths skills

Calculating volumes and rates and using significant figures

It is important to be able to calculate the volumes of several shapes, including the volumes of spheres, cylinders, cubes and rectangular cuboids. You also need to be able to calculate rates confidently and change units.

Worked example

In an experiment, a volume of oxygen has been collected in a photosynthometer (also called the Audus apparatus) (see Figure 8.10) over a period of 5 min. The scale gives a reading for the length of the oxygen bubble but the seaweed has actually released a volume of oxygen. You want to calculate the rate of oxygen production in $mm^3\ s^{-1}$.

The capillary tube has a circular cross-section and so is cylindrical (Figure 8.13).

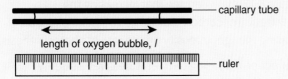

Figure 8.13. Measuring the length of an oxygen bubble.

If you want to calculate the volume of oxygen produced, you need to know the length of the bubble and the radius of the cross-section (Figure 8.14).

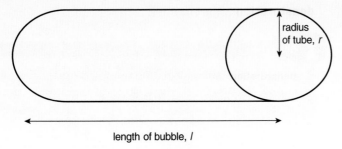

Figure 8.14. Measuring the volume of a cylinder.

The formula for the volume of a cylinder is $\pi r^2 l$

You first need to make sure that you have the same units for all your measurements. So, if the bubble length was 5.00 cm and the radius 1.5 mm, you need to make sure that all the units are in either mm or cm, and then put the values into the equation:

volume = $\pi \times (1.5\ mm)^2 \times 50.0\ mm = 353.25\ mm^3$

In order to decide how many decimal places to use, you need to consider the accuracy of your measurements. When you manipulate data, the general rule is that you can use one more decimal place than the measurements had. So in this example, the measurements were taken to 0.1 of a millimetre, so the final volume of oxygen can be presented as $353.25\ mm^3$.

A rate requires a reference to time. This volume of oxygen was collected over a period of 5 min, so you can now calculate the volume of oxygen released per minute by diving the volume by the time taken (5 min).

rate of oxygen production = $353.25 / 5 = 70.65\ mm^3\ min^{-1}$

Questions

Use the following formulae for the volumes of different shapes to answer the questions.

cylinder: $V = \pi r^2 l$

sphere: $V = 4/3\ \pi r^3$

cube: $V = l^3$ (where l is the length of one side)

rectangular cuboid: $V = \text{length} \times \text{base} \times \text{height}$

1 a   Calculate the rates of oxygen production in $mm^3\ min^{-1}$ by suspensions of diatoms, using a capillary tube of diameter 4 mm, when the length of bubble produced is:

   i   6 cm over 8 min

   ii   4 cm over 6 min

   iii   8 cm over 5 min

   b   Convert each of the rates of oxygen production into $mm^3\ s^{-1}$.

2   A coral grows in the approximate shape of a sphere: calculate its mean rate of growth in $cm^3\ month^{-1}$ if its diameter changes from 50 cm to 58 cm over a year.

3   Determine the density of 75 tilapia fry in tilapia m^{-3} when placed into:

   a   cubic tanks of side lengths:

   i   5 m

   ii   8 m

   iii   225 cm

   b   rectangular cuboid tanks of dimensions:

   i   2 m × 3 m × 8 m

   ii   150 cm × 6 m × 2 m

8.4 Adaptations of different primary producers

Primary producers in the world's seas and oceans come from a range of taxonomic groups, including plants, protoctists and prokaryotes. Different areas of water contain different producers, all specialised for a particular habitat. In all these areas, the main factor that affects producers is access to light, so they have evolved adaptations to maximise how much light is absorbed. Three different areas with different types of producer are:

• open ocean

• shallow waters near coastlines

• intertidal zones, also called littoral zones, where land meets the sea.

Life for producers in each of these areas is very different and as a result requires different specialisations.

Open ocean

The open ocean poses certain problems for most producers. Photosynthesis can only occur down to a depth of approximately 200 m, so not down on deep seabeds. This means that producers are unable to attach to a substrate, and are restricted to the photic zone where light penetration is sufficient and carbon dioxide dissolution from the air is high.

Producers that live in the open ocean must be able to survive in the shifting water currents, which can be very vigorous. There are several different types of producer found in the open ocean.

Phytoplankton

There are many different species of phytoplankton. In the open ocean, most are free floating and are found in the surface water where light intensity is highest. They have no need to settle on a substrate and are carried wherever the ocean currents take them. Several different groups of phytoplankton exist, all with slightly different adaptations and niches.

Diatoms

Diatoms are unicellular phytoplankton found in the oceanic surface water. There are over a hundred different genera but all have intricate cell walls of silica, which often have extraordinarily beautiful designs (Figure 8.15). They are able to reproduce very rapidly when conditions are optimal and blooms are often seen in spring. This is when light intensity and temperature are rising and upwelling of mineral ions into the surface waters occurs. The blooms tend to appear and then rapidly disappear because of consumption by primary consumers such as planktonic crustaceans and krill, and depletion of mineral ions. They are very important in removing carbon dioxide from the atmosphere and form the base of many marine food webs.

Figure 8.15. Diatoms come in a range of sizes and shapes, many of which show extraordinary geometric patterns.

Dinoflagellates

Dinoflagellates are also unicellular protoctists but do not have the silica cell wall that diatoms possess. Like diatoms, they live in the upper surface waters of oceans and can undergo rapid reproduction to produce algal blooms when conditions are optimal. The blooms of some species of dinoflagellate produce toxins that can poison fish and accumulate in shellfish. Contaminated shellfish that are eaten by other organisms, including humans, can cause poisoning. Blooms of dinoflagellates that produce toxins are called harmful algal blooms (HABs) and include red tides, which cause areas of the ocean to turn red. Pollution caused by the run-off of fertiliser from fields is the source of many blooms of dinoflagellates, and as farming has become more intense the number of harmful algal blooms has increased.

Some dinoflagellates bioluminesce, and this can often be seen at night on the ocean or at the coast, when impressive displays can occur in the evening (Figure 8.16). They bioluminesce as a defence mechanism since it tends to attract large predators into the area which then consume predators of the dinoflagellates.

Figure 8.16. Blooms of dinoflagellates often light up coastal waters with their bioluminescence.

Cyanobacteria

Cyanobacteria are photosynthetic bacteria that are one of the earliest known forms of life on Earth. They are found almost everywhere on the planet and are considered to be one of the most successful bacteria. When cyanobacteria evolved, their photosynthetic activity caused a huge increase in the oxygen levels of the planet's atmosphere, which allowed aerobic life to evolve. Planktonic cyanobacteria are filamentous organisms that are found in surface waters (Figure 8.17). Like dinoflagellates and diatoms, they undergo rapid reproduction if the conditions are optimal, producing blooms. Some species produce very harmful cyanotoxins such as BMAA, an altered amino acid, which is now thought to be a possible environmental cause of neurological diseases in humans, such as Alzheimer's and Parkinson's. The blooms are often associated with high levels of pollution from fertilisers and organic waste.

Sargassum

Sargassum is a genus of brown macroalgae (seaweed) in the order Fucales. A piece of *Sargassum* is shown in Figure 8.18. Numerous species are distributed throughout the temperate and tropical oceans of the world, where

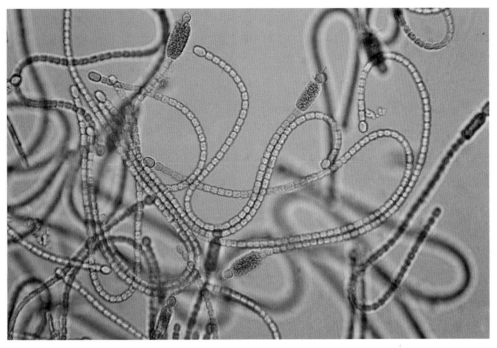

Figure 8.17. Cyanobacteria seen with a light microscope clearly show their filamentous structure.

they generally inhabit shallow water and coral reefs, and the genus is widely known for its planktonic (free-floating) species. Many species that are usually attached to a substrate may also survive as free-floating forms after being detached from reefs during rough weather. Two species (*S. natans* and *S. fluitans*) have become holopelagic: they reproduce vegetatively and never attach to the seabed during their life cycle.

Figure 8.18. A mat of oceanic *Sargassum natans* clearly showing the spherical air bladders used for floatation. Note the turtle swimming between the *Sargassum* and the water surface.

Sargassum was named by the Portuguese sailors who found it in the Atlantic Ocean after a species of rock rose called sargaço that grew in their water wells at home. In turn, the Atlantic Ocean's Sargasso Sea is named after the algae, because it contains large amounts of *Sargassum*. It is thought that the free-floating *S. natans* grows during the spring in the north-west Gulf of Mexico and is then transported into the Atlantic by strong currents. Although it was formerly thought to cover all of the Sargasso Sea, making navigation impossible, it has since been found to occur only in drifts. The Florida Keys and its smaller islands are well known for their high levels of *Sargassum*, which often covers their shores and beaches.

The free-floating forms of *Sargassum* found in the open ocean usually form long floating mats. They have no roots, are composed of very tough, flexible fibres that can resist pounding by the ocean waves, and have air bladders called pneumatocysts that help them stay afloat. These free-floating species provide a food source and serve as a shelter for a rich diversity of marine life, including turtles, puffer fish, crustaceans and the camouflaged Sargassum fish.

Shallow water

In clear coastal waters, light often penetrates to the seabed so producers are able to attach to a substrate and still photosynthesise. They are fixed to the seabed to prevent being washed away by waves and ocean currents. There are several different species that all possess certain adaptations to enable them to survive in this environment. As you have seen earlier in this chapter, as water depth increases, different light wavelengths 'disappear' as they are absorbed by the water. Producers growing in shallow waters have different combinations of pigments depending on the depth of water they live in. Many that live below certain depths have little exposure to red light wavelengths.

KEY TERM

Mutualism: a relationship between two different organisms where both organisms benefit

Zooxanthellae

Zooxanthellae are dinoflagellate protoctistans that are found growing inside other marine organisms. They are found within coral polyps, giant clams, jellyfish and sea anemones. They enter into the cells of their host by a process of endocytosis, or are transferred from parents during reproduction, and remain there in a **mutualistic** relationship. The dinoflagellates photosynthesise and release glucose and amino acids into the coral cells and the coral provides the dinoflagellates with carbon dioxide and minerals. Figure 8.19 shows coral polyps containing zooxanthellae. Many of the host organisms live where there is no red light, so the zooxanthellae contain accessory pigments (for example peridinin and diadinoxanthin) as well as chlorophylls. This means that they are able to maximise the absorption of additional wavelengths of light. These pigments often give corals their red and yellow colours.

Zooxanthellae may also be found as free-living dinoflagellates that are taken up by coral polyps. During the life of a coral, zooxanthellae may be expelled when the coral becomes stressed. This expulsion of the zooxanthellae is known as coral bleaching and can be caused by global warming and pollution. After a coral has undergone bleaching, it may be recolonised by a different species of zooxanthellae. This means that, within its lifetime, an individual coral may be colonised by several species of zooxanthellae, changing colour several times.

Figure 8.19. Coral polyps showing yellow-brown zooxanthellae within them.

Seagrasses

Figure 8.20. Submerged seagrass growing on the seabed.

Seagrasses (Figure 8.20) are not to be confused with seaweeds. They are green, flowering plants that grow on the seabed in shallow waters and look like underwater meadows. There are about 60 different species of seagrass, all of which are restricted to the photic zone and photosynthesise very much like terrestrial flowering plants. They play many important roles in coastal areas, acting as oxygen producers and primary producers for food webs. They are the main food source for organisms such as turtles, manatees and herbivorous fish. They also provide a habitat and nursery for many species of fish and crustaceans, some of which are commercially valuable fishery species. Their root systems stabilise the substrate and prevent coastal erosion and wave damage. It is estimated that seagrass meadows account for more than 10% of the ocean's total carbon storage and, because of their high productivity, they hold twice as much carbon dioxide per hectare as rainforests. Seagrasses are one of many species thought to be under threat from global warming. Seagrasses have many specific adaptations.

- They have well-developed root systems, with thick, horizontal rhizomes that lie up to 25 cm deep in the substrate (Figure 8.21). The root system anchors the seagrass into the seabed so that it is not moved by the shifting water currents and wave actions. The rhizomes also enable seagrasses to reproduce asexually.

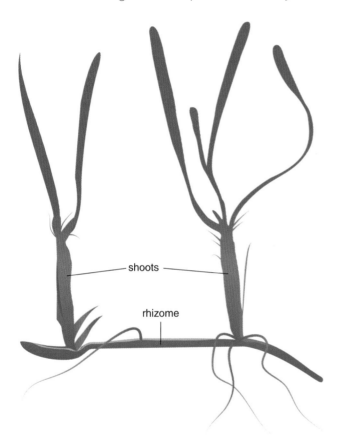

Figure 8.21. Seagrass showing the thick rhizome and two separate shoots.

- They are physiologically adapted to seawater so that their cells are able to exist in salt water without losing water by osmosis.

- They contain a specialised tissue within stems called aerenchyma. This tissue contains air and delivers it to all the submerged areas of the plant.

- The leaf structure is unusual. It has an epidermis layer with chloroplasts (these are absent in the epidermis of most terrestrial plants) to maximise photosynthesis, no

stomata, and a very thin waxy cuticle so that the leaf cells can obtain mineral ions directly from the water. Seagrasses have very few vascular bundles, as there is no need to transport water or minerals through the plant. The leaves are also very flexible so they do not get broken by water currents.

- They are able to reproduce both sexually and asexually. When reproducing sexually, they produce flowers that release pollen that is carried in the water to other flowers.

One species of seagrass that is particularly well known is *Thalassia testudinum,* often called turtle grass. It is found in the Gulf of Mexico, Caribbean Sea and Bermuda, and plays an important role in these areas' ecosystems. It is a vital food source for many rare, endangered species, including turtles.

Kelp forests

Figure 8.22. Giant kelp forests.

Kelp species (Figure 8.22) are giant brown macroalgae that often grow as underwater forests. They require nutrient-rich water and a temperature of between 8 and 16°C. When conditions are optimal, they have a very high rate of growth. One genus, *Macrocystus,* is able to grow up to 0.5 metres a day and can reach lengths up to 80 m. Kelp forests are often considered to be underwater rainforests because they are the base of many food webs generating vast species biodiversity. They also stabilise and create a habitat and shelter for many species of animal, including commercially important fish. Sea urchins are one of the species that eat kelp. Sea otters prey on sea urchins, and where sea otter populations have decreased, kelp forests have also decreased because of a dramatic increase in the sea urchin population. The loss of kelp has then led to a fall in reported fish catches.

Most kelp species have a similar structure that enables them to survive in the water of shallow seas and oceans (Figure 8.23).

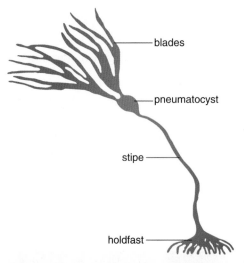

blades

pneumatocyst

stipe

holdfast

Figure 8.23. The basic structure of kelp, showing the holdfast, stipe, pneumatocyst and blades.

The whole body of the kelp is known as a thallus and has three main parts.

- Holdfast: this is a strong, root-like structure that anchors the kelp to the seabed, preventing it from being moved by strong ocean currents or storms. It is for anchorage only and has no function in absorbing minerals.

- Stipe: this is a long, tough, vertical stalk similar to the stem of plants. It extends from the holdfast and reaches up to the blades. It is very tough, to prevent breakage.

- Blades: the blades are broad leaf-like structures that 'hang' in the water. They have a large surface area to absorb light and minerals.

Some kelp species also have structures called **pneumatocysts**, which are gas-filled bladders found underneath the blades. These act as floatation aids to keep the kelp upright.

Because many kelp species live at depths where exposure to red light is restricted, they contain accessory pigments such as xanthophyll and fucoxanthin to absorb additional wavelengths of light.

 KEY TERM

Pneumatocyst: a gas-containing structure that provides buoyancy for some species of seaweed

 KEY TERMS

Intertidal zone: the area of a shore that is above water at low tide and under water at high tide

Littoral zone: the benthic, or bottom, zone between the highest and lowest spring tide shorelines, also referred to as the intertidal zone

Intertidal zones

The **intertidal zone**, or **littoral zone**, is the area of coastline that is underwater at high tide but exposed at low tide. Producers that inhabit this area must overcome particular difficulties:

- exposure to the air creates a problem of desiccation and, in colder regions, the risk of freezing

- submersion in water reduces exposure to light, in particular the red part of the spectrum in deeper water

- tidal movements mean that there is erosion and a constant risk of being washed away.

A vast diversity of green, brown and red algae is found in intertidal zones, all exhibiting adaptations that are suited to a particular habitat. The position on a shore where a particular alga grows has a major effect on the type of adaptation. Algae that live further down the beach spend longer submerged than those higher up. Those that live higher up on the beach need adaptations that enable them to survive prolonged exposure. Those that spend longer submerged in deeper water require adaptations that enable them to trap as much light energy as possible. Algae in the middle of the shore are exposed to strong tidal action so need strong attachment and shelter. Because of the need for anchorage, rocky shores tend to have more algae than sandy shores.

The majority of intertidal algae are brown species, coloured by the presence of xanthophyll, which helps them to survive in water where there is little red light. Red algae species are also found, particularly in regions of deeper water where their pigments of phycoerythrin and phycocyanin are able to absorb green light. There are fewer species of green algae, and the ones that are present tend to be found on the higher parts of the shore rather than in deeper water.

Fucus spiralis (Figure 8.24) is a brown alga found in the middle intertidal zone. It has very thick cell walls to reduce water loss, and the fronds are spiralled in shape to trap water and reduce evaporation. It has a holdfast at the base with which it attaches to rocks to prevent being washed away.

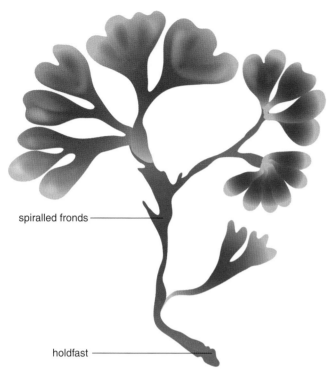

spiralled fronds

holdfast

Figure 8.24. *Fucus spiralis*. The fronds are spiralled to trap water and reduce evaporation.

Chondracanthus exasperates (Figure 8.25) is a red alga that grows low down on the beach and spends most of its time submerged in water up to 20 m in depth. It is able to absorb some of the light wavelengths present in deeper water and has a holdfast to keep it attached.

Figure 8.25. *Chondracanthus exasperates*, a typical red alga.

Ulva lactuca (Figure 8.26) is a green alga that is found throughout the shoreline. It has a small holdfast and tends to grow in more sheltered areas. It can detach and live as a free form that will reattach to suitable substrate. It is very tolerant of high mineral ion concentrations so that it can survive in rock pools in high salinity due to evaporation of water.

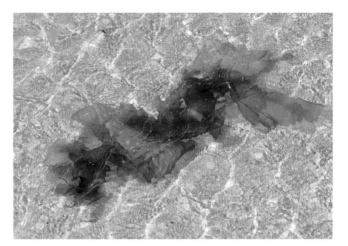

Figure 8.26. *Ulva lactuca*, a green intertidal alga, often called sea lettuce.

165

SELF-ASSESSMENT QUESTIONS

7 State what is limiting the rate of photosynthesis at point A on the graph in Figure 8.12b (page 157).

8 List the adaptations that (a) *Sargassum*, (b) seagrass and (c) *Fucus spiralis* possess to enable them to survive in their particular habitat.

The uses of seaweeds

Humans have harvested seaweed for thousands of years. Some of the reasons for harvesting and farming them are obvious, but there are many others that you would not guess.

- Food: seaweeds have been used as food by coastal communities for years in many countries such as Japan, Korea, Iceland and Wales. In Japan, over 20 species of seaweed are used as food and the red algae species *Porphyra* is dried to make sheets of nori, commonly used as the wrapping for sushi rolls. Nutritionally, seaweed is rich in protein, many vitamins and mineral salts, especially iodine, and is very low in fat.
- Gels and emulsifiers: seaweed is used as a source of three substances that are used to make solid gels and emulsifiers that hold food substances in suspension.
  - Alginate: this substance is extracted from seaweed and is used to form a gelatinous substance. It is used as an additive in many foods such as ice cream and has recently been used to make small gelatinous capsules that contain different flavours, like a synthetic caviar. Alginate gel is also used in burns plasters and firemen's clothing.
  - Agar: this is used to make vegetarian jellies and also the agar plates used frequently in microbiology to grow bacteria.
  - Carrageenan: this is used to make food with a range of different textures, including chocolate milk drinks and milk chocolate bars, because it helps to hold the chocolate in suspension.
- Cosmetics and herbal medicine: seaweed extracts are often found in moisturising skin creams and herbal remedies for a range of conditions including arthritis, tuberculosis and the common cold.

The demand for seaweed has led to the development of seaweed farms in many parts of the world, such as China and Japan. Seaweed is seeded onto nets or ropes, which are then tethered in an area of lagoon that is not shaded, ideally with a temperature between 25 °C and 30 °C. Figure 8.27 shows various depths at which seaweed might be planted. For environmental reasons, spraying fertiliser on the water is not recommended.

(a)   (b)   (c)

Figure 8.27. Depths at which seaweed might be planted.

Questions

1   Explain how the increased demand for seaweed gathered from natural sites could cause environmental problems.

2   Explain why seaweed grows best in the water depth shown in Figure 8.27b.

3   Using your knowledge of the compensation point, suggest why *Eucheumia* grown in very deep, warm water (30 °C) dies rapidly.

4   Explain why use of fertilisers is discouraged when growing seaweed.

Summary

- Photosynthesis is the method that many producers use to synthesise their own food using light, carbon dioxide and water.

- Photosynthesis requires pigments such as chlorophyll to absorb light energy and suitable levels of light, carbon dioxide and warmth.

- Producer organisms bring the energy into ocean food chains, usually from sunlight.

- Producer organisms act as a habitat and provide shelter for animals, often stabilising environments.

- Producer organisms produce oxygen, which is essential for the respiration of other marine organisms.

- Marine producers possess many adaptations that enable them to photosynthesise and survive in their particular habitat.

- In particular, they often have additional photosynthetic pigments, such as xanthophylls and phycobilins, that help them absorb additional wavelengths of light in depths where there is no red light.

Exam-style questions

1 **a** Explain how the depth and location of a body of ocean water affects the rate of photosynthesis of marine primary producers.   **[9]**

   b Describe and explain the potential consequences on the marine environment of allowing unrestricted run-off from fields into a river estuary.   **[6]**

   [Total mark: 15]

2 Kelp are important marine producers often found growing in coastal waters in dense forests. Figure 8.28 shows an individual kelp seaweed.

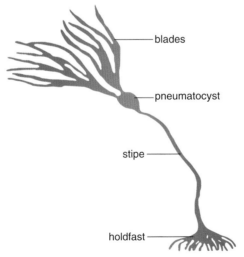

blades

pneumatocyst

stipe

holdfast

Figure 8.28. An individual kelp seaweed.

   a **i** Explain how the pneumatocysts ensure rapid growth of the kelp.   **[3]**

       ii Explain the role of the holdfast.   **[1]**

b In an area of sea off the coast of Scotland, sea urchins graze on kelp and are in turn eaten by sea otters.

i Draw this food chain. **[1]**

ii Fisheries and pollution have caused a reduction in the population of sea otters in some areas. Use the food chain above and your own knowledge to explain how this could affect future harvests of fish. **[4]**

[Total mark: 9]

3 An experiment was carried out into the effect of temperature on the rate of photosynthesis of a seaweed.

The seaweed was placed into a boiling tube containing saline with sodium hydrogencarbonate (a source of carbon dioxide gas) and the boiling tube placed into a water bath as shown in Figure 8.29.

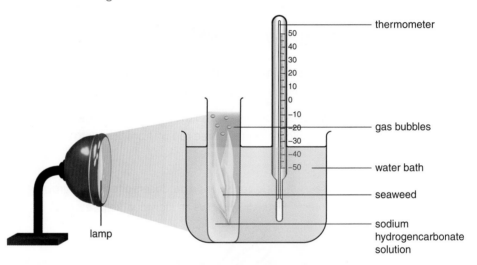

Figure 8.29. Apparatus to investigate the effect of temperature on photosynthesis of seaweed.

The temperature of the water bath was set at 5 °C and a lamp was placed 5 cm away from the beaker. The seaweed was left for 5 min. The seaweed was seen to produce bubbles of gas. The number of bubbles of gas was counted for 5 min.

This was repeated for different temperatures at intervals of 5 °C up to and including 45 °C.

a State how the composition of gases in the bubbles differs from atmospheric air. **[2]**

The results of the experiment are shown as a graph in Figure 8.30.

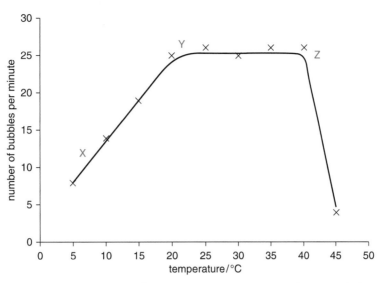

Figure 8.30. The effects of increasing temperature on the rate of photosynthesis of seaweed.

b **i** Suggest what factor may limit the rate of photosynthesis between X and Y on the graph. Explain your reasoning. **[2]**

  ii Suggest what factor may limit the rate of photosynthesis between Y and Z on the graph. Explain your reasoning. **[2]**

  iii Sketch a graph like the figure above to predict the effect of increasing temperature at a lower light intensity. **[2]**

  iv Explain the change in rate of photosynthesis between 40 and 45 °C. **[2]**

c It has been suggested that seaweed could be farmed in an intensive system using artificial lights and heaters. Suggest and explain the optimal temperature that a seaweed farmer would use based on the light intensity used in this experiment. **[2]**

[Total mark: 12]

4 **a** Complete the balanced chemical equation for photosynthesis:

$$\underline{\hspace{2cm}} + 6\,H_2O \longrightarrow \underline{\hspace{2cm}} + 6\,O_2$$ **[2]**

Sargassum is a marine producer that is found floating on the surface of the oceans and can travel many miles across deep ocean. A piece of *Sargassum natans* is shown in Figure 8.31.

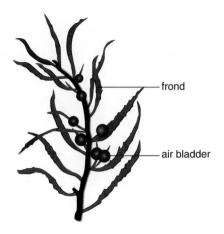

Figure 8.31. *Sargassum natans* showing air bladders.

b **i** Explain how *Sargassum natans* is adapted to maximise its productivity. **[3]**

ii Thick mats of *Sargassum natans* are found on the surface of the Sargasso Sea where it promotes biodiversity. Explain why many other species are dependent on *Sargassum natans*. **[5]**

[Total mark: 11]

Marine algal blooms and red tides: natural causes, pollution and global warming

Algal blooms are rapid, extensive growths of phytoplankton and are common events that occur in the world's seas and oceans. Some of these blooms are so large that they become visible from space. There are many causes: some are natural, seasonal events, while others may be the result of human interference.

A harmful algal bloom (HAB) is an algal bloom that has a negative impact on other organisms, often because of the production of toxins. HABs have been known to cause harmful effects on several species, but in particular marine mammals, turtles, sea birds and predatory fish. In the spring of 2004, at least 107 bottlenose dolphins died off the coast of Florida because they had ingested contaminated menhaden fish with high levels of an algal toxin called brevetoxin. This toxin is produced by the dinoflagellate *Karenia brevis*, which frequently causes 'red tides' in the Gulf of Mexico. Manatees have also been killed as a result of consuming seagrass contaminated with brevetoxin.

Examples of common harmful effects of HABs include:

- the production of neurotoxins killing fish, sea birds, sea turtles and marine mammals
- human illness or death via consumption of seafood contaminated by algal toxins (see Table 8.4)
- suffocation of organisms with gills because of blockage with algae
- death of organisms because of the loss of oxygen after decomposition of dead algae.

condition	symptoms in humans	toxins	affected organisms	some causative algae
amnesic shellfish poisoning	abdominal cramps and diarrhoea, neurological symptoms including dizziness, short-term memory loss, respiratory difficulty and coma	domoic acid	scallops, mussels, some edible crab species	*Pseudo-nitzschia pungens*
ciguatera fish poisoning	diarrhoea, vomiting and abdominal pain, muscular aches, dizziness, sweating, numbness and tingling of the mouth and digits, paralysis and death	ciguatoxin, maitotoxin	grouper, snapper, barracuda, mackerel	*Gambierdiscus toxicus*
diarrhetic shellfish poisoning	diarrhoea, nausea, vomiting, abdominal cramps and chills, rarely fatal	okadaic acid	oysters, mussels, scallops	*Dinophysis* spp.
neurotoxin shellfish poisoning	diarrhoea, dizziness, aches, breathing difficulties	brevetoxins	shellfish, manatees, dolphins, sealions	*Karenia brevis*
paralytic shellfish poisoning	tingling, numbness and drowsiness, fever, rash and staggering	saxitoxins	shellfish, salmon, whales, menhaden, sea otters, sea birds	*Alexandrium* spp.
cyanobacteria poisoning	rashes, allergies, liver disease, effects on nervous system, possible link to neurodegenerative disease	cyanotoxins (including BMAA)	predatory fish, birds, otters	*Lyngbya* spp.

Table 8.4. Some of the effects of algal toxins.

The Gulf of Maine often experiences blooms of the dinoflagellate *Alexandrium fundyense*, an organism that produces saxitoxin, the neurotoxin responsible for paralytic shellfish poisoning. Seasonal blooms of *Pseudo-nitzschia*, a diatom known to produce domoic acid, the neurotoxin responsible for amnesic shellfish poisoning, occurs around California's Pacific coast. Many blooms of cyanobacteria have been recorded, along with poisonings of animals and humans eating shellfish that have accumulated the associated cyanotoxins. One cyanotoxin, BMAA (an altered amino acid), is a powerful neurotoxin and research is now being carried out to determine if it is an environmental cause of some human neurodegenerative conditions such as Parkinson's and Alzheimer's diseases. Because of their negative economic and health impacts, HABs are often carefully monitored by organisations such as the National Oceanic and Atmospheric Administration (NOAA). The NOAA uses weather conditions and known seasonal changes together with known human pollution events to predict the formation of algal blooms, so that measures such as the banning of shellfish fishing can be put into place. Research on preventing HABs and how to clear them quickly is also carried out. In the Gulf of Mexico, NOAA's HAB Forecasting System uses satellite imagery, information about water conditions gathered by weather buoys, and observations from fieldworkers to map blooms and predict how and when they will spread.

Causes of HABs

Some HABs are caused by natural events such as the sudden upwelling of nutrients because of a change in water currents or water temperatures. HABs in the Gulf of Mexico have been reported since the time of early explorers, suggesting they are a natural phenomenon. The growth of marine phytoplankton is generally limited by the availability of nitrates and phosphates. Natural HABs are often predictable seasonal occurrences resulting from coastal upwelling, a natural result of the movement of certain ocean currents. Other factors, such as iron-rich dust influx from large desert areas like the Sahara, are thought to play a role in causing HABs. Some algal blooms on the Pacific coast have been linked to natural occurrences of large-scale climatic oscillations such as El Niño events. The increased frequency of HABs in some parts of the world has, however, been linked with increased nutrient release as a result of human activities. Coastal water pollution caused by agricultural run-off from rivers and increases in seawater temperature have also been suggested as possible contributing factors to HABs.

Some specific examples of HABs are given below.

- *Lingulodinium polyedrum* naturally produces brilliant displays of bioluminescence in warm coastal waters. They have been seen in southern California regularly since at least 1901.
- In 1972, a red tide was caused in New England by a toxic dinoflagellate, *Alexandrium (Gonyaulax) tamarense*.
- The largest algal bloom on record was the 1991 Darling River cyanobacterial bloom in Australia, which affected over 1000 km of the Barwon and Darling Rivers.
- In May 2005, a major HAB led to the temporary suspension of fishing for shellfish in Maine and Massachusetts, leading to a big loss in revenue and also affecting the tourist trade.
- In 2009, Brittany, France, experienced recurring algal blooms caused by the high amounts of fertiliser released into the sea as a result of intensive pig farming. This even caused lethal gas emissions that led to one case of human unconsciousness and three animal deaths.
- In 2010, a major phytoplanktonic bloom occurred in the North Atlantic due to release of iron in ash from the eruption of an Icelandic volcano.
- In 2013, over 19 000 tonnes of sea lettuce algae was removed from beaches around Qingdao in China. The bloom was the size of Connecticut and ended up costing more than $100 million in cleaning costs and loss of fish as a result of suffocation by oxygen loss.
- In 2014, *Myrionecta rubra* caused a major HAB on the south-eastern coast of Brazil.
- In 2014, blue-green algae caused a bloom in the western basin of Lake Erie, poisoning the Toledo, Ohio, water system.

Questions

1 Explain why an algal bloom of *Karenia brevis* led to the death of dolphins and manatees in Florida.
2 Suggest how HABs can lead to reduced oxygen in water resulting in the death of fish.
3 Explain why government agencies will often ban fishing of shellfish when algal blooms are sighted. Also explain the short- and long-term effects of algal blooms on the fishing industry.
4 Explain how farming practices could lead to HABs in marine environments.
5 Using your knowledge of limiting factors, explain why increased atmospheric carbon dioxide could cause an increase in the frequency of HABs.

Chapter 9
Aspects of marine animal physiology

Learning outcomes

By the end of this chapter, you should be able to:

- explain the role of respiration in releasing energy
- explain how organisms need to be able to access the raw materials needed for respiration, and remove the waste products of respiration
- explain how the size and shape of an organism relates to the surface area to volume ratio
- discuss the need for larger and more active animals to have specialised transport systems and gaseous exchange surfaces
- describe the adaptations of marine animals for living in an environment with lower, changing concentrations of oxygen
- describe different methods of gaseous exchange used by marine organisms
- demonstrate the difference in water and ion content between seawater and the body fluids of marine organisms
- describe the process of osmoregulation and explain the terms osmoconformer and euryhaline
- apply what you have learnt to new, unfamiliar contexts.

9.1 A variable environment

The marine environment is a stable environment but that does not mean that it never changes. Temperature, oxygen concentration and salinity are three factors that can vary between different areas of water and over time. This means these factors affect the organisms that live there. The demand for oxygen by each organism also depends on its activity. It is important that these animals are adapted to survive fluctuations in external factors and changes in their own demands for factors such as oxygen in order to survive. This chapter will look at how organisms are adapted to maximise their gaseous exchange and survive different salinities. In a world that may be undergoing some degree of global warming, many physical properties of the marine environment may change and bring new challenges to the organisms that live there.

9.2 Respiration

Respiration is the release of energy from organic molecules. It occurs in every living cell of an organism and is a fundamental property of life. There are two main types of respiration: **aerobic respiration** and **anaerobic respiration**.

> **KEY TERMS**
>
> **Aerobic respiration:** the release of energy from glucose or another organic substrate in the presence of oxygen; the waste products are carbon dioxide and water
>
> **Anaerobic respiration:** the release of energy from glucose or another organic substrate in the absence of oxygen; animals produce lactate as a waste product while plants and fungi produce ethanol and carbon dioxide

Aerobic respiration

During aerobic respiration, energy is released from glucose by oxidation, producing carbon dioxide and water as waste products. Aerobic means that the process uses oxygen. It is the complete combustion of glucose, and the chemical and word equations for this are:

$$C_6H_{12}O_6 + 6\,O_2 \rightarrow 6CO_2 + 6\,H_2O$$

Glucose + oxygen → carbon dioxide + water

The energy that is released is used to form a key, very important molecule called adenosine triphosphate (ATP), which is shown in Figure 9.1.

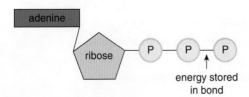

Figure 9.1. The structure of ATP.

An ATP molecule is made up of three main parts:

- a nitrogenous base called adenine, which is also found in DNA and RNA
- a carbohydrate sugar called ribose
- three phosphate groups.

> **KEY TERM**
>
> **Active transport:** the movement of particles (or molecules) from a lower concentration to a higher concentration (against a concentration gradient); it requires additional energy in the form of ATP and the use of membrane protein pumps on the surface of cells

Energy is 'stored' in the bonds between the phosphate groups, in particular between the second and third phosphates, as shown in Figure 9.2. When a cell carries out a process that needs energy, such as muscle contraction or **active transport**, ATP molecules are used. The bond between the second and third phosphates is broken, releasing energy that is then used to power the process. What remains is a molecule with two phosphates called adenosine diphosphate (ADP) and a free phosphate. To reform the ADP, cells respire to release energy from glucose and then use this energy to add the phosphate back onto the ADP, as shown in Figure 9.2.

The levels of ATP in a cell hardly change even if a cell is more or less active. This means that the faster a cell is using up ATP, for example a muscle cell in a fish, the faster the cell must respire to regenerate the ATP. Aerobic respiration is an efficient process, releasing enough energy from one molecule of glucose to produce up to 38 molecules of ATP (although this does depend on the cell type).

In active animals, it is essential to supply oxygen and glucose to the cells as quickly as possible and to remove

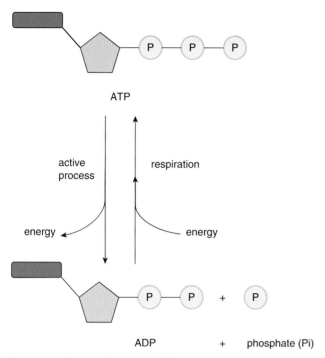

Figure 9.2. The production and breakdown of ATP.

one of the waste products of respiration, carbon dioxide. It is also important that the temperature of an organism is optimal, as respiration is affected by temperature. Like photosynthesis, the process of respiration is a series of chemical reactions that are brought about by enzymes. As the temperature increases, the rate of respiration increases because molecules collide with each other and enzymes more frequently. If the temperature rises too high, enzymes denature and the rate of respiration falls rapidly, as shown in Figure 9.3.

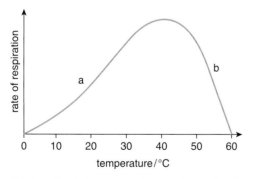

Figure 9.3. The effect of temperature on the rate of respiration. (a) As the temperature increases, the rate of respiration increases as molecules and enzymes collide more frequently. (b) As the temperature continues to increase, the rate of respiration falls steeply as the enzymes denature.

Anaerobic respiration

Cells can continue to respire in the absence of oxygen using a process called anaerobic respiration. This is the incomplete combustion of glucose and only generates two molecules of ATP from one molecule of glucose. The products are different in animals, plants and fungi (Figure 9.4).

In animals, glucose is first broken down into a carbohydrate called pyruvate, which is then converted into lactate, also known as lactic acid. Lactic acid changes the pH of cells and, as a result, other cell processes eventually begin to stop. The lactic acid is removed from the cells and reconverted back into glucose.

In plants and fungi, the glucose is again broken down into pyruvate, but this is then converted to ethanol and carbon dioxide.

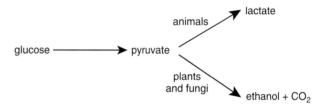

Figure 9.4. Summary of anaerobic respiration in different organisms.

The first stage of aerobic respiration is also the breakdown of glucose into pyruvate, and this occurs in the cytoplasm of cells. If oxygen is present, the pyruvate moves into cell organelles called mitochondria, which complete aerobic respiration. If oxygen is absent, the pyruvate is converted into lactate or ethanol and carbon dioxide in the cytoplasm. Cells that are very active and have a high energy demand, such as the red muscle cells of tuna, have many mitochondria to produce large amounts of ATP.

175

SELF-ASSESSMENT QUESTIONS

1 Draw up a table comparing aerobic and anaerobic respiration.

2 Explain why cold-blooded marine organisms tend to be less active in winter.

9.3 Gaseous exchange

Aerobic respiration requires organisms to obtain a supply of oxygen from the water and remove the waste carbon dioxide produced. This is traditionally known as gaseous exchange (but is also now often called simply gas exchange) and it occurs by the process of **diffusion**.

> **KEY TERM**
>
> **Diffusion:** the random movement of particles (or molecules) from a higher concentration to a lower concentration (down a concentration gradient); it is a passive process, not requiring the input of energy

Diffusion

Molecules are constantly moving in random directions. The energy of movement that they possess is known as kinetic energy. To understand diffusion, it helps if you look at a specific example (Figure 9.5). There is an uneven concentration of a molecule between two places, A and B. There is a concentration gradient between A and B, with a higher concentration in area A.

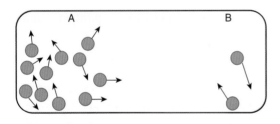

direction of net diffusion

Figure 9.5. Net diffusion of particles from a high concentration to a low concentration. Particles move in random directions.

Because the molecules are all constantly moving in different directions, some of them will move from A to B. Because there are more molecules in area A, there is a higher probability that more of them will move from A to B than from B to A. There is a net diffusion of molecules from A to B. Eventually, the concentration in area A decreases and the concentration in B increases until the two areas are equal. When the two areas are equal, physical diffusion does not actually stop as the molecules are still moving.

The rate of movement in both directions is approximately equal so that the net rate of diffusion is zero (Figure 9.6).

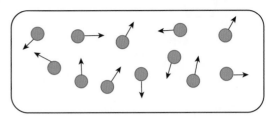

Figure 9.6. Particles are evenly spread and there is equal movement in both directions.

Diffusion is a passive process, requiring no additional input of energy, and is defined as the 'random net movement of particles from a higher concentration to a lower concentration'. It is a very important process by which many substances enter and leave the bodies and cells of organisms. The diffusion of gases in and out of cells and other tissues is affected by several factors, including:

* temperature

* concentration gradient

* distance moved

* surface area of exchange surface.

Temperature

Moving particles possess kinetic energy. As temperature rises, the kinetic energy of the particles rises so the particles move faster. If particles are moving faster, diffusion is faster.

Concentration gradient

A concentration gradient is the difference in concentration of a substance between two places, such as the difference in oxygen concentration between water and blood. The steeper or higher the gradient, the faster the rate of diffusion.

When cells are respiring, it is important to keep a higher concentration of oxygen outside the cells than inside. Respiration uses up the oxygen inside the cells rapidly, maintaining a low concentration inside. The result of this is that the oxygen concentration inside is kept lower than in the fluids outside the cells. There is always a difference in concentration between the inside and outside of the cell, so that oxygen diffuses into the cell. Carbon dioxide is being constantly manufactured inside the cell and is removed outside: the direction of the carbon dioxide gradient is the opposite of oxygen, ensuring a constant net diffusion out of the cell.

The maintenance of concentration gradients for gaseous exchange between blood and water is essential. Maintaining gradients is very important if diffusion is to be rapid, so organisms have evolved transport systems and ventilation movements to ensure delivery and removal of gases.

Marine organisms keep the concentration of oxygen in water higher than inside their blood by both moving the blood and by ventilation movements. Moving the blood brings fresh blood with a low oxygen concentration, and the ventilation movement brings fresh water with a high oxygen concentration.

Diffusion distance

To ensure rapid diffusion, the distance that the gases travel must be as small as possible. Gaseous exchange systems such as gills generally have very thin walls through which gases can diffuse rapidly.

Surface area

Most gaseous exchange organs, such as gills and lungs, have very large surface areas. If a surface area is large, the rate of gaseous exchange is high.

Gaseous exchange in marine organisms

Marine organisms have evolved a range of methods to ensure efficient gaseous exchange that take into account all the factors that affect rates of diffusion and the properties of water.

Water as a gaseous exchange medium

Carrying out gaseous exchange in water is more demanding than in air. The oxygen concentration in water is around 40 times lower than in the air, so gaseous exchange organs have to be highly efficient. The oxygen concentration is also highly variable and affected by both temperature and salinity, as shown in Figure 9.7. The higher the temperature and salinity, the lower the concentration of dissolved oxygen. Water is much denser and more viscous than air, so that moving it through the body of an organism requires more effort. This means that organs such as gills have an inlet and outlet aperture, whereas lungs require only one aperture through which air is breathed in and out.

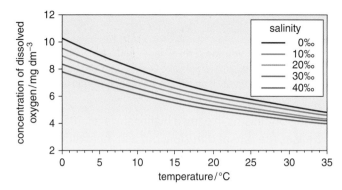

Figure 9.7. The effect of increasing temperature and salinity on the concentration of dissolved oxygen.

3   Explain why rapid respiration in a muscle cell would increase the rate of diffusion of oxygen from the blood into the cell and carbon dioxide out of the cell into the blood.

4   Global warming could lead to an increase in sea temperature and ice cap melting. Suggest and explain how this could affect the dissolved oxygen content of seawater.

Size and shape of marine organisms and gaseous exchange

In order to maximise gaseous exchange, organisms need to have a large surface area. As the size of organisms increases, both the surface area and volume increase, but not in a proportional, linear relationship. If you take a cube and increase the length of each side, the increase in volume is proportionally bigger than the increase in surface area. This is shown in Figure 9.8, where it is clear that the increasing size of the cube results in a much steeper increase in volume than surface area.

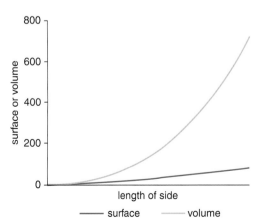

Figure 9.8. Effect of increasing the side length of a cube on the volume and surface area.

> **KEY TERM**
>
> **Surface area : volume ratio** an index that gives a relative measure of both surface area and volume; exchange organs generally have a very high surface area : volume ratio

In living organisms, having a higher surface area increases the rate of diffusion, but a higher volume tends to reduce the rate of diffusion as the distance to the centre of the organism increases. Larger organisms also have more cells so have a higher demand for oxygen. An index that takes into account both the surface area and volume of an organism is called the **surface area: volume ratio** and is calculated using the equation:

$$\text{surface area : volume ratio} = \frac{\text{surface area}}{\text{volume}}$$

- A higher surface area : volume ratio increases the rate of diffusion.

- A lower surface area : volume ratio decreases the rate of diffusion.

As spherical or cubic shapes increase in size, the surface area : volume ratio decreases (Figure 9.9). This means that the rates of diffusion of substances through the surface is lower. Protrusions from the surface (such as the tentacles of sea anemones) help to increase the surface area. This increases the surface area : volume ratio, making diffusion faster.

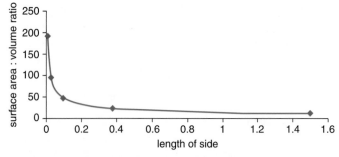

Figure 9.9. The effect of increasing side length of a cube on surface area : volume ratio.

The surface area : volume ratio of organisms affects their ability to carry out gaseous exchange. Very small organisms such as single-celled protozoa have high surface area : volume ratios so have a rapid rate of diffusion through their surface. They have no need for any specialised gaseous exchange organs as the surface area is sufficient for gaseous exchange and the diffusion distance is low. As the size of organisms increases, the surface area : volume ratio decreases and the surface of the organism is no longer sufficient for gaseous exchange. The distance from the outside of the organism to the centre over which gases would have to diffuse also becomes too great. Because of these problems, the majority of larger organisms have specialised gaseous exchange organs such as gills or lungs. Some larger organisms have shapes that increase the surface area and increase the surface area : volume ratio. Coral polyps and anemones have surface projections such as tentacles that increase the surface area : volume ratio.

The surface area : volume ratio is affected by both the overall size of an organism and its shape. More spherical organisms that minimise their surface area tend to have a low surface area : volume ratio, while those that are thinner with a very folded surface have a higher surface : volume ratio.

Circulatory systems

The use of specialised gaseous exchange organs brings with it the problem of how to transport gases. Circulatory systems evolved as a method of delivering oxygen to all tissues. In fish, blood that transports oxygen is pumped through a network of arteries, veins and capillaries by a heart. As in humans, the red blood cells of fish contain the protein hemoglobin, which binds reversibly to oxygen in the gills to form oxyhemoglobin. In areas such as muscles with low oxygen, the oxyhemoglobin releases the oxygen for respiration. The blood also transports dissolved carbon dioxide from the tissues to the gills.

oxyhemoglobin ⇌ hemoglobin + oxygen

gills   tissues

In a typical fish circulatory system such as that shown in Figure 9.10, blood travels in a particular route around the body.

- blood passes through muscles and other body tissues in capillaries, the smallest blood vessels, and releases oxygen and gains carbon dioxide

- blood is then returned to the heart in veins

- blood is then pumped out of the heart in arteries towards the gills

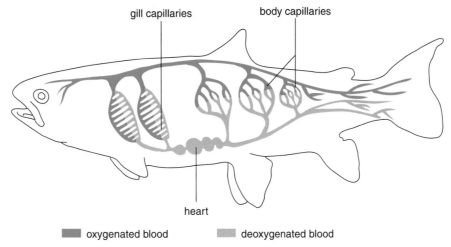

Figure 9.10. The circulatory system of a typical bony fish.

- as the blood passes through capillaries in the gills, it releases carbon dioxide into the water and gains oxygen

- blood leaves the gills in arteries and travels to the muscles in order to deliver oxygen and remove carbon dioxide.

Very active fish such as tuna require rapid respiration in the muscles, so blood is pumped quickly to the muscles. The circulatory system of these active fish is very efficient and maintains a high rate of blood flow.

Fick's Law and gaseous exchange organs

Gaseous exchange organs follow a rule know as Fick's Law. This states that the rate of diffusion of a substance is proportional to the product of the surface area of the organ and the diffusion gradient divided by the diffusion distance.

$$\text{diffusion rate} \propto \frac{\text{surface area} \times \text{concentration gradient}}{\text{diffusion distance}}$$

Fick's Law enables us to predict the following common features of all gaseous exchange surfaces:

- a large surface area

- steep concentration gradients of oxygen / carbon dioxide

- short diffusion distances.

Specific examples of gaseous exchange methods

Coral polyps

Coral polyps do not possess specialised gaseous exchange organs and all gaseous exchange takes place directly across the body surface by diffusion. The surface area : volume ratio of the polyp is sufficient because it has a large number of tentacles (Figure 9.11) and the thickness of the coral polyp epidermis is thin so that diffusion is rapid. Sometimes polyps move their tentacles to generate water currents refreshing the water around the polyp. This movement brings more oxygenated water into contact with the tentacles and maintains the diffusion gradients between the inside of the polyp and the water. Some coral polyps are able to pump oxygenated fluids between each other to ensure an even distribution of oxygen.

Fish gills

Bony fish such as groupers and tuna breathe by taking in water through the mouth, passing it over the gills and then forcing it out through gill openings (Figure 9.12). The gills are covered by a plate called an operculum that can open and close. On either side of the head are four pairs of gill arches, which are bony structures supporting the gills. The gills themselves are made up of many filaments, on the surfaces of which are folds called lamellae that are arranged at a 90° angle to the filaments. The filaments and lamellae provide a very large surface area to maximise gaseous exchange. The lamellae are very thin and contain an extensive capillary network. Blood circulates through

179

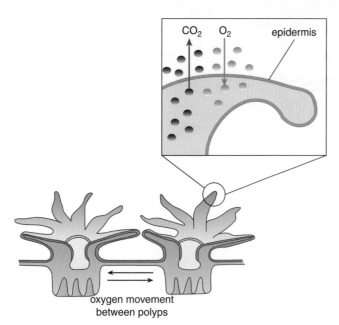

Figure 9.11. The structure of a coral polyp. The tentacles provide a large surface area and the epidermis is thin, reducing the diffusion path. Oxygen can move between polyps.

the capillary network and red blood cells pass through the capillaries very close to the external water, minimising the diffusion path. Pillar cells are found within the secondary lamellae, which help to slow the blood flow and press red blood cells to the surface of the lamella. Deoxygenated blood enters the gills through afferent arterioles and the oxygenated blood leaves through efferent arterioles to then travel to body tissues.

Fish of different species and ages have different gill surface areas according to their oxygen demand. Fast, active swimmers, such as tuna, mackerel and swordfish, have a high oxygen demand (and need to remove carbon dioxide rapidly) because the rate of respiration in the muscles is high. These fish have very large gill surface areas. Less active fish, such as sole and plaice, which often stay stationary for long periods of time, tend to have smaller gill surface areas. These fish move in shorts bursts in order to evade predators or catch food. The energy for this is often obtained by anaerobic respiration so the oxygen demand is lower.

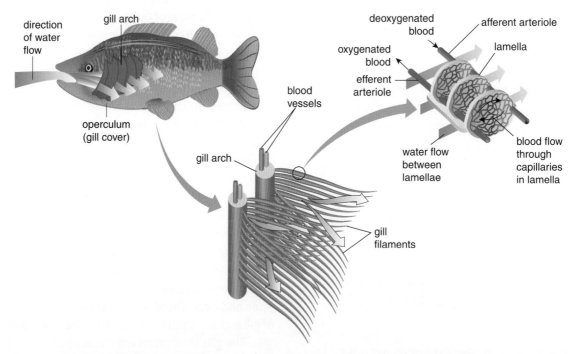

Figure 9.12. The gill structure of bony fish showing filaments, lamellae and direction of water flow.

Counter-current exchanger

Blood flows through the capillaries in the secondary lamellae in the opposite direction to the water. This arrangement in known as a counter-current mechanism. It ensures that gaseous exchange is highly efficient because the diffusion gradient is maintained across the whole gill surface.

If blood and water flow in the same direction, in a concurrent flow (Figure 9.13a), the diffusion gradient occurs until an equilibrium point when the concentration of oxygen in the blood and water is equal. In a counter-current flow (Figure 9.13b), the diffusion gradient is maintained along the full length of the gill so that diffusion is more efficient. In this way, oxygen diffuses into the blood along the whole length of the gill while carbon dioxide diffuses out into the water along the whole length of the gill.

Ventilation movements

In order to maintain the diffusion gradients of oxygen and carbon dioxide, water is constantly passed over the gills. Two different processes are used by fish to ventilate the gills: **ram ventilation** and **pumped ventilation** (Table 9.1).

ram ventilation	pumped ventilation
non-active pumping, saving energy	active pumping, using energy
can only occur when swimming	can occur during swimming and resting

Table 9.1. Differences between ram and pumped ventilation.

Ram ventilation

Fast-swimming fish such as tuna and sharks swim with an open mouth. As they swim, water is forced through the mouth, over the gills and out through the operculum or gill slits. There is no muscle contraction required by the muscles of the mouth and all the force for moving the water is generated by the forward motion of the fish. As no extra effort is made in pumping the water over the gills, energy is saved. One drawback is that fish that only use ram ventilation must keep swimming constantly in order to maintain a constant flow of water over the gills. Some fish species can switch back and forth between ram and pumped ventilation depending on their speed of movement. As fish swim faster, using more energy in their muscles, the rate of water flow over the gills automatically increases so that the rate of gaseous exchange increases. The rapid flow of water generated by high-speed swimming could potentially damage the delicate gill structures. In order to prevent this damage, the gill arches are often reinforced or fused together in tuna species.

> **KEY TERMS**
>
> **Ram ventilation:** ventilation of gills by swimming with the mouth open so that a constant flow of water passes through the mouth and over the gills; it only occurs when a fish is swimming
>
> **Pumped ventilation:** ventilation of gills by the muscle action of the mouth pumping water over the gills; it can occur when the fish is stationary

Pumped ventilation

The majority of fish actively pump water over their gills. This means that even when a fish is stationary, there is a constant flow of water over the gills. Fish that use this method use the muscles of the buccal cavity (mouth region), which requires energy so can be energetically costly. The benefit of pumped ventilation, however, is that fish can continue to breathe when not moving so can remain in one place for extended periods of time. When the fish swim faster, the oxygen demand increases and the rate of pumping also increases.

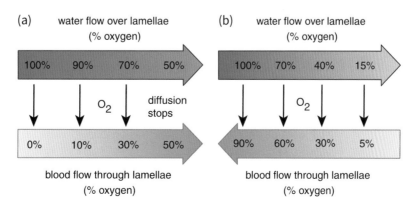

Figure 9.13. (a) A concurrent flow of blood and water and (b) a counter-current flow of blood and water.

When considering pumped ventilation, it is a good idea to remember:

- water always flows from an area of higher pressure to an area of lower pressure

- as the volume of a cavity increases, the pressure decreases, and vice versa.

Figure 9.14 shows the stages of water flow through the buccal cavity of a bony fish.

During inflow of water:

- the mouth opens

- the volume of the buccal cavity is increased by muscle contraction and relaxation

- this lowers the pressure inside the buccal cavity to below the external pressure

- water flows into the buccal cavity down a pressure gradient

- the operculum closes as water tries to flow back across the gills.

During outflow water over the gills:

- the mouth closes

- the volume of buccal cavity is reduced by muscle contraction and relaxation

- pressure inside the buccal cavity rises above the external pressure

- water flows over the gills and the operculum is forced open, allowing the outflow of water.

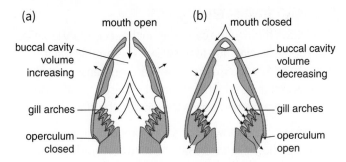

Figure 9.14. Movement of water across gills seen from above. (a) Mouth open, buccal cavity chamber increases in volume, water is drawn into the buccal cavity, operculum is closed; (b) Mouth closed, buccal cavity chamber reduces in volume, operculum opens and water flows over gills.

Gaseous exchange organs of different species all obey Fick's Law (Table 9.2).

SELF-ASSESSMENT QUESTIONS

5   Draw up a table to show the different methods of gaseous exchange used by coral polyps, tuna and grouper, and the advantages and disadvantages of each method.

6   Explain the following.

   a   Highly active fish die more frequently then less active ones when the temperature of the water rises very high.

   b   Gill parasites that eat away parts of the gill lamellae reduce the growth rate of farmed salmon.

   c   If fish are removed from water, they suffocate as the gill lamellae collapse and stick together.

species	gaseous exchange surface	large surface area	short diffusion path	maintenance of diffusion gradient
coral polyp	body surface	large numbers of tentacles	thin epidermis on body surface	none, although tentacles may move
grouper	gill	gill filaments and secondary lamellae	thin epidermis on gills	blood flow through capillaries, pumped ventilation
tuna	gill	gill filaments and secondary lamellae	thin epidermis on gills	blood flow through capillaries, ram ventilation
shark	gill	gill filaments and secondary lamellae	thin epidermis on gills	blood flow through capillaries, ram ventilation

Table 9.2. Summary of how gaseous exchange organs of different species obey Fick's Law.

PRACTICAL ACTIVITY 9.1

Investigating the effect of surface area : volume ratio on the rate of diffusion

Apparatus

- Pink agar blocks
- Scalpel
- Five test tubes
- Stop clock
- Test tube rack
- 2 mol dm^{-3} hydrochloric acid

Method

- Using the scalpel, cut a block of agar of dimensions 20 mm × 10 mm × 10 mm as shown in Figure 9.15. Cut this block in half and reserve one half. Take the other half and cut this in half as shown in Figure 9.15, again reserving one half. Repeat this procedure as shown in Figure 9.15 so that five agar blocks are produced.

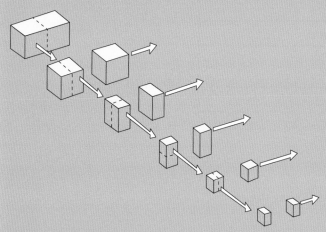

Figure 9.15. Flow chart for cutting agar blocks.

- Fill each test tube with 5 cm^3 2 mol dm^{-3} hydrochloric acid.
- Copy Table 9.3.
- Place the largest block into a test tube and record the time taken for the agar block to change from pink to orange. Repeat this with all the blocks.
- To ensure reliability, the experiment should be repeated two more times using fresh agar blocks.
- Record all the data in the table and calculate the mean time taken for each size of block to change colour.

Preparation

To prepare agar, carry out the following.

- Stir 10 g agar crystals into 100 cm^3 tap water and heat to boiling point.
- Add 5 cm^3 1% cresol red solution and 2 cm^3 bench (2 mol dm^{-3}) ammonium hydroxide.
- Pour the agar to a depth of 10 mm in plastic Petri dishes lightly smeared with a little oil, and when cool cut into blocks of 20 mm × 10 mm × 10 mm.

Risk assessment

- Care should be taken when heating the agar to dissolve it.
- Safety glasses should be worn throughout.
- Hydrochloric acid and ammonium hydroxide are both corrosive. Spills should be wiped up immediately and any splashes on skin washed off.
- Cresol red is an irritant in eyes and on skin, and in the event of contact with eye or skin should be washed off.
- Care should be taken when using a scalpel.

dimensions / mm	surface area / mm²	volume / mm³	surface area : volume ratio	time taken for block to change colour / s			
				1	2	3	mean
10 × 10 × 10	600	1000	0.6				
10 × 10 × 5	400	500	0.8				
10 × 5 × 5	250	250	1.0				
5 × 5 × 5	150	125	1.2				
5 × 5 × 2.5	100	62.5	1.6				

Table 9.3. Results table for the effect of cube size on diffusion rate.

→

Results and data analysis

- Calculate the surface areas, volumes and surface area : volume ratios of each block and record them in the table.
- Plot a graph of surface area : volume ratio against time taken for block to change colour.

Conclusions

1   Describe the effect of increasing surface area : volume ratio on the time taken for the acid to diffuse into the blocks. State whether or not the relationship is linear.

2   Relate the results of the experiment to the need for specialised exchange organs in larger organisms.

Maths skills

Surface area : volume ratios and rearranging formulae

The shape and size of organisms affects their physiology. The surface area of an organism is the area taken up by its entire surface or skin. There are different formulae used to calculate the surface area of shapes (Table 9.4).

Shape	Formula for surface area
cube with side length a	$6a^2$
rectangular cuboid with side lengths of: w, l, h	$2(wl + hl + hw)$
cylinder with height, h, and radius of circular cross section, r	$2\pi r(r + h)$
sphere of radius, r	$4\pi r^2$

Table 9.4. Surface area formulae for different shapes.

Questions

1   Use the formulae above to calculate the surface areas of the following shapes:

   a   cube with side length 5 cm

   b   rectangular cuboid with dimensions of 6 cm × 6 cm × 12 cm

   c   rectangular cuboid with dimensions of 6 cm × 2 cm × 36 cm

   d   sphere with radius 8 cm

   e   cylinder with cross sectional diameter of 4 cm and height of 8 cm.

2   Chapter 8 explains how to calculate the volumes of these shapes. Calculate the volumes of each of the shapes (a) to (e) above. Comment on the difference in the surface area : volume ratios of the two rectangular cuboids.

3   Surface area : volume ratio is calculated by dividing the surface area by the volume. Use your answers to questions (1) and (2) to calculate the surface area : volume ratios for each shape.

It is often necessary to rearrange formulae.

For example, the formula for the surface area of a sphere is:

$$A = 4\pi r^2$$

If we want to find the radius, we can rearrange the formula so that:

$$r = \sqrt{(A/4\pi)}$$

So, the radius of a sphere with a surface area of 160 mm² is

$$r = \sqrt{(160/4\pi)}$$
$$= \sqrt{12.74}$$
$$= \textbf{3.57 mm}$$

4 a Calculate the height of a cylinder with a radius of 3 mm and a total surface area of 250 mm².

   b Determine the radius of a sphere with surface area of 400 cm².

5 Some problems require several steps in order to solve them:

   A coral polyp has 32 cylindrical tentacles each with a radius of 2 mm and length of 10 mm.

   a Calculate the total surface area of the tentacles.

   The polyp was placed into 0.1 dm³ seawater with an oxygen concentration of 9.0 mg dm⁻³. After two hours, the oxygen concentration in the water had fallen to 7.5 mg dm⁻³.

   b Calculate the total mass of oxygen taken up by the coral over the two-hour period.

   c Calculate the rate of oxygen diffusion per mm² polyp membrane in mg mm⁻² hr⁻¹.

9.4 The regulation of salinity

Different bodies of water often have different salinities that may vary both over short and long periods of time. For example, the Red Sea has a very high salinity and the salinity of the Baltic Sea is very low. Estuaries and areas near the outflow of rivers often have brackish water that has a low salinity. In order to survive in media that can have a range of salinities, organisms must possess physiological adaptations.

KEY TERMS

Osmosis: the movement of water from a higher water potential (more dilute solution) to a lower water potential (higher concentration of solute) across a selectively permeable membrane

Water potential: a measure of the potential energy of water in a solution and thus the tendency of water to move from one place to another; the more solute that is dissolved in a solution, the lower the water potential

Osmosis

Osmosis is a process that is of vital importance to all organisms. It is defined as the net movement of water molecules from a region of higher **water potential** to a region of lower water potential across a selectively permeable membrane.

Water potential is a measure of the potential energy of the water molecules in a solution. The more water molecules in a solution, the higher the water potential. If a solute such as salt is dissolved in the water, the proportion of water molecules in the solution decreases so the water potential falls.

In simple terms, the higher the concentration of solutes, such as salt in a solution, the lower the water potential. The highest water potential possible is that of pure water.

If you place two different salt solutions next to each other, separated by a selectively permeable membrane (Figure 9.16), water molecules will move from the weaker, more dilute solution to the more concentrated one.

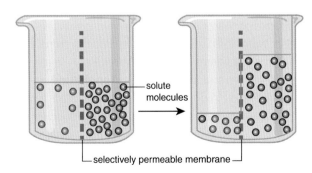

Figure 9.16. Movement of water by osmosis from a dilute solution to a concentrated one.

185

Certain terms are used to describe solutions that have higher or lower water potentials compared with the cells and body fluids of an organism.

- Hypertonic solutions have a lower water potential. They have a higher concentration of solutes and will tend to draw water out of cells.

- Isotonic solutions have a water potential that is equal to the cells. They have an equal concentration of solutes and will result in no net movement of water.

- Hypotonic solutions have a higher water potential. They have a lower concentration of solutes and will tend to pass water into cells.

In living organisms, changing the salt concentration around cells can result in water entering cells or leaving them, causing extensive damage. Organisms such as plants and algae possess cell walls so, if water passes into the cells, the cells will not burst. Animal cells, however, do not possess cell walls and if too much water passes into them, they will burst.

SELF-ASSESSMENT QUESTIONS

7 Rearrange the following in order of increasing water potential: pure water, 2 mol dm^{-3} sodium chloride solution, 1.5 mol dm^{-3} sodium chloride solution, 0.2 mol dm^{-3} sodium chloride solution.

8 Use your knowledge of osmosis to explain why:

   a placing limp vegetables into pure water can 'firm them up'

   b sprinkling sugar on the surface of fruit produces a syrup

   c covering fish with salt preserves it from decay.

Marine organisms usually live in an environment with high salinity and low water potential. This means that there is a danger of water loss from their bodies into the surrounding water. Some organisms are able to survive only in a narrow range of salinities and are classed as **stenohaline** species. Species such as salmon, which are able to tolerate a wide range of salinities, are classed as **euryhaline** species.

Osmoconformers

Osmoconformer organisms have an internal water potential of cells and body fluids that is equal to that of the surrounding water. This means that their fluids are isotonic to the water and there is no net gain or loss of water. The majority of osmoconformers are stenohaline invertebrates and are thus not resistant to major changes in external salinity.

Mussels are euryhaline osmoconformers and frequently live in estuarine areas where the salinity of the water may be very variable. They are able to survive there by using two methods.

- When salinity changes, mussels close their shells tightly to prevent the seawater coming into contact with their body tissue.

- They can increase and decrease the solute concentrations of their cells if the external salinity changes. The solute concentration is matched to the external water so that no net in- or out-flow of water occurs.

Despite some degree of control over **osmoregulation**, most mussel species tend to be restricted to a particular range of salinities. Some species are restricted to brackish waters of estuaries while others are restricted to the more saline waters of the sea.

 KEY TERMS

Stenohaline: description of organisms that are able to tolerate only a narrow range of salinities

Euryhaline: organisms, such as salmon, that are able to tolerate a wide range of salinities

Osmoconformer: organisms that have an ionic and salt concentration that is the same as the surrounding water

Osmoregulation: the process of regulating the internal water and ion content of an organism

Osmoregulator: organisms that regulate their internal salt and ion balance at a constant level, which may differ from the surrounding water

Osmoregulators

Osmoregulators maintain a constant internal osmotic pressure that may differ from the environment they are in. The majority of bony fish species are stenohaline osmoregulators that can only live in a narrow range of salinities. They actively maintain a particular salinity in their cells and body fluids.

Marine fish

In most seas and oceans, the water surrounding fish has a higher salinity (hypertonic) than the cells and body fluids. Water is drawn out of the body from the gills and skin by osmosis and salt diffuses into the body from the water. This constant loss of water could lead to dehydration, resulting in cell damage and death. In order to prevent excess water loss, marine bony fish carry out several processes.

- They constantly drink seawater to replace water that is lost by osmosis.

- Sodium and chloride ions are actively secreted by the gills. Specialised cells on the gill filaments have protein 'pumps' in their membranes that pump the ions into the water, which requires energy in the form of ATP.

- Magnesium and sulfate ions are actively secreted by the kidney into the urine.

- Reabsorption of water by the kidney produces a low volume of very concentrated urine.

These processes are summarised in Figure 9.17.

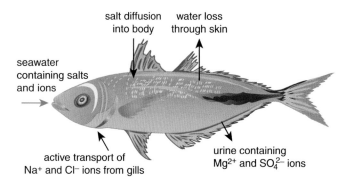

salt diffusion into body water loss through skin

seawater containing salts and ions

active transport of Na^+ and Cl^- ions from gills

urine containing Mg^{2+} and SO_4^{2-} ions

Figure 9.17. Osmoregulation by marine fish.

PRACTICAL ACTIVITY 9.2

Identification of the isotonic point of potato cells

Although not a marine organism, investigating osmosis in potato cells will help your understanding of how osmosis occurs.

Apparatus

- Six McCartney bottles with lids
- 250 cm³ 1 mol dm⁻³ sodium chloride stock solution
- one large potato
- scalpel
- balance

Method

- Use the scalpel to cut six equal rectangular cuboid pieces of potato with dimensions of 10 mm × 10 mm × 50 mm. Ensure that all are the same shape and that there is no peel on the sides.
- Label the McCartney bottles 0.0 mol dm⁻³, 0.2 mol dm⁻³, 0.4 mol dm⁻³, 0.6 mol dm⁻³, 0.8 mol dm⁻³ and 1.0 mol dm⁻³.
- Make up 25 cm³ sodium chloride solutions in each of the bottles as shown in Table 9.5.

Concentration of solution / mol dm⁻³	Volume of water / cm³	Volume of 1 mol dm⁻³ sodium chloride solution / cm³
0.0	25	0
0.2	20	5
0.4	15	10
0.6	10	15
0.8	5	20
1.0	25	0

Table 9.5. Making up the different concentrations of sodium chloride.

- Dry each of the potato pieces, weigh them and record the mass. Place one piece of potato into each bottle and place the lids on the bottles.
- Leave the potatoes for between 2 and 6 h.
- Remove the pieces of potato, dry them on tissue paper and weigh them.

→

Results and data analysis

- Copy Table 9.6, enter your results and carry out the calculations. To calculate the percentage change use the formula:

$$\text{percentage change} = \frac{(\text{finish mass} - \text{start mass})}{\text{start mass}} \times 100$$

concentration of sodium chloride / m	start mass of potato / g	finish mass of potato / g	finish mass – start mass / g	percentage change in mass / %
0.0				
0.2				
0.4				
0.6				
0.8				
1.0				

Table 9.6. Results table for effect of sodium chloride concentration on osmosis.

Some of the percentage changes will be positive and some negative.

- Plot a graph of the concentration of sodium chloride solution against percentage change in mass. Join the points with a ruler.

The axes will need to look like those in Figure 9.18.

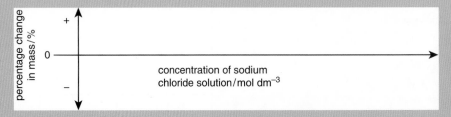

Figure 9.18. Axes with labels for showing your results.

Conclusions

1   Describe and explain the effect of increasing sodium chloride concentration on percentage change in mass of the potatoes.

2   Use the graph to predict the concentration of sodium chloride that is isotonic to the potato cell cytoplasm. Label on the graph the range of concentrations that are hypotonic and hypertonic compared with the potato cell cytoplasm.

3   Explain why the pieces of potato were dried before weighing them.

4   Suggest why lids are placed on the bottles.

Active transport

Active transport is the pumping of substances (often ions) across a membrane by living cells against a concentration gradient. It is carried out by specialised membrane proteins that use the energy in ATP to move the ions against the concentration gradient. Because it requires energy, it can only take place in living, respiring cells.

Fresh-water fish

Fish species that live in fresh water have the opposite problem to marine fish. Fresh water has a very low salinity and high water potential (hypotonic). Water constantly enters the body through the gills and skin by osmosis (Figure 9.19). In order to prevent excess water loss, fresh-water bony fish carry out several processes.

- They drink small amounts of water.

- The gills actively pump sodium and chloride ions into the blood and body fluid. Specialised cells have protein pumps that actively pump the ions from the external water to the internal body fluids. These pumps use ATP, similar to the pumps in marine fish.

- They produce large amounts of very dilute urine.

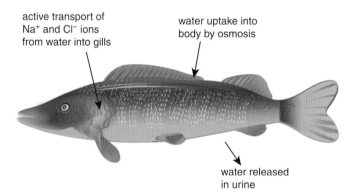

Figure 9.19. Osmoregulation in fresh-water fish.

Euryhaline fish

Euryhaline osmoregulatory species, such as salmon and eels, are able to live in a wide range of salinities, from the fresh water of rivers to the salt water of the oceans. They are able to change direction of ion pumping depending on the salinity of the surrounding water (Table 9.7).

When in salt water, the surrounding water is hypertonic to their body fluids. Salts are pumped out of the gills and they drink water to replace the water that has been lost by osmosis.

When in fresh water, the surrounding water is hypotonic to their body fluids. The ion pumps move the salts in the opposite direction, taking salts into the blood.

	salmon body fluid	ocean water	fresh water
solute concentration / %	1.0	3.5	<0.1

Table 9.7. Comparison of salinity in salmon body fluids, ocean water and fresh water.

SELF-ASSESSMENT QUESTIONS

9 Summarise the osmoregulatory mechanisms a salmon uses as it moves from river water to the sea.

10 Draw up a table to compare diffusion, osmosis and active transport (think about facts such as the direction of movement, the need for energy, the substances moved and the need for a membrane).

Red and white muscles in fish

Fish have two distinct muscles types, red muscle and white muscle. The distribution of the muscle types in a tuna is shown in Figure 9.20.

Figure 9.20. Cross-section through tuna showing muscle types.

The two muscle types have different functions and these different functions are reflected in their composition.

- Red muscle is for continuous swimming. The muscle is red because it contains large quantities of a red, oxygen-binding pigment called myoglobin. Myoglobin is very similar to hemoglobin, the oxygen-transporting molecule found in red blood cells. The muscle also has a high fat content, many mitochondria and a rich blood supply.

- White muscle is for rapid bursts of swimming such as catching prey by surprise or escaping predators. It can perform very strong contractions but can only be used for short periods of time. There is no myoglobin present, fewer mitochondria, a low fat content and fewer blood vessels.

Different fish species have different proportions of the two muscle types. Tuna and swordfish have a high proportion of red muscle, while less active fish such as plaice and cod have far more white muscle. In salmon, the proportions change at different stages in the life cycle. While in the open ocean, the proportion of red muscle is high. When the salmon begin their migration, there is a large increase in the proportion of white muscle.

Questions

1 Using your knowledge of anaerobic and aerobic respiration, explain the roles and structure of the two muscle types.

2 Explain why tuna have such a high proportion of red muscle.

3 Suggest why salmon alter the proportion of the two muscle types when beginning their migration into rivers.

Summary

- Marine organisms have evolved physiologies that enable them to survive in the ocean environment.

- Oxygen is essential for aerobic respiration, and gaseous exchange organs have evolved to maximise the oxygen obtained from the water.

- Salinity in the oceans is variable although often high, so there is a need to maintain internal water balance either through being an osmoconformer or an osmoregulator.

- Both oxygen levels and salinity vary in the world's oceans and seas and also change over time.

- Organisms have evolved and are still evolving to cope with the challenges of these variations.

- Human impact, with the possibility of climate change, agricultural pollution and the use of desalination plants, can affect the levels of oxygen and salt in the water.

- Whether or not organisms in our oceans and seas will cope the advent of greater changes remains to be seen.

Exam-style questions

1 **a** **i** Explain what are meant by the terms:

osmoregulator

osmoconformer

euryhaline. **[3]**

ii Describe how salmon maintain the water balance of their body fluids while swimming in salt water. **[3]**

b Figure 9.21 shows how the numbers of a mussel species and the salinity of the water change along a river, through the estuary and out into the sea.

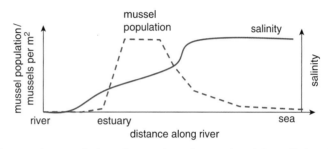

Figure 9.21. Changes in population of a species of mussel and the salinity of water along a riverbed into the sea.

i Describe the changes in the mussel population and the salinity of water as the distance increases. **[2]**

ii Suggest and explain the changes in mussel population. **[4]**

[Total mark: 12]

2 Tilapia are often grown in aquaculture systems. An experiment was carried out to investigate the effect of temperature on the respiration rate of male tilapia. A male tilapia was placed into a tank of salt water and the temperature set at 10 °C. An oxygen probe was placed into the water and the oxygen concentration of the water measured every 15 min for 3 h. This was repeated with a different male tilapia at a temperature of 20 °C. The results are shown in Table 9.8.

time / min	oxygen concentration of water at 10 °C / mg dm^{-3}	oxygen concentration of water at 20 °C / mg dm^{-3}
0	9.2	9.3
15	8.9	8.4
30	8.7	7.9
45	8.5	7.3
60	8.2	6.4
75	7.9	5.6
90	7.5	5.0

time / min	oxygen concentration of water at 10 °C / mg dm^{-3}	oxygen concentration of water at 20 °C / mg dm^{-3}
105	7.2	4.7
120	6.9	4.4
135	6.6	4.1
150	6.4	3.7
165	5.9	3.4
180	5.7	2.9

Table 9.8. Effect of temperature on oxygen uptake by male tilapia.

a **i** State two factors that should have been controlled in the experiment. **[2]**

ii Suggest how the reliability of the experiment could have been improved. **[1]**

iii Calculate the mean rate of oxygen decrease over the 3 h period for both temperatures in mg dm^{-3} h^{-1}. **[2]**

iv Describe and explain the effect of increasing temperature on the rate of oxygen consumption of the tilapia. **[3]**

Table 9.9 shows the effect of increasing temperature on concentration of dissolved oxygen in seawater.

temperature / °C	oxygen solubility / mg dm^{-3}
0	14.6
5	12.8
10	11.3
15	10.2
20	9.2
25	8.6
100	0.0

Table 9.9. Effect of temperature on oxygen concentration.

b Use Tables 9.8 and 9.9 and your own knowledge to explain why intensive aquaculture of tilapia in warmer countries requires the provision of additional oxygen. **[4]**

[Total mark: 12]

3 **a** **i** Complete the equation for aerobic respiration.

glucose + ... ⟶ .... + water **[1]**

ii Use your knowledge of the marine environment and respiration to explain why fish species that are found in deeper areas of the ocean tend to have low activity levels and swim with short rapid bursts. **[4]**

b **i** Explain why small single-celled organisms do not possess specialised gaseous exchange organs. **[3]**

Fick's Law states that diffusion rate is proportional to the product of concentration gradient and surface area divided by the diffusion distance.

$$\text{rate of diffusion} \propto \frac{\text{concentration gradient} \times \text{surface area}}{\text{diffusion distance}}$$

ii Use Fick's Law to explain how the gill system of the grouper is adapted to maximise gaseous exchange. **[3]**

[Total mark: 11]

4 **a** **i** Using named fish species as examples, compare the differences between pumped and ram ventilation. **[6]**

ii Some species of fish use pumped ventilation when swimming at low speeds but switch to ram ventilation when swimming at high speed. Explain why the ability to switch between the two methods of ventilation is advantageous. **[3]**

b During their life cycle, salmon live in both fresh and salt water. Use your knowledge of osmoregulation and osmosis to explain how salmon are able to live in both fresh and salt water. **[6]**

[Total mark: 15]

5 The Baltic Sea is a North European sea that is attached to the North Sea. It is almost entirely surrounded by land and has only a small region between Sweden and Denmark where it connects to the North Sea.

Figure 9.22 shows the salinity of different areas of the Baltic Sea along with the distribution of some species.

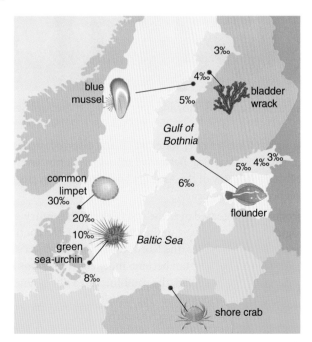

Figure 9.22. Salinity levels of different areas of the Baltic Sea and distribution of some of the species. Salinity is measured in parts per thousand (‰).

a   i   Explain how temperature and river outflow can affect ocean salinity.   **[4]**

ii   Suggest and explain a reason for the difference in salinity of the different parts of the Baltic Sea.   **[3]**

b   The common limpet is an osmoconformer. Use your knowledge of osmosis to explain why the common limpet is not found in the Gulf of Bothnia.   **[3]**

[Total mark: 10]

The Aral Sea, an ecological catastrophe

The Aral Sea (Figure 9.23) is a landlocked lake located in Central Asia on the border of Kazakhstan and Uzbekistan. In 1960, the Aral Sea was the fourth largest lake in the world, with an area of 67 499 km^2. It was a slightly saline lake with an average salinity of about 10 g dm^{-3} and was fed by two rivers, the Amu Darya in the south and the Syr Darya in the east. It was inhabited by at least 12 different fish species and more than 160 invertebrate species. Kazakhstan and Uzbekistan were part of the former Soviet Union, and in the early 1960s the Soviet government decided to divert the feeder rivers in order to build an enormous irrigation network. Over 20 000 miles of canals, 45 dams and more than 80 reservoirs were constructed in an effort to irrigate the desert region for agricultural purposes, particularly the production of cotton and wheat. The irrigation system was poorly constructed, with an estimated 75% of the water that was diverted lost as a result of leaks and evaporation.

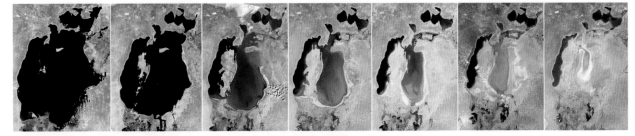

Figure 9.23. Satellite photographs showing the changes in the Aral Sea from 1973 to 2009.

By the mid-1960s, up to 60 km^3 of river water was being diverted each year to the agricultural projects, rather than replenishing the Aral Sea. Between 1961 and 1971, the level of the Aral Sea fell by an average of 10 cm $year^{-1}$. The fishery industry of the Aral Sea began to suffer as stocks of the fresh and brackish water fish it depended on began to disappear.

As agricultural production increased over the rest of the 20th century, the decrease in sea-level declined at a faster rate, averaging over 90 cm $year^{-1}$ in the 1980s. In 1987, the continued loss of water led to the Aral Sea breaking up into two separate seas, the North (or Lesser) Aral Sea and the South (or Greater) Aral Sea. In 1991, Kazakhstan and Uzbekistan became independent nations but large-scale cotton production continued to drain the Aral Sea. By 1998, the combined area of the now two separate seas was 28 687 km^2, with more than an 80% decrease in volume. The salinity had risen to 45 g dm^{-3} (typical seawater salinity is around 35 g dm^{-3}). Many original fish, such as carp, and invertebrate species were completely extinct and were replaced by marine and euryhaline species, such as flounder, that were more adapted to the high salinity.

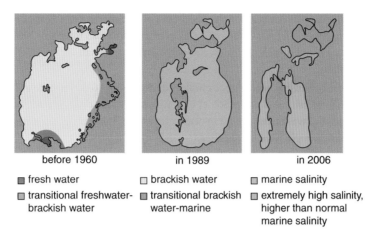

| before 1960 | in 1989 | in 2006 |

■ fresh water □ brackish water ■ marine salinity

□ transitional freshwater-brackish water ■ transitional brackish water-marine ■ extremely high salinity, higher than normal marine salinity

Figure 9.24. Changes in salinity of the Aral Sea over time.

By 2004, the surface area of all parts of the Aral Sea had shrunk to 17 160 km², 25% of its original size (Figure 9.24), and a nearly five-fold increase in salinity had killed nearly all of the native species. Many of the introduced marine species were becoming extinct, unable to cope with the high salinity.

Soviet scientists and the Soviet government considered the loss of the Aral Sea a price worth paying for the mass production of cotton. They often cited the work of the Russian climatologist, Aleksandr Voeikov, who stated that the Aral Sea was a 'mistake of nature' and a 'useless evaporator'. Cotton is Uzbekistan's main cash crop. It produces over 1 million tonnes year^{-1} and accounts for approximately 17% of Uzbekistan's exports. It is the sixth largest producer and second largest exporter of cotton in the world, and the cotton industry employs a significant proportion of the population. The cotton industry in Uzbekistan is, however, controversial. The industry is controlled by the government and a system of forced labour is used to harvest it, including children as young as nine. Some farmers are forced to grow cotton but the profits are often retained by the government. Because of alleged human rights abuses by the Uzbekistan government, several large clothing companies have stopped using cotton from Uzbekistan in their products.

North Aral Sea restoration project

In 2003, the Kazakh government began a project to restore the North Aral Sea. A large concrete dam was built in order to separate the North and South Aral Seas so that water from the north that still had river water flowing into it would not be lost to the south. The dam was completed in 2005 and since then the sea-level of the North Aral Sea has gradually increased, along with a fall in salinity, as shown in Figure 9.24. By 2006, the salinity had fallen to typical estuarine levels and some of the indigenous fish species began to reappear. Fisheries began to report a fall in numbers of marine species such as flounder. Ironically, this has led to a small loss in fishing revenue as people tended to prefer the taste of the marine species.

Sadly, the South Aral Sea has been abandoned to its fate. The dam prevents any overspill from the North Aral Sea entering it and, as a result, by 2007, the sea's area had shrunk to 10% of its original size, and its salinity in the remaining water had increased to over 100 g dm^{-3}. No fish at all now live in the South Aral Sea, and even marine species are unable to tolerate its high salinity. A few invertebrates that can tolerate extreme salinity survive there, but very little else.

Consequences of the destruction of the Aral Sea

The loss of the Aral Sea has had many consequences, both ecological and social.

- Ecological. The South Aral Sea is now almost a 'dead sea'. No fish are left and few invertebrates. Species that depended on fish as part of the food chain are under threat. At one time more than 173 species of animal lived around the Aral Sea, including wild boar, deer, jackals and even tigers; there are now fewer than 38 species.

195

- Human health. Toxic dust storms that contain a high proportion of salt are frequent in the area. This has led to respiratory, liver, kidney and eye diseases. Child mortality is high, at over 75 for every 1000 births. The loss of fish and food crops as a result of lack of fresh water and deposition of salt on the land has led to a loss of food, leading to malnutrition.
- Economic. The Aral Sea fishing industry, which once employed more than 40 000 people and accounted for a huge proportion of the total fish catch of the Soviet Union, has virtually disappeared. Wrecked fishing boats lie on the dried up land that was once covered by water. Unemployment is high, leading to poverty and population loss as so many people have left the area.

Questions

1. Summarise how human impact has led to the loss of the Aral Sea.
2. Explain the changes in salinity of the water over time as shown in Figure 9.24.
3. Explain in detail why stenohaline fresh-water fish have become extinct in the Aral Sea.
4. Explain how marine euryhaline fish were able to survive better in the Aral Sea.
5. Evaluate the impact of growing large quantities of cotton in Kazhakhstan and Uzbekhistan.

Chapter 10
Marine animal reproductive behaviour

Learning outcomes

By the end of this chapter, you should be able to:

- describe the life cycle of a variety of marine organisms
- explain the advantages of the specific habitats used for the different stages of the life cycles
- provide examples of marine organisms that use internal and external fertilisation
- compare the different degrees of parental investment made by different marine organisms
- apply what you have learnt to new, unfamiliar contexts.

10.1 The cycle of life

All life on the planet is driven to reproduce. Evolution by natural selection favours those organisms that can reproduce the most and pass on their genes to future generations. All organisms have evolved life cycles and reproductive methods that solve particular problems associated with their ecosystem and environment.

Charles Darwin made many observations about the natural world. He made three of the most important when writing the *Origin of Species by Natural Selection*.

- Most organisms tend to 'over reproduce' during their lifetime. To replace two sexually reproducing organisms, theoretically only two offspring are needed.

- Most populations tend to remain stable. This must mean that there is a huge struggle to survive and the majority of an organism's offspring die.

- All organisms show enormous variation and only those with the best characteristics or survival strategies survive and breed, passing their characteristics on to the next generation. This is the idea of 'survival of the fittest'.

The problems that all organisms encounter are constantly changing due to numbers of predators, amount of food, climate shifts and changes to habitats. A reproductive strategy that was ideal for one generation may not be ideal for another. Some organisms provide no parental care but produce thousands of offspring (a female Atlantic herring can carry up to 50 000 eggs) in the hope that maybe one or two will survive to breed. Some organisms produce only a few offspring but nurture and guard them in an effort to improve their chances of survival to breeding age. Which reproductive strategy a particular species uses is nature's solution to a particular environmental problem. There are two reasons why studying the life cycles of marine organisms is important to us.

- It can help us create optimal conditions for farming marine creatures such as oysters and salmon.

- It can help us understand why actions such as taking small fish and altering riverbeds can have catastrophic consequences on the populations of marine species.

10.2 Life cycles of marine organisms

Organisms tend to have one of two types of life cycle:

- simple life cycles, where there are no major different stages and metamorphosis does not take place

- complex life cycles, where there are several different stages and forms of organism.

Most marine organisms (other than marine mammals, birds and reptiles) have life cycles that are complex and go through several stages. This means that the majority have larval forms of some description. There are many advantages and disadvantages to having larval forms.

KEY TERM

Larval: the immature form of animals that undergo some metamorphosis, often having different food sources and habitats to avoid competition with the adults

Larval stages

If an organism has several **larval** stages, there must be some form of benefit to the survival of the organism.

- Less competition for food. Often, larvae occupy a different niche or region of ocean compared with the adults. This means that the adults and larvae are not competing for the same food. Zooplankton is made up of many larval forms, some of which eat phytoplankton while others eat other zooplankton. Some species have several larval stages, each of which may exist in a different area and eat a different food source.

- Distribution. Where adults are sessile (fixed to a substrate), a larval stage offers the possibility of moving to another area. The adult giant clam *Tridacna gigas* is usually securely attached to the substrate, but the larvae are free to move in the ocean. When they settle to become an adult, the larvae are often situated away from the parent, which reduces competition with the parent. It also means that the species is more resistant to extinction if a disease, predator or catastrophic event (such as a volcanic eruption) affects one area. If some of the offspring live elsewhere, they may survive.

There are also disadvantages, however.

- There will almost inevitably be less parental care so there is a higher risk of mortality.

- Larval stages tend to be small and free floating, and as a result may be more susceptible to predation and environmental stresses such as pollution and temperature change.

- Lack of substrate. Distribution across different areas does not necessarily mean that there will be a suitable substrate or food source in each area. Many larvae will be lost and simply die because they end up in an inhospitable area.

Salmon life cycle

There are many different species of wild salmon, broadly divided into Atlantic salmon (genus *Salmo*) and Pacific Salmon (genus *Oncorhynchus*). There is one species of Atlantic salmon (*Salmo salar*) but several species of Pacific salmon, including chinook, chum, sockeye and pink.

Most salmon species have a very similar life cycle, which involves spending a significant part of their lives in both fresh water and seawater (Figure 10.1). There are a few species, such as the Danube salmon, that live their lives exclusively in fresh water.

Salmon both begin and end their lives in fresh-water rivers. There are distinct male and female sexes and they do not change sex within their lifetime. In the autumn, sexually mature salmon swim far upstream in the rivers where they were spawned. The females seek out deep, free-flowing water with gravel beds. They dig out a scrape of gravel called a redd and lay their eggs in it. The male then deposits sperm over the eggs. Depending on the species of salmon, the female may lay between 2500 and 7000 eggs. When finished, the female buries the eggs in the gravel using her fins, in order to protect them through the winter. It is essential that the river flow is neither too fast nor too

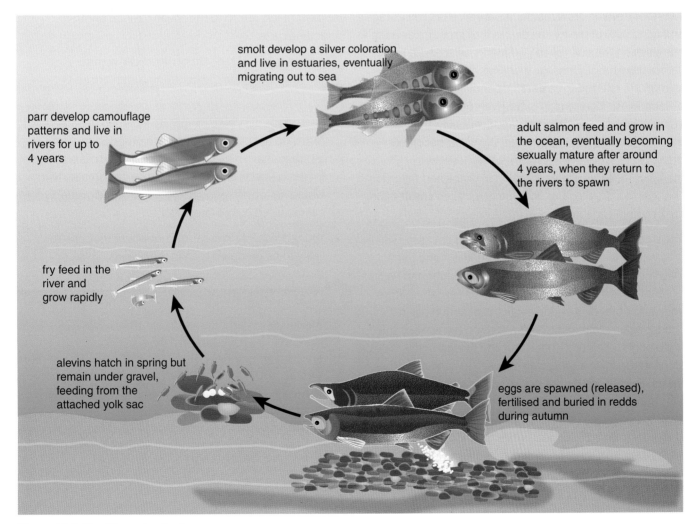

smolt develop a silver coloration and live in estuaries, eventually migrating out to sea

parr develop camouflage patterns and live in rivers for up to 4 years

adult salmon feed and grow in the ocean, eventually becoming sexually mature after around 4 years, when they return to the rivers to spawn

fry feed in the river and grow rapidly

alevins hatch in spring but remain under gravel, feeding from the attached yolk sac

eggs are spawned (released), fertilised and buried in redds during autumn

Figure 10.1. The life cycle of salmon.

slow. Too fast, and the gravel and eggs will be washed away; too slow, and the developing embryos have too little oxygen. The temperature of the water is also critical. Too warm, and the embryos will develop too quickly and hatch at the wrong time of year; too cold, and their development will be delayed.

The eggs develop over winter and hatch into **alevins**. These tiny fish still have an attached yolk sac filled with nutrients and stay hidden within the gravel nest out of reach of most predators. As the alevins grow, the yolk sac decreases in size and the fish have to start finding their own food supply. After the yolk has been completely used up, the salmon are called **fry** and leave the redd. They swim to the surface to fill their swim bladders with air so that they can swim freely throughout the whole depth of the river in an effort to avoid predators. Fry are too weak to swim upstream so tend to be washed downstream, actively seeking out calmer areas of water, which they will defend against other fry. They feed voraciously on invertebrates and grow rapidly. It is a very vulnerable stage and up to 90% of the fry can die. As they grow, fry develop markings on the side called parr marks, which help to camouflage them. Once the markings are complete, the salmon are referred to as **parr**. Depending on the species of salmon, the parr remain in the rivers feeding and growing for between 1 and 4 years. Eventually, the parr move to the river estuaries, where the water becomes more saline. While in the estuaries, they lose their markings, become more elongated in shape and their skin changes to a silver colour; they are now called **smolts** and are becoming adapted for life in the ocean.

The smolts move in shoals into the seas and oceans, where they will remain for between approximately 1 and 5 years. They feed in the rich waters of the north Atlantic and Pacific oceans. While in the sea, the fish become sexually mature and, as the breeding period begins, the salmon begin to change again. Depending on the species, the fish become more brightly coloured (often red) and the jaw of the males elongates to form a kype, which is used to fight with other males. The proportions of red and white muscle in the fish changes so that there is a higher proportion of white muscle. Red muscle contains high levels of myoglobin and more mitochondria than white muscle. Myoglobin stores oxygen in the muscle and, together with the mitochondria, helps aerobic respiration for long-distance

swimming in the oceans. White muscle has less myoglobin and fewer mitochondria and is adapted for sudden bursts of energy, which are necessary for jumping over obstacles in rivers.

The adult fish undertake an extraordinary migration up to the riverbeds where they were hatched. The salmon seem to be able to detect specific chemicals from their 'own' river and move towards it. These mass salmon migrations, called runs, are extremely important in the ecology of many parts of the Northern Hemisphere and salmon are considered a keystone species. As the salmon swim upstream in huge shoals, predators such as bear, otters and osprey lie in wait to eat them during the annual migration. The loss of salmon would be a huge ecological catastrophe because so many food chains depend on them. Eventually, the salmon reach the gravel beds of their river and spawn, continuing the life cycle. All species of Pacific salmon die after spawning. The majority of Atlantic salmon also die after spawning but between 5 and 10% of the females return to the ocean to enter another breeding cycle.

The advantages of the salmon life cycle, with so many stages, include the following (summarised in Table 10.1).

- Each stage occupies a separate niche, so the different forms do not compete with each other. Salmon of all stages have a high food requirement, so if several stages co-occupied the same niche, the smaller fish would not obtain enough food and would probably be cannibalised by the larger fish.

- Younger fish live in areas of river where they are less likely to be predated than in the oceans.

KEY TERMS

Alevin: the first larval form of salmon, they possess a yolk sac and remain within the gravel nests or redds

Fry: the early, small larval stage of many fish, including salmon

Parr: salmon stage between fry and smolt; lives in rivers and has markings along sides of body that act as camouflage

Smolt: form of salmon that occurs when parr lose their markings while in estuaries; they are adapted for marine life by being silver in colour and elongated in shape

stage	habitat	advantages	time duration	other features
fertilisation and embryonic development	gravel beds of rivers	hidden from predators, in running water with plenty of oxygen	c. 4–5 months	must be in deep, flowing water that is cool in temperature
alevin	gravel beds of rivers	hidden from predators, running water with plenty of oxygen	c. 4–6 weeks	nourished by yolk sac so can remain inside gravel nests
fry	flowing water, sheltering behind rocks and other obstacles	food and oxygen is carried in the water, less likely to be swept away by currents because of the shelter	c. 3 months	a phase of rapid growth, fry will defend territories aggressively
parr	deeper pools in river areas	abundant food present in the deeper pools as growth requires more nutrients	c. 1–4 years	the development of camouflaged coloration reduces risk of predation in rivers
smolt	estuaries of rivers	high food abundance and preparation for change in salinity in the oceans, different food sources so not in competition with parr	variable depending on conditions	smolt develop silver colour and streamlined shape for life in the ocean, they also begin to osmoregulate in saline water
adult	oceans and seas	different and rich food source that is not in competition with younger stages	c. 2–4 years	adults feed on rich food such as crustaceans and are voracious predators
sexually mature adult	oceans and seas, and rivers	rich food source in the ocean and appropriate spawning areas in rivers	c. 1 year	males and females change colour and become clearly distinguishable

Table 10.1. A summary of the salmon life cycle.

SELF-ASSESSMENT QUESTIONS

1   List two advantages and two disadvantages of having a larval stage in a life cycle.
2   State why it is important that salmon fry live in moving river water.

Tuna life cycle

There are several different species of true tuna fish, all belonging to the genus *Thunnus*. The main species are:

- Albacore tuna
- southern bluefin tuna
- bigeye tuna
- Pacific bluefin tuna
- Atlantic bluefin tuna.

All these tuna species have a similar life cycle, although some differences occur with spawning grounds and ages at which sexual maturity develops. Sexes appear to be fixed and there are no records of tuna changing sex during their lives.

Male and female tuna migrate to spawning grounds in the Atlantic and Pacific oceans and Mediterranean Sea at certain times of year. The breeding seasons vary for each species and may also depend on the water temperature of the spawning grounds. There are two separate populations

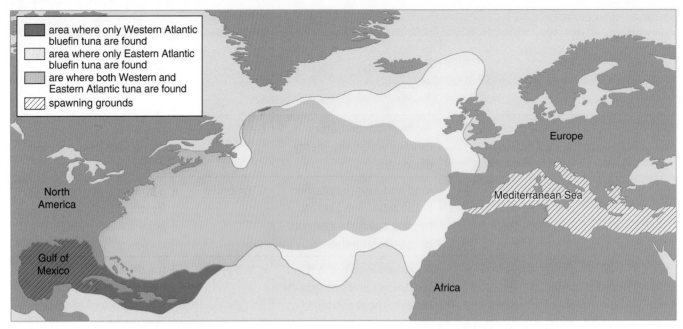

	area where only Western Atlantic bluefin tuna are found
	area where only Eastern Atlantic bluefin tuna are found
	are where both Western and Eastern Atlantic tuna are found
	spawning grounds

Figure 10.2. The ranges of the two groups of Atlantic bluefin tuna and their spawning grounds.

of Atlantic bluefin tuna that either gather in a region of the Mediterranean near the Balearic Islands between May and July, or in the Gulf of Mexico between April and June. Pacific bluefin congregate in distinct spawning grounds in the north-west Philippine Sea and the Sea of Japan between April and August (Figure 10.2). By congregating in the same areas, it increases the likelihood of successful mating and means that genetically different tuna breed together, increasing genetic diversity.

Recent research using tagging has shown that tuna, like salmon, return to the spawning ground in which they themselves were spawned. Males and females swim together during spawning, which generally occurs at night. During spawning, many females release eggs into the water while males release sperm. This is called broadcast spawning because eggs and sperm from many individuals are in the water together. The random, external fertilisation results in increased genetic diversity, although many eggs are lost. The fertilised eggs, which are buoyant because of the presence of oils, float just beneath the surface of the water, where many are eaten by predators.

Each female can produce vast numbers of eggs, depending on their size; a 5-year-old female bluefin tuna releases about 5 million eggs in a year whereas a 20-year-old female can release up to 45 million. Such huge numbers are produced because the majority will fail to fertilise or be eaten as eggs or larvae.

Larvae hatch after about 2 days and live in the planktonic surface waters, where they feed on the larvae of all species. They have disproportionally large heads and jaws to enable easy feeding (Figure 10.3). The larvae remain in the spawning grounds, growing rapidly, until they reach a certain size, when they move out into the open ocean feeding grounds. These **juvenile** fish tend to school together to avoid predators. Different species reach sexual maturity at different ages, typically between 4 and 8 years of age, at which point they will migrate to the spawning grounds to mate.

KEY TERM

Juvenile: the stage of life cycle that is not sexually mature

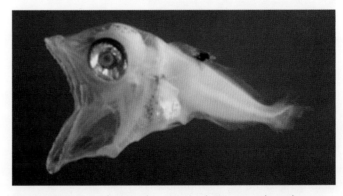

Figure 10.3. Tuna larva, showing its large mouth and head region.

The advantages of the tuna life cycle are as follows.

- It allows synchronisation of male and female tuna in a few areas at one particular time rather than navigation of vast areas of ocean in the hope of finding mates. This means that many males and females are present, increasing the genetic diversity of the population.

- The separate larval stage means that tuna of different ages are not competing for the same food stock.
- The spawning grounds have abundant food for the larvae, which is less available in the adult feeding grounds.

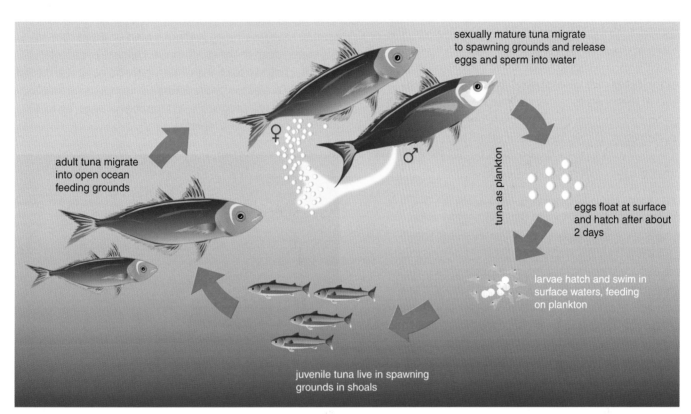

Figure 10.4. The life cycle of tuna.

stage	habitat	advantages	time duration	other features
fertilisation and embryogenesis	spawning ground area of ocean water	allows many males and females to be in close proximity	c. 2–4 days	many unfertilised and fertilised eggs are lost so females lay millions each year
larval stage	planktonic zone of spawning ground	rich feeding area, not in competition with adults	c. 6 months	larvae have large heads and mouthparts to obtain food
juvenile	spawning grounds and open ocean feeding grounds	move in shoals of similar size to evade predators, have different and larger food than larvae	c. 5 years, depending on species	juveniles leave the spawning grounds in shoals and roam the oceans feeding, they have a high growth rate
adult	open ocean feeding grounds	rich diversity of food, not in competition with larvae	5–25 years, depending on species	adults migrate to the spawning grounds where they themselves were spawned during breeding season

Table 10.2. A summary of the tuna life cycle.

Oyster life cycle

Oysters are bivalve molluscs that as adults are sessile (attached to a substrate and unable to move to another region). They have a complex life cycle that has several stages (Figures 10.5 and 10.6). The larval stages allow the oysters to disperse their offspring to different areas, although they tend to settle in beds where there are other oysters already growing.

The majority of oyster species have separate male and female sexes, although most will change sex at some point in their lives. It is thought that individuals can change sex multiple times. Most species live for the first few years of their lives as males and release sperm. As they age and grow bigger they have more energy available to develop eggs, so they become female. They use broadcast spawning, with both males and females releasing gametes into the water, so fertilisation is external.

The factors controlling gamete release are still not fully understood but it is thought that a change in water temperature is a trigger causing the release of sperm from a few males. A synchronising pheromone is probably released into the water at the same time. When one oyster releases its gametes, the others, of both sexes in the local bed, are stimulated to do so in order to synchronise fertilisation. It is common practice to throw a male that is about to spawn into farmed oyster beds in order to stimulate breeding by the whole bed. For many species,

a temperature of 16 °C seems to be critical for breeding, and as soon as the temperature rises above this in spring breeding starts; and conversely breeding stops when the temperature drops below 16 °C in autumn. Many species tend to breed between May and August, hence the old saying that you should only eat oysters when there is an 'r' in the month. This is because, during the breeding season, oysters put most of their energy into their gametes so tend to have less 'meat' in them. External fertilisation in the water, despite the synchronised release of gametes, is very much down to chance; many eggs do not get fertilised and many are eaten by predators. To compensate for this, each female will produce a vast number of eggs, up to 100 million year^{-1} for some species.

Figure 10.5. Oysters releasing gametes.

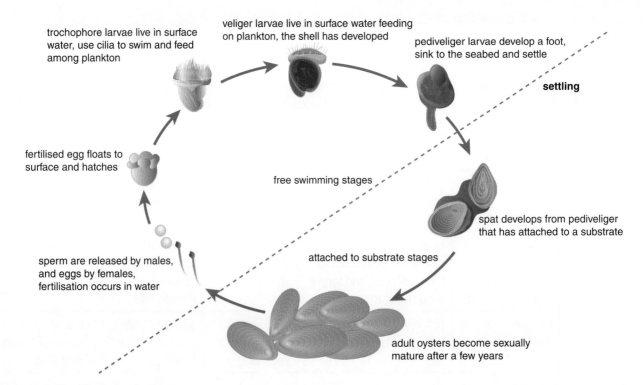

trochophore larvae live in surface water, use cilia to swim and feed among plankton

veliger larvae live in surface water feeding on plankton, the shell has developed

pediveliger larvae develop a foot, sink to the seabed and settle

settling

fertilised egg floats to surface and hatches

free swimming stages

spat develops from pediveliger that has attached to a substrate

sperm are released by males, and eggs by females, fertilisation occurs in water

attached to substrate stages

adult oysters become sexually mature after a few years

Figure 10.6. The life cycle of oysters.

KEY TERMS

Trochophore: the first larval stage of molluscs such as giant clams and oysters, they move using cilia and are planktonic

Veliger: the second-stage larva of molluscs, characterised by the presence of a vellum organ used for feeding and movement, and a shell

Pediveliger: the third-stage larva of molluscs, characterised by the development of a foot

Spat: larval form of oyster, giant clam and other bivalve molluscs that settles and attaches to substrate

The eggs hatch between 6 and 12 h after fertilisation and develop into the first free-swimming larval stage, called a **trochophore**. These larvae have cilia on their surface in order to move through the water while feeding on phytoplankton. After a short time, the trochophore larvae begin to develop a shell and an organ called a vellum, which is coated with cilia and used for movement and feeding. The larva is now called a **veliger** larva. Eventually, the veliger larva begins to grow a foot with which it can attach to a substrate, and is now called a **pediveliger** larva. Pediveligers sink to the seabed and swim over it, dragging their foot on the substratum. The foot is highly sensitive and can detect a suitable site for settling and also seems to be attracted to chemicals from other oysters. When an ideal location is found, glands in the foot release various secretions that stick the pediveliger to the substrate. The byssus thread, a tough material that is produced by many molluscs for attachment, is one such secretion. The larvae then undergo metamorphosis into adults, becoming small oysters or **spats**. Spats spend up to 3 years feeding and growing before reaching sexual maturity. The length of time between fertilisation and settling varies from species to species and is dependent on the conditions of the water, but is typically between 2 and 3 weeks. The whole life cycle is summarised in Table 10.3.

stage	habitat	advantages	time duration	other notes
fertilisation and embryogenesis	water around seabed	oysters grow together so the chance of fertilisation is high	c. 6–12 h	there are separate male and female oysters but oysters change sex during their lives, females release up to 10 million eggs year^{-1}
trochophore	planktonic surface waters	free swimming for dispersal, not competing with adults for food	c. 5–10 h	trochophore are minute, free-swimming larvae that use cilia to move and feed
veliger	planktonic surface waters	free swimming for dispersal, not competing with adults for food	c. 1 week	veliger larvae have a velum that possesses cilia for movement and feeding, and also a shell
pediveliger	planktonic surface waters	free swimming for dispersal, not competing with adults for food, sink to find suitable substrate, attracted to other adult oysters, good food source and mates available	c. 1–2 weeks	the pediveliger is characterised by the development of the foot, which it uses to sense and attach to the substrate
spat	attached to substrate	situated around other oysters that are growing in an area rich in food	2–3 years	the spat is a small version of the adult that grows for several years before becoming sexually mature
adult	attached to substrate	situated with other oysters in an area rich with food and near other individuals for breeding	c. 3+ years	most oyster species begin as males and later become female

Table 10.3. A summary of the oyster life cycle.

Figure 10.7. Giant clam releasing gametes.

Giant clam life cycle

Giant clams are the largest living bivalve molluscs on the Earth. There are several different species, many of which are under threat and are listed as vulnerable by the International Union for Conservation of Nature (IUCN) Red List of Threatened Species.

Like oysters, adult giant clams are sessile and fixed to the seabed. Unlike oysters, giant clams are **hermaphrodites** and can produce both male and female gametes. The ability to produce both sperm and eggs increases the likelihood of being close to a compatible partner and the opportunity to breed. Giant clams reproduce using external fertilisation and broadcast spawning, so that sperm and eggs are ejected into the water, resulting in the mixing of gametes from several different individuals. This mixing of gametes from many individuals results in increased genetic diversity of offspring.

When a clam is ready to breed it suddenly contracts its muscles and ejects a stream of sperm into the water through its siphon (Figure 10.7). The exact trigger for breeding is still unknown but seems to coincide with

the phases of the Moon and the tides. To prevent self-fertilisation occurring, eggs are released some time after the release of sperm.

The life cycle of giant clams is complex, with several stages that enable them to distribute offspring to different areas (Figure 10.8). In order to synchronise gamete release with other clams, a hormone, spawning-induced substance (SIS), is released into the water, which triggers gamete release by clams in the immediate area. Because many eggs are lost, the clams produce huge numbers: a fully

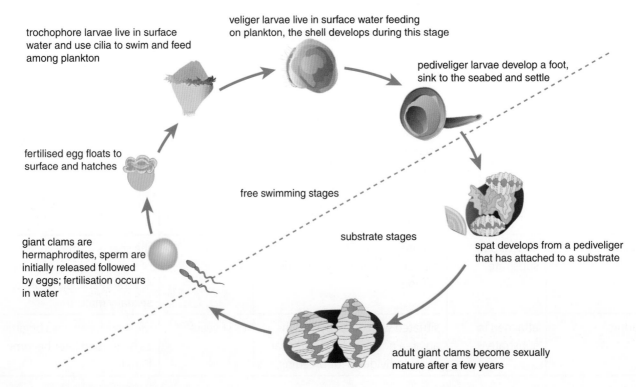

Figure 10.8. The life cycle of giant clams.

grown *Tridacna gigas*, the largest of the giant clams, can produce more than 500 million eggs at a time.

Within approximately 12 h of fertilisation, a trochophore larva hatches from the egg (Figure 10.8). The larval stages of the giant clam are almost identical to those of the oyster. Trochophore larvae possess cilia so that they can swim. They move into the planktonic areas of the surface waters, where they filter feed on phytoplankton. After about 12 h, the trochophore begins to develop a shell and a vellum, and is now considered to be a veliger larva. Over the course of the next week or so, the veliger develops a foot to become a pediveliger, which eventually sinks to the seabed. The pediveliger uses its foot to crawl along the seabed searching for a suitable substrate, such as a coral reef, to attach to. When it finally secretes substances that permanently attach it, metamorphosis occurs turning the pediveliger into a spat, which is a tiny version of an adult clam.

It typically takes between 8 and 25 days from fertilisation to permanent settling on the seabed, depending on how long it takes to find a suitable substrate. The spats grow for 2 or 3 years, at which point they become sexually mature (different species may mature at different ages). Some species mature initially as a male for 2 or 3 years before developing female gonads to become hermaphrodites.

The life cycle is summarised in Table 10.4.

stage	habitat	advantages	time duration	other notes
fertilisation and embryogenesis	water around seabed	giant clams grow together so chance of fertilisation is high	c. 6–12 h	giant clams are hermaphrodites, sperm are released first followed by eggs, the hormone SIS stimulates gamete release from other giant clams
trochophore	planktonic surface waters	free swimming for dispersal, not competing with adults for food	c. 5–10 h	trochophore are minute free-swimming larvae that use cilia to move and feed
veliger	planktonic surface waters	free swimming for dispersal, not competing with adults for food	c. 1 week	veliger larvae possess a velum organ, which has cilia for movement and feeding, and also a shell
pediveliger	planktonic surface waters	free swimming for dispersal, not competing with adults for food, sinks to find suitable substrate, attracted to other adult oysters, good access to food source and mates	c. 1–2 weeks	the pediveliger is characterised by the development of the foot, which it uses to sense and attach to the substrate
spat	attached to substrate	grows on appropriate substrate, such as coral, where other clams grow	2–3 years	the spat is a small version of the adult that grows for several years before becoming sexually mature
adult	attached to substrate	situated with other giant clams in an area rich with food and near other individuals for breeding	c. 3+ years	giant clams tend to spend 2 years as males before becoming hermaphrodites

Table 10.4. A summary of the giant clam life cycle.

Shrimp life cycle

There are hundreds, possibly thousands, of different species of shrimp, many of which have different life cycles. There are certain common themes, however, that occur in the life cycles of all shrimps, so the general principles are given here. Shrimps are decapod crustaceans and are closely related to lobsters and crabs. They are of significant commercial interest, both when fished and farmed, and shrimp farming has led to renewed interest in their reproductive behaviour.

Adult, sexually mature shrimp live in deeper ocean waters (Figure 10.9). Breeding seasons vary from species to species, and breeding may be triggered by a mixture of water temperature and lunar phases. Sex determination is not fully understood in most crustaceans. Some species initially develop as males for 2 or 3 years and then become females; in other species the sexes are fixed for their entire lives.

Figure 10.9. Adult shrimp; the lower shrimp has eggs attached.

Shrimp are not broadcast spawners, and individual males and females mates with each other in deep ocean water (Figure 10.10). During mating, the male attaches a pouch of sperm called a spermatocyst to the underside of the female. As eggs are released by the female, sperm is released onto them from the spermatocyst so that they are fertilised externally. This is a far less wasteful process than broadcast spawning so fewer eggs need to be produced by a female, typically between 900 and 3000. In some species, such as the pink shrimp *Pandalus borealis*, the fertilised eggs remain attached to the female until they hatch 5 or 6 months later. Other species, such as the tiger prawn *Penaeus monodon*, release the fertilised eggs into the water.

 KEY TERMS

Protozoea: the second-stage larva of crustaceans such as shrimp; typically planktonic, these larvae pass through several forms as they grow

Mysis: the later larval form of crustaceans; shrimp mysis larvae drift to coastal areas

A nauplius larva hatches from the egg and moves to the surface waters, where it feeds on plankton. The nauplius larvae are characterised by appendages on their heads that are used for swimming, and the presence of a simple eye. After some time feeding in the plankton, they metamorphose into a different larval stage called a **protozoea**. The protozoea larva continues to feed on plankton and passes through several moults of its exoskeleton as it grows to eventually produce a larger, more typically shrimp-like, larva called a **mysis**. The mysis larvae are carried on ocean currents towards the coast and settle in nutrient-rich areas such as mangrove swamps, estuaries and bays. They move to the estuary floor and feed on detritus and small organisms, and metamorphose into a postlarva, which resembles a small adult shrimp. These postlarvae tend to move to the shallow estuarine waters, where they become increasingly predaceous before growing into juvenile shrimps. The juvenile shrimps move into the deeper estuarine waters in search of larger prey (often being cannibalistic) and more detritus. When the juveniles approach adult size, they begin to migrate back out to the deep sea, where they become sexually mature adults and begin to breed. The life cycle is summarised in Table 10.5.

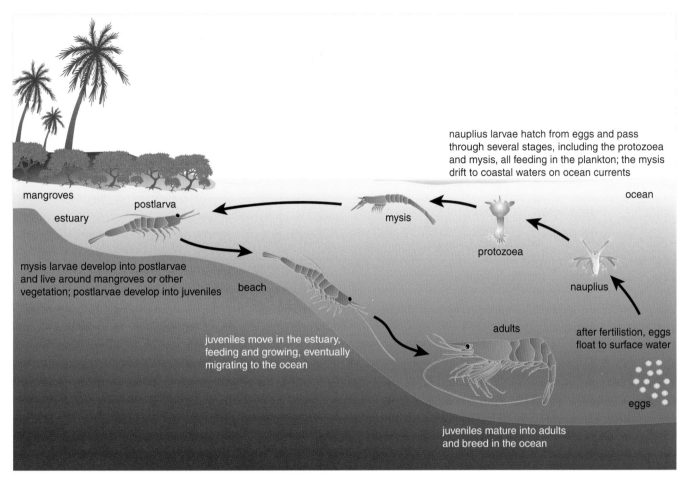

nauplius larvae hatch from eggs and pass through several stages, including the protozoea and mysis, all feeding in the plankton; the mysis drift to coastal waters on ocean currents

ocean

mangroves

estuary

postlarva

mysis

protozoea

nauplius

mysis larvae develop into postlarvae and live around mangroves or other vegetation; postlarvae develop into juveniles

beach

juveniles move in the estuary, feeding and growing, eventually migrating to the ocean

adults

after fertilistion, eggs float to surface water

eggs

juveniles mature into adults and breed in the ocean

Figure 10.10. The life cycle of shrimp.

stage	habitat	advantages	time duration	other notes
fertilisation	deep sea	abundant food for adults and plenty of potential mates	c. 6 months	most shrimp begin life as males and become females after about 3 years, fertilisation is external but males and females pair up
nauplius	planktonic in surface waters	abundant food in plankton and not in competition with later stages, distributed by ocean currents	variable (a few days)	small larva with appendages on head, feeds on phytoplankton
protozoea	planktonic in surface waters	abundant food in plankton and not in competition with later stages, distributed by ocean currents	variable (a few days to weeks)	passes through several stages as it grows and sheds exoskeleton at each stage
mysis	planktonic in surface waters, swept to coastal waters by ocean currents	abundant food in plankton and not in competition with later stages, distributed by ocean currents	variable (a few days to weeks)	begins to resemble the adult shrimp, locates mangrove and seagrass areas, which act as nursery grounds

stage	habitat	advantages	time duration	other notes
postlarva	estuaries / mangroves	abundant food and shelter from predators, not in competition with larvae and adults	variable (a few weeks)	stay in sheltered water until they reach a larger size and move into deeper estuarine areas
juvenile	estuaries, migrate into ocean	abundant food and shelter from predators, larger than postlarva so less vulnerable, not in competition with larvae and adults	1–2 months	live in deeper areas where less susceptible to predation, have a varied diet including cannibalism
adult	deep ocean areas	abundant food and mates, not in competition with younger stages and unlikely to cannibalise them	1–5 years	adults live in deeper oceans where there is abundant food, particularly detritus

Table 10.5. A summary of the life cycle of shrimp.

Grouper life cycle

There are many species of grouper (Figure 10.11) found in the world's oceans and seas. There are many differences in the life cycles of these different species, although certain features are common to all. Most species begin their lives as females and some years later change into males. The length of time spent as each sex varies between species and depends on the size of the fish and the number of other males and females in the area. Groupers seem to have quite complex social structures that differ between species. Fish within a group may occupy different positions in a hierarchy and there are generally far more females than males in any one grouping. If no male is present in an area, the largest females usually spontaneously begin to change into a male; this phenomenon also occurs in other species of fish, such as the moon wrasse.

Figure 10.11. An adult red grouper.

The breeding seasons of most grouper species are triggered by lunar phases and seasons of the year. The nassau grouper, *Epinephelus striatus*, for example, always spawns before a full moon during the winter. Up to 100 000 fish gather at spawning aggregation areas in areas of ocean off the reef shelf (Figure 10.12). By gathering many groupers in one location, the opportunity to increase diversity in the offspring is increased. Mating occurs at night in groups of between 3 and 25 fish. Typically, one or two females are surrounded by several males and, after a courtship routine, the fish release eggs and sperm into the water in a form of broadcast spawning. Fertilisation is external in the water and many eggs are not fertilised, each female releasing up to 1 million in any breeding season.

The fertilised eggs float up to the surface of the water and, after about 24 h, the larvae hatch (Figure 10.12). The early larvae have an attached yolk sac providing nutrients, similar to salmon alevins. The larvae grow through several stages, some of which are characterised by long spines that deter predators while they are in the plankton. They drift in the surface waters for up to 80 days after which they reach coastal areas. Many species, such as the goliath and gag groupers, now find shelter around the roots of mangroves or beds of seagrass, which act as nursery grounds for them. While in coastal waters, the fish pass through the postlarval and juvenile stages, during which extensive growth occurs that can take up to 5 years. When the fish have reached adult size and begin to be sexually mature, they migrate out to coral reefs, where they can live for more than 40 years. With no human interference, the goliath grouper, the largest grouper species, can live for more than 100 years. The life cycle is summarised in Table 10.6.

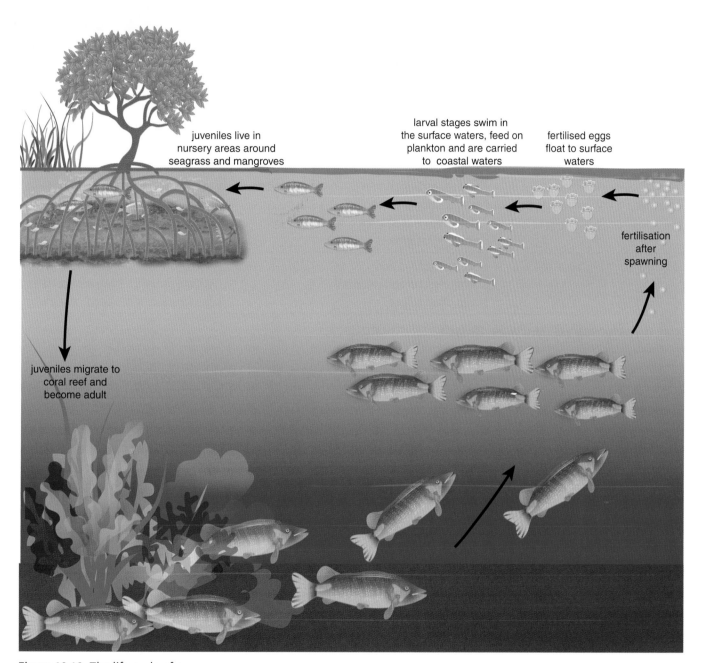

juveniles live in
nursery areas around
seagrass and mangroves

larval stages swim in
the surface waters, feed on
plankton and are carried
to coastal waters

fertilised eggs
float to surface
waters

fertilisation
after
spawning

juveniles migrate to
coral reef and
become adult

Figure 10.12. The life cycle of grouper.

The life cycles of the different species discussed
demonstrate many differences and similarities. These are
summarised in Table 10.7.

SELF-ASSESSMENT QUESTIONS

5 Explain why replanting mangroves is important for
the conservation of groupers.

6 State two similarities and two differences between
the life cycles of shrimp and groupers.

stage	habitat	advantages	time duration	other notes
fertilisation and embryogenesis	spawning aggregation areas off reefs	groupers meet together to ensure fertilisation	c. 24 h	grouper blanket spawn but in groups to help ensure fertilisation
larva	planktonic in surface water	abundant planktonic food, no competition with later stages, ocean currents distribute larvae	c. 80 days	the larvae hatch with a yolk sac to last a few days, some later stages have long spikes to deter predators
postlarva / juvenile	coastal water / mangroves	abundant food, not in competition with adults, shelter from predators around mangroves	c. 5 years	growth occurs around the roots of mangroves, as they reach larger sizes they begin to migrate into the oceans
adult	coral reefs	abundant food and territories, no competition with other stages	40+ years	adults of most species are all initially female, if there are no males the largest females become male

Table 10.6. A summary of the grouper life cycle.

species	sex determination	fertilisation	spawning	egg number per female per breeding season	life stages	different habitats
salmon	fixed male and female at hatching	external	in redds, usually paired mating with several pairings	up to 35 000	alevin, parr, smolt, juvenile, adult	gravel beds of rivers, estuaries, open ocean
oyster	protandrous hermaphrodites	external	broadcast spawning	up to 100 million	trochophore, veliger, pediveliger, spat, adult	marine surface waters in plankton, seabed
giant clam	hermaphrodites	external	broadcast spawning	up to 500 million	trochophore, veliger, pediveliger, spat, adult	marine surface waters in plankton, seabed
shrimp	fixed and protandrous hermaphrodites	external	paired mating	up to 3000	nauplius, protozoea, mysis, post mysis, juvenile, adult	marine surface waters in plankton, estuaries / bays, open ocean seabed

species	sex determination	fertilisation	spawning	egg number per female per breeding season	life stages	different habitats
grouper	protandrous hermaphrodites	external	broadcast spawning with a few individuals	c. 1 million	several stages of larval fish, postlarvae, adult	marine surface waters in plankton, mangroves / estuaries, coral reefs
tuna	fixed	external	broadcast spawning	up to 35 million	several larval fish stages, juvenile, adult	spawning ocean areas, open ocean

Table 10.7. A comparison of life cycle features of different organisms.

PRACTICAL ACTIVITY 10.1

The surface preferences of oyster spats

Several oyster farmers reported that, when growing spats, the majority of them seemed to attach to the underside of existing shells used as a substrate. A scientist set out to test whether or not the pediveligers showed a preference for the orientation of the substrate.

plate angle	plate surface	number of spats on surface
horizontal	A	21
	B	85
vertical	A	1
	B	3
45° angle	A	12
	B	37

Table 10.8. Results of experiment.

Method

Three 50 cm × 50 cm square glass plates were placed near a natural oyster bed and left for 1 month. One plate was placed horizontally, one vertically and one at a 45° angle, as shown in Figure 10.13. On each plate, one surface was labelled A and the other B.

Figure 10.13. Orientation of glass plates placed on oyster beds.

After 1 month, the scientist removed the plates and counted the number of spats found on the surfaces. The results are recorded in Table 10.8.

Conclusions

1. State a hypothesis the scientist could have tested.
2. State the (a) independent and (b) dependent variables.
3. Suggest three variables that the scientist should have controlled.
4. Suggest how the scientist could have made the results more reliable.
5. Explain how the data could be presented so that it is easier to visualise the effect.
6. Explain whether or not the data suggest a preference for any particular surface or angle.

213

Maths skills

Analysing data

When we carry out scientific investigations, you often repeat them to improve reliability. Repeating experiments allows you to identify anomalies and then calculate mean values. Identifying anomalies with biological data can be difficult and it is often never clear whether a value is in fact anomalous or just part of natural variation. If a data point seems clearly anomalous, the general rule is to not include it when calculating the mean and if possible try to repeat the experiment.

Calculating mean values is very simple. All the values are added together after discarding anomalies and then divided by the number of values added together.

Worked example 1

Fifteen samples of zooplankton were taken from an area of ocean. The number of zooplankton per cm^3 of water were determined for each. The values were:

254, 269, 325, 295, 275, 315, 301, 258, 295, 321, 52, 245, 342, 295, 375

There is quite a large range between the maximum and minimum values. The lowest value, 52, seems very different compared with the other values, so would appear anomalous and would be ignored when calculating the mean. The wide range in values could otherwise be the result of variation in the samples.

The mean number of zooplankton per cm^3 =

$$\frac{(254+269+325+295+275+315+301+258+295+321+245+342+295+375)}{14} = 297.5$$

The range for the values is expressed as the lowest to the highest value (with anomalies excluded), which in this example is: 245 to 375. The range can also be expressed as the difference between the lowest and highest value, in other words, 375 – 245 = 130 zooplankton per cm^3.

Question 1

Calculate the means and ranges for the following data series, discounting anomalies:

a   Oyster spats were collected on 12 oyster cages, and the number found in each cage were:
   45, 72, 53, 65, 98, 2, 65, 98, 58, 97, 101, 45

b   The numbers of eggs spawned by eight female salmon were:
   3525, 2974, 3198, 4872, 2956, 3542, 4100, 2954

Worked example 2

Mean values are useful but do not always tell us the whole story. For example, two different experiments were both run twice. The repeat values for one experiment were 14 and 16 and for the second experiment were 30 and 0. The mean value for both experiments is the same, 15. The raw data, however, suggests that the data are more complex. It is often useful to determine how much spread there is about the mean value. This calculation is called the standard deviation. The higher the standard deviation, the greater the spread of the values about the mean (Figure 10.14). For a normal distribution:

* approximately 68% of all values lie within a range of the mean ± 1 standard deviation
* approximately 95% of all values lie within a range of the mean ± 2 standard deviation.

To calculate the standard deviation, you use the formula:

Standard deviation $S = \sqrt{\dfrac{\sum(x-\bar{x})^2}{n-1}}$

Where x = each measurement

$\bar{x}$ = mean
$\sum(x - \bar{x})^2$ = sum of all the $(x - \bar{x})^2$ values
n = number of measurements

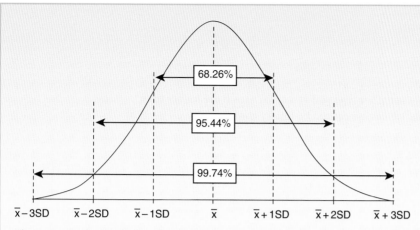

Figure 10.14. Normal distribution showing standard deviation from mean.

Question 2

Calculate the standard deviation for the measurements shown in Table 10.9.

measurements (x)	($x - \bar{x}$)	($x - \bar{x}$)^2
27	(27 – 30.9) = –3.9	15.21
32		
29		
35		
25		
37		
31		

Table 10.9. Standard deviation table.

The mean of the measurements, $\bar{x}$ = (27 + 32 + 29 + 35 + 25 + 37 + 31)/7 = 30.9

- Complete Table 10.9.
- Now calculate the $\Sigma(x - \bar{x})^2$ by adding all of the $(x - \bar{x})^2$ values together.
- The number of values (n) is 7. Now divide your value for $\Sigma(x - \bar{x})^2$ by ($n - 1$).
- Now calculate the standard deviation by finding the square root of this number.
- 68% of the values lie between $\bar{x} \pm 1 \times$ standard deviation. Calculate this range.
- 95% of the values lie between $\bar{x} \pm 2 \times$ standard deviation. Now calculate this range.

Worked example 3

You can use standard deviations to compare mean values in an investigation. For example, the mean numbers of deep sea shrimp in two areas were compared. Area A had 25 shrimp per m^2 of water while area B had 15 shrimp per m^2 of water. If we look only at the means, area A seems to definitely have more shrimps per m^2.

If you then take into account the standard deviations, you can see by how much the two areas really differ. In this example, the standard deviation for area A is 3 and for B is 4.

95% of values will lie between mean $\pm 2 \times$ standard deviation, so

for area A, 95% of values lie between $25 \pm (2 \times 3)$

$= 25 \pm 6$

$= 19$ to 31

215

for area B, 95% of values lie between 15 ± (2 × 4)

= 15 ± 8

= 7 to 23

There is an overlap of the two ranges: some of the higher repeated values for area B are higher than for area A. This means that the means are different but we cannot be totally confident that all parts of area A have more shrimps than area B.

Question 3

Use standard deviation to determine whether or not there is a clear difference between the mean numbers of groupers per square km of two reefs as shown in Table 10.10. Calculate the mean, standard deviation and the ranges within which 95% of values lie.

repeat	number of grouper per square kilometre of reef	
	region A	region B
1	32	18
2	35	19
3	21	12
4	25	24
5	32	27
6	38	19
7	21	18
8	24	27
9	19	18
10	31	12

Table 10.10. Difference in grouper numbers from two reefs.

10.3 Fertilisation methods and parental care

If the cycle of life is to continue, it is essential to ensure that gametes (sperm and eggs) meet. The fusion of sperm and eggs is called fertilisation. There are essentially two options for fertilisation:

- **external fertilisation**, which occurs outside the body

- **internal fertilisation**, which occurs inside the body.

KEY TERMS

External fertilisation: when gametes such as sperm and eggs are released and fuse outside the body

Internal fertilisation: when gametes such as sperm and eggs fuse inside the body of a parent

External fertilisation

When gametes are released outside the body for fertilisation, there is some degree of uncertainty about them meeting. In order to try and improve the odds of successful fertilisation, most species have adapted their physiology or behaviour in a specific way.

Most marine organisms use external fertilisation. Organisms such as giant clams and oysters use broadcast spawning, where gametes are released into the water. It is pure chance whether one gamete meets another, and there is little, if any, choice of mate. Broadcast spawning can be a highly wasteful process because there may be no suitable mates nearby. This means that the majority of eggs and sperm simply drift away in the water currents or are eaten by predators. To compensate for the inefficiency of broadcast spawning, many species release massive numbers of eggs and sperm (up to half a billion eggs from one giant clam, for example). Gamete release is synchronised with other individuals by using chemical signals in the water to help ensure that fertilisation occurs. Tuna maximise the chances of fertilisation by aggregating in the same area to simultaneously release gametes. So why does such an inefficient and seemingly random process exist? The answer is that the potential for so many fertilisations between so many different individuals can generate great genetic diversity, which is important for evolution.

Shrimp and salmon also use external fertilisation but produce far fewer eggs. In both cases, efforts are made to reduce the loss of gametes. Salmon pair up and make redds or nests in gravel, where they deposit the eggs. The sperm are released directly onto them. Male shrimp stick packages that contain sperm onto hairs on the females' bodies. This means that as eggs are released, sperm are already present. The methods used by salmon and shrimp help to make fertilisation far more likely, but there are costs to these adaptations. Individuals need to physically find each other and pair up. Unlike broadcast spawning, each individual has fewer partners so less genetic diversity is the result. This means that species with fewer partners tend to have complex methods of mate choice to make sure individuals choose the 'correct' partner with which to mix their genes.

Internal fertilisation

Internal fertilisation requires one organism to introduce its gametes inside another so that fertilisation can take place inside the body. This means that there is a far higher probability that fertilisation will occur. As animals evolved on land and became less dependent on water, internal fertilisation became more important because externally released gametes would dry up and be lost. Gametes can drift and swim in water, so external fertilisation is more likely to be successful if they are released in aquatic environments than into air or onto land. Marine mammals such as whales and dolphins are ancestors of terrestrial mammals (they are thought to be related to the group of animals that gave rise to hippos) and use internal fertilisation. Male whales, like all mammals, have a penis for introducing sperm into the female vagina. Once deposited in the vagina, the sperm swim up to the fallopian tubes and, if an egg has ovulated, they may fertilise it. During the breeding season, female whales become fertile and, along with the

males, migrate to breeding grounds. Complex courtship routines occur between the sexes and the females choose males to mate with. Most whale species are not monogamous, and both sexes will mate with several different partners during one breeding season. In an effort to gain a competitive advantage, male whales make large quantities of sperm to try and displace a previous male's sperm. If successful fertilisation occurs, a female whale will become pregnant with one calf fathered by one of the males in the breeding group.

Sharks are unusual among fish in having internal fertilisation. The male shark has special adaptations called claspers, which are modified pelvic fins. A tube runs through the claspers through which sperm are ejected. During mating, the male inserts one of the claspers into the female shark's reproductive cavity, called a cloaca, and ejects sperm through the clasper. Internal fertilisation is beneficial for sharks for two main reasons. Some sharks live solitary lives, or live in single-sex groups until the breeding season, and do not often come across a potential mate. It is therefore essential that sharks try to ensure reproductive success by actively transferring the gametes from the male to female. Most species of shark invest a large amount of parental care in their offspring to help ensure their survival.

Parental care

Evolution by natural selection has created two opposing reproductive strategies for passing on genes to the next generation: the **r-strategy** and the **K-strategy**.

 KEY TERMS

r-strategist: an organism that produces large numbers of offspring while providing little parental investment

K-strategist: an organism that produces few offspring but provides a large amount of parental investment

r-strategy

Many marine organisms produce millions of offspring and simply release them without any care or additional nourishment other than a yolk sac or nutrients in the egg. The survival of these offspring relies on chance; mortality rates are high and possibly less than 1% of them will survive. A giant clam may produce half a billion eggs in a breeding season but only one or two may actually survive. There is even the risk that none will survive.

K-strategy

The alternative approach is to produce fewer offspring and invest more energy in nurturing them. It would be impossible to guard and nurture half a billion offspring, but if there are far fewer offspring, it is feasible to make the effort to feed and defend them. However, there is still the risk that with only one or two offspring none will survive.

Tuna

Tuna are r-strategists. A female bluefin tuna can produce up to 25 million eggs every year, of which only a fraction will ever survive to become an adult tuna. No care is given to the larval stages, which have to take their chance within the plankton of the oceans.

Whales

Whales are K-strategists. As mammals, they are viviparous animals, meaning that the offspring develop inside the mother. The developing calf is located in the mother's uterus and obtains its nutrients from her blood via the placenta and umbilical cord. Different whale species have different gestation periods, ranging from 10 months for the humpback whale to 16 months for the sperm whale. Only one calf is born at a time and it is protected and nurtured by its mother, taking from milk from her mammary glands for between 4 and 11 months. The calves often remain with their mother or in family groups until they become sexually mature, which can be anything from 2 to 5 years, depending on the species. Some species, such as the sperm whale, are known to share 'babysitting' duties within their family groups and older calves will sometimes help raise the younger ones.

Sharks

Shark species use a range of reproductive strategies, but most are considered to be K-strategists because a lot of parental care is invested in a few offspring. Three main methods are used by different shark species.

Oviparity

After fertilisation, the females of some shark species lay characteristic eggs often called mermaid's purses. These are attached to rocks or seaweeds and are often guarded by the female. The egg cases contain the developing embryo, which is attached to a yolk sac that contains a high concentration of nutrients. When the yolk sac is depleted of nutrients, the young shark hatches from the egg case as a fully formed, small version of the adult shark.

Ovoviviparity

Some sharks produce live young. In many cases, the eggs are fertilised internally in the female's body and then carried inside her until they hatch, eventually passing out as live young. There is a good supply of oxygen inside the mother and, by being inside her body, there is little chance of the young being eaten by predators. While inside the body of the female, they develop inside their egg cases using a yolk sac for nutrition. Some juvenile sharks are brooded inside the mother's body for longer in order to be protected for longer. This means the young need a further food supply. Thresher and porbeagle shark juveniles eat unfertilised eggs (oophagy) that are continuously ovulated by the mother so that they are born at a larger size. The sandtiger shark and grey nurse shark take this a stage further, with embryophagy or intrauterine cannibalism. Prior to birth, the developing sharks swim around the mother's uterus killing and cannibalising their siblings so that eventually only one or two larger sharks are born. A fully grown sandtiger shark is about 2.5 m long; the juvenile is almost 1 m long when born so is large and strong enough to avoid most predators immediately after birth.

Viviparity

Some shark species, such as hammerheads and bull sharks, are classed as viviparous. They give birth to fully formed live offspring that have been nourished from the mother via a placenta. During their development, these embryos use up the yolk and then parts of the egg covering, and the yolk placenta attaches to the uterine wall in a similar way to the placenta of mammals. A cord containing blood vessels, similar to an umbilical cord, enables blood transport to and from the placenta. The developing shark is able to pass waste products into the mother's blood and gain nutrients such as glucose and amino acids for growth from the mother. When born, these sharks are fully developed and can swim away from their mother to live independently straight away.

SELF-ASSESSMENT QUESTION

7   Summarise the differences between r- and K-strategies, giving named examples of marine organisms for each.

The strange life cycle of the ceratoid deep-sea angler fish

Life in the darker, deeper parts of the ocean is not easy. The pressure of the water is exceptionally high, there is no light and very little life. Fish that live at great depths may only encounter prey and mates very rarely, so need to ensure that when they do these encounters are successful.

Some forms of deep-sea angler fish have adapted to these conditions by having a very unusual life cycle. The male and female fish are very different from each other. The female fish are large, rather ferocious-looking fish with large mouths and teeth, so that any food they encounter is easily caught. Some species have a bioluminescent lure with which they attract other fish and squid. If a meal only passes by once a month, it is essential that it is caught. They also have large ovaries that can produce large numbers of eggs.

The male angler fish are very different. They are very small and have only very rudimentary mouthparts and a poorly developed gut. Their small size means that they need little energy to move around, but they do have extremely well developed olfactory organs and testes. These tiny male fish can sense chemicals released from the females and swim towards them. When they encounter a female they attach themselves to her with their mouth and become a parasitic organism (Figure 10.15).

A blood supply grows from the female into the male so he simply becomes a part of her body, nourished by her blood supply. Once attached he remains part of her body for as long as she lives, and in essence becomes an attached sperm-manufacturing organ that the female always has near. Female angler fish often have several of these parasitic males attached to them.

Questions

1   a   Explain why the male angler fish is small and does not require a fully formed gut.

    b   Explain why it is important that the female fish attracts food towards itself and has well-developed mouthparts.

2   Suggest why this life cycle is a good strategy for the angler fish in the deep oceans.

3   Suggest the benefit to the female of having more than one male angler fish permanently attached.

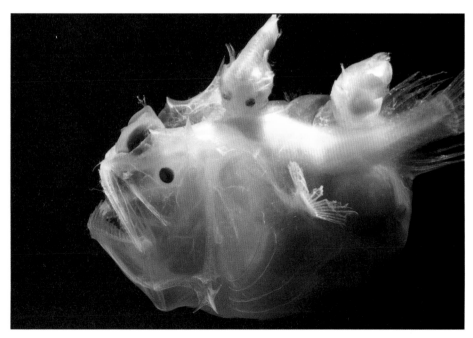

Figure 10.15. A female angler fish with two attached parasitic males.

Summary

- Different species of marine organism have evolved different life cycles as solutions to surviving particular types of environment.

- Many species have larval stages that help them disperse and reduce competition for food.

- Larvae may occupy different habitats from the adults.

- Some species use internal fertilisation to help to ensure that fertilisation is successful, while others scatter their gametes into the water to mix with the gametes of other members of the species.

- Organisms such as whales and sharks produce few offspring but nurture them in an effort to help them to survive to adulthood.

- Other organisms such as tuna and oysters produce extraordinary numbers of offspring and provide little to no care, with only a few surviving.

Exam-style questions

1 **a** Describe the life cycle of the giant clam. **[10]**

   b Explain how the loss of mangroves could affect the populations of shrimps and groupers. **[5]**

                                                    [Total mark: 15]

2 **a** **i** Explain what are meant by the terms internal and external fertilisation. **[2]**

Table 10.11 shows the mean number of fertilised eggs and mean number of offspring that survive to adulthood for one breeding cycle of giant clams and sperm whales.

species	number of fertilised eggs	number of offspring surviving to adulthood
giant clam	354 000 000	5.3
sperm whale	1	0.9

Table 10.11. Survival rates of giant clam and whale fertilised eggs.

     ii Calculate the percentage of fertilised eggs that survive to adulthood for the giant clam and the sperm whale. **[2]**

     iii Explain how parental care strategies determine the number of eggs produced and number of fertilised eggs surviving to adulthood. **[3]**

   b Sandtiger sharks give birth to live young. In the uterus of the mother there are many fertilised eggs that develop into embryos. The embryos actively feed off other embryos until only one or two are left to be born. Suggest and explain how this reproductive strategy is beneficial to the sandtiger sharks. **[4]**

                                                      [Total mark: 11]

3 **a** Figure 10.16 shows the life cycle of Pacific salmon.

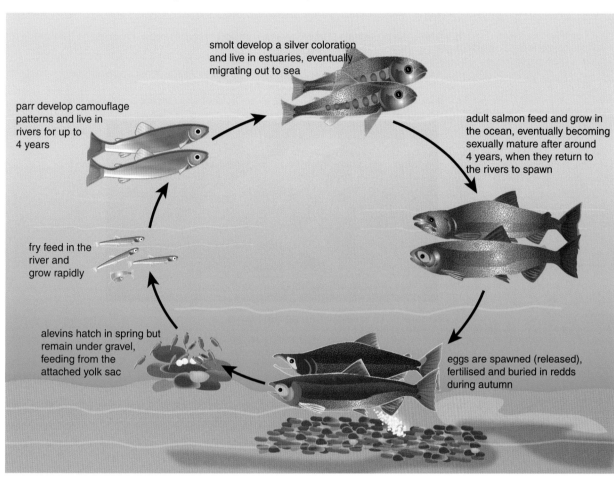

smolt develop a silver coloration and live in estuaries, eventually migrating out to sea

parr develop camouflage patterns and live in rivers for up to 4 years

adult salmon feed and grow in the ocean, eventually becoming sexually mature after around 4 years, when they return to the rivers to spawn

fry feed in the river and grow rapidly

alevins hatch in spring but remain under gravel, feeding from the attached yolk sac

eggs are spawned (released), fertilised and buried in redds during autumn

Figure 10.16. The life cycle of Pacific salmon.

    i Explain why laying eggs in river water that is flowing too slowly or too quickly reduces the number of alevins developing. **[2]**

    ii Explain the benefit of the alevins developing in the gravel redds. **[1]**

    iii Suggest and explain why it is beneficial to the salmon to have life cycle stages in both rivers and oceans. **[3]**

b Pacific salmon are considered a keystone species. Many species such as bears feed on salmon while the salmon are migrating from the oceans up to the rivers.

Using your knowledge of the salmon life cycle, explain how creating a hydroelectric dam across a river could affect the population of bears. **[4]**

[Total mark: 10]

4 Scientists have found that there are two discrete populations of Atlantic bluefin tuna. The populations overlap in the central Atlantic Ocean and then return to spawning grounds in either the Mediterranean Sea or the Gulf of Mexico. Each tuna always returns to the same spawning ground.

→

a Explain why it is advantageous for the tuna to spawn in only two spawning grounds. [3]

b Tuna use broadcast spawning as a method of fertilisation. This means that many tuna aggregate together and simultaneously release gametes into the water. Suggest and explain one advantage and one disadvantage of broadcast spawning. [2]

c Figure 10.17 below shows a tuna larva. Its skin and eye are silver and shiny.

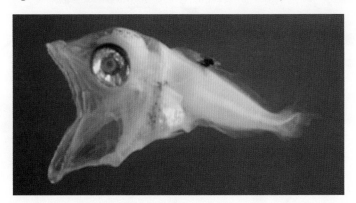

Figure 10.17. Free-swimming tuna larva.

Suggest how the tuna larva is adapted to enable it to survive. [2]

[**Total mark: 7**]

5 Giant clams release a chemical into the water called SIS, which synchronises gamete release from other clams. A scientist investigated the effect of different concentrations of SIS on the release of gametes.

Ten giant clams were placed into a marine tank and exposed to a concentration of 2% SIS. The number of clams that released gametes within 2 s was recorded. The experiment was repeated with different concentrations of SIS, each time using different clams. The results are shown in Table 10.12.

concentration of SIS / %	number of clams that released gametes within 2 s
0	0
2	1
6	1
14	2
22	8
28	9
36	9

Table 10.12. Effect of different concentrations of SIS on release of gametes by giant clams.

a i Plot a line graph of the effect of concentration of SIS on the release of gametes by giant clams. [4]

ii Describe the effect of an increasing concentration of SIS on the release of gametes by giant clams. [2]

b i Suggest two variables that the scientists would need to control. **[2]**

ii The scientists concluded that 22% is the minimum concentration that the giant clams respond to. Explain whether this was a correct conclusion. **[1]**

iii Suggest why the scientists only counted the clams that responded to the SIS within 2 s. **[1]**

c Suggest and explain the advantages of the response by the clams to increasing concentrations of SIS. **[2]**

[Total mark: 12]

The Elwha River Restoration Project

The Elwha River is a 72 km long river located on the Olympic Peninsula in the north-western part of Washington State, USA. The source of the Elwha lies in the Olympic Range of the Olympic National Park. The river was a breeding ground for all species of Pacific salmon, including chinook, pink and sockeye, and at one time it was estimated that up to 400 000 salmon would return to its upper reaches every year. The Olympic National Park area is the ancestral land of a native North American population, the Lower Elwha Klallam Tribe. The Klallam tribe fished the river and its tributaries and their culture is closely linked to the annual salmon runs. The National Park area had a rich diversity of wildlife, including bald eagle, black bear, beaver, bobcat, coyote, raccoon, weasel, mink and river otter, all of which were dependent on the river and annual migration of salmon (Figure 10.18). Pacific salmon are considered to be a keystone species in the area because so many species are dependent on their migration up the rivers.

Figure 10.18. A black bear eating salmon.

The building of the dams

In the late 19th century, pioneers began to settle in the area and interest developed in damming the Elwha River to generate hydroelectric power. In 1889, Thomas Aldwell, a Canadian entrepreneur, began to purchase land along the Elwha and, by 1910, with the financial help of George Glines, a Canadian investor, he began to construct the Elwha Dam. The Elwha Dam was completed in 1912 and a second dam further upstream, the Glines Dam, was completed in 1926 (Figure 10.19). When many hydroelectric dams are built, 'fish ladders' are often included. Fish ladders are artificial stretches of river that bypass the dam and enable migratory fish species to move upstream. Unfortunately, neither the Elwha nor Glines Dam had any route for the salmon, so access to the best upstream river stretches for spawning was totally blocked.

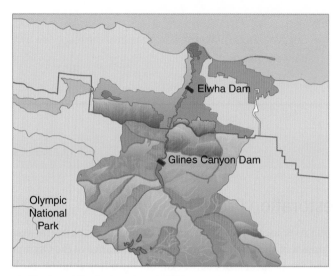

Figure 10.19. A map of Olympic National Park showing the sites of the Elwha and Glines Dams.

The effects of the dams on the ecology of the area

Building the dams caused many ecological problems for the wildlife in the area, along with socio-economic problems for the native Klallam Tribe.

- Two artificial lakes, Lake Aldwell and Lake Mills, were created behind the dams, resulting in the flooding of a large area of land. The temperature of the water was also affected. The normal river temperature was around 0–10 °C, but in the lakes the water remained stationary and warmed up in excess of 16 °C. The warm water was thought to cause an increase in the numbers of fish parasites and diseases.

- The flow rate of the rivers changed upstream of the dams, resulting in flooding of higher reaches of river and no seasonal changes to the flow rate. Rivers normally flow at different speeds during the year, depending on the weather conditions. Many species have life cycles that depend on different flow rates throughout the year. Many of the Klallam people lost their land and were displaced.

- Replacement gravel was no longer washed down past the dams to the lower river reaches, but instead accumulated upstream of the dams. Coastal gravel deposition was reduced, leading to erosion of the coast and loss of beaches around the estuary of the river. Other river sediments that act as food for filter-feeding molluscs such as clams did not reach the estuary and sea.

- Salmon were unable to reach the upper 48 km of river where the best breeding grounds are located. The Klallam people reported seeing thousands of salmon dying at the base of the river unable to pass the dam. An attempt was made to create spawning grounds below the dam but this failed because insufficient gravel was able to accumulate. Salmon fisheries from other areas of the USA and Canada reported reduced catches.

Only a few years after the dams were completed it was recorded that populations of over 22 species of mammals and birds, including beaver, black bear, bobcat, weasel, coyote, bald eagle, raccoon, mink and river otter, had declined. Grazing animals that need grassland and shelter, such as elk and black-tailed deer, also declined. The Klallam people, who had lived in harmony with the river for hundreds of years, also paid a heavy price, with the loss of their homes and livelihoods. Many were displaced to land around the lower reaches of the river, in areas that frequently flooded when the sluice gates of the dams were opened to regulate the flow of the river.

Demolition of the dams and recovery

In the last quarter of the 20th century the amount of electricity generated by the dams became less significant and people became more interested in conservation and ecology. In 1992, the United States Federal Government passed the Elwha River Ecosystem and Fisheries Restoration Act that paved the way for a solution to the problems the dams had created. The Federal Government purchased the dams and debated installing salmon ladders, but eventually decided that the most effective method of restoring the salmon populations and other wildlife would be to demolish both dams entirely (Figure 10.20).

Figure 10.20. Glines Dam (a) before and (b) after demolition.

Removal of the Elwha and Glines Dams began in September 2011 and was completed on 26 August 2014. The total cost of the Elwha River restoration is approximately $351.4 million. After the dams were removed, the two lakes drained, restoring land for wildlife and also releasing more than 10 million tonnes of sediment; this has deposited in the river estuary, reforming the beaches and coastline of the early 20th century. Draining the reservoir also revealed a ceremonial cremation ground of the Lower Elwha Klallam Tribe.

Within months of the removal of the dams, salmon were sighted in the upper reaches of the river. It is now hoped that the populations of salmon, mammals and birds that have declined for 100 years will recover and restore the area to one of rich biodiversity.

Questions

1 Explain why the Pacific salmon is considered to be a keystone species.

2 a Explain the reasons why the dams led to a drastic reduction in numbers of Pacific salmon.

  b Suggest why efforts to breed salmon in the lower reaches of the river below the dam were unsuccessful.

3 Using your knowledge of life cycles, suggest and explain how dams would have affected the marine populations of clams, oysters and shrimps.

4 Draw up a leaflet that could be given to a politician to help lobby for the removal of the dams.

Chapter 11
Fisheries management

Learning outcomes

By the end of this chapter, you should be able to:

- describe the effect modern fishing technology has had on marine habitats and fish stocks
- explain why fish stocks need to be exploited in a sustainable way, and the main methods used to achieve this
- explain the types of information used to understand fish stocks so that they can be used sustainably
- describe the methods used to monitor and enforce sustainable fishing practices
- discuss the short- and long-term sociological impact of restricted and unrestricted fishing
- discuss how effective different methods of sustainable fishing are, and how non-target species can be affected
- describe methods that can be used to redress the damage already done to marine environments
- apply what you have learnt to new, unfamiliar contexts.

11.1 The impact of fishing

Since ancient times, humans have harvested many species from the seas and oceans. Until the beginning of the 20th century, this harvesting of marine stocks was not particularly efficient and, with a lower human population and less advanced transportation networks, the majority of fishing was sustainable. Throughout the 20th century and beyond, however, an ever increasing global population has seen the demand for protein-rich marine organisms rise dramatically. As technology has improved, boats and fishing gear have become increasingly sophisticated, which has led to plundering of the world's oceans on an unprecedented scale, resulting in a serious decline of species. In recent years the need to control our fishing has been recognised. We need to ensure that there will still be stocks for our children and grandchildren to use.

11.2 Sustainable fishing and the North Sea fishing fleet

Sustainable fishing is the harvesting of a particular species so that it will still be present in years to come. It is important that we maintain fish stocks at healthy levels for many reasons, including:

- conservation, to preserve biodiversity in order to maintain food webs

- ethics, to ensure that future generations have food that they can harvest.

A key term that is often referred to in sustainable fishing is the **maximum sustainable yield (MSY)**, which is the rate of fishing that can be carried out without reducing the fish population. If the MSY is exceeded, populations will fall. This can be illustrated by the history of fishing in the North Sea.

KEY TERMS

Sustainable fishing: fishing up to the maximum sustainable yield so that future fish stocks are not at risk of being depleted

Maximum sustainable yield (MSY): the intensity of fishing that can be carried out without reducing future populations

North Sea fishing

The North Sea is a region of the east Atlantic Ocean bordered by many European countries (Figure 11.1). Fishing fleets in the region had harvested fish for hundreds of years without any major effect on fish stocks. In 1970, the

227

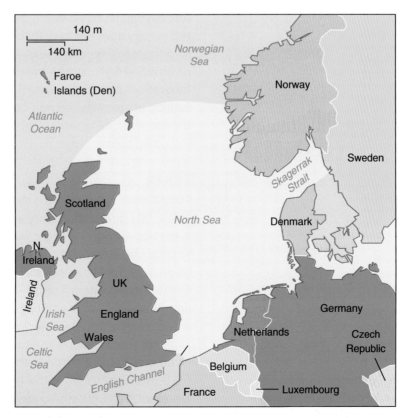

Figure 11.1. Northern Europe and the North Sea.

European Economic Community (EEC), now known as the European Union (EU), created a common fisheries policy (CFP). This declared that fish and coastal waters, apart from small zones around each country, would become a communal resource for all of the EEC. The CFP also created a subsidy system whereby if the price of fish fell, fishing fleets were given money to make up the shortfall.

In the 1960s and 1970s there was a sudden, unexplained increase in populations of certain species, including cod, haddock and whiting. This event, together with EEC subsidies, led to heavy investment in new boats and equipment by fishing fleets. Under the CFP, fishing of the North Sea for whitefish and herring was carried out at unsustainable levels throughout most of the 1970s and 1980s. There were few restrictions on size or age of catch; and young and immature fish were often taken as well as older, sexually mature fish. The eventual consequence of this was a collapse of many of the fish stocks in the 1980s.

North Sea cod dropped to a level that indicated that it was being fished to extinction. Figure 11.2a shows the dramatic fall in cod stocks during this period. The average length of cod caught also decreased, indicating that the number of older fish in the population had fallen and increasingly younger fish were being taken. This trend is shown in Figure 11.2b.

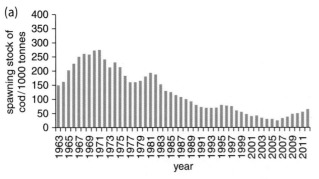

(a)

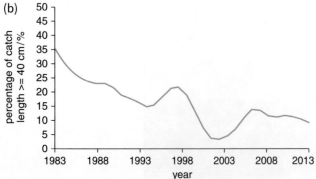

(b)

Figure 11.2. Graphs showing (a) changes in spawning stock of cod and (b) the percentage of cod caught that were longer than 40 cm.

In the 1990s, the EU issued national fishing quotas in an effort to reduce the over-fishing. For political reasons these quotas were still in excess of what was required to save cod stocks. By the early 2000s, after carrying out more surveys of cod populations, scientists called for a ban on cod fishing in the North Sea to allow stocks to recover. At the same time, the CFP was reformed and more focus was placed on protecting fish stocks for the future and preventing over-fishing. Despite the scientific evidence, a ban was not implemented but a big reduction in quotas was agreed. Other measures taken included a reduction in the numbers of days that fishing was allowed and a ban on fishing during breeding seasons.

The much stricter quotas seem to have worked to some extent and by 2015 fish stocks had begun to recover. There are now calls for fishing quotas to be raised because the stocks have improved, but caution is still needed. The stocks are nowhere near the high levels of the 1970s, and quotas and restrictions on boat-days, fishing seasons and fishing areas need to be considered carefully if sustainable fishing in the North Sea is to be achieved.

The impacts of modern fishing technology

Over the last 50 years fishing technology has developed significantly. The methods employed now are highly efficient, which means that we are in danger of fishing well beyond MSYs. However, the use of improved technology does not have to result in a negative effect on our oceans. We can design equipment with less focus on ensuring high catches and more on sustainability. Innovations have been made that can help prevent the capture of juveniles and non-target species. Some of the impacts fishing technologies have had will be discussed below.

SONAR

SONAR (sound navigation) is the method usually used to find fish. Boats either carry a transducer (Figure 11.3) in the hull or drag one under water. The transducer emits sound waves that are reflected by air in the swim bladders of fish like an echo, and this echo is detected by the SONAR system. The fish-finder measures the time interval between emitting the pulse and the pulse rebounding back to the detector. It will take a shorter length of time for sound to return from a fish that is close compared with one that is further away. Information from the SONAR is transmitted to a monitor to provide a visual representation of the fish underwater. Modern SONAR is now so effective that it shows the exact depth of fish and can identify the type of fish. Some SONAR works horizontally enabling ocean areas around a boat to be scanned for shoals.

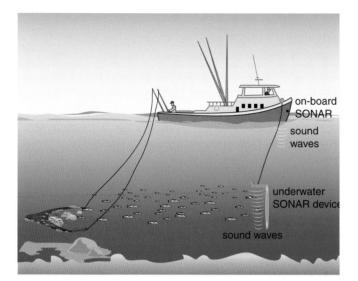

Figure 11.3. SONAR used on a trawler to identify fish.

Before the use of SONAR, identifying fish shoals relied on trial and error and the skill and expertise of the fishers. Experienced crews knew where fish shoals tended to congregate or looked for signs such as pods of dolphins and feeding sea birds. The advent of SONAR has meant that fishing crews can constantly scan for shoals and then efficiently take the fish. This has placed a strain on fish stocks because it is easier to find rare shoals and more time can be spent harvesting the fish than looking for them.

Purse seine fishing

A seine is a fishing net that hangs vertically in the water with its bottom edge held down by weights and its top edge buoyed by floats. A **purse seine** (Figure 11.4) is a type of seine net that can be drawn shut at the bottom to capture fish. It is made of a long wall of netting framed with a float line that floats on the surface, and a weighted lead line that sinks. Purse rings hang from the lower edge of the gear, through which run a purse line made from steel wire or rope. This is used to close the net.

KEY TERM

Purse seine: a seine net used to capture pelagic shoals of fish; it has a series of ropes that are used to close it and trap the fish before hauling them on board

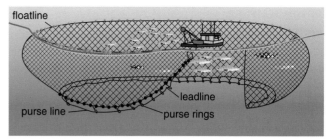

Figure 11.4. Purse seine fishing.

Purse seining is an efficient method for catching **pelagic** fish such as herring and mackerel and can be sustainable when used on a small scale. As net sizes have increased, however, it has been used to take large numbers of fish on an industrial scale (Figure 11.5). This is a problem if fish have vulnerable stocks, and it also takes many non-target species, known as bycatch. Purse seines are often used to capture skipjack tuna and bluefin tuna, both of which have seen dramatic population falls. When capturing skipjack tuna, many other species, such as yellowfin tuna, dolphins, turtles, sharks and rays, are also trapped and killed. Fishers in the Mediterranean wait in spawning areas where bluefin tuna aggregate during the breeding season and trap large numbers using purse seine nets. This practice has led to the collapse of Atlantic bluefin stocks.

Figure 11.5. Purse seine net being hauled on board a trawler.

KEY TERM

Pelagic: zone of open ocean or sea water that is not close to the seabed or shore

Benthic trawling

Benthic trawling uses a large net with heavy weights that is dragged across the seabed, scooping up everything in its path. It is used to catch organisms such as shrimp, sole, flounder and ray, which live on the seabed. Two weighted, wooden or steel otter boards drag along the seabed disturbing sediments and keeping the net open (Figure 11.6). The net has an open front end, and the captured fish collect at the rear of the net, the cod end. Benthic trawling is possibly the most environmentally damaging method of fishing routinely practised. It has been likened to ripping up a forest in an effort to pursue and catch a deer.

> ### KEY TERM
>
> **Benthic trawling:** a fishing method that drags a net along the seabed; wooden boards at the front of the net keep the net open and stir up the seabed, causing damage

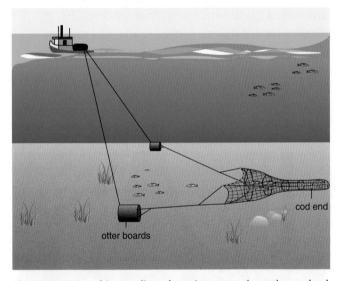

Figure 11.6. Benthic trawling, dragging a net along the seabed.

Dragging the net across the seabed dislodges most of the organisms in its path, breaks coral reefs and severely damages seabed ecosystems. The damage caused by benthic trawling to a coral reef is clearly shown in Figure 11.7: the coral has been smashed to pieces and the reef is no longer capable of functioning as an ecosystem.

Benthic trawling is not selective and up to 90% of a trawl's catch may be bycatch, i.e. non-target organisms. Many of the species caught are of little commercial value and are thrown back overboard already dead or dying. Scientists have estimated that in the Gulf of Mexico, for every pound of shrimp caught, between four and ten pounds of marine resources are thrown away. Shrimp trawls in Panama routinely discard more than 80% of their catch. Juvenile fish of many species are often caught, and in the Caribbean and Gulf of Mexico many juvenile snapper, mackerel and porgy are caught when shrimping. The capture of juvenile fish affects fish populations of target and non-target species, reducing yields for the fishing industries. In Indonesia, increased use of benthic trawling has led to a 40% reduction in catches by local, traditional fishers. In other areas, such as Guinea, benthic trawlers have caused physical damage to other boats and equipment.

Figure 11.7. Seabed (a) before and (b) after benthic trawling.

Tourism is also affected by benthic trawling. Damage to the seabed affects the populations of many species that tourists come to see, such as turtles, coral reefs and sharks.

Benthic trawling is now banned by many countries. The Indonesian government has banned it in an effort to improve catches and income for local fishers. It has also been banned in a 23 000 square mile area of the Atlantic Ocean from North Carolina to Florida, to protect deep-sea coral reefs after it was found that 90% of an area of reef had been destroyed by benthic trawls. The New Zealand government has banned benthic trawling in many ecologically sensitive areas, in particular around hydrothermal vents.

Factory ships

Factory ships are large fish-processing ships. They are designed to exploit areas of ocean far from land and can be at sea many weeks before returning to port. Some factory ships, such as stern trawlers, collect large amounts of fish that is then processed onboard. Others ships act as freezer 'motherships'; other trawlers bring their catch back to the factory ship each day, where it is processed and frozen. The introduction of large factory ships has meant that more fish can be taken on one trip. It has also opened up rich fishing grounds in distant, previously unexploited areas. The Japanese, Korean and Russian fishing fleets have many factory ships and trawl areas such as the south Atlantic Ocean. The use of industrial factory ships has also caused conflict with local fishers who have seen their industries threatened by falling catches.

The original idea for factory ships came from whaling; whalers would sail into distant waters hunting whales and processing them as soon as they were caught. This brought many species of whales to the brink of extinction during the 20th century. Only one whale factory ship now exists, MV *Nisshin Maru*, which is the mothership for the Japanese whaling fleet.

11.3 Regulating sustainable fishing

It is inconceivable for all global fishing to be banned and all fish products to be produced by aquaculture. A realistic aim is to ensure that fishing is sustainable and not putting future stocks at risk. In order to achieve sustainable fishing, certain data need to be collected about the fish populations. When the health of the populations has been determined, restrictions for preventing over-fishing can be put into place and monitoring and enforcement carried out.

Information required for sustainable fishing

Scientists are employed by governments to determine the health of fish stocks and set safe harvesting quotas that will not cause them to fall. Estimating current and predicting future stocks is not easy and scientists must consider several factors in order to recommend accurate quotas.

Figure 11.8 shows a simple population dynamic model for fish stocks. Whether a population increases or decreases depends upon the rate that new fish enter a population (recruitment) and the rate at which fish leave the population. New fish are recruited by reproduction or immigration, while fish leave as a result of mortality or emigration. If fish leave a population faster than they enter, the population will decrease, and vice versa. If fishing is to be sustainable, fewer fish must leave than enter.

KEY TERM

Recruitment: the arrival of new organisms in a population; for fish it is often considered to be the stage at which fish have reached an age when they can be caught in nets

Recruitment

The number of juvenile fish surviving to a particular stage and entering a population is called the **recruitment**. The exact stage that a fish must be at to be classed as successfully recruited into a population varies from species to species and according to who is doing the survey. Most authorities consider this is to be when fish have reached a size when they can be caught and counted in nets.

Recruitment depends upon several factors.

*   **Fecundity**: this is the reproductive rate of the fish and is measured by the number of gametes produced in a set time. It is a measure of fertility. Many species have high fecundity, producing millions of gametes, but only a fraction of these survive to be recruited into the population.

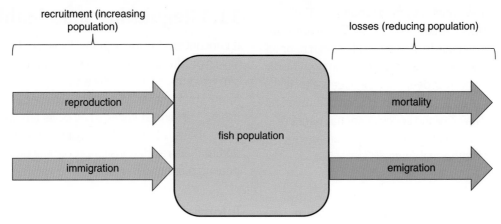

Figure 11.8. Factors affecting fish populations.

- Age of **reproductive maturity**: the control of maturity in fish is complex and there is variation both within and between different species. The age of fish plays an important role in many species. This is complicated by growth rates, masses, population densities and ratios of males and females. There is some evidence that over-fishing can lower the average age of reproductive maturity. The effect of this could be that younger, smaller fish become mature, produce fewer gametes, and overall recruitment falls. Species of fish that take many years to reach reproductive maturity will generally result in slower growing populations. Some species may need many years to re-establish healthy populations after a significant drop in number.

- Growth: the growth rate of fish is the speed at which the length or mass increases. Fish are considered to have been recruited into a population once they have reached a certain stage of development. Growth rates can vary as a result of many factors, such as food availability, temperature, oxygen levels and species of fish. Some species are naturally slow growing, while others grow rapidly. A slow-growing species will generally have a lower rate of recruitment. As already stated, growth rate can also have an impact on age of reproductive maturity and some species only start breeding once they have reached a particular size.

- Habitat dependency: many species of fish have complex life cycles with different stages of development that require different habitats. In Chapter 8, the life cycles of salmon and grouper were described. Both of these species require a range of different habitats for different stages of their life cycle. If one of these habitats is lost, the life cycle is disrupted and recruitment reduced.

KEY TERMS

Fecundity: the rate of reproduction of organisms; in fish the rate of egg production is often considered as a measure of fecundity

Mortality rate: the death rate; natural mortality is the death rate arising from natural causes, while fishing mortality is the death rate caused by fishing

Reproductive maturity: the time when an organism is able to reproduce sexually

Mortality

The rate of mortality is the rate at which the fish are dying. There are two types of **mortality rate**:

- natural mortality

- fishing mortality.

Natural mortality

Fish populations are subject to the normal causes of mortality, such as predation, disease, lack of food, and even chance events such as volcanic eruptions. Large numbers of predators and low amounts of food will directly reduce populations, but other factors can have indirect effects. Predator and food availability can depend on weather conditions, other food web changes, diseases, El Niño and human influence. This means that natural mortality rates can vary from year to year. Because there are so many variables, trying to create a predictive model for population change is almost impossible.

The climate influences how much energy enters a food web by affecting phytoplankton productivity. Phytoplankton growth depends on photosynthesis so is affected by light intensity, carbon dioxide levels and temperature. It also depends on mineral ion concentrations, often from upwelling currents. Human influences such as agricultural run-off and sediment can also have effects.

Diseases can suddenly affect populations. The spread of disease can be increased by high population densities so larger population sizes can appear to fall rapidly.

The majority of fish and shellfish have high fecundity, producing many gametes. The natural attrition rate for larval forms and juveniles is, however, very high. Despite having a high reproductive potential, very few fish are actually recruited into populations.

Fishing mortality

The death of fish as a result of fishing activities is called fishing mortality. It is not simply the number of fish that have been harvested and sold, but includes bycatch, discarded fish and other deaths caused by fishing. The number of fish actually harvested is relatively easy to assess from records of fish sold. Losses as a result of discards and bycatches are more difficult to assess because they rely on reports by fishers and scientific experiments. Fishing industries and scientists often disagree on estimates of bycatch and discards. Because fishers are stakeholders in the industry, they may not feel it is in their short-term interest to report high fishing mortalities. This can lead to reduced estimates of populations and reduced future quotas. An accurate estimate is important for the long-term health of the industry, as unsustainable fishing puts future stocks at risk.

Sustainable fishing models

A simple approach to determining how many fish can be harvested at any one time is that, in order to be sustainable, the population must not be reduced below previous levels. Recruitment in any year must be equal to or greater than the sum of natural mortality and fishing mortality:

recruitment ≥ natural mortality + fishing mortality

If recruitment is lower than the sum of natural mortality and fishing mortality, then the population will fall and the fishing is unsustainable.

In reality, the setting of sustainable fishing quotas is more complicated than this. Predicting the natural mortality is almost impossible and it needs to be measured frequently by scientific surveys. The fishing mortality also has to be as accurate as possible, using scientific methods and not based simply on market sales of fish, which may underestimate discards and bycatch. The age and size

profile of populations needs to be considered. Immature fish, despite being recruited, will not have reproduced so, if they are caught too early, will not contribute to the overall future of the population. Bluefin tuna farming has been problematic in this respect. Juvenile tuna are captured before reproducing and then taken to tuna 'farms'. This means that fish are lost before they have bred so stocks fall. Sudden events that can affect breeding and natural mortality also need to be considered, such as volcanic eruptions and El Niño.

SELF-ASSESSMENT QUESTIONS

2 Explain how the following factors could affect the amount of fish that can be safely harvested without affecting future populations of fish stocks:

   a   migration of large numbers of predator species into an area

   b   reduced age of sexual maturity of the fish

   c   reduced fecundity of the fish.

3 **a**   A population of cod is estimated at 325 000 in one year. The recruitment is estimated to increase the population by 15% $year^{-1}$. The death rate is estimated to be 10% $year^{-1}$. Calculate the number of fish that could be harvested without reducing the population below existing levels.

   b   Explain why it is useful to estimate both number and mass of fish when assessing fish stocks.

Methods to ensure sustainable fishing

In order to ensure that there are stocks of fish for the future, action needs to be taken by national governments to regulate fishing practices. Fish do not respect national boundaries, and there are many areas of our oceans that lie beyond the jurisdiction of any nation. To deal with this problem, intergovernmental agreements have been made by agencies such as the Food and Agriculture Organization (FAO) of the United Nations.

Setting fish quotas

The most basic measure that can be taken is the allocation of specific quotas of fish that may be harvested each year. The aim is to restrict the number of fish taken to let stocks recover. National regulators set an overall quota that may be harvested within a set period of time and then share this allocation between the commercial fishers. These allocations may be used by the fishers or sold on to others. Despite their obvious value and apparent simplicity, implementing quotas is problematic because there are many different fishing vessels and checking catches is not easy. The first use of quotas by the EU for North Sea and Mediterranean fishing was not successful and over-fishing continued illegally in many countries. The quotas also inadvertently encouraged the discarding of dead fish back into the sea if a landing was over its quota. Quotas are, however, very important in regulating how many fish may be harvested each year based on the MSY. In practice, regulators now tend to set quotas and use methods of restriction to achieve those quotas.

Restriction by season

Prohibiting fishing during certain times of year is frequently used to protect stocks. Seasonal restrictions are often linked with area restrictions: bans are imposed on fishing in certain areas at certain times of year. The reasons for seasonal bans include the following.

- Preventing fishing for a period of time enables fish to grow, reach larger sizes and be recruited into the population.

- Restrictions often coincide with breeding seasons, to enable fish to spawn and prevent over-fishing when fish have aggregated for breeding. Fishers found that catches were higher at certain times, usually when fish aggregated for breeding. Fishing efforts used to be increased at those times and had a very negative effect on stocks by disrupting breeding and over-fishing the adult population.

- Restrictions in areas where juveniles are maturing improves their chances of reaching maturity. Many marine organisms have complex life cycles with different stages living in different habitats. In the Gulf of Mexico, shrimp fishing is regulated in this way: fishing seasons are set so that larval and juvenile shrimp are not fished when in coastal areas or in the process of migration out to sea. This allows shrimp to move to open water and grow larger, improving yields for the fishing industry.

- Seasonal restrictions are not only for the benefit of the target fishery organism. Some fishing restrictions in the Caribbean are set to coincide with the migration and breeding of turtles, which can be caught by accident. In some areas, fishing is closed during annual passages of whales and dolphins.

Fishers may object to seasonal restrictions because they reduce the period during which they can work. There is a risk that fishers will then catch other species to make up for shortfall, which can lead to exploitation of other species. If the reasons for the restrictions are explained, however, fishers will often support seasonal (and area) closures in order to help improve fish stocks and secure their long-term future. In many cases they will help prevent boats fishing illegally and help monitor the catch. If local fishers support the bans, it can help to reduce the expense of surveillance of boats and catches.

Imposing restrictions on fishing grounds that span more than one nation requires intergovernmental cooperation. A ban will not work if only fishers from one nation comply, and this can create conflict between fishing fleets. Georges Bank is a fishing ground near New England that is fished by both the US and Canadian fishing fleets. In the 1970s and 1980s it became clear that fish stocks were under severe threat of over-fishing. The US and Canadian governments worked together to impose seasonal and area restrictions in an effort to help restore fish stocks. Despite worries about the threat to their main source of income, the majority of fishers had noticed a fall in their catch and supported the action. They worked with the regulators to put the restrictions in place so helping to restore the stocks of target species.

Advantages of seasonal restrictions are that they:

- allow breeding of fish
- reduce fishing intensity at a time when fish aggregate in specific areas
- reduce overall intensity of fishing, allowing growth of populations
- reduce negative effects on non-target species
- are relative easy to implement.

Disadvantages of seasonal restrictions are that they:

- may require intergovernmental cooperation
- can have high implementation costs
- may face hostility from fishers
- can cause short-term loss of money from reduced catches.

Restriction of location

Areas of sea may be closed for fishing, or restrictions placed on the type of fishing or number of boats that can be used. Restricting fishing in certain locations reduces the number of fish caught, thus increasing populations.

The closure of areas that are known breeding grounds or nursery areas for juveniles helps secure recruitment into the general population. The reasons for restricting fishing within certain locations include the following.

- Allowing depleted populations to recover. It can also help increase populations that are not in the restricted area. In Norway, it was found that banning lobster fishing in protected areas increased populations of lobster in neighbouring areas as well. Some marked lobsters were found to have migrated hundreds of miles away from the protected areas.

- Preventing fishing in a particular breeding or nursery area. Fish aggregate in particular areas to spawn so banning fishing in these areas allows successful breeding. Areas such as mangroves are often nursery grounds, so banning fishing in them allows juveniles to reach adult size.

- Reducing bycatch and damage to other species. Ecologically sensitive areas such as coral reefs, seagrass meadows and mangroves often have bans on fishing to prevent damage to the complex food chains that exist in these areas. They act as a refuge for populations of fish, shellfish and other species.

Refuge zones are often set up as part of general conservation measures, such as the development of marine protected areas (MPAs). MPAs serve as general protectors of biodiversity and, as refuge zones, allow fish to reproduce without threat. The fish then migrate to other areas, increasing the populations of those areas. MPAs and general conservation are discussed further in Chapter 14.

In theory, creating areas where fishing is restricted is a simple tool, as long as fishers respect the restrictions and they can be enforced. If fishers can be convinced of its value to their long-term viability, they will often regulate the areas themselves.

There can be problems, however. Areas that are fished by fleets of different nationalities require intergovernmental agreements across national boundaries. Surveillance and monitoring of an area may be required, and this can be expensive. In the large Phoenix Island Marine Reserve, an MPA around the republic of Kiribati, an illegal shark-fishing vessel reduced shark populations to near-zero levels at one atoll in the early 2000s. In such large MPAs, monitoring and enforcement is very expensive, particularly for countries with low gross domestic products (**GDPs**). Another risk of creating protected areas is that fishers may target and over-exploit other areas instead, thus moving the over-fishing problem to a different area.

Advantages of restrictions on areas are that they:

- create areas where fish populations can recover and increase

- cause population increases in the restricted areas that 'spill over' into other areas, causing a general population increase

- reduce bycatch and damage to other species

- are relatively easy to set up.

Disadvantages of restrictions on areas are that:

- fisheries may lose profits

- fisheries may begin to damage other areas

- expensive surveillance and enforcement is required

- they can causes disputes within the fishing industry.

Restriction of method

Certain fishing methods are far more damaging than others. Restrictions may be placed on which methods are permitted at different times of year and in different areas.

Table 11.2 summarises the environmental effects of different fishing methods. The use of nets when purse seining (Figure 11.4) and benthic trawling (Figure 11.6) can have potentially major impacts on fish stocks. Both methods can take large numbers of fish at any one time, and if not used carefully do not discriminate between adult and juveniles and other species. Regulating mesh sizes can help reduce the catch of smaller, juvenile fish and smaller non-target species but is not perfect. Theoretically, setting larger minimum mesh sizes should allow smaller fish to slip through the net. When fish gather at the cod end of a trawl, however, they are crowded together and juveniles may not be able to reach the mesh where they could pass through to escape.

Purse seine fishing can be sustainable when used carefully but only when a shoal of target fish has been located. It should be used with turtle escape devices and dolphin deterrents. Almost all methods of benthic trawling are unsustainable, severely reducing stocks of target and non-target species and damaging habitats. Many fishing regulators have now placed restrictions on benthic trawling because of its potential to cause damage.

KEY TERM

Gross Domestic Product (GDP): a measure of a nation's total economic activity

235

fishing method	example target species	effect on target species	effect on non-target species	effect on habitat	other information
purse seine	mackerel, tuna, herring, sardines	• risk of overfishing • mesh size restrictions can reduce catch of juveniles	• loss of tuna, turtles and dolphins	• low impact on habitat	• sustainable methods can be used but require smaller nets. Measures must be taken to reduce bycatch of dolphins and turtles
benthic trawl	plaice, sole, rays	• Risk of overfishing • Mesh and net size restrictions can reduce catch of juveniles and prevent over-fishing	• severe impact on other species • very non-selective method of harvesting	• severe impact on seabed, damaging reefs and habitats	• one of the most all-round damaging fishing methods
rod and line	tuna, swordfish	• lower risk of overfishing • less intensive than using nets	• low risk of bycatch	• little or no impact on habitat	• one of the most sustainable methods
long-lines	tuna, hake, cod, swordfish	• medium risk of overfishing if lines are not long and have few hooks	• demersal long-lines are a sustainable method if lines are secured to the seabed away from sea birds and turtles • demersal long-lines can catch and kill sharks • pelagic long-lines catch and kill sea birds, turtles, sharks and other non-target species	• impact on habitat	• demersal long-lines are sustainable methods if used with carefully selected bait and do not come loose • pelagic long-lines are unsustainable as they tend to be longer, carry many hooks and catch large amounts of bycatch

Table 11.2. A summary of the environmental effects of different fishing methods.

Rod and line fishing (often called pole-and-line) is used for catching pelagic predator species such as tuna and swordfish (Figure 11.9). It is a much more sustainable method than using nets. As it is less efficient than net fishing, fewer fish are caught so there is less impact on populations. If bait is used selectively, there is little risk of bycatch and there is almost no impact on the habitat. Many regulators ban all methods other than rod and line fishing for tuna.

Long-line fishing is a controversial method. Two types are practised, **demersal** (or bottom) long-line fishing and pelagic long-line fishing (Figure 11.10). In both methods, large numbers of baited hooks hang on long lines. In demersal long-lining, the lines are weighed down at the seabed between marker buoys and left to catch fish such as cod. This method, as long as the lines are carefully secured, are not too long, do not have too many hooks, and the bait is carefully selected, is a sustainable method. The use of pelagic long-lines is much more damaging. When used to catch fish such as tuna, the lines are towed behind boats in the surface water. Lines can stretch for hundreds of metres and have many hooks. Unfortunately, the bait not only attracts tuna but many other species, such as sharks, sea turtles and sea birds. Pelagic long-lining is not a sustainable method, although research is being carried out into methods of weighting the hooks to take them out of the range of sea birds and turtles and making bait unappetising to non-target species.

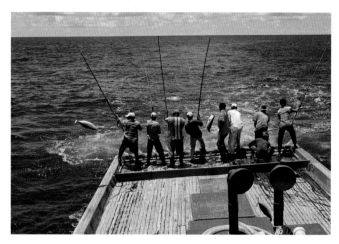

Figure 11.9. Pole-and-line fishing for tuna around the Maldives.

KEY TERM

Demersal: region of sea close to seabed, demersal fish live on or close to the seabed

Advantages of restricting fishing methods are that they prevent:

- over-exploitation of target species by reducing net sizes and using less efficient methods such as rod and line fishing

- bycatch by restricting the use of benthic trawling and pelagic long-lines and setting minimum mesh sizes

- catch of smaller, immature fish by setting minimum mesh sizes.

237

(a)

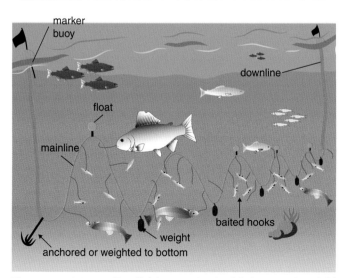

(b)

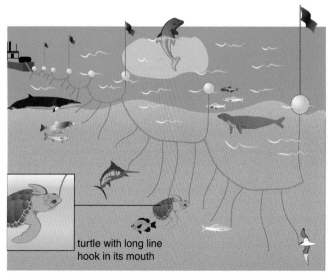

Figure 11.10. Long-line fishing methods: (a) demersal and (b) pelagic. Pelagic long-line fishing can cause the deaths of turtles, sea birds and sharks.

Disadvantages of restricting fishing methods are that:

- more labour-intensive methods, such as rod and line, are required

- there can be resistance from fisheries

- there is a cost to enforcing them.

Restrictions on the size of fish that can be retained

If fish are removed from a population before they have reproduced, populations decline rapidly. Determining accurately whether a fish is reproductively mature is almost impossible while at sea, so a basic measure of whether or not it has reached reproductive maturity is its size. Large fish are more likely to be older and to have already had at least one breeding season. Many national and supranational regulators set minimum sizes for the fish and shellfish that may be kept. Fish need to be measured at the point of catch and thrown back into the sea immediately if they are undersize. This requires a quick measurement of length (usually the end of the snout to the end of the tail). Table 11.3 shows the minimum sizes for some North Sea fish. One of the problems with setting minimum sizes is that the fish may have already been killed or damaged by the time they are measured. Enforcing restrictions on fish size is costly and requires spot checks on fishing vessels, landings on the quayside and also the markets for undersize fish. What should be done with dead undersize fish is a difficult question. These fish are often discarded into the sea and not added to the quota of fish landed, and are a hidden cause of fish mortality. It is better to ensure that undersize fish are not caught in the first place.

species of fish	minimum landing size / cm
bass	42
cod	35
dover sole	24
haddock	30
hake	27
herring	20
whiting	27
plaice	27

Table 11.3. Minimum sizes of North Sea fish.

Advantages of setting minimum fish sizes are that:

- immature fish are returned to the sea to breed, increasing populations

- fish stocks increase.

Disadvantages of setting minimum fish sizes are that:

- the enforcement of fish size restrictions is costly

- damaged and dead fish are returned to the sea, which may not be included in the landing quota.

Restriction of fishing intensity

If we are to ensure that fishing is sustainable, there needs to be regulation of how many fish are caught. Harvesting of fish needs to be below the MSY. Setting quotas for fish landings to ensure that we harvest below the MSY may seem simple, but in practice it is difficult to enforce and monitor. As already discussed, imposing quotas has, at times, led to dumping of dead fish that have been caught over quota, and these dead, undeclared fish are a hidden cause of fish mortality. Illegal catches are estimated to amount to between 11 and 26 million tonnes of fish annually. Rather than stipulating how many can be caught, it can be easier to control the intensity of fishing by restricting factors such as the number of boats in a fleet, boat sizes, engine sizes, number of boat-days and fishing gear sizes. In many countries, boat owners must apply for a commercial fishing licence or permit. This enables regulators to control the number of boats that are permitted to fish each year. The licence system also enables regulators to stipulate the maximum boat and engine sizes, fish quotas, permissible fishing gear and number of boat-days the licensee is entitled to. Licences can be revoked if the holder is not adhering to the rules and fines may be issued.

Restricting the number of boats in a fishing fleet will help prevent over-fishing but has to be carried out in conjunction with other control measures. One factory ship can take many more fish than three small inshore trawlers, so not only does the size of the fleet have to be controlled, but also the size of individual boats. Engine size is another factor, as larger engines allow trawlers to reach more distant fishing grounds and move between fishing grounds more quickly in order to exploit more stocks. The aim of regulating boat numbers, sizes and engines is to create a system that ensures there is a fair allocation for all fishers in a fleet.

Restricting the size of nets and the lengths of lines used will help prevent over-fishing. Less fishing intensity reduces the intensity of effort, so more trawls need to be carried out to achieve the same catch. Rod and line fishing is far less intensive than using nets, and in many parts of the world, such as the Maldives and Seychelles, this method is encouraged.

The number of days that boats are able to fish is also often restricted. Each fishing vessel owner is allocated an annual number of boat-days for fishing. Fishers need to keep detailed boat logbooks that can be inspected by regulators, stating the times they have been out at sea. One disadvantage of setting boat-days is that if trawlers are at sea for days without a reasonable catch, they will have used their boat-day allocation but at a loss.

Restricting fishing intensity requires regulation by governments and needs to be done in a way that does not disadvantage any particular fishers. In some countries, such as Indonesia and Malaysia, restrictions on fishing intensity have benefitted medium- and small-scale fisheries by reducing the share of large companies. The number of licences and permissible boat numbers and sizes needs to be evaluated annually depending on fish stocks, which requires constant scientific monitoring and enforcement. Care also has to be taken not to suddenly increase fleet capacity in a year when stocks are large, but then have to reverse this when stocks are lower, causing unemployment. Some regulators such as the EU operate subsidy systems to help fishers when fleet sizes need to be reduced. This has caused problems when subsidies have been spent on fewer, larger vessels with more equipment.

Advantages of restricting fishing intensity are that:

- less fish are harvested, increasing stocks
- careful restrictions on boat and engine sizes can help small- and medium-scale fisheries
- licencing can help monitoring of boat numbers and make enforcement easier
- it is easier to regulate than simply setting quotas, which are difficult to monitor.

Disadvantages of restricting fishing intensity are that:

- there is a possibility of unemployment and loss of earnings for fisheries and local communities
- it can be expensive to monitor and enforce, and may require subsidies for boats that are no longer used
- different years require different-sized fleets, causing fluctuations in employment and income each year.

Market-oriented tools, including the labelling of tuna as dolphin-friendly

A major factor in ensuring that fishing is sustainable is consumer awareness. Consumers are becoming increasingly interested in the origin of their food, how it is obtained, and how environmentally friendly it is. Tuna that has been caught by pole-and-line, a dolphin friendly method, is now often labelled as such to inform consumers.

There are many organisations that issue guidelines to consumers and put ratings on different products to advise on sustainability. Unfortunately, having so many different organisations offering 'accreditation' for different products can be confusing for consumers. The criteria that each organisation uses to classify food as sustainable can vary, meaning that a fishery may be classed as sustainable by one organisation but not another. Some of the current organisations accrediting seafood include:

- Marine Stewardship Council
- Ocean Wise
- SeaChoice
- Seafood Watch.

If consumers choose to buy seafood that has been harvested using sustainable, environmentally aware methods, those fisheries will make more profit and expand. In theory, companies that continue to use unsustainable methods will not sell as much produce so will reduce in size. However, food that is certified as sustainable also often carries a price premium to cover the additional costs of lower intensity harvests. Unfortunately, not all consumers are prepared to pay more for food that has been harvested in a sustainable way. Bulk buyers of food, such as restaurants, workplaces and hospitals, may not always make informed choices, and processed products such as fish meal may be used. Table 11.4 illustrates some of the advice given by four different groups for different North American species and methods of fishing.

Advantages of market-oriented tools are that:

- consumers are advised on sustainable food and make informed decisions
- market forces increase production of sustainable seafood rather than unsustainable methods.

Disadvantage of market-oriented tools are that:

- it only works where consumers are informed; several bodies offer accreditation and there may be conflicting advice
- not all consumers are prepared to pay more for sustainable food
- large-scale buyers, such as workplaces and restaurants, may not engage with the schemes
- industrial, processed products such as fish meal may not be included.

Table 11.5 summarises the advantages and disadvantages of the principal methods used to protect fish stocks.

239

fish species and location	Marine Stewardship Council (MSC)	Ocean Wise	Seafood Watch	SeaChoice
sablefish by hook and line – British Colombia	●	●	●	●
halibut by hook and line – Alaska	●	●	●	●
sockeye salmon – British Colombia	●	●	▲	▲
halibut by hook and line – British Colombia	●	●	▲	▲
haddock by hook and line – Atlantic Canada	●	●	▲	▲
haddock by bottom trawl – Atlantic Canada	●	●	▲	▲
lobster by trap – Atlantic Canada	●	⬡	▲	▲
spiny dogfish by long-line – British Colombia	●	⬡	▲	▲
shrimp by bottom trawl – Atlantic Canada	●	⬡	▲	▲
scallop by dredge – Atlantic Canada	●	⬡	▲	▲

Table 11.4. Consumer advice from four different organisations for North American seafood.

● = MSC certified; Ocean Wise recommended; Seafood Watch best choice; SeaChoice best choice

⬡ = Seafood Watch good alternative; SeaChoice some concerns

▲ = Ocean Wise not recommended; Seafood Watch avoid; SeaChoice avoid

SELF-ASSESSMENT QUESTIONS

4   Use these words to complete the sentences:

market-oriented, sustainable, season, rod and line, area, mesh

The principal tools that can be used to achieve _____ fishing include restricting fishing by _____ and _____. Restrictions on fishing gear can also be imposed such as enforcing the use of _____ fishing and increasing the minimum _____ size of nets. Labelling seafood as dolphin-friendly is an example of a _____ tool enabling consumers to make informed choices.

5   Explain why reducing the number of boats in a fleet may actually help secure employment in the future.

tool for maintaining fish stocks	advantages	disadvantages
restricting seasons	• allows breeding time for fish • reduces fishing intensity at a time when fish are aggregated in specific areas • reduces overall intensity of fishing, allowing growth of populations • reduces effect on non-target species • relative easy to implement	• may require intergovernmental cooperation • cost of implementation • may face hostility from fisheries • short-term loss of money from reduced catches
restricting areas	• creates areas where fish populations can recover and increase • population increases in restricted areas extend into other areas, causing a general population increase • reduces bycatch and damage to other species • relatively easy to set up	• fisheries may lose profits • fisheries may begin to damage other areas • expensive surveillance and enforcement are required
restricting fishing methods	• prevents over-exploitation of target species by reducing net sizes and using less efficient methods such as rod and line fishing • prevents bycatch by restricting use of benthic trawling, pelagic long-lines and setting minimum mesh size • prevents catch of smaller, immature fish by setting minimum mesh sizes	• more labour intensive methods such as rod and line are required • resistance from fisheries • cost of enforcing
restricting fish size	• immature fish are returned to the sea to breed, increasing populations • fish stocks increase	• enforcement of fish size restrictions is costly • damaged and dead fish are returned to the sea, which are not part of the landing quota
restricting boat and gear sizes	• fewer fish are harvested, increasing stocks • careful restrictions on boat and engine sizes can help small- and medium-scale fisheries • licencing can help monitoring of boat numbers and make enforcement easier • easier to regulate than simply setting quotas, which are difficult to monitor	• possibility of unemployment and loss of earnings for fisheries and local communities • expensive to monitor and enforce, may require subsidies for unused boats • different years require different sized fleets, changing the employment and income status each year
market-oriented tools	• consumers are advised on sustainable food and can make informed decisions • market forces increase production of sustainable seafood rather than unsustainable methods	• only works where consumers are informed, does not affect industrial fish products such as fish meal • several bodies offer accreditation and the advice may conflict • not all consumers are prepared to pay more for sustainable food • large-scale buyers such as workplaces and restaurants may not engage • processed products such as fish meal may not be included

Table 11.5. Advantages and disadvantages of methods for protecting fish stocks.

PRACTICAL ACTIVITY 11.1

Estimating fish ages in a population

Certain fish structures, including teeth, bones called otoliths and scales, have annual growth rings. Every year when a fish grows, another ring is laid down. If you look carefully at these structures using a microscope, you can count the rings and estimate the age of a fish. For example, if there are four rings present in the structure, the fish was 4 years old when caught. The easiest of these structures to obtain are scales.

Apparatus

- Scales from a range of different species and several individuals of the same species; these are best collected from a fish market: ask for offcuts of fish from particular species that have scales attached
- microscope
- glass slides
- coverslips
- forceps

Method

- Using the forceps, carefully removed a scale from the fish without breaking it.
- Place the scale on the slide in a drop of water and cover with the glass coverslip.
- Use the microscope to view the scale.
- Count the number of rings present (Figure 11.11) and record the age of the fish.

Figure 11.11. Scale from a guppy showing growth rings.

Results

Draw up a results table to show the number of fish within each species for a particular age. Table 11.6 provides a suitable example.

species	number of fish of particular age / years old					
	1	2	3	4	5	6

Table 11.6. Example results table showing the age of fish.

Draw a bar chart to display the number of fish in each age group for each species.

Conclusions

1 Discuss what use a fishing regulator could make of growth ring data from fish scales collected randomly from market stalls.

2 Table 11.7 shows data about the ages of plaice collected from fish market stalls every year for 4 years. The fish were aged by counting the number of growth rings on the scales. The scale samples were taken during March each year.

year	number of fish of particular age / years old					
	2–5	6–9	10–13	14–17	18–21	22–25
2010	0	2	7	6	4	1
2011	0	2	6	4	5	1
2012	1	3	5	3	3	0
2013	0	3	3	2	0	0

Table 11.7. Number of plaice of different ages collected over a 4-year period.

a Explain why the scale samples were always taken in March.

b The regulator stated that the fish stock was under threat and measures would need to be taken to reduce over-fishing of plaice. Discuss whether or not the data suggest that restrictions on fishing should be put in place.

11.4 Methods of monitoring and enforcement

If restrictions are placed on fishing, they need to be monitored and enforced fairly. Illegal fishing needs to be prevented, so the best way of maintaining a restriction is if fishers are in agreement with the measures being taken. Most fishers want to be able to continue to harvest fish in the future. They will often be open to measures taken to protect stocks, as long as they are involved in the decision making and their needs and views considered. Fishers that are in agreement with restrictions will self-monitor and help to police and report transgressions. Rather than imposing what may seem to be draconian measures on the fishing industry from remote governmental organisations, a more successful policy is to bring all parties together for discussions.

Monitoring and surveillance

In order to monitor restrictions, several methods are available.

Air and sea patrolling

The area covered by fishing boats can be very large so monitoring can be difficult and costly. Coastguards and fishery inspection teams use low-flying aeroplanes and surface boats to observe fishing boats randomly. If aerial observers are concerned about the activity of a particular boat, they will radio for a surface boat with boarding crew, who will intercept the ship. Aerial and sea patrols are useful because they can spot unusual activity, and can watch for boats that seem to be at sea too frequently. They are, however, expensive and it is impossible to cover large areas of ocean. Even if ships are seen breaking fishing laws, it can be difficult to obtain evidence. If a crew knows that it has been spotted, excess catch or gear can be disposed of before inspectors arrive.

Advantages of air and sea patrolling are that they can be used to:

- monitor 'real-time' fishing
- place observers on boats with little warning
- work together as a team.

Disadvantages of air and sea patrolling are that:

- there is a high financial cost
- trained staff are required

- they cannot cover all fishing areas
- they can be spotted, and ships may then discard evidence.

Inspection of catch

In many countries, owners of all licensed fishing boats have to keep detailed logbooks as a form of self-monitoring. In the US and EU, paper logbooks are gradually being replaced by electronic logbooks for ease of use and instant data access. These new e-logbooks instantly transmit information about catch weights via satellite links to regulators. The logbooks contain details such as:

- the number of hours spent at sea
- the number of hours spent fishing
- the fishing grounds and coordinates where fishing took place
- the catch taken from the sea before discards
- the catch taken after discards
- the catch that was landed on the quayside
- the catch that was sold at market.

In some countries, regulators ask to see logbooks as part of a system of random spot checks, and logbooks are submitted at regular intervals.

Catch inspections also take place. Inspectors may arrive without notice before a boat sets sail and observe fishing practices during a trip. They also travel to fishing grounds in fisheries support vessels to make spot checks on fishing boats and ensure that the logbook records are correct. Catches are checked on the quayside after unloading and again at markets. Inspectors often examine the size of fish on sale in fish markets and note any that are undersized and the boat from which they came. All fish sold now have a record of where and when they were caught, and by which ship, so it is easy to trace back to where they were fished. When inspectors work with fishers and help them to fish legally, it generates an open, realistic picture of what is happening on ships. When inspectors are considered to be remote and punitive, they are mistrusted and some fishing practices remain hidden.

Advantages of catch inspections include:

- self-monitoring with licences, which encourages ownership of fishing regulation by the fishers

- random checks, which allow quotas and fishing methods to be monitored

- fish records, which means that it is easy to trace illegally caught fish back to a particular ship.

Disadvantages of catch inspections include:

- records may be falsified

- if inspectors are present on a ship, fishing practices may be modified

- they are expensive to carry out

- fisheries may distrust the inspectors.

 KEY TERM

Catch per unit effort (CPUE): a measure of fish abundance calculated from the catch size divided by the fishing effort

Catch per unit effort

The **catch per unit effort (CPUE)** is a measure of how much fishing effort has gone into harvesting a particular catch. It is a measure of the abundance of a target species and is calculated by dividing the total catch by the effort used to harvest it:

$$CPUE = \frac{\text{fish catch}}{\text{fishing effort}}$$

Fish catch is easy to measure from ships' logbooks and fish markets. The concept of fishing effort is, however, much harder to standardise and different authorities use different measurements. Factors that may be taken into account for fishing effort include:

- days spent fishing

- size of engines

- size of boats

- number of traps set.

In order to be consistent when comparing CPUE from year to year, the same measurement of fishing effort must always be used.

CPUE can be used as a monitoring tool to assess the health of fish stocks and whether tougher restrictions need to be enforced.

- If CPUE decreases, it indicates that either the catch is decreasing and / or the effort needed to harvest the

catch is increasing. This would suggest that fish stocks are decreasing.

- If CPUE increases, it indicates that either the catch is increasing and / or the effort needed to gain the harvest the catch is decreasing. This would suggest that fish stocks are increasing.

If scientific surveys estimate that a fish population is low and a fishing company consistently declares a high CPUE, it may be that they have been underestimating their fishing effort and more investigations will be undertaken. In this way, CPUE can be used to monitor fishing vessels as well as the health of fish stocks.

Advantages of using CPUE are it:

- is easy to assess because data are readily available

- is a relatively simple measure of stock abundance and changes can be easily monitored

- can be used as a starting point for further investigations if there are concerns about fishing practices.

Disadvantages of using CPUE are:

- fishing effort is very difficult to standardise

- if used to monitor fishing methods, it is a very basic measure and changes in CPUE may be caused by natural population fluctuations.

Satellite monitoring

The majority of ships use the Automatic Identification System (AIS), which is a satellite communication method originally used for maritime safety and security. It uses navigation and communication satellites so that ships can 'talk' electronically to each other and with authorities on shore. It broadcasts information such as vessel identification data, position, course and speed. Fishing regulators now use AIS as part of a vessel detection system (VDS) as it can transmit real-time information about the activities of each ship. If a ship is causing concern, air and sea patrols can be sent out with inspectors to obtain further information. The full integrated inspection system is shown in Figure 11.12. As part of satellite monitoring, electronic logbooks send information via satellite to the regulators so that real-time data of catches made at sea can be seen immediately.

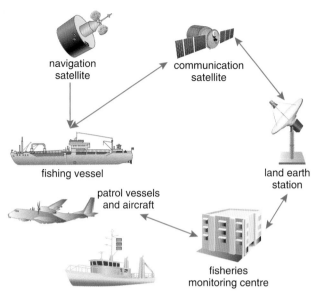

Figure 11.12. The integrated vessel management system (VMS) for monitoring fishing activity.

Satellite monitoring makes it possible to carry out surveillance in areas of ocean that are too distant for air and sea patrols. It also means that ships are visible at all times, even in the dark.

A project called Global Fishing Watch is being developed that brings together satellite technology with the internet. It is the product of a technology partnership between SkyTruth, Oceana and Google. Its aim is to use AIS to show all trackable fishing activity in all the oceans on the planet. The information will be available via a website and open to the general public.

While satellite monitoring is a highly effective method, it cannot totally replace human monitoring. Fishing boats and catches still need to be checked by inspection teams once a boat has been identified as needing further investigation.

Advantages of satellite monitoring are it:

- rapidly transfers information about fishing boats to regulators
- gathers detailed information about boats
- can reach all areas of the ocean at all times
- can gather data about catches as soon as they are taken.

Disadvantages of satellite monitoring are that:

- it can be costly
- not every boat has the technology
- it does not replace manual inspections, which still need to be carried out.

Table 11.8 summarises methods of monitoring fishing restrictions.

monitoring method	advantages	disadvantages
air and sea patrols	• monitors real-time fishing • sends observers on boats with little warning • air and surface teams work together	• high cost and requires trained staff • unable to cover all fishing areas • ships may discard evidence
monitoring of catches	• self-monitoring with licences encourages ownership of fishing regulation by fishers • random checks allow quotas and fishing methods to be checked • fish records make it easy to trace illegally caught fish to a ship	• records may be falsified • if inspectors are present, fishing practices may be modified • expensive to carry out • fishers may distrust inspectors
CPUE	• easy to assess as data are readily available • simple measure of stock abundance and changes can be easily monitored • starting point for further investigations if there are concerns about fishing practices	• fishing effort is very difficult to standardise • if used to monitor fishing methods it is a very basic measure and CPUE changes may be the result of natural population fluctuations
satellite monitoring	• rapid transfer of information about fishing boats to regulators • gathers detailed information about boats • reaches all areas of ocean at all times • can gather data about catches as soon as they are taken	• costly • not all boats have the technology • manual inspections still need to be carried out

Table 11.8. Advantages and disadvantages of monitoring methods.

Maths skills

Comparing data

Catch data from trawlers are often presented as 'mass of fish landed'. When comparing data from year to year, or from area to area, however, simply stating the mass of fish landed is not enough. To make data comparable you need to take into account variables such as time, number of boats, boat-days and size of fishing ground.

Worked example

Three fishing areas have released data about haddock catches:

- Area A, a total catch of 624 000 haddock over 3 years.

- Area B, a total catch of 470 000 haddock in 2 years.

- Area C, a total catch of 435 000 haddock over 5 years.

If you just look at the raw data, you cannot make a fair comparison. You need to take into account the time period over which the catch was gathered to obtain a mean annual catch. This is calculated by dividing the catch by the number of years it was gathered over:

- Area A mean catch per year, $624\,000 \div 3 = 208\,000$ tonnes year^{-1}

- Area B mean catch per year, $470\,000 \div 2 = 235\,000$ tonnes year^{-1}

- Area C mean catch per year, $435\,000 \div 5 = 87\,000$ tonnes year^{-1}.

From the mean annual catch rates, it looks like fishing ground C has a much lower yield than the other two grounds. This lower yield could be due to lower fish stocks, a smaller fishing ground or simply less fishing effort.

Measuring the area of a fishing ground is not easy but you can get an approximation by looking at the water surface area in km^2. If you want to compare the health of fish stocks in different fishing areas, the fishing effort is usually taken into account. Larger areas will generally have more boats, so have higher fishing efforts. Fishing effort is difficult to measure but the concept of boat-days is usually used (although some authorities use boat sizes and engine capacities).

You now divide the mean annual catch by the number of boat-days. This is the CPUE.

The number of boat-days for each fishing area is:

- Area A, 2000 boat-days

- Area B, 2200 boat-days

- Area C, 1500 boat-days.

The CPUE value for each fishing area is:

- Area A CPUE, $208\,000 \div 2000 = 104$ tonnes year^{-1} boat-day^{-1}

- Area B CPUE, $235\,000 \div 2200 = 107$ tonnes year^{-1} boat-day^{-1}

- Area C CPUE, $87\,000 \div 1500 = 58$ tonnes year^{-1} boat-day^{-1}

When looking at fishery data, you also often need to compare trends in two or more sets of data. Different data sets may have very different units of measurement, or may have very different magnitudes. Rather than plotting two separate graphs, it is helpful to use the same x-axis but two different y-axes.

Figure 11.13 shows the changes over time in the amount of groundfish brought to market in New England and the market values of these groundfish. The two measures have different units so use different *y*-axes. The left *y*-axis is the amount of fish and the right *y*-axis is the market value. Always take care when using these types of graph to read values from the correct *y*-axis.

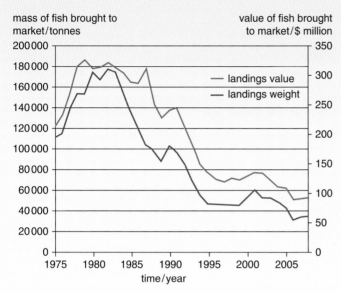

Figure 11.13. Change in market stock and value of stock of New England groundfish between 1975 and 2010.

year	total annual catch / 000 tonnes	number of fishing boats in fleet
1985	125	70
1990	105	72
1995	85	74
2000	80	75
2005	65	60
2010	70	55
2015	65	45

Table 11.9. Total annual catch and number of fishing boats between 1985 and 2015.

Follow the steps below to draw a line graph of the data in Table 11.9.

- On the left-hand side, draw a *y*-axis, select a continuous scale, and label it 'total annual catch / 000 tonnes'.

- Draw an *x*-axis with a continuous scale and label it 'year'.

- On the right-hand side, draw a second *y*-axis, select a continuous scale and label it 'number of fishing boats in fleet'.

- Using the left-hand axis, plot the points for the total annual catch and join them with straight, ruler-drawn lines.

- Using the right-hand axis, plot the points for the number of fishing boats in the fleet and join them with straight, ruler-drawn lines. Use a different style of line, for example by using different colours or dots and dashes.

- Add a key for the lines.

Questions

1 Calculate the CPUEs for the following sets of data.

    a   A catch of 365 000 over 6 years with a fishing intensity of 2135 boat-days.

    b   A catch of 275 000 over 3 years with a fishing intensity of 3282 boat-days.

2 Determine the fishing effort in boat-days that would be required to produce the following CPUE and total catches:

    a   CPUE = 25 tonnes year^{-1} boat-day^{-1}; mean annual catch = 168 000 tonnes year^{-1}

    b   CPUE = 15 tonnes year^{-1} boat-day^{-1}; mean annual catch = 125 000 tonnes year^{-1}

3 Check that the figure you drew for the worked example looks like the one provided in the answers.

Enforcement

In order to ensure that fishers follow restrictions and report their catches and activity accurately, there are several possible methods of enforcement (Table 11.10). The procedures and penalties for fisheries found breaking the law vary between different countries. The EU has instigated a points system whereby penalty points are added to fishing licences after committing offences. As transgressions are logged, more points are added to the licence. When a certain number of points is reached, a range of penalties is imposed. Some of the penalties that different countries use for breaking fishing laws include:

- bans on fishing for stated periods of time
- imposition of fines
- confiscation of boats and fishing gear
- imprisonment.

Penalties are designed to act as deterrents. They also help fishers that work within the law see that they are not losing out to those who fish illegally. Minor infringements are often punished by short bans and fines. Fishers that are repeat offenders, and those guilty of major infringements, can be punished more harshly, including long bans, the confiscation of their boats and fishing gear, and even imprisonment. These measures will cause a major loss of income and could lead to the complete loss of their livelihood. Similarly to monitoring, it is best if regulators work with the fishers to advise and help them to work within the law and educate them about the need for sustainability. If penalties are too severe for genuine mistakes, people could lose their livelihoods and their whole future could be at risk. There has to be an awareness that larger fishing companies can cope with harsher penalties that could ruin small and medium-scale companies. Table 11.10 summarises the methods that can be used to enforce fishing restrictions.

enforcement method	advantages	disadvantages
bans	• deterrent • prevents over-fishing for a period	• may be hard to enforce • small fisheries may lose all income
fines	• deterrent • loss of money to equate to any extra gained from illegal fishing	• may not affect very large fishery businesses • may cause poverty to small fisheries and lead to unemployment
confiscation of boats and gear	• deterrent • prevents over-fishing for a period	• may not affect very large fishery businesses • may cause poverty to small fisheries and lead to unemployment
imprisonment	• deterrent • prevents over-fishing for a period	• may lead to loss of career and future, resulting in unemployment and poverty

Table 11.10. Methods for enforcing fishing restrictions.

11.5 Sociological impacts of fishing policies

Fishing regulations obviously have major impacts on the fishers, who are the principal stakeholders in the industry. It is not only the direct employees who are affected, however. In some areas fishing is the main industry that fuels the local economy, and large service industries develop around it. Boat yards, fishing gear manufacturers and repairers, transport services, shops and other services can all be under threat if a fishing company closes. The local economy of an area is like a food chain, with the fishing industry filling the role of producer and the other industries being ultimately dependent on it. If the fishing industry fails, all the other industries are affected, which can result in unemployment, poverty and the loss of a whole community.

If restrictions are placed on fishing activity, this can lead to loss of revenue and unemployment in the short term (Table 11.11). A reduction in fleet size and fishing intensity would cause a sudden reduction in employment within the industry, and less money in the local economy. Protecting fish stocks could, however, be essential for securing the long-term future of fishing and employment in the area. In order to help local communities after reductions in the fishing intensity, governments need to help. They, along with local planners, need to explore ways of encouraging the development of alternative businesses and finding financial support.

If no restrictions are placed on fishing activity, in the short term the fishing industry would continue to generate revenue and the local economy would not suffer. However, in the long term fish stocks will begin to fall, and if fish stocks collapse completely there would be no fishing industry, leading to mass unemployment, loss of income and poverty. The economic future of the whole area could be in serious jeopardy.

Placing restrictions on fishing is not intended to punish the fishing industry. If used carefully and correctly, they are a way of securing its future. It is important, however, that governments and fishing regulators work with the industries and develop a strategic plan to safeguard employment and prosperity in affected areas.

11.6 Rehabilitation of stocks

When fish stocks have fallen, restrictions on fishing may not be enough to ensure that populations become fully rehabilitated. In the North Sea, restrictions have helped improve the numbers of cod and haddock, but they are still far from the levels of 50 years ago. Other methods can be employed to try to increase the numbers of fish, such as replanting mangroves, building artificial reefs and introducing cultivated stock to the wild.

Replanting mangroves

Mangrove forests are areas of rich biodiversity and exceptional ecological importance. They prevent coastal erosion and act as nursery grounds for large numbers of fish and crustacean species. Between 1980 and 2005, it was estimated that the global area covered by mangroves fell from 188 000 km^2 to 125 000 km^2, an approximately 20% fall. The majority of mangroves were cleared for shrimp farming, industrial development, housing, tourist resorts and agriculture. This has led to a problems with coastal erosion and a reported reduction in wild fish and crustacean stocks.

	restrictions	no restrictions
short term	<ul><li>reduced fishing intensity</li><li>fewer boats</li><li>increased unemployment</li><li>reduced earnings</li></ul>	<ul><li>continued high intensity fishing</li><li>continued employment</li><li>no reduction in earnings</li></ul>
long term	<ul><li>sustainable future fishing</li><li>ensures future employment and income</li></ul>	<ul><li>fish stocks collapse</li><li>total loss of fishing industry</li><li>mass unemployment and loss of income</li></ul>

Table 11.11. Long- and short-term sociological effects of restricted and non-restricted fishing.

Over the last ten years, there have been efforts in many countries, such as Guyana, Philippines, Indonesia and Malaysia, to rehabilitate areas of mangrove forest (Figure 11.14). Early attempts at replanting mangroves in Indonesia were not always successful. However, many lessons were learnt about the conditions needed, such as water depth and methods of rooting, and it was realised that it is essential to involve local communities in the projects. Mangrove rehabilitation is expensive and this has made it difficult for many less economically developed nations. In an effort to help, other countries, such as Canada, the USA and the UK, along with charitable organisations have helped provide funding. Restoring mangrove forests and their areas to their former state will take many years if they have been very badly damaged. There are some signs of success, however, with fishers in the Philippines and Guyana reporting increased catches of fish and shellfish after mangrove reconstruction.

Figure 11.14. Replanting mangrove as part of a restoration project in Grenada.

Building artificial reefs

Coral reefs are natural habitats for a rich diversity of marine life. They act as refuge areas for many fish species and help to increase populations. Artificial reefs have been successfully constructed in areas of the Mediterranean Sea for many years in an effort to increase fish stocks. Fishers have known for a long time that good catches are found around these artificial reefs, and many have now been built to improve the fishing industry. A range of materials have been used, including concrete blocks, old ships, cars and even old tanks. The use of old wrecked ships as artificial reefs is discussed in Chapter 14. The reefs certainly do increase fish stocks but care needs to be taken to make sure that the materials used are non-toxic, do not threaten shipping and do not damage other habitats.

Introduction of cultivated stock into the wild

The highest mortality rate during the life cycle of most marine species occurs in the period between egg and adult. Theoretically, if fish are bred and raised to a later stage by aquaculture, these fish could then be released back into the wild to help rehabilitate wild stocks. This practice has been used for many years to increase wild salmon populations in Alaska. Large numbers of king salmon are raised in tanks and then released into rivers to help to keep stocks high. There has to be strict regulation, however, as there are several risks.

- Released fish need to be disease free. Raising fish by aquaculture requires high stocking densities, which means there is a high risk of disease transfer. Aquaculture fish are often vaccinated and treated with medicines, but wild fish are not. Aquaculture fish can transfer diseases to the wild fish.

- Care has to be taken to not affect the gene pool in the wild. Fish that are raised in aquaculture may be from a particular genetic strain and can become inbred. If large numbers of these fish are released into the wild, it can affect the gene pool of wild fish and cause genetic weaknesses.

- Cultured fish may outcompete the wild fish. In Norway, it was discovered that many salmon caught by anglers from rivers and the sea were not wild salmon but escapees from farms. The escaped salmon were also found to feed more ferociously than wild salmon and they may have had other ecological impacts. There is concern that the salmon that are often thought of as wild in many North American fisheries are actually mainly cultivated salmon. The true, wild salmon may be decreasing in number.

- The number of fish released needs to be carefully regulated. Too many could affect other food chains that exist in the wild and outcompete other organisms.

Table 11.12 summarises a variety of methods that can be used to increase the numbers of fish.

rehabilitation method	advantages	disadvantages
replanting mangroves	• increases fish stocks • acts as nursery ground for many species • reduces costal erosion	• financially costly • requires research and skilled workers • may not grow successfully if not planted correctly
building artificial reefs	• increases fish stocks • increases biodiversity of marine species	• may have harmful chemicals • may damage other habitats
releasing cultivated fish	• increases fish stocks	• may affect gene pool of wild fish • may introduce disease • may affect other food chains

Table 11.12. Advantages and disadvantages of different methods for rehabilitating fish stocks.

SELF-ASSESSMENT QUESTIONS

6 Compare and contrast the effectiveness of replanting mangroves and the introduction of cultivated fish in order to rehabilitate fish stocks.

7 Explain how the following could be monitored.

   a Illegal shark fishing far from land in the mid-Atlantic Ocean.

   b Concerns about the size of fish being sold by a fishing business.

   c Concern about the fishing methods being employed by a group of inshore trawlers.

CASE STUDY

Salmon hatcheries in North America

The first recorded instance of breeding salmon in hatcheries for release into the wild was in Canada in 1857. The aim was to increase wild populations and introduce salmon to new areas. This practice soon spread into the USA and Alaska and became a common method for reversing the trend of falling salmon populations. In 1938, the US government provided money for the construction of large-scale hatcheries to replace salmon spawning grounds that were blocked or flooded behind dams. More than 80 hatcheries were built in the Columbia River basin alone, and throughout the US more and more salmon hatcheries appeared. Washington State, USA, has more than 24 salmon breeding centres that raise millions of Pacific salmon for release every year (Figure 11.15). These fish are vital to the sport-fishing industry in Washington State which is worth over $850 million per year. It has been estimated that between 70% and 90% of

'wild salmon' caught by recreational and commercial fishers are in fact salmon that have been initially bred in captivity and released.

Figure 11.15. Coho salmon hatchery.

Between the 1950s and early 1970s, scientists found evidence that releasing hatchery salmon was harming wild salmon populations. It now seems clear that the process has had major ecological and genetic impacts on wild salmon populations. There has been a reduction of genetic diversity in salmon populations, altered behaviour of fish, and ecological imbalances. Some scientists consider that the release of salmon has caused more harm than good to native salmon populations and this could be irreversible. In the 1990s, there was a sharp decline in the price of salmon because of a succession of high catches. This sharp decline caused many salmon fisheries to go out of business. It may be that, by trying to increase the harvest, the policy of releasing extra fish has led to the decline of the industry.

Environmental groups have become increasingly concerned with the volume of artificially raised salmon that have been released into the wild. In 2004, the Hatchery Review Group issued a new set of guidelines for hatcheries. The document contained more than 1000 recommendations for improving the industry. Some of the main recommendations included:

- closing substandard hatcheries
- limiting the number of hatchery fish released
- putting in place safeguards for the genetic health of wild stocks and preventing the spread of infectious disease.

There are now strict guidelines on checking fish for disease before release. Hatcheries can only release eggs from local wild salmon and may not transport eggs or fish around the area.

Questions

1 Explain the environmental and economic reasons for releasing salmon bred in hatcheries.

2 State why many salmon fishing companies went out of business in the 1990s. Suggest **one** other factor that may have contributed.

3 Summarise the risks to the environment that releasing the salmon could cause.

Summary

- Our seas and oceans have provided us with a rich source of food for much of our history.

- The intensity of harvesting has increased over the last hundred years to such an extent that if we are not careful there will be no more fish left for us to take.

- If we are to continue to enjoy fish and shellfish as food we need to fish sustainably.

- This means that stocks need regular monitoring and regulating bodies need to put restrictions in place to protect the future of these stocks.

- Restrictions can be enforced through constant surveillance of fishing by inspections and satellite technology.

- Governments and regulators need to work with fishers, not against them, and offer support and help when incomes fall.

- It is in everyone's interests that fish stocks remain healthy for future generations, and as such everyone needs to work together to preserve them.

Exam-style questions

1 a i Explain why fishing regulators can use the catch per unit effort (CPUE) to determine the health of fish stocks. **[4]**

ii Discuss the advantages and disadvantages of placing restrictions on seasons and areas as methods of protecting fish populations. **[6]**

b Explain how replanting of mangroves can be beneficial to a coastal area. **[5]**

[Total mark: 15]

2 Catch per unit effort (CPUE) is defined as the catch in a year divided by the fishing effort. It is often used as a tool to determine whether fish stocks are healthy.

Fishing effort was measured in number of boat-days, which is the total of number of days during which fishing took place.

Table 11.13 shows the changes in CPUE for two species of North Sea fish, cod and pollock, over a period of 10 years.

year	CPUE / tonnes boat-day $^{-1}$	
	cod	pollock
2000	55	64
2001	32	62
2002	25	54
2003	12	49
2004	8	45
2005	9	24
2006	15	21
2007	18	15
2008	22	14
2009	25	12

Table 11.13. Change in CPUE for cod and pollock in North Sea over a 10-year period.

a   i   Plot a graph to show the changes in CPUE of cod and pollock over the 10-year period. **[5]**

    ii Calculate the percentage change in CPUE for cod between 2000 and 2004. **[2]**

    iii Compare the changes in CPUE for both species. **[3]**

b   i   In an effort to conserve stocks, restrictions on fishing effort for cod were introduced in 2005. Discuss the conclusion that the restrictions have helped the health of populations of North Sea fish. **[4]**

[Total mark: 14]

3 If fish stocks are under threat, restrictions are often used to help protect populations.

a   i   State three types of restriction that can be used to preserve fish populations. **[3]**

    ii Explain short- and long-term sociological effects of fishing restrictions on a coastal area where fishing is the major industry. **[4]**

b   In 2003, restrictions on scallop fishing were introduced in a coastal area of Australia in an effort to protect the population. The restrictions included a reduction in the number of boats that could fish and a reduction in the number of scallops that each boat could harvest.

Table 11.14 shows the effect on the mean annual profits made by fishing for the scallops per boat.

year	mean annual profit per boat per year / A\$ boat^{-1} year^{-1}
2001	4500
2002	3700
2003	4800
2004	4700
2005	5100
2006	5300
2007	5300

Table 11.14. Annual profit per boat per year in Australian \$ from scallop fishing.

i   Describe the impact of the restrictions on the profits made from scallop fishing. **[2]**

ii   Suggest and explain reasons for the effect of the restrictions on the mean annual profits made per boat. **[4]**

[Total mark: 13]

4   Different methods of fishing have different impacts on habitats and other non-target species organisms.

   a   i   Describe the negative impacts of benthic trawling. **[3]**

      ii   Explain why purse seine fishing is often replaced by rod and line fishing. **[3]**

In an effort to investigate the effects of fishing on the age profile of a population of cod, scientists sampled fish in 1985 and 2005. The percentage of fish in different age groups was determined in both years.

The scientists sampled the cod for the same lengths of time and using the same equipment each year.

The results are shown in Figure 11.16 and Table 11.15.

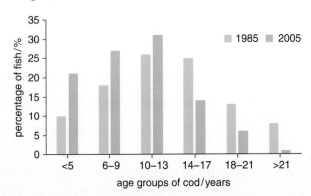

Figure 11.16. Graph showing percentages of cod in different age groups in 1985 and 2005.

year	total number of fish sampled
1985	2524
2005	1414

Table 11.15. Sample sizes of fish in 1985 and 2005.

b **i** Calculate the difference in the numbers of fish sampled in the 10–13 age group between 1985 and 2005. **[3]**

ii Describe and explain the differences in the cod populations between 1985 and 2005. **[3]**

iii The scientists recommended that a range of fishing restrictions needed to be imposed. One of the recommendations was that there should be an increase in the minimum mesh size used in the nets. Explain how increasing the minimum mesh size could improve the health of the population. **[2]**

[Total mark: 14]

Sustainable rock lobster fishing in West Australia

The coastal waters off the state of Western Australia (Figure 11.17) contain rich stocks of fish and shellfish. Commercial fishing companies operate in the area and it is very popular with recreational fishers. Commercial fishing, including pearling and aquaculture, contributes around 1 billion dollars to Western Australia's economy each year. It also provides direct employment for 5000 people, plus many more in-linked industries. Commercial fishing is based mainly on small family businesses, and 85% of commercial fishing activity is conducted in remote coastal communities. Over the years, Western Australia has been considered to be an example of excellent practice for the regulation of sustainable fisheries. It has achieved this by careful implementation of several policies.

Methods employed to ensure sustainable fishing

An integrated fish management programme is used so that the state government works with representatives from commercial fisheries, recreational fishers and scientists. Fish management programmes are discussed by all stakeholders to produce quotas and policies that are fair for everyone.

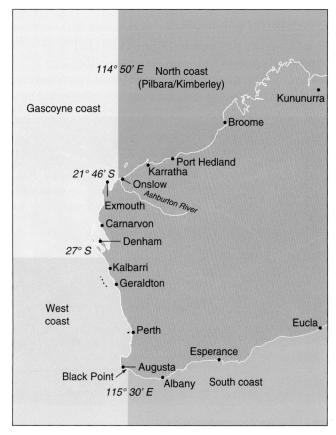

Figure 11.17. Western Australia, showing marine bioregions.

Western Australia operates a very strict licencing policy for both commercial and recreational fishers. Fishing licences must be purchased, and the revenue raised from the sale of licences is used to pay for the development of sustainable fishing projects and sustainable aquaculture. Projects have included the building of artificial reefs and fish-attracting devices, the restocking of prawns, mulloway and barramundi, training programmes, research projects and surveillance programmes.

There are strict rules and regulations for recreational fishing:

- only certain areas may be fished
- fish that are kept and not returned must be above a certain size
- there are limits on the number of each species that can be kept
- certain fishing gear is not permitted
- at some times of year fishing is prohibited in some areas.

There are also strict rules and regulations for commercial fishing:

- restrictions on the number of licences issued, gear restrictions, seasonal closures and limits on total fishing time
- quotas to limit the quantity of fish that can be landed
- permanent and temporary area closures to protect important habitats
- specific measures to protect juvenile or breeding fish (such as size limits and seasonal and area closures)
- nearly all boats carry AIS as a part of the VMS.

The measures taken to safeguard the future of Western Australia's fish and shellfish have proved to be some of the most effective in the world and are an example of good practice. Efforts to safeguard one species in particular, the western rock lobster, are seen as a good model for other species.

The western rock lobster

In the wild, western rock lobsters (Figure 11.18) can live for up to 20 years and grow to sizes of over 5 kg. They mature at around six or seven years of age. They are a very commercially important species and were initially exploited at the end of the Second World War, when small fisheries were set up to produce canned lobster for soldiers. The lobsters were caught by using baited lobster traps.

Figure 11.18. Western rock lobster.

Throughout the 1950s, lobster fishing expanded rapidly, with many more mechanised boats being used. By the early 1960s, lobster populations were beginning to decline and the average size of lobster caught was also decreasing. In 1963, the first restrictions on lobster fishing were introduced. No more new fishing licences were issued and restrictions were placed on the number of lobster traps allowed on each boat. Legislation controlling lobster fishing has continued to evolve and current measures include:

- restricted access to fishing grounds
- minimum legal size of 76 mm in length
- closed season from 1 July to 15 November each year
- escape gap of 54 mm in all pots to allow escape of smaller lobsters
- ban on taking spawning female rock lobsters and those in a pre-spawning condition
- annual quotas based on population estimates; if catch per unit effort is low, quotas are reduced
- maximum holding of 150 lobster pots per boat
- constant scientific surveys to assess numbers of juvenile lobsters in order to predict future stocks.

Recruitment of lobsters varies enormously and is affected by many natural factors, including the strength of the winds and water currents. Scientists have managed to produce a population model that takes into account many biotic and abiotic factors. This helps to predict future populations and set fishing quotas.

Lobster fishing is actively managed. Before 2008, a period of very low juvenile settlement was recorded so that fishing effort reductions were introduced for the 2008–2009 season. Trap numbers and fishing periods were limited and the number of vessels decreased from 460 to 294 over 2 years. The reduced fishing effort was associated with an overall increase in profit compared with what would have been achieved if all 460 vessels had still been operating at the previous effort levels. After the restrictions, commercial catch rates improved and rock lobster egg production moved to record-high levels. The success of the measures, both environmentally and economically, has pleased both the scientists and the fisheries. By working together they have developed a model for sustainable fishing that can be copied elsewhere.

In recognition of its success, the West Coast Rock Lobster Managed Fishery was the first fishery in the world to be certified as ecologically sustainable by the Marine Stewardship Council (MSC). The state of Western Australia continues to work hard to promote sustainable fishing methods. It monitors and controls all fishing in its waters and carefully implements restrictions that take into consideration both the industry and the long-term health of fish populations. It continues to fund research: new lobster pots have been designed to prevent sealion pups getting trapped in them. Continuing and extensive consultation, in addition to a long-term science programme, has resulted in the western rock lobster being one of the best managed fisheries in the world.

Questions

1. Explain why the integrated management system that regulates fishing in Western Australia makes the regulation more effective.
2. Explain how three of the general commercial fishing rules help to preserve fish stocks.
3. Suggest how biotic and abiotic factors can affect the population of the lobsters.
4. Suggest why putting restrictions on lobster fishing has actually resulted in an increase in profits.
5. Make a summary of the reasons why the fisheries management by the state of Western Australia is considered an example of good practice for others to follow.

Chapter 12
Aquaculture

Learning outcomes

By the end of this chapter, you should be able to:

- describe the intensive and extensive methods of aquaculture used for different marine organisms, and what is needed to make the methods sustainable
- describe the positive and negative impacts of aquaculture
- assess the requirements and impact of potential aquaculture projects
- explain what aquaculture projects need to consider in order to be sustainable and minimise any negative impact
- apply what you have learnt to new, unfamiliar contexts.

12.1 Feeding the world

It is estimated that the global population of humans reached 1 billion in 1804 and, 123 years later, in 1927 it reached 2 billion. By 1960, 33 years later, it reached 3 billion and by 1999, 6 billion. Current projections suggest that the global population will reach 8 billion sometime around 2030, and this ever-increasing human population needs more and more food. As the years have gone by, the increased demand for food from our oceans, along with more efficient fishing methods, has led to a dramatic reduction in many species of fish. The oceans alone cannot meet the consumer demand for fish so it has become increasingly important to use methods of **aquaculture** to farm fish. However, we have to be aware that aquaculture, if not regulated carefully, can have adverse effects on environments and human communities.

KEY TERM

Aquaculture: the rearing of aquatic animals and plants for human consumption or use

12.2 Extensive and intensive aquaculture

In order to produce fish and shellfish successfully by aquaculture, there are several requirements.

- Food source: there must be sufficient food to maximise growth.
- Oxygen: the water must contain sufficient oxygen for respiration.
- Clean water: waste must be removed before it becomes toxic.
- Space: with more predatory species, there must be sufficient space to prevent cannibalism.
- Separation of ages and sizes: with predatory species, smaller fish must be kept away from larger fish.
- Disease prevention: large numbers of a single species encourage the spread of disease, so methods of prevention and control must be used.

Aquaculture is usually carried out using one of three systems (Figure 12.1).

- Cages: organisms are placed into nets or cages within open, natural water (Figure 12.1a). The natural water flow flushes waste out of the cages and brings oxygen and some natural food into the cage. Molluscs such as mussels are often grown on free ropes in the water.
- Ponds: organisms are placed into specially dug outdoor ponds. The ponds may be made out of a range of materials, such as earth or concrete, and may be totally or partially separated from natural water. In some cases, they are simply areas of coastal water separated by ditches. Raceway ponds are a particular type of shallow pond that extend over a large area and are often used for the production of shrimp.
- Indoor tanks: species are placed into plastic or metal indoor tanks. They are isolated from natural water and water is pumped in. Waste water is passed through filtration systems.

KEY TERMS

Intensive aquaculture: aquaculture that uses intensive methods such as high stocking densities and artificial feeding to maximise production

Extensive aquaculture: aquaculture that uses little technology, low stocking densities and no artificial feeding

Aquaculture is broadly divided into two main types based on the amount of 'effort' used: **intensive aquaculture** and **extensive aquaculture**. A fully extensive method relies totally on the natural productivity of a body of water with no artificial feeding or maintenance. The water provides all food, oxygen and waste removal. A fully intensive method requires much more capital investment and ongoing maintenance, with feeding regimes, an artificial oxygen supply and water filtration. Intensive aquaculture is often carried out in closed containers rather than open water. The method used depends on factors such as the demand for the fish, the requirements of a particular species and the level of investment that is available. The two systems have different effects on the environment, depending on the methods used. In practice, most methods of aquaculture lie somewhere between the two extremes.

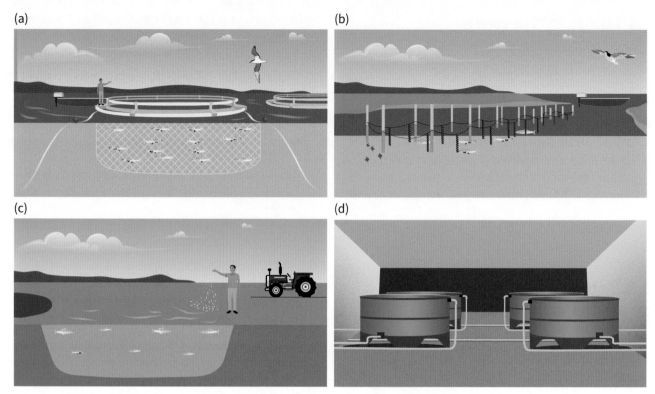

Figure 12.1. Basic methods of aquaculture: (a) a cage system, where the cage is placed into open water; (b) hanging mussels on ropes in open water; (c) a pond, where fish are placed in a specially dug pond that can be made of earth or synthetic substances such as concrete; (d) indoor tanks, where fish are totally separated from natural water.

Extensive aquaculture

Extensive aquaculture is less labour intensive and usually requires less capital investment. Fish and shellfish are grown in the ocean, lakes or rivers rather than in tanks, and in fully extensive systems there is no use of additional fertilisers or artificial feeding. Stocking densities are kept low. The capital investment required to set up an extensive system is usually low, as are the day-to-day running costs.

Productivity tends to be lower than in intensive systems because the food available is dependent on natural productivity, and oxygenation and waste removal are dependent on natural water flow. However, the low food usage and low stocking densities help reduce the threat of disease and pollution. There is little human involvement other than stocking and harvesting fish, so there is some risk of water pollution and disease due to waste accumulation. Fish that grow well in fully extensive systems tend to be very hardy. For example, tilapia can live in a range of salinities and can tolerate high waste accumulation and low oxygen levels.

There are both marine and fresh-water extensive systems for a diverse range of species, such as carp, tilapia, tuna, salmon and shrimp. The methods for each may vary, for example some use a simple pond that is stocked with fish, while others rely on placing cages or nets filled with fish into an area of natural water. Figure 12.1b shows mussels and clams growing on ropes in an estuary, where they feed on the natural food present in the water.

Tilapia are often produced by extensive methods on rice farms. Fish are released into the channels of water where rice grows. They feed on floating plants such as duckweed, eliminating plant competitors. They require little maintenance, although it could be argued that the fertilisers given to the rice encourage the growth of weeds upon which the tilapia feed.

Intensive aquaculture

Intensive aquaculture requires much more human input. Stocking densities are high and frequent feeding is carried out. In tanks and ponds, water filtration systems are used to remove waste, and an oxygen supply is necessary. High stocking densities encourage the spread of disease so pesticides and antibiotics are frequently used. Productivity is high, although this can be reduced by high setting up and running costs and losses as a result of disease. The cage method, pioneered in Japan, is often a semi-intensive method that uses natural water but with intensive feeding and monitoring of the water quality. Care must be taken with these forms of semi-intensive methods in natural water because they can cause pollution. Food that is not consumed may fall through the cages, causing eutrophication. Pesticides and antibiotics can be released into the water, and pests that grow within the cages can be transferred to wild organisms. The fish and shellfish may also escape into the natural water.

Extensive and intensive methods are compared in Table 12.1.

feature	extensive	intensive
feeding	natural food with no additional feed	frequent addition of artificial food
stocking density	low	high
start-up costs	low	high
running costs	low	high
management	low	high
productivity	low	high
risk of disease	low	high
use of pesticides / antibiotics	low	high

Table 12.1. Extensive and intensive methods.

SELF-ASSESSMENT QUESTIONS

1   State whether the following aquacultures are extensive, semi-intensive or intensive.

   a   Seabass grown in cages that are placed into the ocean. Natural food is brought in by tidal movements, although some extra food is added.

   b   Mussels grown on ropes. The mussels are hung in estuaries but no artificial feeding is carried out. No antibiotics or pesticides are used and the yield is low.

   c   Halibut raised in indoor tanks. Water is recirculated by pumps and is purified. The stocking density is high so feed is frequently added, as are pesticides and antibiotics.

   d   Clams grown in cages. The clams are placed into open water and monitored. Most feeding is natural because of the flow of the water, but if growth rates are low artificial feed is added.

2   Compare the use of tanks with open-water cages in aquaculture.

12.3 Specific examples of aquaculture

Many different species of fish and shellfish are produced by aquaculture. Although there are certain general principals of aquaculture common to producing any species, each species often has its own particular requirements. The specific methods used in the aquaculture of grouper, tuna, shrimp and giant clams are discussed below.

Grouper aquaculture

A few species of grouper, such as the orange spotted grouper (*Epinephelus coioides*), have been farmed in Asian countries such as Malaysia for several years. Despite being a relatively slow-growing fish, the grouper is very resilient and responds well to aquaculture. There is high consumer demand and aquaculture has helped to reduce over-fishing of wild stocks. There are now plans to extend the methods of aquaculture to other parts of the world where groupers are fished, such as the Bahamas.

There are several slight variations in grouper aquaculture methods, depending on the size of the venture, the country and the species of grouper. Some methods of aquaculture use brood fish to produce the juveniles, while others collect eggs or fry from the wild. Producing the fry from brood fish does not cause a reduction of wild fish so is more sustainable (Figure 12.2).

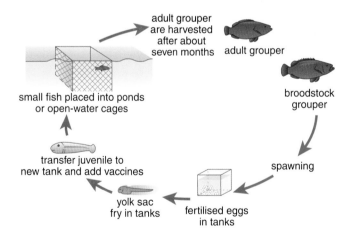

Figure 12.2. Grouper aquaculture.

Adult fish are collected from the natural environment to act as brood fish. The brood fish are kept in 50 m³ tanks of seawater at a temperature between 27 °C and 28 °C. Groupers begin their lives as female fish, and once they reach a larger size and the number of males is low some will turn male (usually between 4 and 6 years of age). These fish are fed with a high protein and cholesterol diet of fish and shellfish such as squid, sardines and mackerel.

Spawning occurs by one of two methods.

- Natural spawning: male and female groupers are placed into tanks and allowed to spawn naturally. Spawning occurs nocturnally when the water temperature is between 27 °C and 28 °C, for 1 week before and 1 week after a new moon. After spawning has occurred, the fertilised eggs are removed using nets in order to prevent the eggs being eaten by the adult fish.

- Induced spawning: more intensive farming methods inject the male and female brood fish with a hormone called hCG. After the injections, they are placed into 50 m³ tanks at a temperature between 28.0 °C and 28.5 °C. Spawning usually occurs between 36 and 48 h after injection.

The fertilised eggs are placed into tanks of seawater (Figure 12.2) at a density of 600 000 eggs m⁻³. The water is aerated to provide oxygen for respiration and circulated constantly in order to remove toxins. Approximately 3 h after hatching, the yolk sac fry are removed from the surface water using glass beakers and placed into 20 m³ concrete larval-rearing tanks. The fry develop through several larval stages, and begin to feed at 3 days of age. The larvae are placed under artificial illumination for 7 days, after which natural lighting is used. They are fed intensively with different types of food, such as rotifers (small invertebrates), according to their age and size. It is essential that the larvae are fed frequently with sufficient food otherwise cannibalism becomes a problem that would reduce the yield. Once the fish have reached about 2–3 cm in length they are ready to be transferred to nursery tanks.

The small fish, known as fingerlings, are placed into either indoor nursery tanks or outdoor nursery ponds. In outdoor systems, they are placed in nets within the pond and fed a high protein diet four to six times a day, until they reach around 6 cm in length. Lighting is placed over the pond to encourage the growth of live food for the grouper. Indoor systems use a similar regime, the fish being placed in tanks that have a continuous supply of fresh, filtered water and oxygen. The fish are sorted by size daily in order to reduce cannibalism. Vaccines and antibiotics may be added to the water to reduce disease spread.

Once the fish have reached about 6 cm in length, they are moved to outdoor, earthen ponds or placed in floating cages in natural coastal waters. In both cases, the fish are fed at least twice a day with high-protein pellets. Water filtration and oxygenation is usually done naturally, as in an extensive system. In some cases, adult tilapia are placed into the ponds to breed and produce tilapia fry,

which are a source of live food for the groupers. This stage in known as growing on.

The fully grown groupers are harvested after about 7 months of growing on, depending on the size required. They are netted carefully and processed for consumption on site or packaged live into cool water for transportation.

Tuna aquaculture

Stocks of all species of bluefin tuna (Southern, Atlantic and Pacific) have declined dramatically throughout the 20th century because of over-fishing (Figure 12.3).

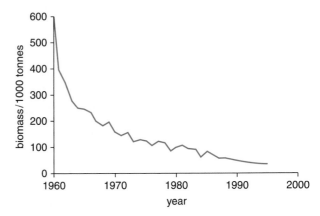

Figure 12.3. Decline of breeding South Pacific bluefin tuna biomass between 1960 and 2000.

Because bluefin tuna is a high-demand species and can be sold at high prices, bluefin tuna aquaculture has been practised for more than 20 years. The method employed is not based entirely aquaculture, as it relies upon the collection of wild juvenile tuna, and is often referred to as 'ranching'. The first Atlantic bluefin tuna farming started in 1996 in Spain, and is now practised commonly in the Mediterranean and around South Australia. The following stages are involved.

Juvenile fish are trapped using purse seine nets from spawning areas and then transferred to specialised towing cages. Tugboats slowly tow the cages to the farm sites. The towing is slow in order to reduce damage to the fish, although this often means that the fish require daily feeding during their long journey.

The juvenile fish are transferred into large farming cages, where they remain for up to 8 months. The cages consist of free-floating nets with a diameter of between 30 and 90 m and depth of up to 50 m (Figure 12.4). The tuna must be able to swim freely in order to stop them damaging each other. They are fed 1–3 times a day with fish and shellfish such as sardines, pilchards, herring, mackerel and squid, which are usually obtained from the local marine environment. In most farms, a scuba diver swims in the cage during feeding and signals to stop the feeding when the tuna stop feeding.

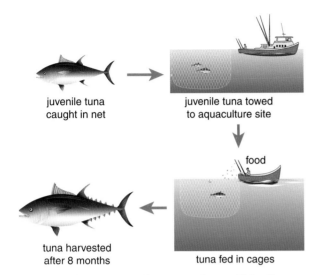

Figure 12.4. The stages in the aquaculture of bluefin tuna.

Bluefin tuna farming is controversial as it may do more harm than good to the environment. Because the tuna are initially caught in the wild as juveniles, they have not had the opportunity to reproduce so large-scale harvests threaten the wild populations. As a predatory fish, tuna require large quantities of other fish species for food, which are removed from the sea, depleting the populations of those fish species. The tuna are often overfed, with excess food falling through the cages and causing pollution, and because the fish are rapid swimming, large predators, many are killed as a result of collisions within the nets.

Recently, scientists have developed a hormonal therapy that induces spawning in adult brood stock tuna. This would enable the larvae to be generated within an aquaculture system, avoiding the need to trap wild fish. The method is still under development but would offer a way of producing tuna without affecting wild populations.

SELF-ASSESSMENT QUESTIONS

3 Give two similarities and two differences between grouper and bluefin tuna aquaculture.

4 Suggest why the bluefin tuna population has declined and why the method of ranching is unlikely to stop the decline.

Shrimp aquaculture

Shrimp have been farmed in China and South-East Asia for hundreds of years using extensive, low-density methods. Juvenile shrimp were often trapped in salt-water ponds or the waters around mangrove forests. Food was supplied naturally by the water currents, which also removed waste and brought in fresh oxygen. In the late 20th century, the global demand for shrimps increased, leading to the development of intensive and semi-intensive methods of aquaculture around the coastlines of Asia and Central and South America. A range of methods are now used, from fully extensive to highly intensive (Figure 12.5), in the farming of two main species of shrimp, the Pacific white shrimp and the giant tiger prawn. All the methods have some general procedures and particular stages in common.

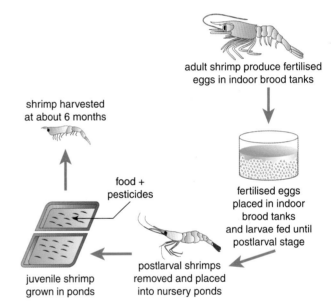

Figure 12.5. The stages of intensive shrimp aquaculture.

- Breeding and hatcheries. Before the 1980s, most shrimp farms relied on the collection of shrimp postlarvae (see Chapter 10) from estuaries. This put pressure on wild stocks, and methods have now been developed to breed shrimp within the aquaculture farms. The shrimp are bred in indoor hatchery tanks and, after hatching, the larvae are fed initially on algae and later on zooplankton and brine shrimps. Disease outbreaks are common and difficult to contain, so antibiotics and pesticides are often included in the feed. All tanks are routinely rinsed with disinfectant. Despite these measures, there is still a high mortality rate of larvae.

- Nursery. Postlarval shrimps are transferred into separate long, shallow, rectangular tanks called raceway ponds. There is continuous water flow through the tanks and the shrimp are fed on a high-protein diet for approximately 3 weeks, before being transferred into grow-out ponds. The water temperature and salinity of the raceway ponds are gradually adjusted to that of the grow-out ponds to enable the shrimp to acclimatise.

- Grow-out ponds. The juvenile shrimp are transferred into grow-out ponds, where they are fed for 3–6 months until they reach marketable size. Harvesting is performed by either draining the ponds or fishing with nets. A variety of pond structures are used, ranging from blocked off areas of coastal water, fields flooded with water to concrete walled tanks.

Depending on the farm, shrimp farming uses extensive, semi-intensive and intensive farming methods, especially for grow-out ponds.

- Extensive systems require low investment, are usually located on a coastal or mangrove area, and stock shrimp at low density. In their simplest form, they are areas of coastal water or mangrove roots surrounded by a ditch or netting. Water is refreshed by the sea and the shrimp feed on naturally occurring organisms. Rather than breeding the shrimp, they are often obtained by trapping wild larvae within the ponds. Yields tend to be low but production costs and the technical skill required are also low, and because stocking densities are low the risk of disease is low.

- Semi-intensive methods are more separated from the coastal water and do not rely on the tide for water flow. Pumps are used to move fresh water, often from the sea, and remove the waste water (Figure 12.6). The shrimp are stocked at higher densities so require additional food, although the natural growth of food is also encouraged. Productivity is higher than in extensive farms, but production costs are higher.

- Intensive methods, at fully intensive shrimp farms, isolate the shrimp from the marine environment. The shrimp are usually bred on the aquaculture site or bought in from suppliers, and are stocked at high density. Water is constantly circulated by pumps and filtration systems, and oxygen is supplied by aerators. Because of the high stocking densities, disease outbreaks are common so pesticides and antibiotics are frequently used. Feeding is intensive and uses artificially manufactured high-protein feedstocks. Productivity is

high but is coupled with a high initial capital investment, high running costs and a need for skilled technicians.

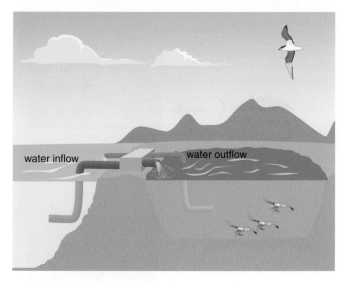

Figure 12.6. A semi-intensive method of shrimp aquaculture, using a pumping system to bring fresh seawater into the ponds and release waste water into the sea.

Most studies estimate that about 55–60% of all shrimp farms worldwide are extensive farms, 25–30% are semi-intensive and the remaining 20–10% are intensive farms.

Giant clam aquaculture

Giant clam aquaculture has developed in Micronesia for several reasons. The populations of many species of giant clam have declined rapidly, and aquaculture is helping to restore them. In Japan and other parts of Asia, giant clams are in demand as a food and for aquaria. The Republic of Palau was one of the first countries to develop methods of farming clams, including intensive and extensive methods.

Brood clams are taken from the wild and placed into disinfected concrete tanks that contain seawater. The gonad of one mature clam is extracted and placed near each clam in the water. The gonad releases a hormone called spawning induced substance (SIS) and this triggers the release of sperm and eggs from the brood clams (Chapter 10). The larvae are allowed to develop in the tanks and phytoplankton is added to the water as a food source. The larvae pass through the trochophore, veliger and pediveliger stages and settle to the bottom of the tanks. After 2–3 weeks, juvenile clams (spats) are removed from the tank and transferred into nursery tanks.

The spats are placed in trays containing gravel for them to settle on. The trays are then laid in large nursery tanks of seawater and fed intensively (Figure 12.7). Because of the high density of the juvenile clams, the water is aerated to provide oxygen for respiration. Fertiliser is added to the water in order to speed up growth. After about 3 months, the clams are removed from the water. Some of the clams are sold on at this stage for the aquarium trade or exported live to countries where they are required for food.

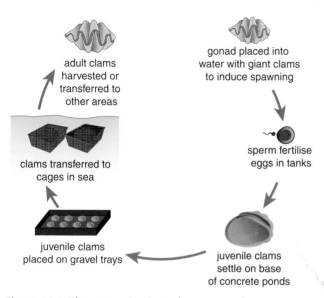

Figure 12.7. The stages in giant clam aquaculture.

adult clams harvested or transferred to other areas

clams transferred to cages in sea

juvenile clams placed on gravel trays

gonad placed into water with giant clams to induce spawning

sperm fertilise eggs in tanks

juvenile clams settle on base of concrete ponds

The clams are placed into cages that prevent the entry of predators, and these cages are tethered to the seabed in coastal areas. They are then left to grow in the cages using a semi-extensive method. Divers inspect the clams twice a week to check the rate of growth and presence of predators. As they grow they are thinned out in order to prevent overcrowding. When they reach a size that will not be eaten by predators, the lids of the cages are removed and the clams allowed to grow in the water. Food may be supplemented artificially but because clams are now in open seawater, care must be taken to not give surplus food. The clams are sized and, when the desired size is reached, they are harvested. They are used for food, the shells are sold in tourist markets, or live clams may be placed in reef areas as part of conservation programmes.

SELF-ASSESSMENT QUESTIONS

5 Explain why intensive shrimp farming may be harmful to the environment.

6 List three uses for giant clams produced by aquaculture.

265

PRACTICAL ACTIVITY 12.1

The effects of aquaculture conditions on the growth rate of fish

The effects of different conditions such as salinity, temperature and feeding routine can be investigated using rapidly growing fish such as tilapia. This requires an aquaculture system consisting of tanks, water purification systems and heating systems. If a suitable aquaculture system is available, it is possible to design and carry out experiments on fish growth rate.

Using live animals in an experiment raises animal welfare issues, so careful thought and planning must be carried out.

In the absence of aquaculture equipment, you can still plan how you would carry out the following experiments:

- An investigation into the effect of water temperature on the growth of tilapia, which normally grow in water temperatures of between 15 and 25 °C.
- An investigation into the effect of feeding frequency on the growth rate of tilapia and water pollution. Water

pollution can be assessed by measuring the biological oxygen demand (BOD) of the water. BOD is a measure of the microbial content of the water: the higher the BOD, the more decomposer microbes are present.

Plan a full experimental investigation separated into the following parts.

Hypothesis

Think of a hypothesis for the experiment, based on scientific reasoning.

Method

This part should state:

- the independent variable, the range you will use and how you will alter it
- the dependent variable and how you will measure it
- the control variables and how you will control them
- how many repeats you will carry out
- the details of your method, describing what you will do.

Results

This part should include:

- the calculations you will carry out
- how you will present the data (for example graphs and charts).

Conclusions

1 Present your hypothesis and methods and how you would display your results for an investigation into the effect of water temperature on the growth of tilapia.

2 Present your hypothesis and methods and how you would display your results for an investigation into the effect of feeding frequency on the growth rate of tilapia and water pollution, using BOD.

Maths skills

Frequency tables, pie charts and histograms

When you are collecting data about numbers of individuals in different categories, it is best to collate them in a frequency table. Pie charts are circular charts that show proportions easily. A histogram is a form of bar chart that is used to display frequency data when the independent variable is continuous.

Worked example

- The variation in mass of 25 salmon was investigated after 1 year of aquaculture. The data are shown in Table 12.2.

Mass / g			
1260	1760	2100	2275
1265	1765	2050	2280
1525	1800	2125	2450
1525	1850	2075	2575
1600	1865	2165	
1605	1875	2200	
1700	1950	2255	

Table 12.2. Mass of 25 salmon after 1 year of aquaculture.

To determine the frequency of different categories, a frequency table needs to be made. If large amounts of data are being processed, it is useful to use a tally chart, as shown in Table 12.3.

To create a pie chart, you need to calculate the angles that each category will represent. To do that, you need to determine the percentage of the total for each category.

For example, five of the salmon have a mass in the range of 1501–1750 g. As there are 25 fish, the percentage of fish that have a mass between 1501 g and 1750 g is:

$5 \div 25 \times 100 = 20\%$

To determine the angle required for the pie chart, you need to calculate 20% of 360°:

$20 \div 100 \times 360 = 72°$

The rest of the percentages and angles for the salmon are shown in Table 12.3. The angles should all add up to 360°.

mass range categories	tally	frequency	percentage in category / %	angle on pie chart / °
1251–1500	||	2	8	29
1501–1750	⊞	5	20	72
1751–2000	⊞ ||	7	28	101
2001–2250	⊞ |	6	24	86
2251–2500	||||	4	16	58
2501–2750	|	1	4	14

Table 12.3. Tally chart and frequency table showing the masses of 25 salmon after 1 year of aquaculture.

The pie chart can then be drawn using a protractor, and should look like Figure 12.8.

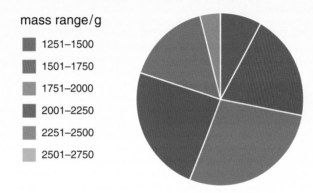

mass range/g

- 1251–1500
- 1501–1750
- 1751–2000
- 2001–2250
- 2251–2500
- 2501–2750

Figure 12.8. Pie chart showing the frequencies of different masses of salmon after 1 year of aquaculture.

Histograms are very similar to bar charts but are used when the x-axis shows continuous data and the y-axis shows frequency. The bars in histograms touch, unlike bar charts, in which the bars are separate from each other. The category intervals for the bars should ideally be equal.

The histogram for the salmon data is shown in Figure 12.9.

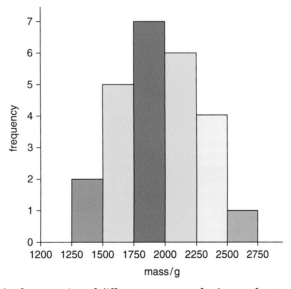

Figure 12.9. Histogram showing the frequencies of different masses of salmon after 1 year of aquaculture.

Questions

1   An aquaculture company earns profits for five different products, as shown in Table 12.4.

product	profit / £
grouper	150 000
lobster	125 000
crab	25 000
scallops	75 000
seaweed	10 000

Table 12.4. Profits for five different products.

Display the profits for the products in the form of a pie chart.

2   A hundred tilapia were split into two tanks, which were placed at different temperatures for 4 months. The masses of the tilapia were measured and frequency categories determined. The results are shown in Table 12.5.

mass category / g	tilapia kept at 15 °C	tilapia kept at 20 °C
251–500	6	1
501–750	13	4
751–1000	21	15
1001–1250	8	18
1251–1500	2	8
1501–1750	0	4

Table 12.5. Effect of temperature on tilapia masses.

Draw histograms to display the two sets of data.

12.4 Sustainable aquaculture

Sustainable aquaculture must address three main issues (Figure 12.10).

> **KEY TERM**
>
> **Sustainable aquaculture:** aquaculture that causes less short- and long-term damage to the environment, economy and local community

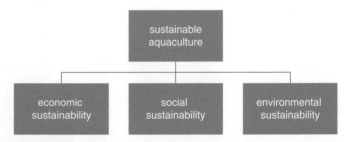

Figure 12.10. Factors that must be considered when setting up a sustainable aquaculture business.

- Economic sustainability: aquaculture ventures must be able to generate a profit over the long term. It may not necessarily develop large profits initially because of start-up costs, but if the business is to continue and grow over time, it will need to have some of the profits reinvested into its further development.

- Social sustainability: aquaculture ventures have the potential to benefit local communities, but they can also have negative impacts. To be fully sustainable, a venture will have to benefit the local community.

- Environmental sustainability: aquaculture ventures can be beneficial to wild stocks of fish and shellfish but care has to be taken. Pollution, removal of juveniles for farming and removal of organisms for feed can all have a negative impact. If aquaculture is to be sustainable, it must lessen the negative impacts on the environment.

Economic sustainability

It is a simple rule of business that if any business continues to make a financial loss, it is not sustainable. Aquaculture ventures are set up for different reasons, including:

- the conservation of fish stocks

- the re-establishment of stocks in the environment

- providing a food source for populations that lack protein in their diets

- to make a profit, either for small, local businesses or large international companies.

In every case, if an aquaculture venture operates at a major financial loss, it will not be able to continue.

All successful aquaculture ventures have basic economic requirements:

- availability of stock

- availability of clean water

- availability of feed

- efficiency of feeding

- disease management

- availability of location

- market demand

- access to market

- return on investment.

Availability of stock

There must be a source of juvenile organisms to provide the stock. This can be achieved by:

- keeping brood-stock adults, which provide a source of young offspring

- buying in fertilised eggs or larvae from other companies that produce them

- removing juveniles from the wild and bringing them into the aquaculture.

Most ventures aim to keep brood stock or buy in fertilised eggs, which requires capital outlay, as breeding tanks and more technically demanding methods and equipment are required. The majority of fully intensive farms breed their own stock and will often sell a proportion on to smaller producers. Breeding the stock on site also benefits the wild population, as removing juveniles from the wild can have devastating effects on the wild populations.

Availability of clean water

In order to reduce mortality rates caused by disease and accumulation of toxins, it is essential that the water is cleaned and replaced regularly. In extensive systems, natural water movements are used. This is not a problem for species that are grown in cages in open water but for species that are in semi-landlocked ponds, tidal movements can limit the population densities. In intensive farming, when tanks are not connected to a natural water source, constant running water is needed. At the same time, a filtration system is required to remove waste.

Availability of feed

Fully extensive systems use food provided naturally by the water. For example, in extensive shrimp farming, the tide brings water carrying food substances into areas partially sealed off from the coastal water. In semi-intensive systems, the growth of live food may be encouraged. Fertilisers are added to water to stimulate the growth of the phytoplankton that giant clam spats feed on. In fully intensive farming, fish and shellfish are stocked at high densities so food has to be added in order to maximise **growth rates**. The extra food can

KEY TERM

Growth rate: the speed of growth of a population in terms of numbers or size of individual fish

269

come from environmentally sustainable and relatively inexpensive sources. Protein pellets made from waste food (such as fish-processing trimmings) are often used to feed carnivorous species. Other sources of food can be environmentally damaging and costly. The aquaculture of predatory species such as bluefin tuna requires large quantities of fish and shellfish, which are usually removed from the environment, damaging wild stocks. If the feed fish are farmed, the financial costs of the venture rise. Highly active predatory species are particularly costly to feed because they need food from relatively high trophic levels.

Efficiency of feeding

In extensive aquaculture, the feeding is natural so that there is no waste. In intensive systems, it would be financially inefficient and environmentally damaging to overfeed. An optimal strategy for feeding is needed on intensive farms. If fish and shellfish are underfed, growth rates will not be optimal and, in predatory species, cannibalism can occur. If feeding is excessive, food is wasted, which increases costs and causes pollution. Most farms tend to operate a little-and-often policy in order to reduce wastage, by constantly monitoring growth rates.

It is also important to control the type of food. Food that is highly indigestible will produce larger amounts of faecal waste and, because less is absorbed into the organism, slower growth. The addition of easily digested and absorbed substances, such as protein and fat, is a common practice in order to increase productivity.

Disease management

The high-density populations that are produced in aquaculture, particularly in highly intensive systems, encourages the growth and spread of parasites and pathogens. Antibiotics are frequently added to tanks in order to suppress the growth of bacteria, which is financially costly and can affect the environment. Fungicides and pesticides are also added and, in intensive systems that are sited in natural water, these can be lost into the environment. Vaccines are often added to help fish such as groupers develop immunity to certain viral conditions. Nursery tanks in particular must be scrubbed and washed out with disinfectants because eggs and early stage larvae are particularly vulnerable to infection. In shrimp aquaculture, the mortality rate of early embryos can reach 60% as a result of infections such as white spot disease (Figure 12.11) unless strict precautions are taken. The costs of chemicals required to reduce disease can be

high but this is generally outweighed by the cost of losing an entire harvest of a species.

Figure 12.11. Shrimp with white spot disease, a common infection found in shrimp aquaculture.

Availability of location

Extensive aquaculture ventures require an area of natural water that is easily accessible and suitable for the species being produced. There must be appropriate food present, a suitable substrate and water at suitable temperatures. Tropical species need warmer conditions while those from colder regions of the world need cooler temperatures. Most small, extensive systems in developing nations do not have a major impact on the environment and the land is not classed as premium. However, as farms expand, more space is required and more coastal habitats such as mangrove regions are removed. In more developed nations, in particular where tourism is a major part of the economy, the land may be premium and expensive to buy, increasing the amount of capital needed for aquaculture.

Intensive systems require far more support and are costly to build. Larger areas of land need to be purchased and more ponds and tanks constructed alongside pumping stations and water filtration units. Storage facilities for food and equipment are required. If harvests are large, processing facilities are needed on the site. Electricity needs to be installed, along with good transport links such as roads and rail links. One advantage of many highly intensive systems is that, by using separate tanks and ponds, they are less dependent on the natural condition of the water. The conditions of the tanks can be controlled according to the demands of the particular species being produced. For example, a species such as grouper can be produced in a location that is naturally cooler than the optimum for grouper growth by placing the fish in heated tanks. However, the cost both in terms of capital investment and maintenance is high so the product must be able to be sold for a high price.

Market demand

Figure 12.12 shows how the global demand for marine products has risen since 1950 and is predicted to continue to rise until 2050. Harvesting fish from natural stocks in the world's seas and oceans is no longer sufficient to meet the rising consumer demands for fish and shellfish. Aquaculture is needed to fill the gap between what is taken by fisheries (which, because of quotas and falling fish stocks, may decrease). However, if aquaculture ventures are to be sustainable in the long term, there must be continued, sufficient consumer demand for the products. As already discussed, if a venture is to be a long-term success, the profits must exceed the start-up and running costs. Like any other product, aquaculture obeys the commercial laws of supply and demand. If the demand for a product is high, the price for that product will tend to be high and bring higher profits. Prices do not, however, remain constant, and if production exceeds the demand (especially as more aquaculture ventures are developed) the prices will fall, reducing profit margins. Highly intensive systems that produce one product are often at risk from falling prices and need to ensure that the market demand is sufficient to meet operating costs.

Many aquaculture ventures now produce more than one product, for example by integrated production, so that if the demand for one species falls, profits may be generated from another.

Market access

When an aquaculture venture is set up, it must have easy access to fish markets. This requires a transport network, which may include road, rail and air transportation. In most of the ventures set up in developing nations, the products are primarily produced for export. Fish and shellfish spoil rapidly, so they must be transported soon after harvest. Some larger businesses process the food at source and then export it as frozen food. Other businesses chill or freeze whole fish once harvested. There is a high demand for live fish in Asia, so aquaculture sites need facilities for packaging live fish and shellfish in chilled water. Refrigeration units and ice plants are needed, along with fresh, clean water. Road networks must be able to transport the products rapidly to airports, which are often situated close by. The need for efficient transport means that ventures are often too costly to set up in remote areas of developing nations without government intervention to build an efficient network. Building transport networks, however, may cost the environment in terms of pollution and loss of land.

Return on investment

If a business is to remain viable, it must be able to generate a profit over the long term. It is accepted that a new aquaculture venture may operate at a loss for the first few years because of initial start-up costs. Loans may be required to purchase equipment, stock, feed

271

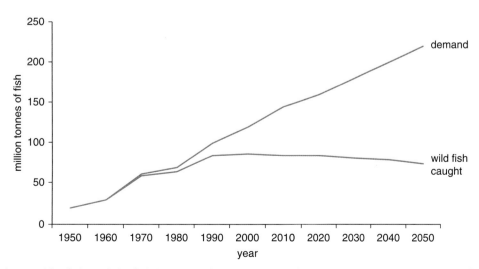

Figure 12.12. The demand for fish and the fish harvest. The growing gap between the two will have to be filled by aquaculture. Predicted demands and catches are shown for years 2020 to 2050.

and other items, and paying back these loans can affect profits for several years. All ventures need a business plan in order to ensure they meet the necessary costs and are able to reinvest money into updating and expanding the business. As businesses age, equipment such as water pumps and filtration units require maintenance, which incurs more cost. Any successful aquaculture venture will have to consider the replacement and updating of equipment over time.

Large-scale aquaculture ventures are vulnerable to economic changes both within a nation and globally (Figure 12.13). If the currency of a particular country rises in value in world markets, a farm selling tilapia from that country will find its product harder to sell internationally as it becomes more expensive for other countries. Likewise, if a currency falls, it is easier to sell and export. A weak currency is not always good for production: raw materials that have to be bought in from other countries become more expensive. Large multinational aquaculture companies are able to regulate production in the different countries they operate, but small- and medium-sized businesses are more vulnerable to world economic events. If the world economy goes through a period of weakness, there may be less money to buy premium brands such as bluefin tuna. On the other hand, if less money is available there may be more demand for less expensive products, such as tilapia.

SELF-ASSESSMENT QUESTIONS

7 Explain why high premium fish aquaculture, such as bluefin tuna, becomes more profitable when the global economy is strong.

8 Explain why aquaculture feed is often highly digestible and supplied frequently in small amounts rather than adding large amounts at any one time.

Social sustainability

Aquaculture ventures can have positive and negative impacts on local people. They can bring employment, wealth and food, but may also cause loss of traditional fishing jobs, land and other species that are used as food. If not practised in an ethical, sustainable way, local communities may receive very few of the benefits of aquaculture.

All aquaculture ventures have an impact on local labour forces and social systems.

Availability of labour

Any aquaculture venture requires a labour force. Extensive systems generally do not require a great deal of human input other than setting up the initial site, minimal

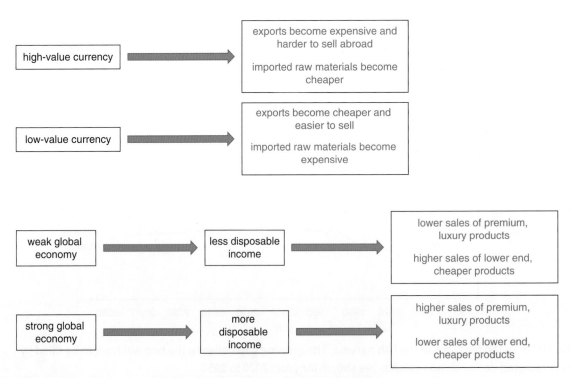

Figure 12.13. Effects of currency and economic conditions on the sale of goods.

maintenance and harvesting. As the level of intensive practice increases, there is a higher requirement for both numbers of people to work on the site and level of technical skill. A fully intensive system will need to employ people in different areas of the venture, such as breeding, maintenance, harvesting, feeding and processing. As a venture grows, more people are needed and with that comes the need for tiers of management and organisation. Complicated systems require skilled, trained staff, and this training can be carried out locally or at special training centres run by multinational aquaculture companies.

If an area used to develop an aquaculture venture has a limited population, new people are brought into the area and will often settle there, requiring more housing and other infrastructures. Labour costs will fluctuate according to supply and demand. In areas where there are few industries and few opportunities for employment, labour costs will be cheap. In areas where there is competition for employers, labour costs are high and this increases the cost of the products.

Social impact

An aquaculture business can have many short- and long-term social impacts on the local population. If it is to be successful and socially sustainable, all possible outcomes need to be considered.

Positive social outcomes

Increased employment opportunities are particularly important in areas with low employment and few opportunities for people to work and train. A successful business can provide higher incomes for local people and the opportunity for people to be trained in skills that can be transferable to other employment sectors. There can be improved employment prospects not only in the primary aquaculture business but also in secondary services such as transport, housing construction, food businesses and retail. As a business grows, it employs more people, many of whom may move into the area and require housing and will also buy goods and services from local businesses.

In areas with low wealth, the development of an aquaculture business that generates more money from exports can increase local wealth. Increased wealth can raise the standard of living for local people. For this to happen, however, the money must reach all parts of the local community.

If a major aquaculture venture is planned, local people may benefit from an improved infrastructure, such as increased road and rail links. If money from the venture is invested in a growing local community, better facilities, such as housing, schools and medical services, can be developed.

In regions where malnutrition is high, the development of aquaculture ventures may offer a cheaper and more abundant source of food that is rich in protein and several vitamins. This requires the venture to be used for local food production rather than exporting all the products.

Negative social outcomes

Despite employing more people in the sector, some aquaculture ventures can actually cause more unemployment. Local fishing industries can become less cost effective and unable to compete with the lower prices of farmed products. If an intensive system is built, smaller, less efficient extensive farms may close because they cannot compete. Intensive farms that use food that is taken from the sea may impact upon local fish stocks and so reduce the yield of fisheries.

If a large aquaculture production site is built, more people may move into the area and bring more wealth. The increased wealth of one group of people may lead to a rise in local prices that results in food and goods becoming too expensive for locals.

An aquaculture venture can also put pressure on housing. It may use building land, reducing the land available for housing (and raising the price of building land). If more people are attracted into an area, there will be a higher demand for housing and as a result many could become homeless or unable to afford houses because of increasing prices. If a population grows too rapidly without careful planning, the infrastructure is placed under strain. Schools, roads, medical care, sewerage and water supplies become inadequate and, if not improved, this can lead to social problems.

When one employment sector becomes dominant in an area and there is a shortage of labour, other, less attractive, industries may suffer a decline. There will be competition between different sectors for sufficient staff which may cause some businesses to close because of higher wage demands. Older industries that may be perceived as old fashioned, may be less able to attract staff and go out of business. When traditional businesses begin to close, local traditions can be lost. If aquaculture

273

becomes the only business in an area, it could become a problem in the future if it fails. This is often a problem with larger international companies, who will open and close businesses in different parts of the world according to profitability at a particular time.

If a venture is to be sustainable, the local population should benefit from it. Intensive systems that do not benefit a local population are less likely to be sustainable. Imagine a situation where a large international company buys an area of coastal water and begins to farm shrimp.

- If the company employs few local people, exports the produce and does not allow profits to benefit the local area, it will not be popular. It is unlikely to be sustainable in the long term. Local people will not feel any loyalty to the company.

- If the company has a well-designed aquaculture system, employs local people, produces food for local people as well as export, and puts profits into the local area, it will be highly regarded. Local people will benefit from the company and become stakeholders in its success: in the long term this should prove to be more sustainable.

Environmental sustainability and impacts

One of the aims of aquaculture is to make up the shortfall in fish and shellfish between global demand and what can be harvested from the seas. By reducing what is taken from the seas, the stocks of fish and shellfish should be protected and allowed to increase. This means that the environment can benefit from aquaculture. If not set up carefully, however, aquaculture can cause extensive damage to habitats, which are often delicate and ecologically important areas.

Factors that must be addressed to ensure environmental sustainability include:

- habitat destruction
- over-exploitation of feedstocks
- pollution
- introduction of **exotic species**
- spread of disease
- competition for resources.

KEY TERM

Exotic species: species that are not native to a particular location

Habitat destruction

Building a new aquaculture venture will inevitably lead to land development. Even extensive systems may lead to the loss of habitats. For example, if an area of mangrove forest is sealed off from the sea to culture shrimp, it may lead to the loss of mangroves or other coastal habitats. Intensive systems that use cage methods or raceway ponds are often built in coastal areas. Intensive shrimp farming (Figure 12.14) has led to the loss of large areas of mangrove forest, resulting in a loss of biodiversity. Many coastal areas are already under threat from tourist resort development and further losses could lead to the extinction of many species. Indoor tank systems are less likely to damage fragile coastal ecosystems but still cause habitat loss because of their construction.

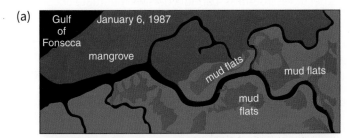

Figure 12.14. Effects of shrimp farming on areas of mangrove forest and mud flats in Nicaragua between (a) 1987 and (b) 1999.

Overexploitation of feedstocks

Intensive farming of fish and shellfish requires a large quantity of food. In many cases, such as bluefin tuna farming, the food is harvested from the oceans. Bluefin tuna is a highly active, top predator so requires intensive feeding. Sardines, mackerel, other fish and squid are harvested from the sea and fed to the tuna. The harvesting of these species may lead to a fall in their populations and further effects on food chains.

Pollution

There are many types of pollution that can occur as a result of aquaculture. Extensive systems are less polluting because there is little to no additional feeding and there

274

is less use of pesticides and other chemicals. Intensive systems, particularly cage systems in open water, have the potential to release large quantities of pollutants, including the following.

- Waste food that is not consumed and faecal waste: these can cause eutrophication (Chapter 13), leading to oxygen depletion in the water as a result of microbial decay. This has happened in the Philippines as a result of tilapia farming (Figure 12.15).

- Fertilisers that have been added to encourage plant growth: these can leach into the water and cause eutrophication.

- Pesticides that have been added to kill parasites: these can pass into the water and kill native species or generate resistance in native species.

- Antibiotics and antifungals that have been added to kill bacteria and fungi: these can also pass into the water and affect the natural bacteria and fungi.

Closed systems where fish and shellfish are grown in sealed tanks require filtration units before waste water is released into the sea. Open-water cage systems are more difficult to control and procedures are needed to avoid over-feeding, overuse of chemicals and excessive production of waste.

Figure 12.15. Eutrophication in the Philippines caused by waste from tilapia farming.

Introduction of exotic species

Exotic species are species that are not native to a particular area. Aquaculture has often resulted in the introduction of exotic species, when culture organisms escape into the wild. The impact of exotic species are varied. In South-East Asia, introduced species such as tilapia and common carp have established populations that have brought socio-economic benefits in terms of dietary protein and money. But the same species can have a negative environmental impact.

In Cambodia, the population of the native bronze featherback fish (*Notopterus notopterus*) has declined in rivers and lakes as the exotic Nile tilapia populations have increased. In Laos, the decline of the native prawn and a native snail species has been linked to the introduction of exotic species. If introduced species have no natural predators, their populations will increase unchecked and they have the potential to over-consume prey species and outcompete native species. Chapter 15 discusses the animal and plant life in Australia that has suffered greatly because of the introduction of exotic species.

Exotic species may bring diseases with them that escape and adversely affect native species. In Thailand, three fish diseases have entered the country with introduced fish. The viral white spot disease that infects shrimp is thought to have been introduced by imported shrimp larvae.

Spread of disease

Intensive farming tends to rely on stocking fish and shellfish at very high densities. Keeping large numbers of one species at a high density encourages the development and spread of disease, so aquaculture can provide a breeding ground for disease. It is estimated that up to $6 billion is lost annually by disease in aquaculture. If open-water cage systems used, there is a risk that the diseases will spread to natural populations. One notable example is that of parasitic sea lice, which feed on salmon skin, mucus and blood and can kill the fish. Recent research in British Columbia suggests that sea lice infestation resulting from farms will cause local pink salmon populations to fall by 99% within four generations.

Waste water from tank systems is filtered and disinfected, and pesticides, fungicides and antibiotics are frequently used to reduce the spread of disease. Fish must be continuously monitored for the presence of disease and treated accordingly. White spot disease affecting shrimp is one of the most damaging diseases, and it is estimated that the early death of shrimp has cost over $2 billion. Research into remote, rapid DNA diagnosis of the disease is being carried out to help to reduce its effects.

Competition for resources

The development of an aquaculture venture requires many raw materials from the local environment. If the venture is inland, away from major water bodies, large quantities of water need to be provided. Diverting large volumes of water to the venture can create competition within the local environment and with businesses such as traditional crop farms that need water for irrigation. If large quantities of water are taken from lakes and rivers, the water levels will drop, plant growth around the margins can be reduced and the ecosystem disturbed.

A large intensive aquaculture farm can potentially buy such large quantities of fertiliser and other raw materials that local farmers are unable to meet their needs. This can ultimately lead to loss of crops.

Intensive shrimp farming in ponds requires a considerable amount of fresh water to maintain the pond water at the optimum salinity for shrimp growth. Typically, this involves pumping water from nearby rivers or groundwater supplies, and this can deplete local fresh-water resources. Furthermore, if aquifers are pumped excessively, salt water seeps in from the nearby sea, causing salinisation and making the water unfit for human consumption. For example, in Sri Lanka, 74% of people living in coastal shrimp farming areas no longer have ready access to drinking water. Shrimp farming can also cause increased soil salinity in nearby agricultural areas, leading to declines in crops. In Bangladesh there have been reports of crop loss because of the salinisation of land around shrimp farms.

12.5 Minimising the negative effects of aquaculture

A poorly planned aquaculture venture can have many negative impacts on the environment and the local human population. In order to reduce the overall impact, extensive planning is needed. Certain precautions should be taken, including:

- reducing pollution

- using resources sustainably

- preventing escape

- conserving habitats

- minimising social impacts.

Reducing pollution

For tanks and ponds that are physically separated from the natural water, there must be a source of clean water

and removal of waste water. The waste water will carry with it waste food and faecal waste, together with any chemicals such as pesticides that have been used. There is also a risk of infectious organisms and pests from the tanks being released into the natural water. Figure 12.16 shows an aquaculture plant with a water purification system. The water is passed through a series of tanks that remove inorganic wastes such as carbon dioxide, nitrates and ammonia. Solid waste is allowed to settle out in other tanks and then passed into anaerobic digesters to produce methane gas, which can be used as an energy source.

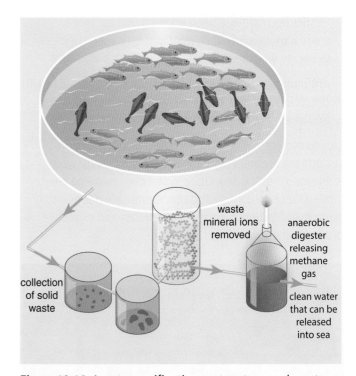

Figure 12.16. A water purification system to recycle water for aquaculture.

Reducing pollution from open-cage systems is more difficult because they are not physically separated from the natural water. Where fish are kept in cages in estuaries and coastal waters, it is important not to overfeed them as uneaten food can pass into the water and cause pollution. Care has to be taken to treat infections and parasite infestations before they can spread to wild populations, but treatment chemicals should not be used excessively to reduce leakage into the local water. Recently, integrated multi-trophic aquaculture (IMTA) systems have been developed (Figure 12.17). Fish are kept in open-water cages and detritus feeders such as lobsters and crabs are grown underneath. The detritus feeders consume the excess food and faeces from the fish. Filter-feeding molluscs such as mussels are grown on ropes in order to remove particulate waste in the water, and seaweed is grown in order to extract excess mineral ions from the water. These systems reduce pollution and also generate more profits by growing several different products.

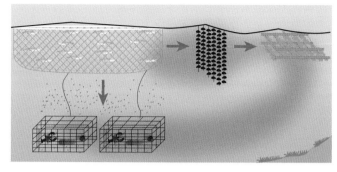

Figure 12.17. Integrated multi-trophic aquaculture (IMTA). Waste from the cage falls through to feed detritus feeders such as lobsters, sea urchins and sea cucumbers. Mussels and other molluscs are grown on ropes to remove small particulate matter, and seaweeds remove mineral ions such as nitrates and phosphates.

A company in the Netherlands called *Happy Shrimp* uses waste from its shrimp farms to grow vegetables. The shrimp are fed on algae and bacteria as well as on aquaculture feed containing a high proportion of plant protein. They are cultivated in greenhouses that are heated in an environmentally sustainable way, and no shrimp juveniles are extracted from the wild.

Figure 12.18 illustrates a practice called integrated rice culture, where tilapia are grown in rice fields. The fish control weeds and pests and the faeces they produce fertilises the rice plants.

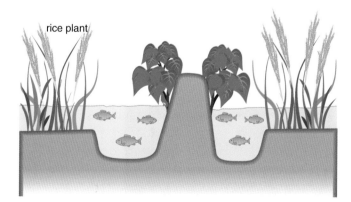

Figure 12.18. Integrated rice culture. This system puts tilapia into rice fields where they reduce weed numbers.

Not using high stocking densities helps to reduce the spread of pests and diseases and the use of chemical pesticides and antibiotics.

Sustainably using resources

Harvesting marine species, both plant and animal, to use as aquaculture feed is not a sustainable practice. Populations of species such as herring and sardines have declined in some parts of the world where they have been heavily fished for use in the aquaculture industry. Recently, plant species such as soybeans, barley, corn and peas have been used successfully to make feed pellets for herbivorous and omnivorous fish and shellfish. Carnivore species such as tuna are problematic because they require large quantities of other fish and fishmeal to feed on. They also need a source of omega 3 oils. Using the fish trimmings from fish-processing plants to make high protein and oil feed pellets is a possible sustainable source of feed for carnivorous species.

Inland aquaculture sites that require a water source need to recycle the water they use back into rivers and lakes rather than simply disposing of it through sewers. The water should be cleaned, filtered and, if necessary, desalinated before being released.

Preventing escape

If species, particularly exotics, escape from aquaculture, they can have an impact on the ecology of the area. Food chains can be disrupted and native species may be outcompeted by the escaped organisms. Escaped tilapia have caused the decline of native fish species in many parts of the world, including Nevada and Arizona in the United States, and in Madagascar and Nicaragua. Farmed species should be isolated from natural waters by using either tanks or closed pools. Where cages are used, there should be strong netting with an appropriate mesh size. The production of exotics in cage systems that are in contact with natural water should be discouraged.

Conserving habitats

Figure 12.14 shows the loss of mangrove forest to the development of shrimp farms. Careful planning is needed before aquaculture sites are built, in order to minimise the loss of coastal habitats. Research should be undertaken into the likely effects on local ecosystems, and no aquaculture should be permitted in marine reserves.

Minimising the social impacts

The development of a new aquaculture site has the potential to bring many benefits to a local community but can also cause many social problems. It can provide employment, increased standards of living and a high protein food at a low price. If not planned carefully, however, there will be little benefit to the local community. Existing industries such as fisheries may fail, inflation may occur increasing the cost of food, all the products may be used for export so that none is available locally, the area may become polluted and land lost. Care should be taken that existing industries are not affected and that the venture brings money into the local area so that the local community benefits. If local people become stakeholders in the venture, it will become a far more sustainable concern and will be more successful in the long term. Responsible employment will ensure that the needs of the workforce are met so that they are not exploited with low wages, and health and safety should be of paramount importance.

SELF-ASSESSMENT QUESTIONS

9   Summarise the possible negative effects that aquaculture can have on the environment.

10 Explain how integrated multi-trophic aquaculture methods reduce the pollution generated by aquaculture.

CASE STUDY

278

Saving the mangroves of Vietnam with organic shrimp farming

The area of Cà Mau in Vietnam is home to half of Vietnam's shrimp production, an industry estimated to be worth more than US $3.1 billion. In response to the rising demand for shrimp of the last few decades, large quantities of Vietnam's natural mangrove forest have been cleared to make way for shrimp farms. Shrimp were farmed in shallow ponds in very intensive systems; stocking densities were high and large quantities of feed were used (Figure 12.19).

Management costs were high, the farms caused high levels of pollution and disease outbreaks were common, leading to the loss of many shrimp. The move to highly intensive methods left the area with many failed shrimp ponds as a result of pollution and disease. The development of intensive shrimp aquaculture came at the expense of the mangrove ecosystem and also reduced the average income of the local people. The high rates of disease and pollution threatened the livelihoods of the shrimp farmers themselves.

Cà Mau's mangroves forests act as nursery grounds for fish and shrimp and protect the area against storm

Figure 12.19. Intensive shrimp farming in Vietnam.

surges and coastal erosion. They also act as carbon sinks, locking up carbon in the vegetation and soil. The global greenhouse gas emissions from the destruction of mangrove forests worldwide are estimated to be equivalent to the annual fossil fuel emissions of the UK.

The Netherlands Development Organisation has recently begun the Mangroves and Markets (MAM) project in Cà Mau. They have trained local people to integrate sustainable shrimp aquaculture with restoration of mangrove forests. The MAM project uses an extensive method of shrimp farming that requires at least 50%

sold by the farmers at a premium price, strengthening this small-scale aquaculture. Since the project's start in 2012, MAM has trained more than 1300 shrimp farmers in organic shrimp farming practices (Figure 12.20).

The mangrove forests of Cà Mau are no longer in decline, pollution has been reduced and the once regular outbreaks of shrimp disease have almost stopped. Even though shrimp aquaculture is no longer intensive, employment in the industry has increased and, because of the organic certification, the profits for the farmers are higher. Working with nature rather than against it seems to be more beneficial for all parties.

Figure 12.20. Extensive, organic shrimp farming in Cà Mau.

mangrove cover. The shrimp grow and reproduce around the mangroves, where they are protected from predators and find shelter. The shrimp are farmed at low densities and artificial feeding is not carried out, so management costs are low and small-scale farmers are able to make a successful living. Pollution is low and disease outbreaks are less frequent, so no pesticides or antibiotics are used. The shrimp are certified as organic and are

Questions

1 Explain why intensive farming in Cà Mau encouraged pollution and disease.

2 Summarise the benefits of the integrated sustainable shrimp aquaculture method.

3 Explain what is meant by the term carbon sink.

Summary

- At the current rate of global population increase, the demand for fish and shellfish will continue to increase.

- Harvesting our oceans cannot provide enough food to meet the demand of the global population.

- Aquaculture will become increasingly important as a method of feeding the world and preventing the loss of fish populations.

- Responsible, sustainable aquaculture can help conserve marine stocks.

- If not carried out with proper planning and concern for the environment and local population, aquaculture can cause more harm than good.

- We need to work with our environment to increase fish productivity, not against it.

Exam-style questions

1 **a** Describe the differences between extensive and intensive aquaculture. **[3]**

b Figure 12.21 shows an enclosed aquaculture system used for growing grouper.

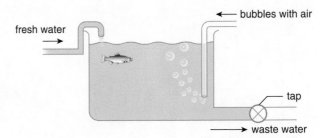

Figure 12.21. Tank aquaculture system used for producing grouper.

i Explain the purpose of the bubbler. **[2]**

ii Explain why fresh water is pumped through the tanks. **[2]**

iii Suggest and explain the effects on the environment that could occur if the filtration tank that waste water passes through before release was removed. **[5]**

[Total mark: 12]

2 **a** Outline the aquaculture method for grouper. **[8]**

b Shrimp aquaculture ponds are often sited in areas of mangrove forests. This leads to the destruction of areas of the mangroves. Suggest and explain how the development of the shrimp farms could affect the local environment and human population. **[7]**

[Total mark: 15]

3 Figure 12.22 shows the map of a coastline where a new intensive shrimp aquaculture facility is proposed.

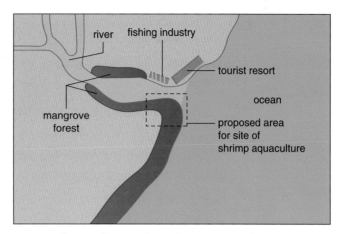

Figure 12.22. Map of coastal area where shrimp aquaculture venue is proposed.

a   Suggest and explain the negative consequences of developing the
    aquaculture venture.   **[6]**

b   Suggest and explain what the company should do to minimise negative
    effects on the local community.   **[5]**

c   Bluefin tuna is a carnivorous species of fish that is often produced by
    aquaculture. Explain why it is less sustainable to farm large carnivorous species
    rather than herbivore species such as carp.   **[3]**

                                                          [Total mark: 14]

4   a   Outline the stages involved in the aquaculture of giant clams.   **[6]**

  b   Explain the factors that a local government would need to consider before
         approving the development of a sustainable aquaculture venture for shrimp.   **[9]**

                                                          [Total mark: 15]

5   The demand for fish is increasing as the global human population increases. Harvesting fish
     from the seas will be increasingly unable to meet the demand for fish in the future.

     Table 12.6 shows the demand for fish since 1970 and the predicted demand up to 2050. It
     also shows the quantity of fish that may be harvested from the sea.

year	demand / million tonnes	harvest from sea / million tonnes
1970	60	60
1990	80	70
2010	140	80
2030	180	85
2050	220	80

Table 12.6. Changes in demand for fish and harvest of fish between 1970 and 2050.

a **i** Plot line graphs on the same axes of the demand for fish and fish that may be harvested from the sea. **[5]**

ii The difference in the total demand for a year and what may be harvested is the mass of fish that will have to be produced by aquaculture.

Calculate the mass of fish that will have to be produced by aquaculture in 2050. **[1]**

b Different types of fish feed are more or less digestible. This means that fish may be able to absorb them more or less efficiently, so growing more or less rapidly and producing more or less faecal waste.

Describe an experiment that would produce valid data to investigate the effect of different feed types on the rate of tilapia growth and faeces production. **[6]**

[Total mark: 12]

Offshore cobia and mutton snapper production in the Bahamas

The sustainable production of large predatory carnivorous fish by aquaculture has proved difficult. Bluefin tuna is a top predator that has been produced by aquaculture for several decades. The aquaculture methods used to produce bluefin tuna, however, are not environmentally sustainable for several reasons.

- The fishmeal used for feed is from the unsustainable harvest of other species.
- The tuna are not spawned as part of the process: juveniles are captured from the wild.
- The tuna are kept in cages, which are often too small for fast swimming, large fish, resulting in damage to the fish.
- The tuna produce large quantities of waste that causes pollution.

Recently, research has been carried out into the sustainable production of two carnivorous species, cobia and mutton snapper.

Adult cobia grow up to 2 m in length and weigh over 68 kg; mutton snapper are smaller, with a length of up to 95 cm and weight up to 16 kg. Brood-stock fish are captured and checked for parasites and disease before being transferred to inland controlled tanks or ponds. To reduce infection, the tanks contain cleaner fish in order to minimise the use of pesticides and antibiotics. The brood stock produce fertilised eggs that are then collected and transferred to sterilised hatchery tanks. Once hatched, they are fed sustainably produced feed such as live rotifers (microscopic invertebrates). As they pass through different larval stages, the juvenile fish are transferred to different tanks and fed on protein- and fat-rich food. The feed pellets used contain a combination of protein-rich soya, sustainably raised prey fish and waste trimmings of processed fish. After several weeks in the hatcheries, the fish are taken to offshore aquaculture sites, where they are placed into large submerged cages called sea stations, which have a volume of approximately 3000 m³. The sea stations are anchored to the seabed well away from the coast, as shown in Figure 12.23.

The anchorage needs to be very secure to prevent the sea stations being dislodged by storms. The sea stations are made of strong netting to reduce shark

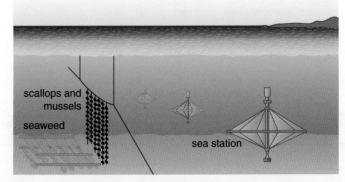

Figure 12.23. Offshore aquaculture using sea stations.

attacks, and their volume is high to prevent collision damage to the fish. Tidal currents flush water and wastes through the cages and bring oxygen. Controlled feeding is carried out to prevent waste food falling through the cages, and the feed used is the same as that used in the hatcheries. In order to minimise the risk of eutrophication, ropes of scallops and mussels are hung in the water to collect organic waste in the water. Seaweeds are also grown, to remove excess mineral ions such as nitrates and phosphates.

In a study into the effects of sea stations on water pollution, the dissolved nutrient and organic matter content was measured in the water and the sediment on the seabed. Chlorophyll *a* concentration was also measured in the water at various distances from the sea station over a year. The results of the study are shown in Figure 12.24.

The results of the pollution assessment of the offshore aquaculture of the cobia and mutton snapper are encouraging. The system offers an environmentally sustainable method of producing high trophic level predatory fish and could be extended to other species such as tuna. The main drawbacks are the logistics of working offshore. The sea stations need to be attached very securely to the seabed to prevent strong ocean currents and storms dislodging them. Sharks are attracted by the high density of fish and feed and have damaged some of the netting. Skilled and experienced divers and technicians are required to operate the system, and the conditions can be hazardous.

Questions

1   Evaluate the results of the study into the effects of the sea stations on pollution.

2   Explain the benefits of this method of aquaculture for producing cobia and mutton snapper.

3   Explain why the level of chlorophyll *a* in the water is an indicator of pollution.

4   Cobia and mutton snapper are fish that can be sold at high prices. Suggest and explain why offshore aquaculture methods are likely to be used more frequently for expensive fish.

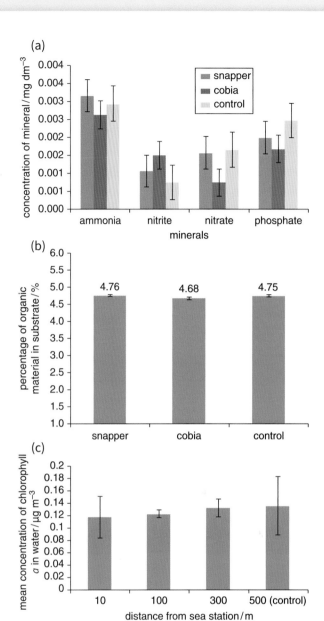

Figure 12.24. Effects of offshore aquaculture on pollution indicators. (a) Dissolved minerals in the water around the sea station; (b) Percentage of organic matter in seabed sediment underneath sea station; (c) Mean concentration of chlorophyll *a* in the water at different distances from the sea station. Error bars represent standard deviation.

283

Chapter 13
Human impact on marine ecosystems

Learning outcomes

By the end of this chapter, you should be able to:

- describe the ecological impact of human activities, particularly industrial and large-scale activities, on the abiotic and biotic components of the marine environment
- discuss the relationship between toxins accumulating in marine food chains and the safety of fish and shellfish as human food
- discuss the evidence for global warming, particularly the role of human activities, and its impact on marine ecosystems
- describe the positive impact that some human activities can have on the marine ecosystems
- apply what you have learnt to new, unfamiliar contexts.

13.1 The impact of humans

All species alter the environment around them. The changes inflicted on the environment by one species in particular, however, far outweigh all other species. That species is ours: *Homo sapiens*.

Human activities, particularly during the 20th and 21st centuries, have had a major impact on marine ecosystems. Food webs have been disrupted, habitats destroyed and biodiversity lost, along with changes to the physical and chemical nature of the water. A range of agricultural and industrial activities have affected the ecosystems of our oceans, both directly by altering the properties of the water and adding poisons, and indirectly by global warming. Some of our activities, such as the sinking of ships for wreck diving, can increase biodiversity; while others, such as the release of mercury, have a negative impact.

Our influence affects the organisms in the oceans and, by passing poisons through marine food chains, we risk poisoning ourselves. We are the dominant species on the planet and, as such, have a responsibility to maintain the ocean ecosystems for the future.

13.2 The oil industry

Oil is the main source of fuel for ships, cars, trucks and aeroplanes around the world. It is a mixture of many different compounds, including gasoline, diesel, kerosene and bitumen. It was formed millions of years ago and is the remains of the anaerobic decomposition of marine organisms as phytoplankton and zooplankton. Over time, these remains became buried under layers of sediment and subjected to heat and pressure, resulting in their conversion into crude oil. Crude oil is the product of living organisms, but many of the chemicals within it are toxic.

Oil from deep deposits is brought to the surface by drilling on land or at sea on oil rigs. It is then transported in large oil tankers to refineries where different fuels are produced. The exploration, drilling, transport and use of oil causes many environmental issues.

Exploratory drilling and setting up offshore oil platforms

In order to identify oil reserves, survey ships map the seabed by emitting high decibel explosive impulses. The noise from these surveys has been reported to kill fish eggs and larvae, and damage the vibration detection mechanisms of fish. Damaged fish are less able to escape predators and are often unable to find mates. Whales and other fish divert from their normal migration routes.

Drilling through the seabed releases toxins such as benzene, zinc and arsenic into the water. These can pass through food chains by **bioaccumulation**. Disrupted sediment can block the gills of invertebrates and fish, causing suffocation. Sediment can also block the light in the water, reducing phytoplankton productivity. The fragile seabed habitat can be physically damaged, resulting in organisms being dislodged and killed.

 KEY TERM

Bioaccumulation: the accumulation of substances, such as pesticides, or other chemicals in an organism.

Oil spillage

Oil spills can be caused by leakage from oil tankers or drilling sites. Oil spillage may be a major, sudden event, such as the *Deepwater Horizon* disaster in 2010, caused by the explosion of an oil rig in the Gulf of Mexico. Such sudden spills release vast quantities of oil into the sea that then spread quickly onto coastlines (Figure 13.1). Continuous leakage from drilling sites or tankers is also a problem, leading to an on-going flow of oil into the sea.

Figure 13.1. A beach in Alaska coated with oil after the *Exxon Valdez* supertanker spillage in 1989.

Oil spills can ruin entire ecosystems in oceans and on coastlines. They can take many years to clean up; they are very costly, both financially and environmentally, and the clean-up operations can sometimes cause as much damage as the oil spill. Since the transportation of oil began in the 20th century, there have been many spillages and it is estimated that every year more than 880 000 gallons of oil are released into the water from drilling operations alone.

Marine oil spills have a range of effects, including:

- toxicity to organisms

- physical damage to organisms and ecosystems

- disrupted food webs

- clean-up damage

- dead zones.

Oil toxicity

Crude oil contains many chemicals that are toxic when ingested by marine organisms. After the *Deepwater Horizon* explosion in 2010, many organisms were poisoned, including dolphins, turtles, bluefin tuna and sea birds. Dolphins were found to have sustained serious damage to their lungs and fish larvae had undergone mutations.

Physical damage to organisms

When whales and dolphins come to the surface to breathe, oil can cover their blowholes and enter their lungs, damaging the tissue or causing suffocation. Oil can also get into the animals' eyes, potentially damaging vision. When oil reaches coastal water, it can prevent hatchlings and juvenile turtles from surfacing to breathe. Fish, especially pelagic fish such as bluefin tuna, can take in oil through their mouths, damaging their gills.

Sea birds such as pelicans become covered with oil when diving into oily water to feed (Figure 13.2). Once birds are covered with oil, they are unable to fly, making feeding and escaping predators impossible. Their natural buoyancy and insulation from cold are also lost, causing death by drowning or hypothermia. When oil washes up onto beaches, nests and eggs get covered, often killing the chicks and causing adult birds to abandon the nesting areas. Some birds exposed to crude oil show hormonal changes that disrupt breeding.

Figure 13.2. Oil-coated pelicans after the *Deepwater Horizon* oil spill.

Furred marine mammals, such as sea otters and seals, often get coated in oil. The fur then loses its insulating properties and as a result the animals can die from hypothermia.

Effects on food webs and productivity

Oil on the surface of the water reduces light penetration, decreasing phytoplankton productivity. Because of its toxic effect, oil also kills organisms from different trophic levels, causing food chains and webs to become unbalanced.

Damage to coastal ecosystems

Water currents drive oil spills onto coastlines and beach areas, resulting in a thick coating of oil on sand and rocks. This poisons and suffocates coastal organisms and can kill plants, including mangroves. The loss of mangroves is particularly damaging to ecosystems because mangrove roots anchor soil and prevent coastal erosion. Mangroves are nesting areas for many birds and the water around their roots is a nursery ground for many marine species. Rocky beach animals such as crabs and sea anemones are often killed and seaweeds are lost.

Sun and wind turn oil into a hard, asphalt-like substance that eventually breaks up and is washed away. On sandy beaches, oil can sink through to lower layers of sand, causing contamination that can last for years. Nesting sites for birds and turtles can be destroyed, leading to the loss of many breeding seasons. If an oil spill coincides with the hatching of turtle eggs, a whole generation can be lost. It can take many years for established food webs to recover, and sometimes it is impossible because erosion of the substrate results in habitat loss.

Damage caused by cleaning-up oil spills

Oil does not dissolve in water so tends to aggregate as a slick across the water surface. The natural movement of the sea breaks up the oil into smaller droplets, which then fall down through the water column to the seabed or spread further afield. Some methods, such as the use of booms to collect surface oil, do not affect the environment. The use of bacteria is discussed in Chapter 15. Many other methods have environmental consequences.

Controlled burning of the surface oil involves igniting it by adding accelerants. This can only be carried out in calm weather and generates large quantities of smoke and air pollution, including sulfur dioxide gas, which causes acid rain.

Dispersants are sprayed onto the oil, helping to break it up into smaller droplets so that it is scattered. This helps prevent the oil contaminating coastlines but does not remove it. Corexit, a frequently used dispersant, is toxic to plankton and other marine organisms. Recent evidence suggests that it passes through food chains, accumulating and harming top predators such as dolphins and birds. Many dolphins seem to have been poisoned in this way after the *Deepwater Horizon* disaster and there have been reports that plankton biomass in the Gulf of Mexico has been reduced. Dispersants cause oil to sink to the seabed where, because of the cold, it persists for a long time, slowly leaking toxins into the water. Filter-feeder organisms such as mussels and oysters concentrate the dispersant in their bodies when they collect dead organic matter.

Oxygen dead zones

When oil sinks to the seabed, it is decomposed by bacteria that use it as a source of energy. The Gulf of Mexico contains many microbes that consume the natural seepage of oil from rocks. After the *Deepwater Horizon* disaster, these bacteria appeared to be one of the main processes by which the oil was broken down and removed. However, if large quantities of oil are released, the bacteria increase in number and their high rate of respiration removes oxygen from the ecosystem. This produces dead zones where most organisms are unable to live. Recent research suggests that the oxygen

levels in some areas of the Gulf of Mexico were reduced dramatically after the *Deepwater Horizon* spill.

> **KEY TERM**
>
> **Global warming:** the observed and projected increases in the average temperature of Earth's atmosphere and oceans due to an enhanced greenhouse effect

Indirect effects of the oil industry

When oil is burnt, it produces many waste gases, including carbon dioxide and sulfur dioxide. Carbon dioxide is a greenhouse gas and has potential effects on **global warming** and ocean acidification.

Sulfur dioxide dissolves in rainwater to produce sulfurous and sulfuric acids. These fall as acid rain on land and sea. On land, acid rain is known to cause deforestation and loss of fish from fresh-water lakes. High quantities of acid rain at sea have the potential to lower the pH of seawater, affecting the physiology of marine organisms such as coral reefs and bivalve molluscs. Tables 13.1 summarises the effects of the oil industry on marine ecosystems.

> **SELF-ASSESSMENT QUESTIONS**
>
> 1 Explain three ways in which animals may be harmed directly by oil spills.
>
> 2 Use the following words to complete the sentences.
>
> **bioremediation, bacteria, dispersants, droplets, respiration, temperature**
>
> One method for protecting the coast from oil spills to spray on _____. This causes the oil to break up into smaller _____ and sink to the seabed. Once it has sunk, _____ begin to break down the oil. The _____ at the seabed is low so that the rate of bacterial _____ is slow. This means that it can take many years for the oil to finally be removed by this process of _____.

factor affected by oil industry	effects of oil contamination
water quality	• toxins such heavy metals released from drilling • oil emulsion in water column • loss of oxygen in deep water • surface coated with oil
habitat	• physical damage to seabed from exploration and drilling • coverage of beaches and coast areas with oil • loss of reefs and nesting sites • loss of mangroves, leading to coastal erosion and loss of nursery sites
biodiversity	• reduction in biodiversity • loss of phytoplankton • loss of all species at all trophic levels due to ingestion of toxic oil, suffocation, loss of insulation, breeding
food webs	• food webs disrupted at all levels • loss of producers reduces energy available • loss of top predators causes increases in some prey • overgrowth of decomposer bacteria
chemical composition of water	• toxins such as mercury and arsenic present from drilling • presence of many toxic hydrocarbons • presence of dissolved, toxic dispersants • increased acidity due to acid rain and carbon dioxide • oxygen levels may fall
physical properties of water	• high turbidity causing less light penetration • surface tension affected due to oil

Table 13.1. Effects of the oil industry on marine ecosystems.

13.3 Desalination plants

The rapid increase in the human population over the last hundred years has brought with it increased demands for fresh water. Farming requires large quantities of fresh water, and the higher standards of living that people demand necessitates fresh water for things such as golf courses and swimming pools. The high demand for fresh water cannot be met in many parts of the world by natural sources alone, so increasing numbers of desalination plants have been built to extract fresh water from seawater.

Desalination plants can cause several problems to marine ecosystems (Table 13.2). Most of these problems are linked to the effluent that is released. There are two main types of desalination plant: distillation plants that boil seawater and collect fresh water by condensation, and reverse osmosis plants that pump water at high pressure through membranes to remove the salt. Both types generate similar pollutants that affect the water quality.

High salinity brine

Desalination plants release a very concentrated salt solution (brine) back into the sea. The brine from distillation plants is also very hot. It has a high density so sinks to lower depths and increases the salinity of the water there. Organisms that are osmoconformers are often killed by osmotic water loss, and even many osmoregulatory species are unable to survive. When the water temperature is high, it can kill organisms by causing overheating or can affect organisms' respiration rate. The productivity of phytoplankton is reduced by higher salinity and higher temperatures, and this reduces the energy available to food webs. Higher temperatures also reduce the solubility of oxygen, causing organisms to suffocate. The higher salinity can affect water currents because it alters natural haloclines.

Pollution due to waste chemicals

Chlorine is added to water in desalination plants to prevent the growth of algae within the machinery. Waste chlorine in the effluent water can be highly toxic to organisms in the sea. Heavy metals such as copper, iron, nickel and chromium are known to leak from the equipment into the waste water. These metals tend to aggregate in sediment on the seabed, where they are taken up by filter-feeding organisms and pass through food chains, accumulating in the body tissues of top predators. Desalination plants are cleaned every 3–6 months using harsh, toxic cleaning solutions that are often acidic or alkaline. When released, these solutions can poison marine organisms and alter the pH of the water, affecting their physiology.

Sediment movement

The outflow from desalination plants may agitate the seabed when pumped out at high pressure. This dislodges sediment, which can reduce light penetration for producers and damage the gills of fish and invertebrates.

Direct risks to organisms

In addition to the problem of water pollution, there is a risk that organisms are taken into the desalination plant with the seawater. To prevent fish and other species being sucked into the plant, filters are placed on inflow tubes, but smaller organisms, including planktonic larval forms, will still be drawn in. To reduce loss of plankton, only deeper water should be used. Harvesting water during spawning times can also remove eggs and larvae from the water column, reducing the populations of some species. Table 13.2 summarises the effects of desalination on marine ecosystems.

factor affected by desalination plants	effects of desalination plants
water quality	• increase in salinity as salt is dumped into water • toxic cleaning agents released into water • toxic heavy metal ions released from corrosion • acids and alkalis released from cleaning equipment • detergents released from cleaning fluids • increased sediment in water from pumping of waste water • reduced oxygen content
habitat	• physical damage to seabed from release of water • loss of phytoplankton due to high salinity and temperature • agitation of sediment
biodiversity	• reduction in biodiversity • loss of many species, especially sessile osmoconformers such as shellfish, because of higher salinity, toxins and heat • loss of smaller organisms and eggs into the desalination plant
food webs	• food webs disrupted at several levels • loss of producers due to salinity change • loss of many sessile osmoconformers, such as molluscs, reducing food for higher trophic levels • loss of planktonic larvae and eggs lowers populations
chemical composition of water	• increase in salinity as salt is dumped into water • toxic cleaning agents released into water • toxic heavy metal ions released by corrosion • acids and alkalis released from cleaning equipment • detergents released from cleaning fluids • reduced oxygen content due to high temperatures
physical properties of water	• raised water temperature • altered haloclines due to higher density of saline water

Table 13.2. Effects of desalination plants on marine ecosystems.

13.4 Agriculture

The effect of mineral ions such as nitrates and phosphates on algal blooms and producer productivity is discussed in Chapter 8. Using fertilisers on fields close to coastal areas and rivers can cause algal blooms in the sea. Overgrowth of algae can then lead to the establishment of dead zones in the sea, where oxygen is very low and virtually no life is present. This process is called **eutrophication** and consists of several stages (Figure 13.3).

- To maximise crop yields, farmers often add inorganic fertiliser to their fields. This dissolves in rainwater and runs off into rivers. The loss of the fertilisers into the rivers is called leaching.

- The rivers develop high concentrations of mineral ions, which are carried into estuaries and seas. These mineral ions encourage the overgrowth of phytoplankton, known as algal blooms.

- The overgrowth of algae produces a population that over-competes for light so many organisms die and sink down to the seabed.

🔑 **KEY TERM**

Eutrophication: the process by which a body of water becomes enriched in dissolved nutrients (such as nitrates and phosphates) that stimulate the growth of producers, usually resulting in the depletion of dissolved oxygen

- Decomposer bacteria break down the dead phytoplankton and respire at a high rate, reducing the concentration of oxygen in the water.

- The low oxygen concentration in the water leads to the death of aerobic organisms by suffocation.

The loss of organic matter, such as animal faeces or dead plant material, into rivers and seas also provides decomposer bacteria with nutrition and can lead to oxygen depletion. Dead zones can be catastrophic for sessile marine organisms such as mussels and oysters, and can affect coastal communities that rely on such organisms for their economy.

Not only is fertiliser and dead organic waste passed into the sea from agriculture, but pesticides, herbicides and fungicides may also be lost into the water. These substances can poison marine organisms and may accumulate along food chains, killing top predators.

In a recent investigation, the effect of agriculture on algal blooms in the Gulf of California was carried out. The Yaqui Valley is a 225 000 hectare area of Mexico where intensive farming is practised. The whole valley is fertilised and irrigated, causing excessive run-off of fertiliser into rivers, and eventually into the Gulf of California. Satellite images of water in the gulf were analysed between 1998 and 2002. It was found that in each year there were four periods when fertiliser was added to the wheat and, in each case, an algal bloom of up to 570 km^2 would appear in the Gulf of California days after the fertiliser was added. Table 13.3 summarises the effects of agriculture on marine ecosystems.

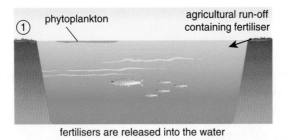

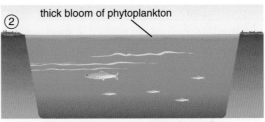

Figure 13.3. Stages in the eutrophication of a body of water.

factor affected by agriculture	effects of agriculture
water quality	• increase in sediments from run-off • increase in mineral ions such as nitrates and phosphates from fertilisers • reduced oxygen in water due to decomposition of organic waste and dead plants • increased algal blooms
habitat	• large quantities of algae can wash up on shores • dead organic matter can accumulate on the seabed
biodiversity	• reduction in biodiversity due to low oxygen • loss of many species, especially those that require higher levels of oxygen in water • some species die due to escape of pesticides into water • poisoning of some species by algal toxins
food webs	• food webs disrupted at several levels • loss of pelagic predator fish species due to low oxygen • over-growth of phytoplankton causing algal blooms
chemical composition of water	• increase mineral ion content, especially nitrate and phosphates • reduced oxygen concentration • possible increase in dissolved pesticides
physical properties of water	• increased turbidity due to sediment and algal bloom • reduced light penetration

Table 13.3. Effects of agriculture on marine ecosystems.

291

PRACTICAL ACTIVITY 13.1

The effect of mineral ions on eutrophication

This experiment requires the use of pond water that has been established outside for at least 2 or 3 months.

Apparatus

• 4 × 1 dm³ plastic drinks bottles (or four separate fish tanks, or any similar sized containers)
• Samples of pond water
• Liquid plant fertiliser
• pH indicator paper
• Nitrate testing kit
• Phosphate testing kit (these can be purchased from aquarium suppliers or garden centres)
• Oxygen meter

Method

• Fill each of the bottles or tanks with pond water and label them 1, 2, 3 and 4.
• Bottle 1 is the control experiment and has no fertiliser.
• Place 40 drops of liquid fertiliser into bottle 2, 80 drops into bottle 3 and 120 drops into bottle 4.

• Use the test kits, pH paper and oxygen meter to measure the starting levels of pH, oxygen concentration, nitrate and phosphate in the water.
• Place all four bottles in an area that has plenty of sunlight.
• Every 2 days for the next 4 weeks, record the appearance of the water in each bottle and the levels of nitrate, pH, phosphate and oxygen. (Depending on the conditions, it may take longer to see the effects of decomposition because of over-population with phytoplankton.)

Risk assessment

Safety glasses should be worn when handling all solutions, as the testing solutions may be irritants. After handling the bottled water where phytoplankton has been growing, wash your hands thoroughly.

Results and analysis

Record your results in a suitable table and think of a way to present the data.

Conclusions

1. Explain any changes in colour of the water.
2. Explain any changes in oxygen, nitrate, phosphate and pH.
3. Why might oxygen levels increase for the first few days in the bottles with more fertiliser and then decrease?
4. Why might nitrate and phosphate levels decrease for the first few days and then begin to increase in the bottles with more fertiliser?
5. Why might the pH rise over the first few days and fall towards the end of the experiment?

13.5 Sewage and refuse

Sewage

Sewage is water that carries waste materials. It is usually channelled through plumbing pipes and a series of underground sewers. In most developed nations, sewage is sent to water treatment plants where it is cleaned by removing toxins and organic material before being released into lakes, rivers and the sea. In many countries, however, there is little or no purification of the water before it is released back into natural water bodies. There are several different sources of sewage.

Domestic sewage is waste water generated by human residences. It carries faeces, urine, washing water and laundry waste. Waste water from large institutions such as hospitals and schools may come under this category if it is similar to domestic waste water. It is usually channelled through underground sewers.

Surface run-off is rainwater that runs over the ground, picking up particulate matter and dissolving mineral ions as it flows. It may carry sediment and mineral ions such as nitrates and phosphates.

Industrial waste water is liquid waste generated by factories that is washed into the sewerage system, although technically it is not defined as sewage. Companies have a duty to avoid releasing hazardous waste directly and should ensure that water is treated before release. Industrial waste water may contain substances such as detergents, heavy metals and pesticides, which pose a risk to living organisms.

Untreated sewage poses several risks to the marine environment because of its content.

Faeces and other organic wastes provide a source of food for decomposer bacteria. If large quantities are dumped into the water, it has a similar effect to agricultural run-off, resulting in an increase in bacterial populations in the water. The bacteria respire rapidly, reducing the oxygen in the water so that other organisms die by suffocation.

If sewage contained only purely organic waste, it could be used as a fertiliser. However, it can contain chemicals including detergents, fertilisers and toxins. Detergents often contain phosphates, which can promote eutrophication and have been linked with algal blooms. Detergents also contain chemicals called surfactants, which reduce the surface tension of water. Surfactants are toxic to aquatic life, persist in the environment and have been found to break down the protective mucus layer that coats fish, making them vulnerable to parasites and bacteria. Medicinal drugs taken by humans can pass into the sewerage system in human urine, and affect marine organisms. Steroid hormones from contraceptive pills may have altered the ratios of male to female fish around sewage outflow pipes, although this research is controversial.

Untreated sewage can contain pathogens such as viruses that can affect marine organisms, particularly mammals. In 2015, large numbers of grey seal pups off the Welsh coast died from infection with campylobacter bacteria, which cause human gastroenteritis. The infected seals had symptoms consistent with human gastroenteritis and it is thought they were infected from sewage.

Refuse

Marine refuse is made up of discarded objects from coastal areas and ships. Typical examples include waste from beach users, waste from sewers, shipping debris and fishing waste such as old lines and nets. It is estimated that more than 10 000 containers are lost every year from ships during storms, with one notable event occurring in 1992 when a cargo of yellow plastic toy ducks were lost in transit from Japan. These ducks have been found all over the world and are known as the 'friendly floatees'. Their movements have helped reveal the path of the world's ocean currents (Figure 13.4).

The majority of litter found in the seas is plastic, is not biodegradable and may persist for thousands of years. Exposure to sunlight and constant wave action breaks the plastics up into small microparticles that float in the surface waters of the sea. Ocean currents move the microparticles and concentrate them in 'garbage patches'. The Great Pacific Garbage Patch is a collection of marine debris in the north Pacific Ocean that is created by ocean currents (Figure 13.5). There are also larger

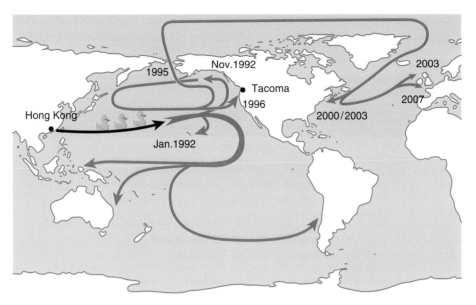

Figure 13.4. Ocean currents shown by the movement of a lost cargo of plastic ducks.

pieces of debris and even old, floating computer screens have been seen. About 80% of the debris in the Great Pacific Garbage Patch comes from land-based activities in North America and Asia. The remaining 20% comes mainly from shipping, the majority of which is discarded fishing nets, which are particularly hazardous to wildlife. It takes about 6 years for refuse from North America to the reach the Great Pacific Garbage Patch, while refuse from Japan takes about a year. Most other ocean garbage patches are located in the centre of gyres (Figure 13.5).

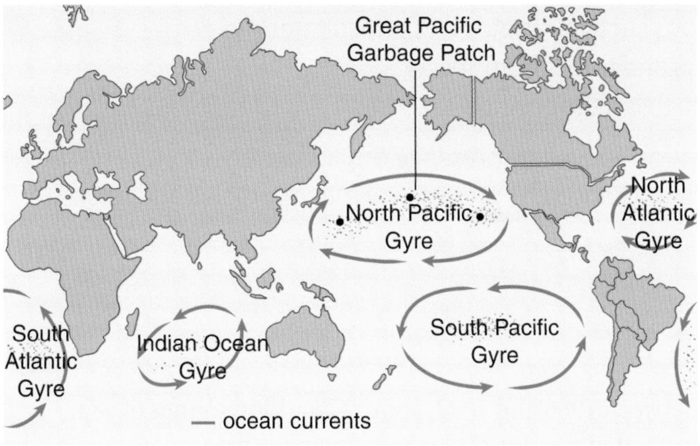

Figure 13.5. The location of five ocean gyres where refuse has accumulated.

Refuse has several potential negative effects upon the marine environment.

Sea birds, turtles, mammals and fish can become entangled in old fishing nets, fishing lines and other objects, causing them to drown, become more susceptible to predation or die from starvation. Refuse can physically damage animals, killing them directly or wounding them, leading to infection and incapacity.

Many animals that live on or in the sea consume refuse by mistake, because it can look similar to their natural prey. Plastic can become stuck in the digestive system of animals, blocking the passage of food and causing death by starvation or infection (Figure 13.6). Tiny floating plastic particles resemble zooplankton, which are eaten by animals and then travel up the food chain. Loggerhead sea turtles often mistake plastic bags for jellyfish and albatrosses can mistake plastic resin pellets for fish eggs, which they feed to their chicks.

Figure 13.6. The body of albatross showing ingested refuse.

Many plastics release toxins, such as bisphenol, into water. These can be absorbed by organisms directly from the water or from ingested plastics. The plastics can themselves absorb toxic substances from the water, such as PCBs, which are then passed on to organisms when eaten.

293

Once PCBs have entered one organism, they have entered the food chain and can travel up to the top predators.

Microparticles in the water reduce the penetration of sunlight so reduce the rate of photosynthesis by phytoplankton, reducing primary productivity. If producers such as phytoplankton have a reduced biomass, there is less energy entering the food web. Table 13.4 summarises the effects of sewage and refuse on marine ecosystems.

factor affected by sewage and refuse	effects of sewage and refuse
water quality	• increase in sediments • increase in detergents and toxins from waste water • increase in toxins from run-off water • increase in suspended microparticles of plastics • reduced oxygen concentrations due to decomposition • reduced mineral ion concentrations • presence of harmful microbes
habitat	• sediment settling on seabed • refuse such as plastic damaging habitats • refuse and microparticles blocking upper water habitats
biodiversity	• reduction in biodiversity • loss of many species due to low oxygen levels, especially organisms with higher oxygen demands • loss of species due to infection by harmful microbes • loss of fish, mammals, birds and turtles due to physical damage from refuse such as nets and ingestion • reduced phytoplankton due to reduced light penetration caused by microparticles
food webs	• disrupted at several levels by toxins and detergents • loss of predators due to physical damage by refuse and ingestion of refuse • loss of predators due to infection
chemical composition of water	• increase in mineral ions such as nitrates and phosphates • increase in detergents and toxins from sewage • oxygen depletion due to decomposition
physical properties of water	• reduced light penetration caused by presence of sediments • reduced light penetration caused by presence of microparticles and refuse

Table 13.4. Effects of sewage and refuse on marine ecosystems.

Dumping New York's sewage into the north-west Atlantic

Until 1992, the sewage of New Jersey and New York was collected and the solid parts allowed to settle out in tanks. The resulting semi-solid sludge was then placed onto sewage ships that sailed out to sites in the north-west Atlantic, and dumped into the sea. One such site was located 106 miles out to sea at a depth of 2500 m. It is estimated that between 1986 and 1992, about 42 million tonnes of wet, untreated, sewage sludge was dumped there.

A survey of the seabed at the site was carried out in the late 1980s. Oxygen levels in the water around the site were extremely low, and high concentrations of toxic metals such as cadmium and mercury, along with organic compounds, were found in the sediment. Sea urchins and sea cucumbers in the area were analysed for concentrations of radioactive isotopes of carbon, hydrogen and sulfur, which are very rare in the marine environment but are found in human faeces. The animals had high concentrations of these isotopes, indicating that substances from the sewage were entering the food chains. Traces of one potentially harmful bacterium that causes food poisoning were also found in the sediment.

During the time that the sewage was being dumped, there were several algal bloom events in the sea around New York. Cases of food poisoning were recorded in people who swam in the sea or visited the beaches, and refuse such as used syringes was found washed up on beaches. Some shellfish beds died because of pollution and lack of oxygen, and others were often closed for fishing because of worries about the presence of pathogens. Beaches were shut for days each year because of harmful microbes.

The sewage dumping was stopped in 1992, after which the seabed at the dumping site began to change rapidly. Oxygen levels increased and species of organisms that require higher oxygen levels appeared. The waters around New York improved, with more species of fish present and much more biodiversity. Algal blooms still occur but the beaches are much cleaner, are rarely closed and are safer for bathers. The fisheries have also benefitted with higher catches and less frequent closure of the oyster beds.

Questions

1 Explain why the oxygen levels were low at the base of the dumping site.

2 Explain how the radioactive tracers show that substances from the sewage were entering the food chain.

3 Suggest why the presence of mercury in the sewage sludge could be a problem for fisheries.

13.6 Dredging

Dredging is the process of physically gathering up sediment from the bottom of shallow areas of sea. It is often used to keep shipping routes open but is also used when building the foundations for new structures or to harvest sand or minerals. There are several methods of dredging.

- Suction dredging: specialised dredging ships carry giant suction tubes that operate like very strong vacuum cleaners (Figure 13.7). As the ships move through the water, they suck up the sediment from the seabed through tubes and deposit the sediment into large metal tanks on the ship or neighbouring barges, to be deposited later in other areas. Some suction dredgers use cutting equipment that breaks up the rocky seabed and dislodges underwater obstacles.

- Mechanical dredging: bucket dredgers carry a series of buckets on a rotating belt that scrape the seabed. They can be carried on ships and in some cases are strong enough to cut through coral. Clamshell dredgers use a large mechanical grab that can be lowered into the water in order to remove sediment.

- Water-injection dredging: ships have large hosepipe-like structures that force water along the seabed. This dislodges the sediment, scattering it out of shipping lanes.

All forms of dredging can have negative impacts. The physical nature of the process has the potential to damage the seabed and sessile organisms, and generate sediment.

Physical damage to benthic communities

All forms of dredging involve removal of the seabed. This obviously has the potential to destroy coral reefs, and dislodge sessile organisms such as oysters and mussels. Breeding grounds for fish can be affected, and estuarine environments may become uninhabitable for species that prefer sandy seabeds with high levels of sediment. The loss of many filter-feeding organisms can have an effect on food webs, because they are a food source for other organisms. If the population of filter feeders decreases, organic waste that is washed down rivers is not removed and decomposes, resulting in loss of oxygen. It can take several years for communities to recover from dredging, particularly when the rocky seabed has been extensively altered.

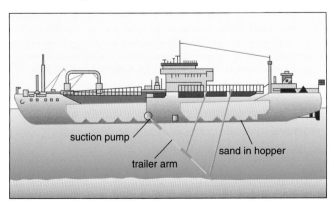

Figure 13.7. A typical suction dredger: sediment is taken from the seabed and stored in the hull of the ship.

295

Sediment release

Stirring up the sediment from the seabed causes an increase in water turbidity. Light penetration is reduced, lowering the productivity of producers so that less energy is available to the food web. Coral can become covered in sediment, reducing the amount of light available for zooxanthellae. Sediment can cover organisms that live over the seabed, getting caught in their delicate gill structures and eventually causing suffocation. Sessile organisms can become totally smothered so that they are unable to obtain sufficient oxygen or food. The sediment can also interfere with the spawning of fish and shellfish by killing eggs and sperm: in many countries dredging is prohibited during spawning seasons. In some cases, however, there have been reports that limited dredging has caused an increase in populations of shellfish such as oysters, mussels and even edible crabs, suggesting these organisms may benefit from some agitation of the water.

The effect of dredging on oxygen levels in the water is unpredictable. If sediment is released into the water, it has the potential to increase the rate of bacterial decomposition and thus reduce oxygen levels in the water. The release of nitrates and phosphates can cause eutrophication, which will also reduce oxygen levels. In some cases, however, the removal of large amounts of organic waste that has accumulated from sewage and rivers actually reduces the rate of decay so increases the oxygen levels.

Release of chemicals from sediments

Sediment from harbours and estuaries often contains toxins such as heavy metals ions, oil, tributyltin (TBT), PCBs and pesticides from shipping and coastal activities. These chemicals are embedded in the sediment and are dislodged when dredging is carried out. Some substances are directly toxic to marine organisms and also accumulate through food chains, harming top predators. If sediment is dumped into other areas of the sea, chemicals can seep out in those areas. Careful planning is needed before dumping sediment, to minimise damage to other communities. Tables 13.5 summarises the effects of dredging on marine ecosystems.

factor affected by dredging	effects of dredging
water quality	• increase in sediment • increase in heavy metals and toxins • possible change in oxygen concentrations
habitat	• physical damage to seabed from scraping • destruction of reefs • destruction of shellfish breeding grounds • sediment covers areas of seabed
biodiversity	• reduction in biodiversity • loss of coral and sessile reef organisms • loss of sessile shellfish beds, such as oyster, due to physical damage or smothering with sediment • possible loss of species due to lack of oxygen • possible increase in algal blooms due to release of mineral ions
food webs	• food webs disrupted by loss of lower trophic levels such as coral and molluscs • loss of higher predators due to loss of lower levels • possible increase in algal blooms
chemical composition of water	• increase in toxins, heavy metals and minerals from disturbing seabed • possible reduction in oxygen levels due to decomposition
physical properties of water	• increased turbidity due to sediment • reduced light penetration

Table 13.5. Effects of dredging on marine ecosystems.

3   List human activities that can cause: (a) reduced oxygen content of water, (b) accumulation of toxins through food chains, (c) increased turbidity in the water.

4   Suggest two measures that could be taken to reduce the effects of pollution from (a) agriculture, (b) sewage and (c) refuse.

13.7 The bioaccumulation and biomagnification of toxins

Chapter 3 discusses how energy passes through food chains. Similarly, toxins eaten at low trophic levels in a food chain are often passed from one organism to another, eventually ending up in top predators.

When organisms ingest toxins that are not excreted from their bodies, the toxins accumulate as they eat more of them: this process is called bioaccumulation. As the toxins pass along the food chain, the concentration found in

the bodies of the organisms tends to increase with each trophic level: this process is known as **biomagnification**. Toxins that do not break down or are not flushed out of an organism's body tend to undergo biomagnification along food chains and can reach dangerously high levels in top predators.

Figure 13.8 shows a simple marine food chain. If each phytoplankton picks up 0.001 µg of a toxin and each zooplankton consumes 100 phytoplankton, then the zooplankton gain 100 doses of 0.001 µg of toxin (0.1 µg of toxin) each. Each anchovy consumes 100 zooplankton, gaining 10 µg (100 × 0.1 µg) of toxin. Each herring eats 100 anchovies, gaining 1 mg of toxin, and the tuna eats 100 herring, gaining a massive 100 mg of toxin.

The organisms most affected by toxins tend to be top predators, and this is a problem not just for the marine organisms. Many of the species harvested for human consumption, such as tuna and shark, can contain high concentrations of toxins such as mercury.

Mercury accumulation

During the 1950s, animals in the seaside town of Minamata on Kyushu Island in Japan began to exhibit a series of strange behaviours. Cats developed nervous tremors, convulsions and screamed loudly, and birds fell out of the sky or tress without warning. Doctors were treating humans with tremors, seizures and other neurological symptoms. An enquiry was launched and it was found that

Biomagnification: the increasing concentration of a substance, such as a toxic chemical, in the tissues of organisms at successively higher levels in a food chain

297

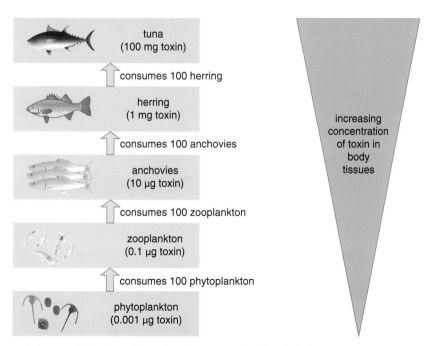

Figure 13.8. The process of biomagnification of a toxin along a marine food chain.

an industrial company called Chisso Corporation had been discharging heavy metal waste including mercury into the sea. The mercury had formed methylmercury, a highly toxic form of mercury, which had accumulated in the marine food chain. Humans and animals such as cats had consumed marine food that contained the methylmercury.

Methylmercury is present at very low concentrations in seawater but is absorbed by algae at the start of food chains. It is not excreted, but remains in the bodies of organisms, especially the liver, fatty tissues and muscles, and is passed along the food chain, increasing in concentration at each trophic level (Figure 13.9). Many fish and shellfish contain methylmercury in their bodies, and species that are long lived and top predators, such as tuna, shark, swordfish and marlin, tend to have the highest concentrations. Methylmercury is a neurotoxin and caused the symptoms seen in the animals and humans of Minamata Bay.

The US Food and Drug Administration (FDA) advises that the risk of mercury poisoning from eating fish and shellfish is not a health concern for most people. However, certain seafood can contain levels of mercury that can harm unborn babies or young children, because of their small body sizes.

The FDA advice is that young children, pregnant women and women of child-bearing age can safely eat two or three portions of fish or shellfish a week. Good choices of fish and shellfish include salmon, shrimp, pollock, tuna, tilapia, catfish and cod. Fish that are best avoided are tilefish (from the Gulf of Mexico), shark, swordfish and king mackerel. The FDA also advises that white tuna should only be eaten once a week.

Mercury gets into the oceans from three main sources:

- 30% from human industries, mainly coal and oil burning and gold mining

- 60% from flooded land and forest fires, often as a result of human activities

- 10% from natural sources, such as volcanic activity and leaching from rocks.

In an effort to reduce emissions of mercury into the marine environment, countries such as Japan and the USA began to regulate industries in the 1970s. To reduce the global emissions requires international collaboration, and on 19th January 2013, 140 countries signed a treaty called The Minamata Convention on Mercury. This treaty represents a global commitment to protecting human health and the environment from mercury. It took 3 years of meetings and negotiations before the convention was signed, but provides hope for the future.

Tributyltin (TBT)

When any physical structure is placed into the sea for any length of time, organisms attach to it and begin to create a community. This attachment is called biofouling. A diverse range of organisms, such as barnacles, molluscs, tube worms, seaweeds, sponges and many others, biofoul ships (Figure 13.10). This causes increased drag in the water for ships, leading to increased fuel use, which is estimated to cost the global shipping industry up to $1 billion each year. The increased fuel use leads to increased output of carbon dioxide and sulfur dioxide, potentially contributing to global warming and acid rain.

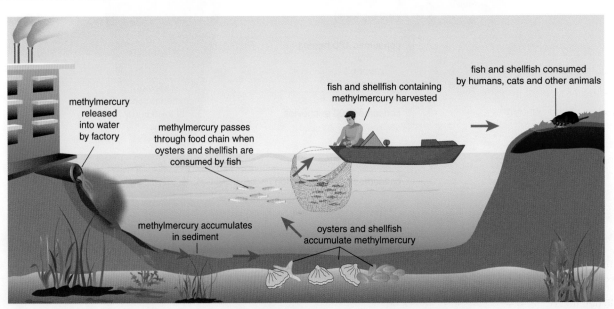

Figure 13.9. The transfer of methylmercury to humans and shellfish.

Figure 13.10. Biofouling of a ship's hull with a range of marine organisms.

TBT is an anti-fouling chemical that was developed in the 1950s. It was added to paint used on the hulls of ships and other structures. It is highly effective but leaks out of the paint into the water. Once in the water, it attaches to sediments and sinks to the seabed, where it can remain for up to 30 years.

TBT is highly toxic for many species of marine organisms, often at very low concentrations. Besides the biofouling species it is targeted at, it has far reaching effects on other organisms as a result of bioaccumulation. It enters food chains at lower trophic levels, through organisms such as barnacles and molluscs, and then passes upwards. TBT

concentrations increase in organisms as it moves through the food chain, eventually poisoning top predators such as tuna, dolphins and sea otters. Specific effects of TBT include:

- altered invertebrate development, for example TBT causes deformities in oysters and the masculinisation of dog whelks, which results in fewer fertile females so reducing the population

- reduced immune response, for example high concentrations of TBT have been recorded in the livers of top predators such as tuna, sea otters and dolphins, which has reportedly led to their deaths from infection because of a weakened immune response.

Because of its harmful effects on the environment, there have been efforts to ban the use of TBT. The International Convention on the Control of Harmful Anti-fouling Systems is an International Maritime Organisation (IMO) treaty that bans the use of TBT by all nations that sign up to it. By 2015, 71 states, representing more than 85% of global shipping, had signed the treaty, but there are still reports of the illegal use of TBT in many areas and monitoring the ban is not easy.

SELF-ASSESSMENT QUESTIONS

5   Explain why it is recommended that pregnant women do not eat top predator fish such as swordfish.

6   Outline why TBT has been used on ships and explain why there are campaigns for it to be banned.

Maths skills

Standard form, decimal places and accuracy

Standard form is a useful way of writing down very big or very small numbers. A number in standard form is always written in the form of:

$$A \times 10^n$$

where A is a number between 1 and 10 and n is the number of places a decimal point needs to move.

Worked example

750 000 000 is actually the same as $7.5 \times 10 \times 10 \times 10 \times 10 \times 10 \times 10 \times 10 \times 10$

It is written in standard form as 7.5×10^8

An easy way of working this out is to count how many 'jumps' the decimal point must make to the left to get to a number between 1 and 10, in this case eight:

750 000 000.0 $\longrightarrow$ 7.5×10^8

When the number is a very small number, the decimal point moves in the other direction (to the right) to get to a number between 1 and 10, so the index is negative.

0.0000056 in standard form is 5.6×10^{-6}

0.0000056 $\longrightarrow$ 5.6×10^{-6}

If you need to add or subtract two numbers in standard form, it is easiest to convert them first into ordinary numbers and then change them back into standard form. For example:

$3 \times 10^4 + 6 \times 10^5 = 30\,000 + 600\,000 = 630\,000$, which is the same as 6.3×10^5

If you want to multiply and divide numbers in standard form there are rules to follow:

- to multiply you add the powers

- to divide you subtract the powers

$(3 \times 10^3) \times (6 \times 10^4) = (3 \times 6) \times (10^{3+4}) = 18 \times 10^7$, which is the same as 1.8×10^8

$(9 \times 10^4) \div (3 \times 10^2) = (9/3) \times (10^{4-2})$, which is the same as 3×10^2

The number of decimal places a number is given is the number of places after the decimal point. The number 5.621 has three decimal places.

If, for example, you are asked to give a number to two decimal places, you may have to round the number: 6.372 to two decimal places is 6.37.

If you are asked to give a number to a certain number of decimal places, you may have to add zeroes after the decimal point: 0.2 to two decimal places is 0.20.

In experimental results tables you need to have a consistent number of decimal places, and you should always use the number of decimal places your equipment was capable of measuring to.

Table 13.6 compares two presentations of the masses of four mussels.

mass of mussel / g
5.35
5.00
5.20
5.35

☑

mass of mussel / g
5.35
5
5.2
5.35

☒

Table 13.6. Setting up results tables to the correct number of decimal places.

The column on the left is correct because each value has been given to two decimal places.

Questions

1 a Write the following in standard form.

    i   35 000 000

    ii   0.0000352

    iii   45 000

    iv   0.00000000435

  b Work out the following:

    i $(3 \times 10^5) + (6 \times 10^6)$

    ii $(1.2 \times 10^{-2}) + (1.1 \times 10^{-3})$

    iii $(2.3 \times 10^3) \times (1.2 \times 10^2)$

iv $(4 \times 10^3) \times (3 \times 10^4)$

v $(6 \times 10^6) \div (3 \times 10^3)$

2 a Round the following to 2 decimal places:

i 0.3267

ii 1.234

iii 1.378

iv 3.599

b Present the following lengths of juvenile groupers in a table; they were measured with a ruler that had 1 mm increments: 10.3 cm, 12 cm, 4.56 cm, 5 cm, 7.6 cm.

13.8 Global warming and human activity

One of the indirect consequences of the oil industry is the production of large volumes of carbon dioxide gas as a result of burning fossil fuel. Increased atmospheric carbon dioxide may be leading to an enhanced **greenhouse effect** and increase in global temperature, which could pose many problems for our oceans.

Greenhouse effect

The greenhouse effect is a natural phenomenon and is not wholly the result of human influence. Short wavelength solar radiation penetrates through the Earth's atmosphere and warms the planet when it hits the surface. Some of this radiation is reflected as longer wavelength infrared light. Some of this longer wavelength infrared light passes back through the atmosphere into space, but some of it is reflected back to Earth by certain greenhouse gases (Figure 13.11). The greenhouse gases in the Earth's atmosphere include:

- carbon dioxide
- methane
- water vapour
- chlorofluorocarbons (CFCs)
- nitrous oxide.

This natural greenhouse effect maintains the Earth's temperature within the range required for life.

All the greenhouse gases, apart from water vapour, are generated by both natural and human activities. During the 20th and 21st centuries, the increasing global population and increased burning of fossil fuels has

caused an increase in the production of these gases. This has led to an imbalance in the carbon cycle, with too much carbon dioxide being released into the atmosphere and too little removed. It is believed that if the Earth's atmosphere contains more greenhouse gases, the amount of infrared light trapped within the atmosphere will increase, resulting in an enhanced greenhouse effect and global warming.

KEY TERM

Greenhouse effect: the heating of the atmosphere due to the presence of carbon dioxide and other gases; these gases prevent infrared radiation being re-emitted into space

301

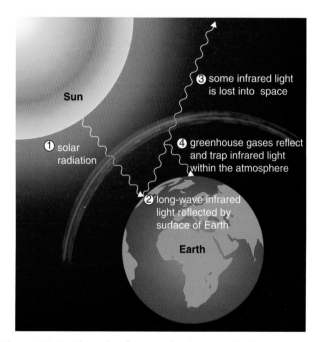

Figure 13.11. The role of atmospheric gases in the greenhouse effect.

Evidence for global warming

It is difficult to prove that human activities producing greenhouse gases are leading directly to global warming. There is, however, a great deal of evidence to indicate that the amount of greenhouse gases in the atmosphere has increased and that the average global temperature has also increased.

Increasing global temperatures

Four main institutions have monitored average global temperatures, the NASA Goddard Institute for Space Studies (GISS), the UK Meteorological Office, the NOAA National Climatic Data Center and the Japanese Meteorological Agency. These institutions set a baseline average temperature and then determine how far the average temperature for a particular year deviates from the baseline. This value is called a temperature anomaly. The baseline used is slightly different for each agency. Figure 13.12 shows the temperature anomalies determined by each agency since 1880. It is clear that, despite small variations, the overall trend indicated by all of them is upwards.

Increasing levels of atmospheric carbon dioxide

Since 1958, the atmospheric concentration of carbon dioxide has been monitored by observatories on a volcano called Mauna Loa in Hawaii. Figure 13.13 shows the change in atmospheric carbon dioxide since then. It is clear that there is an overall upwards trend. Each year shows a seasonal increase and decrease in carbon dioxide levels as a result of changes in the rate of photosynthesis through the year.

It is possible to analyse atmospheric carbon dioxide concentrations from much earlier time periods by analysing ice cores. Ice cores are cylinders of ice drilled out of an ice sheet or glacier, which can be up to 3 km deep. The oldest ice core records from Antarctica extend back for 800 \ 000 years. Within the frozen ice core are small bubbles of air that were trapped when the ice froze. These bubbles can give us a direct measure of the gas composition at different periods of time. It is also possible to determine the temperature at the time of deposition by analysing other gases. Figure 13.14 shows that carbon dioxide and methane concentrations remained stable over much of the last 1000 years but increased rapidly over the 20th century.

If you look at older ice core data, the results can seem confusing. Figure 13.15 shows that there have been periods of high and low carbon dioxide concentrations. Temperatures also show fluctuations through colder and warmer periods. What is clear, however, is that carbon dioxide and temperature fluctuate together and show a positive correlation.

Some people think that the fluctuations over time show that the current global warming is simply part of a natural cycle of heating up and cooling down and that it is nothing to do with human activity. What we must not forget, however, is that the current global increases in carbon dioxide, methane and temperature are all linked with a period of industrialisation, and that the steepness of the increases now seen is almost without precedent.

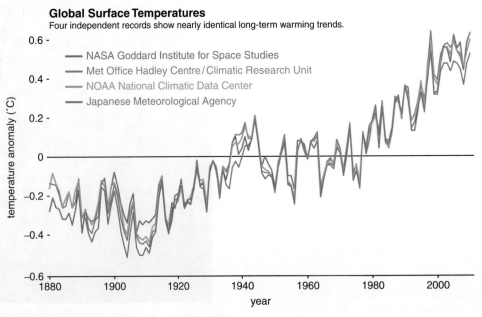

Credit: NASA Earth Observation / Robert Simmon
Data Source: NASA Goddard Institute for Space Studies, NOAA National Data Center, Met Office Hadley Centre / Climate Research Unit, and the Japanese Meteorological Agency.

Figure 13.12. Change in global temperature between 1880 and 2000.

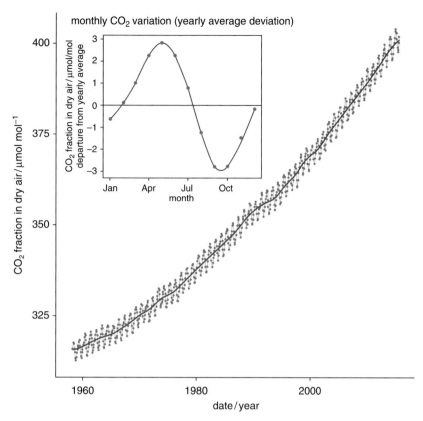

Figure 13.13. Change in atmospheric carbon dioxide levels from 1958 measured on Mauna Loa, Hawaii.

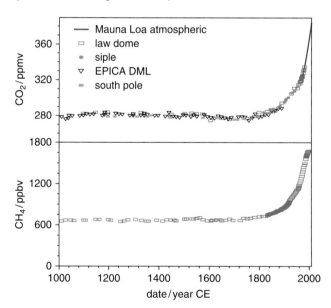

Figure 13.14. Ice core data showing changes in atmospheric carbon dioxide and methane between 1000 and 2000 CE.

Melting of ice and sea-level rises

One of the possible effects of global warming is the melting of ice, both at sea and on land. The Arctic sea ice stretches to its minimum extent each September, after the warm summer. Satellite images show that the minimum extent of the ice has been getting less each year.

Figure 13.16 shows that the mass of land ice in the Antarctic ice sheet has lost about 134 billion tonnes of ice per year since 2002, while the Greenland ice sheet has lost an estimated 287 billion tonnes per year. The graphs show that the mass of ice is decreasing each year.

As ice melts and the water enters the oceans, it causes an increase in sea-levels. In the last century, the global sea-level rose about 17 cm but the rate over the first decade of the 21st century has been nearly double that.

Climate change

As the global temperature has risen, there have been noticable effects upon our climate. There are reports of changes in the seasons, with winters in the Northern Hemisphere ending earlier and the volume of snow decreasing. The ranges of some organisms are changing, with species such as barracuda and Pacific cod being found in more northerly latitudes. There have been more extreme weather events, such as major storms and floods. Many species of plant have flowered earlier in the year, and animals have emerged from hibernation earlier. In Canada, the mountain pine beetle, which consumes pine trees and is normally killed off by cold winters, is spreading further northwards as the winters become warmer.

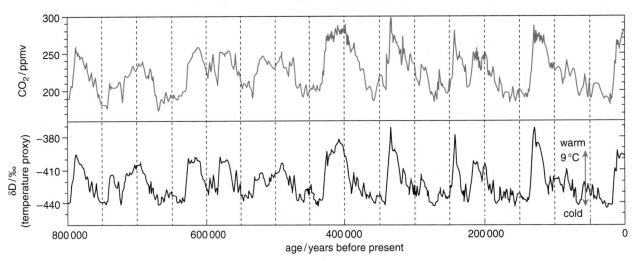

Figure 13.15. Ice core data showing fluctuations in carbon dioxide and temperature over 800 000 years.

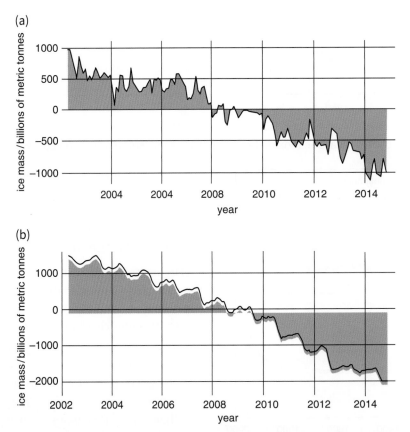

Figure 13.16. Changes of mass of ice in (a) Antarctic and (b) Greenland ice sheets since 2002. The baseline is set for an average between 2008 and 2010.

Possible alternative theories

Despite the evidence suggesting that global warming is occurring, and that it is in large part now due to human activity, it is very difficult to prove. Critics often point out several problems with the evidence.

- Carbon dioxide levels and temperature do show a positive correlation but it is difficult to show if one causes the other. If the planet is warming, the solubility of carbon dioxide in the oceans decreases, so carbon dioxide is released into the atmosphere increasing the atmospheric concentration.

- Ice core data show that the planet goes through periodic heating and cooling cycles and that the same occurs with carbon dioxide levels. We may be in a natural cooling cycle.

- Some recent temperature measurements have conflicted with the current model of global warming, suggesting that the rate of temperature increase has slowed.

- Global temperature may correlate with solar activity rather than carbon dioxide concentrations. Comparisons of historic global climate warming and sunspot activity suggest a correlation. However, data comparing the solar energy reaching the planet with the global temperature indicates no significant correlation.

Consequences of global warming

Global warming could have many far-reaching consequences for our oceans and marine communities. There are already indications that some ecosystems are under threat.

Melting of ice sheets

Satellite images have demonstrated that the Arctic sea ice is at much lower levels than in the past and that the land ice sheets of Antarctica and Greenland are in retreat. The release of vast quantities of fresh water into the ocean could have many consequences.

- Increase in sea-level. The rate of sea-level increase has doubled over the last decade and, if temperatures continue to rise, will increase further. Low-lying land will be far more prone to flooding, resulting in coastal erosion and loss of both human and animal coastal communities. Coastal soils will become more saline, affecting plant growth and the growth of crops. Many low-lying atolls could disappear altogether, causing species extinction and leaving people without a home.

- Reduction in seawater salinity. The release of large amounts of fresh water would lower seawater salinity. This would harm osmoconformers, which can only tolerate narrow ranges of salinity. It could also affect breeding, as eggs and sperm are sensitive to changes in salinity. The world's great ocean currents are generated by differences in water density as a result of variations in temperature and salinity. If the salinity falls in the Arctic and Antarctic regions, the direction of these currents could change.

- Habitat loss. The ice sheets of the Arctic and Antarctic are an important habitat for many organisms. If the ice melts, especially in the Arctic where there is no land under the ice sheet, organisms such as polar bears, which rely on the ice, will lose their habitat.

Acidification of the water

Carbon dioxide is an acidic gas that dissolves in water. As the concentration of carbon dioxide in the atmosphere increases, so does the acidity of the oceans. It is estimated that the pH of oceanic surface water is now 30% more acidic than in the 18th century. Acidification of water is a problem for organisms such as corals, molluscs and sea urchins, which secrete calcium carbonate to build skeletons and shells. When water is very acidic the shells, skeletons and coral reefs erode.

KEY TERM

Coral bleaching: the loss of symbiotic algae from the tissues of corals as a result of environmental factors

Increased water temperature

The oceans absorb a great deal of heat and there are already reports that the mean water temperature has increased. This temperature rise could have many direct and indirect effects on marine life.

- **Coral bleaching**. Increased water temperatures can cause corals to eject their zooxanthellae, as described in Chapter 5.

- Changes in ranges of organisms. As waters warm, the habitat a particular organism lives in may no longer be suitable, but other areas may be. Warm-water fish could extend their ranges further towards the poles and then come into competition with other species in these areas. Original species could become extinct as a result of competition with the new invasive species. Food sources may die out, leaving predators little to feed on. Krill is important for many ocean food chains and reproduces at a lower rate when in warmer water.

- Phytoplankton productivity. Photosynthesis rates increase at higher temperatures, so there may be an increase in productivity of algae. This may be counterbalanced by changes in acidity and salinity. Harmful algal blooms releasing toxins and causing anoxic areas of ocean because of their decay could also occur.

- Animal physiology. The majority of marine animals, other than birds and mammals, are cold-blooded and have a body temperature that is the same as the water. If their body temperature rises, processes such as respiration will increase, raising the demand for food and oxygen in the water.

- Changes to breeding seasons. Breeding seasons are regulated by many things including day length, lunar

305

periods, tides and temperature. If temperatures rise, some organisms may breed earlier, causing their offspring to mature at the wrong time. Many spawning seasons and migrations are timed so that the organisms arrive at locations when food sources increase. If different species' breeding seasons become out of phase with each other, there is a risk that food chains would be very badly affected.

- Changes in ocean currents. Ocean currents are the product of differences in density of water. The density of water is influenced by salinity and temperature. If the oceans increase in temperature, the density gradients would be disrupted, altering ocean currents.

Climate change

Global warming may already be causing the climate to change. The last 20 years has seen an increase in severe weather episodes such as storms and hurricanes. Increases in storms can cause physical damage to reefs and coastal areas, breaking coral and stirring up sediments from the seabed. Coastal areas such as estuaries will experience more flooding from high tides, leading to increased salinity of land. Inland storms can increase run-off, which brings more mineral ions and sediment down to the coast. The sediment could smother estuarine organisms and the mineral ions contribute to eutrophication.

SELF-ASSESSMENT QUESTIONS

7 Draw up a two-column table to summarise the evidence that global warming is occurring. Use the column headings 'factor' and 'source of evidence'.

8 Use these words to complete the sentences below:

extinct, ranges, food webs, bleaching, salinity, sea-levels

Global warming could have serious consequences for our oceans. An increased temperature could lead to the _____ of organisms changing which may bring them into conflict with other species. As a result of this, species may become _____ and that could have effects on other organisms in _____. Acidification of the water and increased temperatures could cause coral _____. In addition, ice sheets could melt, raising _____ and reducing the _____ of the water which could kill organisms that cannot osmoregulate.

13.9 Effects of wrecking ships for dive sites

There are up to 3 million shipwrecks on the floors of our oceans. When a ship sinks it may initially disrupt the seabed when it lands. Within weeks of sinking, the habitat of a wreck begins to undergo the process of succession: pioneer species start to colonise it and eventually turn it into an artificial reef. In an effort to observe the process of succession, British marine scientists sank the HMS *Scylla*, an old Royal Navy frigate, just off the south coast of the UK. The frigate was observed over the next few years to see how the biodiversity changed.

- Within 1 week, fish such as cod were sheltering within the wreck, and crabs, barnacles and tube worms began to settle and grow.

- Within 18 weeks, brown algae and sea kelp had become established. Barnacles and tube worms were well established and sea squirts, sea anemones and scallops had also arrived.

- Within 48 weeks, green sea urchins and starfish arrived and sponges were growing. The mussel and barnacle populations began to decline because of predation by the starfish. Wrasse were found to be defending the wreck as a territory.

- Within 3 years, HMS *Scylla* had developed coral and a diverse community of organisms. A complex food web was established within the wreck site.

Sunken ships are now left where they are and allowed to become part of the marine ecosystem. They have slightly different species present than natural coral reefs but still offer a valuable method of improving biodiversity. Any metal or solid structures can be sunk in order to create an artificial reef. In North Carolina, USA, as well as ships, old vehicles and even tanks have been sunk, with the same effects. These artificial reefs also protect the coastline from erosion by dissipating wave energy.

When deliberately sinking ships and old vehicles, it is important to ensure that any potentially toxic components are removed. Oils and fuels must be drained off, and pieces of metal that are coated in antifouling paint or have deeply ingrained oil removed. Electrical equipment, such as batteries, can leak when they begin to corrode so they are also removed. Ships that have been sunk unintentionally will retain many of these potential hazards so they do represent an environmental risk. Deliberately sinking old, clean ships helps improve biodiversity over both the short and long term, but the accidental sinking of an oil tanker can cause a great deal of harm. Table 13.7 summarises the effects of deliberately and accidentally sunk ships on marine ecosystems.

Wrecked ships that act as reefs are not only beneficial to marine ecology but also local economies. Wreck diving is a popular pursuit and many people are attracted by the beauty of the artificial reefs. Most wreck divers are responsible, environmentally aware people, but care still needs to be taken with the industry. Careless diving could damage the reefs and there have been reports of coral being removed as souvenirs. Large numbers of boats sailing to an area can also cause pollution. Many wrecks are sunken military vessels, designated as war graves, and should be treated with respect and not as tourist attractions. Some wrecks are archaeological sites and need protection to prevent looting. As fish tend to aggregate near the wrecks, fishermen often trawl around the areas and this needs monitoring to prevent physical damage.

oil tanker	deliberately wrecked cleaned ship
• leaks vast quantities of toxic oil • oil poisons fish, mammals, birds and other species • oil reduces light penetration through water • reduces biodiversity • causes pollution due to use of dispersants and burning • damages beaches and coastlines • causes damage to local economy due to loss of fishing industry and tourist industry	• if cleaned does not leak toxic chemicals • acts as a substrate for organisms to settle • acts as a shelter for fish • increases biodiversity • generates food webs • protects coastlines from erosion • benefits local economy by acting as a tourist attraction and may improve fish stocks

Table 13.7. A comparison of a wrecked oil tanker and a deliberately wrecked cleaned ship intended as an artificial reef.

307

Summary

- Our oceans and coasts are under threat from a range of human activities.

- Over the years, oceans have been treated as a dumping ground for refuse and sewage and industries have given little thought to the ecological health of these areas.

- The need for fuel has led to oil spills that have devastated areas around the world, and the ever-increasing demand for food has increased agricultural pollution.

- Desalination plants are being built to meet our need for fresh water, and by burning more and more fossil fuels we may well be causing the planet to warm up.

- We have poisoned ourselves by eating fish that has accumulated poisons from our own activities.

- Now that we have begun to suffer from the effects of pollution, we have begun to try to improve the health of our oceans.

- Many steps are being taken to try to reverse some of the damage. It is to be hoped that we are not too late.

Exam-style questions

1 a State what is meant by the greenhouse effect. **[3]**

b i Describe the possible causes of global warming. **[5]**

ii Explain the potential consequences of global warming on marine ecosystems. **[7]**

[Total mark: 15]

2 The concentration of mercury found in body tissues was analysed for different species of marine fish. Concentrations were compared against the mean trophic level of the fish. The mean trophic level takes account of the different types of food a fish eats.

The results are shown in Table 13.8.

species	mean mercury concentration / ppm	SD	mean trophic level
swordfish	0.995	0.870	4.5
bigeye tuna	0.689	0.341	4.5
grouper	0.448	0.278	4.2
Patagonian toothfish	0.354	0.303	4.3
halibut	0.241	0.157	3.8
monkfish	0.181	0.139	4.5
skipjack tuna	0.144	0.119	3.8
jacksmelt	0.081	0.050	3.1
sardine	0.013	0.015	2.7
oyster	0.012	0.035	*

Table 13.8. Mercury concentrations in body tissues of different fish species.

* The trophic level of oysters is difficult to assess because they filter feed on dead organic remains.

a Describe how mercury concentration changes as mean trophic level increases. **[2]**

b Suggest and explain reasons why some fish species have larger standard deviations than others. **[3]**

c Give an explanation for the differences in mercury concentrations of the different fish species. **[4]**

[Total mark: 9]

3 Dredging is sometimes used to clear harmful waste, such as heavy metals, from sediments at the base of estuaries. Figure 13.17 shows the effect of dredging contaminated sediment from the bottom of an estuary on the rate of cancers found in fish. The estuary once had effluent entering it from an industrial plant. The industrial plant was closed in 1983 and the river was dredged between 1989 and 1990.

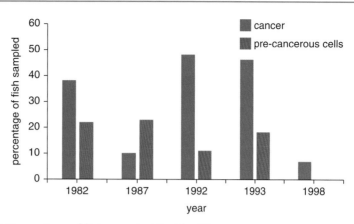

Figure 13.17. Percentage of fish sampled that had liver cancer or pre-cancerous cells.

a i In 1992, 84 fish were sampled. Calculate the number of fish found to have liver cancer. [2]

ii Describe the change in number of fish with cancer and pre-cancerous cells over time. [2]

iii Suggest an explanation for the changes in fish with cancer and pre-cancerous cells. [4]

b Discuss other potential effects of dredging the bottom of an estuary on marine life in an estuary. [4]

[Total mark: 12]

4 Read the following information about agriculture and marine pollution.

Farms destroy Asian oyster industry

In a coastal region of south-east Asia, oysters were once abundant. Fed by organic particles brought by the rivers from miles inland and deposited in the estuary, the oysters grew rapidly. Fisheries made a good living from harvesting the oysters to be exported and sold in restaurants all over Asia. Recently, however, the oyster beds have begun to die off and the fisheries are going out of business bringing high unemployment to the area.

The culprit seems not to be anything local but from inland. Far away from the oyster beds, intensive farming of crops has begun. Areas of once forested land have been removed to grow more and more crops. Many of the fields are on slopes that lead down into the very rivers that run down to the coast to feed the oysters. Growing conditions are good and many farmers have begun to add fertiliser onto the fields. The fertiliser has found its way into the rivers and then out to the estuary where the oysters grow. Scientists have said that the oysters are suffocating due to lack of oxygen and being covered in sediment.

The highest death rates of the oysters occurs during the monsoon seasons when algal blooms occur. It is also feared that global warming could make the situation worse and lead to their eventual extinction from the area. There is now conflict between the stakeholders of the farming and fisheries industries, so resolving it could be very difficult.

a i Explain, using an example, what is meant by the term stakeholder. [2]

ii Explain how the use of fertilisers by the farms has led to the death of the oysters. [4]

b **i** Explain what is meant by the term global warming. **[2]**

ii Suggest why the death rates are higher during the monsoon. **[2]**

iii Suggest why global warming could lead to a higher death rate of oysters. **[3]**

[Total mark: 13]

5 An investigation into the effects of a desalination plant sited on the Mediterranean coast on the diversity of invertebrate animal species was carried out. Species were randomly sampled on one day in the waters near the outflow from the desalination plant and at a similar, control area further up the coast. The number of each type of species found was recorded along with several abiotic factors. The results are shown in Tables 13.9 and 13.10.

species	number of individual animals in each location	
	desalination plant	control area
red sea squirt	5	27
yellow sea squirt	7	24
common brittlestar	4	5
rock crab	15	8
feather star	2	17
common sea urchin	15	7
purple sea urchin	0	16

Table 13.9. Numbers of species found in water around a desalination plant and a control area.

abiotic factor	desalination plant water	control area water
pH	6.7	7.2
mean 10 m depth temperature / °C	16	12
oxygen concentration / mg dm^{-3}	6	9
light penetration	low	high
salinity / %	4.0	3.4

Table 13.10. Some abiotic data for water around a desalination plant and control area.

a **i** Explain why the invertebrate animals were sampled at random. **[1]**

ii Explain the purpose of the control site. **[1]**

iii State what is meant by the term abiotic factors. **[1]**

b i Describe the general effects of the desalination plant on the invertebrate species. **[3]**

ii Calculate the percentage difference in rock crabs in the water around the desalination plant compared with the control area. **[2]**

iii Suggest and explain reasons for the effect of the desalination plant on the abiotic factors. **[3]**

iv Suggest and explain reasons for the differences in numbers of species found in the water around the desalination plant compared to the control area. **[3]**

[Total mark: 14]

EXTENDED CASE STUDY

The *Deepwater Horizon* oil spill in the Gulf of Mexico

The *Deepwater Horizon* oil rig was a modern, high-tech oil rig designed for exploratory drilling of oil fields in deep-water, long-distance areas of the sea. It had been used successfully in several drilling operations in the Gulf of Mexico. The well it drilled in the Tiber field was the deepest ever drilled, being below 1259 m of seawater with a measured depth of 10 683 m. In February 2010, *Deepwater Horizon* began drilling in the Macondo in the Gulf of Mexico, about 41 miles off the south-east coast of Louisiana, at a water depth of more than 1500 m.

The explosion and leak

On 20th April 2010, at approximately 9.45 p.m., the BP *Deepwater Horizon* oil platform in the Gulf of Mexico burst into flames and exploded. Eleven crew members died in the explosion. The fire continued to burn until, on the morning of the 22nd April, *Deepwater Horizon* finally sank. By the afternoon it became clear that there was a huge oil leak coming from the broken oil platform and that a major environmental disaster was beginning to unfold.

It took 87 days to stop the flow of oil from the broken platform, and there is still controversy over the actual flow rate of oil from the well. Original estimates by BP were that the oil was flowing at a rate of 790 m^3 day^{-1}. This estimate was challenged by scientists working for the US government, who estimated that the actual flow could be up to 9900 m^3 day^{-1}. There may have been up to 780 000 m^3 of oil lost in total, making it the world's biggest ever accidental oil spill, although the exact figure of how much oil was lost into the ocean is still disputed. BP argue that much of the oil loss was contained or burnt off at source. What was never in doubt was that the oil would have dramatic effects on the ecosystems of the local area.

Containing the oil

Initial attempts to seal the well head using submersible craft failed and, instead, a containment dome was placed over the largest leak. Oil was piped into a specialised ship called the *Discovery Enterprise*. This ship burnt off the gas that had been released and stored the collected oil, to be taken later to storage tanks. More containment domes were placed over other leaks and more ships employed to burn off and transport the collected oil. These measures did prevent large quantities of oil entering the Gulf of Mexico, but US government officials estimated that only about half the leaking oil was collected in this way. Over the next few months more efforts were made to permanently cap the leaking well heads, and by September 19th 2010, the well was declared 'dead' and fresh leakage of oil stopped.

Clearing up the spill

The oil spill was at such a large scale that an equally large-scale response was required. This response focused on four approaches: containment, dispersal, removal and bioremediation.

Containment

To prevent the oil from spreading to beaches, mangrove forests and other coastal areas, more than 1300 km of containment booms were used (Figure 13.18). Booms are floating barriers that attempt to contain the oil in one area, from where it can be removed. They act as a physical barrier but only work well in calm water and low wind.

Figure 13.18. Booms containing the oil spill from *Deepwater Horizon*.

Dispersal

Dispersants are chemicals that cause oil to break up into smaller droplets, forming an emulsion in the water. The oil droplets then disperse throughout the water column and sink to the bottom rather than staying on the surface. Dispersants are used to protect beaches, and it has been suggested that the oil is broken up faster by bacteria when it is scattered by dispersants. The dispersant used was called Corexit. It was sprayed from aeroplanes flying over the oil slick, and directly injected into oil coming from the underwater well. The use of this dispersant is controversial, because it may have added to the toxicity of the spill and caused a build-up of oil on the seabed. Injection of Corexit under water seems to have caused the oil to remain in the depths. Because of the cold temperature of these waters, it will take longer for the oil to be digested by bacteria. The toxic effects may last for many years.

Removal

Oil was removed from the water by collection or burning. Specialised ships with water skimmers were used to skim off the surface oil. This oil was then taken to on-shore tanks for storage and reprocessing. Burning was also used to remove oil from the water surface. This released vast quantities of smoke, carbon dioxide and other hazardous gases. Sandy beaches that were contaminated by oil were cleaned manually by sifting sand and digging out tar using mechanical diggers. Dispersants may have hindered the beach clean-up because oil mixed with dispersant sank to lower depths of sand. In marshy areas, vegetation and soil was hosed down with water and the waste extracted by vacuum devices.

Bioremediation

In theory, microbes will ultimately remove all traces of oil from the Gulf of Mexico. Many species of oil-digesting microbe live naturally in the sea, feeding on naturally leaked oil. The cold temperatures on the seabed where much of the oil has gathered will slow the rate of digestion, and some scientists have suggested that the ability of microbes to break down all oil is exaggerated. A genetically modified variety of oil-digesting bacteria, *Alcanivorax borkumensis*, was released into the water and also sprayed onto coastal areas.

The cost to the environment

The *Deepwater Horizon* oil spill caused both short- and long-term damage to the Gulf of Mexico. Eight US National Parks were threatened along with thousands of kilometres of coastline that provide habitats for a rich diversity of plants and animals. By November 2010, nearly 7000 dead animals had been collected, including birds, mammals and turtles. The actual number directly killed by the oil will be far in excess of this, as most will not have been collected and recorded. There are few data about the number of invertebrate casualties of the leak and it will have had considerable effects on microscopic species such as phytoplankton and zooplankton. Many birds such as pelicans, ducks and gannets were coated with oil and died as a result of loss of buoyancy or insulation. Many deaths were due to direct ingestion of oil from the water or inhalation of toxic fumes. Fish deaths are also difficult to record, but many were poisoned due to ingestion of oil or suffocated due to gill damage.

Areas of dead coral reef close to the leak site have been found that seem to have been directly affected by the oil. Toxins from the oil and the dispersants have worked their way through the food chains. Many dead dolphin have been washed up on beaches and post mortems have found traces of oil in their bodies. There have been frequent reports of sick dolphins in the years after the spill, with conditions such as liver cancer and lung disorders. Pregnant dolphins carrying dead fetuses have been reported, along with dolphins having miscarriages. Mutant fish, crabs and shrimp with traces of Corexit and oil-derived chemicals in their bodies have been caught.

Habitat loss has been severe in some areas, with the loss of plants such as mangroves. Figure 13.19 shows Cat Island in Baratria Bay, Louisiana. It was once full of mangroves, which held the soil together with their root systems, and was an important nesting place for pelicans. The island has now undergone severe erosion because of the death of the mangroves, and the pelicans have gone, probably never to return. Marhes and wetlands still have traces of oil, and the use of Corexit seems to have encouraged an oil-Corexit mixture to sink deep into the soil, where it may remain for many years.

Figure 13.19. Cat island, Baratria Bay, Louisiana (a) before and (b) after the oil spill. All that remains of the mangroves are a few dead roots.

The economic cost

The oil spill has had a serious impact on fisheries in the area. Stocks of commercially important shellfish such as oysters and crabs may never fully recover, and many fishers have gone out of business. Fish stocks are thought to have decreased in many areas, in particular stocks of valuable top predator fish such as bluefin tuna. Even when bans have been lifted on fishing, there has been resistance from consumers to buy fish products from the Gulf because of the risk of toxin accumulation in species such as oysters.

Tourism suffered greatly after the oil spill. The images of oil-covered beaches and burning oil caused many people to cancel trips, and it has taken time for the tourist trade to recover.

Local people have paid a heavy economic and social price for the oil spill. There are also concerns about the health effects of oil residues and Corexit that may have contaminated local water systems.

The future

It will take a great deal of time for the area to recover fully. Balls of congealed oil still wash up on beaches, especially when there have been storms out at sea. There are still oil deposits in the soil of marshlands. Dead dolphins and other organisms wash up on shores. There may still be large quantities of oil on the seabed that will continue to leak toxins into the water for many years. Some of the species affected may never fully recover.

There is, however, hope for the future of the Gulf of Mexico. In July 2015, BP agreed in principle to a financial settlement for the *Deepwater Horizon* oil disaster. There are many restoration projects for the affected coastline planned that will be funded by this money. Research into the long-term effects of the oil spill can be funded along with regeneration of the industries that have been affected. Local people from all the affected states, stretching from Texas in the west to Florida in the east, have risen to the challenge. Many of them have worked tirelessly over the years since the spill to rescue animals and plants and protect the fragile ecosystems of the Gulf. Without their help, the ecological disaster would have been far worse.

The *Deepwater Horizon* oil spill was an environmental, economic and social disaster. It is impossible to undo what happened, but we can learn many lessons from it to both try and prevent such an accident happening again, and respond more efficiently if one does.

Questions

1   Summarise the methods used to remove the oil.
2   Explain how oil could have led to death of sea birds and mammals in the weeks immediately after the spill.
3   Explain why dolphins and bluefin tuna are affected by oil and Corexit many years after the spill.
4   Dead zones, with low oxygen and very little life, have been recorded in areas around the oil spill. Explain how oil leakage could have caused these.
5   Explain why the loss of mangroves could be costly for both the environment and fishing industries.

Chapter 14
Marine conservation and ecotourism

Learning outcomes

By the end of this chapter, you should be able to:

- explain what is meant by conservation and ecological linkages
- describe the need to conserve marine species and ecosystems
- explain the possible negative impact of conservation programmes
- discuss the conflict of interests that can exist between different stakeholders in coastal activities
- describe the potential benefits and negative impacts of sustainable ecotourism in coastal communities
- apply what you have learnt to new, unfamiliar contexts.

14.1 Successful conservation

Chapter 13 explored ways in which humans have damaged the marine environment. If we are to remedy this and stop further damage, we need to think of ways of conserving species and their habitats. **Conservation** is often easy in theory but more difficult in practice. If they are to be successful, conservation projects need careful consideration and the support of local people. Projects that could affect local and national economies need to ensure that people retain employment and have the opportunity to improve their living standards. **Ecotourism** is an increasingly popular way of making conservation pay, but it needs careful regulation and a responsible approach from all concerned. If ecotourism is managed carefully, it is a valuable method from which the environment and local people benefit.

KEY TERMS

Conservation: the protection of plants, animals and other organisms along with their habitats from extinction

Ecotourism: sustainable tourism that is associated with an appreciation of the natural world and that minimises damage to the environment; it can benefit both environment and local populations

14.2 Conservation: what it is and why it is necessary

Most people are aware of at least one example of a conservation project, for example to conserve areas of rainforest, or to prevent a species such as the blue whale from extinction. Formally defining conservation, however, is actually quite difficult. It is best thought of as an ethical philosophy, the main aim being the maintenance of the health of the natural world. Many things are included in conservation, such as the Earth's habitats, biological diversity, fisheries, energy and non-renewable resources. In the preceding chapters you will have read about the human impact on fish stocks and our marine habitats. The aim of conservation is to prevent further damage, and in some way begin to rectify it. The people who try to protect nature are called conservationists. They have many roles and many types of people are involved. Some of these roles include:

- carrying out scientific research on how humans are affecting the planet and suggesting methods for protecting it

- raising awareness of conservation issues with the general public, businesses and governments

- carrying out practical conservation projects, such as the replanting of mangroves.

Why do we need conservation?

There are many arguments for conserving species and habitats, four of which are discussed below.

Ethical reasons

We are currently in the grip of a mass global extinction of species. There have been mass extinctions in the past (Figure 14.1), but the current mass extinction is different. In the past, mass extinctions have been caused by sudden, cataclysmic events. The extinction of the dinosaurs at the end of the Cretaceous period is thought to have been caused by an asteroid collision. The Ordovician–Silurian extinction, about 440 million years ago, was probably due to the formation of massive glaciers. This glaciation caused much of the world's water to turn to ice and sea-levels fell dramatically. The eruption of super-volcanoes is thought to be the cause of other extinctions.

Figure 14.1 shows how the rate of extinction shows a positive correlation with the human population. It is estimated that if we do nothing, by the year 2100 our activities will have led to the extinction of almost half of the world's current species. At the present time, we are the dominant species on the planet and have a moral duty to stop the damage that we are causing.

Future generations

We are the custodians of the planet for our descendants. Our activities now will shape the world of the future. If large areas of habitat continue to be lost, we will deprive our descendants of the opportunity to witness the beauty of nature. Their only knowledge of the beauty of coral reefs or unusual species will be through textbooks or films. There are already many species, such as the dodo and the Tasmanian tiger, that now only exist as drawings or museum specimens. If we continue to allow extinctions, many more species will become simply a page in a book or an image on a screen.

Our planet also provides our food and many other resources such as oil. If we use all the fish in the seas and all the non-renewable energy sources without finding

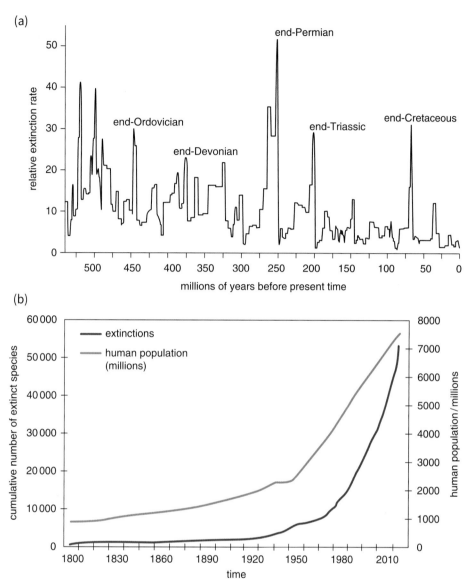

Figure 14.1. (a) The change in extinction rate, showing periods of mass extinction. The peaks represent periods of mass extinction; (b) The change in human population and number of species becoming extinct since 1800.

alternatives, there will be nothing left for our descendants. If they have no food, we will soon be on the road to extinction; ourselves.

Preserving ecosystems

An ecosystem consists of many species of interacting organisms and their habitats. Organisms are highly dependent on each other in many ways. They provide food for each other, can transport each other from place to place, and can provide and alter habitats for each other.

Food webs are complicated interactions between organisms, and if one species is lost from a food web, other trophic levels are affected. Some species are keystone species and have particularly important roles

in maintaining ecosystems (Chapter 2). If these keystone species are lost, the ecological effects are massive. Salmon feed in the oceans, obtaining their energy from a food chain based on phytoplankton. When the salmon migrate up rivers to breed, they are eaten by inland species such as bears and birds of prey. This means that the energy for many inland food chains comes ultimately from phytoplankton in the oceans. If salmon do not migrate, the energy for these food chains is lost.

Kelp forests are areas of rich biodiversity (Chapter 8). Figure 14.2 shows part of the food web in a kelp forest. Sea otters eat sea urchins, which in turn eat kelp. If sea otters numbers fall, the sea urchin population would increase and the amount of kelp decrease.

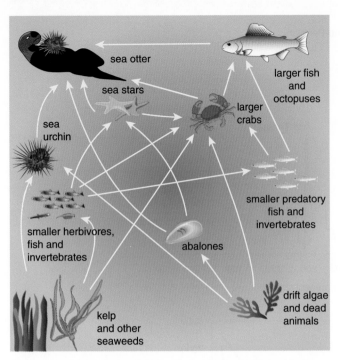

Figure 14.2. A complex food web that exists within a kelp forest. Sea otters are at the top of the food web and their numbers affect the diversity of the other species.

Some species depend on others for distribution. Barnacles attach themselves to humpback whales, so travel across oceans to spawn in different places. If humpback whales became extinct, barnacles would lose their distribution network.

Parrotfish live around coral reefs eating old coral. They grind up coral and release sand in their faeces that helps make sandy beaches and small islands. They also rasp away algae from the surface of the coral and remove sponges, helping to preserve the reefs. If parrotfish become extinct, the reefs would become overgrown with algae and sponges.

Benefits for ourselves

Our oceans provide us with many things that improve our lives, and more than 350 million jobs depend on them. We have harvested them for food for hundreds of years, and they have enriched our lives for recreational purposes. People are attracted by the beauty and diversity of the marine world. Diving, recreational fishing, whale watching, sailing and just the peaceful pleasure of sitting by the sea all form part of our enjoyment.

Marine organisms can also provide us with medicines. Organisms found on coral reefs have formed the basis of drugs for asthma, arthritis, lung cancer and skin cancer. Scientists suspect that there are many more potential drugs yet to be discovered.

If we allow biodiversity to fall and habitats to be destroyed, we will lose a food source, a place of enjoyment and the potential to treat many diseases.

Opposition to conservation

Some people argue that there is no point in conservation, particularly of species that are already well on their way to extinction. Several arguments are used to promote this opinion, four of which are discussed below.

Extinction and change is a natural part of life

Species have been going extinct since life began on the planet, and in fact the majority of species that have existed have become extinct. Evolution by natural selection is driven by competition and death. Individuals compete with each other and the consequence is that some species make other species extinct. Figure 14.1 shows the extinction rate of species based on fossil evidence, indicating that there have been several mass extinctions. It is argued that some species are not well adapted to their environment and it is natural for them to become extinct. Some people even argue that by protecting such species we are allowing weak organisms to survive, negatively affecting gene pools.

Expense

Conservation projects can be very costly. It is estimated that the cost of conserving all the threatened species in the world is in excess of $80 billion. If a species or habitat that is being conserved is unlikely to survive anyway, it can be argued that it is not worth the cost and the money should be spent on more realistic projects. Supporting a species or habitat that is a hopeless cause could put other species, that have more chance of survival, at risk.

 KEY TERM

Marine protected area (MPA): an area of ocean or coastline where restrictions have been placed on activities; the levels of restriction may vary, some may be no-take areas where no fishing is permitted, others may allow some fishing, some may ban all access to unauthorised people, while others may allow restricted access

Loss of income

Marine protected areas (MPAs) are areas of conservation where fishing is often prohibited, and in some cases no humans are allowed to enter unless as part of a research programme. Opposition to MPAs has come from groups whose livelihoods are threatened by them, including commercial and recreational fishers, tourists and people who have lived in an area for many years. Some industries have argued that MPAs only have a limited effect, and that the loss of income and increased unemployment does not justify their creation. Many people think that conserving nature can stand in the way of progress, industrial development and wealth creation.

Excessive conservation

If protection for one species is put in place and its population increases, it will have an effect on other organisms in food webs. In the 1970s, Scotland placed a ban on killing grey seals and the population gradually rose to over 30 000. Despite being a success, conservation of the seal population may have hampered other conservation measures. The seals eat a range of fish species, including large amounts of sand eels and cod, and they have few predators (sharks and killer whales). There have been reports of grey seals killing harbour porpoises and harbour seals, and they may be preventing the recovery of cod stocks.

SELF-ASSESSMENT QUESTIONS

1 **a** List three reasons why conservation is important and three reasons why it may not be necessary.

   b Explain why the current mass extinction is different from previous mass extinctions.

2 In many areas of ocean, the number of top predators is very low because of over-fishing. Explain why the conservation measures used to protect the grey seals should also include measures to protect sharks and killer whales.

Human activities that have resulted in a need for conservation

In Chapters 11 and 13, the effect of human activities on fish stocks and marine pollution was discussed. Our activities over the past 100 years have placed pressure on many species, causing their populations to fall. Habitat loss due to a range of human activities, such fishing, industry, tourist development and mining, has had a major impact. Intensive fishing has led directly to the reduction of many commercially valuable species and has affected many non-target species, which have been caught as bycatch and affected by changes in the food chains.

The impact of human activities on biodiversity can be considered from two points of view: loss of habitat and direct effects on species.

Habitat loss

Many marine habitats are under threat. If a habitat is damaged, the species that live there and depend on it will be threatened with extinction. Large areas of coastal habitats have been lost all around the world to make way for aquaculture ventures, tourist resorts, marinas and industries. Any loss of habitat will negatively affect the species that live there, but this is easiest to understand when considering specific types of habitat. Mangrove forests, coral reefs and seagrass meadows all support high biodiversity and are under threat because of human activity.

Mangroves

Mangrove forests around the world are under severe threat (Figure 14.3). They are important habitats, acting as nursery grounds for many species, preventing coastal erosion, reducing wave energy and acting as a carbon dioxide sink. The United Nations Food and Agriculture Organization (FAO) estimates that approximately 150 000 hectares of the world's mangrove forests are lost every year. Since 1960, Thailand has lost more than half of its mangrove forests. In the Philippines, mangroves have declined from an estimated 448 000 hectares in the 1920s to only 110 000 hectares by 1990, and in Ecuador up to 50% of the nation's mangrove forest has been lost.

Figure 14.3. Mangrove deforestation in South-East Asia.

Mangrove loss is caused in various ways. Shrimp farming has had a devastating effect, with large areas being removed to make way for aquaculture businesses (Chapter 12). Many mangrove areas have been dug up for easier boat access and to build tourist resorts. Pollution from industrial waste, oil spills and agricultural run-off and climate change have also destroyed many areas.

Coral reefs

Coral reef areas are extremely important areas of biodiversity that help to maintain fish stocks of many species and play an important role in preventing coastal erosion. A survey in 2008 stated that the planet's coral reefs were in a critical state and estimated that already:

- 19% of the world's reefs had been lost
- 15% were seriously threatened with loss within the next 10–30 years
- 20% were under threat of loss within the next 20–40 years.

Many human activities have negative impacts on coral reefs. Benthic trawling physically wrecks coral and other fishing practices, such as the use of dynamite, break and shatter it. In many countries, coral has been mined to use as a building material. Irresponsible tourism has caused physical damage by boats and diving, and damage caused by the sewage and refuse released from tourist resorts. Toxic pollutants from industry, sediment from dredging and agricultural run-off can all cause eutrophication, which also damages coral.

The main threat to coral may be from climate change because of the increased emission of greenhouse gases. Corals cannot survive if the water temperature is too high or the pH is too acidic. High atmospheric carbon dioxide levels cause an increase in both these factors and this seems to have led to increased coral bleaching in many areas.

The state of coral in Australia's Great Barrier Reef is monitored carefully. Between 1985 and 2012, coral cover was found to have declined from 28.0% to 13.8%. Suggestions for the causes of this decline include climate change, storm damage (possibly a result of climate change) and high populations of the predatory crown-of-thorns starfish.

Seagrass meadows

Seagrass meadows are, like mangroves and coral reefs, very important habitats with high biodiversity. They provide food and shelter for many species and are the primary producers for many food webs. They also stabilise the substrate and act as carbon sinks. In 2009, a research project demonstrated that, since 1980, seagrass has been lost at a mean rate of 110 km² year⁻¹. It has also been estimated that 29% of the area covered by seagrass has disappeared since recording began in 1879 (Figure 14.4).

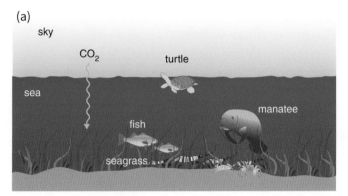

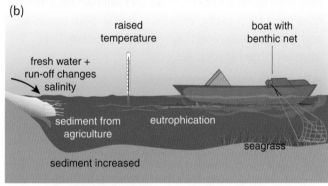

Figure 14.4. (a) The importance of seagrass as a nursery area for fish and other organisms and a food source for animals such as manatees and turtles; (b) Activities that threaten seagrass.

The principal causes of seagrass loss are related to human activity. Destructive fishing practices, boat propellers, anchors and coastal development for industry and tourism cause direct and immediate seagrass loss. Pollution from industry and oil spills has killed large areas. High levels of sediment from agricultural run-off and dredging are also damaging, as they reduce light penetration in the water, reducing photosynthesis. Irrigation of agricultural land with fresh water that runs into the sea has killed seagrass by causing changes in salinity. Over-fishing of predators such as sharks has caused increases in populations of herbivores that eat seagrass.

Invasive species may also have affected seagrass meadows. It is estimated that at least 56 non-native species, primarily invertebrates, non-native seagrasses and seaweeds, have been introduced to seagrass beds. These species have been introduced through shipping and aquaculture and have outcompeted or consumed native seagrasses. Increasing water temperatures as a result of climate change are also thought to be placing areas of seagrass under pressure.

Direct effects on species

As well as altering habitats, human activity has directly affected organisms.

Over-fishing and hunting

The negative effects of over-fishing species have been discussed in Chapter 11. The hunting of many species such as bluefin tuna and cod has led to collapses in their populations to almost unsustainable levels. In the 20th century, whaling was responsible for bringing many species of whale close to the point of extinction. Figure 14.5 shows the estimated population of blue whales through the 20th century. Before the onset of industrial whaling, the population was estimated to be around 275 000 animals. By 1964 the global population had fallen to between 650 and 2000. This catastrophic fall was due almost entirely to unrestricted hunting, and a global ban on hunting blue whales was brought into effect in 1965. The population of blue whales has gradually begun to recover but, as

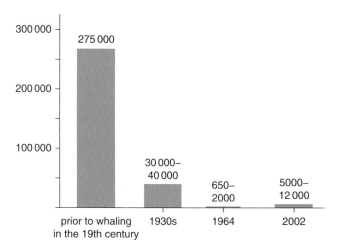

Figure 14.5. Change in populations of blue whales in the 20th century.

they breed slowly, it will take a long time for them to recover to previous levels.

As well as reducing the populations of species by specifically targeting them, human activity has accidentally affected many others. Certain fishing methods, such as pelagic long-lining, purse seining and benthic trawling have a high risk of bycatch (Chapter 11). Other non-target organisms, such as dolphins, turtles and sea birds, are often trapped. Collisions with boats has led to the deaths of organisms, particularly large mammals such as whales and manatees. When examined carefully, scars due to propeller damage can often be seen on the sides of these animals.

Pollution and refuse

In Chapter 13, the effects of many marine pollutants were discussed. Every day, large quantities of different pollutants are released into the water.

- Toxins such as mercury and TBT accumulate through food chains, killing top predator species.

- Fertilisers and sewage can cause eutrophication, lowering oxygen concentrations and suffocating organisms.

- Coastal industries have released heavy metal ions into the water along with their effluent.

- Sewage can contain toxins, and its decomposition leads to oxygen loss.

- Aquaculture produces large amounts of waste that can contain toxins and minerals that lead to eutrophication.

- Tourist resorts in coastal areas can release large amounts of sewage, and refuse such as plastic, into the sea. Large amounts of plastic from ships, coastal communities and tourist resorts have killed thousands of sea birds, marine mammals and turtles as a result of ingestion and entanglement.

- Oil spills from container ships and oil platforms has poisoned and suffocated many species and damaged coastlines, and may persist for many years.

- Increased carbon dioxide emissions leading to global warming has directly affected many species. Increased sea-levels, increased temperatures, changes to salinity and pH, along with food chain effects, have the potential to cause catastrophic effects.

321

Coastal development

Tourist resorts have been built on crucial habitats such as nesting sites and migration routes, and boat trips can damage coral reefs. They can also release refuse and sewage into the sea. Cluttered, busy beaches hinder the movement of turtles along beaches when laying eggs and the movement of hatchlings from eggs to sea.

In Costa Rica in 2015, tourists gathered on beaches to see olive ridley sea turtles migrate from the sea up the beach to lay eggs. Unfortunately, there were so many tourists that the turtles were deterred from leaving the sea, and egg laying was prevented.

KEY TERM

Ecological linkages: the ecological relationships that exist between species and their environment within an ecosystem

Invasive species

We have accidentally and deliberately introduced species into areas where they are not native. Organisms such as sponges and barnacles attach onto the hulls of boats and migrate around the world. It has been estimated that up to 3000 different species are transferred around the world in the ballast water of ships.

Some invasive species have escaped from aquaculture. These species may have no natural predators and so can reproduce rapidly and consume or outcompete native species, affecting **ecological linkages**. The Nile tilapia and common carp are invasive species in areas of South-East Asia.

The bluestripe snapper (Figure 14.6) was introduced into Hawaii for aquaculture and has become established in the surrounding coral reefs. There are concerns that it is outcompeting native coral reef fish species.

Figure 14.6. Shoal of bluestripe snapper by a coral reef.

If we continue to ignore the health of our marine habitats and species, many of them will become extinct. Conservation aims to reduce the effect of damaging activities and reverse the damage that has already been done.

14.3 Successful conservation

There have been many successful conservation programmes carried out to restore and protect habitats and individual species. Successful conservation is not just about releasing more individuals of a particular species into the wild and hoping that they will survive and breed. If certain conditions are not met, populations will not increase and they could even damage other species. Below is a summary of the main general methods used in conservation.

- Protecting a species by banning or restricting hunting or fishing. The success of this method is illustrated by the slow recovery of some populations of whales after the International Whaling Commission placed a ban on hunting.

- Increasing population sizes by increasing the amount of food present. If a species is under pressure because of food loss, efforts may be made to increase the food source. To do this in a sustainable way, the habitat has to be conserved in order to boost productivity. Grouper populations have been increased by conserving areas of mangrove where the juveniles feed.

- Conservation of a habitat to protect biodiversity and the variety of species in an area. Preserving coral reefs will not only protect the reefs but also the species that depend on them as a food source and habitat. This can be done by reducing tourist damage on beaches where birds and turtles nest, controlling shipping and reducing dredging and tourist boat activities.

- Enhancing and restoring habitats to increase populations. Building artificial reefs increases the populations of many fish. Replanting mangroves in areas where shrimp farming has reduced mangrove forests can help to restore mangrove populations.

- Removing sources of local pollution that threaten species and habitats. Local restrictions can be placed on waste released by industrial plants and agriculture. Water treatment plants can be built to reduce the release of sewage. Recycling programmes can reduce the amount of refuse that is lost into the seas, and more environmentally sound methods of disposal can be encouraged.

- Controlling global pollution. Many of the threats facing species are the result of global emissions rather than local issues. Global warming poses a threat to many habitats and species and can only be tackled by international cooperation. Legally binding treaties aim to set targets for reducing emissions such as carbon dioxide and methane in order to reduce global warming. Bans on importing the remains of endangered species, such as whale meat, reduces the demand for illegal hunting of these species.

There are many different scales of conservation projects, ranging from global involvement to local community volunteers. Global ocean treaties are set at international meetings. Charities such as the World Wide Fund for Nature (WWF) and the Marine Conservation Society increase public awareness of the need for conservation, lobby governments for action and fund projects themselves. National governments set up conservation projects for their coastal waters and employ scientists and professional conservation workers. Many charities and governments from more economically developed nations help fund conservation work in less economically developed nations. There are also many small-scale conservation projects that are run by volunteers. Many people spend their time preserving habitats, clearing litter and monitoring biodiversity. Despite the global international treaties signed by world leaders, it is often the efforts of local people who are aware of the need for a particular project that have the highest impact. Many habitats and species are still flourishing thanks to the efforts of people who give up their time.

Ecological linkages

If a population is to recover, we need to ensure that all the necessary ecological linkages are secure. This means that all elements of a food web must be present and that the habitat is optimal for survival. In practice, this means that there needs to be sufficient food and a variety of food types, and that the habitat has the correct shelter and other necessary features such as nursery grounds and breeding sites. Attempting to repopulate a species of coral-ingesting parrotfish will be unsuccessful if the coral reefs have been badly damaged. The reefs need protecting along with the parrotfish if the project is to be successful.

If other organisms or diseases are causing the loss of a species or habitat, those species need to be controlled. The crown-of-thorns starfish has caused the loss of large areas of the Great Barrier Reef near Australia. To help the reef recover, the starfish population needs to be reduced. Understanding the reasons for the high population of starfish will help, and recent research has pointed towards agricultural run-off of fertilisers, so conservation efforts need to focus on reducing the use of fertilisers.

Sea turtle conservation

Successful conservation programmes do not put other organisms at risk. Research in India and Florida has suggested that care must be taken when conserving populations of turtles to prevent damage to seagrasses.

Sea turtles eat seagrasses. A healthy population of sea turtles grazing on the seagrasses encourages good seagrass growth, increases the fertility of the seabed and helps disperse the seagrass. If turtle populations are too low, seagrass dies off and is replaced by algae. If turtle populations are too high, seagrass is overconsumed and dies off. Juvenile sea turtles are consumed by sharks. In many parts of the world, sharks have been over-fished.

The problem with sea turtle conservation projects is that the ecological balance of many areas has been affected. Turtle populations are threatened, but shark populations are also very low because of over-fishing. Strategies that successfully increase the sea turtle populations alone could lead to the loss of seagrasses and other species that feed on them (Figure 14.7). To be effective, a turtle conservation project would need to:

- increase turtle populations via habitat conservation and regulation of fishing methods

- place a ban, or restrictions, on shark fishing.

Conservation measures can have unforeseen effects on other organisms. When whaling bans were put in place for many species of large whale, species of smaller whales such as sei whales began to fall because whalers started to hunt them.

Local engagement

If conservation is to be successful, there has to be engagement with local people because the preservation

323

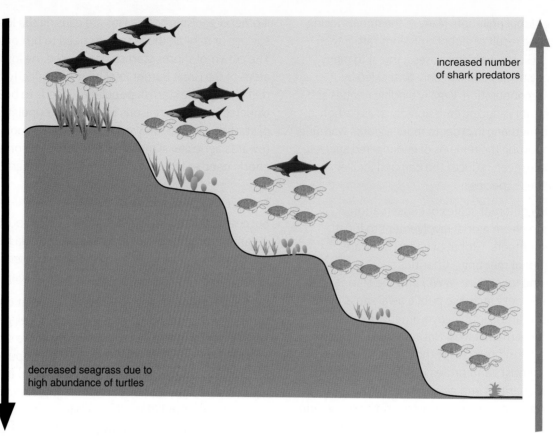

increased number
of shark predators

decreased seagrass due to
high abundance of turtles

Figure 14.7. Possible effects of sea turtle conservation on seagrass. A healthy balance in the populations of sea turtles and sharks must be maintained.

of areas and species could have negative impacts on their lifestyles and wealth. If bans are placed on traditional fishing areas, it is obvious that many people could lose their livelihood or recreational areas. It is essential that local people become **stakeholders** in conservation projects and benefit from them. If a project is seen only as a cost that has been imposed from a remote government, there is little incentive to adhere to the rules and regulations. If the project offers direct benefits to local communities, there is an incentive for them to support it.

In parts of Indonesia where mangrove replanting projects were carried out, those areas that were replanted by non-local workers failed to become established. Where local people were paid to take part in the project, and were incentivised by financial rewards for survival of the mangroves, the success rate was far higher.

KEY TERM

Stakeholder: a person who has a vested interest, for any reason, in an area or project

SELF-ASSESSMENT QUESTIONS

3 Use these words to complete the text below.

**invasive species   conservation   bycatch
bioaccumulate   TBT   seagrass**

Many human activities have damaged the environment and produced a need for _____. There has been extensive damage to habitats such as mangrove forests, coral reefs and _____. The fishing industry has caused fish stocks to be reduced due to over-fishing and the catching of _____. Humans have released pollutants into the oceans such as _____ and mercury which _____ along food chains. The escape of fish from aquaculture has led to _____ affecting native populations.

4 Explain why (a) establishing ecological linkages and (b) ensuring local engagement are essential for a successful conservation project.

Marine protected areas (MPAs)

MPAs are conservation areas of ocean and coasts that are tightly regulated. Their purpose is to provide areas where species can breed without human interference and increase their populations. They range in size, for example, from Echo Bay Marine Provincial Park, BC, Canada at 0.004 km² to the Pacific Remote Islands Marine National Monument at 1 271 500 km². Some MPAs are shown in Figure 14.8.

The activities permitted in different MPAs vary. Some areas offer general protection for all species, while others focus on a specific group of species such as sharks. Shark sanctuaries ban commercial fishing of sharks and provide areas where sharks can breed without being hunted. The governments of Congo-Brazzaville, Maldives, French Polynesia, Palau, Israel and Honduras have banned all types of shark fishing within their territorial waters, including recreational fishing.

The most highly protected MPAs are 'no-take' reserves where all fishing is prohibited. In practice, only a fraction of MPAs enforce a no-take policy, with most allowing certain restricted forms of fishing in specially reserved areas. In some MPAs, no fishing, diving, agriculture or tourism is allowed and entry is restricted to official research teams.

It is estimated that MPAs account for only between 1.8 and 2.8% of our oceans (Figure 14.9). International agreements, such as the Convention on Biological Diversity's 2011 Aichi Biodiversity Targets, have set a target for conservation at 10% coverage of the oceans by MPAs. Several scientific studies have indicated that to safeguard marine life, we actually need to have between 20 and 30% of marine areas in reserves. The concern is that it may not be until 2100 that we even reach the 10% target.

Effectiveness of MPAs

MPAs aim to create high populations of fish within the protected areas. These fish then spill over into fished areas. If healthy populations are maintained in an MPA, this can have positive effects on catches and profits for the fishing industry. New Zealand was one of the first countries to create no-take MPAs. An MPA established in 1977 at Goat Island Bay, New Zealand, successfully conserved fish stocks in the area and caused millions of eggs and larvae to drift into neighbouring areas. This increased fish catches for local fishers and helped popularise the creation of MPAs with the fishing industry. Other surveys on the effects of MPAs have found that, within the MPAs, there were twice as many large (>250 mm total length) fish

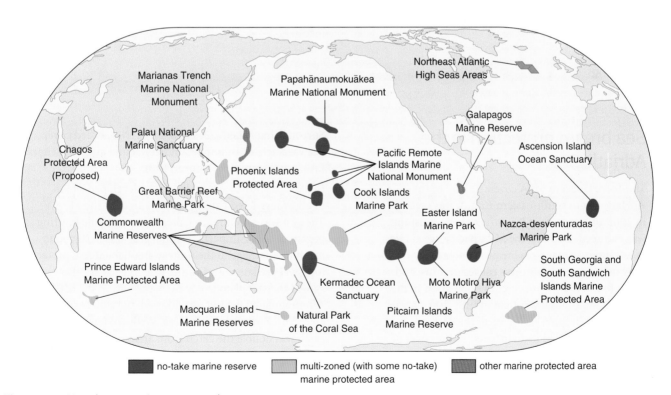

Figure 14.8. Very large marine protected areas.

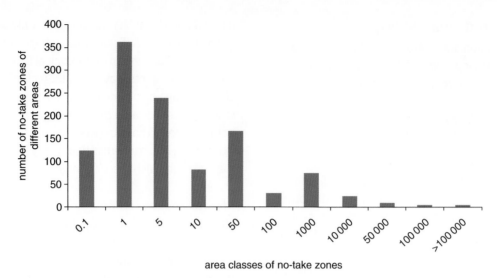

Figure 14.9. The number of marine no-take zones of different sizes in 2012.

species per transect, and up to fourteen times more shark biomass than in fished areas.

The ecology of MPAs needs careful monitoring as there can be unexpected impacts on food chains. In the Leigh Marine Reserve in New Zealand, predator species increased, causing a decrease in primary consumers and a subsequent increase in plants and producers. This caused the seabed to become covered with large amounts of seaweed.

Large MPAs are very costly to monitor. Preventing illegal fishing requires surveillance that can be too expensive for less economically developed nations. Local sensitivities also need to be taken into account. The UK government has set up one of the largest MPAs in the world around the Chagos Islands in the Indian Ocean. This MPA is proving to be highly controversial because it prevents people from any form of fishing or tourism, thus denying them any income.

Sea bream protection in the Adriatic Sea

The Torre Guaceto MPA covers 22 km² of the Adriatic Sea in south-eastern Italy. It was created in 2001 and in parts of it a no-take ban on fishing was enforced. By 2003, the MPA had between two to ten times as many sea breams compared with a fully fished area. Sea breams eat sea urchins, and it was found that the sea urchin population in the area was ten times lower than in fully fished areas. Because sea urchins eat seaweed, the decrease in their population led to an increase in the cover of seaweed to 47% of the seabed inside the reserve.

Surrounding fished areas had only 15% seaweed cover. Seaweed acts as an important habitat and area of shelter for many organisms (Figure 14.10).

In 2005, scientists and local fishers developed a plan to allow restricted fishing in some areas of the MPA. The aim was to maintain fishers' income while limiting negative fishing impacts. Fishing gear was designed to minimise damage to the underwater habitat and protect top-level predators and young fish. The fishers also agreed to fish only one day per week within the MPA. After regulated fishing was allowed, the fishers reported an increase in catch in the area. Within a few years, the catch was double the catch from areas outside the MPA

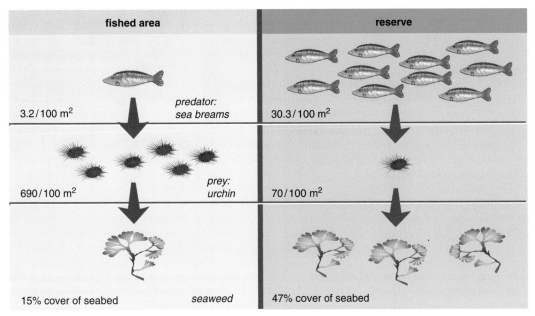

Figure 14.10. Effect of sea bream conservation on sea urchin and seaweed populations.

and the income of the fishers was considerably higher than before the MPA was established.

The success of the project has made the fishers supportive of the MPA and has also increased trust between fishers and scientists. It has shown that collaboration between scientists and the fishing industry is crucial to the success of marine conservation.

Questions

1 Explain what is meant by a 'no-take' area.

2 a Explain why the MPA had more seaweed than the fully fished area.

   b Suggest why the higher amounts of seaweed could help increase biodiversity.

3 Explain why the fishers are now supportive of MPAs.

14.4 Coastal communities

Many large coastal towns and urban areas began as small fishing communities. Hundreds of years ago people who lived in these communities fished for food for themselves and sold any surplus fish to make a small profit. Over time, these communities grew in size, with more people employed in fishing and a growing service industry to serve the needs of the fishers. Docks to unload catches developed, along with boat yards and industries manufacturing fishing gear. More houses were built and, as populations grew, more shops and local services such as schools and medical centres followed. Larger populations need more food so agriculture in the surrounding areas developed to fulfil those needs. As areas expand and grow, hotels and resorts are constructed, along with improved roads and transport facilities. As fish stocks have dwindled over the 20th century, alternative industries such as aquaculture have filled the gaps in food and employment (Figure 14.11).

The activities in coastal communities interact with each other in complex ways. They are dependent on each other but also come into conflict and compete for resources. For example, the roads and transport networks built to transport tourists also transport fish and food to markets. Pollution from a tourist resort could reduce fish stocks, harm sales and reduce profits for the fishing industry. As communities expand, they also have negative effects on the environment, damaging habitats and animal populations. This brings a need for conservation, which may conflict with many of the activities.

1. A simple fishing village develops on the coast.

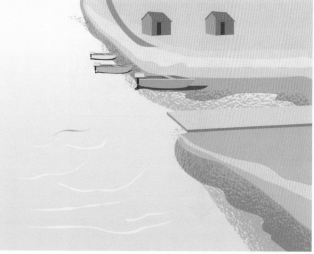

2. As the fishing industry increases in size. More houses and roads are built along with service industries such as boat yards.

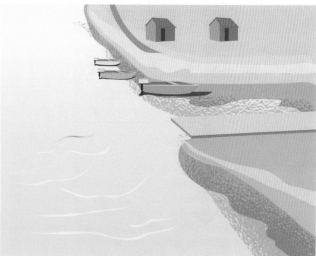

3. As the town continues to expand, more industry develops and hotels are built to service a growing tourist industry

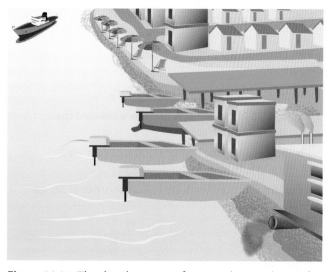

4. The town continues to grow. More houses, roads and factories are built. Air transport is developed and new industries such as aquaculture are established.

Figure 14.11. The development of a typical coastal town from a simple fishing village.

The interactions of different coastal activities are detailed below.

Agriculture

As we have already seen in Chapter 13, agriculture can have negative impacts on marine environments as a result of run-off of fertilisers and pesticides but it may also help industries such as tourism.

Positive interactions of agriculture with other activities include:

- provision of food for people employed in other activities in the area

- provision of food for the tourist industry to expand

- production of food for feeding fish in aquaculture.

Negative interactions of agriculture with other activities include:

- release of organic waste and fertiliser into water, causing eutrophication and depleting fish stocks which reduces the catches and profits of the fishing industry

- pollution damage of habitats, leading to loss of tourist attractions and a fall in tourist revenue

- competition for land with resorts, aquaculture and industries, which can have an inflationary effect on the price of land

- conflict with conservationists as a result of expansion of agriculture into areas with sensitive habitats, which can lead to clearance of land such as marshes and wetlands.

Industry

Many different industries can grow up in coastal areas. Some of these industries, such as boat building and fishing gear manufacture, can be linked with the primary fishing industry. Some are situated by the coast for easy access to marine water and for easy waste disposal. Power plants and oil refineries can be built to provide electricity, oil and gas for the community.

Positive interactions of industry with other activities include:

- an increased workforce, providing a market for fish from fishing and aquaculture

- employment if the fishing industry is adversely affected

- provision of technology, electricity and power for fishing, agriculture, tourist and aquaculture industries

- provision of oil, diesel and petrol for transport involved with tourism, shipping and fishing.

Negative interactions of industry with other activities include:

- release of pollution and waste such as heavy metal ions including mercury, toxic organic waste and radioactivity, which reduce fish stocks, catches and profits for the fishing industry

- pollution that contaminates shellfish beds and fish, causing bans and a drop in sales

- pollution affecting beaches and causing closure of tourist areas, resulting in a loss of tourism, for example the *Deepwater Horizon* oil spill in the Gulf of Mexico led to a big decrease in tourist revenue in many local beach resorts

- competition for employment, driving up local wages

- more people living in the area, placing pressure on houses, schools and inflation

- pollution damaging agriculture

- competition for land with agriculture, tourist and aquaculture industries, resulting in price inflation

- damage to habitats and loss of species, conflicting with conservation efforts.

Shipping

Coastal towns usually contain docks for ships. The ships that use these docks may be fishing vessels, tourist ships and boats, ferries and cargo ships.

Positive interactions of shipping with other activities include:

- provision of a means of exporting fish harvested by fishers and produced by aquaculture

- provision of a means of exporting agricultural and industrial products

- provision of a means of importing raw materials for industry and agriculture

- improved roads for moving materials of all industries in and out of the area

- easy movement for tourists and recreational trips for tourists, increasing profit

- better dock facilities, with mooring for fishing and tourist vessels.

Negative interactions of shipping with other activities include:

- reducing dock space for fishing fleets, reducing their ability to land catches

- unattractive areas for tourists, lowering income from tourists

- pollution from oil and ships, such as TBT, killing species and damaging habitats

- introduciton of invasive species brought in via ballast water

- oil spillages, killing marine organisms, damaging habitats and affecting conservation efforts

- dredging to keep shipping lanes open, damaging the seabed and coral reefs

- increased shipping, damaging coral reefs by scraping over their surfaces.

Sewage and refuse disposal

If untreated sewage and refuse is dumped straight into the water it can be very damaging and affect many activities. If refuse is disposed of properly and recycling is encouraged, it can be beneficial to other activities.

Positive interactions of sewage and refuse disposal with other activities include:

- clean, disease-free beaches that have no litter, attracting tourists and bringing in more revenue

- an effective sewage and refuse disposal facility that can process wastes from agriculture, tourism, aquaculture

329

and industry, which can increase in size without damage to the environment, bringing in more revenue

- effective disposal, resulting in fewer deaths of animals from sewage and harmful plastics, helping conservation efforts

- production of useful products such as gas and fertiliser, the gas providing an energy source for tourist resorts, industries and aquaculture, and the fertiliser being used in agriculture and aquaculture

- good disposal, enabling communities to increase in size, and allowing more people to live in the area to work in industry, fishing, tourism, agriculture and aquaculture.

Negative interactions of sewage and refuse disposal with other activities include:

- unsightly sewage treatment plants, which can cause bad smells, reducing tourism

- release of untreated sewage, causing dead zones, the death of marine organisms reducing fish catches and affecting conservation projects

- spread of harmful diseases into the water, killing fish and conflicting with conservation projects, killing fish and shellfish stock in open-water aquaculture, causing bans on fishing, reducing fishing income, causing food poisoning in humans, and causing the closure of beaches, losing tourist revenue

- refuse in the water, killing many marine organisms and affecting conservation efforts

- unsightly refuse on beaches, deterring tourists and losing revenue.

Aquaculture

As fish stocks have begun to fall, the use of aquaculture has increased to ease the pressure off wild stocks and generate revenue. Aquaculture can be beneficial because it can offer employment to people when the fishing industry contracts, and can keep the price of fish low and affordable for local people. Over-production of fish by aquaculture, however, can lower fish prices so that fishing yields lower profits. This can increase poverty levels and cause unemployment.

Positive interactions of aquaculture with other activities include:

- helping conserve wild fish stocks so that sustainable fishing can still occur

- providing other employment opportunities for unemployed fishers

- cheaper food that can be produced on demand for workers and tourists visiting the area.

Negative interactions of aquaculture with other activities include:

- pollution, causing eutrophication that can lower fish stocks and harm other species, leading to less profit for the fishing industry because of loss of fish, and conflicting with conservation efforts to preserve species

- competition for employment with other activities, driving up wage demands and making it difficult for other industries to make a profit, and taking the work force away from the fishing industry and agriculture

- spreading disease to fish in the wild, reducing wild fish stocks and causing the loss of fishing income and affecting conservation efforts

- loss of habitats and competition for land with other activities, especially agriculture and tourism, with a reduction in fish stocks damaging the fishing industry and impacting on conservation

- large unsightly, smelly aquaculture ventures and associated fish-processing factories, deterring tourists and reducing tourist income.

Fisheries

Coastal communities often started out as fishing villages that gradually grew over time. In many areas, the fishing industry is still the primary industry and employer. As the activities in these areas have become more diverse, their interactions with the fishing industry have become increasingly complex.

Positive interactions of fisheries with other activities include:

- commercial fishing becoming the primary industry, bringing money into the area upon which service industries depend

- commercial fishing supplying food that is used in tourist resorts and hotels

- docks that are used to unload catches can be used by shipping and help other industries to import and export goods

- recreational fishing, attracting tourists.

Negative interactions of fisheries with other activities include:

- commercial fishing boats getting in the way of tourist boats and looking unsightly
- smelly fish docks, reducing tourism
- commercial fishing impacting on conservation because of over-fishing, damage to reefs and habitats and pollution, the damage also reducing tourist numbers
- commercial fishing boats getting in the way of cargo ships
- high catches reducing fish prices, lowering aquaculture profits.

Tourism

People have always been drawn to seaside areas for recreation. They visit them for many reasons, including relaxation, diving, animal watching, water sports and cultural understanding. The tourist industry can be financially rewarding and provide a very welcome input of currency for many less economically developed nations. In many areas, it has integrated well with established activities but it can also cause competition and conflict. The problems tourism can cause are accentuated when the tour companies and hotel chains are multinational companies that do not contribute greatly to local economies.

Positive interactions of tourism with other activities include:

- increased sales of food from fishing, aquaculture and agriculture, improving profits for those industries
- tourists taking part in recreational fishing and buying products from fishing gear manufacturers
- bring money into the local economy with the purchase of goods
- the development of a tourist resort, which can include road, rail and other transport improvements, even new airports; all this means that all other industries can export and import goods more easily
- dependence on and therefore maintenance of habitats such as coral reefs, to the benefit of conservation.

Negative interactions of tourism with other activities include:

- increased numbers of tourists, causing price inflation for items such as food, making the area less affordable for local people

- competition for employment with other industries such as fishing, agriculture and aquaculture, as people employed in the tourist industry are often paid more than in the traditional sectors and it is often seen to be a more glamorous job
- competition for land, with large areas taken for tourist resorts that may have been agricultural land or areas of important habitat such as mangroves; multinational tourist companies are able to afford land more easily than local industries, leading to a loss of habitat and space for agriculture and aquaculture, a reduction in biodiversity and falling fish stocks, which affects conservation efforts and the fishing industry
- competition for resources such as timber and water
- negative impacts on conservation. Important habitats can be built on, litter and sewage can be released, recreational fishing can reduce fish stocks, tourist boats and divers can damage reefs and scare animals. On some beaches deckchairs and beach equipment can prevent turtle hatchlings reaching the sea or adult females moving up the beach to lay eggs.

Conservation

Serious damage to habitats and biodiversity will occur if coastal communities are allowed to increase in size without restrictions. Conservation activities aim to prevent further damage being done and reverse any damage already done. Imposing conservation measures on an area is often thought to have only negative impacts on other activities because it can reduce profits. In fact, if conservation is carried out carefully and after discussion with everyone in the area, it can increase the profits of other activities.

Positive interactions of conservation with other activities include:

- maintaining fish stocks and habitats, preserving the fishing industry
- encouraging more environmentally friendly aquaculture practices, reducing disease outbreaks and increasing yields
- conserving areas of natural beauty and their organisms, encouraging tourism
- achieving a premium price for food if low impact agriculture and aquaculture are marketed carefully
- keeping the water clean by treating sewage and reducing litter. This would curb disease spread, and keep shellfish

beds open, providing healthy fish for consumers. Profits for fishing industries increase and tourism is encouraged by open, attractive and clean beaches.

Negative interactions of conservation with other activities include:

- restricting access to some areas, preventing tourist access and fishing access, lowering tourist numbers and reducing fishers' catches and profits
- reductions in quotas and fishing activities, reducing catches and profits for fishers
- restricting the number of hotels that can be built, reducing tourism
- restricting the scale of aquaculture, reducing profits
- restricting transport and dredging, reducing the number of ships that can enter and leave, and affecting the import and export of other businesses.

Stakeholders

Any person who has an interest in a building, activity or area is a stakeholder. In coastal communities there are many different stakeholders who have a range of interests that can come into conflict. Livelihoods, such as fishing, may depend on the area and the habitat may be an area of natural beauty. When conflicts do arise, they are best resolved by discussions involving representatives of all stakeholder activities. The most successful conservation projects have the involvement of local communities. A top-down approach, where decisions are made remotely and imposed on people, rarely works and can cause more conflict. Education is essential as it can help people see how proposed conservation measures will benefit them. If a project offers benefits for everyone, they all have a vested interest in seeing it succeed. If the project is seen as punitive with no local support, it will ultimately fail.

SELF-ASSESSMENT QUESTIONS

5 State why the following activities could come into conflict with each other in a coastal community: (a) tourist and fishing industries, (b) aquaculture and fishing industries, (c) agriculture and tourist industry.

6 Outline why conservation may (a) negatively impact on fishing and tourist industries in the short term and (b) positively impact on fishing and tourism in the long term.

Ecotourism

Since the 1970s, there has been a rise in tourism that is based on an appreciation of the natural environment. This form of tourism is called ecotourism (Figure 14.12). The aim of ecotourism is to ensure that travel is responsible, conserves the environment, sustains the well-being of local people and is also educational. The key principles of ecotourism are to:

- minimise the physical, social, behavioural and psychological impacts on the environment and local people
- build environmental and cultural awareness and respect
- provide positive experiences for visitors and hosts
- provide direct financial benefits for conservation
- generate financial benefits for both local people and private industry

Figure 14.12. Comparison of (a) a sustainable ecotourist lodge in a coastal area of Tanzania and (b) a typical unsustainable mass tourist resort.

- deliver memorable interpretative experiences to visitors that help raise sensitivity of the host countries' political, environmental and social climates

- design, construct and operate low-impact facilities

- recognise the rights and spiritual beliefs of indigenous people and work in partnership with them to create empowerment.

Ecotourism can offer local communities a means of making a profit from tourism and reducing harmful activities such as intensive aquaculture and over-fishing. If the conservation of the natural environment becomes essential to the income of a local community, people will engage with it. For example, sea otters could be seen by fishers as a nuisance predator that reduce fish catches. If ecotourism depends on the survival of the sea otters and their habitats, and this ecotourism generates higher profits, there is more incentive to conserve them.

Different types of ecotourism

One of the problems with the idea of ecotourism is that it has been defined in many different ways. Most environmental organisations suggest that ecotourism is a nature-based, sustainably managed, conservation supporting and environmentally educating tourism. The tourist industry and governments often create the idea that ecotourism is any tourism that is linked to nature. This means that many tourist resorts that are not sustainable or environmentally sensitive are classed as ecotourist resorts. Other types of tourism are often confused with ecotourism but may be not be as environmentally sustainable.

Wildlife or nature tourism is when tourists travel to see animals and plants in their natural habitats. It can include activities such as whale watching or trips to Antarctica to see the diversity of wildlife. Although these activities are involved with nature, they are often not sustainable. Tourists may stay in large hotels, affect the behaviour of animals, interfere with breeding sites and damage local habitats.

Adventure tourism is when tourists take part in activities such as jungle trekking and whitewater rafting. It also includes reaching parts of the world that are difficult to get to. Despite being immersed in the natural world, these activities are not necessarily examples of ecotourism.

However, ecotourists can engage in many different types of activities, all of which attempt to benefit the environment and local community.

Ecolodging is when tourists stay in accommodation that has been built with environmental awareness. It may range from small hotels built using sustainable materials to remote camps where tents and small lodges are carefully sited in areas of ecological importance. The accommodation is close to the area of interest so that it can be reached easily by, for example, walking or canoeing. The tourists usually want to see species in their natural habitats, learn about local cultures and immerse themselves in the area.

Agrotourism is when tourists stay on small rural farms. They may witness sustainable farming methods, and in some cases take part in the farming to help local people. Agrotourism encourages local people to practise sustainable farming methods and helps them make additional money.

Community development can be part of ecotourism if organisations offer opportunities to tourists to join projects that protect the land of communities threatened by industry or deforestation. Tourists stay with local people and help with projects such as tree planting or building sustainable housing. They gain a better understanding of the local people and the communities benefit from the help and additional income.

Factors that must taken into account

If ecotourism is to be truly sustainable and beneficial to nature and local people, there are several factors that have to be considered. There must be balance between the acceptable risk of these factors and helping local people gain an income. Factors to be considered include the fact that:

- ecotourists often go to environmentally fragile areas

- visits may occur during sensitive periods, such as during breeding or hatching periods

- ecotourism could lead to mass tourism at the site if the attraction becomes better known

- distant locations require long flights, which cause high carbon dioxide emissions

- if there are many visits, there may be impacts on ecosystems such as soil erosion, disturbance of wildlife, trampling of plants, removal of vegetation (for example collection of plants or firewood) and the introduction of exotic species on clothing or equipment

333

- even though most ecotourists are interested in conservation, there is a risk that litter and refuse will be dropped unintentionally and water polluted

- as more tourists arrive, more accommodation needs to be built, which requires resources such as wood and the clearance of areas to provide more space

- some tourists may purchase souvenirs from threatened or endangered species, such as coral.

> **KEY TERMS**
>
> **Sustainable development:** development that meets the needs of the present without compromising the ability of future generations to meet their needs
>
> **Carbon footprint:** the total amount of carbon dioxide released into the atmosphere by a particular activity

Responsible tourism

Unrestricted development of tourist resorts with no consideration of their impact on the marine environment is potentially very damaging and unsustainable. The goal should be responsible tourism, in which both the tourist industry and the environment benefit. When a new tourist business is being developed, certain factors should be taken into account, including **sustainable development**.

Energy conservation

Tourists fly to remote locations and then use road or boat connections to take them from the airport to the resort. This creates a large **carbon footprint** that needs to be minimised. Flights should be organised so that there are fewer of them but operating at maximal capacity. Tourists are encouraged to use energy-efficient public transport, such as electric trams, wherever possible rather than cars. Many ecotourists travel locally by bicycle or trek. Some ecotourist companies offset their carbon footprint from the flight by planting mangroves or trees for every tour party that is flown there.

Accommodation should be energy efficient. In colder regions, buildings should be fully insulated to reduce heat loss. In warmer regions, the air conditioning should be minimised and buildings designed to maximise natural cooling. Low-energy light bulbs and similar technology can reduce electricity consumption. Rather than using energy that is based on non-renewable fossil fuels, electricity can be generated using more environmentally friendly methods. Solar panels, wind power and wave power are used in many ecoresorts.

Figure 14.13. The Laguna Lodge in the Tzantizotz nature reserve, Guatemala, is built from local materials, including walls made from adobe and clay and lampshades from corn paper. It is a zero-carbon resort, with electricity for lighting, hot water and wifi generated by 180 solar panels.

Recycling

Even though they may be careful, large numbers of visitors produce large amounts of refuse. Disposal of it, particularly plastic, is problematic but can be done responsibly. Hotels and other service industries should have recycling policies, and tourists and local people should be encouraged to place their refuse in the appropriate recycling bins. Glass, metals, paper and many forms of plastic can be recycled into other products rather than being discarded. This also creates more revenue from waste. Old plant material and food can be recycled to make fertilisers for agriculture.

Sustainable materials

Building accommodation requires raw materials such as stone, concrete and wood. Developers should be careful to harvest these in a sustainable way. It is easy to chop down forest trees to produce timber for building, but this would quickly cause deforestation and loss of biodiversity. Ideally, locally produced materials should be used. Timber should be from sites where new trees are planted, and stones and bricks from demolished buildings can be used. Figure 14.13 shows the Laguna Lodge in the Tzantizotz nature reserve, Guatemala, which is built with locally sourced sustainable materials such as adobe, clay and even locally made corn paper. Similarly, structures such as new roads should be built with sustainable materials. Rather than large, concrete hotels, most ecotourist resorts tend to have small lodges that are built in the style of the local area.

Sponsorship of conservation

Tourist resorts have the potential to help conservation efforts. When visiting a nature area, even the most environmentally aware tourists can potentially affect plants and wildlife negatively. Their presence may scare animals or affect migration routes, and hiking through areas can damage habitats. However, if some of the profits generated by the tourism are used for local conservation projects and to help local people, tourism can have a very positive effect on conservation efforts. Costa Rica has a well-developed ecotourist industry and businesses use money made from tourism to sponsor conservation projects. Money is also used to sponsor the education of local people and improve resources such as sanitation and plumbing systems.

The Bosca del Cabo Rainforest Lodge

Figure 14.14. The Bosca del Cabo Rainforest Lodge in Costa Rica.

The Bosca del Cabo Rainforest Lodge on the Osa Peninsula, Costa Rica (Figure 14.14), is an excellent example of a sustainable tourism project. It is a lodge from which tourists can visit areas of outstanding natural beauty around the coasts and forests of Costa Rica. It advertises itself as providing many environmentally and culturally friendly activities, as indicated below.

Educational activities include:

- providing forums for guests to learn about local conservation, wildlife programmes and general information about rainforests
- providing guidelines for workers regarding recycling at the lodge and in their own homes
- educating staff on hunting and the conservation of natural resources
- sponsoring clean-up projects and promoting beach health and raising awareness of the need to keep beaches pristine and natural
- hosting interns from around the world so that they can learn about sustainable tourism
- exposing guests to local culture, for example through dance classes, local crafts and reading materials about the area
- sponsoring three children of Bosque employees to attend the local bilingual school (Nueva Hoja).

Waste management policies include:

- reusing building materials from previous structures for new constructions whenever possible
- providing receptacles and transportation to recycling centres for plastic, aluminium and glass, for both staff and guests
- recycling paper, envelopes, packing materials, newspapers and any other feasible products
- reusing fresh food scraps as compost for the gardens
- donating cooked food scraps to a local farmer for feeding his pigs.

Low or zero impact practices include the:

- implementation of a constructed wetlands filtration system for processing of grey water
- use of organic compost as fertiliser
- use of mainly bamboo and plantation-grown wood for construction
- use of biodegradable soaps and cleaning products whenever possible
- creation of drainage around the lodge by taking erosion control measures and planting

- provision of carpools for workers to decrease the number of vehicles coming and going from the town
- reduction of the number of vehicles going into town by combining guest transfers whenever possible
- creation of reusable bags for transporting laundry, etc., to and from town
- provision of signage in the cabins asking for cooperation in reducing water use, power use and unnecessary laundry
- use of biodegradable straws and stir sticks at the bar
- participation with the Costa Rica Tourism Board in their Certificate for Sustainable Tourism (CST), a programme to protect the country's cultural and natural treasures through responsible tourism.

Alternative energy is used by:

- generating most of the lodges' power from micro-hydro and solar systems
- installing low-power consuming LED and compact florescent light bulbs for fixed lights and flashlights
- installing a non-chemical ionising system and solar-powered pool pump for pool maintenance.

There is a focus on the local community by:

- cooking with local ingredients
- preparing local dishes and typical food to encourage local Costa Rican culture and traditions
- buying the majority of food supplies locally

- buying and cooking with organically grown food when possible
- hiring local Costa Ricans as staff
- selling primarily locally or nationally crafted souvenirs in the shop
- hosting a local artisan once a week to display and sell her work directly to the guests.

Support and participation is provided by:

- hosting the annual Bosque del Cabo Jungle Golf Tournament, with all proceeds going to the Women of the Osa
- hosting of the annual science meeting of the Friends of the Osa
- actively participating in Friends of the Osa and their related projects
- donating to multiple projects led by local and international organisations focused mostly on community development and conservation.

336

SELF-ASSESSMENT QUESTIONS

7 Define the terms (a) ecotourism and (b) stakeholder.

8 Explain why the following activities would help ensure that ecotourism is sustainable: (a) recycling refuse, (b) using solar power to generate electricity for hotels, (c) using local wood and materials.

PRACTICAL ACTIVITY 14.1

Reporting on the effectiveness of a conservation project

To understand how effective conservation measures can be, it is useful to visit an area where conservation is being carried out. Many coastal areas have projects that welcome visits from students and schools in order to explain their work. If there is no local marine conservation project you can visit, lots of marine conservation groups advertise and explain their work on the internet. Costa Rica and the Bahamas in particular have many ongoing projects that have websites containing lots of information.

Method

Visit a conservation area or read about one using the internet. Compile a report about the project including the following:

- the species that are being conserved and the reasons for the conservation
- the methods of conservation being employed, identifying long-term strategies such as the maintenance of ecological links and suitable habitat or nesting sites
- the methods used to monitor the success of the project
- any data available about effects on the target species and other species
- identifying other stakeholders in the area and how they have been affected by the conservation project, explaining any opposition to the project and how it is being resolved
- a description of the long-term future of the project and how it is impacting on local finance.

Maths skills

Significant figures and when to use them

Any measurement has some uncertainty in it, and it does not make sense to give values to a level of accuracy that could not have actually been measured. If you measure the length of a fish with a metre ruler, it is not sensible to give a measurement of 23.34235 cm. The ruler could realistically only measure with any accuracy to 23.3 cm. The number of figures used that makes sense is called a significant figure.

In Chapter 13, you looked at using the correct number of decimal places in calculations and tables. When you are asked to give numbers to a certain number of significant figures, it is similar to using decimal places but not quite the same. It is very common for people to mix up significant figures and decimal places. There are certain rules to remember when using significant figures.

- All non-zero digits are significant, which means that 34 has two significant figures while 21.325 has five significant figures.

- Zeros between non-zero digits are significant. For example, 2045 has four significant figures: 2, 0, 4 and 5.

- In a number with a decimal point, trailing zeros (those to the right of the last non-zero digit) are significant. For example, 0.0034500 has five significant figures: 3, 4, 5, 0 and 0 (the two zeroes to the right of the number five)

- In a number without a decimal point, trailing zeros may or may not be significant. For example, 2300 may have four significant figures: 2, 3, 0 and 0. However, it may be considered to only have two significant figures if it is the product of another number that has been rounded up or down. For example, the raw (actual) result may have been 2311; if this is rounded to two significant figures it will be 2300.

- Leading zeros are never significant. For example, 0.0000346 has three significant figures: 3, 4 and 6.

Worked example

You can compare the numbers of decimal places and significant figures. An example of 98.766 is shown in Table 14.1

number of:	decimal places	significant figures
5	98.76600	98.766
4	98.7660	98.77
3	98.766	98.8
2	98.77	99
1	98.8	100

Table 14.1. Difference between decimal places and significant figures for the value 98.766.

The easiest way to determine the number of significant figures is to use scientific notation.

For example, the number 7500 in scientific notation is 7.5×10^3. This is quoted to two significant figures. The number 0.00006751 is the same as 6.751×10^{-5}. This is quoted to four significant figures.

When carrying out calculations using different numbers, the rule is that the final answer should only be quoted to the same number of significant figures as the least accurate measure.

For example, $23.450 \times 1.31 = 30.7195$

30.7195 should be written to three significant figures because the least accurate input number is 1.31, which is three significant figures. The correct answer is therefore 30.7.

Questions

1 a Determine the number of significant figures that are used in the following numbers:

   i   34.501

   ii 3.050

   iii 0.000340

   iv 6400

   b Write the number 674.13 to 1, 2, 3 and 4 significant figures.

2 Calculate the following to the correct number of significant figures:

   a 432.00×22

   b $32.31 \div 7.2$

   c 6.002×213

Summary

- Our oceans are not in a healthy state. Industry, agriculture, over-fishing and pollution have strained their habitats and populations. We are now beginning to realise the extent of the damage and what the future could hold if we do nothing.

- Conservation is essential if we are not to witness the extinction of many of our marine species. However, conservation projects must ensure that ecological linkages are intact and that they have the support of local stakeholders.

- In coastal communities, there are many activities that can conflict with each other and with conservation efforts. The best way for conservation projects to succeed is for all the stakeholders to meet and discuss how to work for each other's benefit.

- Ecotourism is a useful way for tourists to help preserve habitats and species while bringing in money for local communities. When building ecotourist resorts, we must be careful to ensure they are environmentally sustainable.

- Our relationship with the marine environment is at a crossroads. The steps we take now will have a big effect on the relationships that our descendants can have with it. We must work hard and carefully to ensure that they are able to experience the enjoyment and benefits from it in the same way we have.

Exam-style questions

1 Coho and chinook salmon populations have declined throughout the 20th century. In 2003, a conservation programme was set up in a North American river to stop the decline in numbers of the two species of salmon. The measures taken included:

- three river passages past a large dam were created, to allow salmon access to upstream areas of the river
- restrictions were placed on the use of fertilisers on agricultural land in the upstream areas
- land near the river was purchased to prevent the expansion of industries
- salmon fry were cultivated in hatcheries and released into the river.

The numbers of both species of salmon found in the upstream areas each year are shown in Figure 14.15.

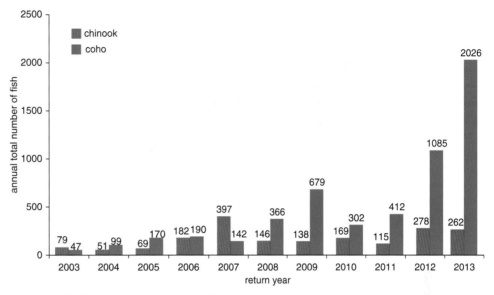

Figure 14.15. Numbers of coho and chinook salmon passing upstream of dam.

a **i** Compare the effect of the conservation measures on the coho and chinook salmon. **[3]**

ii Calculate the mean rate of increase in chinook salmon between 2003 and 2013. **[2]**

iii Discuss the success of the conservation project for both species of salmon. **[3]**

b **i** Explain why creating the river passages could help conserve the salmon. **[2]**

ii Suggest why restrictions were placed on the use of fertilisers. **[3]**

iii State one risk of introducing cultivated salmon from hatcheries. **[1]**

[Total mark: 14]

2 **a** Explain what is meant by:

i conservation **[2]**

ii ecotourism **[2]**

b Explain how the establishment of a conservation area around a coastal community could cause conflict with the fishing and tourist industries. **[5]**

c Explain how a tourist resort could be developed responsibly in order to minimise damage to the environment. **[6]**

[Total mark: 15]

3 Figure 14.16 shows the abundance of commercially important fish at different distances from the centre of a marine protected area (MPA). The central area of the MPA is a region

339

with no fishing and the outer regions of the MPA have limited regulated fishing. Outside the MPA, the sea is fully fished with few restrictions.

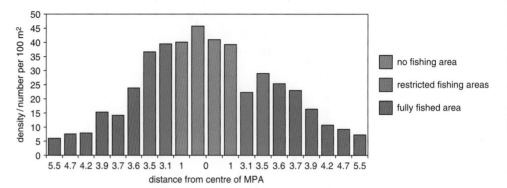

Figure 14.16. Fish density at increasing distances from the centre of a marine protected area.

a **i**   Describe how the density of fish changes with distance from the centre of the MPA.   **[2]**

   ii   Explain the change in density of fish as distance from the centre of the MPA increases.   **[3]**

b **i**   Suggest why the local fishing industry would object to the setting up of more MPAs.   **[2]**

   ii   Suggest why the MPA could be of benefit to the local fishing industry.   **[3]**

[Total mark: 10]

4   Table 14.2 shows the number of ecotourists that visited some countries in 1990 and 1999.

country	number of visits × 1000	
	1990	1999
South Africa	1028	6026
Costa Rica	435	1027
Indonesia	2178	4700
Belize	88	157
Ecuador	362	509
Botswana	543	740

Table 14.2. Number of ecotourists visiting countries in 1990 and 1999.

a **i**   Calculate the percentage increase in ecotourist visits to Costa Rica between 1990 and 1999.   **[2]**

   ii   Plot a bar chart of the data in Table 14.2.   **[5]**

b   Explain how ecotourism can be beneficial for conservation and local communities.   **[5]**

[Total mark: 12]

5 Figure 4.17 shows the change in area of kelp forest in a marine reserve where fishing is prohibited, and a control area that is fully fished over a period of 18 years.

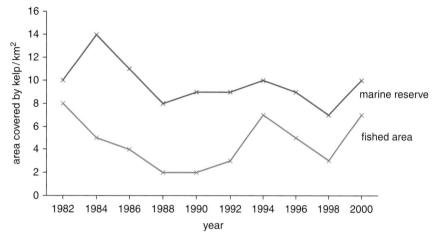

Figure 14.17. The change in area of seabed covered by kelp in a marine reserve and fully fished area.

a Compare the changes in area covered by kelp in the marine reserve and the fished area. **[3]**

b Figure 4.18 shows part of the food web in the kelp forest. Use Figure 4.18 to explain the difference in area covered by kelp in the marine reserve and the protected area. **[2]**

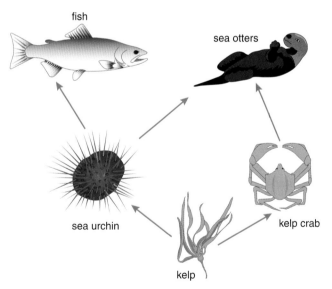

Figure 14.18. Part of kelp forest food web.

c Suggest two other factors that could cause the change in area covered by kelp over time. **[2]**

[Total mark: 7]

341

Trouble in paradise, the Chagos Islands marine protected area

The Chagos archipelago is a collection of 55 islands in the central Indian Ocean (Figure 14.19). It is part of the British Indian Ocean Territory (BIOT). On 1st April, 2010, the British government announced that Chagos would become the world's largest marine protected area (MPA). It would comprise a total surface area of 640 000 km² and would be a no-take reserve, with no fishing permitted, and there would be minimal human disturbance of the islands, beaches and ocean.

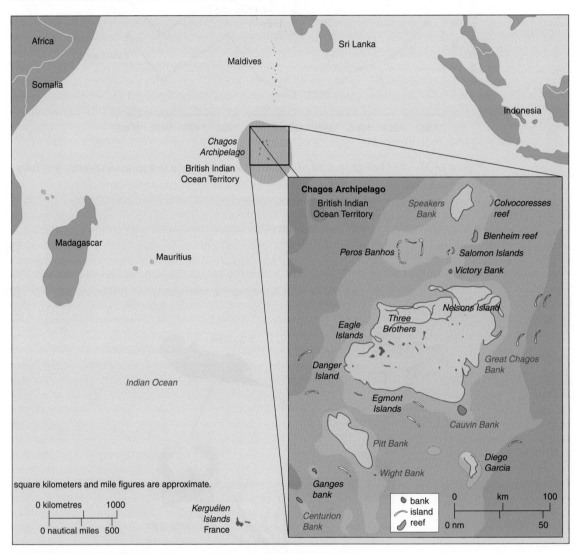

Figure 14.19. Map of the proposed Chagos marine protected area.

The area has one of the healthiest reef systems in the world, the largest coral atoll in the world and some of the cleanest waters, with exceptionally high biodiversity. Many endangered and protected species inhabit the area.

There are more than 200 different species of coral, some of which are very rare. The reefs are very healthy and bleaching is low. Coral reefs in the Indian Ocean are under pressure from human activities, but the Chagos archipelago is an exception. The Chagos archipelago acts as a link between reefs in the east and west Indian Ocean.

There are more than 784 different species of fish found in the area. Some species, such as the Chagos clownfish, are only found in this area and it is a refuge for species of wrasse and grouper that have been hunted to extinction in other parts of the Indian Ocean. There are large populations of manta rays, sharks and tuna. Prior to the establishment of the reserve, large numbers of these fish were harvested, resulting in a collapse of their populations. The 'no-take' reserve would act as a refuge for them.

The islands are nursery sites for green and hawksbill turtles. Green turtles are classed as endangered and hawksbill turtles as critically endangered. Between 300 and 700 hawksbill and 400 to 800 green turtles are estimated to nest there annually.

The Chagos archipelago has a high diversity of sea birds. Ten of the islands are formally designated as Important Bird Areas by the conservation group Birdlife International. Protection of their habitat increases the number of nesting areas and the no-take fishing policy ensures a rich food source. In the past, rats were accidentally introduced to the islands by humans and efforts have been made to control their population because they eat eggs and chicks.

Coconut crabs are giant crustaceans that can reach more than 1 m in leg span and 3.5–5 kg in weight (Figure 14.20). The juveniles use empty coconut shells as protection, in a similar way to hermit crabs, and the adults climb trees using their claws to crack through coconuts. Coconut crabs are widely distributed but actually quite rare. They have been hunted for food, tourist souvenirs and as a fishing bait. They have also suffered from habitat loss and predation by introduced rats. The Chagos crabs are one of the most intact populations and act as an important source of crabs for other Indian Ocean islands.

Figure 14.20. A coconut crab descending a tree.

The conservation of the area had several objectives.

- Creating one of the world's greatest conservation areas. The Chagos archipelago has a massive range of biodiversity and is as important as the Galapagos Islands or the Great Barrier Reef in ecological importance.
- Saving coral reefs. Millions of people who live in the countries bordering the Indian Ocean are dependent on coral reefs as a source for food, building materials, coastal protection and tourism revenue. The Chagos reefs are very healthy and could act as an area from which corals can be used to seed other ocean reefs that have been badly damaged.
- Saving marine wildlife and rebuilding fish stocks. The no-take zone would be a refuge area where turtles, birds and fish could breed without human impact. Animals that breed in these areas would spill over into surrounding areas, maintaining other populations.
- Food and jobs for people in the region. If the islands are protected, fishing in surrounding areas could be maintained because of the overspill of fish from the MPA. If reefs in other areas are improved, tourism would be maintained.

- Scientific research. A protected marine area with such a high biodiversity and range of habitats offers an unrivalled opportunity for scientific research, and could provide a comparison of areas with little human activity with polluted and damaged areas.

The creation of the MPA seems to be an important and highly valuable tool for global conservation. However, it has proved to be extremely controversial and there has been opposition to it. To appreciate the controversy fully, you need to understand some of the history of the islands, and know who the stakeholders in the area are.

History of the Chagos Islands

According to Maldivian tradition, fishers occasionally became stranded on some of the islands of the Chagos. They were considered to be too far from the Maldives to be colonised and remained uninhabited for many years. The first Europeans to discover them in the 1500s were Portuguese explorers who named the island group Bassas de Chagas. They were not considered to be important, and eventually the French laid claim to them in the 1700s. Coconut oil plantations were developed in the 1770s and slave labourers were brought over to work on them. In 1814, after the defeat of Napoleon, the islands passed to Great Britain and in 1840 slavery was abolished.

Many of the freed slaves remained on the island as free inhabitants, along with other people from different nationalities who moved there for work. The islands were administered from the Seychelles until 1903, when they became classed as being part of Mauritius. In 1965, the British government removed the Chagos archipelago from Mauritius to become the British Indian Ocean Territories prior to the establishment of independence in Mauritius in 1968. Mauritius retained fishing rights to the waters of the area and has disputed the sovereignty of the Chagos archipelago ever since independence.

By the late 1960s, the coconut plantations had become less profitable because of competition with larger plantations in the Far East. At this time, the Cold War was at its peak and the US was looking for a military base in the Indian Ocean. In 1966, the UK government granted a 50-year permit (until 2016), followed by an optional 20-year extension (until 2036) for the US government to use any island for defence purposes. In return for the permit, the UK government was able to purchase Polaris nuclear missiles at reduced price. Part of the agreement insisted that there was an uninhabited island on which to build a military base. Between 1967 and 1973, the entire population of native Chagossians was forcibly removed from the islands to make way for a military base on the island of Diego Garcia. More than 2000 people who had resided in the area for over 100 years were displaced to Mauritius, the Seychelles and the UK and were officially prevented from ever returning.

The displaced Chagossian people have spent many years campaigning for the right to return. In the 1990s, conservation groups began to call for the area to be designated as an area of conservation, and restrictions were placed on fishing and visitations. By 2009, the idea of designating the whole area as a no-take MPA was formulated, leading to its formal declaration in 2010. This was welcomed by conservation groups such as Greenpeace as a major step forwards in the campaign to preserve biodiversity. In response, the government of Mauritius began a legal campaign against the MPA stating that it breached its long-established fishing rights. Conflict occurred between the Mauritian government and Greenpeace, with Mauritius at onepoint refusing access to Greenpeace ships. To clarify their position, Greenpeace issued a statement declaring their support for the no-take MPA. They also stated that they did not condone the existence of the Diego Garcia military base, and supported the right of the Chagossians to return.

In 2010, the politics of the MPA took another unexpected turn. The 50-year lease was due to expire in 2016 and Diego Garcia had become increasingly important because of the increased risk of global terrorism. According to the WikiLeaks Cablegate documents, the UK government suggested that the creation of the marine reserve would safeguard the US and UK interests in these strategically important islands, and make it difficult for the Chagossian people to return to their islands. If they were not permitted to fish, farm, develop tourism or any other industry, it would be all but impossible for them to make a living on the islands. This suggested that the reasons for setting up the MPA were not entirely for marine conservation.

The current situation

On 18 March 2015, the Permanent Court of Arbitration in The Hague unanimously held that the MPA was illegal under the UN Convention on the Law of the Sea. It upheld the legal right of Mauritius to fish in the waters surrounding the Chagos Archipelago. Currently, the UK and Mauritius continue to negotiate on permissible levels of fishing in the area and how best to conserve the area. The Chagossian people continue to campaign for a return to the islands. In 2015, a UK government report stated that the return of the Chagossians would have minimal negative environmental impact and that they could establish good relations with any military presence on Diego Garcia.

The Chagossian people are still waiting.

Questions

1   Summarise the (a) environmental and (b) political reasons for setting up the Chagos MPA.

2   List the stakeholders who could (a) benefit from the MPA (b) be negatively affected by the MPA.

3   Explain the conflicts between (a) conservation groups and the Mauritian government, and (b) the UK and US governments and the Mauritian government.

4   Suggest a strategy that could benefit all the stakeholders.

Chapter 15
Marine biotechnology

Learning objectives

At the end of this chapter you should be able to:

- describe the use of microorganisms as biotechnology to clean up oil spills
- explain the relationship between genotype and phenotype
- explain the differences between genetic engineering and selective breeding
- describe the processes of gene transfer and use of promoters in genetic engineering
- discuss the possible benefits and negative impacts of using genetically modified marine species in aquaculture
- explain the precautionary principle
- apply what you have learnt to new, unfamiliar contexts.

15.1 The biotechnological age

Biotechnology is the industrial application of biological processes. Humans have been using biotechnology for many years. Electron micrographs have revealed that the remains of bread made by ancient Egyptians contain yeast. Records from India and Persia dating back thousands of years indicate the manufacture of yoghurt using bacteria. Most crops and farm animals are the products of **selective breeding** over many generations. In recent times, the development of new genetic technologies has enabled us to take biotechnology to a new level, by allowing the transfer of genes from one organism to another. This new approach to biotechnology may help preserve the stocks of our oceans and reduce malnutrition, but there may be a high cost to pay if we do not regulate its use carefully.

KEY TERMS

Biotechnology: the application of biological processes for industrial and other purposes, which can be the use of substances from living organisms, such as enzymes, or the use of the organisms themselves

Selective breeding: the process by which humans use animal and plant breeding to develop particular characteristics selectively, choosing which animals or plants are used for sexual reproduction and then selecting the offspring that are required; this is also known as artificial selection

15.2 Biotechnology

There are many examples of how biotechnology has been and is being used. Here are some examples.

- Bacteria that digest oil can be used to help remove the oil from areas polluted by oil spillages.

- Selective breeding of organisms can be used to produce organisms with particular properties, such as rapid growth.

- The products of organisms, such as enzymes, can be used for industrial processes.

- Genes can be transferred from one organism to another to make organisms with particular characteristics and uses.

Oil-digesting bacteria

As discussed in Chapter 14, oil spills from offshore drilling platforms and oil tankers can have devastating effects on the marine environment, injuring and killing many species of organism. Many methods are employed to contain, disperse and remove the oil, but ultimately the oil is removed by a microbial process called bioremediation. Bioremediation is the name given to the decomposition of pollutants by microbes.

Crude oil is a natural, organic product formed from the fossilised remains of zooplankton and algae. These organisms were buried under rock without oxygen and subjected to high pressures and temperatures, resulting in the formation of crude oil or petroleum. Crude oil contains a mixture of many different hydrocarbons. Several species of naturally occurring bacteria can use the hydrocarbons found in crude oil as an energy source so naturally break down and remove oil present in water. Different species of bacteria tend to 'specialise' in metabolising or breaking down just a few of the different components of oil. They use the hydrocarbons in respiration, breaking them down to release carbon dioxide and water as waste products. In order to remove an oil spill completely, several different bacteria are necessary. Several factors affect the speed at which the bacteria are able to break down and remove an oil spill.

- Oxygen concentration: the bacteria are aerobic and break down oil faster when oxygen concentrations are high. The breakdown is fastest in surface waters, where oxygen concentrations are higher, and slowest in deep water. Water movements speed up oil removal by preventing the oil settling to lower depths where the oxygen concentrations are lower. When artificially adding bacteria to an oil spill, it is important to monitor the oxygen concentration of the water: the bacteria respire rapidly and can cause oxygen levels to fall.

- Mineral ion concentration: bacteria require mineral ions, including nitrates and phosphates. If mineral ion concentrations are low, bacterial growth rates are low and oil breakdown is slow. Fertilisers that contain mineral ions are often added to help remove oil spills by increasing bacterial growth, although care has to be taken not to cause eutrophication.

347

- Water temperature: oil is usually broken down faster in warmer water. The enzymes that catalyse the metabolism of the oil work faster in higher temperatures but will denature if the temperature becomes too high. In colder areas such as the Arctic, the naturally occurring bacteria have evolved to break down the oil rapidly at low temperatures. Cold water can, however, cause surface oil to evaporate more slowly so that there is more oil for the bacteria to break down. Oil also becomes more viscous when cold and clumps together, reducing the surface area exposed to the bacteria.

- Chemical and physical properties of oil: crude oil from different parts of the world can vary in hydrocarbon composition. Some hydrocarbons are decomposed more quickly than others. If the oil is concentrated in one large slick rather than dispersed, the surface area exposed to the microbes is lower and the decomposition rate is slower. Heavy viscous oils also take longer to decompose than light oils.

- pH and salinity: in most marine environments, the pH and salinity do not vary enough to affect the rate of oil breakdown. Laboratory investigations have shown, however, that extreme pH fluctuations do slow the rate of decomposition, and highly saline waters tend to reduce bacterial activity.

Using bacteria to remove oil spills

When an oil spill has occurred, in addition to the physical methods that may be employed to contain and remove the spill, bacterial growth is often encouraged. Several methods are employed to do this.

- Suspensions of live bacteria are sprayed onto affected beaches and directly into affected water.

- Dispersants are used, often by spraying from aeroplanes (Figure 15.1). These are chemicals that help to break up the oil spill and are often used to protect beaches and coastlines from the oil. By physically breaking up the oil slick and dispersing it in the water, they increase the contact of bacteria with the oil, speeding up chemical breakdown. Care has to be taken when using dispersants because many of them are toxic. Environmental campaigners suggest that dispersants may cause the death of more animals, such as turtles, whales and dolphins, than the oil itself.

- Fertilisers are sprayed onto the beaches and in the water. This encourages microbe growth and speeds up the breakdown of the oil.

Figure 15.1. Aerial spraying of dispersant over an oil slick.

What happens to the oil and bacteria?

The hydrocarbons in oil are broken down by the bacteria and used in aerobic respiration; the waste products are carbon dioxide and water. The bacteria are a natural part of marine food chains so are consumed by other organisms. Chapter 14 discussed the *Deepwater Horizon* oil spill that occurred in 2010 in the Gulf of Mexico. By 2015, large quantities of the oil had been removed and digested by bacteria, although much remained on the seabed in deep-water areas. The long-term effects of the oil spill and the dispersants are not yet know, although there are reports that bioaccumulation of toxins has occurred, adversely affecting top predators such as dolphins.

> **SELF-ASSESSMENT QUESTIONS**
>
> 1 Explain why oil spills in cold, still waters can often take longer to be removed than those in warm, turbulent waters.
>
> 2 Suggest why adding fertiliser can speed up oil removal, but why adding too much may lead to the death of animals because of lack of oxygen.

15.3 Selective breeding

Selective breeding has been used to develop plant and animal species for thousands of years. Humans select organisms with desirable characteristics and repeatedly breed these organisms together over several generations to develop the characteristics. The characteristics are encoded by genes, so selective breeding is a form of genetic engineering that retains or introduces desirable genes. Most of the food species that we are familiar with today are the products of many years of selective breeding from wild species. Crop plants from the brassica family (Figure 15.2) have been selectively bred from the wild mustard plant. Farmers repeatedly selected plants over successive generations in order to enhance certain characteristics.

> **KEY TERMS**
>
> **Genotype:** the genetic constitution of an individual organism
>
> **Phenotype:** the observable characteristics of an individual resulting from the interaction of its genotype with the environment

By selecting organisms for particular characteristics, you are selecting aspects of their **phenotype**. The phenotype of an organism is the set of observable characteristics resulting from the interaction of its genotype with the environment. A common misunderstanding is that the phenotype of an organism is what it looks like. It is partly the appearance of the organism but can also be aspects of physiology and behaviour. The genetic constitution of an organism is known as its **genotype**. An organism's genotype is inherited as a combination of genes from both its parents.

Selective breeding is used in marine aquaculture programmes in order to improve organisms for several reasons.

- Increased growth rate: fish and shellfish that grow more rapidly or more efficiently are more commercially viable. They reach market size more rapidly and waste less food.

- Disease and stress resistance: because of high stocking densities, aquaculture increases the risk of disease transmission, can lead to stress as a result of over-competition for oxygen, and can cause accumulation of toxins. Organisms that have some resistance to these stressors grow more rapidly and have a lower death rate.

- Product quality: the quality of fish or shellfish meat, such as the colour, flavour and nutritional composition, is commercially very important. Products that are appealing to consumers generate higher profits.

- Age of sexual maturation: delayed sexual maturation is often desirable because it ensures that organisms put more energy into growth rather than gamete production, so can maximise profits.

349

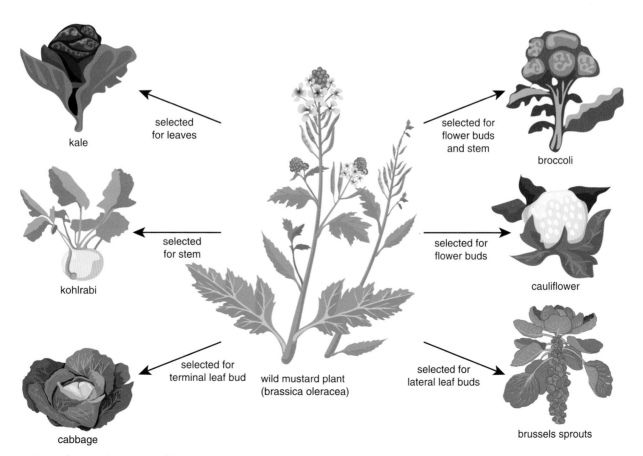

kale — selected for leaves

kohlrabi — selected for stem

cabbage — selected for terminal leaf bud

wild mustard plant (brassica oleracea)

broccoli — selected for flower buds and stem

cauliflower — selected for flower buds

brussels sprouts — selected for lateral leaf buds

Figure 15.2. Selective breeding of brassicas.

DNA, genes and alleles

To understand how selective breeding and genetic engineering work, you need to understand some of the basic principles of genetics.

Nucleotides

The molecule of heredity is deoxyribonucleic acid (DNA). This very important molecule is a polymer, which means that it is made up of long sequences of smaller molecules joined together. These smaller molecules are called nucleotides and are themselves made up of three smaller parts:

- a five-carbon sugar called deoxyribose
- a phosphate group
- a nitrogen-containing base.

There are four different types of nitrogen-containing base in DNA: adenine, thymine, cytosine and guanine. These four different bases and the nucleotides they are found in are shown in Figure 15.3.

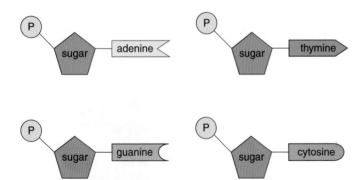

Figure 15.3. The four DNA nucleotides. A nucleotide is made up of a sugar, a nitrogen-containing base and a phosphate.

Polynucleotides and the double helix

The nucleotides of DNA are joined together in a long lines called polynucleotide strands. Within a polynucleotide strand, the nucleotides are joined by chemical bonds between the sugar of one nucleotide and the phosphate of the next (Figure 15.4). DNA molecules are made of two polynucleotide strands that lie side by side and are held together by bonds between the bases, called hydrogen bonds. The way the strands line up is very precise. Adenine (A) always joins with thymine (T), while cytosine (C) always joins with guanine (G). Bases that join are said to be complementary to each other. The two strands of DNA form a spiral structure that is called a double helix.

Chromosomes and genes

Long lengths of DNA are arranged into structures known as chromosomes, which are found in the cytoplasm of bacteria and the nuclei of cells of other organisms. When cell division occurs in organisms other than bacteria, the chromosomes undergo a process known as supercoiling. When this happens, the DNA molecules coil up around proteins called histones and the chromosomes become condensed and visible with a microscope. By looking at dividing cells with a microscope you can produce a map of the chromosomes called a karyotype. Figure 15.5 shows a karyotype of a coho salmon, which has 60 chromosomes in its body cells.

Organisms other than bacteria contain two sets of chromosomes in all their body cells, one set of chromosomes from each parent. For example, coho salmon have two sets of 30 chromosomes, one set that comes from the mother's egg, the other the father's sperm. Humans have 46 chromosomes in their body cells, one set of 23 comes from the mother, the other set of 23 comes from the father.

Genes are sections of DNA along the chromosomes that code for polypeptides. These polypeptides control the characteristics of an organism. Because a cell has two copies of each chromosome, there are two copies of each gene, one from the mother and one from the father. Within populations, there are often many different forms of a particular gene. These different forms of a particular gene are called **alleles**. For example, Figure 15.6 shows some of the variety of skin colour found in koi carp, indicating that there are many different alleles present for skin colour within the koi carp species.

Different alleles may be **dominant** or **recessive**. Dominant alleles exert their effect in the phenotype when only one copy is present, recessive alleles require the presence of two copies to exert their effect. If an organism possesses two copies of the same allele, it is said to be **homozygous**, and if it possesses two different alleles, it is said to be **heterozygous**.

KEY TERMS

Allele: a particular variety of a gene

Dominant: an allele is said to be dominant when its effect on the phenotype of a organisms is the same in a heterozygote and a homozygote

Gene: a sequence of nucleotides in an organism's DNA that codes for the production of a particular protein; it is the hereditary unit that codes for a characteristic of an organism

Heterozygous: possessing two different alleles of a gene

Homozygous: possessing two identical alleles of a gene

Recessive: an allele is said to be recessive when it only exerts an effect on the phenotype of an organism when no dominant allele is present

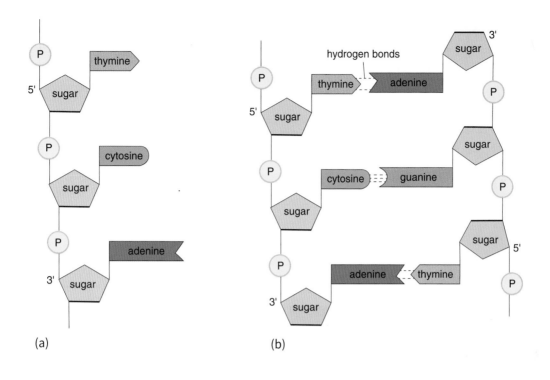

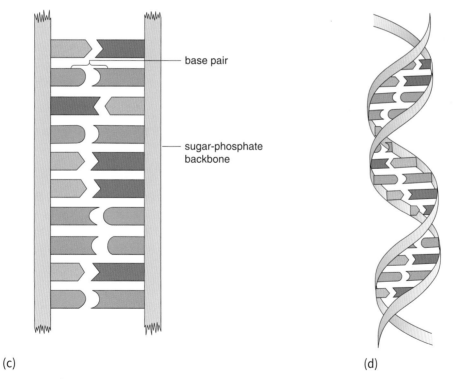

Figure 15.4. The structure of DNA.

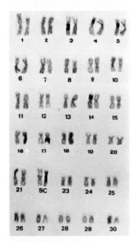

Figure 15.5. Coho salmon karyotype. There are 60 chromosomes in total, 30 pairs.

Figure 15.6. Variation in colour of koi carp.

For example, in a particular species of fish, the allele for striping on the skin, **B**, is dominant to the allele for lacking stripes, **b**. This means that three different genotypes are possible:

BB, Bb, bb

Because the striping allele is dominant to no-striping, only two phenotypes will result from these genotypes (Figure 15.7).

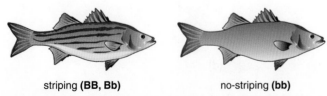

striping (BB, Bb)   no-striping (bb)

Figure 15.7. Phenotypes and genotypes of fish with and without the striping allele.

You can use your knowledge of the genotypes of organisms to help predict or explain the result of breeding programmes. For example, consider a cross between a homozygous striped fish with an unstriped fish. The genotypes of the fish are:

BB – striped

bb – unstriped

The gametes (sperm and eggs) that the fish produce have one copy of the gene. All gametes from the striped fish will carry **B** and all gametes from the unstriped fish will carry **b**. You can set up the cross using a grid known as a Punnett square:

		gametes	
		B	**B**
gametes	**b**	Bb	Bb
	b	Bb	Bb

All the offspring are heterozygotes and will be striped.

Now consider what could happen if you take two of these heterozygous offspring and cross them together. The genotypes of the two parents would both be **Bb** and both will produce gametes carrying either the **B** or **b** allele. The cross would be:

		gametes	
		B	**b**
gametes	**B**	BB	Bb
	b	Bb	bb

The genotypes of the offspring are **BB**, **Bb**, **bb**. The phenotypes of the offspring would be striped (**BB**, **Bb**) and unstriped (**bb**). The predicted ratio of the offspring phenotypes would be three striped to one unstriped. This ratio is a theoretical prediction and not definitive. It predicts that there is a probability of 0.25 of producing an unstriped fish each time an egg is fertilised.

The genetics of selective breeding

Selective breeding programmes often work by selectively culling individual fish that possess a phenotype that is not required. For example, if you are aiming to breed tilapia with a longer average length, you would selectively cull those fish that have a lower length than required. This means that fish with alleles for shorter body length are removed from the population. The remaining fish that have alleles for longer body length are allowed to breed with each other. The offspring are allowed to develop, and those that are below a certain length are again culled. The remaining fish are allowed to breed together. This is repeated over several generations until fish with the desired body length are obtained. The frequency of alleles for longer body length in the population increases, while the frequency of alleles for a shorter body length decreases.

Selective breeding is sometimes used to introduce new genetic characteristics into organisms. This is often called **cross-breeding**. For example, suppose two varieties of farmed Atlantic salmon have been developed. One variety has been bred for rapid growth, the other for disease resistance. Fish from both varieties could be bred with each other and the offspring allowed to develop. Offspring that showed both resistance and rapid growth could be selected and crossed with each other. This process is repeated over several generations until the fish 'breed true', meaning that all fish show both traits.

Risks of selective breeding

Inbreeding depression

Selective breeding carries a risk of inbreeding depression. All organisms carry 'hidden' recessive alleles that have no effect because in the heterozygous condition they are masked by a dominant allele. When organisms that are genetically very different breed together, the possibility of both organisms having a particular recessive allele is low so it is unlikely that the offspring will gain two harmful, recessive alleles. When populations become inbred and genetically very similar, because of continuous breeding from a few individuals, the chance of two parents carrying similar recessive alleles becomes higher. The consequence of this is that selective breeding carries a risk of passing on harmful recessive conditions that appear in the offspring (Figure 15.8).

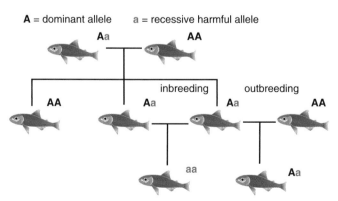

A = dominant allele   a = recessive harmful allele

Figure 15.8. Effect of inbreeding on the chance of passing on harmful alleles to offspring.

Escape into the wild

Studies carried out in Norway have suggested that a significant proportion of 'wild' salmon caught by fishers is actually escaped farmed salmon. These salmon interbreed with the wild salmon and may have negative impacts on the wild populations, affecting their genetic variability. In laboratory research, farmed and hybrid salmon (farmed salmon mated with wild salmon) grow faster, are more competitive when feeding, and are more aggressive than the wild-type salmon. They are, however, less likely to avoid predators.

If organisms have been selectively bred for characteristics such as rapid growth rate, high fecundity and disease resistance, there are environmental risks if they escape into the wild. They could disrupt food chains and mating patterns by competing more fiercely than native species. There is also the possibility of these individuals breeding with wild members of the same species and transferring their genetic background into the wild population. This could have two effects: the addition of low genetic variation from inbred fish or the introduction of advantageous alleles. In order to reduce the risks, fish such as salmon and tilapia are kept in enclosures to prevent escape. Farming the fish in areas where there are no native populations also means that if they did escape, they will not be able to breed with wild individuals. Shellfish that have been selective bred are more difficult to enclose because of their external fertilisation and blanket spawning. However, most selectively bred fish and shellfish do not pose a large threat to the environment, because they are natural organisms that have simply been bred in a particular way and are still very similar to wild populations.

SELF-ASSESSMENT QUESTIONS

3 Describe the differences between (a) alleles and genes; (b) phenotype and genotype; (c) dominant allele and recessive allele; (d) homozygous and heterozygous.

4 Describe and explain how you would set up a selective breeding programme to produce tilapia that grow rapidly from a stock of fish that have a range of growth rates.

KEY TERM

Cross-breeding: mating together different varieties of organism

PRACTICAL ACTIVITY 15.1

Extracting DNA from organisms

Apparatus

- Pestle and mortar
- Test tube
- Ice
- Table salt (sodium chloride)
- Glass funnel
- Droppers or 1 cm³ syringe
- Pasteur pipette
- 10 cm³ pipette
- Glass rod
- 20–30 g caviar (lumpfish, capelin or salmon, or, if no caviar is available, fish roe, peas or onion)
- Distilled water
- Washing-up liquid (diluted 1 : 10 with distilled water)
- Ice-cold ethanol
- Protease enzyme (e.g. Novozymes Neutrase®)
- coffee filter paper

Method

- Store the ethanol and pestle and mortar in the freezer for at least 2 h before use.
- Place the caviar along with about 5 g sodium chloride salt into the mortar and crush with the pestle. This breaks open the eggs and precipitates the proteins.
- Add the 15 cm³ 1 : 10 dilution of washing-up liquid and 3–4 drops of protease to the mixture in the mortar. Stir with the glass rod.
- Place the coffee filter paper into the funnel and pour the mixture through it into a clean test tube.
- Holding the test tube at an angle, use the syringe or pipette to gently pour a layer of ice-cold ethanol on to the surface of the egg extract, as shown in Figure 15.9. White DNA fibres should appear at the interface between the extract and the ethanol.
- Use the glass rod to gently spool the DNA out of the tube, as shown in Figure 15.9.

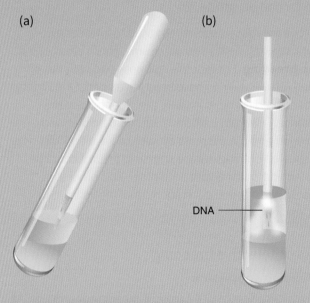

Figure 15.9. (a) Adding ethanol to precipitate the DNA and (b) spooling the DNA out using the glass rod.

Risk assessment

Ethanol is flammable so should only be used if no naked flames are present.

Safety glasses should be worn as the ethanol, protease and washing-up liquid are potential irritants.

Fish caviar can cause an allergic reaction.

KEY TERMS

Genetic engineering: the modification of organisms by changing their genetic material; this can be the addition of genes from other species or the editing of genes that are already present

Transgenic organism: an organism that contains genetic material into which DNA from an unrelated organism has been introduced

15.4 Genetic engineering

During the latter part of the 20th century, scientists developed the technology to be able to genetically alter species in the laboratory. It has now become possible to alter the structure of genes and move genes from one species to another to create organisms. Although selective breeding is a form of **genetic engineering**, it is 'low-tech': it is the mixing of existing alleles between members of the same species. Modern genetic engineering to make genetically modified (GM) organisms uses more sophisticated technology and can alter the genetic makeup of organisms by adding genes from other species or artificially constructed genes. An organism that has had the gene of another organism added to it is known as a **transgenic organism**.

As technology improves, increasing numbers of GM organisms are being developed for a variety of reasons, such as disease resistance, improved products and rapid growth rates. By 2015, there had been approximately 50 different varieties of GM fish produced, although only one has been approved for human consumption. The reasons for producing these transgenic fish include:

- making models for investigating animal development and physiology
- making models for medical research
- improving the yield of fish
- producing disease-resistant fish
- detecting environmental pollution
- producing novelty pets.

KEY TERMS

DNA ligase: an enzyme that joins the sugar–phosphate backbone of sections of DNA, it is used to recombine pieces of DNA

Plasmid: a small circular DNA strand in the cytoplasm of a bacterium; they are used as vectors in the laboratory manipulation of genes

Promoter: a section of DNA that is often located in front of a gene, and is responsible for the 'switching on and off' of a gene

Restriction endonuclease: enzyme that cuts DNA at specific internal, palindromic sequences; they are used in genetic engineering

Transformation: the genetic altering of a cell by taking up DNA. Bacterial transformation occurs when bacteria are induced to take up plasmids

Vector: a section of DNA, typically a plasmid, that is used to transfer DNA from one organism to another

Comparing Selective Breeding with Genetic Engineering

It is very easy to confuse selective breeding and genetic engineering. Both processes have some similarities but there are also many fundamental differences.

Similarities

- Both processes are carried out by humans.
- Both processes are used to "design organisms" for our own requirements.

Differences

- Selective breeding has been carried out for a very long time, possibly 10 000 years and has led to the production of most of the domestic animals and crops that we recognise today. Genetic engineering is a recent technique that has only been practised over the last fifty years or so.

- Selective breeding involves the selection of organisms of the same species with 'desired characteristics' which are then mated. The offspring with the 'desired characteristics' are then selected. This is repeated over many generations. Although it requires skill, it does not need high level technology and is not usually carried out in laboratories.

- Genetic engineering is the transfer of genes (DNA) from organisms of one species to a different species. This requires a great deal of expertise and is done using sophisticated technology in the laboratory.

General principles and tools of genetic engineering

There are certain key techniques and substances that are used to genetically engineer organisms.

- **Restriction endonucleases** are enzymes that cut DNA at specific sequences of nucleotides. The sequences they recognise are usually palindromes, which means that they read the same in both directions on opposite strands of DNA (Figure 15.10). When they cut the DNA, they tend to leave small sections of single-stranded DNA that will bind to a complementary sequence. These ends are called sticky ends.

355

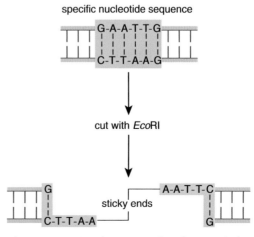

Figure 15.10. Cutting DNA using the restriction endonuclease *Eco*R1.

- **DNA ligase** is an enzyme that joins the sugar–phosphate backbone of DNA. It is used to 'glue' sections of DNA together. The DNA that is joined together is known as recombinant DNA.

- **Plasmids** are small circles of DNA found in bacteria that can copy themselves within the bacteria. They can be used as **vectors** to transfer pieces of DNA from one cell to another.

- Gene **promoters** are sections of DNA found 'upstream' of the part of the gene that codes for a polypeptide. They control when a gene is switched on and off.

Figure 15.11 shows how recombinant plasmids containing a foreign gene are produced. The key steps are as follows.

- The required gene is cut out by using a restriction endonuclease, leaving 'sticky ends' capable of binding to complementary DNA sequences.

- A plasmid vector is cut using the same restriction endonuclease and the gene added to it. The sticky ends of the gene and plasmid are complementary to each other and so bind.

- DNA ligase is used to join the sugar phosphate backbone of the gene and plasmid. The plasmid now carries an extra gene and is called a recombinant plasmid.

- The recombinant plasmid is placed into bacteria, in a process called **transformation**. The bacteria can be

grown in large numbers to make large quantities of the plasmid. Some plasmids carry a promoter sequence that 'switches on' the gene so that the protein is manufactured by the bacteria. This is used if a protein product, such as the hormone insulin, is required. The bacteria are then grown continuously and, for example, constantly produce insulin. In some cases large quantities of the plasmid are required to be introduced into animals and plants in order to genetically modify them. One example of this is the production of the AquAdvantage salmon.

The AquAdvantage GM salmon

In November 2015, the Food and Drug Administration (FDA) of the USA approved the AquAdvantage salmon created by AquaBounty for commercial production, sale and consumption. It is the first GM animal to be approved for human consumption.

Atlantic salmon normally produce growth hormone only when the water temperature is warm. The AquAdvantage salmon has been genetically engineered to produce growth hormone all the time, so that it grows all year. The fish (Figure 15.12) grow much faster and can be harvested sooner. Two extra sections have been added to the salmon DNA:

- a growth hormone gene from the chinook salmon (the production of growth hormone stimulates growth of body tissues)

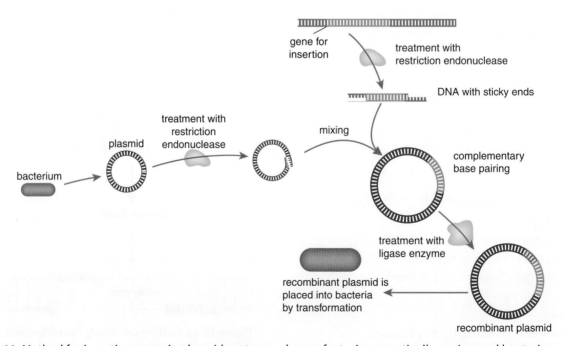

Figure 15.11. Method for inserting genes in plasmid vectors and manufacturing genetically engineered bacteria.

Figure 15.12. The AquAdvantage salmon, with normal salmon of same age in front

- a gene promoter for antifreeze proteins from an ocean pout (this promoter switches on the antifreeze genes when the temperature is low). The gene terminator found at the end of the antifreeze protein genes is also used.

Gene promoters switch genes on and off. The normal growth hormone gene promoter is sensitive to environmental factors such as temperature and day length. This means that growth hormone is only produced under certain environmental conditions. As a consequence, the salmon do not grow all year round. The ocean pout promoter switches on the growth hormone gene all the time so that the growth hormone is produced continuously and the salmon will grow all year round.

Procedure

The procedure used to generate the AquAdvantage salmon (Figure 15.13) has several steps.

- DNA for the growth hormone gene is obtained from the chinook salmon and 'cut out' using restriction endonucleases.

- The promoter and gene terminator from the ocean pout are also cut out using restriction endonucleases.

- The promoter, growth hormone gene and terminator gene are joined together and placed into a plasmid vector, also cut with restriction endonucleases. The DNA fragments are joined using DNA ligase.

- The recombinant plasmid is placed into bacteria to manufacture large quantities of it. The recombinant

plasmids are then purified and microinjected into fertilised salmon eggs. The salmon are allowed to hatch and then grown in tanks. Salmon that have taken up the transgene are selected and kept. The promoter and terminator sequences ensure that the growth hormone gene is switched on constantly, so that the salmon grow throughout the year.

- Male fish that carry the transgene are selected and used to produce sperm that will also carry the transgene. Sperm from these males are used to fertilise female, non-transgenic eggs (Figure 15.14). The eggs are then 'pressure shocked'. Pressure shocking interferes with the final stages of egg meiosis, resulting in a fertilised egg with three sets of chromosomes rather than two. The resulting fish have a triploid number of chromosomes (three sets of chromosomes) rather than the usual diploid number (two sets of chromosomes). Female fish are selected and grown to adulthood, as the majority of triploid females are sterile. This means they will not be able to reproduce if they escape.

Successful microinjection of the DNA is an inefficient process and only a relatively small percentage of eggs will integrate the DNA into the genome. Even when the DNA integrates into the genome, it may attach to regions of DNA that are not active so will not function. It is not easy to target the DNA to an area of the salmon egg DNA that is active, so it is important to select fish that have got the transgene and are able to switch on production of growth hormone.

357

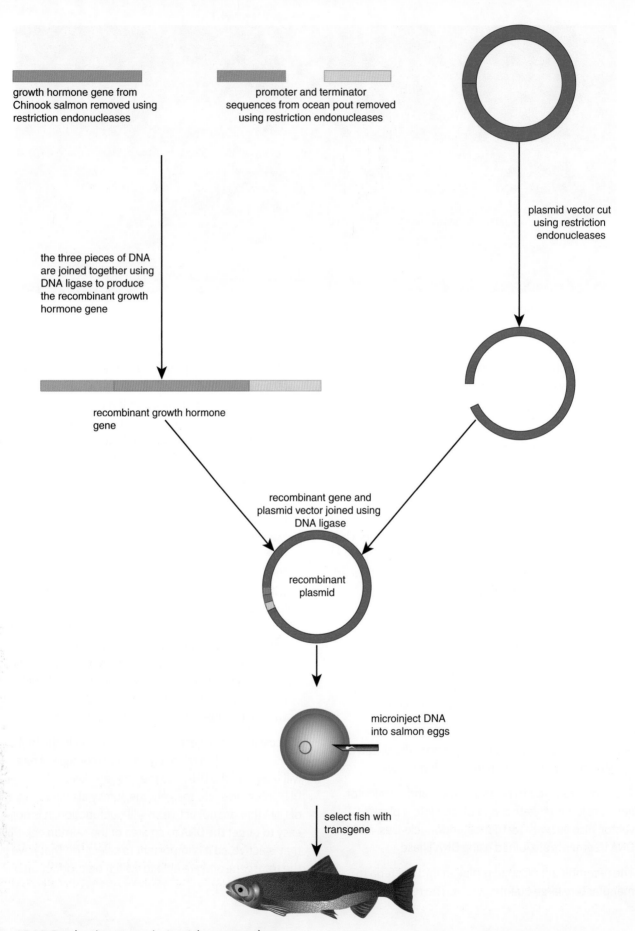

Figure 15.13. Production stages in AquAdvantage salmon.

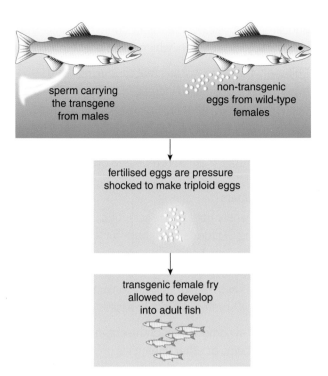

Figure 15.14. Using transgenic male fish to produce sterile rapidly growing fish.

The benefits and risks of genetically engineering fish and shellfish

The production of genetically engineered organisms could have many benefits. It could also create many problems with far-reaching consequences if their use is not managed carefully.

Benefits

Commercial benefits (higher profits) can be achieved with GM organisms as a result of the following.

*   Faster growth rate: fish and shellfish can be genetically modified to mature faster (the AquAdvantage salmon is a good example of this, and a comparison of growth rates is shown in Figure 15.15). This means that they reach market size faster and so more can be produced in a shorter time.

*   Improved product: if GM fish and shellfish have a desirable nutritional composition or more attractive appearance, consumer demand will be higher.

*   Guaranteed availability of product: GM fish can be generated that will mature and grow at all times of the year, so there will be year-round availability.

*   Efficient energy conversion: GM organisms could be developed that convert energy more efficiently, resulting in less food wastage. A reduction in food requirements would increase profit margins.

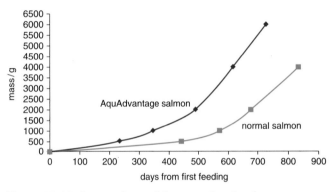

Figure 15.15. Comparison of the growth rate of AquAdvantage and normal salmon.

Humanitarian benefits (improved source of protein in developing nations) of GM fish and shellfish include the following.

*   Resistant organisms: organisms that have been genetically modified to be resistant to harsh conditions could help provide a source of protein in developing nations.

*   Efficient energy conversion: GM fish that require less food could be grown in larger numbers, providing additional, affordable dietary protein for people.

Environmental benefits of GM fish and shellfish include them the following.

*   Reduced pressure on wild stocks: if GM fish and shellfish can be grown rapidly, production will at least meet consumer demand. Fewer wild fish will need to be taken so that the wild populations will increase.

*   Efficient energy conversion: if fish and shellfish require less continuous feeding, there is less uneaten food and / or faeces that can otherwise cause water pollution.

Risks and consequences

Genetically modifying fish and shellfish does, however, bring with it potential risks. At the present time, different nations have different approaches to permitting the use of GM foods. In most cases consideration is given to the risk of GM organisms escaping and the risks to consumers.

Risk of escape

Some GM organisms are more likely to cause problems if they escape than others. If GM cattle escaped, they are quite unlikely to cross-breed with native cattle. They are not likely to escape in large numbers and, because of their relatively large size, they are generally easier to keep within a restricted area. Plants are more difficult to contain because it is almost impossible to prevent pollen being scattered beyond field boundaries by wind or insects. This could result in cross-breeding with native plants, so any genetic modifications could be introduced into wild plants. Finding and removing any GM plants that have escaped would also be difficult. Fish and shellfish are similarly difficult to contain. Many would be farmed in extensive systems and there would be a high risk of escape. Many shellfish species in particular are broadcast spawners, releasing microscopic gametes into the water that could easily get past nets. Larval stages are small and could also easily pass through small nets. Once out, tracking down any GM fish or shellfish would be almost impossible.

The consequences of escape

If GM organisms were to escape, they could potentially cause a range of problems.

- Food chain effects: GM organisms that are designed to grow rapidly and feed more efficiently would have the potential to outcompete wild species. For example, rapidly growing salmon would grow faster than wild salmon and outcompete them for food, territory and mates. They could reduce the food sources for wild salmon and other fish. The escape of GM organisms therefore has the potential to cause the extinction of their wild counterparts, the food sources and other organisms dependent on those food sources.

- Cross-breeding with wild species: if GM organisms escaped, they could potentially breed with wild organisms of the same species, transferring the genetic modifications into the wild population. Genes for phenotypes such as disease resistance, pest resistance

and altered physical appearance could be transferred into the wild population, which could affect food chains.

- Pollution: there are worries that producing GM organisms could lead to increased pollution. The use of glyphosate-resistant (weedkiller-resistant) crops, such as maize and soya, has led to an increased use of weedkiller. The loss of native plants (weeds) may reduce the populations of animals that feed on them.

Risks to consumers

The belief generally held by the scientific community is that consuming GM foods is not harmful to human health. There have, however, been some negative reactions by consumers regarding the safety of GM foods. Before a new GM food is allowed for human consumption, it goes through several studies in order to assess its safety.

- The chemical composition of the organism, including any GM proteins or other chemicals produced, is determined.

- The risk of allergy to all aspects of the organism is assessed.

- The risk of genetic transfer from the organism to human cells or microorganisms in the human gut is tested.

- Tests to measure toxicity are carried out.

- The probable composition of the organism in a typical human diet is determined.

Minimising the risks

Before genetically engineered organisms are released into the environment or allowed to be consumed or kept by the general public, they must be thoroughly tested.

The **precautionary principle** is applied to any new application for the use of genetically engineered organisms. The idea is that if an action or policy could cause any harm to people or the environment, it is best avoided. When there is no scientific proof that an action is not harmful, law-makers have a responsibility to think carefully about the safety, risk, cost and feasibility of the proposed action.

Genetically engineered organisms could pose risks to human health and the environment. Because very few have been released, the only evidence of harm comes from laboratory experiments rather than field work.

A great deal of consideration must be given to all possible outcomes before legalising the use of GM organisms.

The AquAdvantage salmon is currently the only genetically engineered animal that is licenced for human consumption in the United States. The FDA approved the AquAdvantage salmon to US consumers on 19 November 2015, almost 20 years after the first submission of data to the FDA. Extensive rounds of research and consultations were carried out and the nutritional composition of the fish was tested thoroughly. One area of controversy is the labelling of the salmon. Because the AquAdvantage salmon does not have a markedly different composition to wild salmon, it is not necessary to label the salmon so that consumers know which type they are eating.

Production of the AquAdvantage salmon is still tightly regulated and several precautions are taken in order to minimise the risk of escape and breeding with wild salmon.

The salmon are farmed at two land-based locations. The breeding stock are kept in a special indoor facility on Prince Edward Island, Canada (Figure 15.16). The fertilised eggs from Canada are transported to an outdoor facility in Panama, where they are hatched and grown into fish for the marketplace. Both facilities have extensive filtration units and fine mesh netting to prevent any escape of the fish. All waste water is chemically treated to kill any eggs or fry. In Panama, netting is placed above the fish farm to prevent predators removing fish.

Figure 15.16. AquAdvantage salmon breeding tanks at the Prince Edward Island location.

At the Panama facility, it is highly unlikely that an escaped salmon would survive in the wild because of the high river and ocean water temperatures. Wild Atlantic salmon are not found in the seas around Panama, so if salmon escaped there are no wild salmon to interbreed with.

KEY TERM

Precautionary principle: a strategy to cope with possible risks where scientific understanding is yet incomplete, such as the risks of releasing genetically modified organisms; it tries to ensure that all possible consequences of a new technology are considered before allowing it to be used

Fertilised eggs are rendered infertile by pressure shocking. Applying high pressure to fish eggs prevents the final round of cell division occurring, so that after fertilisation the fish eggs have three sets of chromosomes (triploid) rather than the normal two sets (diploid). Triploid salmon are infertile so would not be able to breed if they did escape. In addition, only female fish are farmed, reducing the risk of breeding colonies occurring.

SELF-ASSESSMENT QUESTIONS

7 **a** Summarise the potential risks to the environment from producing GM fish and shellfish.

   b Describe the precautions taken by AquaBounty when developing the AquAdvantage salmon and explain how they help to prevent escape of the fish.

8 **a** Describe the similarities and differences between selective breeding and genetic engineering.

   b Imagine a scenario whereby a company has applied for a licence to develop and produce for human consumption a variety of shrimp genetically engineered to have pest resistance. Suggest some of the procedures that the company would have to carry out in order to convince a government to issue a licence.

361

Pollution indicators and pets: the story of the GloFish

In 2006, a company called Yorktown Technologies released the first genetically engineered organisms available for sale to the general public in the United States. The fish was a genetically engineered zebrafish (a fish that is native to India and Bangladesh) called the GloFish. It contained a gene for the green fluorescent protein (GFP), originally extracted from a jellyfish, that results in bright green fluorescence in the cells. Figure 15.17 shows a bioluminescent jellyfish that naturally produces GFP. The GloFish was initially developed by Dr Zhiyuan Gong and his colleagues at the National University of Singapore. They extracted the gene from the jellyfish DNA, placed it into a plasmid vector and then microinjected this into zebrafish eggs, where it integrated into the zebrafish genome. The fish were developed with the intention of using them as pollution indicators. The aim was to attach pollutant-specific gene promoters in front of the GFP gene so that the gene would be switched on if the fish were placed in the presence of a specific pollutant such as oestrogen.

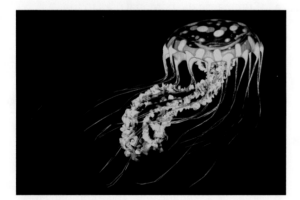

Figure 15.17. Naturally bioluminescent jellyfish.

The US FDA carried out 2 years of research into the safety of the GloFish before issuing a licence for their sale. The fish eggs are pressure shocked to render the majority of GloFish infertile, although there have been reports that some fish have been able to breed in captivity. Wild zebrafish are only found in south Asia, and studies with the GloFish demonstrated that they were eaten more frequently by predators than wild-type fish. Other research suggested that the GloFish offer no more threat to the environment than normal zebrafish. Some environmental groups objected to the sale of the GloFish, and their sale is still not permitted in Canada, the UK and the countries within the European Union.

The original green GloFish has now been joined by more genetically engineered species, such as tiger barbs and tetras, and more fluorescent colours, such as pink, red, blue, orange and purple (Figure 15.18).

Figure 15.18. Some examples of different colours of GloFish

Questions

1. Outline how the genetically engineered zebrafish were produced.

2. Explain why the GloFish is unlikely to be a risk to the environment or to humans in the United States. Suggest why keeping the GloFish as pets in southern Asia may represent more of a risk to the environment.

3. Explain why environmental groups may object to the GloFish being available to the general public.

4. Suggest how the GloFish could be used to detect environmental pollution.

Maths skills

Measuring gradients of straight lines and curves

You need to be able to use line graphs where the x-axis represents time to determine the rate of change of a variable. For example, Figure 15.19 shows the mean increase in mass of a group of farmed salmon over a period of 6 months. A line of best fit has been drawn through the points and the relationship is linear over the 6 month period. This means that the rate of increase is the same over the time period. You can calculate the mean rate of growth by determining the gradient of the line.

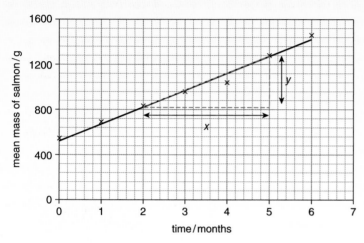

Figure 15.19. Calculating growth rate of salmon.

To calculate the gradient of the line, draw a triangle anywhere on the line of best fit, as shown in Figure 15.19.

Gradient of a straight line = y/x

In this case, the gradient of the line = y grams $/ x$ months, so this is in fact a rate of increase in mass.

The graph shows that in the period between 2 months and 5 months, the mean increase in mass was
$y = 1280$ g – 800 g = 480 g

The time period, x, equals 5 months – 2 months = 3 months

The gradient, y/x, = $480/3 = 26.7$ g month^{-1}

If a graph does not show a linear relationship, and the rate of increase or decrease changes, you need to draw a tangent to the curve in order to calculate the gradients at different points. For example, Figure 15.20 shows the increase in length of farmed tilapia over a 10 month period. It is clear that the curve of best fit is steepest at the start from month 0 up to month 2, and that it gradually levels off to a plateau as time increases.

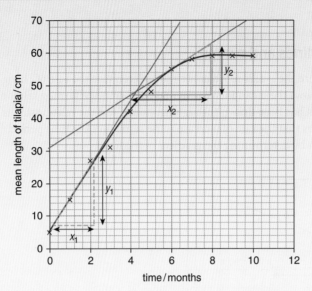

Figure 15.20. Calculating growth rate of tilapia with a variable growth rate.

In order to calculate the gradient at a particular point, use a ruler to draw a line with the same gradient as the curve at that point. You can now calculate the gradient of the tangent at the point.

For this example, the gradient at 1 month is:

$y_1/x_1 = (25\ cm – 4\ cm)/(2\ months – 0\ months) = 21/2 = 10.5\ cm\ month^{-1}$

At 6 months, the rate of growth is:

$y_2/x_2 = (63\ cm – 47\ cm)/(8\ months – 4\ months) = 26/4 = 6.5\ cm\ month^{-1}$

Questions

1   The population growth of oysters in two estuaries is shown in Figure 15.21.

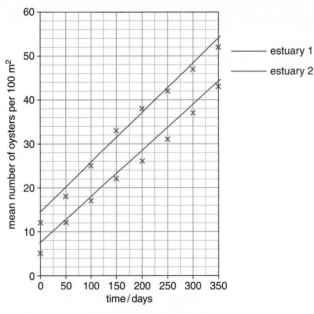

Figure 15.21. Growth of oyster populations in two estuaries.

Use the graph to calculate and compare the rates of growth of the two oyster populations over the 350-day period.

2 The growth rates of a group of genetically engineered salmon was compared with a group of non-genetically engineered salmon. The mean mass of each group of salmon was determined each month over a period of 750 days. The results are shown in Table 15.1.

time / days	mean mass of genetically engineered salmon / g	mean mass of non-genetically engineered salmon / g
0	0	0
250	500	275
350	1000	450
450	1500	550
500	2000	800
550	2500	950
600	3200	1100
650	4200	1700
700	5000	2100
750	6000	2900

Table 15.1. Comparison of growth rates of genetically engineered and non-genetically engineered salmon.

a Draw a graph to compare the growth rate of the two groups of salmon. Make sure that your axes are linear and that you draw two curves of best fit.

b Calculate the rates of growth of each group of salmon by drawing tangents to the lines at (i) 250 days and (ii) 550 days.

Summary

- As we progress through the 21st century, biotechnology is playing an increasing role in our day-to-day lives.

- We have seen the power of bacteria to remove oil pollution, and how over centuries we have shaped our food stocks by selective breeding.

- As genetic technologies become increasingly sophisticated and more powerful, there are more and more opportunities to design organisms for our own purposes.

- Changing the fundamental genetic makeup of organisms brings with it a responsibility to think through the consequences carefully.

- The genetic constituents of the organisms on this planet are the results of millions of years of evolution. We must consider the effects of interfering with this very carefully.

Exam-style questions

1   The effect of different factors on the rate of digestion of oil by bacteria was investigated. A culture of oil-digesting bacteria was added to a suspension of oil and the mixture incubated at 15 °C. After 1 month, the relative amount of undigested oil was determined by using a technique called colorimetry. The effects of changing the temperature and addition of dispersant chemicals and fertiliser were then investigated. Colorimetry is a method whereby light is passed through a liquid and the percentage that is transmitted is measured. The higher the quantity of oil in the suspension, the lower the percentage transmission. Dispersants are chemicals that physically break up the droplets of oil in the water. The results are shown in Table 15.2.

temperature / °C	presence or absence of dispersant	presence or absence of fertiliser	% transmission of light / %
15	absent	absent	15
15	present	absent	23
15	absent	present	54
15	present	present	62
25	absent	absent	17
25	present	absent	27
25	absent	present	49
25	present	present	65

Table 15.2. Effect of different factors on the digestion of oil by bacteria.

a   i   Describe the relative effects of increased temperature and adding dispersant and fertiliser on removal of the oil. **[4]**

   ii   Suggest reasons for the effects of adding the fertiliser and dispersant on removal of the oil. **[4]**

   iii   State two factors that would need to be controlled in the experiment. **[1]**

b   Explain why adding fertilisers containing nitrates and phosphates to oil-polluted water could result in the death of organisms as a result of lack of oxygen. **[4]**

[Total mark: 13]

2   a   Explain what is meant by the terms:

   i   selective breeding **[2]**

   ii   genetic engineering **[2]**

b   Describe how salmon can be genetically engineered to increase their rate of growth. **[7]**

c   Explain the environmental risks that could be associated with the production of genetically engineered salmon. **[4]**

[Total mark: 15]

3 The growth rate of a variety of genetically engineered salmon was investigated. The fish were genetically engineered by adding a growth hormone gene to salmon eggs. Ten genetically engineered Atlantic salmon were kept in a marine tank and the mass of the salmon determined every month for 8 months. The mean mass of the salmon was determined along with the standard deviation. The experiment was repeated with ten normal Atlantic salmon. The results are shown in Table 15.3.

time / months	genetically engineered salmon		normal salmon	
	mass / g	standard deviation	mass / g	standard deviation
0	200	34	190	12
1	640	45	450	21
2	860	41	680	45
3	1110	76	790	65
4	1300	125	850	74
5	1510	102	990	75
6	1690	154	1060	84
7	1780	187	1280	75
8	1800	176	1370	76

Table 15.3. Growth rate of genetically engineered and normal salmon.

a **i** Plot a graph to show the increase in mass of the genetically engineered salmon and normal salmon over the 8 months. Draw curves of best fit for both groups of salmon. Do not add error bars for standard deviations. **[4]**

ii Use tangents to the curves to determine the growth rates of both groups of salmon at 1 month. **[2]**

iii When carrying out genetic engineering, the introduced genes do not always integrate into active parts of the genome. Compare and suggest explanations for the differences in standard deviations between the genetically engineered fish and the normal salmon. **[4]**

b Use the results in Table 15.3 and your graph to explain how genetic engineering in relation to salmon could be beneficial to salmon farmers. **[3]**

[Total mark: 13]

4 Figure 15.22 shows some of the stages that occur when producing genetically engineered salmon that have rapid growth rates.

a Complete Figure 15.22 by naming the DNA that is taken from the ocean pout fish and chinook salmon and used to genetically engineer the salmon eggs. **[2]**

367

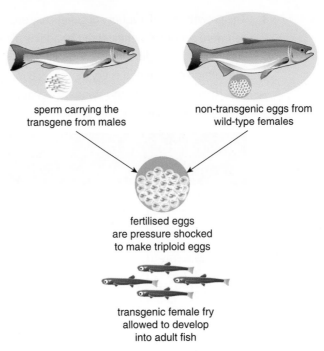

sperm carrying the
transgene from males

non-transgenic eggs from
wild-type females

fertilised eggs
are pressure shocked
to make triploid eggs

transgenic female fry
allowed to develop
into adult fish

Figure 15.22. Production of genetically engineered salmon.

b Before the salmon eggs are fertilised, they are pressure shocked in an effort to make the salmon they produce infertile. It is estimated that 1% of salmon produced from these eggs are fertile.

i Calculate how many eggs from a group of 50 000 eggs would produce fish that are fertile. **[1]**

ii Explain why it is important that farmed transgenic salmon are infertile. **[3]**

iii Explain what is meant by the precautionary principle and why it is important to consider it when releasing GM organisms. **[4]**

[Total mark: 10]

Using genetic engineering to control invasive species

Australia is currently in the grip of an extinction event. It is a nation that has one of the highest amounts of biodiversity and has many plants and animals that are not found anywhere else in the world. Approximately 87% of Australia's mammal species, 93% of reptiles, 94% of frogs and 45% of bird species are found only in Australia. Unfortunately, many of these native species are now dying out and are threatened with extinction. In fact, over 1700 species of animals and plants are listed by the Australian government as threatened with extinction. The main cause of this is the arrival of humans in the country.

Plate tectonics can explain the unique biodiversity of Australia. Over 180 million years ago, Australia, along with Antarctica, India, South America and Africa, was part of the southern supercontinent of Gondwanaland (Figure 15.23). North America, Europe and Asia were part of the northern supercontinent of Laurasia. Between 160 and 170 million years ago, plate movements caused the breakup of Gondwanaland. India was the first land mass to separate, followed by Africa and New Zealand. South America, Antarctica and Australia remained in contact until about 65 million years ago, when South America began to detach. Antarctica and Australia separated approximately 50 million years ago.

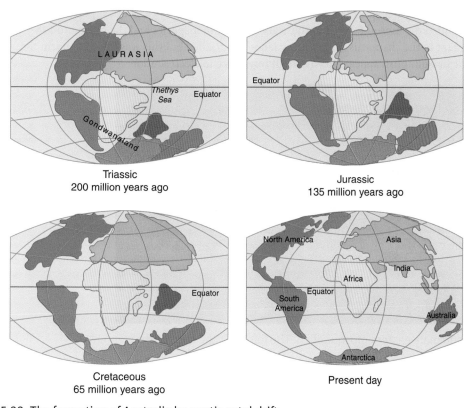

Figure 15.23. The formation of Australia by continental drift.

Some of the animals and plants in Australia that had existed in Gondwanaland now evolved in isolation from the other continents. When Australia reached the area of Indonesia, a few species such as bats and rats began to arrive and spread throughout the country. The largest invasions, however, occurred with the arrival of humans, initially between 40 000 and 60 000 years ago with the Aboriginal population and later after the 1788 colonisation by Europeans. The colonists set out to reproduce the landscape of England by bringing with them familiar animals such as goats, rabbits, cats and even foxes. Unfortunately, these invasive animals had few natural predators and the animals and plants of Australia were an easy source of food for them. In subsequent years, other species were introduced, both intentionally and accidentally, including the now infamous cane toad, which was introduced in 1935 to keep a sugar cane beetle in check. It ate almost everything except the beetle, including small birds and marsupials, and this poisonous toad is still spreading across Australia destroying native populations of animals. A number of marine pests have arrived in the ballast water of cargo ships. These include the black-striped mussel, the Asian mussel, the New Zealand green-lipped mussel and the European shore crab. Many of the waterways of Australia are now populated by invasive fish such as the European carp, brown trout, rainbow trout, redfin perch and the mosquitofish. These fish have caused the loss of native species as a result of competition for food and predation. Research is now being carried out to try and find a way of reducing the spread and threat of these invasive fish.

Eastern mosquitofish

The eastern mosquitofish (*Gambusia holbrooki*) (Figure 15.24) is native to the eastern and southern United States. It was introduced into New South Wales, Australia, in the 1920s to control mosquito larvae in the water, but failed to have any effect. They are predatory fish that consume native invertebrates and fish species that have aquatic larval stages. They are aggressive and cause fin and scale damage to other fish. They cause unbalanced food webs because they often eat the larvae of top predators. Several native fish and amphibian species are now extinct because of the spread of this fish. Conservation efforts have been made to try and prevent further spread and control the current populations. Chemical pesticides were used that initially killed the mosquitofish, but these also killed other species and the mosquito fish eventually became tolerant to the chemicals. Electrifying lakes was trialled but this was found to harm the native species more: the mosquitofish appears to have high resistance to electrocution.

Figure 15.24. Female and male eastern mosquitofish. The female is the larger fish.

European carp

The exact date that the European carp (*Cyprinus carpio*) was introduced into the waterways of Australia is unknown but is thought to have been between the 1850s and 1870s. They were introduced as a food source for people and rapidly spread. They have an extremely high reproduction rate (a single female can produce between 80 000 and 1 500 000 eggs), are voracious feeders and have a habit of grubbing through sediment looking for food. While feeding, they cause extensive damage by uprooting and eating submerged vegetation, resulting in the loss of food and nesting areas for other species of fish, amphibians and water birds such as ducks. They have relatively inefficient digestive systems so produce large quantities of faeces, which decay and cause eutrophication.

In the country's largest river system, the Murray-Darling River Basin in south-east Australia, carp now account for 90% of the fish (Figure 15.25). This puts about half of the native species at risk of extinction. Controlling the spread of the carp has been almost impossible and methods such as the release of carp-specific viruses have been controversial. In the state of Victoria, fishers can take unlimited quantities of carp and in South Australia is it illegal to release carp that have been captured back into the rivers.

Figure 15.25. Dense population of carp in Murray-Darling River Basin, Australia.

Carp have been successfully eradicated in Lake Crescent in Tasmania by using a combination of control methods, including electronic fish tracking, netting and high use of pesticides to kill unhatched embryos.

Using genetic engineering to control the mosquitofish and carp

In an effort to control the populations of mosquitofish and carp, scientists are turning to genetic engineering. Transgenic zebrafish have been produced that do not produce female fish. To develop as female fish, embryos need to produce the hormone oestrogen. An enzyme called aromatase is needed to make the oestrogen. In the absence of oestrogen, fish develop as males.

Scientists added a gene called *daughterless* to zebrafish eggs. The *daughterless* gene blocks the production of the aromatase enzyme. Most of the fish that developed from the eggs were male. The male offspring that carried copies of the *daughterless* gene were then selected and bred with female zebrafish. Almost all of the offspring of these transgenic fish were again male.

The use of the *daughterless* gene is now being extended to the mosquitofish and carp. The ultimate aim is to generate male fish carrying copies of the *daughterless* gene and then release these into rivers and lakes that have invasive fish. These male fish will breed with the invasive carp and mosquitofish but produce only fish that are male in the next generation. In time, the population of female fish should decrease so that the overall carp and mosquitofish populations should decline.

Risks and possible problems

It has been suggested that transgenic fish will have to be released every year for up to 20 years to eradicate the invasive populations fully. As the gene impairs the reproductive ability of the fish, scientists have suggested that it should naturally prevent the transgenic fish becoming a new invasive organism themselves. There is concern, however, that the gene could cross species boundaries in some way to affect native fish. If the transgenic carp or mosquitofish were released into rivers and lakes where the native species live, they could transfer the *daughterless* gene into native fish and affect their reproductive efficiency. The nation of Australia has had several bad experiences with the release of non-native species so approach the release of a genetically engineered species with great caution.

Questions

1 Explain why the native animals and plants of Australia are particularly vulnerable to threats from invasive species.

2 Explain how the *daughterless* gene could be used to help control the carp and mosquitofish in Australia and why it might be preferable to conventional methods such as pesticides.

3 Suggest and explain why using the *daughterless* gene to control carp and mosquitofish in Australia is unlikely to have adverse effects on the environment.

4 Suggest why accidental release of carp carrying the *daughterless* gene in Europe and Asia could have a major effect on the environment.

Chapter 1

1

type of variable	description
independent	the variable that is changed by the experimenter
dependent	the variable that is measured by the experimenter
control	variables that are kept constant so that the dependent variable is not affected
confounding	a variable in a field experiment that cannot be controlled but that could affect the dependent variable; these variables should be recorded and measured

2 Suggested hypotheses:
  - Algae grow better in the fish tank at higher temperatures
  - Algae grow better in the fish tank in the summer because there is more light

  Suggested predictions:
  - The higher the temperature, the greater the growth of algae
  - The higher the light intensity, the greater the growth of algae

3 **a** 100 cm³ measuring cylinder
  b 1 cm³ pipette or syringe
  c Measure the area using a tape measure and the mass using a balance or weighing scales

4 The eyes must be level with the surface of the meniscus. The volumes shown are:
  a 88.5 cm³
  b 92.0 cm³
  c 90.0 cm³
  Note that it is important to be consistent in the number of decimal places shown, so 92 and 90 would be inaccurate compared with 88.5.

5 An anomalous result is one that does not fit the pattern. In experiments, it is normally one of a series of repeated results for one value of the independent variable.

6 If the results support the hypothesis, it is highly likely that they will match the original prediction because this was based on the hypothesis.

7 A hypothesis is an idea to explain an observation that can be tested experimentally. A theory is a well-substantiated explanation of an aspect of the natural world that has been repeatedly tested and confirmed through observation and experimentation.

8 **a** Any two from salinity, light intensity, wavelength of light, nutrient levels, pH, initial number or mass of algae, time the algae are left for, oxygen concentration, carbon dioxide concentration
  b Any two from salinity, light intensity, wavelength of light, nutrient levels, temperature, initial number or mass of zooplankton, time the zooplankton are left for, oxygen concentration, carbon dioxide concentration
  c Any two from salinity, wavelength of light, nutrient levels, temperature, initial size of seagrass, time the seagrass is left for, pH, carbon dioxide concentration, oxygen concentration

Chapter 2

1

	host	symbiont
mutualism	+	+
parasitism	–	+
competition	–	–
predation	+	–

2 Similarities: use energy source to fix carbon / CO_2 / inorganic molecules into 'food' energy / carbohydrates / glucose / organic molecules

Differences: must have both sides of the following table

	photosynthesis	chemosynthesis
example	plants, algae, bacteria, seagrass	chemosynthetic bacteria
energy source	light energy	chemical energy
marine habitat	photic zone / surface water	aphotic zone / deep-sea vent

3
- Light intensity decreases further from the equator. The lower light intensity inhibits the light-dependent stage of photosynthesis.
- Ocean temperatures are lower in polar oceans. The low ocean temperature slows down the rate of diffusion of molecules involved in photosynthesis
- Lower temperatures mean a lower rate of reaction for the enzymes that catalyse photosynthesis.

4
- Decreased lobster population size
- Fewer places for lobsters to live / nest
- Less protection from predators / less prey to feed on

5
- Decrease lobster and fish catches
- Increase harvesting of sea urchins

6 Similarities
- Both extreme environments, i.e. great depth, increased pressure, high temperatures
- No light for photosynthesis
- Chemosynthetic bacteria present
- Tube worms, mussels, clams and crabs present

Differences
- The source of energy and carbon at whale falls is organic 'food' energy fixed by photosynthesis from the photic zone, while hydrothermal vents rely on chemosynthesis in the aphotic zone.
- Different consumers: sharks, hagfish and amphipods feed directly on whale fall, while tube worms feed directly on 'food' energy from chemosynthetic bacteria near hydrothermal vents.
- Inorganic nutrients are produced by whale decomposition in whale falls whereas they are released directly from hydrothermal vents.

7 Primary succession occurs when a new deep-sea vent emerges, i.e. this is a newly formed habitat where there has never been a community before. Secondary succession occurs after hydrothermal vents, which previously supported a community, have been destroyed by a volcanic eruption.

8 Extreme environment
- Any two extreme conditions: high temperature, high pressure, low pH
- Few organisms are adapted to survive
- Species example: tube worms, clams, mussels

- No light / no photosynthesis / little energy for consumers

9 Rocky shores are less extreme than hydrothermal vents having a more optimum pH, temperature and pressure for marine organisms to live in. The stable substrate and high light intensity allows photoautotrophs to be abundant ensuring that there is lots of food energy for consumers. The larger range of habitats and niches leads to a higher biodiversity.

Chapter 3

1 New biomass can be added to the ocean through photosynthesis or chemosynthesis.

2 Below 200 m all the light has either been scattered or absorbed by the water. Light is essential for photosynthesis and therefore productivity.

3 Hydrothermal vents are a very inhospitable environment. The temperature varies from near freezing to 400 °C and there is high pressure.

4

	process	
feature	chemosynthesis	photosynthesis
energy source	chemicals such as hydrogen sulfide	light energy
products	sulfur, water and sugar	oxygen and sugar/ glucose
type of organism	chemoautotroph/ bacteria	photoautotroph/ phytoplankton/ algae/seagrass
main location in ocean	hydrothermal vents at seabed	upper layers of ocean/photic zone

5 Gross primary production is the amount of energy fixed by producers. Net primary production is the amount of energy that the producers can use to build new biomass after respiration has been taken into account. NPP = GPP – R

6 a R = 22 kJ m^{-2} year^{-1} because NPP = GPP – R
so 31 = 53 – R

b Organisms respire in order to release energy from stored carbohydrate. The energy is used for life processes such as reproduction and movement.

7 a Include at least one good and one bad point for each method.

method	good point	bad point
light/dark bottle method	relatively easy to do, measures gross and net productivity, allows comparison at different depths so that compensation point can be found	will be inaccurate if heterotrophic organisms are not removed, results may have to be converted from oxygen produced to a different unit, assumes rate of respiration remains the same in the dark and the light, requires samples to be taken and incubated
accumulation of biomass	relatively easy to do, allows different ecosystems to be compared, can be used for producers which are too big to fit into a bottle	only gives an estimate of NPP, does not take into account biomass that has already been eaten
chlorophyll concentrations	enables us to compare worldwide productivity, many images are available so that productivity can be compared at different times of year	chlorophyll concentration will depend on the species of producer being measured, satellites cannot penetrate the entire euphotic zone

b The water in an iceberg contains dissolved nutrients. As the iceberg drifts through slightly warmer waters, some of it melts, releasing the nutrients. This allows more phytoplankton to grow and increases the productivity.

8 a If nutrient levels increase too much, this can cause an algal bloom. This can directly damage organisms, e.g. by clogging fish gills. It can also produce high levels of toxins causing poisoning. When the algae die, bacteria populations increase and use up the oxygen in the water in respiration. This can lead to anoxic conditions.

b Tropical waters are clear because they have low levels of nutrients. This limits the rate of photosynthesis and therefore the productivity. Water at higher latitudes has a small thermocline (the temperature gradient between shallow and deep waters) so there is more mixing of nutrients from the deeper water.

9 a 1% of 1 000 000 is 10 000 so the GPP is 10 000 kJ m^{-2} year^{-1}

b NPP = GPP – respiration

if respiration = 30%, NPP = 70%

70/100 × 10 000 = 7000 kJ m^{-2} year^{-1}

10 Efficiency of energy transfer depends on:

- how much food is eaten
- how easy it is for the consumer to digest and assimilate the nutrients
- how much energy is used for movement
- how much is lost in waste products of metabolism
- whether organisms in the food chain are ectothermic or endothermic.

11 Difficult to find the numbers of organisms present in each trophic level; hard to find a scale that allows numbers to be plotted accurately; organisms such as parasites are tiny, so there will be more of them than the organism they feed on; pyramids can be an odd shape. Phytoplankton can be eaten before they are counted but still be very productive because they have a high reproductive rate.

12 The wet mass is unreliable (e.g. amount of water will be higher if an animal has recently eaten). Water is not part of the biomass (mass of living material) and should not be counted.

13 An inverted pyramid is upside down: the bottom layer (producers) is the smallest and not the largest. This can happen if the producer is very large and the consumers are small (e.g. beetles feeding on an oak tree). In aquatic ecosystems, it normally occurs because a standing crop has been used: the number of phytoplankton present at a particular moment in time. Much of the phytoplankton is eaten very quickly but because they have a high reproductive rate, they can still support large numbers of zooplankton.

Chapter 4

1 a Biotic part means the living part of the nutrient cycle; any part of the cycle where the nutrient is found within a living organism. Abiotic means the non-living part of the nutrient cycle; any part of the cycle where the nutrient is present as an inorganic molecule.

b Nutrients move from the abiotic to the biotic part when they are absorbed and assimilated by producers. For example, carbon dioxide (abiotic / inorganic) is fixed during photosynthesis into glucose (biotic / organic).

2 a Within the biotic part of the cycle nutrients move by feeding – they move through the food chain when consumers eat the producers.

b Nutrients are found in rocks, sediments, dissolved in water (in soil or in rivers, lakes and oceans) and in the atmosphere during the abiotic part of the cycle.

3 Upwelling increases the nutrients available to the phytoplankton and therefore increases the rate of photosynthesis. Productivity increases and there is more food for the consumers. So, the numbers of both producers and consumers increase.

4 Nitrogen and carbon dioxide gases are both present in the atmosphere so can dissolve in water. Phosphate is not present in atmospheric gas so cannot dissolve in water.

5 Nutrients are removed from the water by uptake and assimilation by producers. They can then be eaten by consumers and thus enter the food chain.

6 Marine snow is formed from faeces and dead and decaying organic matter that falls from the surface layer to the deeper ocean. The majority of marine snow ends up at the bottom of the ocean in the sediment.

7 Coral shells are made from calcium carbonate so the two important nutrients involved are calcium and carbon.

8 Harvesting is important to marine nutrient cycles because it removes nutrients that have entered the food chain from the oceans. This means there are fewer nutrients in the surface water. This could be limiting the productivity of producers which would be harmful. However, it could be beneficial by preventing the nutrient levels reaching very high levels and causing eutrophication and harmful algal blooms. It can also be argued that the harvest feeds huge numbers of people worldwide. Clearly this is beneficial to those people.

9 The positive effect of more carbon dioxide is increased productivity due to more photosynthesis by phytoplankton. The negative effect is decreased pH affecting shell formation by organisms such as coral.

10

type of microorganism	function in the nitrogen cycle
diazotrophs	fix nitrogen gas into ammonia
saprophytic bacteria	break down proteins in dead matter into amino acids
ammonifying bacteria	break down amino acids into ammonia
nitrifying bacteria	oxidise ammonia into nitrite and nitrate
denitrifying bacteria	convert nitrates and ammonia back into nitrogen gas

11

nutrient	biological use
nitrogen	proteins
carbon	all organic materials (e.g. glucose, lipids, proteins)
magnesium	chlorophyll
calcium	bones, shell and coral
phosphorus	bones and DNA

12 More than average rainfall will mean that there is more surface run-off as less of the water will be able to infiltrate the soil.

Chapter 5

1 Coral reefs are most commonly found between 30 °N and 30 °S of the equator because these tropical waters have the warmest temperatures, low levels of nutrients and clear waters.

2 The physical factor linked most closely with coral's symbiotic relationship is sunlight. The zooxanthellae need sunlight in order to photosynthesise. The products of photosynthesis are then given to the coral, allowing it to have enough energy to build its coral skeleton, so creating the reef. Other factors tied to sunlight are reef depth and water clarity.

3 The youngest of the reef types is the fringing reef, which forms early along the edge of an oceanic volcano. If present, the lagoon in a fringing reef is very narrow, unlike those of the slightly older (geologically speaking) barrier reefs that tend to have deeper and wider lagoons. Atolls tend to form a circular pattern with a lagoon in the centre that can be very wide and deep. They form far away from land and tend to be the oldest of the reefs.

4 The evidence used to support the Darwin–Dana–Daly theory of atoll formation comes primarily from the fossilised coral existing at the very bottom of atolls. Because healthy coral growth happens within 20 m of the surface, these fossilised corals indicate that at one time the surface was much closer. The best explanation for fossilised corals at the base of a coral reef 1200 m deep is that the land has slowly sunk into the seabed, taking the coral down with it.

5 The major factors leading to reef erosion include predation by animals like the crown-of-thorns starfish, damage from tropical cyclones, exposure to air at low tides and ocean acidification.

6 Artificial reefs work to protect the shoreline by creating a natural breakwater. By slowing down waves and reducing their height, the artificial reef is able to reduce the amount of sand the water is able to hold thereby preserving the shoreline.

7 Surfers tend to like large waves to surf on. Artificial reefs are designed to reduce wave height and power, making the waves less fun to surf.

8 Deep drilling allows scientists to take core samples from corals that can show the different species that have inhabited the reef over time. The results of carbon dating the corals in the samples support the theory that the oldest corals are the deepest. These data provide evidence supporting the Darwin–Dana–Daly theory of atoll formation.

Chapter 6

1 Continental drift theory (CDT) is an earlier version of plate tectonics (PT). In both theories, fossil evidence, fit of the coastlines, and geological structures on multiple continents are used to show that the planet's continents are moving apart. CDT failed to provide the mechanism for the movement, thus making it an incomplete theory.

2 PT is supported by evidence such as SONAR maps, convection currents in the mantle and magnetic stripes on the ocean floor.

3 Tsunamis form when submarine earthquakes or volcanoes erupt releasing large amounts of stored energy that move the water above them. This movement creates a long-wavelength wave that builds until it reaches shallow water. At that point, the wave increases in size and crashes onto the shore causing great damage.

4 New rock is created at divergent boundaries as magma emerges from the crust, cools and solidifies. Old rock is destroyed at convergent boundaries as oceanic crust sinks into the asthenosphere and slides under continental crust.

5 Technology had to be invented to withstand the amount of pressure located that deep within the ocean.

6 This environment is classified as extreme. The incredible pressure and lack of light are major physical factors an organism has to adapt to, and the range of temperatures and toxicity of the water make this an extreme habitat. Organisms that live here have to contend with temperatures changing from 4 °C to over 300 °C over just a few metres. Additionally, the minerals spewing from the vents make the water uninhabitable for organisms not adapted to it.

7 Continental shelves near convergent plates tend to be narrow because these boundaries tend to create trenches with steep sides.

8 During times when water is not frozen into large glaciers, it covers the continental shelf. Because the continental shelf has a lower density than the oceanic crust, it floats higher on the mantle, creating a raised area for the water to settle on and create a shallow sea.

9 Estuaries are semi-enclosed and protected, reducing the amount of erosion that occurs, whereas deltas are places of direct contact between river and sea and face a great deal of erosion.

10 Rocky shores provide a stable substrate for attachment and places to hide from predators. Sandy shores are susceptible to erosion and wave action so it is difficult to survive there. More organisms are capable of adapting to life in a rocky shore.

11 The prop roots of the red mangrove act as a cage slowing building up land through sedimentation. These roots also act as protective cages for fish, crabs and other invertebrates from larger predators.

Chapter 7

1 Oxygen, carbon dioxide, and nitrogen. Oxygen is used by consumers for respiration; carbon dioxide is used by producers for photosynthesis and also by corals to create the calcium carbonate necessary for their skeletons; nitrogen is used by all organisms in the production of proteins and DNA.

2 Volcanoes add many ions into the ocean, particularly chloride ions. Scientists believe underwater volcanoes may be the reason why chloride ions outnumber all of the other ions in today's oceans. Run-off is capable of bringing nutrients like nitrogen and phosphorus into the ocean, but also of bringing in pollutants like pesticide and fertiliser.

3 Temperature and density have an inverse relationship or negative correlation: as temperature increases, density decreases. Salinity and density have a positive correlation: as salinity increases, density increases. When taken together, temperature has a greater impact on density than salinity.

4

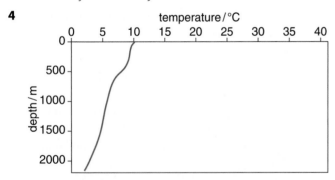

5 Answers should indicate that a quarter moon would be preferable because a neap tide is occurring, so the highest tide is lower than normal. A lower tide means less of a storm surge, so there will be less flooding and erosion of the shore.

6 Currents at the surface are masses of water blowing in the same direction caused by the wind. Deep-water currents are moved by density changes. Tides are the predictable movement of water based on the gravitational effects of the Moon and Sun. Tides are not affected by winds, density, or temperature.

7 Wind patterns in the Southern Pacific Ocean typically blow from east to west along the equator. During El Niño, these wind patterns are reduced. This causes warm water to spread back east, preventing the upwelling of nutrient-rich bottom water. These changes in weather patterns and sea surface temperature are called the El Niño Southern Oscillation.

8 El Niño causes excessive warm water to build up along the equator, so tropical cyclones form more easily than usual. Tropical cyclones in the Pacific have greater access to warm water and high winds.

Chapter 8

1 *Absorption spectrum:* a graph of the absorbance of different wavelengths of light by a compound such as a photosynthetic pigment

Action spectrum: a graph showing the effect of different wavelengths of light on a process, e.g. on the rate of photosynthesis

2 a They will show where photosynthesis is occurring along the algal filament and so which wavelengths of light are used in photosynthesis

b Areas that are undergoing photosynthesis

c Algae only photosynthesise using light at the red and blue ends of the spectrum / not with green. The bacteria have moved towards those regions illuminated with red and blue light and that is where the oxygen is being produced.

3 In deeper water there is no red light, only blue and green parts of the spectrum. A red object will absorb all colours of light except red so the red tank absorbs blue and green light and as there is no red light to reflect, it appears black.

4 All colours of light are present at the surface so there is no 'need' to absorb green light. The cost of producing the phycobilins must be greater than the gain in absorbing other areas of the spectrum.

5 Coastal waters have more run-off of soil from rivers and beaches. The wave action moves the sand and other particulate material on beaches, increasing water turbidity and reducing light penetration.

6 Having two readings increases the accuracy and reliability of the mean. Only recording the depth once could cause the risk of an anomalous reading.

7 Light intensity must have been limiting the rate of photosynthesis. By repeating the experiment at 10 arbitrary units of light, the rate of photosynthesis increases.

8 *Sargassum:*
- Pneumatocysts / air bladders/ floats – for distribution and to enable *Sargassum* to remain at the surface water where light, CO_2 and warmth are optimal. The water is too deep to allow anchorage.
- No roots / vascular transport tissue needed as minerals are taken up directly by fronds

Seagrass:
- Deep roots and rhizomes for anchorage and asexual reproduction.
- Aerenchyma tissue present to provide oxygen
- Flexible leaves to move in currents
- Physiologically adapted to saline to prevent osmotic damage
- Thin epidermis in leaves with chloroplasts
- Stomata are absent
- Leaves have little vascular tissue as they take up minerals directly from water

Fucus spiralis
- Holdfast to attach to rock
- Spiral fronds to reduce water loss by evaporation and trap water
- Phycoerythrin and phycocyanin pigments to trap areas of spectrum in deeper water where there is less red light

Chapter 9

1

	aerobic respiration	anaerobic respiration
use of oxygen	yes	no
products	carbon dioxide and water	lactate (animals) ethanol and carbon dioxide (plants and fungi)
energy yield	high (up to 38 ATP)	low (2 ATP)
occurs in mitochondria	yes	no

2
- The body temperature of cold-blooded organisms is equal to the water temperature which is colder in winter
- Therefore the kinetic energy of intracellular molecules and enzymes is low
- Therefore the collision frequency of molecules and enzymes involved in respiration is low
- Low respiration rate means that energy release is low
- Therefore there is less energy for muscle contraction

3
- Rapid aerobic respiration uses oxygen at a high rate
- Concentration of oxygen inside cells is therefore kept low
- Maintains a diffusion gradient of oxygen from outside cell to inside
- Rapid production of carbon dioxide in the cell
- Maintains a diffusion gradient of carbon dioxide from inside to outside

4
- Oxygen concentration of water could fall
- As warmer water has a reduced concentration of oxygen
- It is also possible that oxygen concentration could rise
- As salinity will reduce due to ice cap melting
- And lower salinity water can have a higher oxygen concentration

379

5

species	method of gas exchange	advantages	disadvantages
coral polyp	passive diffusion over body surface	no energy expenditure	limited ability to maintain diffusion gradient by movements/blood circulation; low speed of gas exchange so activity levels are limited
tuna	ram ventilation	little or no energy expenditure enables rapid movement of water over gills	fish must swim continuously so cannot remain hidden from predators speed of water movement requires gill adaptations for strength
grouper	pumped ventilation	fish does not have to swim constantly so can hide from predators/eq	speed of ventilation is not as fast as ram ventilation; muscle contraction requires use of energy

6 a • Warmer water has less dissolved oxygen
 • Active fish have a higher respiration rate
 • A higher respiration rate uses up oxygen faster
 • Therefore the highly active fish run out of available oxygen
 • (accept converse)

b • Gill parasites damage surface of gills
 • This reduces gill surface area
 • Reduced surface area of gills reduces rate/volume of oxygen diffused into blood
 • Therefore the growth rate of the salmon is reduced

c • When lamellae stick together, the surface area exposed to oxygen/air is reduced
 • Therefore less oxygen diffuses into blood so there is less respiration in muscles
 • The fish suffocate

7 2 mol dm^{-3} sodium chloride solution, 1.5 mol dm^{-3} sodium chloride solution, 0.2 mol dm^{-3} sodium chloride solution, pure water

8 a • Water potential outside cells is higher than inside cells
 • Water enters cells by osmosis
 • Increasing pressure on cell walls (turgor) so cells press against each other

b • Sugar dissolves in water on surface of fruit
 • Water potential inside cells is higher than outside
 • Water leaves cells by osmosis so a syrup forms outside the cells

c • Salt dissolves in water producing very high salt concentration
 • Water potential in fish cells/bacterial cells is higher inside cells so water exits cells by osmosis into salt
 • Therefore, no water present for bacterial decay/bacteria are killed due to water loss

9 • In river, water potential of river water is higher than fish body fluids
 • Fish actively pumps salts into body fluid/cells
 • Fish produces large urine volume to remove excess water
 • In sea, water potential of sea is lower than body fluids
 • Water leaves fish cells by osmosis and salts diffuse in.
 • Fish drinks to replace lost water
 • Fish actively pumps salts out of blood and releases salts in urine
 • Fish produces small volume of urine

10

process	substances moved	direction of gradient	additional energy	membrane required
diffusion	any small molecules	higher concentration to lower concentration	no	no
osmosis	water only	higher water potential to lower water potential (lower concentration of solute to higher concentration of solute)	no	yes
active transport	any small molecules, typically ions	lower concentration to higher concentration	yes	yes

Chapter 10

1 Advantages: dispersal of organism, reduced competition for food, reduced risk of cannibalism in predatory species,

Disadvantages: often reduced parent care so risk of mortality, more susceptible to pollution / environmental changes

2 Supply of oxygen for respiration and bringing food

3 Advantages: random fertilisation increasing genetic diversity;

Disadvantages: many eggs remain unfertilised / are lost / eaten

4 Difference: giant clams are hermaphrodites / oysters have separate sexes;

Similarities: broadcast spawning; external fertilisation; planktonic larvae; trochophore larvae; veliger larvae; pediveliger larvae with foot; settling occurs; sessile adults

5 Mangroves act as nursery grounds providing food and shelter for juveniles

6 Similarities: several larval stages; adults in open sea; both have planktonic larvae; juvenile stage in mangrove / estuarine regions; both change sex;

Differences: shrimp start as male and become female / groupers start as female and become male; shrimp have more larval stages; shrimp mate in pairs / groupers use a form of blanket spawning

7 *r*-strategists: many offspring, very little parental care, e.g. tuna, giant clams, oyster

K-strategists: few offspring, high levels of parental care, e.g. sharks, whales

Chapter 11

1

fishing method	negative effects on fish stocks and habitats
purse seine	• reduces fish stocks by taking many fish • risk of bycatch of other species such as sharks, tuna, dolphins, turtles
benthic trawl	• risk of over-fishing • high risk of bycatch • severe damage to seabed habitats disrupting ecosystems
factory ship	• risk of over-fishing • risk of over-fishing in previously unexploited areas

2 a • Reduced catch
  • Higher natural mortality due to predation

b • Increased catch
  • More fish are able to reproduce
  • Increasing recruitment
  • May be a consequence of reduced population
  • So catches would reduce

c • Reduce catch
  • Reduced recruitment

3 a Population increase from recruitment = (15/100) × 325 000 = 48 750

Population decrease from natural mortality = (10/100) × 325 000 = 32 750

Net increase = 48 750 – 32 750 = 16 000

Possible fish harvest = 16 000 fish

381

b • High mass could be due to fewer, larger fish or many smaller fish

• Number does not give an idea of sizes of fish and there may be large numbers of immature, smaller fish

4 The principal tools that can be used to achieve sustainable fishing include restricting fishing by area and season. Restrictions on fishing gear can also be imposed such as enforcing the use of rod and line fishing and increasing the minimum mesh size of nets. Labelling seafood as dolphin-friendly is an example of a market-oriented tool enabling consumers to make informed choices.

5 • Reduces pressure on fish stocks

• Fish stocks are maintained at a healthy level

• Recruitment increases

• So that fishing at a lower intensity can continue

(Idea is that it will enable fishing at a lower intensity in the future, rather than high intensity for a short period followed by no fishing)

6 Mangroves:

• Try to recreate / restore habitat

• Create food chains and links

• For long-term preservation of stocks

• Take time to establish

• Helps wild fish breed and increase

• May not grow if planted incorrectly

• Also protects from coastal erosion

Introducing cultivated fish:

• Increases fish population

• Using hatched fish

• May damage existing wild fish by altering gene pool / introducing disease

• May be a short-term measure as habitat may not sustain the population

7 a By satellite / VMS monitoring followed by targeted air / sea patrols

b By random checks by inspector of catch at sea, on landing and at fish markets

c By air and sea patrols, random checks at sea, sending inspectors onto boats during fishing trips

Chapter 12

1 a Semi-intensive

b Extensive

c Intensive

d Semi-intensive

2 • Tanks are separated from natural water, cages are placed into natural water.

• Tanks have fresh water pumping system, cages have tidal flow

• Tanks have waste removal system, cages rely on tidal flow

• Tanks have regulated salinity / temperature, cages have salinity / temperature of natural water

• Cages have water currents bringing natural food

• Tanks and cages may have extra food added

• Tanks and cages may have pesticides and antibiotics added but they are easier to control in tanks

3 Similarities:

• Both are kept in nets / cages

• In some cages, both use trapped juveniles

• Both require added feed

• both require fish / live food

Differences:

• grouper has different stages

• groupers may be spawned rather than trapped

• juvenile tuna are towed to the site in open ocean, juvenile groupers are placed in ponds

4 • High demand for Bluefin tuna

• High price paid for Bluefin tuna

• Overfishing / catching more than can be reproduced

• Juveniles are collected before breeding

5 • Pollution from faeces / food / pesticides / antibiotics

• Leads to eutrophication / bioaccumulation / bacterial resistance

• Spread of disease to wild shrimp

• Loss of habitat – mangroves

6 • Food product

• Conservation programmes

• Aquaria

7 • More disposable income
- More demand for luxury products
- Prices of bluefin tuna rise
- More wealth

8 • Less faeces produced / less waste
- All feed eaten / feed not wasted
- Less organic waste
- So less algal growth / decay / eutrophication

9 • Loss of habitat
- Escape of fish
- Loss of ecological niches
- Disruption to food chains
- Competition with wild species
- Spread of disease
  Pollution (eutrophication / pesticide release)

10 • Organic waste is removed by crabs / lobster on base
- Seaweed grown to remove nitrates and phosphates
- Mussels and molluscs grown on ropes to remove small particles of organic waste

Chapter 13

1 Any three of (suggested possibilities as there may be other correct answers):
- Poisoned by ingestion
- Suffocated by covered blowhole / gills damaged
- Lungs damaged by fumes
- Poisoned by dispersant
- Immobilised by oil in feathers / fur so drown / eaten by predators
- Die of hypothermia due to feathers / fur covered by oil
- Die due to lack of food
- Die due to loss of nest site

2 One method for protecting the coast from oil spills to spray on dispersants. This causes the oil to break up into smaller droplets and sink to the seabed. Once it has sunk, bacteria begin to breakdown the oil. The temperature at the seabed is low so that the rate of bacterial respiration is slow. This means that it can

take many years for the oil to finally be removed by this process of bioremediation

3 a • Agricultural run-off of fertilisers and organic waste
- Oil spills being broken down by respiring bacteria
- Organic sediment dispersal into the water during dredging
- Sewage release containing organic waste into the water
- High temperature of brine from desalination plants

b • Oil spills from chemicals in oil and dispersant
- Pesticides from agriculture
- Toxins absorbed by waste plastic that is ingested by marine organisms
- Toxins in sewage dumped in sea
- Toxins and cleaning substances from desalination plant
- Toxin release from sediment during dredging

c • Crude oil spill on water surface blocking light
- Sediment disturbance when waste brine released from desalination plant
- Sediment disturbance during dredging
- Organic waste from agricultural run-off and algal blooms blocking light
- Microparticles of plastic from refuse
- Organic material in sewage

4 a Suggested examples:
- Reduce fertiliser use
- Site farms away from rivers
- Prevent dumping of waste in rivers
- Do not use fertilisers during rainy periods
- Do not use fertilisers when crops are not growing

b Suggested examples:
- Purify water / send through treatment plant before release into sea
- Improve sewerage so waste is not directly released into sea / river
- Separate organic sewage from detergents / toxic wastes
- Collect industrial sewage separately

383

c Suggested examples:
  - Use biodegradable plastics
  - Fines to prevent dumping old nets
  - Encourage recycling
  - Reduce use of plastic bags / bottles
  - Introduce taxes on disposable plastics
  - Secure cargo on ships better

5 • Swordfish contain high levels of mercury and other toxins
  - Due to bioaccumulation and biomagnification
  - The developing baby has a smaller mass so toxins will have a higher relative concentration

6 • TBT was used as an antifouling agent
  - Ships accumulate living organisms that affect the hydrodynamics / affect drag
  - Which uses more fuel and costs increase
  - TBT is highly toxic to many species
  - It accumulates in food chains affecting non-target organisms
  - Causes deformities in molluscs

7

factor	source of evidence
global temperature rise	• weather monitoring stations • ice core data
atmospheric carbon dioxide and methane levels rise	• Mauna Loa data • ice core data
ice sheet loss	• satellite monitoring
changes of animal and plant ranges	• (scientific monitoring)
weather pattern changes / climate change	• weather monitoring stations (meteorological data)
coral bleaching	• reports from scientists / divers

8 Global warming could have serious consequences for our oceans. An increased temperature could lead to the ranges of organisms changing which may bring them into conflict with other species. As a result of this, species may become extinct and that could have effects on other organisms in food webs. Acidification of the water and increased temperatures could cause coral bleaching. In addition, ice sheets could melt, raising sea-levels and reducing the salinity of the water which could kill organisms that cannot osmoregulate.

Chapter 14

1 a • Ethics / responsibility to the planet
  - For future generations
  - To maintain ecosystems / food chains / webs
  - Our recreation / maintain fishing / medicines
  - Extinction is a natural event
  - Not worth conserving species that are nearly extinct
  - Costs are too high
  - Prevents progress / revenue
  - Can damage other species and habitats

  b The current mass extinction is caused by human activity while previous extinctions were probably sudden catastrophic events such as meteorite collision.

2 If top predators are absent, the conservation of the conserved species can lead to over-population of the conserved species. This can then cause over-predation or over-grazing of lower trophic levels reducing their populations.

3 Many human activities have damaged the environment and produced a need for conservation. There has been extensive damage to habitats such as mangrove forests, coral reefs and seagrass. The fishing industry has caused fish stocks to be reduced due to overfishing and the catching of bycatch. Humans have released pollutants into the oceans such as TBT and mercury which bioaccumulate along food chains. The escape of fish from aquaculture has led to invasive species affecting native populations.

4 a • ensures adequate food source
  - correct predator population to ensure overpopulation does not occur
  - ensures correct habitat/nesting sites

  b • Locals gain financial benefit from the conservation
  - More likely to ensure it succeeds if their livelihood depends on it

5 a • Smell of fish deters tourists
  - Fishing boats interfere with tourist boats / beaches / diving / activities
  - Fishing reduces fish stocks / damages reefs that tourists come to see

- Tourism scares fish
- The two create competition for employment
- Tourism cause price inflation
- Tourist boats damage fishing areas / get in way of fishing boats / damage nets

b • Pollution from aquaculture kills wild fish reducing catches
- Fish prices are reduced due to competition
- Parasites released into wild affect wild stocks
- Competition for employment
- Damage to traditional shellfish fishing areas such as mangroves

c • Run-off pollution damages reefs / reduces fish stocks
- Sediment from agricultural run-off damages reefs / benthic organisms
- Tourists are less likely to visit if reefs / marine attractions are damaged
- Competition for land between agriculture and tourist resorts
- Competition for employment

6 a • Restrictions on catches and methods reduces catch and profits
- No-take areas prevent fishing
- Restrictions on building / number of visitors / restricted access areas reduces tourism profits

b • Preservation of fish stocks maintains future of the industry
- Spill over of fish from no-take zone into fished zones increases catches
- Maintaining the area increases tourist numbers
- Ecotourism brings more revenue

7 a Visiting a natural area in a sustainable manner without damaging the habitats, species or local communities

b Individuals who have an interest in an area, project or activity

8 a • Prevents accumulation of plastics and other refuse in a natural area
- Prevents damage to species due to ingestion or being trapped in refuse
- Produces useful products that can be used in the resort reducing need to manufacture new items or import them

b • Reduces fossil fuel burning
- Sustainable method of producing electricity
- Reduces carbon dioxide emissions
- Reduces global warming

c • Minimises imports reducing fuel use and carbon emissions
- Provides locals with employment and keeps money in the area
- Reduces non-sustainable, non-renewable materials

Chapter 15

1 • Slower bacterial respiration and reproduction rates
- Due to less frequent collision of particle with enzymes
- Less dispersal / mixing of oil due to increased viscosity and less turbulence
- Less surface area exposed to the bacteria

2 • Bacteria require mineral ions such as phosphates and nitrates
- For rapid growth which will occur when nutrients such as oil are present
- So the minerals could limit bacterial growth
- Large numbers of bacteria would have a high respiration rate
- Reducing oxygen levels for other organisms
- High mineral ions would also encourage algal blooms
- Which would undergo eutrophication eventually reducing oxygen

3 a Alleles are different forms of particular genes. A gene is a section of DNA that codes for a protein / characteristic. Organisms have two copies of each gene, these two copies could carry the same or different alleles.

b Phenotype is the physical effect of the genotype of an organism and its interaction with the environment; genotype is the genetic composition of an organism.

c Dominant allele only requires one copy to see the effect in the phenotype; recessive alleles require two copies to see the effects in the phenotype.

d Homozygous is the possession of two identical alleles; heterozygous is the possession of two different alleles.

4
- Select rapidly growing fish
- Cull / discard all slow-growing fish
- Allow rapidly growing fish to spawn / mate
- Check offspring and select rapidly growing individuals to breed from, discarding slow-growing individuals.
- Repeat over several generations

5 a Ensure that fish do not become inbred and become weaker for some characteristics / more disease susceptible. Check fish for abnormalities / keep logs of breeding / occasionally rebreed with different stocks.

b Ensure that fish escape is prevented by using nets / tanks / preventing predators getting in / using sterile fish.

6 Flow chart should include the following steps:
- Remove promoter (and terminator) DNA from ocean pout using restriction endonucleases.
- Remove growth hormone gene from chinook salmon using restriction endonucleases.
- Cut plasmid vector with same restriction endonuclease
- Attach plasmid vector, growth hormone gene and promoter (and terminator) together using DNA ligase.
- Inject DNA into salmon eggs.
- Select transgenic male salmon that have active gene.
- Fertilise female eggs with sperm from transgenic male salmon.
- Pressure shock eggs to make them into infertile fish.
- Grow on fish.

7 a
- Escape
- Outcompete native species for food and mates leading to extinction.
- Over-predation of food sources causing extinction of the food organisms and other organisms that depend upon them.
- Reduced predation by predators, affecting predator populations.
- Cross-breeding with the wild fish.
- Transferring the transgene into the wild populations.

b
- Indoor tanks to keep breeding fish on Prince Edward Island – keeping fish away from rivers / sea.
- Netting to prevent fish escape and predator entry.
- Filtering all waste water to prevent escape of fish eggs / fry.
- Chemical pesticides used to kill any eggs in waste water.
- Growing fish in Panama where climate would not allow escaped salmon to survive / no wild fish to interbreed with.
- Pressure shocking eggs to make them triploid so adult fish will be sterile.
- Only using female eggs to reduce breeding if they escape.

8 a Similarities:
- Both aim to improve stock.
- Both involve introduction / manipulation of genes.

Differences:
- Selective breeding uses mate choice.
- No need for advanced technology in selective breeding.
- Selective breeding only uses genes already present within a species / genetic engineering involves the transfer of genes from different species.

b Possible factors include:
- Safety for human consumption would have to be proved.
- No chance of escape of the shrimp or the gametes / larvae.
- Fine mesh nets used / method for preventing escape.
- Method for killing off shrimp / eggs / larvae in waste water.
- Shrimp rendered infertile so cannot breed if they escape.
- The potential effects on the environment would need evaluating and modelling.
- The cost-effectiveness of the programme and how it might affect other fishing industries.

Chapter 3

Practical activity 3.1

1 The indicator is very sensitive to changes in pH so the equipment must be rinsed to make sure it is not contaminated by any residue.

2 As a control, to allow comparison with the other tubes and to show what happens to the indicator without any pondweed.

3 To make sure changes in atmospheric carbon dioxide (for example from someone breathing out) did not affect the results.

4 Answers depend on results and predictions.

5 Unwrapped with pondweed – should turn purple because the rate of photosynthesis is greater than the rate of respiration, so amount of carbon dioxide decreases.

   Wrapped in muslin – should stay red because the rate of photosynthesis is equal to the rate of respiration, so no net change in the amount of carbon dioxide. It is at the compensation point.

   Wrapped in foil – should turn yellow because it is in the dark and unable to photosynthesise. Rate of respiration is greater than rate of photosynthesis, so the amount of carbon dioxide increases.

   Unwrapped but no pondweed – depending on how long the tubes are left for it either remains red because there is no change in carbon dioxide or turns orange/yellow because it absorbs carbon dioxide from the air within the tube.

6 Suitable suggestions
   • Measure the colour of the hydrogencarbonate with a colorimeter. This allows the amount of carbon dioxide to be assessed more accurately and objectively.
   • Use a wider range of light intensities and a light meter to find the actual light intensity that corresponds to the compensation point.
   • Use different wavelengths of light.
   • Repeat the experiment with an algal culture to find its compensation point.
   • Any other sensible suggestion.

Practical activity 3.2

Sample results and calculations

	light tray	dark tray
initial wet mass/g	57	n/a
final wet mass/g	74	54
initial dry mass/g	24	n/a
final dry mass/g	36	22

Final mass in the light – initial mass = net primary productivity

Dry 36 – 24 = 12 g   Wet 74 – 57 = 17 g

Final mass in the dark – initial mass = respiration (negative because the plants lose mass)

Dry 22 – 24 = –2 g   Wet 54 – 57 = –3 g

Gross primary productivity = net primary productivity + respiration (ignore the – sign)

Dry 12 + 2 = 14 g   Wet 17 + 3 = 20 g

These figures could be multiplied by 400 to give results in g m^{-2} week^{-1}

1 The wet masses are bigger and possibly more variable.

2 The rate of respiration – these plants are unable to photosynthesise and will almost certainly lose mass. Any gain is due to stored carbohydrates.

3 This gives the biomass at the beginning of the experiment.

4 The dry mass should be more reliable (similar results in each group in the class). This is because the water content of the plant varies depending on the availability of water.

5 You have assumed that the rate of respiration is the same in the light as it is in the dark. Also that the only two processes that could affect the mass of the plants are photosynthesis and respiration.

Chapter 4

Practical activity 4.1

1 After being placed in acid, some or all of the eggshell dissolves. The egg is much softer than normal. If handled too roughly, the egg may burst, releasing the yolk.

2 As the ocean becomes more acidic, there is a risk that marine organisms that rely on calcium carbonate shells will be damaged as their shells are weakened by dissolving. This leaves them more vulnerable to damage.

3 Exhaled air contains carbon dioxide. When this dissolves in the water it forms carbonic acid. Universal indicator turns yellow in the presence of an acid.

4 The seawater should take longer to become acidic suggesting that it can absorb more carbon dioxide before it becomes acidic.

5 This suggests that seawater is a more important carbon dioxide sink as it is able to absorb more atmospheric carbon dioxide without changing the pH of the water.

6 First, because there is a much higher volume of water. Second, because there are living organisms present which are able to use the carbon dioxide and its dissolved forms which removes carbon dioxide from the water.

7 You could investigate the time taken for water to become acidic at different temperatures or test different volumes of water. You could also measure the acidity more accurately using a pH meter or use a colorimeter to determine accurately changes in the colour with universal indicators.

Practical activity 4.2

1 Shape of graphs depends on student results but there should be an initial rise in ammonia levels, followed by decreasing ammonia levels and increasing nitrite. The nitrite should then decrease as the nitrate increases.

2 The ammonia increases as the fish or prawns which were added to the tank rot. The proteins in the fish are broken down by decomposers into amino acids. Ammonifying bacteria then convert the amino acids into ammonia so the levels of ammonia initially increase. Later, nitrifying bacteria start to convert the ammonia into nitrite so the ammonia levels decrease and the nitrite levels increase. Finally, different nitrifying bacteria convert the nitrite into nitrate so the nitrite levels fall and the nitrate levels rise.

3 To provide a source of ammonia as they decompose.

4 Bacteria are naturally present in the water which was added to the tank.

5 This depends on student results.

6 If there are anomalous results, this is probably due to problems with the test kits or human error in reading the concentration. If there are no anomalous results, the answer should focus on all of the results fitting the expected pattern and perhaps being close to the line of best fit on the graph.

7 Since ammonia is damaging to fish, they should not be introduced before there has been a period of time longer than it took for the ammonia concentration to increase and then decrease during this investigation. This is normally 2 to 3 weeks.

Chapter 5

Practical activity 5.1

1 The independent variable is the pH of the solution used. The dependent variable is the percentage difference in mass of the limestone.

2 The water acts as your control group because it is at a neutral pH.

3 Answers will vary, but you should see a greater loss of mass in limestone after exposure to the vinegar solution.

4 These data can be used to generalise about the impacts of pH change in the oceans on coral reefs. The data illustrate how a reduction in pH leads to an increase in reef erosion.

Chapter 6

Practical activity 6.1

1 The tube demonstrates the settling rates on the different types of shore. The pebbles represent rocky shores; the sand represents sandy shores; and the diatomaceous earth represents the fine silt on a muddy shore.

2 Rocky shore, sandy shore, muddy shore. The pebbles, like larger rocks, settle quickly and are able to withstand a greater amount of wave action without being eroded. The diatomaceous earth takes a very long time to settle and the slightest movement of water stirs it up again. Therefore, a muddy shore needs to have little or no wave action in order to have a substrate.

3 Mangroves help to calm water and capture sediment. By reducing wave action, the mangrove roots slow the water movement enough for fine grains of sand to settle within the root structure. These plants stabilise the shore and reduce erosion.

Chapter 7

Practical activity 7.1

1 The salt water sinks below the fresh water with very little mixing.

2 The salt water is denser than the fresh water.

3 Answers will vary, but should suggest that hot, salty water would sit higher in the water column than cold, salty water.

4 Answers will vary. Sketch should label the halocline as the area between the fresh and salt water.

Chapter 8

Practical activity 8.2

1 To allow the photosynthesis rate for a particular light intensity to stabilise.

2 • Ideally this should show higher rates of photosynthesis when using light of blue and red colours rather than green and orange.

 • Chlorophyll, carotene and xanthophyll collectively absorb light in the red and blue areas of the spectrum but not in the green area.

3 • Bubble sizes are very variable, the photosynthometer measures volume of oxygen produced and so is more accurate.

 • The photosynthometer has a heat shield so the water temperature will not be altered by the lamp.

4 • Brown and red algae have additional pigments such as the phycobilins and xanthophyll. These are able to absorb green light and other parts of the spectrum that the chlorophylls do not. Green algae do not possess these pigments so in deeper waters where there is no red light they are only able to absorb blue light.

Chapter 9

Practical activity 9.1

1 As the surface area : volume ratio decreases, the time take for acid to diffuse increases. The relationship is not linear.

2 As surface area : volume ratio decreases in larger organisms, the body surface is not sufficient for gas exchange. Gills and lungs have evolved to increase gas exchange.

Practical activity 9.2

1 As the concentration initially decreases, the percentage increase in mass should fall. As the concentration continues to increase, there should be an increasing percentage decrease in mass. The graph may or may not level off at the higher concentrations.

2 The graph is shown below.

3 To remove surface water that would increase mass. This water has not entered the cells so has not undergone osmosis.

4 To prevent evaporation of water, which would increase the concentration of the solutions.

Chapter 10

Practical activity 10.1

1 Oyster spats have a preference for the upper or lower surface of the glass sheet/oyster spats have a preference for horizontal/angled/vertical/a particular angle of glass sheet.

2 **a** Independent variable: upper/lower surface of the glass; orientation of the glass.

 b Dependent variable: number of spats on the surface of glass.

3 Location in the oyster bed; wave action/exposure; depth of the glass sheet; exposure to Sun; colour of glass sheet; coating on glass surface.

4 Repeat each glass sheet and calculate a mean.

5 Bar chart or a pie chart as the data is categoric data.

6 The oyster spats settle mainly on the lower surface (B) but also on the horizontal glass. The fewest settle on the vertical surface.

Chapter 11

Practical activity 11.1

1 • Calculate number of fish of different ages on sale at market.

 • Identify underage fish illegally caught.

 • Calculate age structures of fish stocks.

 • Identify if fish are being overexploited and few older fish are being caught.

 • Restrictions can be put into place based on evidence.

389

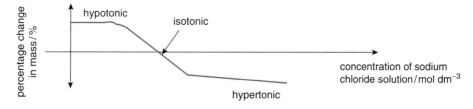

2 a Answers should include the following points:

- ensures a fair test
- so that the years can be compared
- because they are all at same growth stage in life cycles.

b Answers should include the following points:

- fewer fish are sampled in later years
- could reflect lower stocks
- or too low a sample
- ages seem to be declining
- suggesting the fish population is under stress
- there is no evidence about where the fish is obtained and in different years the market may have bought them from different fleets
- the population changes may be due to natural events
- fishing methods may have changed and are not collecting as many older fish
- the days on which samples were taken may have had different sized fish due to consumer demands.

Chapter 12

Practical activity 12.1

1 Investigate the effect of water temperature on the growth of tilapia which normally grow in water temperatures of between 15 and 25 °C.

- Hypothesis: 'As temperature increases, rate of growth of tilapia will increase as metabolic rate increases'.
- Independent variable: temperature, altered by using thermostatically controlled water heater, temperatures between 5 °C and 30 °C at even intervals. Repeats made for reliability.
- Dependent variable: mass or length of tilapia using a balance or ruler; set time for experiment, e.g. two months
- The control variables: food, same quantities, type and feeding frequency; tank size; light intensity, same lighting; salinity, ensure that water is made up

to the same salinity; waste accumulation, water is constantly filtered.

- How many repeats would be made: ideally, three sets of data.
- How the data would be presented: in the form of a line graph with temperature on the x-axis and mass/length/growth rate on the y-axis.

2 Investigate the effect of feeding frequency on the growth rate of tilapia and water pollution. Water pollution can be assessed by measuring the biochemical oxygen demand (BOD) of the water. BOD is a measure of the microbial content of the water; the higher the BOD, the more decomposer microbes are present.

- Hypothesis: 'As feeding frequency increases, rate of growth increases until it levels off and pollution increases'.
- Independent variable: frequency that feed is added, e.g. once each hour, once every two hours.
- Dependent variables: growth rate, mass or length in set time; water pollution, BOD measured over set times.
- The control variables: temperature, thermostatically controlled heater; tank size; light intensity, same lighting; salinity, ensure that water is made up to the same salinity; waste accumulation, water is constantly filtered.
- How many repeats would be made: ideally three sets of data.
- How the data would be presented: line graph with two separate y-axes for growth rate and pollution; if independent variable is categoric (e.g. high feed rate vs low feed rate) bar chart should be plotted, if it is linear, a line graph should be plotted.

Chapter 13

Practical activity 13.1

Sample results

A table for each variable with the independent variable (number of drops of fertiliser) in the left column.

number of drops of fertiliser in water	nitrate concentration for each day / mg dm^{-3}								
	day 0	day 2	day 4	day 6	day 8	day 10	day 12	day 14	day 16
0									
40									
80									
120									

The data could be presented as a series of graphs for each factor. Each graph should have the number of days on the x-axis and the dependent variable (e.g. nitrate concentration) on the y-axis. Four lines or sets of bars can then be plotted on the same axes, one for each fertiliser concentration.

1   The water may go green due to the reproduction of phytoplankton in the water. The higher concentration of fertiliser would be expected to go more deeply green. Towards the end of the experiment, the bottles with higher concentrations of fertiliser may accumulate dead sediment in the bottom/appear to have a browner coloration.

2   Oxygen may increase in the flasks over the first few days as phytoplankton photosynthesise. The bottles with higher concentrations of fertiliser should initially have more oxygen. As time progresses and the algae die in the bottles with higher fertiliser concentration, the oxygen levels may begin to decline.

Nitrate and phosphate will be higher initially in the bottles with high fertiliser concentrations (they are in the fertiliser itself). There should be a decrease in nitrate and phosphate content in all the flasks as time progresses. During the later period, the weaker fertiliser concentrations will have nitrate and phosphate concentrations that continue to fall while the higher concentration fertiliser may show an increase.

pH should increase gradually in all flasks for the first few days. In the bottles with higher fertiliser concentrations, the pH will begin to begin to decrease towards the end of the experiment.

3   Oxygen will increase as the amount of photosynthesising phytoplankton increases and releases oxygen. As the experiment progresses, the amount of oxygen will begin to fall as the phytoplankton die and the decomposer bacteria begin to use up the oxygen.

4   As the phytoplankton grow, the nitrate and phosphate is used up. Towards the end of the experiment as the phytoplankton die and decompose, the nitrogen and phosphorus cycles will cause the nitrate and phosphate to be released back into the water.

5   As the phytoplankton grow initially they photosynthesise rapidly using up carbon dioxide in the water and raising the pH. As the phytoplankton are decomposed by respiring bacteria towards the end of the experiment, carbon dioxide is released causing the pH to fall.

Chapter 1

1 The independent variable (the variable that is changed) is the distance from the low water mark. The dependent variable (the variable that is measured) is the percentage cover of each barnacle species.

2 The student controlled the size of the area being tested (given in the question). She could also have controlled the time of day she sampled each species, and the method of identifying the species. She could have attempted to control the other species present by choosing areas that mainly contained only barnacles.

3 The percentage cover of *Chthamalus stellatus* at 5 m appears to be anomalous because it does not fit into the rest of the pattern.

4 It might have been caused by misidentification of the barnacle species, mistakes in recording the results, or differences in the actual shoreline at that point. There may have been a rockpool present or changes in the pH, temperature or amount of sunlight.

5 The student could repeat her experiment to make it easier to identify anomalies. She should measure the confounding variables, for example temperature, light intensity and pH. She could decrease the distance between her readings so that there are more data to make a pattern or a trend. She could increase the size of the area being tested so that more organisms were sampled in each case.

6 Yes: there do seem to be more *Chthamalus stellatus* further away from the low-water mark, which suggests this species might be more resistant to drying out.

No: there are no repeats, there is an anomalous result, none of the confounding variables was measured, the distance between the samples is too big, there is too much uncertainty in the results.

Chapter 2

1 Mean, 100/6 = 17%

2 Bacteria: produce drugs that protect sponges against predators or pathogens.

Sponge: provides bacteria with a sheltered habitat and nutrients.

3 Strain E is most effective as it has the largest zone of inhibition of the bacterial lawn.

Chapter 3

1 A lack of nutrients limits the rate of photosynthesis and therefore the primary productivity. There is less energy available to pass down the food chain by feeding. Numbers of zooplankton decrease as they have less food and numbers of anchoveta decrease because there is less zooplankton to feed on. The fish may migrate to other areas where more food is available so fewer are caught in the original area (there may also be fewer in the overall population).

2 As the sardines feed directly on the phytoplankton there is more energy available to them; less has been used by other animals in respiration and excretion. Even though fewer phytoplankton are available, they still obtain enough energy to grow.

3 Any two years of: 1965, 1969, 1977, 1983, 1987, 1991, 1995 or 1997 [these are not *all* El Niño years but from the information given in the graph they *could* be]. There are fewer anchoveta in these years: this is associated with an El Niño event because of the decrease in productivity of the waters.

Chapter 4

1 If excess nitrates enter the water, the N part of the ratio increases so the ratio gets bigger. (The normal ratio of N : P is 16 : 1; if it changes to 21 : 1, that is a bigger ratio.) Conversely, the ratio of carbon to nitrogen is normally 106 : 16, so if the nitrogen increases, this ratio decreases.

2 The phytoplankton which grow in conditions of increased nitrogen are those adapted to rapid growth under high nutrient conditions. Their ratio of N : P is lower than normal.

3 Scientists continue to monitor the ratio in the water because it can be changed by increased levels of nutrients. Monitoring allows scientists to see if excess nutrients are being allowed to run off from coastal areas. Changes to the ratio can also be caused by alterations to nitrogen-fixing and denitrification. This could be caused by important changes to the populations of organisms which carry out these processes. So monitoring the ratio allows scientists to monitor the nutrient cycles within the marine environment.

Chapter 5

1 Since most slow-growing corals only add millimetres of new growth to their skeletons each year, the amount of coral damaged in 2006 may not recover for hundreds or thousands of years, even assuming no new damage is done in the meantime.

2 When fishermen take too many fish from the reef, it leaves the reef vulnerable to other species that are normally kept in check. For example, if too many herbivorous fish are taken, there are not enough fish to prevent fast-growing algae spreading on top of a healthy reef. When this encrusting algae grows over the reef, it can create the beginning of a new ecosystem and lead to succession of the area.

3 Hermatypic corals because they create a limestone skeleton that hardens and does not decay, unlike ahermatypic corals, which form a protein skeleton that begins to break down shortly after death.

Chapter 6

1 Mangrove forests collect carbon dioxide within their tissues, particularly their roots, and act as a carbon sink in the carbon cycle. This means they effectively lock the carbon out of the atmosphere temporarily. Carbon dioxide is a greenhouse gas; it is responsible for maintaining the warming effect of reradiated heat from the Sun. When too much carbon dioxide builds up, so does the heat, causing climate change. The more carbon dioxide mangroves can remove from the atmosphere, the better for slowing or reducing the impacts of climate change.

2 $(823 + 35\,696) - (8340 + (-5443)) = 33\,622$
Net difference: \$33 622

3 Answers will vary, but could include references to the ecological benefits of mangroves, costs of shoreline erosion, and how local fisheries will be more stable.

Chapter 7

1 You would expect to find primarily sodium, chloride, magnesium, sulfates, and calcium.

2 Evaporation plays much the same role in the ocean as it does in the Dead Sea. This is why salinity levels are highest in the surface layer of tropical oceans compared to other oceans and depths.

3 Such high levels of salinity prevent most organisms, with the exception of a few archaea, from surviving in the Dead Sea.

Chapter 8

1 • Less food for primary consumers / less energy available for food webs
  • Less oxygen produced in coastal water
  • Less habitat / nursery areas for animals
  • Reduced carbon dioxide removal leading to water acidification and linked to global warming

2 • Depth (a) is too deep – there is less light intensity and red light will have been lost
  • Depth (c) is too shallow – there will be exposure of the seaweed to the air resulting in dehydration

3 • In deep water, light intensity is low
  • So photosynthesis rate is low
  • Warmth increases rate of respiration
  • So respiration rate is greater than photosynthesis rate
  • So *Eucheumia* uses up glucose faster than it is made

4 • Fertilisers contain high nitrate and phosphate levels
  • Leading to rapid growth of producers
  • Over-competition to light occurs
  • Producers die and are decomposed by bacteria
  • Bacteria respire aerobically reducing the oxygen concentration so animals suffocate

Chapter 9

1 Red muscle:
  • For continuous 'cruising' swimming
  • Has many mitochondria for aerobic respiration
  • Has myoglobin to store oxygen for aerobic respiration
  • Fat is a longer-term energy store for endurance swimming
  • Aerobic respiration releases more energy than anaerobic

White muscle:
  • For sprints / short bursts of swimming
  • Few mitochondria
  • No myoglobin so no oxygen storage
  • Little fat so less long-term energy storage
  • Anaerobic respiration releases less energy for short bursts

2 Tuna swim continuously for ram ventilation and for continuous feeding. This requires aerobic respiration and large quantities of red muscle.

3 In the oceans, the salmon swim for long distances continuously so require red muscle with aerobic respiration. As the salmon migrate along the rivers they require short, rapid bursts to jump over obstacles and climb salmon ladders. The short bursts are done by white, anaerobic muscles.

Chapter 10

1 a The male angler fish has no need to actively feed as it is a parasitic organism that gains nutrition from female. As it cannot feed, it has a small size thus requiring less food.

b There is little prey in the deep ocean so using a lure helps to ensure food presence and they have large mouths and teeth to maximise the chance of catching the food.

2 There are few fish in the deep ocean so that the chance meeting a mate is low. By attaching, the fish are ensuring that each time eggs are released, they will be fertilised.

3 The eggs will be fertilised by the sperm of more than one male increasing genetic diversity in the offspring.

Chapter 11

1 • To increase natural populations after reductions due to fishing and loss due to dams and other human activities
  • To increase populations for recreational fishing which boosts the local economy

2 • Population of salmon was very high due to release of large numbers of salmon from hatcheries
  • High harvests
  • Large amounts of salmon on sale
  • Salmon price falls
  • Other factors include: high production from aquaculture, natural increase in recruitment, natural fall in mortality rate, cheap imports of salmon

3 • Loss of true wild salmon
  • Overpopulation of salmon affecting food chains
  • Changes to salmon behaviour
  • Risk of changes to gene pool
  • Risk of introduction of diseases

Chapter 12

1 • High stocking densities
  • High transmission of viruses / bacteria / fungi / pests
  • High use of food
  • Waste food / faeces / dead shrimp decays and causes eutrophication
  • Pollution from pesticides and antibiotics used due to high densities

2 • Mangroves are preserved
  • More habitats, nursery grounds for other species
  • Protection from coastal erosion
  • Low stocking densities
  • Less pollution and disease
  • Less transfer of disease to wild shrimp
  • More employment for smaller farmers
  • Less disease wiping out farmed stock
  • More income from organically labelled shrimp

3 • Producers that take in carbon dioxide from environment
  • Usually by photosynthesis
  • Lock up the carbon in the form of carbohydrates / organic compounds
  • Reducing atmospheric carbon dioxide

Chapter 13

1 • Large amounts of organic waste / human faeces
  • Providing food for decomposer organisms
  • Increased respiration rate
  • Reducing oxygen levels

2 • Tracers not found in species that live away from the site (control experiment)
  • Radioactive isotopes are found in human faeces in higher amounts than in normal sediment
  • Radioactive substances have passed into filter feeders and detritus feeders from human faeces and passed along to other organisms via food chain

3 • Mercury is a serious toxin
  • High concentration in sewage that is dumped
  • Taken up by filter feeders and passed along food chain
  • Eventually concentrates in bodies of higher trophic level fish

- Fish / oysters / shellfish are not safe for human consumption
- Oyster beds and fishing face periodic bans resulting in lost profit

Chapter 14

1   Areas of marine protected zones where no fishing is permitted.

2   **a**   Sea bream eat sea urchins. The higher number of sea bream means that there are fewer sea urchins so that less seaweed is consumed.

   b   Seaweed can provide food for more herbivores encouraging more variety. It also acts as a shelter and nursery for other species.

3   Catches have increased in surrounding areas and restricted fishing has been permitted in the area. Profits have also risen.

Chapter 15

1   - GFP gene extracted from jellyfish
   - GFP placed into a plasmid and injected into zebrafish eggs

- Green, fluorescent zebrafish selected and used for breeding

2   - No native zebrafish present to interbreed with
   - They are not intended for human consumption
   - Laboratory trials have shown they are more easily predated
   - Unlikely to survive as no food sources for them
   - Zebrafish is native to south Asia so would have correct environment / food to survive and could interbreed with wild zebrafish

3   - Worries it could affect populations of native fish species / harm native fish
   - No predation could cause it to spread
   - Could transfer the gene into other species
   - Could be the start of other, more dangerous organisms being released

4   - Place a pollutant-specific promoter in front of the GFP gene
   - The fish would then only luminesce when a pollutant is present
   - Water samples would be taken and brought to laboratory and fish placed into them

Chapter 2

1 a 2000/10 000 × 100 = 20%

b 200/2000 × 100 = 10%

c 1/20 × 100 = 5%

2 Mean: (4 + 4 + 4 + 4 + 8 + 10 + 10 + 10 + 12 + 15 + 20)/11
= 101/11 = 9%
Median: 10%
Mode: 4%
Range: 20−4 = 16%

Chapter 3

1 a Energy in = 6421

Energy out to decomposers = 2389

Energy passed to secondary consumers = 598

6421 − (2389 + 598) = 3434 kJ m^{-2} year^{-1}

b Energy transferred to primary consumers = 6421

Energy present in producers = 72 567

6421 / 72 567 × 100 = 8.8%

2 a Energy in phytoplankton = 8000

Energy in zooplankton = 912

912/8000 × 100 = 11.4

b Energy in zooplankton = 912

Energy in fish = 86

86 / 912 × 100 = 8.8

c Single-celled phytoplankton are more easily digested than terrestrial plants; less cellulose; less energy lost in respiration/heat; entire organism eaten/more of terrestrial plant will not be eaten (e.g. roots).

Chapter 4

1 a Year should be on the *x*-axis with the phosphate used in tonnes on the *y*-axis. The scale must fill ¾ of the graph paper and be easy to read. Each point must be plotted correctly and the points should be joined with straight lines.

b There is a fairly steady decrease between 1975 and 1990 with the amount of phosphate fertiliser used decreasing from 124 000 to 38 000. The rate of decrease then slows – the graph levels off and by 2005 it has decreased to 22 000.

2 a There is a gradual increase in the amount of carbon dioxide. In 1970, there were 1350 million metric tonnes of carbon dioxide, this rose to 2300 million metric tonnes by 2005.

b Burning fossil fuels (allow respiration)

c Increased amounts of carbon dioxide in the atmosphere mean that more is able to dissolve in the seawater.

Chapter 5

1

half-lives that have passed	years from present	percent of original ^{14}C remaining	amount of original ^{14}C remaining / g
0	0	100	5000
1	5730	50	2500
2	11 460	25	1250
3	17 190	12.5	625
4	22 920	6.25	312.5
5	28 650	3.13	156.25
6	34 380	1.56	78.13

2

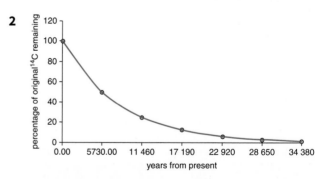

3 The sample is approximately 4500–5000 years old. This can be determined by locating the point on the created line graph where the curve intersects with 60%.

Chapter 6

1 a Mussels: 34.3 m^{-2}

b

sample area	1	2	3	4	5	6	7	8	9	10	mean
number of mussels in 1 m²	20	49	9	47	12	100	48	10	16	32	34.3
$(x_i - \mu)^2$	204.5	216.1	640.1	161.3	497.3	4316.5	187.7	590.5	334.9	5.3	**715.4**

Standard deviation for Pacific blue mussels is 26.7 m^{-2}

2 Quadrats with the highest numbers of organisms (2, 4, 6 and 7) were most likely to be in the lower intertidal zone where the organisms would spend most of their time submerged. Quadrats 3 and 8 are probably located in the mid to high intertidal zone where the organisms may be unable to tolerate the conditions.

Chapter 7

1

date	high tide level/m	low tide level/m	tidal range/m
1 June	0.55	0.50	0.05
2 June	0.59	0.46	0.13
3 June	0.66	0.31	0.35
4 June	0.76	0.13	0.63
5 June	0.90	−0.06	0.96
6 June	0.98	−0.23	1.21
7 June	1.05	−0.37	1.42
8 June	1.13	−0.46	1.59
9 June	1.18	−0.50	1.68
10 June	1.19	−0.48	1.67
11 June	1.15	−0.42	1.57
12 June	1.05	−0.31	1.36
13 June	0.90	−0.17	1.07
14 June	0.72	−0.02	0.74
15 June	0.53	0.12	0.41
16 June	0.34	0.25	0.09

2 a

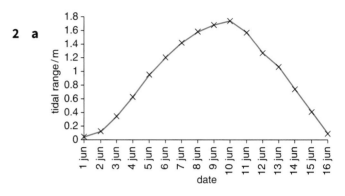

b 9 June should be circled because tidal range is the highest during spring tides.

c 1 June and 16 June should have a square around them because tidal range is the lowest during neap tides.

Chapter 8

1 a i $(60 \times \pi \times 2^2)/8 = 94.2$ mm³ min^{-1}

ii $(40 \times \pi \times 2^2)/6 = 83.7$ mm³ min^{-1}

iii $(80 \times \pi \times 2^2)/5 = 201.0$ mm³ min^{-1}

b i $94.2/60 = 1.57$ mm³ s^{-1}

ii $83.7/60 = 1.4$ mm³ s^{-1}

iii $201.0/60 = 3.4$ mm³ s^{-1}

2 start volume = $4/3 \times \pi \times 25^3 = 65\ 416.6$ cm³

finish volume = $4/3 \times \pi \times 29^3 = 102\ 108.6$ cm³

increase in volume in one year = $102\ 108.6 - 65\ 416.6$
= 36 692 cm³

mean increase per month = 36 692/12
= 3057.7 cm³ month^{-1}

3 a i volume of tank = 5^3 = 125 m³; density of tilapia = 75/125 = 0.6 tilapia m⁻³

ii volume of tank = 8^3 = 512 m³; density of tilapia = 75/512 = 0.15 tilapia m⁻³

iii volume of tank = 2.25^3 = 11.4 m³; density of tilapia = 75/11.4 = 6.6 tilapia m⁻³

b i volume of tank = 2 × 3 × 8 = 48 m³; density of tilapia = 75/48 = 1.6 tilapia m⁻³

ii volume of tank = 1.5 × 6 × 2 = 18 m³; density of tilapia = 75/18 = 4.2 tilapia m⁻³

Chapter 9

1 a $6 × 5^2$ = 150 cm²;

b 2 × (6 × 6 + 12 × 6 + 12 × 6) = 360 cm²;

c 2 × (6 × 2 + 6 × 36 + 2 × 36) = 600 cm²;

d $4 × 3.14 × 8^2$ = 803.84 cm²;

e 2 × 3.14 × 2(2 + 8) = 125.6 cm²

2 a 5 × 5 × 5 = 125 cm³;

b 6 × 6 × 12 = 432 cm³;

c 6 × 2 × 36 = 432 cm³;

d $4/3 × 3.14 × 8^3$ = 2143.6 cm³;

e 3.14 × 8 × 2 × 2 = 100.48 cm³

The two rectangular cuboids have the same volumes but different surface areas. (c) is flatter and wider than (b) resulting in a higher surface area and higher surface area : volume ratio.

3 a 150/125 = 1.2;

b 360/432 = 0.83;

c 600/432 = 1.34;

d 803.84/2143.6 = 0.37;

e 125.6/100.48 = 1.25;

4 a $h = (A/2\pi r) – r$, so $h = (250/2 × 3.14 × 3) – 3$; h = 10.3 mm;

b $r = \sqrt{(A/4\pi)}$, so $r = \sqrt{(400/(4 × 3.14))}$ r = 5.64 cm;

5 a surface area of one tentacle = $2\pi r (r + h)$ = 2 × 3.14 × 2 (2 + 10) = 150.7 mm², 32 tentacles have a total area of 32 × 150.7 = 4822.4 mm²

b mass of oxygen at start = 9 mg dm⁻³ × 0.1 dm³ = 0.90 mg,

mass of oxygen at finish = 7.5 mg dm⁻³ × 0.1 dm³ = 0.75 mg,

mass of oxygen removed by polyp = 0.90 – 0.75 = 0.15 mg

c Rate of oxygen removal for polyp = 0.15 mg/2 hours = 0.075 mg h⁻¹ polyp⁻¹.

Rate of oxygen removal per mm² of polyp is 0.075 mg/4822.4 mm² = 0.0000155 mg mm⁻² h⁻¹

Chapter 10

1 a 72.4 (value of 2 discounted as an anomaly); range = 2–101 (45–101 without anomalies)

b 3515.1 (no anomalies); range: 2954–4872

2

measurements (x)	($x – \bar{x}$)	($x – \bar{x}$)²
27	(27 – 30.9) = –3.9	15.21
32	(32 – 30.9) = 1.1	1.21
29	(29 – 30.9) = –1.9	3.61
35	(35 – 30.9) = 4.1	16.81
25	(25 – 30.9) = –5.9	34.81
37	(37 – 30.9) = 6.1	37.21
31	(31 – 30.9) = 0.1	0.01

$\sum(x – \bar{x})^2$ = 108.87

$\sum(x – \bar{x})^2/n – 1$ = 108.87/6 = 18.15

Standard deviation = $\sqrt{18.15}$ = 4.26

68% of values lie between 30.9 ± 4.26; (range: 26.64–35.16)

95% of values lie between 30.9 ± 8.52; (range: 22.38–39.42)

3

number of grouper per square kilometre of reef A(x)	($x – \bar{x}$)	($x – \bar{x}$)²
32	4.2	17.64
35	7.2	51.84
21	–6.8	46.24
25	–2.8	7.84
32	4.2	17.64
38	10.2	104.04
21	–6.8	46.24
24	–3.8	14.44
19	–8.8	77.44
31	3.2	10.24
		$\sum(x – \bar{x})^2$= 393.6

Mean number of groupers per square kilometre of reef A = 27.8

Standard deviation = 6.61

95% of values lie between 27.8 ± (2 × 6.61) = 27.8 ± 13.2; (range: 14.6–41.0)

number of grouper per square kilometre of reef B(x)	$(x - \bar{x})$	$(x - \bar{x})^2$
18	−1.4	1.96
19	−0.4	0.16
12	−7.4	54.76
24	4.6	21.16
27	7.6	57.76
19	−0.4	0.16
18	−1.4	1.96
27	7.6	57.76
18	−1.4	1.96
12	−7.4	54.76
		$\sum(x - \bar{x})^2 = 252.4$

Mean number of groupers per square kilometre of reef B = 19.4

Standard deviation = 5.30

95% of values lie between 19.4 ± (2 × 5.30) = 19.4 ± 10.6; (range: 8.8–30.0)

Chapter 11

1 **a** (365 000 ÷ 6) ÷ 2135 = 28.5 tonnes year⁻¹ boat-day⁻¹

   b (275 000 ÷ 3) ÷ 3282 = 27.9 tonnes year⁻¹ boat-day⁻¹

2 **a** fishing intensity = 168 000 ÷ 25 = 6720 boat-days

   b fishing intensity = 125 000 ÷ 15 = 8333 boat-days

3

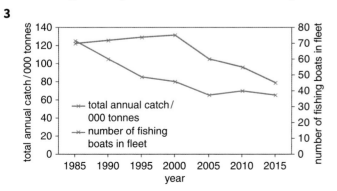

Chapter 12

1

product	profit/£	percentage	angle on pie chart/°
grouper	150 000	39	140.4
lobster	125 000	32	115.2
crab	25 000	7	25.2
scallops	75 000	19	68.4
seaweed	10 000	3	10.8

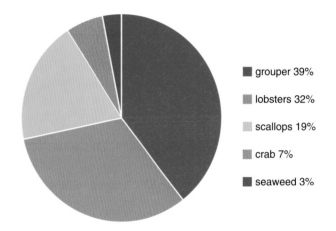

grouper 39%

lobsters 32%

scallops 19%

crab 7%

seaweed 3%

2

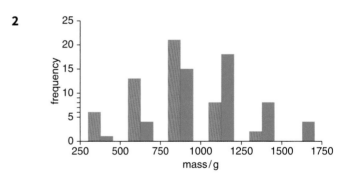

Chapter 13

1 **a** **i** 3.5×10^7;

      ii 3.52×10^{-5};

      iii 4.5×10^4;

      iv 4.35×10^{-9}

   b **i** $300\,000 + 6\,000\,000 = 6.3 \times 10^6$;

      ii $0.012 + 0.0011 = 1.31 \times 10^{-2}$;

      iii $(2.3 \times 1.2) \times 10^{2+3} = 2.76 \times 10^5$;

      iv $(4 \times 3) \times 10^{3+4} = 1.2 \times 10^8$;

      v $(6 \div 3) \times 10^{6-3} = 2 \times 10^3$

2 a i 0.33;

  ii 1.23;

  iii 1.38;

  iv 3.60

b

grouper number	length of grouper / cm
1	10.3
2	12.0
3	4.6
4	5.0
5	7.6

Chapter 14

1 a i 5;

  ii 4;

  iii 3;

  iv 2 or 4 depending on whether the number has been rounded

b 1 sig fig = 700; 2 sig fig = 670; 3 sig fig = 674; 4 sig fig = 674.1

2 a 9500;

b 4.5;

c 1280

Chapter 15

1 The answer may be reached in several ways, the answers given are suggested calculations.

Estuary 1: $(31 – 20)/(150 – 50) = 9/100 = 0.09$ oysters 100 m^{-2} day^{-1}

Estuary 2: $(22 – 11)/(150 – 50) = 11/100 = 0.11$ oysters 100 m^{-2} day^{-1}

Although estuary 1 has consistently more oysters, the rate of increase is approximately the same for both estuaries.

2 a

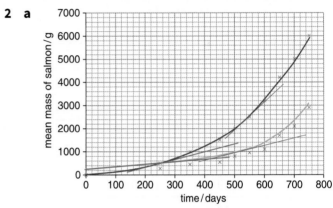

× mass of genetically engineered salmon / g
× mass of non-genetically engineered salmon / g

b The gradients are dependent on the lines of best fit, so some tolerance must be allowed.

There should be a tangent drawn at each point and the gradient of each calculated correctly.

  i GM salmon: 1000 g/360 days = 2.8 g day^{-1}

    Non-GM salmon: 200 g/200 days = 1.0 g day^{-1}

  ii GM salmon: 1200 g/100 days = 12.0 g day^{-1}

    Non-GM salmon: 400 g/100 days = 4.00 g day^{-1}

Answers to exam-style questions

Chapter 1

1 Range of light intensities **[1]**

Same number/mass of cells at the start **[1]**

Reference to time left for (e.g. 3 days) **[1]**

Reference to counting the cells **[1]**

Two control variables, e.g. pH, salinity, temperature, CO_2 concentration, O_2 concentration, light wavelength **[2]**

Reference to repeated measurements **[1]**

Reference to calculating a mean value **[2]**

[Total mark: 6]

2 a i 0.67 **[2]**

Incorrect answer but evidence of dividing by 3 **[1]**

[max 2]

ii 0.1 at 20 °C/Trial 2 at 20 °C **[1]**

iii As the temperature increases so does the growth of coral. **[1]**

Up to 22 °C when it levels off **[1]**

b i The results support the hypothesis because the coral did grow faster at the higher temperatures. **[1]**

Reference to the anomalous result/ uncertainties **[1]**

Reference to 24 °C being the same as 22 °C **[1]**

[max 2]

ii Any two from pH/salinity/CO_2 concentration, O_2 concentration, light wavelength/light intensity **[2]**

c Range of salinities **[1]**

Reference to NaOH/sodium chloride **[1]**

Reference to time left for/1 week **[1]**

Reference to repeats **[1]**

Two correct control variables, e.g. pH/temperature/ CO_2 concentration, O_2 concentration, light wavelength/light intensity **[1]**

Reference to calculating a mean **[1]**

[Total mark: 15]

3 a Any three from temperature, availability of food, competition, predation, pH, O_2 concentration **[3]**

b Environmental factors should be measured **[1]**

Results should be recorded and used to analyse the results **[1]**

Reference to confounding variables **[1]**

[Total mark: 2]

Chapter 2

1 a i A group of interbreeding organisms of the same species **[1]**

ii All the organisms in a specific area or habitat **[1]**

iii The feeding position or level in a food chain **[1]**

iv A group of organisms that share similar characteristics and can interbreed to produce fertile offspring **[1]**

v The living organisms (biotic factors) and the physical and chemical environment (abiotic factors) with which they interact. **[1]**

b i Increased swimming speed/hydrodynamic efficiency/decreased drag

Improved navigation

Increased foraging efficiency

Protection from predators

Increased reproduction, e.g. finding of mates/ fertilisation **[4]**

ii Some predators are better at attacking shoals (e.g. jacks)

Increased toxic waste

Decreased dissolved oxygen for aerobic respiration **[2]**

[Total mark: 11]

2 a 10.8 °C – 6.0 °C = 4.8 °C **[1]**

b Increase in population size as the temperatures of the ocean rise. **[1]**

c Green crabs are predators of the clams/clams are prey of the green crabs.

As green crabs increase, clams decrease

There is a time lag between changes in the predator and prey populations **[3]**

d Predators follow prey

Prey hide from their predators [2]

e Quadrats

Random sampling

Sampling a suitable area

Sampling over time

Counting

Repeated sampling

Calculating mean numbers [4]

[Total mark: 11]

3 a Sun/light [1]

b Phytoplankton → clam → crab → bass/grackle/sanderling/turtle

Arrows in correct direction (left to right) [2]

c Transfer of energy between trophic levels

Transfer of biomass between trophic levels [2]

d An animal that kills/hunts and eats other animals

Any named predator species from Fig 2.19 (terrapin/crab/bass/turtle/sanderling/grackle) [2]

e Disease/fishing/change in food supply [1]

f An interrelationship between species/between crabs and ciliates

Host (crab) suffers.

Parasite (ciliate) feeds on host (crab)/benefits [3]

[Total mark:11]

4 a Mutualism (ignore symbiosis)

Both organisms benefit

Zooxanthellae get protection/inorganic substrates for photosynthesis

Coral get organic products from photosynthesis [3]

b Change in community structure over a period of time [1]

c Bare rock/volcanic eruption

Colonising/pioneer species – first to arrive

Succession/seral stages – as new species become successfully established

Climax community – complex and stable final community [3]

d Coral reefs are stable and not extreme environments

High biodiversity/species richness

Organisms have specialised niches

Niches have little overlap

Decreased interspecific competition [4]

[Total mark: 11]

5 a Ice algae/phytoplankton – zooplankton – small fish – ringed seal – polar bear [1]

b Arctic cod increase as there is less predation by beluga whales.

Small fish decrease as there is more predation by Arctic cod.

Zooplankton increase as there is less predation by small fish.

Phytoplankton decrease as there is more predation by zooplankton.

c Mean = sum of each invertebrate type/number of invertebrate types

Mean = (73+ 55 + 47 + 32 + 18)/5 = 225/5 = 45 [1]

d i Polar bear: less ice for breeding/hunting [1]

ii Ice algae: less ice so decreased habitat size [1]

e Reduced ice or less time on ice for moulting.

Seals unable to grow adequate healthy coats.

Coats protect seals' skin from abrasions and infections. [2]

f Less ice for seals to breed/moult on.

Harder for hunters to walk on ice

Seals had already migrated further north to more stable ice [1]

[Total mark: 11]

Chapter 3

1 a i Amount of biomass [1]

Produced by plants/algae/phytoplankton/bacteria [1]

Through photosynthesis/chemosynthesis [1]

Per unit time [1]

Per unit area [1]

[max 3]

ii Any three of: Temperature [1]

Light intensity/amount of light [1]

Carbon dioxide [1]

Nutrient levels/availability/concentration/amount [1]

pH [1]

[max 3]

iii Either:

Measure photosynthesis [1]

By production of oxygen [1]

Or reduction in carbon dioxide [1]

Light bottle/dark bottle method [1]

Or:

Measure change in biomass [1]

Harvest producers [1]

After a set time [1]

Use dry mass [1]

[max 3]

b In spring the temperature increases [1]

There is more light/longer daylength [1]

More photosynthesis/rate of photosynthesis increases [1]

Growth rate increases/more biomass [1]

More nutrients present in water [1]

Faster growth rate (linked to nutrients) [1]

[max 4]

[Total mark: 13]

2 a Energy from the Sun [1]

Captured/absorbed by chlorophyll [1]

In algae/green plants/phytoplankton/seaweeds/ seagrasses [1]

Carbon dioxide and water are used [1]

Glucose produced [1]

Oxygen produced [1]

[max 4]

b i No light [1]

No producers present [1]

ii Chemosynthesis [1]

Chemical energy/dissolved chemicals [1]

Bacteria [1]

Symbiotic relationships [1]

Example of species with symbionts e.g. *Riftia/Tevnia* [1]

[max 4]

c i correct answer of 1.1/1.10% [2]

1% [1]

Incorrect answer but principle of dividing by 1.7×10^6 [1]

c ii Light reflected by water or plants/algae [1]

Wrong wavelength for chlorophyll/pigment [1]

Water absorbs/scatters light [1]

Light misses chlorophyll/pigment/not absorbed/transmitted [1]

[max 3]

[Total mark: 15]

3 a Gradual increase in chlorophyll concentration until early April [1]

Rapid increase between March and April [1]

Fluctuates/variable but staying high until July [1]

Decreases between July and December [1]

[max 3]

b Increased temperature/warmer [1]

Increased amounts of light/daylength [1]

More photosynthesis [1]

Higher growth rate/more reproduction [1]

Of phytoplankton/algae [1]

[max 5]

c Population increases/more zooplankton/amount increases [1]

Because there is more food/more producers/ more phytoplankton to eat [1]

d Drawn to scale [1]

Organisms in correct order (phytoplankton at bottom) [1]

Bars labelled correctly with phytoplankton, zooplankton, herring then mackerel [1]

[Total mark: 13]

4 a Shape [1]

Bars labelled correctly [1]

b Loss of energy from phytoplankton [1]

Through respiration/heat loss [1]

Some parts may be undigested/not eaten/ excreted [1]

c Inverted/upside down/accept sketch of this [1]

More zooplankton than phytoplankton [1]

d Phytoplankton reproduce very rapidly/zooplankton eat phytoplankton before they can be weighed to work out biomass/standing crop [1]

[Total mark: 8]

5 a Correct answer of 11.8/11.78% [2]

12 [1]

Incorrect answer but principle of dividing by 5000 [1]

b Energy is lost from phytoplankton [1]

Not all of the phytoplankton is eaten [1]

Energy used in respiration/heat loss [1]

Some of the phytoplankton eaten is not digested/excreted [1]

[max 3]

c i More phytoplankton [1]

So more zooplankton/sardines/tuna [1]

Because there is more food [1]

[max 3]

ii Either:

Increased nutrient levels [1]

More photosynthesis [1]

More phytoplankton therefore more zooplankton etc. [1]

Or:

Increased nutrient levels/nitrates/phosphates [1]

Algal bloom [1]

Decrease in oxygen/hypoxia [1]

Zooplankton and fish die [1]

[max 3]

[Total mark: 11]

6 a i GPP is the amount of light/chemical energy fixed [1]

By producers [1]

In a given length of time [1]

In a given area [1]

NPP is GPP – respiration/takes respiration into account [1]

[max 3]

a ii Correct answer of 55 261 [2]

Incorrect answer but principle of subtracting respiration [1]

b Biomass can be standing crop/particular time/ one day [1]

Biomass of phytoplankton can be very small [1]

Because they are eaten very quickly [1]

Energy is measured for the whole year [1]

[max 2]

[Total mark: 7]

Chapter 4

1 a Upwelling [1]

b Erosion/rain/leaching/run-off [1]

Water drains/flows to ocean [1]

Taken up/uptake by phytoplankton/producers [1]

Moves through food chain by feeding [1]

Death of producers/consumers [1]

Sinks to the bottom/marine snow [1]

[max 4]

c i Stays the same/constant/equal [1]

ii The same amount of magnesium enters the water [1]

Through run-off/upwelling [1]

As is removed [1]

Through sinking and harvesting [1]

Equilibrium [1]

[max 3]

[Total mark: 9]

2 a i Upwelling [1]

Caused by ocean currents/wind [1]

Pushing surface water away from land [1]

[max 2]

ii Run-off [1]

Dissolving from the atmosphere [1]

b i Increased productivity/growth rate [1]

Example of nutrient provided [1]

ii Algal bloom [1]

Blocks light to coral and other organisms [1]

Reduces the amount of oxygen in the water [1]

Because of decomposition of dead organisms by bacteria [1]

[max 2]

[Total mark: 8]

3 a i Dissolving [1]

ii pH decreases/becomes more acidic [1]

Because carbonic acid/bicarbonate ions are formed [1]

iii Any organic compound, e.g. glucose, cellulose, DNA, phospholipid **[1]**

b i Run-off **[1]**

Upwelling **[1]**

ii More phosphate taken up by producers **[1]**

Increased growth rate/productivity **[1]**

Reference to photosynthesis **[1]**

[Total mark: 9]

4 a Nitrogen – for proteins/amino acids **[1]**

Calcium – for bones/coral/shells **[1]**

Phosphorus – for DNA and bone **[1]**

b i Draining/flow of water from land **[1]**

Into the sea/ocean/river/lake **[1]**

Carrying nutrients/named nutrient **[1]**

Caused by rain/snow melt/irrigation water **[1]**

[max 3]

ii More nitrates taken up/assimilated **[1]**

Increased growth/productivity **[1]**

Reference to photosynthesis **[1]**

Allow reference to too many nitrates **[1]**

Allow reference to algal bloom **[1]**

[max 3]

iii Increased availability of food/biomass of producers **[1]**

Increased growth rate of consumers/biomass of consumers **[1]**

Allow reference to decreased growth IF algal blooms were used in part **ii** **[1]**

Allow reference to reduced oxygen levels IF algal blooms were used in part **ii** **[1]**

[max 2]

[Total mark: 11]

5 a Erosion of limestone/dissolving/leaching **[1]**

Run-off/drains to ocean **[1]**

Taken up by producers/phytoplankton **[1]**

Phytoplankton/producers eaten by zooplankton **[1]**

Corals feed on zooplankton **[1]**

Calcium used to form coral skeleton **[1]**

Reference to calcium carbonate **[1]**

[max 5]

b i Bones/shells of other organisms **[1]**

ii Same amount added to the water as is removed **[1]**

Reference to equilibrium **[1]**

Removed by sinking to seabed/corals/bones/shells **[1]**

Added by upwelling/run-off **[1]**

Added through decomposition/breakdown of organisms after death **[1]**

[max 4]

c i carbon **[1]**

Accept nitrogen or phosphorus **[1]**

ii More carbon dioxide in the atmosphere **[1]**

From burning fossil fuels **[1]**

More carbon dioxide dissolves in the water **[1]**

Accept explanations linked to increased use of fertilisers if nitrogen or phosphorus named in **i** **[1]**

Accept more run-off linked to fertiliser use and nitrogen/phosphorus **[1]**

[max 2]

[Total mark: 13]

Chapter 5

1 a i A shallow reef that forms along a coastline, with little or no lagoon **[2]**

ii A reef separated from land by a lagoon that may be many kilometres wide **[2]**

iii A circular coral reef in the deep waters of the Indo-Pacific with a centralised deep lagoon **[2]**

b An oceanic volcano surfaces; hermatypic coral colonise the coastline of this volcano; this volcano begins to sink as a result of subsidence, causing vertical growth of the coral reef and the development of a lagoon between the reef and the shore; the volcano continues sinking until it is below the surface and all that remains is a circular reef with a central lagoon. **[4]**

[Total mark: 10]

2 a Any three of:

Reduce wave height and strength

Reduce erosion

Protect coastal development

Protect anchorages for boats

Provide economic benefits [6]

b For healthy coral growth, developers must place artifical reefs in clear water of appropriate depth (20 m or less) so sunlight can reach the zooxanthellae in the coral polyps for photosynthesis. They must also ensure the water temperature will remain between 23-25 °C for optimal growth and reduced stress and that coral will have a hard stable substrate for best attachment. [6]

c Coral are very susceptible to reduced pH and tend to do best in a slightly basic environment. Truck tyres, planes and ships all contain chemicals that may alter the pH or contaminate the water (e.g. oil and rust). Therefore a pH neutral material allows the coral to grow on a substrate that is very similar to the basaltic rocks it prefers and offers little chance of chemical damage. [4]

[Total mark: 16]

3 a Both locations saw a decrease of coral cover. However, Key West showed a 25% decrease compared with Islamorada's 19%. [2]

b [(57 – 43)/43] × 100 = 32.55% [2]

c Given the popularity of Key West, it is possible that there is greater tourism in the area that is preventing a swift recovery. The coral in Key West may also be less sheltered, suffer from greater pollution (e.g. run-off, oil, pesticides) or have been damaged by another storm in the intervening years. [2]

[Total mark: 6]

4 a i This relationship is symbiotic/mutualistic because the zooxanthellae give the coral carbohydrates from photosynthesis and the coral provides nitrogen, phosphorus, and carbon dioxide to the zooxanthellae, creating a benefit to each. [2]

ii This is a predator-prey relationship because the butterflyfish eats the coral polyps. [2]

b In order to graze for the symbiotic algae, parrotfish take bites of living coral and the limestone skeleton. These causes erosion as a result of loss of calcium carbonate. [3]

[Total mark: 7]

5 a As the carbon dioxide in our atmosphere increases, it dissolves more quickly into our oceans through dissolution. Once in the ocean, carbon dioxide combines with water to form a weak form of carbonic acid making the ocean more acidic. [3]

b The impacts of limiting nutrients on coral is all relative to the amount present in the environment. When the levels of nutrients are in balance, zooxanthellae are able to grow well and provide corals with more nutrients to build their skeletons. When the concentration of nutrients is too high, it leads to a plankton bloom. A plankton bloom can cause turbidity in the water preventing sunlight from reaching zooxanthellae and reducing photosynthesis thereby lessening the availability of energy to coral. Another side-effect of increased nutrients is the increased number of crown-of-thorns starfish larvae able to survive due to an increase in food source (phytoplankton). If these reach adulthood, they may cause an outbreak. [4]

c Upwelling is the rise of cold, nutrient-rich water to the surface. Both the presence of cold, instead of warm, water and a heavy load of nutrients is not healthy for coral growth. [1]

[Total mark: 8]

Chapter 6

1 a The intertidal zone is the area of a shoreline that is submerged during high tide and exposed during low tide. [1]

b On a rocky shore, organisms have to deal with increased wave action and weathering from the exposed shoreline. Organisms living here tend to be those capable of attaching themselves to the rocks in some way. On a sandy shore, the organisms must contend with the large amounts of erosion occurring on the shore. The best adaptation for doing so is burrowing, which is why the majority of organisms on this shore tend to be infauna. [4]

c i Vertical zonation is when organisms within an ecosystem organise themselves into definite bands according to biological and physical factors. [1]

ii In areas where zonation is common, typically physical factors like exposure to air and temperature tolerance determine an organism's upper limit in the ecosystem. Meanwhile, biological factors like predation and competition determine the organism's lower limit in the ecosystem. [2]

[Total mark: 8]

2 a Any three of the following: magnetic reversals in the rocks on the seabed, fit of the continents, fossil evidence on multiple continents, geological structures on multiple continents, and seabed spreading. **[3]**

b i The tectonic plates are sliding past one another; abyssal plains. **[2]**

ii The tectonic plates are moving toward each other; ocean trenches. **[2]**

iii The tectonic plates are moving away from each other; mid-ocean ridges. **[2]**

[Total mark: 9]

3 a Hydrothermal vents are found in mid-ocean ridges along divergent plate boundaries. **[1]**

b Hydrothermal vents form when cold water along the ocean floor sinks through cracks in the Earth's crust. The water moves through the crust, dissolving minerals, until it finds a magma chamber at which point the water is superheated and escapes through a vent in the seabed. As the water quickly cools, many of the minerals fall out of solution and build up the chimney of the hydrothermal vent. **[4]**

c Hydrothermal vents are considered extreme environments due to the physical factors associated with living there. Organisms must be adapted to severe fluctuations in temperature – from near-freezing at the base of the vent to over 300 °C at the top – as well as incredible pressure due to the depth, and the presence of toxic chemicals in the water that is expelled from the vent. **[3]**

[Total mark: 8]

4 a Mangrove trees are found in tropical and subtropical coastal regions. They typically inhabit brackish muddy areas where there is a mix of salt and fresh water and low oxygen concentration within the sediment, like an estuary. **[3]**

b Mangroves need adaptations for dealing with soil that is anoxic. Black mangroves have pneumatophores that perform oxygen exchange at high tide, while red mangroves absorb oxygen through the bark. The prop roots of red mangroves hold the plants above the high water mark.. Mangroves also have to deal with high salt levels, so red mangroves have a filtration system that is highly efficient at keeping out salt of the roots while black mangroves excrete salt onto their leaves. **[2]**

c Red mangroves benefit coastal ecosystems by providing habitats for juvenile fish and invertebrates among their roots, by trapping sediments and building land, by creating a wave break and reducing wave energy, and by preventing erosion. **[4]**

[Total mark: 9]

5 a As pressure increases, so do the number of tube worm larvae that settle. With an increase of 250 atm, you see an increase of 533% [((95 – 15)/15) × 100] in larval settlement. **[2]**

b Three containers of seawater were set up. Each container was kept at a constant temperature and pressure of 250 atm. The pH in each container varied: container 1 = 7.0 pH; container 2 = 5.0 pH; container 3 = 3.0 pH. Approximately 250 larvae were released into each container. After 3 days, the numbers of larvae that had settled within each container were counted. The experiment was repeated three times and means were calculated for each container. **[5]**

[Total mark: 7]

Chapter 7

1 a As the Earth rotates, objects that are moving in a straight line across Earth's surface are actually deflected 45° from their original path. In the Northern Hemisphere, objects deflect to the right. In the Southern Hemisphere, objects deflect to the left. **[4]**

b As tropical cyclones form, air rises from a low-pressure centre, cools and sinks again. This movement is affected by the Coriolis Effect which causes the air masses to rotate in a clockwise fashion in the Northern Hemisphere and a counter-clockwise fashion in the Southern Hemisphere. These storms are also blown across the ocean by the wind and therefore begin to turn to either the right or the left. **[3]**

c i **[4]**

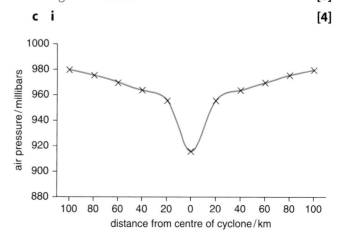

ii The lowest pressure is at the centre of the graph cyclone because that is where the greatest rates of rising air and evaporation are occurring. As the warm air rises, the air pressure drops. **[2]**

[Total mark: 13]

2 a i During El Niño, the westerly wind slows and reduces in strength. Rains move from over Asia/Australia to over the Pacific Ocean. The thermocline also flattens out preventing upwelling from occurring. **[2]**

ii During El Niño, the thermocline flattens out. This means that more warm water is kept near the surface off the coast of South America. Colder, nutrient-rich waters are prevented from upwelling. The lack of nutrients reduces the ability of phytoplankton to produce biomass through photosynthesis. Fewer producers means fewer fish due to lack of food. Fewer fish means a smaller fish harvest by fishermen. **[6]**

b The mass of warm water sitting at the surface during an El Niño year acts as fuel for tropical cyclones. Tropical cyclones need warm water and low pressure areas to form, both of which are prevalent in an El Niño year. However, reduced winds may make it harder for the cyclone to create the rotating winds needed. **[3]**

[Total mark: 11]

3 a During a summer monsoon, the air over the Indian landmass is much warmer than that of over the ocean. This creates a low-pressure zone as the warm air rises. The low-pressure zone pulls in cooler, moist air from over the Indian Ocean towards the land. Once the moist air reaches the landmass, it begins to release the water vapour in the form of torrential rains. During the winter, the low-pressure zone is over the warmer ocean. This means drought conditions for the Indian landmass, instead of rains. **(8)**

b The summer rains cause massive flooding in many parts of India, but they also bring much needed water for agriculture. **[2]**

[Total mark: 10]

4 a i The oxygen minimum layer forms between 200 and 500 m deep. At this depth, levels of photosynthesis are low due to lack of sunlight. Thus oxygen production by producers is low. There is very little mixing in this region, so turbulence has little impact on incoming oxygen. However, organisms do live in the region and they consume oxygen through cellular respiration. **[5]**

ii Carbon dioxide levels at the surface are low, with an increase around 500 m deep. The levels of carbon dioxide decrease after this peak. **[2]**

iii At the surface, producers are using carbon dioxide in order to photosynthesise. At 500 m, there are no producers, but consumers in the region are creating carbon dioxide through cellular respiration. **[2]**

[Total mark: 9]

Chapter 8

1 a Photosynthesis rate is limited by light intensity and carbon dioxide concentration and temperature;

Deeper water has less light intensity;

Less red light;

As red light is absorbed by the surface waters;

So less light energy is available for photosynthesis;

Temperature is lower in deeper water;

So photosynthetic enzymatic reactions are slower;

Carbon dioxide levels are lower in deeper water;

As there are fewer animals respiring;

So there are less raw materials for photosynthesis

Coastal waters are more turbid/cloudy accept converse;

So less light penetration reducing depth to which photosynthesis can occur

(max 9)

b (run-off) contains nitrates and phosphates;

Which promote producer growth

Leading to overcompetition for light

Producers die and are decomposed;

By bacteria;

(Bacterial) aerobic respiration rate is high/accept respiration with oxygen;

Reducing oxygen levels of water causing animals to suffocate

(max 6)

[Total mark: 15]

2 a i (Pneumatocysts) help blades/kelp to float;

Keeping the blades in contact with light;

(so) photosynthesis can occur making carbohydrates for growth **[3]**

    ii to stop the kelp being dislodged **[1]**

b i Kelp → sea urchin → sea otter **[1]**

    ii More sea urchins;

      (so) more kelp is eaten (by sea urchins)

      Less kelp acting as food for fish;

      Or reduced nursery grounds/shelter

      Causing reduction of fish populations

      (max 4)

      [Total mark: 9]

3 **a** higher oxygen; lower carbon dioxide; lower nitrogen; more water/humidity; accept for one mark one other correctly named rare gas (e.g. helium) **(max 2)**

  b i Temperature; increasing temperature increases the rate **[2]**

    ii Light intensity/carbon dioxide concentration; increasing temperature has no effect on rate **[2]**

    iii A line that rises, stays flat and then decreases; levels off at a lower temperature **[2]**

    iv Enzymes; denature **[2]**

  c 19 °C22 °C; higher temperature does not increase the rate any more so costs money for no gain **[2]**

      [Total mark: 12]

4 **a** 6 CO_2 (on left); 6 H_2O (on right); **[2]**

  b i Air bladders help floatation of fronds; to maximise surface area exposed to sunlight for (maximal) photosynthesis; in surface water where all light wavelengths are present; no holdfast as ocean is too deep to anchor to **[3]**

    ii Fixes carbon/produces carbohydrates (idea of) base of food chain; acts as a shelter/nursery ground keeps organisms/eggs safe from predators; other organisms can attach to it and be dispersed; produces oxygen; for respiration; acts as shade **[5]**

      [Total mark: 11]

Chapter 9

1 **a** i Osmoregulator: (animal) that alters internal water content/salt content when placed in different concentration of salt **[1]**

Osmoconformer: (animal) that has same {body fluid/cell/cytoplasm} concentration as the surrounding water **[1]**

Euryhaline: (animal) that can live in a wide range of salinities/can live in fresh water and salt water/rivers and seas **[1]**

    ii Drinking water;

      Excreting salt from gills/urine;

      By active transport/pumping **[3]**

  b i Mussel population increases, stays constant, falls; as the salinity of water increases **[2]**

    ii Mussels are osmoconformers;

      Adapted to live with salt concentration/salinity of estuary/brackish water/medium salinity

      In {fresh water/river water} water enters cells

      By osmosis (credit once);

      In {highly saline water/seawater water leaves

      By osmosis (credit once);

      Estuary/brackish water is isotonic **(max 4)**

      [Total mark: 12]

2 **a** i (any two of):

      Age of fish/mass/weight/health of fish;

      Starting oxygen concentration;

      Previous food given;

      Light levels;

      Volume of tank

      Salinity of water

      Movement of fish **(max 2)**

    ii Repeat and take mean **[1]**

    iii 1.17 and 2.13 **[2]**

      One mark for calculating 3.5 and 6.4 **[2]**

    iv Increasing temperature increases rate of oxygen use;

      Due to increased aerobic respiration rate;

      Due to collision frequencies/increased kinetic energy;

      Reference to enzymes **(max 3)**

  b Increased temperature reduces dissolved oxygen concentration;

    Increased temperature increases respiration rate of fish/tilapia;

    (which) increases rate of removal of oxygen;

409

Leading to inadequate oxygen in the water;

Fish suffocate **(max 4)**

[Total mark: 12]

3 a i Oxygen

Carbon dioxide **[1]**

ii Less oxygen in lower depths;

(due to) lack of producers/lack of surface dissolution

Oxygen is required for respiration;

Providing energy/ATP;

For muscle contraction **(max 4)**

b i Large surface area : volume ratio;

Gas exchange by diffusion;

Short diffusion path **[3]**

ii Concentration gradient: maintained by blood movement/ventilation movement/pumped ventilation

Large surface area: many filaments/primary lamellae/secondary lamellae;

Diffusion distance: thin gill epithelium/wall **[3]**

[Total mark: 11]

4 a i Pumped:

Grouper

Muscle contraction (of mouth)

Pushes water over gills

Reference to pressure gradients

Ram:

Tuna/shark

Ref to open mouth and swimming

Forward movement forces water over gills **(max 6)**

ii Pumped enables ventilation while stationary

To hide from predators/stay in area with food

Ram ventilation reduces energy use

Increased rate of ventilation **(max 3)**

b In fresh water, water potential is higher outside body/salinity is lower outside body

In seawater, water potential is lower outside body/salinity is higher outside body

Water moves from high water potential to a low water potential across membrane

(In fresh water) active pumping of ions into body fluids;

(in fresh water) large urine volume produced;

(in salt water) active pumping of ions out of body (by gills/kidney);

(in salt water) drink water;

(in salt water) produce low urine volume with high salt/ion concentration;

Credit ref to membrane protein pumps **(max 6)**

[Total mark: 15]

5 a i Higher temperature increases evaporation;

Increasing salinity/salt concentration

(river water) brings fresh water;

Lowering salinity/reducing salt concentration **[4]**

ii Bay areas

Have rivers reducing salinity

Bay areas have glacial meltwater reducing salinity;

Region near North Sea has ocean water mixing increasing salinity;

Due to tidal action **(max 3)**

b Limpet has body fluid/cells at concentration equal to marine water;

In (Bothnia) water will be hypotonic

Water enters limpet by osmosis;

Cell damage/bursting **(max 3)**

[Total mark: 10]

Chapter 10

1 a Hermaphrodite clam releases gametes into water/ broadcast spawn;

Spawning inducing substance (SIS) is released coordinating release of gametes from other clams;

External fertilisation occurs;

Trochophore larva (hatches);

Lives/feeds among plankton;

Shell/vellum develops;

(changes into) veliger;

Foot grows;

To develop into a pediveliger;

(pediveliger) settles/sinks;

Attaches to substrate and metamorphoses into a juvenile;

Juvenile grows;

Begins as a male and becomes a hermaphrodite
(max 10)

b Both populations would reduce;

Mangroves are a nursery ground;

Mysis shrimp larvae settle in mangroves

Grouper larvae are brought to mangroves by ocean currents;

Providing food and shelter;

(for) juvenile groupers and shrimp **(max 5)**

[Total mark:15]

2 a i Fertilisation is the fusion of gametes/sperm and eggs;

Internal fertilisation occurs inside the body and external outside the body; **[2]**

ii 1.49×10^{-6} (%) and 90 (%);

Award one mark for correct method **[2]**

iii Whale is a *K*-strategist/produces few offspring but has high levels of parental care;

Giant clam is an *r*-strategist/produces many offspring but has no/low parental care;

It is impossible to care for/add nutrients for so many offspring as a giant clam;

Whale has only one egg (so it) is important to care to help survival **(max 3)**

b Sharks are born at a large size/fully formed;

So less likely to be predated;

Other offspring/siblings provide nutrients;

Such as protein;

For growth;

Selection occurs (in utero) to only allow strongest offspring to survive **(max 4)**

[Total mark: 11]

3 a i Too slow: insufficient oxygen (accept converse);

Too fast: fry are washed away **[2]**

ii Alevins are hidden from predators/not washed away **[1]**

iii Different food sources in river and ocean;

Different stages are not competing with each other

Prevents cannibalism;

Young fish would be more easily predated/die in the ocean **(max 3)**

b Dam prevents adult salmon migrating upstream;

(to) gravel beds;

Fewer eggs fertilised/young salmon produced;

Less food for bears so bear population drops **[4]**

[Total mark: 10]

4 a Many tuna accumulate in the same area;

Higher probability of fertilisation occurring;

An individual tuna will fertilise gametes from several other tuna

Increased genetic diversity of offspring; **(max 3)**

b Wasteful as many gametes are lost;

Random fertilisation increasing genetic diversity **[2]**

c Large mouth/many teeth to catch prey;

Shiny/silver colour to camouflage from predators **[2]**

[Total mark: 7]

5 a i Axes labelled correctly;

Linear scales on both axes;

Plots correct;

Straight line joining the points/correct curve of best fit **[4]**

ii Increasing concentration increases number of clams releasing gametes;

(almost) no effect up to and including 14, steep increase at 22 **[2]**

b i (two from) temperature/water volume/species of clam/age of clam/sunlight/salinity; **[2]**

ii No – any percentage between 14% and 22% could be the value **[1]**

iii When clams release gametes they will release more SIS **[1]**

c Low concentrations do not elicit response as it means the clam is distant/wasting gametes;

SIS synchronising gamete release helping to ensure fertilisation **[2]**

[Total mark: 12]

Chapter 11

1 a i Catch divided by fishing effort;

Fishing effort is a measure of intensity/boat days/boat sizes

Low CPUE indicates low catch and/or high effort;

So fish stocks are declining;

Accept converse for last two points **[4]**

411

ii Reduced catch;

Increased population/recruitment;

No fishing during breeding season;

When fish aggregate;

No fishing in nursery areas;

Allowing juveniles/larval forms to mature;

No fishing during migrations;

Protects other species in certain areas/during their breeding

Cost of monitoring;

Reduced income of fishers **(max 6)**

b Increased primary productivity;

For food chains

Protection against erosion;

Nursery grounds;

For named species (grouper/shrimp)

More larvae develop

Increased recruitment to protect stocks;

More income for fishers **(max 5)**

[Total mark: 15]

2 a i Linear x-and y-axes;

Both axes labelled and with units;

Plots correct;

Points joined with straight lines;

Key for both lines **[5]**

ii 85.5%;

One mark for 55–8 or reference to 47 **[2]**

iii CPUE for both fall;

Cod increases after falling;

Cod falls more steeply;

Cod falls earlier

Credit manipulated numerical comparison **(max 3)**

b CPUE increases after restrictions/2005;

So stocks are increasing;

Idea of delayed effect;

Fishers turned to pollock when restricted from cod;

As pollock CPUE falls after the ban;

So restriction has harmed other species **(max 4)**

[Total mark: 14]

3 a i Any three from:

Restriction of areas;

Restriction of seasons;

Restriction of fishing method/gear types;

Restriction of boat number/sizes/engine sizes;

Restriction of fish sizes **[3]**

ii Short-term:

Reduced income;

Some unemployment;

Effect on life quality

Long-term:

Stocks are retained;

So fishing industry continues;

Guarantee of future incomes/employment **(max 4)**

b i Initially a small fall/no effect;

Rise in profits (from 2005) **[2]**

ii Fewer scallops harvested;

As fewer boats/lower quotas

Prices of scallops rise

Scallop population eventually rises due to management **[4]**

[Total mark: 13]

4 a i Over fishing

High amounts of bycatch

Damage to habitat/seabed **[3]**

ii Purse seine takes large quantities/rod and line less efficient;

Purse seine is less selective/rod and line is very selective;

No damage to dolphins/turtles **[3]**

b i 218;

One mark for correctly calculating a number of fish using the percentages;

One mark for subtracting number of fish in 2005 from number of fish in 1985 **[3]**

ii Peak at 10–13 for both years;

Fewer older fish in 2005/converse;

Higher proportion of smaller fish in 2005;

Overfishing means that fewer fish survive to older ages **(max 3)**

iii Smaller fish/immature fish escape;

Can then mature and breed **[2]**

[Total mark: 14]

Chapter 12

1 a Any three of:

Extensive is in open water (or converse for intensive);

Extensive has food supplied by natural water/intensive requires extra feeding

Extensive has wastes removed by natural water/intensive requires filtering of water

Extensive has little management/intensive has more human input **(max 3)**

b i Provides oxygen;

For respiration **[2]**

ii Flushing through waste

That would cause pollution/disease **[2]**

iii Faeces/wastes/ammonium/old food released into sea;

(wastes) are broken down into nitrates/phosphates/named mineral ions;

Causing growth of algae/plants/eutrophication;

Over-competition for light amongst algae causing algal death

Decomposition by bacteria;

Respiration (by bacteria) using oxygen;

Suffocation of organisms **(max 5)**

[Total mark: 12]

2 a Collect adult fish/brood fish from wild;

Allow fish to spawn and collect fertilised eggs;

Ref to injection of hCG to induce spawning;

Place eggs into tanks with seawater/salt water;

Aerate to provide oxygen

Feed with invertebrates/rotifers

Ref to illumination to encourage natural food

Transfer to nursery tanks (at 2–3 cm length);

High protein diet for juveniles;

Transfer to floating cages/ponds;

Use of natural water currents to filter water and oxygenate;

Ref to addition of adult tilapia to produce larval tilapia as food source **(max 8)**

b Loss of nursery areas for other species;

Spread of disease into wild populations;

Pollution/eutrophication

Loss of habitats for species;

Coastal erosion

Reduced catch of fish;

Competition for products with fishers;

Loss of fishing employment;

Conflict over land;

Inflationary prices **(max 7)**

[Total mark: 15]

3 a Loss of habitats for native species/nursery grounds;

Waste food/faeces release into river/ocean;

Eutrophication

Reducing oxygen levels in water causing suffocation/eq of species;

Disease affecting wild organisms;

Escape of shrimp affecting food chains

Reduced fish/wild shrimp catch;

Loss of revenue/employment for fishing industry;

Loss of tourism as area is no longer desirable **(max 6)**

b Ensure that areas of mangrove are protected;

Low stocking densities

Filter water to remove wastes;

Minimise use of pesticides/eq;

Nets/eq to prevent escape of shrimp;

Use food that has not been collected from ocean/river **(max 5)**

c Requires fish/other animals as food/herbivores require plants

Which are collected from natural water/plants can be grown in farms;

Causing depletion of stocks of other species/plant products can be grown in farms **[3]**

[Total mark: 14]

4 a Brood clams taken from wild

Placed into (concrete) tanks;

Ref to use of disinfectants

Gonad/SIS placed into water to start spawning;

Larvae fed with phytoplankton;

Spats collected and transferred to gravel trays (gravel trays) placed into nursery tanks;

Ref to use of fertiliser;

Placed in cages in open water **(max 6)**

b Risk of damage to habitat;

Availability of feed/risk of environmental damage due to taking feed from ocean

Availability of clean water;

Risk of pollution;

Risk of disease spread;

Risk of escape;

Competition with other industries/people for resources such as water;

Availability of employment;

Risk of damage to employment;

Economic impact

Access to market **(max 9)**

[Total mark: 9]

5 a i

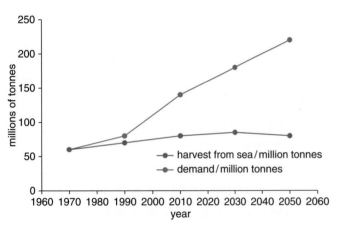

Axes labelled with units;

Linear scales used;

Plots correct;

Points joined by straight lines;

Key for each line **[5]**

ii 140 million tonnes **[1]**

b Two or more different feed types used;

Measure change in mass of fish/length of fish;

Measure mass of faeces;

Ref to stated time;

Ref to repeats and means;

Ref to two control variables, e.g. temperature/other food types/oxygen/light/water volume/tank size **[6]**

[Total mark: 12]

Chapter 13

1 a Solar radiation warms the planet;

Greenhouse gases (carbon dioxide/methane

Prevent infrared light leaving/reflect infrared light back to the surface

Resulting in a retention of heat **(max 3)**

b i Increased burning of fossil fuel;

From power stations/transport

Releasing carbon dioxide;

Increased rice farming/cattle;

Increasing methane production;

Credit ref to CFC/nitrous oxide;

More infrared light is trapped;

Causing an enhanced greenhouse effect **(max 5)**

ii Global temperature rise;

Ice sheet melting;

Loss of habitats/flooding;

Increase in sea-levels;

Reduction in salinity;

Change in water currents;

Change in ranges;

Change in producer productivity;

Extinction;

Effects on food chains

Coral bleaching;

Climate change/storms **(max 7)**

[Total mark: 15]

2 a As mean trophic level increases, mercury concentration increases;

different species at different trophic levels have different mercury concentrations (e.g. swordfish and bigeye tuna have same trophic level but different mercury concentrations) ; some species (e.g. monkfish) have lower amounts of mercury than their trophic level would suggest / eq ; **(max 2)**

b Standard deviation shows variation between individuals;

(two from) Different diets/ages of fish/food webs/locations fish taken from **[2]**

c Mercury is not broken down/lost from bodies/tissues;

Bioaccumulates;

Enters low trophic levels at low concentrations;

Predators eat many doses of mercury

Concentration increases along food chain/
biomagnifies   **(max 4)**

[Total mark: 9]

3 a i 48/100 × 84 = 40 fish ;

(one mark for 48%)   **[2]**

ii Decrease, increase, decrease;

Credit correct manipulated data   **[2]**

iii After factory closed, less waste released so fewer
cancers;

Toxins present in the sediment;

Dredging releases toxins from sediment;

So cancer increases in 1992

Rates eventually fall as dredging has removed
bulk of toxins   **(max 4)**

b Physical damage to habitat

Loss of benthic/eq organisms;

Sediment agitation

Damaging gills/suffocation/settling on benthic
organisms;

Eutrophication due to organic matter release;

Loss of oxygen in water   **(max 4)**

[Total mark: 12]

4 a i Individuals with vested interest in an industry/area

Fisheries employees/farmers   **[2]**

ii Nitrates/phosphates

Increased algal growth/algal blooms;

Decomposition of dead algae;

Bacterial respiration;

Using oxygen   **(max 4)**

b i Increased mean global temperature;

Due to human influences   **[2]**

ii Rain dissolves fertilisers;

More run-off   **[2]**

iii Climate change;

More rain/storms

More pathogens;

Spread of other organisms to area;

Spawning affected by temperature change

(max 3)

[Total mark: 13]

5 a i Preventing bias/representative sample

[1]

ii To compare/set base line   **[1]**

iii Physical/environmental factors   **[1]**

b i General decrease in numbers;

Most species reduced;

One species (brittlestar) unchanged;

One species (rock crab) increased   **(max 3)**

ii (15 − 8)/8 × 100 = 87.5%;

One mark for 15 − 8 = 7   **[2]**

iii Waste brine increases salinity;

Action of waste water agitates seabed reducing
light penetration;

Waste water is hot;

Hot water reduces oxygen concentration;

Cleaning fluid is acidic   **(max 3)**

iv Inability to osmoregulate for most species

(one from) poisoned by acidity/suffocate due to
low oxygen/gills damaged by sediment/lack of
food;

Rock crabs increased as less competition/
vacant niche   **(max 3)**

[Total mark: 14]

Chapter 14

1 a i Increase in both from 2003;

Higher increase in coho salmon;

Coho salmon continue to increase/Chinook
salmon do not continuously increase

Credit manipulated numerical answer

(max 3)

ii accept 231% for two marks;

(262–79) or 183 for one mark   **[2]**

iii Far more successful for coho salmon;

Some success but other factors must limit
chinook salmon;

Some periods when chinook salmon population
have fallen;

May be some competition between chinook and
coho salmon

(which) reduces the chinook population

(max 3)

b i Salmon able to reach upstream areas;

More spawning/breeding **[2]**

ii Prevent run-off into upstream areas/areas salmon spawn;

Causing eutrophication/loss of oxygen

Which would kill salmon fry/eggs/alevins **[3]**

iii One of: infection/genetic weakness/different genetic strains **[1]**

[Total mark: 14]

2 a i Preservation/preventing extinction

Of natural areas/species/habitats **[2]**

ii Visiting natural areas without damage

To ecology/habitat/species/local communities **[2]**

b Ban on fishing;

Reducing catches;

Loss of historical/cultural fishing sites;

Ban on visits to sensitive areas;

Ban on hotel building;

Restrictions on number of tourists **(max 5)**

c Restrict size/capacity/tourist number;

Use local materials;

Use sustainable building materials/wood from sustainable sources;

Reduce fossil fuel transport methods/encourage more sustainable transport methods

Plant trees for each visitor to offset carbon footprint;

Use solar power;

Wind power/wave power

Recycling facilities for refuse;

Sewage treatment facilities;

Education programmes for tourists;

Use locally raised food;

Other valid points **(max 6)**

[Total mark: 15]

3 a i Small decrease from centre/restricted areas;

Steep decrease in fully fished areas **[2]**

ii Fished area has more fish taken;

Highest level in centre as fish do not migrate out;

Higher in fished area near to MPA as fish spill over from MPA **[3]**

b i Loss of catch/restrictions

Loss of revenue/unemployment

Loss of historically important fishing area **(max 2)**

ii Refuge for fish breeding;

Spill over into fished areas;

Ensures that fishing is a long-term prospect **[3]**

[Total mark: 10]

4 a i 136%;

One mark for 59 200 **[2]**

ii Continuous scale on *y*-axis;

Both axes labelled;

Bar chart drawn;

Correct plotting of bars on bar chart;

Bars labelled **[5]**

b Provides money for projects;

Stops other activities destroying the areas;

Employs people so that they do not join non-sustainable industries;

Educates so that people are aware of conservation issues;

Provides employment

Provides revenue for service industries/eq;

Preserves local areas **(max 5)**

[Total mark: 12]

5 a Both decline and then increase from 1994;

between 1982 and 1984, kelp increases in the marine reserve but decreases in the fished area;

marine reserve kelp is always higher than fished area

Both increase from 1988 to 1994;

Fished area has a sharper increase between 1992 and 1994 **(max 3)**

b Fishing reduces number of fish so less predation of sea urchins;

Sea urchin population increases and eats more kelp **[2]**

c Any two from:

El Niño/sea otter populations/crab populations/climate change/light intensity/sedimentation/new predators/nitrate or phosphate levels/run-off **[2]**

[Total mark: 7]

Chapter 15

1 a i Increasing temperature generates a small increase on oil digestion/increased transmission;

Adding fertiliser generates the largest increase on the oil digestion/increased transmission;

Adding dispersant generates a small increase on the oil digestion/increased transmission;

There is a combined effect of increasing all factors together;

Credit manipulated numerical comparison **(max 4)**

ii (Any factors) increase rate of bacterial activity/ digestion

(Temperature) increases respiration rate of bacteria/enzyme kinetics

(Dispersant) increases surface area in contact with bacteria

(Fertiliser) increases bacterial growth rate/ prevents minerals limiting bacterial growth **[4]**

iii any two from: bacterial number/ concentration; salinity; pH; agitation; volume of oil; type of oil/eq; light intensity **[1]**

b Increased plant/algae growth;

Over-competition for light

Death and decomposition of plants/algae;

Bacterial growth;

Increased rate of aerobic respiration (by bacteria) **(max 4)**

[Total mark: 13]

2 a i Humans select (organism) with characteristics;

Mate together and select offspring **[2]**

ii Introducing new genes;

That have come from other species **[2]**

b Growth hormone gene;

From chinook salmon;

Promoter;

From ocean pout;

(Use of) plasmid vector;

Correct reference to restriction endonuclease;

Correct reference to DNA ligase;

Injection into salmon eggs;

Selection of fish that contain the gene **(max 7)**

c Escape of salmon;

Out-competing wild salmon;

Over-consumption of food sources

effect on food chains;

Interbreeding with wild salmon **(max 4)**

[Total mark: 15]

3 a i Use of linear scales for x-and y-axes;

Correct plots;

Correct curves of best fit with key/lines labelled;

Axes labelled with units **[4]**

ii Tangents drawn to both curves at one month;

Correct calculations of gradients consistent with the tangent drawn **[2]**

iii Genetically engineered salmon have higher standard deviations;

So there is more variation in masses;

Suggests that in some cases the gene has not integrated/integrates into an inactive section of genome;

So some salmon have no additional growth **[4]**

b Salmon can be harvested sooner;

More salmon can be grown in each year;

Can meet demand more easily **[3]**

[Total mark: 13]

4 a (pout) promoter; (chinook salmon) growth hormone **[2]**

b i 500 **[1]**

ii In case of escape;

Will not breed with wild salmon;

Will not pass gene onto wild salmon;

Will not reproduce with other GM salmon **(max 3)**

iii (In the event of) no full scientific consensus on safety

All possible risks are considered

GM organisms could have risks on food chains

Cause extinction of native species

Outcompete native species **(max 4)**

[Total mark: 10]

417

Chapter 2

1 a Light does not easily penetrate the ice.

Light intensity under the ice is too low for phytoplankton

Algae can photosynthesise at lower light intensity

b Snow blown away decreases the distance for light to penetrate.

Increased light intensity under ice.

Increased photosynthesis.

Increased oxygen production: $CO_2 + H_2O = glucose + O_2$

c Cracks allow access to the water to feed/avoid predation

Cracks allow access to the ice to nest/avoid predation

2 a algae → krill → lantern fish → squid → killer whales/seals

b Krill are a vital part of food chains for a variety of Antarctic consumers including fish, birds, squid, whales, seals and Emperor penguins. A decrease in krill populations has a significant negative effect on the health and abundance of these consumers. Krill are therefore indicators of the overall health of the Southern Ocean ecosystem.

3 a 10 000 pairs = 20 000 penguins

20 000 penguins = 0.7 × original number of penguins

Original number of penguins = 20 000/0.7

Original number of penguins = 28 571 penguins

29 000 penguins to the nearest 1000

b Adelie penguins: specialised niche – krill – less able to adapt to changes in food supply – at risk of starving if krill is low in abundance

Gentoo penguins: generalised niche – feed on a wider range of species – able to change food supply when one species of prey is low in abundance – less chance of starving.

c Less sea ice – less space/time for penguins to moult

Less moult leads to increase death due to disease/hypothermia

d In cold periods there is more time to moult – more penguins survive.

In cold periods there is less food so less nutrients for laying eggs.

4 Less photosynthesis by phytoplankton – less oxygen – reduced oxygen for benthic aerobic respiration

Less phytoplankton producers for consumers in benthic food chains

Reduced detritus (snow fall) for benthic decomposers

Chapter 3

1 Excess nutrients wash into the water; especially nitrates and phosphates; this leads to an algal bloom; blue-green algae grow; when they die they sink to the bottom; bacteria feed on the dead algae; respiration by increased numbers of bacteria uses up the dissolved oxygen; the water becomes hypoxic; marine life either dies or has to migrate to different waters

2 Increased population sizes means more treated sewage; increased reliance on inorganic fertilisers; more flooding and therefore erosion due to global warming; allow more research has taken place so more have been found

3 The size depends on the levels of nutrients washed into the Mississippi River; droughts mean less water in the river; flooding means more water and also more leaching of nutrients; the amount of fertiliser used can also vary.

4 In spring and summer the water is more stratified with a less dense layer on top; there is less mixing between the layers so no more oxygen can enter the deeper waters; higher levels of light and higher temperatures increase the productivity of algae and make algal blooms more likely

5 Reduced use of inorganic fertilisers – fewer nutrients present to wash into the river

Timing the use of fertilisers – to avoid heavy rain and therefore reducing leaching and run-off

Increasing the area of flood plains – so that sediment is left behind when the flood recedes and the nutrients in the sediment do not make their way into the Gulf

Avoiding draining wetlands – avoids flooding and means that soil is less likely to wash away

Reducing discharge of animal waste and treated sewage into the water – reduces the concentration of nutrients reaching the Gulf of Mexico

Chapter 4

1 **a** Growth of trees is important to the survival of salmon because the trees shade the water, keeping it at the optimum temperature for the salmon eggs and ensuring that enough oxygen remains dissolved in the water for respiration. The trees also prevent soil erosion and so prevent sediment from entering the water.

   b Salmon increase the growth of trees by providing a flow of nitrogen compounds which originate in the ocean. When the salmon are killed by the bears, their carcasses are left in the forest where they rot down and eventually provide nitrates for the trees. Since nitrate is a limiting factor for the trees, increasing the amount of nitrate increases growth.

2 **a** Ammonia is taken up by phytoplankton and used to build proteins; phytoplankton are eaten by zooplankton and the radioactive nitrogen is incorporated into zooplankton protein. The zooplankton is eaten by juvenile salmon and the radioactive isotope is assimilated into salmon protein. When the salmon return to the stream to spawn, they may be caught by bears and the carcasses left to rot in the forest. The amino acids containing the radioactive isotope are released during decomposition. Amino acids are converted into ammonia, then nitrite and nitrate, which can be taken up by the trees.

   [There are alternative routes which are equally valid, for example the ammonia could be converted into nitrate in the ocean before being taken up by phytoplankton, zooplankton could be eaten by smaller fish which are then eaten by adult salmon]

   b The faeces and urine from the bears contain nitrogen-containing compounds from the salmon; these are broken down in the same way as the salmon carcasses. When the bears die, their bodies also rot and the nutrients from the salmon which were assimilated into bear biomass are broken down. This is true for any other species (e.g. eagles) which might feed on the salmon.

3 Any of:
   - carbon – in any named organic molecule (e.g. glucose, lipids, DNA)
   - calcium – in bones and teeth
   - phosphorus – in DNA and bone
   - magnesium – in all living cells and in bone (do not allow chlorophyll since salmon are not photosynthetic)

4 Eagles, wolves, crows, pine martens, gulls, which eat the salmon; also any species that feeds on part of the tree (e.g. insects)

5 **a** Nitrogen in the forest is returned to the marine ecosystem through excretion, death and decomposition followed by surface run-off. For example, when the trees die, they are decomposed and eventually the nitrogen-containing compounds are nitrified into nitrates. Nitrates are soluble and can be leached from the soil by heavy rain and flow back to the ocean. The same is true for the bodies of any animals that feed on the salmon when they die and decompose. The urine and faeces from the bears and from any other species that feed on the salmon also decompose to eventually release nitrates into the soil.

   b Since the salmon and the trees in the forest rely on each other for survival it is not possible to focus on conservation of one without the other. Trees are necessary for salmon reproduction and salmon are necessary for successful growth of the trees.

Chapter 5

1 Causes of crown-of-thorns starfish outbreak include nutrient pollution causing plankton blooms and over-fishing of their predators.

2 Tropical cyclones may lead to outbreaks in two ways: (1) they can introduce excess fertiliser into the water causing plankton blooms; (2) the damage done during the cyclone harms the coral, making it harder to recover from crown-of-thorns outbreaks, creating a positive-feedback loop.

3 When a reef is over-fished, predators of the crown-of-thorns are removed, making survival much easier for this predator of coral. Additionally, poor waste management, particularly in island nations, leads to excess nutrients in the form of run-off and fertilisers being introduced into the ocean. As previously

419

mentioned, these nutrients create plankton blooms making it easier for the larval form of this starfish to survive.

4   When the crown-of-thorns starfish is not in outbreak status it helps coral reefs. By eating fast-growing corals, it makes room for the slower growing corals to survive. Without these predators, the slow-growing corals would be taken over by the faster growing species reducing overall coral diversity on the reef.

Chapter 6

1   If the outflow of fresh water is high enough, it may push further into the ocean and affect organisms that are not used to the lower salinity levels of estuaries. Also, estuaries act as nurseries, so if the young fish die off because of the low salinity levels or raised pollution levels, the overall population size of that species will decrease. This will impact upon the food chain.

2   Answers will vary, but both sides are negatively impacted by the failing infrastructure of the lake. Estuary incomes include tourism, fishing, boat charters, snorkelling, restaurants, and hotels – all are negatively impacted because of the appearance and quality of the water entering the ecosystem. Agricultural economies rely on fields that are not flooded and people who can get to work. The economies of both systems are fragile and need a better system to ensure their survival.

3   Seagrasses and phytoplankton are the dominant producers in estuary habitats. Massive die-offs of producers reduce the overall energy available for the consumers in the ecosystems. Consumers that rely on seagrasses because they do not eat plankton are especially harmed.

4   Answers will vary, but some suggestions for improved water quality and quantity include:
   * increasing the flow of water from Lake Okeechobee south toward Florida Bay
   * building additional reservoirs to the east and west
   * restoring the Caloosahatchee and St Lucie river systems to their natural slower-moving, meandering path rather than the deep, fast-paced canals they have become.

Chapter 7

1   Answer may vary: oyster → grey mullet → china fish → crab → humans

2   Because Minamata Bay is secluded, the contaminated water tended to stay within the confines of the bay. This made the levels of methylmercury much higher than if the waters had poured directly into the ocean where they would have been diluted. The higher levels of methylmercury then had a better chance of entering the food web.

3   Answers will vary, but a general idea of toxins being greatest at the top of the food chain should be present.

4   The concentrations of methylmercury doubled in nearly every organism as it made its way through the food chain.

Chapter 8

1   Possible reasons:
   * *Karenia brevis* releases brevetoxin. *Karenia* will be ingested by filter feeders such as scallops and accumulate. This will pass up through the food chain so that by the time it reaches dolphins it will be toxic.
   * Brevetoxins affect the respiratory system directly so reducing the ability of marine mammals to breathe.
   * Manatees will eat large quantities of seagrass that will have *Karenia* deposited on it thus accumulating large quantities of the toxin.
   * Diarrhoea occurs in marine mammals due to brevetoxin leading to dehydration.

2   * Algal growth is high so that there is over-competition for light.
   * Many algae die and are decomposed.
   * The decomposer bacteria respire aerobically
   * Using up oxygen so that oxygen levels are reduced
   * Fish that require high levels of oxygen die due to suffocation

3   * Shellfish accumulate large quantities of algae due to filter feeding
   * The shellfish will contain toxins that will cause human poisoning
   * The short-term effect is to reduce fish populations reducing income immediately. Closure of fishing grounds will reduce income
   * If recurrent poisonings of humans occur there will be a loss of confidence in the products so less demand resulting in reduced prices and less income for fishing

4 • Agricultural farming uses fertilisers which are usually soluble

• Fertilisers contain nitrates, phosphates and other minerals

• The minerals dissolve and leach into rivers and eventually the sea

• Nitrate and phosphate are essential for the production of chlorophyll, ATP and other many other substances in algae.

• Animal farming produces large amounts of farmyard slurry (organic waste)

• Organic waste washes into rivers and then decomposes

• Decomposition releases minerals for algal growth

5 • Carbon dioxide is a raw material for photosynthesis

• Carbon dioxide will not be a limiting factor/more carbon dioxide results in more photosynthesis increasing algal growth

• Carbon dioxide may cause global warming

• Higher temperature will increase rate of photosynthesis so that algal productivity is higher

Chapter 9

1 • Increasing cotton and agricultural farming by Soviet Union

• Diverting of two rivers to move water to take water to irrigate crops

• Inefficient irrigation led to large scale water loss

• Lack of water entering the rivers led to gradual reduction in the volume of water

• Evaporation of water from surface loses water

2 • Before 1960, the salinity was low being mainly fresh water – brackish with areas of fresh water where rivers empty into the sea. Some slightly higher salinity to the eastern part of the sea.

• In 1989, lack of fresh water entering the river results in increase in salinity across all of sea. Little fresh water enters the sea. Evaporation of water leads to water loss and increase in salinity.

• In 2006, the sea has split into several parts. The North Aral Sea salinity has reduced due to creation of dam preventing water loss into the South Aral Sea. Some fresh water still enters from the river. The South Aral Sea is hyperhaline as there is now no flow of water from the North Aral Sea and little/no fresh water entering from the rivers. There is increased

evaporation of water from the South Aral Sea increasing salinity further.

3 • Stenolhaline fish can only tolerate a narrow range of salinities.

• Water in the Aral Sea became hypertonic compared to body fluids.

• Water is drawn out of fish via gills and skin into the water by osmosis.

• Fresh-water fish are not adapted to drink water to replace lost water and their ion pumps pump ions into the fish rather than excreting excess ions.

• Fish dehydrate, cells shrink resulting in death

4 • Euryhaline fish can tolerate a broader range of salinities.

• As the lake becomes increasingly saline, fish drink water to replace lost water and actively excrete ions through gills and kidney by reversing the direction of ion pumping.

• Euryhaline fish can alter the amount of ion pumping according to the external water salinity.

5 Pros:

• Cotton is a major cash crop bringing foreign revenue for the country

• Provides employment for people

Cons:

• Loss of fishing industry due to extinction of fish.

• Displacement of local population due to lack of employment

• Health effects on people

• Ecological effects on food chains due to loss of fish

• Toxicity of salt to crops

• Controversial labour system that many regard as exploitation

Chapter 10

1 • Pacific salmon take nutrients from the ocean in order to grow

• The salmon migrate up the rivers to spawn

• Many species rely on the salmon migration for food, e.g. bears, eagles

• Salmon are a key component of the river and land food chain from which energy originates in ocean

• Without the annual salmon migration, many species will have little/no food

2 a • Salmon cannot swim upstream past the dam
  • The best breeding grounds are in the higher river reaches
  • Less spawning results in fewer of all stages of salmon so fewer smolts migrate into the ocean to grow into adults.
 b • The water moves slowly, warming up and having less oxygen
  • The embryos/fry are able to respire less and die
  • The temperature is too high for optimal alevin/fry development
  • Higher temperature results in more disease
  • The river does not wash gravel from upstream so there are no nesting sites

3 • Less organic matter is washed down to estuary
  • Less food for filter feeders such as clams and oysters
  • Less sand/gravel is deposited in the estuary leading to coastal erosion
  • Less habitat space for juvenile shrimp
  • All populations will reduce

4 Leaflet should contain information explaining:
  • how the dam has led to loss of salmon, affecting food chains and ecosystem
  • how and why salmon is a keystone species
  • effect on the salmon fishing industry
  • effect on commercial species such as clams, shrimps and oysters
  • effect on habitat loss for elk and other species
  • effect on coastal erosion
  • socio-economic effects on the local people
  • effects of regenerating the area on tourism

Chapter 11

1 Idea that agreement is reached between all stakeholders: recreational fishers, commercial fishers, government representatives and scientists. Fishing quotas are set with full agreement and discussion and they have been effective in the past so there is trust between all groups.

2 Any three from:
  • License number: reduces number of boats fishing, lowering catches
  • Gear restrictions: preventing damaging methods such as benthic trawling/intense purse seining to reduce damage to environment and prevent loss of stock
  • Seasonal closure: allowing breeding of fish/allowing periods of time with low pressure on stocks which allows recovery
  • Limits on fishing time: reduces amount of catch
  • Limiting the quantity of fish that can be landed/quota: reduces amount of catch
  • Permanently closing areas/area closures: protects nursery grounds/breeding grounds to allow recruitment
  • Size limits: prevent capture of juveniles
  • AIS/VMS: fishing is monitored constantly by satellite

3 • Biotic factors (examples of)
  • Predation by other species, particularly of young and larval forms
  • Food presence (linked to overall productivity of ecosystem)
  • Disease spread suddenly causing loss of lobsters
 Abiotic factors (examples of)
  • Temperature of water affecting breeding seasons/growth rates
  • Water currents distributing juveniles/bringing food/sediment
  • Wind/storms distributing juveniles/food/sediment/disturbing habitats
  • Light affecting overall productivity of ecosystem

4 • Boat number decrease reduces catch
  • Market price of fewer lobsters increases
  • Increased lobster populations
  • So quotas eventually rise
  • Fewer boats then exist with more lobsters present

5 Points could include, among others:
  • Active management of the fish population
  • Strict licencing rules for both recreational and commercial fishers
  • Money from licencing used to help sustainable projects
  • Methods to increase stocks are used such as artificial reef building
  • Many measures employed such as area closures/gear restrictions, etc.
  • VMS is used to monitor all vessels

- Involvement of all stakeholders in decision making with clear, transparent decisions made
- Policies work for all stakeholders
- Lobster fishing is still highly profitable due to management
- Decisions are made yearly and there is constant stock assessment.

Chapter 12

1.
- Sea stations do not cause significant pollution
- Ammonia is highest for snapper and control. Cobia has lowest ammonia but standard deviations overlap so there is not a definite difference.
- Cobia has least nitrate and phosphate (lower than snapper and control) and most nitrite but standard deviations overlap so no difference from control
- None of the mineral ions show great difference from control as error bars overlap
- Percentage organic material in the seabed is the same for snapper, cobia and the control
- Chlorophyll a content increases slightly with distance from the sea station but error bars overlap so there may be no real difference.

2.
- Feed is sustainable so does not cause depletion of other fish stocks
- Snapper and cobia are produced by using brood fish to produce eggs so this not reducing wild fish populations
- Pollution levels are low and are away from the coast so less coastal eutrophication
- Less need for pesticides and antibiotics
- Large tanks reduce damage to fish so less loss of the stocks increasing profits

3.
- Chlorophyll a is a photosynthetic pigment.
- Found in algae
- Eutrophication results in algal blooms thus increasing chlorophyll a concentration in the water

4.
- Costs are high due to expensive equipment
- High maintenance costs due to hazardous, more hostile offshore conditions
- Low-value fish would not raise enough money when sold
- So profits would be lower
- High-value, premium fish will raise more money than is spent

Chapter 13

1.
- Cap over the well and pumping into ships for disposal
- Containment by using booms
- Burning
- Use of Corexit dispersant
- Skimming ships
- Oil–water separation equipment
- Washing down beaches and removing contaminated sand and tar
- Adding genetically engineered bacteria for bioremediation

2.
- Ingestion causing poisoning
- Damage to eyes
- Suffocation due to lung damage/blowhole blockage of whales and dolphins
- Hypothermia due to loss of insulation
- Inability to fly away from predators/escape from water
- Taking poisoned fish back to chicks, killing chicks

3.
- Corexit and oil products taken up by filter feeders/plankton
- Are not lost from body tissues so bioaccumulate
- Pass through food chains and biomagnify at higher trophic levels
- Oil and Corexit sink to seabeds and is only slowly broken down due to cold
- Constant leakage of toxins into seawater which are taken up directly by dolphins or by other organisms

4.
- Oil-digesting bacteria use oil as a source of energy
- Increased oil increases population of these bacteria
- Respiration rate of bacteria increases
- Using up oxygen in water
- Animals suffocate

5.
- Roots stabilise soil/substrate so prevent erosion
- So habitats could be lost
- Removing nesting sites for birds and other organisms
- Mangroves act as a nursery ground for juvenile fish and invertebrates such as shrimp and crabs
- Loss of juvenile stages causes reduced populations of commercial stocks
- Reducing catch for fisheries
- Loss of species in mangroves that are prey for other commercially important stocks

423

Chapter 14

1 a • Protection of large areas of coral reef
  • Protection of over-fished species such as manta rays, sharks and tuna
  • Act as an area for restoration of other Indian Ocean reefs
  • Protection of many species of sea birds
  • Protection of rare species of turtles
  • Protection of coconut crabs
  • Protection of this area will allow the spillover of species to other areas of Indian Ocean

b • The Chagos Islands have large US/UK military base
  • Preventing access of the area to other groups
  • Preventing the return of the native Chagossians as they would not be able to make a living in the area

2 a • Fishing industry in other areas of Indian Ocean (due to increased fish stocks)
  • Conservation groups such as Greenpeace
  • US/UK governments

b • Chagossian people who would be prevented from returning
  • Mauritian fishing industry which has historical rights to the area
  • Mauritian government which has territorial claims to the area

3 a • Conservation groups want the MPA set up as a no-take area
  • The area would be a model area for other MPAs
  • The environmental effects could be very positive and far reaching, preserving fish stocks for many areas of the Indian Ocean
  • It would be a big step forward in meeting the targets for areas of ocean covered under MPAs
  • Mauritius fishing industry has historical fishing rights in the area
  • Chagos was part of Mauritius and the government should have a say in the project
  • Many Chagossians live in Mauritius and the government would help them to return if possible

b • UK and US governments wish to see the MPA established
  • Preventing access to the waters around the islands and the return of the Chagossians

• So that a military base can be maintained
  • The Mauritian government has territorial claims over the Chagos Islands
  • Fishing industry in Mauritius has fishing rights to the area which would be lost

4 (These are suggestions and there may be many correct answers for this!)
  • Talks held between all stakeholders: UK and US governments, Mauritian government, Chagossian representatives, fishing industry representatives, conservation groups.
  • It is suggested that the Chagossian people could co-exist happily with the base on Diego Garcia if they are allowed a restricted level of fishing and other activities such as coconut farming. They and the military staff could help each other economically.
  • Talks should focus on several aspects:
    • Possible return of islands to Mauritius
    • Some degree of limited fishing in certain areas whilst some areas are no-take
    • Possible leasing of base to US/UK from Mauritian government
    • Return of Chagossian people to the islands with the ability to make a living from the fishing and farming

Chapter 15

1 Australia has fauna that date back to Gondwanaland. Australia and Antarctica separated from India, Africa and South America and the plants and animals evolved in isolation from the organisms on other continents. After Australia reached the area around Indonesia, other organisms, including humans, were able to colonise it and introduce animals that outcompeted the native species. The original species in Australia had not evolved alongside the new organisms so had less ability to compete.

2 • The *daughterless* gene is removed using restriction endonucleases and placed into a plasmid vector using DNA ligase.
  • The gene would then be injected into carp and mosquitofish eggs.
  • Male fish that contain the gene would be selected.
  • Male fish containing copies of the gene could be used to breed other transgenic male fish, which would be placed into rivers and lakes.

- The transgenic male fish would breed with the normal females but the offspring would all be male, some of which will carry the transgene.
- Eventually, the population will be largely male resulting in a reduced breeding rate.
- *daughterless* will not affect other species
- Pesticides and other methods are non-specific and affect other species
- Pesticides can bio-accumulate through food chains

3 • Neither carp nor mosquitofish are native to Australia so if fish did escape they would be unable to interbreed with wild fish.
- The *daughterless* gene negatively affects the population of carp and mosquitofish so it is highly

unlikely to give them any competitive advantage. They would be expected to die off.

4 • In Asia and Europe, carp are a native species.
- Escaped carp could interbreed with the wild carp.
- The *daughterless* gene could be transferred into the wild population.
- The ratio of males to females would increase leading to reduced breeding.
- Carp populations would decrease.
- Food chains would be affected; river and lake plants would increase and predators of carp would decrease.

Glossary

Abiotic: the environment's geological, physical and chemical features, the non-living part of an ecosystem

Absorption spectrum: a graph of the absorbance of different wavelengths of light by a compound such as a photosynthetic pigment

Abyssal plain: a flat, sandy region of the ocean floor found between trenches and the continental rise

Accessory pigment: a pigment that is not essential for photosynthesis but that absorbs light of different wavelengths and passes the energy to chlorophyll *a*, such as chlorophyll b, xanthophylls and phycobilins

Action spectrum: a graph showing the effect of different wavelengths of light on a process, e.g. on the rate of photosynthesis

Active transport: the movement of particles (or molecules) from a lower concentration to a higher concentration (against a concentration gradient), it requires additional energy in the form of ATP and the use of membrane protein pumps on the surface of cells

Aerobic respiration: the release of energy from glucose or another organic substrate in the presence of oxygen, the waste products are carbon dioxide and water

Ahermatypic: soft corals that do not build reefs

Alevin: the first larval form of salmon, they possess a yolk sac and remain within the gravel nests or redds

Algal bloom: a rapid increase in a population of algae

Anaerobic respiration: the release of energy from glucose or another organic substrate in the absence of oxygen, animals produce lactate as a waster product while plants and fungi produce ethanol and carbon dioxide

Anchorage: [boats] the portion of a harbour or estuary used for ships to anchor; [organisms] location on a substrate where a sessile organism attaches and lives

Anomaly: a result or observation that deviates from what is normal or expected. In experimental results it normally refers to one repeated result that does not fit the pattern of the others

Aquaculture: the rearing of aquatic animals and plants for human consumption or use

Artificial reef: an artificial underwater structure built to mimic the characteristics of a natural reef

Assimilated: the conversion of a nutrient into a useable form that can be incorporated into the tissues of an organism

Asthenosphere: a nearly liquid layer made of the uppermost part of the mantle

Atoll: a coral reef somewhat circular in shape with a central lagoon

Autotroph (autotrophic): an organism that can capture the energy in light or chemicals and use it to produce carbohydrates from simple molecules such as carbon dioxide

Barrier reef: a reef separated by a lagoon from the land mass with which it is associated

Beach renourishment: the process of dumping sand from another location onto an eroding shoreline to create a new beach or to widen the existing beach.

Benthic trawling: a fishing method that drags a net along the seabed; wooden boards at the front of the net keep the net open and stir up the seabed, causing damage

Bioaccumulation: the accumulation of substances, such as pesticides or other chemicals, in an organism

Biodiversity: a measure of the numbers of different species present

Biomagnification: the increasing concentration of a substance, such as a toxic chemical, in the tissues of organisms at successively higher levels in a food chain

Biomass: the mass of living material in an area, it can be measured as dry mass (without the water) or wet mass

Biotechnology: the application of biological processes for industrial and other purposes, which can be the use of substances from living organisms, such as enzymes, or the use of the organisms themselves

Biotic: the living parts of an ecosystem, which includes the organisms and their effects on each other

Carbohydrate: organic compounds occurring in living tissues that contain carbon, hydrogen and oxygen, for example starch, cellulose and sugars; carbohydrates can be broken down in the process of respiration to release energy

Catch per unit effort: a measure of fish abundance calculated from the catch size divided by the fishing effort

Chemoautotroph: a producer that uses chemical energy to produce its own food energy

Chemosynthesis (chemosynthetic): the production of organic compounds by bacteria or other living organisms using the energy derived from reactions with inorganic chemicals

Chlorophyll: a pigment found in plants and algae that is used to absorb sunlight for photosynthesis

Chloroplast: the photosynthetic cell organelle found in eukaryotes

Climate change: changes in global or regional climate patterns, especially changes that have been seen since the late 20th century

Community: all the different populations occupying a habitat at the same time

Compensation point: the light intensity at which the rate of photosynthesis and the rate of respiration are equal

Competition: a relationship between two organisms where both species are negatively affected by trying to fill the same ecological niche

Condensation (condense): when water changes from vapour to liquid; the energy needed to maintain the vapour state is released into the atmosphere

Confounding variable: a variable that could affect the dependent variable. In laboratory experiments these are the variables that must be controlled. In field experiments they are normally just measured and recorded

Conservation: the protection of plants, animals and other organisms along with their habitats from extinction

Consumer: an animal that feeds on other organisms to gain its food energy

Continental drift: a theory supporting the possibility that continents are able to move over Earth's surface

Continental margin: the submerged area next to a continent, which includes the continental shelf, continental slope and continental rise

Continental rise: a gently sloping surface at the base of the continental slope where sand deposits

Continental shelf: a gently sloping surface that extends from the low tide line to the continental slope, typically where a great deal of sand deposits

Continental slope: a relatively steep sloping surface between the continental shelf and the continental rise

Control group: a group within an experiment or study that receives exactly the same treatment as the experimental groups with the exception of the variable being tested

Control variables: variables that are not being tested but that must be kept the same in case they affect the experiment

Convection current: the movement of fluids or air based on density differences caused by differing temperatures

Convergent boundary: when two or more tectonic plates come together

Coral bleaching: the loss of symbiotic algae from the tissues of corals as a result of environmental factors

Coriolis Effect: a force that results from the Earth's rotation that causes objects or particles in motion to deflect to the right in the Northern Hemisphere and to the left in the Southern Hemisphere

Current: a continuous physical movement of water caused by wind or density

Cyanobacteria: group of photosynthetic bacteria found in marine and fresh water

Decomposers: bacteria and fungi that break down dead organic matter and release the nutrients back into the environment

Deep chlorophyll maximum: the maximum concentration of chlorophyll below the surface of a body of water

Delta: a low-lying triangular area at the mouth of a river formed by the deposition of sediments

Denaturation: the loss of shape of enzymes resulting in a loss of activity, usually the result of heating to a high temperature

Density: the mass per unit volume of a substance

Dependent variable: the variable being measured in an experiment

Deposition: a geological process where sediments, soil and rocks are added to a landform or land mass

Desiccation: the process of drying out or losing moisture

Diatom: group of unicellular algae found in phytoplankton characterised by silica skeletons

427

Diazotroph: an organism that is able to grow without external sources of fixed nitrogen because it is able to fix nitrogen gas into substances like ammonia

Diffusion: the random movement of particles (or molecules) from a higher concentration to a lower concentration (down a concentration gradient); it is a passive process, not requiring the input of energy

Dinoflagellate: group of unicellular algae found in phytoplankton characterised by the presence of two flagella

Dissociation (dissociates): a reversible chemical change where the molecules of a single compound separate into two or more other substances

Dissolution: the dissolving of a solute into a solvent

Dissolved oxygen (DO): oxygen that has dissolved into water

Diurnal: occurring daily

Divergent boundary: where two tectonic plates are moving away from each other

DNA ligase: an enzyme that joins the sugar–phosphate backbone of sections of DNA, it is used to recombine pieces of DNA

Earthquake: a sudden release of energy inside the Earth that creates seismic waves usually caused by movement of tectonic plates or volcanic activity

Ecological linkages: the ecological relationships that exist between species and their environment within an ecosystem

Ecological niche: the role of a species within an ecosystem

Ecosystem: the living organisms and the environment with which they interact

Ecotourism: sustainable tourism that is associated with an appreciation of the natural world and that minimises damage to the environment; it can benefit both environment and local populations

Ectothermic: an organism that maintains its body temperature by exchanging heat with its surroundings

El Niño: a warm current that develops off the coast of Ecuador around December, which can cause widespread death within local food chains

Endosymbiosis: a theory that suggest that chloroplasts were originally independent photosynthetic bacteria that were taken in by other cells

Endothermic: an organism that maintains its body temperature by generating heat in metabolic processes

Enzyme: a protein produced by a living organism that acts as a catalyst in a specific reaction

Erosion: a natural process where material is worn away from the Earth's surface and transported elsewhere

Estuary: a partially enclosed, tidal, coastal body of water where fresh water from a river meets the salt water of the ocean

Euryhaline: organisms, such as salmon, that are able to tolerate a wide range of salinities

Eutrophication: the process by which a body of water becomes enriched in dissolved nutrients (such as nitrates and phosphates) that stimulate the growth of producers, usually resulting in the depletion of dissolved oxygen

Evaporation: a change in state from liquid to gas below the boiling point of a substance

Exotic species: species that are not native to a particular location

Extensive aquaculture: aquaculture that uses little technology, low stocking densities and no artificial feeding

External fertilisation: when gametes such as sperm and eggs are released and fuse outside the body

Extremophile: an organism that is adapted to survive extreme temperature, pressure, salinity or pH

Fecundity: the rate of reproduction of organisms, in fish the rate of egg production is often considered as a measure of fecundity

Fish: vertebrates that live in water and have gills and fins

Food chain: a way of describing the feeding relationships between organisms

Food web: a way of describing how food chains are interrelated in an ecosystem

Fringing reef: a reef close to and surrounding newer volcanic islands or that borders continental landmasses

Fry: the early, small larval stage of many fish, including salmon

Gene: a sequence of nucleotides in an organism's DNA that codes for the production of a particular protein, it is the hereditary unit that codes for a characteristic of an organism

Genetic engineering: the modification of organisms by changing their genetic material, this can be the addition of genes from other species or the editing of genes that are already present

Genotype: the genetic constitution of an individual organism

Geomorphology: the study of the characteristics, origin and development of landforms

Global warming: the observed and projected increases in the average temperature of Earth's atmosphere and oceans due to an enhanced greenhouse effect

Gradient: the rate of increase or decrease of a characteristic relative to another

Greenhouse effect: the heating of the atmosphere due to the presence of carbon dioxide and other gases, these gases prevent infrared radiation being re-emitted into space

Gross primary production: the amount of light or chemical energy fixed by producers in a given length of time in a given area

Growth rate: the speed of growth of a population in terms of numbers or size of individual fish

Habitat: the natural environment where an organism lives

Halocline: a layer of water below the mixed surface layer where a rapid change in salinity can be measured as depth increases

Hermaphroditism: able to produce both male and female gametes

Hermatypic: hard corals capable of reef-building

Heterotroph (heterotrophic): an organism that cannot make its own food and instead relies on consuming other organisms; all animals, fungi and protozoans are heterotrophic, as well as most bacteria

Hurricane: a tropical cyclone with wind speeds of more than 120 km h^{-1}, generally applied to those occurring in the Atlantic Ocean and northern Pacific Ocean

Hydrothermal vent: an area where cold ocean water that has seeped into the Earth's crust is superheated by underlying magma and forced through vents in the ocean floor

Hypersaline: when a body of water has a salinity level greater than 35‰

Hypothesis: an explanation of an observation that can be tested through experimentation

Hypoxic: an area of water with a low concentration of dissolved oxygen

Independent variable: the variable being changed in an experiment

Infauna: animals living within the sediments of the ocean floor, river or lake beds

Infiltration: part of the water cycle where water soaks into the soil from ground level and moves underground

Intensive aquaculture: aquaculture that uses intensive methods such as high stocking densities and artificial feeding to maximise production

Internal fertilisation: when gametes such as sperm and eggs fuse inside the body of a parent

Isostasy: a process similar to buoyancy but related to the Earth's crust floating on the flexible mantle

Juvenile: the stage of life cycle that is not sexually mature

Keystone species: a consumer that affects biodiversity to a greater extent than would be expected from its population numbers

***K*-strategist:** an organism that produces few offspring but provides a large amount of parental investment

Larval: the immature form of animals that undergo some metamorphosis, often having different food sources and habitats to avoid competition with the adults

Latent heat: the quantity of heat gained or lost per unit of mass as a substance undergoes a change of state (e.g. vapour to liquid)

Leaching: a process during which water-soluble nutrients are removed from the soil and dissolve in water that is flowing to the sea (run-off)

Lithosphere: the outermost layer of the Earth's crust

Littoral zone: the benthic, or bottom, zone between the highest and lowest spring tide shorelines, also referred to as the intertidal zone

Mantle: a region of molten rock within the interior of the Earth, between the core and the crust

Marine protected area (MPA): an area of ocean or coastline where restrictions have been placed on activities, the levels of restriction may vary, some may be no-take areas where no fishing is permitted, others may allow some fishing, some may ban all access to unauthorised people while others may allow restricted access

Marine snow: particles of organic material that fall from surface waters to the deeper ocean

Maximum sustainable yield (MSY): the intensity of fishing that can be carried out without reducing future populations

Meniscus: the curve in the upper surface of a liquid inside a container. It is caused by surface tension and can be concave or convex

Mid-ocean ridge: a mountain range with a central valley on an ocean floor at the boundary between two diverging tectonic plates, where new crust forms from upwelling magma

Monsoon: seasonal winds in India that blow from the south-west during the summer and the north-east during the winter

Morphology: the study of the forms of things

Mortality rate: the death rate; natural mortality is the death rate arising from natural causes, while fishing mortality is the death rate caused by fishing

Mutualism: a relationship between two different organisms where both organisms benefit

Mysis: the later larval form of crustaceans, shrimp mysis larvae drift to coastal areas

Neap tide: a tide that occurs when the Moon and Sun are at right angles from each other, causing the smallest tidal range

Net primary production: the amount of energy that is left over after respiration to be made into new plant biomass

Nursery ground: important habitats of oceanic water where young fish and other species find food and shelter from predators, e.g. mangroves

Nutrient: a chemical that provides what is needed for organisms to live and grow

Nutrient cycles: the movement and exchange of elements that are essential to life, from inorganic molecules, through fixation and then into living organisms before being decomposed back into inorganic molecules

Ocean: a continuous mass of seawater on the Earth's surface, its boundaries formed by continental land masses, ridges on the ocean floor or the equator

Ocean acidification: a reduction in the pH of the ocean over an extended period time, caused primarily by uptake of carbon dioxide from the atmosphere

Osmoconformer: organisms that have an ionic and salt concentration that is the same as the surrounding water

Osmoregulation: the process of regulating the internal water and ion content of an organism

Osmoregulator: organisms that regulate their internal salt and ion balance at a constant level, which may differ from the surrounding water

Osmosis: the movement of water from a higher water potential (more dilute solution) to a lower water potential (higher concentration of solute) across a selectively permeable membrane

Oxygen minimum layer: the layer within the ocean where the concentration of dissolved oxygen is at its lowest, typically found between 100 and 1000 m deep

Parasitism: a relationship between two organisms where the parasite obtains benefit at the expense of the host

Parental investment: the amount of care and nutrition that parent organisms give to offspring

Patch reef: small, isolated reef usually located within the lagoon of a barrier reef

Pediveliger: the third-stage larva of molluscs, characterised by the development of a foot

Phenotype: the observable characteristics of an individual resulting from the interaction of its genotype with the environment

Photoautotroph: a producer that uses light energy to produce its own food energy

Photosynthesis (photosynthetic): the process of using light energy to synthesis glucose from carbon dioxide and water

Phytoplankton: microscopic photosynthetic organisms that live in the upper, sunlit layers of water

Plasmid: a small circular DNA strand in the cytoplasm of a bacterium, they are used as vectors in the laboratory manipulation of genes

Plate tectonics: the process where large sections ('plates') of the Earth's crust are in constant movement over the fluid mantle, causing earthquakes and volcanoes at the borders between the plates

Population: all the individuals of the same species that live at the same place and time

Precautionary principle: a strategy to cope with possible risks where scientific understanding is yet incomplete, such as the risks of releasing genetically modified organisms; it tries to ensure that all possible consequences of a new technology are considered before allowing it to be used

Precipitation: water that falls from the atmosphere to the Earth's surface as rain, sleet, snow or hail

Predation: a relationship between two organisms where a predator hunts, kills and eats a prey animal.

Predator: an animal that kills and eats animals for food

Prediction: a statement of the expected results in an experiment based on the hypothesis being tested

Prey: an animal that is eaten by predators

Primary pigment: photosynthetic pigment that is directly involved with photosynthesis

Primary producer: organisms that produce biomass from inorganic compounds, in almost all cases these are photosynthetically active organisms

Primary productivity: the rate of production of new biomass through photosynthesis or chemosynthesis

Producer: an organism that can produce its own food energy

Promoter: a section of DNA that is often located in front of a gene, it is responsible for the 'switching on and off' a gene

Protozoea: the second-stage larva of crustaceans such as shrimp, typically planktonic these larvae pass through several forms as they grow

Pumped ventilation: ventilation of gills by the muscle action of the mouth pumping water over the gills, it can occur when the fish is stationary

Purse seine: a seine net used capture pelagic shoals of fish, it has a series of ropes that are used to close it and trap the fish before hauling them on board

Pycnocline: a boundary between two layers of water with different densities

Pyramid of biomass: a diagram that shows the biomass present in each trophic level of a food chain

Pyramid of energy: a diagram that shows the amount of energy in each trophic level of a food chain

Pyramid of numbers: a diagram that shows the number of organisms in each trophic level of a food chain

Qualitative data: descriptive data about a variable, for example colour or behaviour

Quantitative data: numerical data that give the quantity, amount or range of a variable, for example concentration of oxygen or number of eggs laid

Radiocarbon dating: process used to estimate the age of organic material by measuring the radioactivity of its carbon content (also called carbon dating)

Ram ventilation: ventilation of gills by swimming with the mouth open so that a constant flow of water passes through the mouth and over the gills, it only occurs when a fish is swimming

Recruitment: the arrival of new organisms in a population, for fish it is often considered to be the stage at which fish have reached an age when then they can to be caught in nets

Reef erosion: the gradual wearing away of a coral reef by the action of living organisms (bioerosion) and physical factors, such as storms

Refute (a hypothesis): submitting evidence that shows that a hypothesis is not correct

Reliable: results that can be replicated by other people

Reproductive maturity: the time when an organism is able to reproduce sexually

Reservoir: part of the abiotic phase of the nutrient cycle where nutrients can remain for long periods of time

Residence time: the average time that a particle spends in a particular system

Respiration: the process by which all living things release energy from their food by oxidising glucose

Restriction endonuclease: enzyme that cuts DNA at specific internals, palindromic sequences, they are used in genetic engineering

Ribosome: cell organelle involved in protein synthesis

r-strategist: an organism that produces large numbers of offspring while providing little parental investment

Run-off: the flow of water from land caused by precipitation

Salinity: a measure of the quantity of dissolved solids in ocean water, represented by parts per thousand, ppt or ‰

Saprophytic (saprophyte): decomposers that feed on dead organic matter ('death eater')

Sea: a continuous mass of seawater on the Earth's surface, part of the ocean, that is partially enclosed by land, so seas are found where the ocean and land meet

Secondary production: the rate of production of new biomass by consumers, using the energy gained by eating producers

Sedimentation: the act or process of depositing sediment from a solution (e.g. seawater)

Selective breeding: the process by which humans use animal and plant breeding to develop particular characteristics selectively, choosing which animals or plants are used for sexual reproduction and then selecting the offspring that are required; this is also known as artificial selection

Semi-diurnal: occurring twice daily

Shellfish: aquatic invertebrates that are used as food, including shelled molluscs, crustaceans and echinoderms, such as bivalves, crabs, lobsters and sea urchins

Shoaling: when fish swim together in a group

Sink: an area where there is a net loss of material (for example where more gas dissolves into the ocean than diffuses into the atmosphere)

Smolt: form of salmon that occurs when parr lose their markings while in estuaries, they are adapted for marine life by being silver in colour and elongated in shape

Solubility: the ability of a solute to dissolve into a solvent

Source: an area where there is a net gain of material (for example where more gas diffuses into the atmosphere than dissolves in the ocean)

Species: a group of similar organisms that can interbreed naturally to produce fertile offspring

Spring tide: a tide that occurs when the Sun and Moon are aligned, causing the largest tidal range

Stakeholder: a person who has a vested interest, for any reason, in an area or project

Stroma: the fluid part of a chloroplast in which the carbohydrates are synthesised

Subduction: the process where one lithospheric plate slides below another at a convergent plate boundary

Subsidence: sinking of land

Succession: the change in community structure over time

Surface area: volume ratio an index that gives a relative measure of both surface area and volume, exchange organs generally have a very high surface area : volume ratio

Sustainable aquaculture: aquaculture that causes less short- and long-term damage to the environment, economy and local community

Sustainable development: development that meets the needs of the present without compromising the ability of future generations to meet their needs

Sustainable fishing: fishing up to the maximum sustainable yield so that future fish stocks are not at risk of being depleted

Theory: a well-substantiated explanation of an aspect of the natural world that has been repeatedly tested and confirmed through observation and experimentation

Thermocline: a boundary between two layers of water with different temperatures

Thylakoid: a flattened, membrane-bound, fluid-filled sac that is the site of the light-dependent reactions of photosynthesis in a chloroplast

Tidal range: the difference in height between the high-tide mark and the low-tide mark over the course of a day, also called the tidal amplitude

Tidal surge: the coastal flood or tsunami-like phenomenon of rising water, associated with low pressure weather systems, also called a storm surge

Tide: the periodic rise and fall of the surface of the ocean resulting from the gravitational pull of the Moon and Sun

Transform boundary: when two plates are moving in an antiparallel direction, creating friction between them

Transgenic organism: an organism that contains genetic material into which DNA from an unrelated organism has been introduced

Trench: a long, narrow and deep depression on the ocean floor with relatively steep sides, caused by convergent plate boundaries

Trochophore: the first larval stage of molluscs such as giant clams and oysters, they move using cilia and are planktonic

Trophic level: a position in a food chain or food web

Tropical cyclone: a localised, intense low-pressure wind system that forms over tropical oceans with strong winds

Tsunami: a seismic sea wave created by an underwater earthquake or volcanic event, not noticeable in the open ocean but building to great heights in shallow water

Typhoon: a tropical cyclone in the Indian Ocean or western Pacific Ocean

Upwelling: the movement of cold, nutrient-rich water from deep in the ocean to the surface

Variable: a condition in an experiment that can be controlled or changed

Vector: a section of DNA, typically a plasmid, that is used to transfer DNA from one organism to another

Veliger: the second-stage larva of molluscs, characterised by the presence of a vellum organ used for feeding and movement, and a shell

Volcano: a mountain or hill with a crater or vent through which lava, rock fragments, hot vapour and gas are being forced from the Earth's crust

Water potential: a measure of the potential energy of water in a solution and thus the tendency of water to move from one place to another; the more solute that is dissolved in a solution, the lower the water potential

Zonation: a separation of organisms in a habitat into definite zones or bands according to biological and physical factors, common in rocky shore habitats

Zooxanthellae: symbiotic, photosynthetic dinoflagellates living within the tissues of many invertebrates

Acknowledgements

The authors and publishers acknowledge the following sources of copyright material and are grateful for the permissions granted. While every effort has been made, it has not always been possible to identify the sources of all the material used, or to trace all copyright holders. If any omissions are brought to our notice, we will be happy to include the appropriate acknowledgements on reprinting.

Chap 1 Scientific method: Greg Johnston/Getty Images; Fig 1.4: Nature Picture Library/Getty Images; Chap 2 Marine ecosystems and biodiversity: Alexander Safonov/Getty Images; Fig 2.3: Salvatore Mele; Fig 2.4a: plovets/Getty Images; Fig 2.4b: Daniela Dirscherl/Getty Images; Fig 2.7: Jules Robson; Fig 2.10: Dave Fleetham/Getty Images; Fig 2.16: Biophotos Associates/Science Photo Library; Fig 2.17: by wildestanimal/Getty Images; Fig 2.22: Dave Fleetham / Design Pics/Getty Images; Fig 2.23: Norbert Wu/Minden Pictures/ Getty Images; Chap 3 Energetics of marine ecosystems: Dave Fleetham/Design Pics/Getty Images; Fig 3.1a: D.P. Wilson/FLPA/Getty Images; Fig 3.1b: Pete Atkinson/Getty Images; Fig 3.1c: paule858/Getty Images; Fig 3.2: Nancy Nehring/Getty Images; Fig 3.4: Jeff Rotman / Alamy Stock Photo; Fig 3.7: Image courtesy SeaWiFS Project; Fig 3.8: De Agostini Picture Library/Getty Images; chap 4 Nutrient cycles in marine ecosystems: Westend61/Getty Images; Fig 4.2: from Climate Change 2007: The Physical Science Basis. Working Group I Contribution to the Fourth Assessment Report of the Intergovernmental Panel on Climate Change [Solomon, S., D. Qin, M. Manning, Z. Chen, M. Marquis, K.B. Averyt, M. Tignor and H.L. Miller (eds.)]. Cambridge University Press, Cambridge, United Kingdom and New York, NY, USA; Fig 4.5: Dr Ken Macdonald/Science Photo Library; Fig 4.6: James Brunson-Smith / EyeEm/Getty Images; Fig 4.9: Abigail Heithoff/ Woods Hole Oceanographic Institution/Visuals Unlimited /Science Photo Library; Fig 4.12: Steve Gschmeissner/Science Photo Library; Fig 4.14: Don Klumpp/Getty Images; Fig 4.20: Bill Schaefer/Getty Images; Fig 4.21: Yva Momatiuk & John Eastcott/Getty Images; Fig 4.22: Barrett Hedges/Getty Images: Fig 4.23: Paul Damien/Getty Images; chap 5 Coral reefs and lagoons: Iryna Rieber/EyeEm/Getty Images; Fig 5.5a: Daniela Dirscherl/Getty Images: Fig 5.5b: Franco Banfi/Getty Images; Fig 5.6: WILDLIFE GmbH / Alamy Stock Photo; Fig 5.7a: Pete Oxford/Minden Pictures/Getty Images; Fig 5.7b: Carlos Villoch - MagicSea.com / Alamy Stock Photo; Fig 5.8: age fotostock / Alamy Stock Photo; Fig 5.10a: Images & Stories / Alamy Stock Photo; Fig 5.11: Visuals Unlimited, Inc./David Fleetham/Getty Images; chap 6: Iryna Rieber/EyeEm/Getty Image; Fig 6.2: De Agostini Picture Library/Getty Images; Fig 6.6: Ralph White/Getty Images; Fig 6.10: Melissa Lorenz; Fig 6.11: Planet Observer/Getty Images; Fig 6.12: Melissa Lorenz; Fig 6.15: Roger de la Harpe/Getty Images; Fig: 6.18: epa european pressphoto agency b.v. / Alamy Stock Photo chap 7 Physical and chemical oceanography: Jan Maguire Photography/ Getty Images; Fig 7.3: Maxime VIGE/Getty Images; Fig 7.4: NASA/Science Photo Library; chap 8 Physiology of marine primary producers: Johner Images/Getty Images; Fig 8.15: Wim Van Egmond/Science Photo Library; Fig 8.16: Nature Picture Library / Alamy Stock Photo; Fig 8.17: Nancy Nehring/Getty Images; Fig 8.18: Masa Ushioda / Alamy Stock Photo; Fig 8.19: Oxford Scientific/Getty Images; Fig 8.20: Ethan Daniels/Stocktrek Images/Getty Images; Fig 8.22: Douglas Klug/Getty Images; Fig 8.25: Fotosearch/Getty Images: Fig 8.26: blickwinkel / Alamy Stock Photo; chap 9 Aspects of marine animal physiology: Siegfried Gehlhaar/EyeEm/Getty Images; Fig 9.20: Marayok/Getty Images; Fig 9.23: NASA/Science Photo Library; chap 10 Marine animal reproductive behaviour: Steve Proehl/Getty Images; Fig 10.3 & Fig 10.17: Benjamin Victor, Coralreeffish.com; Fig 10.5: Robert F. Sisson/Getty Images; Fig 10.7: D. Parer & E. Parer-Cook/Getty Images: Fig 10.9: Scott Groth, Oregon Department of Fish and Wildlife; Fig 10.11: WaterFrame / Alamy Stock Photo; Fig 10.15: Dr Clive Bromhall/Getty Images; Fig 10.18: John E Marriott/Getty Images; Fig 10.20a: George Ostertag / Alamy Stock Photo; chap 11 Fisheries management: Adrian Peacock/Getty Images; Fig 11.5: Jim Brandenburg/Getty Images; Fig 11.7a: Jason Edwards/Getty Images; Fig 11.7b: Undersea Vehicles Program/UNCW; Fig 11.9: WaterFrame / Alamy Stock Photo; Fig 11.11: Dr Keith Wheeler/Science Photo Library; Fig 11.14: Romeo Gacad/Getty Images; Fig 11.15: Mint Images - Frans Lanting/Getty Images; Fig 11.18: Eye Ubiquitous/ Getty Images; chap 12 Aquaculture: Westend61/Getty Images; Fig 12.15: National Geographic Creative / Alamy Stock Photo; Fig 12.19: Hoang Dinh Nam/Getty Images; Fig 12.20: Harald Franzen; chap 13 Human impact on marine ecosystems: Frank and Helena/Getty Images; Fig 13.1: Anchorage Daily News/Getty Images; Fig 13.2: Saul Loeb/Getty Images; Fig 13.6: Rosanne Tackaberry / Alamy Stock Photo; Fig 13.10: Jonathan Eastland/Getty Images; Fig 13.12: NASA Earth Observatory; Fig 13.13: Data from Dr. Pieter Tans, NOAA/ESRL and Dr. Ralph Keeling, Scripps Institution of Oceanography. licensed under the Creative Commons Attribution-ShareAlike 3.0 license; Fig 13.18: Saul Loeb/Getty Images; Fig 13.19a: Gerald Herbert AP/Press Association Images; Fig 13.19b: Joel Sartore/Getty Images; chap 14 Marine conservation and ecotourism: Reinhard Dirscherl/Getty Images; Fig 14.3: Cyril Ruoso/Getty Images; Fig 14.6: Dave Fleetham / Design Pics/Getty Images; Fig 14.12a: Michel de Nijs/Getty Images; Fig 14.12b: Angelo Cavalli/Getty Images; Fig 14.13a: Laguna Lodge Eco-Resort and Nature Reserve; Fig 14.13b: Laguna Lodge Eco-Resort and Nature Reserve; Fig 14.14: Roy Toft; Fig 14.20: Gary Roberts / Alamy Stock Photo; chap 15 Marine biotechnology: Jeff Rotman/Getty Images; Fig 15.1: US Air Force Photo / Alamy Stock Photo; Fig 15.5: Genet. Mol. Biol. vol.22 n.1 São Paulo Mar. 1999. Copyright SBG; Fig 15.6: Wolfgang Kaehler/Getty Images; Fig 15.12: AquaBounty Technologies; Fig 15.16: AquaBounty Technologies; Fig 15.17: Catmando/Shutterstock.com; Fig 15.18: Sam Yeh/Getty Images; Fig 15.24: Joel Sartore/Getty Images; Fig 15.25: Benjamin F. Haith/Shutterstock.com.

Index

Note: The letters 'f' and 't' following locators refer to figures and tables respectively

abiotic, 10, 59
absorption spectrum, 150
abyssal plains, 105
accessory pigments, 148
action spectrum, 150
active transport, 174
aerobic respiration, 174
agriculture, 290–291
ahermatypic corals, 83
alevins, 200
algal bloom, 46
alleles, 350
anaerobic respiration, 174
analysing results, 5
anchorages, 91
anomalous, 4
aquaculture
    examples, 261–276
    extensive and intensive, 260–261
    negative effects of, 276–279
aquatic home, 10
artificial reefs, 91
assimilated, 59
asthenosphere, 101
atolls, 86
autotrophic nutrition, 147
autotrophic organisms, 37

barrier reefs, 86
benthic trawling, 229
bioaccumulation, 285
biodiversity, 11
biomagnification of toxins
    and bioaccumulation, 297
    mercury accumulation, 297–298
    Tributyltin (TBT), 298–299
biotechnology, 347
    bacteria to remove oil spills, 348
    oil and bacteria, 348
    oil-digesting bacteria, 347–348
biotic, 10, 59
breeding
    DNA, genes and alleles, 350–352
        chromosomes, 350–352
        double helix, 350
        nucleotides, 350
        polynucleotides, 350
    genetics of selective, 352–353
    risk of selective
        escape into world, 353
        inbreeding depression, 353

carbohydrates, 37, 147
carbon footprint, 334

catch per unit eff ort (CPUE), 244
chemical oceanography
    chemical composition of water, 123
    ocean layers
        density, 130
        mixing of, 131
    salinity
        atmospheric dissolution on, 124–125
        dissolved oxygen, 126–129
        evaporation effects, 126
        oxygen minimum layer, 126–129
        precipitation on, 126
        run-off on chemical composition, 125–126
        seawater composition, 123–124
        volcanoes on, 125
chemoautotrophs, 14
chemosynthetic, 37
chlorophyll *a,* 148
chlorophyll *b,* 148
chloroplasts, 147
climate change, 90
coastal communities
    agriculture, 328
    aquaculture, 330
    Bosca del Cabo Rainforest Lodge, 335–336
    conservation, 331–332
    ecotourism
        factors, 333–334
        types, 333
    fisheries, 330–331
    industry, 329
    responsible
        energy, 334
        recycling, 334
        sponsorship of conservation, 335
        sustainable materials, 334–335
    sewage and refuse disposal, 329–330
    shipping, 329
    stakeholders, 332
    tourism, 331
community, 11
compensation point, 43
competition, 12
condenses, 140
confounding variables, 4
conservation, 316
    human activities
        direct effects on species, 321–322
        habitat loss, 319–321
    need
        benefits for ourselves, 318
        ethical reasons, 316
        future generations, 316–317
        preserving ecosystems, 317–318
    opposition to
        excessive, 319
        expense, 318

loss of income, 318–319
natural part of life, 318
consumer, 14
continental drift, 100
continental margin, 106
continental rise, 107
continental shelf, 106
continental slope, 106
control group, 3
control variables, 3
convection currents, 102
convergent boundaries, 103
coral and zooxanthellae, 12
coral bleaching, 83, 305
coral growth, 84–85
coral physiology, 83–84
coral reefs reconstructing, 92–93
coriolis effect, 135
CPUE. *See* catch per unit effort (CPUE)
cross-breeding, 353
currents, 135
cyanobacteria, 147

Darwin–Dana–Daly theory of atoll formation, 86
decomposers, 59
deep chlorophyll maximum, 39
deltas, 109
demersal, 237
density, 130
salinity, 130
temperature, 130
dependent variable, 3
deposition, 109
desalination plants
high salinity brine, 288
organisms risk, 289
sediment movement, 289
waste chemicals, 288–290
desiccation, 110
diatoms, 147
diazotrophs, 68
diffusion, 176
dinoflagellates, 147
dissociates, 65
dissolution, 124
dissolved oxygen (Do), 126
diurnal, 132
divergent boundaries, 104
DNA ligase, 356
dominant alleles, 350
dredging
chemicals from sediments, 296
physical damage to benthic communities, 295
sediment release, 296

earthquakes, 103
ecological linkages, 322
ecological niche, 11
ecosystems, 10
ecotourism, 316
ectoparasites, 13

ectothermic, 49
el niño, 137
endocytosis, 162
endoparasites, 13
endosymbiosis, 147
endothermic, 49
energy transfer, efficiency of, 48–49
enzymes, 147
erosion, 109
estuaries, 10, 109
euryhaline, 186
eutrophication, 290
evaporates, 123
examples of aquaculture
economic sustainability
clean water availability, 269
disease management, 270
feed availability, 269–270
feeding efficiency, 270
location availability, 270–271
market access, 271
market demand, 271
return investment, 271–272
stock availability, 269
giant clam, 264–265
grouper, 261–262
shrimp, 263–264
social sustainability
disease spread, 275
exotic species, 275
habitat destruction, 274
labour availability, 272–273
overexploitation of feedstocks, 274
pollution, 274–275
resources competition, 276
social impact, 273–274
tuna, 262–263
exotic species, 274
extensive aquaculture, 259, 260
external fertilisation, 216
extremophiles, 40

fecundity, 231
feeding relationships
pyramids of biomass, 51–52
pyramids of energy, 52
pyramids of number, 51
fertilisation methods
external, 216–217
internal, 217
parental care
K-strategy, 218
r-strategy, 217
sharks, 218
tuna, 218
whales, 218
and parental care, 216
fish quotas
fishing methods, 236*t*
restriction by season, 234
restriction intensity , 238–239

restriction of location, 234–235
restriction of method, 235
restrictions on size, 238
fisheries management
enforcement, 243–248
monitoring, 243–248
North sea fleet, 227–231
regulating sustainable, 231–242
rehabilitation of stocks, 249–251
sociological impacts, 249
fishing policy, 249
food chain, 15
food web, 15
fringing reefs, 86
fry, salmon, 200

gaseous exchange
diffusion
concentration gradient, 176–177
distance, 177
surface area, 177
temperature, 176
Fick's Law and, 179
in marine organisms
circulatory systems, 178–179
size and shape, 177–178
water as, 177
methods
coral polyps, 179
counter-current exchanger, 181
fish gills, 179–180
ventilation movements, 181–184
GDPs. *See* gross domestic products (GDPs)
genes, 350
genetic engineering, 354
aquadvantage GM salmon procedure, 357
fish and shellfish
benefits, 359
risk and consequences, 360
risk minimising, 360–362
selective breeding
differences, 355
similarities, 355
tools of, 355–356
genotype, 349
global warming, 287
alternative theories, 304–305
consequences
climate change, 306
melting ice sheets, 305
water temperature increased, 305–306
evidence
atmospheric carbon dioxide, 302–303
climate change, 303
increasing global temperatures, 302
melting of ice and sea-level rises, 303
greehouse effect, 301
and human activity, 301
GPP. *See* gross primary productivity (GPP)
gradient, 130
greenhouse effect, 301

gross domestic products (GDPs), 235
gross primary productivity (GPP), 155
growth rates, 269

habitat loss
coral reefs, 320
mangroves, 319–320
seagrass meadows, 320–321
halocline, 130
hermaphrodites, 206
hermatypic, 83
heterotrophic, 37
heterozygous, 350
homozygous, 350
host, 12
hurricanes, 139
hydrothermal vent, 105
hydrothermal vents, formation of, 105*f*
hypersaline, 126
hypothesis, 2
hypothesis evaluation, 5
hypoxic, 46

independent variable, 3
infauna, 112
infiltration, 62
intensive aquaculture, 259, 260–261
internal fertilisation, 216
intertidal zone, 164
isostasy, 107–108

juvenile, 200

keystone species, 17
K-strategy, 217

laboratory-based experiments, 6
larval stages, 198
latent heat, 140
law of limiting factors, 156
leaches, 63
life cycle of tuna, 203*f*
lithosphere, 101
littoral zone, 108, 164
ecosystems
mangroves, 114–115
rocky shores, 110–112
sandy shores, 112–114
morphology of
deltas, 109
estuaries, 109
muddy shores, 109
rocky shores, 108–109
sandy shores, 109

mangroves
anoxic soil, 115
high salt content, 114–115
mantle, 101
marine animal physiology
gaseous exchange, 176–184

respiration, 174–175
salinity regulation, 185–190
marine ecology, principles of, 10–12
marine ecosystems
    agriculture, 290–291
    bioaccumulation, 297–299
    biomagnification of toxins, 297–299
    desalination plants, 288–289
    dredging, 295–296
    energy transfer, 47–50
    feeding relationships, 51–53
        consumers, 14–15
        producers, 14
    food chains/food webs
        keystone species, 17
        predator–prey, 15–17
    global warming, 301–306
    oil industry, 285–288
    productivity, 37–46
    sewage and refuse, 292–295
    symbiosis within, 12
    wrecking ships dive sites, 306–307
marine fish, 187
marine mutualism
    chemosynthetic bacteria and tube worms, 12–13
    cleaner fish, 13
    coral and zooxanthellae, 12
    grouper, 13
    shrimps, 13
marine nutrient cycles
    calcium, 71
    carbon, 65–67
    magnesium, 69
    nitrogen, 68–69
    phosphorus, 71–73
marine organisms
    giant clam life cycle, 206–207
    grouper life cycle, 210–213
    larval stages, 198–199
    life cycles, 198
    oyster life cycle, 204–205
    Salmon life cycle, 199–200
    shrimp life cycle, 208–209
    tuna life cycle, 201–203, 203f
marine parasitism
    ectoparasites, 13
    endoparasites, 13
marine primary producers
    adaptations, 159–165
    photosynthesis, 155–158
    productivity basics, 147–155
marine protected areas (MPAs), 318, 325
marine refuse, 292
marine snow, 64
maximum sustainable yield (MSY), 227
meniscus, 4
mid-ocean ridges, 104
monitoring
    enforcement, 248
    and enforcement, 243
    and surveillance
        air and sea patrolling, 243
        catch inspection, 243–244
        catch per unit effort (CPUE), 244
        satellite, 244–245
monsoon, 139
morphology, 108
mortality rate, 232
MPAs. See marine protected areas (MPAs)
MSY. See maximum sustainable yield (MSY)
mutualism, 12
mutualistic, 162
mysis, 206

neap tides, 133
negative effect of aquaculture
    conserving habitats, 277
    preventing escape, 277
    social impacts, 278
    sustainably using resources, 277
net primary production, 41
net primary productivity (NPP), 155
NPP. See net primary productivity (NPP)
nursery grounds, 147
nutrient cycles, 59
    abiotic phases, 60f
    reservoirs in, 60–61
nutrients, 59
nutrients removing
    coral reefs, 64
    harvesting, 64–65
    marine snow, 64
    from surface layer, 63

ocean acidification, 88
oceans, 10
oil industry
    indirect effects, 287
    setting up off shore platforms, 285
    spillage
        cleaning-up oil spills, 287
        coastal ecosystems, 286
        food webs and productivity, 286
        oxygen dead zones, 287
        physical damage to organisms, 286
        toxicity, 286
osmoconformer, 186
osmoregulators, 186
osmosis, 185
oxygen minimum layer, 129

parasitism, 12
parr, 200
patch reefs, 86
pediveliger, 205
pelagic, 229
phenotype, 349
photoautotrophs, 14
photosynthesis, 147
    chloroplasts, 147–148
    law of limiting factors
        carbon dioxide, 156–157
        light intensity, 156
        light wavelength, 156

temperature, 156
    water concentrations, 156–157
  primary and accessory pigments
    absorption, 150–151
    action spectra, 150–151
    productivity and depth of water, 154–155
    turbidity, 151
    wavelength, 151
photosynthetic, 37
physical oceanography
  currents
    deep, 135–136
    surface, 135
  El Niño southern oscillation
    major, 138–139
    normal conditions, 137
  monsoons, 139
  tides range, 132–135
  tropical cyclones
    coastal communities, 141
    formation, 140–141
  upwelling, 137
phytoplankton, 37
  cyanobacteria, 160
  diatoms, 160
  dinoflagellates, 160
plasmids, 356
plate boundaries
  convergent, 103
  divergent, 104
  transform, 104–105
plate tectonics, 101
  evidence supporting
    magnetic polarity reversal, 101–102
    seabed spreading, 101
  history of, 100
  theory of, 101
pneumatocysts, 164
population, 11
precautionary principle, 360
precipitation, 125
predation, 12
predator, 15
prediction, 2
prey, 15
primary pigment, 148
primary producers, 147
primary producers, adaptations
  intertidal zones, 164–165
  open ocean
    phytoplankton, 159–160
    sargassum, 160–161
  shallow water
    kelp forests, 163–164
    seagrasses, 162–163
    zooxanthellae, 162
primary production, 41
primary productivity, 37
  chemosynthesis, 39–40
  photosynthesis
    light, 38–39

nutrients, 38
    temperature and carbon dioxide, 38
  photosynthesis and chemosynthesis, 40
  photosynthesis *vs.* respiration, 41
  productivity measuring
    changes in biomass, 43–44
    food chain, 45–46
    rate of photosynthesis, 42–43
    satellite imagery, 44
  respiration, 40
producers, 14
promoters, 356
protozoea, 206
pumped ventilation, 181
purse seine, 229
pycnocline, 39
pyramid of biomass, 52
pyramid of energy, 52
pyramid of numbers, 51

qualitative data, 2
quantitative data, 2

radiocarbon dating, 93
ram ventilation, 181
recessive alleles, 350
recruitment, 231
reef eroison
  and artificial reefs, 91
  coral bleaching and climate change, 90
reef types, 85–86
refute, 2
reliable, 4
reproductive maturity, 232
reservoir, 59
residence time, 60
respiration, 40
  aerobic, 174–175
  anaerobic, 175
respire, 147
restriction endonucleases, 355
ribosomes, 148
rocky shores
  high-tide zone, 111
  low-tide zone, 111–112
  middle-tide zone, 111
r-strategy, 217
run-off, 59, 125

salinity, 123
salinity regulations
  active transport
    euryhaline fish, 189–190
    fresh-water fish, 189
  osmosis
    osmoconformers, 186
    osmoregulators, 186–188
saprophytic, 68
scientific method
  data uncertainty, 4
  history of, 2

hypothesis, testing, 2–3
laboratory-based experiments, 6
scientific theories, 6
seabed, 106–107
seas, 10
secondary production, 41
sedimentation, 115
selective breeding, 347
semi-diurnal, 132
sewage, 292
sharks
    oviparity, 218
    ovoviviparity, 218
    viviparity, 218
shellfish, 15
shoaling, 21
sinks, 61
smolts, 200
social impact, aquaculture
    negative social outcomes, 273–274
    positive social outcomes, 273
solubility, 124
sources, 61
spats, 205
species, 11
    coastal development, 322
    hunting, 321
    over-fishing, 321
    pollution and refuse, 321
spring tides, 132
stakeholders, 324
stenohaline, 186
stock rehabilitation
    artificial reefs, 250
    cultivated stock, 250
    replanting mangroves, 249–250
stroma, 148
subsidence, 94
successful conservation
    ecological linkages
        local engagement, 323–324
        sea turtle, 323
    marine protected areas (MPAs)
        effectiveness of, 325–326
succession, 22
surface area, 178
surface water
    add nutrients, 61
    atmospheric gases, dissolving, 61
    run-off, 62–63
    upwelling, 61–62
sustainable aquaculture, 268
sustainable development, 334
sustainable fishing, 227
    information required
        models, 233
        mortality, 232–233
        recruitment, 231–232

methods
    market-oriented tools, 239–242
    setting fish quotas, 233–239
modern technology
    benthic trawling, 230–231
    factory ships, 231
    purse seine fishing, 229
    sonar, 228–229
North sea fishing, 227–228
symbiont, 12

TDS. *See* Total dissolved solids (TDS)
theory, 2
thermocline, 39, 130
thylakoids, 148
tidal range, 132
tidal surge, 133
tide, 132
tides
    factors affecting, 133
    lakes, 133
    neap, 133
    open ocean, 133
    range, 132
    seas, 133
    spring, 132
Total dissolved solids (TDS), 123
transform boundaries, 104
transformation, 356
transgenic organism, 355
trenches, 103
trochophore, 205
trophic level, 15
tropical cyclones, 139
tsunamis, 103
tube worms, 12–13
turbidity, 152
typhoons, 139

upwelling, 59, 137

vectors, 356
veliger, 205
volcanoes, 103

water potential, 185
wavelength
    light, 151–152
    and turbidity, 151
WHOI. *See* Woods Hole Oceanographic Institute (WHOI)
Woods Hole Oceanographic Institute (WHOI), 105
wrecking ships for dive sites, 306–307

zonation, 110
zooxanthellae, 83